From Underdevelopment
to Affluence

From Underdevelopment
to Affluence

Western, Soviet, and Chinese Views

Edited by

HARRY G. SHAFFER

University of Kansas

and

JAN S. PRYBYLA

The Pennsylvania State University

APPLETON-CENTURY-CROFTS
EDUCATIONAL DIVISION
New York   MEREDITH CORPORATION

PREFACE

Since the end of World War II, over sixty new countries with more than a billion inhabitants have joined the family of independent nations— almost forty of them during the first half of the 1960's. The list of these newly independent nations includes such familiar names as Algeria, Burma, Pakistan, and the Philippines, but also such little known ones as Gabon, Rwanda, Upper Volta, and the Republic of Chad. They vary in size from little Antigua with about 65,000 inhabitants, to India, whose population approaches the half billion mark. Almost all these new nations with their rapidly growing voice in the United Nations are in the group of underdeveloped (or, if one prefers, "less developed" or "developing") countries, a group which *in toto* encompasses two thirds of the human race. Half of these—one third of the people on earth—live in underdeveloped countries which have not aligned themselves with any of the major power blocs. So far at least, they remain uncommitted.

In the underdeveloped parts of our globe, hundreds of millions of people live in abject poverty and destitution. So wretched are their living standards, so great is their deprivation, that it defies the comprehension of most inhabitants of Western lands. Few in the industrially advanced countries can picture the lot of a person who is born, lives out his short life, and dies without ever having known a day without hunger, without ever having tasted a piece of meat, having sat in a chair, slept in a bed, learned to spell his own name, or received medical treatment for his ills. Yet, the number of such persons is still legion. Moreover, there is growing evidence that the gap between the have and the have-not nations is widening and that increases in food production are inadequate to keep up with increasing population. There is hardly a problem more urgent today than the plight of these underdeveloped regions, nor one more challenging to the human mind.

Throughout the history of mankind, the masses of people almost everywhere have had to labor hard and diligently for at best a bare minimum of existence, and with no hope for a better future—at least not on this earth. In modern times, however, it has become evident that it does not necessarily have to be that way, that it is possible to build a society in which the good life can be shared by most, and, in time, perhaps by all people. The underdeveloped parts of the world are desperately seeking the road that leads to this better life, seeking it with a sense of urgency and of growing impatience.

Looking toward the West, the inhabitants of the uncommitted, underdeveloped countries find societies that have traveled the road from underdevelopment to affluence. Industrialization by means of private initiative, based on private entrepreneurship, with the market as the guide and profit as the goal—this has been the itinerary, modified only toward the end of the road when an increasing economic role for the government seems to have become the order of the day. Whatever the shortcomings of this road may have been, whatever inequities may remain, there is no gainsaying that in Western Europe, in Australia, in New Zealand, in Canada, and—first and foremost—in the United States it has led to living standards for the majority of inhabitants beyond the fondest dreams of previous generations or of most people in the rest of the world today. Moreover, this phenomenal increase in economic well being has been accompanied by substantial advances in democracy and freedom. The abolition of slavery and of indentured servitude, universal suffrage, enhanced equality of opportunity irrespective of race or creed—these are but some of the characteristics of life in the West towards the end of the 1960's. Much still needs to be done to wipe out age-old economic and political inequities, but surely great progress has been made.

There are other societies which have taken a different road from underdevelopment to affluence. A crash industrialization program guided by a central plan, implemented by strictly enforced commands from above, and based on the social ownership of the means of production—this essentially has been the itinerary of the fourteen communist countries. Only very recently has this itinerary been modified in varying degrees in the Soviet Union and in most of the communist countries of Eastern Europe by the introduction of decentralization measures and of the use of techniques hitherto associated primarily with market economies. None of the fourteen has attained the living standards of the advanced industrialized nations of the West; but there is no gainsaying that the Communist world can boast of imposing economic achievements, accomplished in impressively short spans of time. Moreover, economic progress has recently been accompanied in the majority of the countries by substantial progress toward political and cultural liberalization: coercion, tyranny, and the ever-present fear of the secret police—once the primary tools to exact economic performance and political conformity—have largely given way to enhanced emphasis on material incentives and political persuasion; increased numbers of citizens participate in the decision making process; and relatively open discussion of many (though by no means all) issues is not only tolerated but invited.

In the two major camps in the world today, typified to some extent by the United States and the Soviet Union respectively, the uncommitted countries find two different models of industrialization and economic development. The Western system, originally based on a blueprint of a competitive free market economy, has matured almost everywhere into modified, progressive capitalism. The Soviet system, for a quarter of a century functioning as a highly centralized command economy, has now started to mature into a less centralized, somewhat more liberal, socialism. There is, however, a third giant among world powers, still weak as compared with the other two but evolving: Communist China. China offers the underdeveloped countries an example of a course of economic development, reminiscent of that followed by the Soviet Union during the 1930's. Rejecting both Western "imperialism" and Soviet "revisionism" China has taken a dogmatic stand in favor of a Stalinist-type command economy, and has contemptuously repudiated all economic, political, social, cultural, and ideological positions not directly promulgated by Mao Tse-tung. Be it clothing, music, or street names—if not "revolutionary" and symbolic of the "New China" they are condemned by the "cultural revolution." Though itself still an underdeveloped country, barely at the beginning of the road toward affluence, China has yet made remarkable and undeniable progress during the less than two decades of Mao's leadership. The diet of the average Chinese may still be meager and well below the minimum considered necessary in the West for the maintenance of health; but recurrent periods of mass starvation which often left hundreds of thousands dead appear to be a thing of the past. Living standards may still be pitifully low as compared with those of the more advanced nations, but for many years no Western observer has reported having seen even a single hungry child, a single barefoot man or woman, a single indigent sleeping in a city street, or a single beggar—quite a difference from the sight confronting the traveler to countries such as India. And in education and scientific achievements, China, though still in its early stages, has already taken important steps forward—has even become the fifth nation to have atomic weapons.

What road or roads toward economic development and political evolution will be chosen by that third of the human race that inhabits the uncommitted, underdeveloped parts of the world? Undoubtedly their choices will have not only great impacts upon their own futures but also great repercussions on economic and political developments throughout the rest of the world. No wonder that the United States, the Soviet Union, Communist China, and their respective allies vie for the alignment of these neutral countries! Surely, the social science student in the West, be his major interest in economics, political science, sociology, history, or related subjects, should gain an understanding of the various socio-economic-political models proffered to these countries for their consideration. These proposed models, these various roads from underdevelopment to affluence suggested to the uncommitted, underdeveloped countries are the topic of this book.

The West, and especially the United States, tends to emphasize the achievement of high living standards and of great degrees of political and cultural freedom as proof of the effectiveness of the Western road. Yet, underdeveloped countries are not advised to follow that road exactly as traveled by the industrial West. No Western scholar would propose that the underdeveloped countries reach their ambitious goals with the aid of such institutions as slave labor, child labor, indentured servitude, voting restricted to adult, white, property owning males, education limited to the children of those who can pay for it, etc. As is to be expected in a poly-centric society, there is today considerable disagreement about the precise road that should be taken. There is, for instance, substantial disagreement on such issues as the economic functions of government, the relative importance of foreign capital investments, the required emphasis on heavy industry, or the degree of universality to which one or another of the Western prescriptions is applicable under varying conditions. However, Western scholars seem in general agreed that the process of development is necessarily slow and laborious, and that endeavors to achieve substantial shortcuts are likely to prove disappointing.

The Soviet Union points with pride to her own economic accomplishments and the rapidity of her economic growth; yet the recommended road is not a precise replica either of that taken by the Soviet Union during her half century of existence. Collectivization of agricultural lands irrespective of cost and of peasant readiness to accept it, total economic planning from the center, Stalinist political repressions—these are no longer part of the recipe. Contrary to the West, there is an official Party line on most issues connected with policies advocated for the underdeveloped countries, and disagreement with that Party line is strongly discouraged, to put it mildly. However, communist ideology is no longer as monolithic as it used to be. There is at least a certain degree of disagreement among the Party lines of some of the countries on such issues as the necessity of so-called "wars of national liberation," the desirability of nationalist, non-communist governments as stepping stones on the road towards socialism, or the functions of the Communist Party in newly independent, non-communist countries. Such disagreements are more than simply a matter of degree between the Soviet Union on the one side and China (and her only faithful ally, Albania) on the other. While the United States and the Soviet Union recommend models of development different in varying degrees from their own, China—still young, more dogmatic, and more rigid—has hitherto shown little inclination for constructive self-criticism or for compromise. China's prescription for one and all is, in essence: "Do as we have done!"

The first chapter of the book is devoted to an analysis of the crucial problem of overpopulation, often referred to in common parlance as "the population explosion." The views of a Western scholar are confronted with those of Soviet social scientists who, interestingly enough, are not in complete agreement on the issue.

Chapter II consists of representative (and somewhat divergent) Western endeavors to outline the laborious path from underdevelopment to affluence. Chapters III and IV reflect respectively the official Soviet and Chinese views on the subject.

The search for the proper way of reaching high standards of economic performance has led most of the recently emerging nations to choose a path that corresponds to a mixture of private and government planning and of private and social ownership of the means of production. To enable the student to gain a rudimentary understanding of the efforts of some of these countries, five have been chosen for discussion in an appendix. These five—Japan, India, Israel, Egypt, and Yugoslavia—are at different stages in their economic development and show great variations in their political and social institutions. Some tend to lean more toward the Western models, others toward those proposed by the adherents to Marxism-Leninism. One, Yugoslavia, officially proclaims to be embarked on its "own road to [Marxist] socialism." Whether the divergence of that country's economic and political institutions from those of the other communist countries is merely one of degree, or whether the Yugoslav system is tantamount to a fundamentally and basically different socio-economic-political structure, is a question of dispute.

The co-editors would like to take this opportunity to express their sincere appreciation to all the authors, publishers, and agencies who have granted permission for material to be reproduced in this book.

H. G. S.
J. S. P.

CONTENTS

Preface   v

Chapter 1   *POPULATION PRESSURE AND*
UNDERDEVELOPMENT: WESTERN AND SOVIET
VIEWS   1

1. The Population Explosion and the Underdeveloped
    Countries: Past Effects and Prospective Dangers.
    A Western View
    ROY D. LAIRD   5

2. Yesterday, Today, Tomorrow: A Thirst for Perspective.
    A Soviet View
    VLADIMIR KELLER   14

3. Overpopulation Does not Threaten our Planet.
    A Soviet View
    STANISLAV STRUMILIN   17

4. Rapid Economic Development, Profound Social
    Transformation, and a Scientific Population Policy.
    A Soviet View
    ARAB OGLY   20

5. Population Problems in Developing Countries.
    A Soviet View
    V. GUZEVATY   25

    Suggested Reading   31

Chapter 2   *FROM UNDERDEVELOPMENT TO*
AFFLUENCE: WESTERN VIEWS   33

1. The Struggle for Economic Development in Our Time
    ROBERT L. HEILBRONER   37

2. Rich Lands, Poor Lands, and the Widening Gap
    GUNNAR MYRDAL   45

3. What Is the Third World?
    IRVING LOUIS HOROWITZ   49

4. Stages of Economic Growth
    W. W. ROSTOW   60

5. There Are No Simple Answers
   ROBERT E. BALDWIN   67

6. Bread and Freedom: The Pluralistic Approach
   WILLIAM McCORD   71

Appendix to Chapter 2: Selected Economic Data for the Less
   Developed Countries.   91

   Suggested Reading   106

Chapter 3   FROM UNDERDEVELOPMENT TO
AFFLUENCE: SOVIET VIEWS   107

1. The Changing Soviet Perception of the Development
   Process in Underdeveloped Countries. A Western
   Non-Marxist Analysis
   DONALD S. CARLISLE   112

2. The Recent Soviet Reassessment of Developments in the
   Third World. A Western Non-Marxist Analysis
   ROGER E. KANET   132

3. The Breakup of the Colonial System
   K. BRUTENTS   143

4. What Disarmament Will Give to Developing Countries
   K. IVANOV and B. BATSANOV   145

5. They Will Not Choose the Capitalist Path
   O. V. KUUSINEN and OTHERS   152

6. The Non-Capitalist Way of Development
   V. YEGOROV and I. PRONICHEV   153

7. Vital Problems of Non-Capitalist Development
   R. AVAKOV and OTHERS   156

8. The Transition to Socialism
   R. AVAKOV, I. PRONICHEV, and OTHERS   173

9. The Developing Countries Can Count on Aid and
   Assistance From the Socialist Camp.
   A. TKACHENKO   176

   Suggested Reading   181

Chapter 4   *FROM UNDERDEVELOPMENT TO*
AFFLUENCE: CHINESE VIEWS   183

1. China's Prescription for Economic Growth
        JAN S. PRYBYLA   183

2. What Are the Fundamental Contradictions in the
    Contemporary World?   190

3. Contradictions in the Contemporary World Are
    Concentrated in Asia, Africa, and Latin America: The
    Storm Centers of World Revolution   192

4. First Task for Peoples of Asia, Africa, and Latin America:
    National-Democratic Struggle Against Imperialism,
    Colonialism, and Neocolonialism   195

5. The Chinese Revolution Points the Way to the Emancipation
    of Other Asian as Well as African and Latin American
    Countries   197

6. Liberation From Colonialism (National Democratic
    Revolution) on the Chinese Model Means People's Liberation
    Wars Waged in the Countryside by Peasant Guerrilla Armies
    Under the Leaderships of the Communists   202

7. The Economic Program of the National Democratic
    (New Democratic) Revolution   211

8. The Peasant Question and Agricultural Development Are
    Basic to Socialist Construction Once the National
    Democratic Revolution Is Completed   213

9. The People's Communes Are China's Contribution to the
    Question of Transition From Collective Ownership to
    Ownership by the Whole People—An Important Step in
    the Direction of Full Communism   218

10. Self-Reliance Based on Correct Thought Is the Way to
    National Liberation and Socialist Development   223

11. Underdeveloped Countries and Foreign Economic Aid
    From Capitalist Countries   225

12. Even During the Period of Socialist Construction
    Class Struggles Continue   228

13. Politics Must Be Put in Command of Economics and
    All Other Work   235

14. Correct Leadership Is Important at All Stages of the
    Revolution   239

15. Those Who Oppose China's Prescription for National
    Liberation and Socialist Development are Lackeys of
    Imperialism. All Opposition Must Be Silenced   243

Appendix to Chapter 4   247

1. China: A Revolution for Export.   247

2. War and Revolution
   PAUL M. SWEEZY and LEO HUBERMAN   255

   Suggested Reading   264

*APPENDIX: CASE STUDIES OF FIVE
DEVELOPING COUNTRIES*   265

Japan   268

1. The Economic Development of Japan
   WILLIAM W. LOCKWOOD   269

2. Japan's Economic Expansion: Achievements and Prospects
   G. C. ALLEN   287

3. Japan's Economic Cooperation With the Developing
   Countries
   SHIGEO HORIE   300

   Suggested Reading   303

India   304

1. India's Painful Experiment
   DILIP MUKERJEE   305

2. Politicians, Bureaucrats, and Development in India
   WAYNE WILCOX   315

3. Recent Economic Experience in India and Communist
   China: Another Interpretation
   SIDNEY KLEIN, with excerpts
   from a discussion by
   WILFRED MALENBAUM   324

   Suggested Reading   336

Contents

Israel   337

1. The Israeli Road From Underdevelopment to Affluence
     LEONARD J. FEIN   338

    Suggested Reading   365

Egypt   366

1. Egypt: The Way Out of Poverty
     PETER MANSFIELD   367

2. Egypt's Economy Analyzed
     WILLY LINDER   408

    Suggested Reading   416

Yugoslavia   417

1. Economic Development and Planning in Yugoslavia
     MILOS SAMARDZIJA   419

2. Constitutional Socialism in Yugoslavia
     IVAN MAKSIMOVIĆ   429

    Suggested Reading   441

Chapter *1*

Population Pressure and Underdevelopment

WESTERN AND SOVIET VIEWS

One hundred seventy years ago, a British political economist, Thomas Robert Malthus,[1] wrote a book (*Essay on the Principles of Population, 1789*) in which he painted a dismal picture of mankind's future. Because of a universal and unalterable propensity of the world's population to outrun the world's food supply, he contended, the broad masses of people would forever be condemned to languish at a bare minimum of existence. Diseases, famines, wars—positive checks, as Malthus called them—would periodically kill off surplus population. No redistribution of wealth, no reform of the economic system, no advance in technology could ever change this fundamental truth. Increases in food production could at best lead to temporary improvements in overall living standards, for they would only enable more offspring to survive which in turn would again reduce the masses to the subsistence level. Malthus did talk about the possibility of "preventive checks" (such as late marriage and abstention) which would reduce birth rates instead of increasing death rates;[2] but he had little faith that people would ever be sensible or steadfast enough to employ these to an extent adequate to cope with the problem.

The wealthy classes wholeheartedly welcomed Malthus's thesis, for here was a theory which absolved them from all guilt for the misery of Eng-

[1] Reverend Thomas Robert Malthus (1766-1834) was an early member of the classical school of economic thought. Founded by Adam Smith (1723-1790), this school advocated a competitive free enterprise society based on the principle of laissez-faire, the "obvious and simple system of natural liberty."

[2] For religious reasons, Malthus refrained from advocating birth control, but most modern-day neo-Malthusians base their hopes on it.

1

land's masses. It wasn't the conversion of farms into grazing land for sheep, it wasn't the replacement of workers by machinery, it wasn't profit or exploitation that could be blamed for ubiquitous poverty. England's common people were poor simply because there were too many of them—too many job seekers for the number of jobs available, too many mouths for the amount of food society could provide. Were the middle and upper classes to heed proposed schemes for sharing wealth and income, they could only reduce their own living standards to a common level of poverty, without any long-run benefit to the lower classes.

Malthus was apparently wrong with respect to his predicted positive correlation between wealth (and especially food supplies) and population. As countries industrialized and living standards improved, birth rates showed declining tendencies almost everywhere.[3] There is an almost universal tendency for urban population to grow more slowly than rural, and the poorest seem to spawn the most children. But while, at least for the time being, there appears to be no danger of the population outrunning the food supply in the wealthier countries, much of the world still lives under the shadow of Malthus.

The world's population as a whole is presently increasing at the net rate of 180,000 every twenty-four hours, and birth rates in the underdeveloped countries—those least able to feed their growing populations—are twice those of the industrialized nations.[4] In much of Asia, and in most of Africa and Latin America, hundreds of millions of woefully wretched people—illiterate, undernourished, and destitute—are struggling desperately to keep food production ahead of increases in their numbers.

In the Western world, a substantial number of scholars concerned with the problems of underdevelopment see in the predictions of Malthus the real specter, the sword of Damocles that hangs by a hair over the inhabitants of the underdeveloped countries. Rapid population growth tends to outrun food producing capacities, leading to semistarvation conditions; semistarvation conditions make it imperative that hands be kept on the land; and as long as most hands are kept on the land, economic growth is impeded, labor productivity remains low, economic growth fails to surge ahead of population increases, and semistarvation conditions persist. Unable to divert people from the farm to the city, unable even to dispense with the labor of children so that they may go to school to learn the ways and methods of modern society, the future looks bleak for the underdeveloped countries.

Although not all Western scholars subscribe to the idea that the "pop-

---

[3] This tendency for birth rates to decline may be reversed after a nation has reached very high living standards. In the United States, in any case, such a reversal has taken place, but it is probably too early to draw long-run and universal conclusions.

[4] 40 per 1,000 per year, as compared with 20 per 1,000. See "Births Outracing World's Food Production," *New York Times,* January 20, 1967.

ulation explosion" represents such a menacing portent, the view is surely widespread and important enough to merit consideration in a book such as this. It is therefore given a hearing, before the Western, Soviet, and Chinese models for the development of the "Third World" are presented. In the first selection, Roy Laird makes a strong case for the predominance of population pressure and the corresponding food shortages among the problems facing the underdeveloped countries and the world. He sees the communist exploitation of peasant discontent as the major dynamic of world affairs since 1917, and he warns the West of dire consequences unless a way is found to cope with the problem.

Marx, Engels, and Lenin[5] denied the existence of a universal, invariable law of population; they treated excess population and subsistence-level living standards not as perennial components of life on earth, but as inevitable adjuncts of capitalist modes of production and distribution. Marx and Engels referred to the Malthusian doctrine as a "vile, low, loathsome mockery of nature and of mankind," and Lenin criticized advocates of preventive checks "who would like to instill in the proletariat the false idea that workers can better their status under capitalism by curtailing the size of their families."[6] Not an official birth control policy, but increased output while on a non-capitalist path of development—this is, then, the fundamental recipe for the solution of population problems. Moreover, orthodox Marxist-Leninists point to historic evidence that even under capitalism increasing living standards have been accompanied not by increasing, but by diminishing, birth rates; and they express their conviction that under socialism a healthy relationship between population growth and growth in production will establish itself of its own accord.

From August 30 to September 10, 1965, a World Population Conference was held in Belgrade, Yugoslavia. While still endorsing the official Marxist-Leninist position on the matter, several Soviet social scientists declared that the population problem of underdeveloped countries was quite real, at least in its present context. Ever since the conference, the issue has been discussed openly and frankly in the Soviet Union. In December, 1965, for instance, K. Kolganov, a Senior Scientific Worker at the Institute of Economics of the U.S.S.R. Academy of Sciences, expressed his view that "the world's rapid population growth engenders many problems," and he

[5] Karl Marx (1818-1883), German-born economist and philosopher, was the first to expound the ideology of present-day communism. Friedrich Engels (1820-1895), son of a wealthy British textile manufacturer, was Marx's lifelong friend and collaborator; he co-authored *The Communist Manifesto,* and after Marx's death he edited the second and third volumes of Marx's major scientific work, *Das Kapital (Capital).* V. I. Lenin (born Vladimir Ilyich Ulyanov, 1870-1924) led the 1917 October Revolution in Russia against Kerensky's moderate provisional government, and became the first premier and uncontested head of the new Soviet state.

[6] Cited by Peter Podyachikh, Deputy Chief of the Central Statistical Administration in Moscow, in *Literaturnaya gazeta,* January 13, 1966.

charged that only "a short while ago the accusation of being guilty of Malthusianism made it difficult to analyze in a calm and scientific manner one of the present day's urgent questions, namely the population problem."[7]

The first two Soviet selections, by Vladimir Keler and Stanislav Strumilin, represent the orthodox Marxist-Leninist position: the former emphasizing that the world could easily support ten times its present population; the latter (written a full nine months after the debate had been started at the World Population Conference), that population growth will automatically decline as socialist society advances. The last two Soviet selections, by Arab Ogly and V. Guzevaty, represent the new approach. While still adhering to the orthodox view that the population problem is socioeconomic and not biological in nature and that economic and political solutions must therefore be given priority above all others, these authors nevertheless see the problem as a serious one and advocate birth control. Ogly emphasizes that rapid population increases would be undesirable, even if accompanied by corresponding increases in output, since such population increases would necessarily be achieved at the expense of rapidly rising living standards. Guzevaty's conclusion that population pressure forces young, underdeveloped nations to turn to capitalist countries for help, thereby strengthening the position of the "imperialist states" and the "reactionary forces" within the recipient countries, is interesting because it is in direct contradiction to Laird's view that the population explosion plays into the hands of the forces of world communism.

The views expressed in the latter two Soviet selections do not amount to an about-face; they represent, rather, a slow and cautious shift in emphasis. Should the Soviet government decide to alter its approach to the population problem, policy changes would probably be introduced gradually. After all, as one American expert recently explained, "The United States government spent several years evolving a new policy on this very question. It would be unrealistic to expect the Soviet Union to change more rapidly on a question with such deep ideological implications for them."[8]

---

[7] *Literaturnaya gazeta,* December 25, 1965. By mid-1967, Soviet authors felt free to publish statements such as the following by Isaac Asimov which appeared in the May 1, 1967, issue of *Literaturnaya gazeta,* p. 11: "Perhaps by 1990, governments in all countries will have taken stringent measures to control the birthrate. If they succeed in stopping the enormous population growth . . . let us hope the writers of 1990 will be able to make more cheerful predictions for the world of 2000."

[8] From a paper prepared for the annual meeting of the Population Association of America, Cincinnati, Ohio, April 28-29, 1967, by James W. Brackett of the Foreign Demographic Analysis Division, U.S. Bureau of the Census.

1. *The Population Explosion and the Underdeveloped Countries: Past Effects and Prospective Dangers. A Western View*

ROY D. LAIRD

A July 12, 1965, press account of a U.S. A.I.D. (Agency for International Development) study indicates that some "70 percent of children in less developed countries were undernourished or malnourished . . . [And] about 50 percent of all children up to 6 years old [in these countries] . . . were labeled . . . 'seriously malnourished.' "[1] This human tragedy is deepening, for in recent years, the growth rate of population in the developing nations has outstripped the growth rate of food supplies. Moreover, the people in these nations comprise some seventy percent of the total world population.[2] The assumption of this study is that on humanitarian grounds the crisis in food production as related to the population explosion is, and will continue to be for the foreseeable future, mankind's greatest problem. The thesis which the material that follows will support is that from a pragmatic viewpoint the world crisis (which exhibits many elements of a revolution) may well have become the single most important factor determining the course of international relations, including relations among the major powers.

Whatever the proper place may be for hunger and peasant unrest on a spectrum of factors that determine contemporary international politics, there is reason to conclude that only since World War II has this factor challenged such traditionally recognized forces as nationalism and power politics as a major cause of conflict and accommodation among the major world powers. Therefore, not only has the post-World War II scene produced a new array of super-powers (the triangle of the United States, the

From Roy D. Laird, "The Triangle and the Agrarian Revolution," in Jan S. Prybyla (Ed.), *The Triangle of Power, Conflict and Accommodation: The United States, The Soviet Union and Communist China,* Papers presented at a Conference on Controversies in American Society, held at The Pennsylvania State University, November 1966. The Pennsylvania State University Center for Continuing Liberal Education, Slavic and Soviet Languages and Area Center, 1967. Reprinted by permission of the author and the publisher.

[1] *Associated Press.*

[2] *Third World Food Survey,* Freedom from Hunger Campaign, Rome, Italy: Food and Agriculture Organization of the United Nations, Basic No. 11 Study, 1963, p. 24.

Soviet Union, and Mainland China) but the array of factors that govern power relationships has changed as well.

Mass hunger is not new. The ancestors of today's inhabitants of Asia, Latin America, and Africa have long known recurring hunger and famine. However, mass starvation largely has disappeared from Europe and North America in the present century (Stalin's man-made famine in Russia during the 1930's was an exception). Thus, the absolute difference between the persistent hunger of large numbers of peoples in the developing world and the nutritional well being of peoples of the industrialized nations is a relatively recent phenomenon. In addition, the technical feasibility of transporting massive quantities of food to starving nations is also a recent development. Perhaps most important, for present purposes, has been the very recent, very rapid growth among the have-not peoples of a self awareness that their plight is unjust. Modern technology not only has produced the enormous gap between the living standards of the have and have-not nations, but it also has evolved communications systems that tie all of mankind together, systems which surely have been key to stimulating the growth of the "revolution in rising expectations" at an epidemic rate. Even though they may remain predominantly illiterate, the hungry of the world can no longer accept their suffering as just nature or a God-ordained inevitability, when at the least they have been exposed to local leaders who have seen or heard of Western standards.

Before we explore the impact of the food crisis upon international relations, and particularly the relations among the three major powers, the nature of the crisis itself deserves further examination.

For the world as a whole (excluding Mainland China, because of a lack of available statistics), the United Nations Food and Agricultural Organization (FAO) reports that the "combined production index for agriculture, fisheries and forestry . . . shows clearly how since about the middle of the [1950-59] decade there has been no further gain in production in relation to populations, and thus no margin for better levels of living."[3] (See Table 1.) Indices for food products alone in the developing countries of Latin America, Far East (excluding Mainland China), Near East, and Africa show a steady decline in recent years in the per capita production of food. With an average of 1952/53–1956/57 = 100, a peak index of 104 was reached in 1959/60 with a decline to 103 in 1963/64, and a preliminary estimate of 101 for 1964/65; these numbers can be contrasted with the index number of 102 for the average of the pre-World War II years.[4] In sum, therefore, although agricultural production has continued to rise in these regions of the world, "this advantage has been entirely

---

[3] *The State of Food and Agriculture 1965*, Rome, Italy: Food and Agriculture Organization of the United Nations, 1965, p. inside front cover.
[4] *Ibid.*, p. 15.

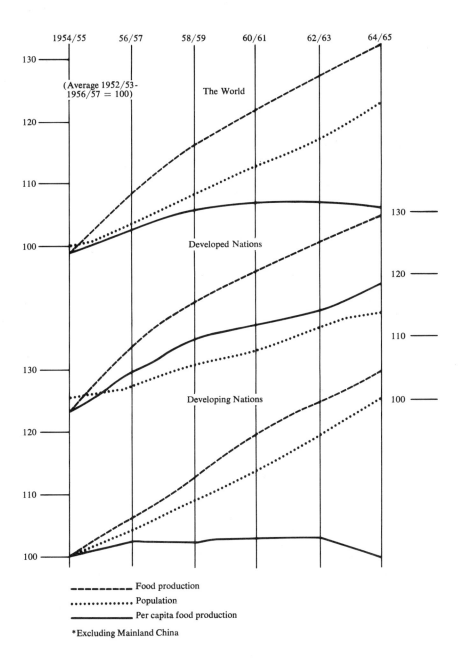

Adapted from the *State of Food and Agriculture 1965* FAO, 1965, pp. 14, 15, 17, and cover page.

Figure 1. Food vs. Population: 1954–1964*

wiped out by their much more rapid population growth."[5] Indeed, estimates of future population expansion in the developing nations imply a rate of growth between now and 1980 that is roughly double that of the industrialized states.[6] A United Nations study of the population outburst in Asia and the Far East notes that "The sheer bulk of the population in the . . . region . . . which (already) holds just over half of humanity in less than one-eighth of the earth's land area—confronts it with problems of unparalleled proportions."[7] Latin America, which many might assume to be least hurt by the population explosion, actually is one of the worst off regions of the world. Dr. Alberto Lleras Camargo, former president of Columbia, testified in 1965 before a United States Senate subcommittee that "Latin America is breeding misery, revolutionary pressures, famine and many other potentially disastrous problems in proportions that exceed our imagination even in the age of thermonuclear war."[8] Similarly, the Swedish economist, Professor Gunnar Myrdal, has argued that "the world is moving swiftly toward something more than crisis—a world calamity."[9]

Even among the three major world powers, only the United States is in a secure position in the production of food. China, with a population of some 700,000,000, has one of the world's most serious agricultural problems. Although Russia under the Tsars was a grain exporting nation, the Soviet Union's nutritional standards have remained below the level of Western standards, and in recent years she has needed to import large quantities of grain. A projection of future needs published by this author, indicates that in spite of encouraging economic reforms in recent years, the U.S.S.R. can be expected to continue to import grains for the foreseeable future.[10]

While the failure to produce adequate quantities of food is by far the most serious aspect of the world's human problem, in a sense, hunger is only the major symptom of a much broader crisis. The average North American and Western European is an urban resident who has not only an adequate diet, but decent housing, labor-saving appliances, and good transportation (often his own car), and he is literate. In contrast, the average citizen of that seventy percent of mankind that live in the developing nations is a peasant with an inadequate diet, earth for the floor in his hut, and at best burros or oxen to help till his fields and provide some transportation, and he is illiterate. More than this, the average peasant's fields probably are not his own, and, most of all, even with his best efforts they are too tiny to support him and his family decently. Thus, under existing political and

[5] *Ibid.,* p. 14.
[6] *Some Important Issues in Foreign Aid,* Committee on Foreign Relations, United States Senate, Washington: U.S. Government Printing Office, August 4, 1966, p. 45.
[7] *Associated Press,* April 1, 1965.
[8] *Associated Press,* July 12, 1965.
[9] *Some Important Issues in Foreign Aid, op. cit.,* p. 45.
[10] "Soviet Agricultural Output in 1980: An Appraisal," *Ost Europa Wirtschaft,* 1965, No. 2 (July), pp. 90-104.

economic conditions, the majority of mankind is without even the means for hope in the improvement of their and their children's future. Even Mexico, the most advanced of the Latin American nations, and a nation justly proud of the land reform of the 1930's, continues to have a most serious agricultural problem. During the past summer this author conducted a survey in several parts of rural Mexico. Widespread rural poverty is still serious. The failure of continuing agricultural advances to keep up with rising peasant expectations could become explosive. Dedicated governmental officials trained in agriculture and working in the farming regions are seriously concerned over the need for faster advance. Indeed, one key agricultural official emphatically agreed that I correctly summarized much of what he had been saying with the following question: "You mean that the Mexican government must continue to run like Hell, just to keep ahead of serious rural unrest that could well precipitate another revolution?"

Although communism has made little headway in Mexico, hunger and agrarian unrest in other underdeveloped nations have provided the media in which communist systems have been able to come to life during the twentieth century. The British writer David Mitrany was the first to describe vividly this causal relationship when he wrote the following in 1951:

The startling fact is that communism has only come to power [by revolution] where by all Marxist tenets it might have been least expected that it could. In every instance, from 1917 in Russia to 1949 in China, Communism has ridden to victory on the back of disaffected peasantries; in no instance has it come near to victory in industrialized "proletarian" countries. So far it has always been a "proletarian" revolution without a proletariat; a matter of Communist management of peasant discontent.[11]

Communist successful exploitation of agrarian revolutionary situations has continued since 1949. Castro's Cuba fits the general pattern. Whatever the changed character of the war in Vietnam, the early widespread support of the revolt in rural South Vietnam came from "disaffected peasantries" who may not have known the difference between Karl Marx and Charles de Gaulle, but who were receptive to a Marxist-Leninist inspired leadership that convincingly promised agrarian revolution.[12] To date, leadership in the

---

[11] *Marx Against the Peasant,* Chapel Hill: The University of North Carolina Press, 1951, pp. 205-206.

[12] Agrarian revolution is used herein to describe a view of the state of unrest in the developing nations. What needs to be done in response goes much further than just land reform (as implied by many observers). This point is brilliantly presented by Professor T. Lynn Smith in the introduction to the book he has edited, *Agrarian Reform in Latin America,* New York: Alfred A. Knopf, 1965. On page 46 Professor Smith outlines the three principal objectives of agrarian reform:

(1) A genuine agrarian reform should effect substantial improvement in the abilities, capacities, and performances of those who cultivate the land to bring them more in line with human potentialities.

(2) Any worthwhile agrarian reform should result in a substantial increase in

major Western powers has failed to answer this communist challenge. Moreover, within the developing nations themselves, local leadership also has failed, with such rare exceptions as Mexico, the Philippines, and, ironically, Formosa—after Chiang had learned his lesson and had been driven from the mainland. Therefore, as of now, although communist leaders often fail, their successes have been notable, and they have retained a virtual monopoly among those bidding for leadership in the developing nations by convincingly promising genuine agrarian reform.

One of Lenin's two major revisions of Marxism was to point to the peasants in the colonies existing during the early part of the present century as major sources of revolutionary ferment.[13] Therefore, Lenin must be credited with perceiving the beginnings of a phenomenon that constitutes a subthesis of this paper. The agrarian revolution of the twentieth century is having a cumulative impact on political and social life that in the end will equal the changes wrought by the industrial revolution during the nineteenth century. In its essence, the industrial revolution altered the fundamental manufacturing process that, in turn, produced a profound sociopolitical change in urban society. Of course, the industrial revolution also has had an enormous and continuing impact upon rural production and populations as well, but as important as its gifts of modern machines and chemical aids have been, in most realms of agriculture, the production process has not changed fundamentally. All over the world, far too many city born and educated economists and public leaders continue to speak and make decisions based upon expectations in agricultural production that are in contradiction to this truth. As Brewster and Wunderlich of the Agricultural Research Service, United States Department of Agriculture have recorded, "With minor exceptions of certain specialized poultry and livestock operations, a shift to machine farming leaves relatively undisturbed the sequential pattern of operations that has prevailed in farming since the domestication of plants and animals." These authors continue, "in farming, the 'Industrial Revolution' is merely a spectacular change in the gadgets with which operations are performed, whereas in industry it is a further revolution in the sequence of productive operations."[14] The meaning of this reality for any hoped for increase in food production is profound.

---

the amount of agricultural and livestock products secured from a given amount of land and the efforts of those who work it.

(3) A real agrarian reform should result in the replacement of wasteful, inefficient, demeaning, and stultifying ways of producing agricultural and livestock products by methods of agriculture that are efficient, dignifying, or ennobling to those engaged in agriculture and stock-raising.

[13] The other major revision was the leadership role Lenin assigned to the Party. For an excellent discussion of Leninism see Alfred G. Meyer, *Leninism,* Cambridge, Massachusetts: Harvard University Press, 1957.

[14] John M. Brewster and Gene Wunderlich, "Farm Size, Capital and Tenure Requirements," *Adjustments in Agriculture—a National Basebook,* Carlton F. Christian (ed.), Iowa University Press, Ames, Iowa, 1961, p. 207.

Borrowing from Malthus, the industrial revolution has resulted in a rate of increase in urban factory output that is a multiple of the rate of increase in the output of food, independent of the stage of development. Thus, for every increase of agricultural product in the developed countries from 1950 through 1963 there is an index of a 2.56 increase in industrial product. The ratio in the developing countries for the same period was a very similar 1-2.78. However, during this period an index of the absolute growth of the industrial product in the developed countries is only 1.82 times as contrasted with a growth in the developing countries of 2.28 times. Yet indices of the absolute agricultural product in the developed nations grew by only 1.32 times and in the developing countries a strikingly similar growth of only 1.46 times occurred. If the United States had not imposed a relative holdback on agricultural production advance during the period, these indices undoubtedly would be even closer together.

From the above, one sees that regardless of the level of development, the rate of industrial growth has been more than two and a half times that of agriculture in recent years. More than this, while many factors may have been responsible for the relative similarity of rate of agricultural growth in the two world regions, neither the rate of growth nor the level of industrial development seems to have been a significant factor in agricultural growth.[15]

With the exception of the fortunate regions of the world where past history has been kind to the rural populations, agriculture has long needed the revolution that now seems to be upon it. Moreover, the introduction into agriculture of the valuable aids of the industrial revolution is not enough in itself. Most developing nations can be characterized as being land poor and labor rich. Most of all they need increased yields from the soil. Therefore, beyond humanitarian considerations, pragmatic demands arising from the particular character of agricultural production are such that critical shortcomings in education, systems of land tenure, and related factors of rural sociology comprise the most serious impediment to output increases. Profound social and administrative changes must come first, or at least simultaneously, if the now predominantly illiterate and largely unorganized peasants in the developing nations are efficiently to exploit the new scientific and technical aids to production.

Both the enormity and the character of the problems outlined above have been described by previous observers, but rarely the two together. Moreover, although the standard and vitally important influences upon international affairs are recited repeatedly (e.g., the rise and fall of states as powers, conflicts of nationalisms, and the challenge of the new communist

---

[15] These calculations are based upon United Nations "Index Numbers of Gross Domestic Product by Industrial Origin, World Excluding USSR and Eastern Europe." The developed countries include "North America, Europe, Oceania, together with Japan and South Africa." The developing countries include "Latin America, Asia and the Far East (except Japan), and the Middle East and Africa (except South Africa)." See, *Statistical Yearbook, 1965,* United Nations, New York, 1966, pp. 27, 31.

states), only communists seem to have recognized fully that peasant needs and aspirations may be the most important force shaping world events. Ironically, the widespread failure of Western students of politics to recognize such a possibility contradicts three important axioms of political science.

1. Basic economic needs are the primary determinants of political policies.
2. International politics are primarily an extension of domestic interests on the world scene.
3. If the basic wants and needs of society's masses are continually ignored, a revolutionary situation is produced.

Traditionally the urban half of the world (48% in 1960)[16] has seemed to be the dynamic center of human life and direction, for the cities possess the great share of mankind's wealth. But the food of the world is controlled by the farmers, and as Lenin learned in 1921, peasant majorities are capable of dictating policy. To have asserted, at the beginning of the present century, that the long-run needs and interests of the world's peasants would become the most important factor determining international affairs would have seemed absurd; this, however, would have been before modern communications and transport technology had reduced the worlds' distances to hours and economic exchanges had made the world a highly interdependent unit. What has been said above, then, is the major evidence supporting the conclusion implicit in the title of this piece. The mass of the world's rural poor collectively comprise an interest group whose indirect pressures may well be the major force determining the course of world affairs. More specifically, the pressures and responses of this interest group are the key force determining the course of Soviet, Chinese, and United States foreign policies. A review of some of the major events of twentieth century history will support this conclusion.

1. *Communist exploitation of peasant discontent has constituted the major dynamic of world affairs since 1917.* While the Westerner tends to view World Wars I and II as the most important events of the century, these momentous events largely marked the end of an era. In contrast, the strange alliance between communism and peasant disaffection, that started in 1917, has continued to spread, and its impact has been increasingly felt all over the world.

2. *Ironically, peasant agricultural problems continue to be the most serious area of concern within China and the U.S.S.R.* Lenin's New Economic Policy of 1921 ("one step backwards for two steps forward"), primarily granted concessions to the peasants' interests, largely in order to forestall the possibility of another revolt. Stalin's forced collectivization of

---

[16] The agricultural population of the world for 1960 was expressed as 52%. See, *Production Yearbook 1965,* Food and Agriculture Organization of the United Nations, Rome, Italy, 1966, p. 20.

the 1930's ("a revolution from above") left both Khrushchev and his successors with one of the world's most inefficient agricultural systems. In China, the primary cause of the enormous failure of the 1957-58 "Great Leap Forward" was peasant unadaptability to the agricultural communes.

3. *The communist-led Huk rebellion was succeeding in the Philippines until the government turned a serious ear to peasant wants and needs.*

4. *The origins of the Vietnam War are deeply rooted in peasant discontent.*

5. *There is widespread belief, both in the East and the West, that the eventual fate of predominantly peasant India could be decisive in world affairs.*

6. *The major key to the success of the Mexican revolution was an acceptable program of agrarian reform put through by a non-communist leadership.*

7. *Peasant support of Castro in the beginning, and their lack of support for the invading forces during the Bay of Pigs fiasco later, have been decisive factors influencing the recent fate of Cuba.*

8. *Soviet unwillingness and inability to give massive aid (particularly, food) to China may have been a major factor in precipitating the Sino-Soviet split.* The "split" is, of course, a highly complex affair involving conflicting nationalisms, ideological disputes, power conflicts, and leadership jealousies, but the provision of massive aid to China surely would have reduced greatly the pressures in the rift.

9. Finally, *the major clashes of arms between communist systems and the West have been in predominantly peasant Korea and predominantly peasant Vietnam.*

Although the focus of attention during the early post-World War II years centered upon such events as guerrilla action in Greece, the early Berlin crises, and the Hungarian uprising, the stage of confrontation has shifted elsewhere—e.g., Thailand, the Congo, Rhodesia, Laos, Vietnam, India-Pakistan, India-China, Indonesia, China, and Cuba. The major initiative in world affairs no longer rests in London, Paris, Berlin, Washington, or even Moscow. Capitals of largely peasant nations such as Peking, New Delhi, Saigon, and Havana increasingly have monopolized world attention, since it is largely the actions and reactions of their rural masses that have determined the tide of human events. True, Moscow and Washington retain the initiative of ending peaceful international relations through their ability to unleash their great clutches of nuclear destruction, but on most other counts, nations beset at the various stages of the rising tide of the agrarian revolution have left the major powers frantically searching for desirable courses of reaction to a new green uprising.

2. Yesterday, Today, Tomorrow: A Thirst for Perspective. A Soviet View

VLADIMIR KELER

. . . The Malthusians have grown much more active in recent years. They flourish statistics and estimates to prove their point. Sometimes their arguments seem to make sense.

Just what does an unbiased picture of population growth look like?

Of the 33 billion acres of the earth's surface (without Antarctica) only 3.2 billion acres, or less than 10 per cent, is now plowland, plantation and orchard. By developing virgin land, clearing and draining marsh-ridden areas, irrigating arid land, and making intelligent use of part of what is now jungle and forest, the cultivated portion could be very considerably enlarged.

How much? Opinions differ. The eminent economist Professor Fritz Baade, director of the Institute of Underdeveloped Countries in the Federal Republic of Germany, says by as much as 10 billion acres. Colin Clark of Great Britain thinks it could be 17 billion.

How densely is the earth populated?

If we take the 47 million square miles of the earth's surface that is suitable for habitation and divide it by the 3.3 billion people in the world, we obtain an average density of 70 persons per square mile. This is not much when you consider that population density in some European countries is 932 persons to the square mile. . . .

How many inhabitants will the world have by the year 2000? According to the latest UN demographic forecast (October 1965), approximately 7.4 billion. That means the ninth doubling will take place in the nineties, that is, in 30 years' time.

A table of the population increase would look something like this: (See Table 2.)

What after that? Will the rate of growth continue to increase as it did for the tens of thousands of years of human history?

Certainly not. A simple estimate shows that to be . . . [impossible].[1]

From *Soviet Life,* August 1966, pp. 62-63. Excerpts reprinted by permission of the Soviet Embassy, Washington, D.C.

[1] Brackets indicate words added by the editors for clarification. In this particular case, for instance, the word in the original translation was "incredible." That word was omitted (indicated by . . .) and replaced by "impossible" [Editors' note].

Table 2.

Year	Population (in millions)	Number of years it took to double
7000 B.C.	12.5	
4500 B.C.	25	2,500
2700 B.C.	50	1,800
1300 B.C.	100	1,400
0 A.D.	200	1,300
1200 A.D.	400	1,200
1800	800	600
1890	1,600	90
1963	3,200	73
1990's	6,400	30

Even if the rate remained what it is today, with the population doubling every 30 years, it would still be beyond reason. After doubling 17 more times the population would reach all of 416 trillion somewhere around the year 2500. There would not be enough standing room on the earth's surface, even including Antarctica. . . .

The typical population capacity of our stage is most likely from 35 to 40 billion. A lower figure is unreal. Mankind is not merely moving but flying toward that limit. To speak of a higher figure is premature. That is for the more distant future, the next stage.

True, some scholars believe that science has advanced to a high enough level to make the land feed very great numbers of people. Clark places the figure at 90 billion. The late Academician Abram Ioffe calculated that new growing methods would produce yields so high that an area the size of Moscow Region could feed the population of the whole world. Ioffe's estimates applied worldwide would give us the impressive figure of three trillion people.

Man does not live by bread alone, however. I do not believe we need to equate possible population capacity with possible grain harvest. It is quite likely that the better human society is organized, the more food will be planned per head of population. And not merely to give each person more and better food than his parents or grandparents had. The goal of all humanistic progress is abundance. Any food product that is good for man must be as abundant as air or water.

Relieving man of some of his material concerns would set his mind free to create and enjoy spiritual values.

In recent years scientists in various countries have been studying the population problem. The fact that some 500 papers were read at the Second World Population Conference in Belgrade in September 1965 shows how keen interest in the problem is. The conference was devoted, in great measure, to a search for solutions to the problem facing the underdeveloped countries. Many of the speakers expressed neo-Malthusian views, implying that population growth is a *biological* law and therefore extremely difficult to control.

That population growth is a problem goes without saying. It is, however, one of many problems, among them hunger, unemployment, widespread disease due to working conditions, the consequences of urbanization, illiteracy. These are not imaginary but very real problems, said Professor Boris Urlanis, prominent Soviet demographer. They may not exist at all in some countries, in some they are approaching, in some they are already knocking at the door, and in some they have already "entered" and are really making themselves felt. . . . [However,] these problems are based not on biological but on *socioeconomic* laws. Biological laws operate through socioeconomic laws that can exert a considerable influence on biological processes.

If, by applying common sense and scientific premises, we set a reasonable population limit in the contemporary world (until mankind takes off for other planets on a mass scale) at from 35 to 40 billion people, as we assume, or at some other figure, we could, by proper organization, painlessly regulate the increase in the numbers of people. "It is not a matter of 'planned quotas in child-bearing,' " says Professor Mikhail Kolganov. "The population can be regulated by a complex of measures. First, rational utilization of the earth's riches and an increase in soil fertility, crop yields and livestock productivity. The second important step is to replace agricultural raw materials with synthetic materials." Professor Kolganov also speaks of raising the cultural level of the population and making women more active participants in the life of their community and country. This is a precondition for conscious motherhood, when birth would no longer be merely a biological act, would always bring the parents joy, and would give every child the promise of a full, happy life. There are other steps as well, such as a natural drop in the birthrate through an increase in life expectancy. . . .

Mankind is increasing in numbers more and more rapidly. But this is not the acceleration of an avalanche rushing irresistibly toward disaster. The evolution of man bears a greater resemblance to the growth of a plant that gathers strength in winter and flowers rapidly in spring. The trunk grows while the crown spreads and thickens.

3. Overpopulation Does Not Threaten Our Planet. A Soviet View

STANISLAV STRUMILIN

Back in 1913, Vladimir Lenin wrote with full conviction that: ". . . we are unconditional enemies of Neo-Malthusianism, which suits only those unfeeling and egotistic petty-bourgeois couples who whisper in scared voices: 'God grant we may manage somehow, by ourselves. If we have no children, so much the better'." The overpopulation danger many scientists are now writing about is, in my opinion, not a real danger at all.

There is no need for us to meddle in intimate family relations, to advocate or forbid the use of certain tablets. Pills, after all, are hardly the means for solving major social problems. But the social theory of Neo-Malthusianism is inimical to us. Lenin was right when he wrote: "Class-conscious workers will always wage the most ruthless struggle against attempts to impose this reactionary and cowardly theory on the most progressive and strongest class in modern society, the class that is best prepared for great changes."

On the basis of existing birth rates, the world population is expected to double in the next 35 years. Is this so terrible? We know that on the average world population density did not exceed 24 persons per square kilometer by the beginning of 1965. But even suppose this figure were to double by the year 2000—there are after all quite a few countries which already have far exceeded this rate. Let us examine the conditions there.

For instance, by 1965 population density per square kilometer stood at 88 in France, 157 in the German Democratic Republic, 177 in Italy, 222 in Great Britain, 264 in Japan, and over 300 in the Netherlands and Belgium. Would a single one of these countries change places with any of the African republics where there are less than two persons per square kilometer? . . . There is no need to fear a high population density if this is accompanied by a sufficient rise in labor productivity and living standards. But first we must have a clear idea of the basic trends of population growth and the laws governing it.

From *Literaturnaya gazeta,* May 28, 1966. Published in English translation in *Reprints from the Soviet Press,* August 4, 1966, pp. 37-42, under the title "Does Overpopulation Threaten Our Planet?" Reprinted by permission of the publisher, Compass Publications, Inc.

In this respect the Malthusian principle, according to which the population has a tendency to grow in geometric progression while the means of subsistence grow only in arithmetic progression, should be weighed against another, the one established by Karl Marx in the first volume of "Capital." Marx assumed that each mode of production had its own special laws of population and formulated the following law as governing the increase of the working class: "Not only the number of births and deaths, but the absolute size of families stand in inverse proportion to wage levels, and therefore to the amount of means of subsistence of which the different categories of laborers dispose." But the laboring population becomes "a relative surplus population," with all the ensuing evils of mass unemployment, poverty and starvation, only under the definite conditions of growth of capitalist accumulations at the expense of cuts in the workers' means of subsistence. . . .

. . . "Malthusianism is a law of population peculiar to the capitalist mode of production," Marx asserted. In order to deprive such a law of all its force it is necessary to root out capitalism, which sustains it. This is most strikingly borne out by the experience of the USSR, where the birth rate has already dropped more than 2.5 times since 1913, following the extirpation of capitalism and a rise in living standards. The percentage drop in the birth rate is also very appreciable in the other socialist countries.

A noticeable drop in the birth rate has also been observed here and there in the capitalist countries during the past few years, following the successes scored by the labor movement and a rise in wages; but as a general rule, it has been much more modest there than in the socialist countries, notwithstanding the great profusion of pills and tablets so intensively advertised in the West. For instance, the birth rate has dropped by 37 per cent in Italy and by 22 per cent in Great Britain in the course of 52 years and by only 15 per cent in the United States over a period of 50 years; it has remained at the same level in France and, since 1950, has even continued to mount in the Federal German Republic. But the general trend everywhere is toward a drop in the birth rate, with a corresponding rise in living standards, in full conformity with Marx's formulation that the number of births stands in inverse proportion to wage levels. And if living standards continue to rise while the boundaries of socialism continue to expand, and the strength and power of the world labor movement grows, a further decrease in the birth rate will inevitably shortly face us with the converse problem. Given the existing birth rate, instead of a frightening *surplus* of hungry mouths, the ample *reproduction* of labor may become the real concern.

Heretofore, we had no such concern in our country simply because under conditions of socialism, the rapid drop in the birth rate was accompanied by a still more rapid drop in the death rate. But there is a limit under which the death rate cannot drop, and in the past decade we have already approached it. In fact, during the 1960-65 period the death rate even rose from 7.1 to 7.3 per 1,000 of the population. The birth rate, on the other hand has continued to drop. This alone clearly shows how credible are the conjectures of certain authors regarding the population doubling in the course of 35 years, especially if we fail to take into account the wholly realistic and natural tendency of the birth rate to drop while a steady rise in living standards is taking place, as observed in our country.

We reject the pretentious wisdom of Malthusian practice, for having once acknowledged the geometric rates of population growth to be an eternal and immutable law of nature, it is ridiculous to try to annul it by means of a couple of Malthusian prescriptions. As for conditions where slower population growth has now become a law, the law itself is hardly in need of such artificial bolstering. And these prescriptions are least of all opportune in the USSR where, in conditions of competition with capitalism, every worker is on record and a high birth rate is deliberately encouraged by the Party and the Government. Here mass birth control—a practice obviously detrimental to both the health instincts of motherhood and the interests of the country—though not prohibited, is hardly deserving of public approval.

Malthus' principle . . . is thus doubly refuted, not only because, with technological expansion, the means of subsistence are growing faster than the population, but also because in these conditions the population itself grows not in mounting geometric progression as Malthus asserted, but in *a progression known to be diminishing,* so that ultimately there will be no population increment. . . .

The groundlessness of Neo-Malthusianism is obvious. This ideology is inimical in principle to the social gains of our country. What is most needed to combat it is a knowledge of the actual tendencies of population growth in our day.

4. Rapid Economic Development, Profound Social Transformation, and a Scientific Population Policy. A Soviet View

ARAB OGLY

The rapid growth of our planet's population is a result of the so-called "demographic revolution" taking place in the world today. Scientists use this term to characterize the process of the population passing from one qualitative state to another.

This process of transition involves much more than just a redistribution of the population by age groups; it is also marked by an enormous absolute population growth. The "demographic revolution" obviously does not come about spontaneously and certainly not as a result of mathematical formulas and proportions, which merely serve to describe it. It is the result of profound economic and social changes initially caused by the industrial revolution. In our revolutionary time (revolutionary in every respect), it has already spread all over the world, as may be seen from the table below.

Table 3. Phases of "Demographic Revolution"

	Initial	Intermediate	Final
	Western Europe before 19th century; rest of the world until mid-20th century	Western Europe in 19th century; rest of the world in the mid-20th century	Britain, FRG, France, Sweden in mid-20th century[a]
Birth rate (per 1,000 pop.)	35–40	35–45	15–18
Death rate (per 1,000 pop.)	35–40	10–25	10–12
Life span	30 yrs. (approx.)	40–50 yrs.	70–73 yrs.
Population ratios:			
Children	40% (approx.) to	40%	22–25%
Old people	less than 7%	5–10%	16–18%

[a] The rest of the world has not yet reached this phase.

From *Literaturnaya gazeta,* June 11, 1966. Published in English translation in *Reprints from the Soviet Press,* August 4, 1966, pp. 43-48, under the title "Scientific Calculations or Spontaneity?" Reprinted by permission of the publisher, Compass Publications, Inc.

There arises the logical question: does the human race have at its disposal sufficient resources on our planet to provide the growing population in the coming decades with the means of subsistence? The overwhelming majority of scientists answer this question in the affirmative. Moreover, they cite data on the possibility of providing with food ten times more people than exist on the earth today.

Unfortunately, among the convinced optimists there are also men whose optimism reminds one of a telling episode from Lewis Carroll's "Alice in Wonderland," where the March Hare and the Mad Hatter work out an original solution to their food problem: every time they want to eat, they simply move on to the next seat at the dinner table. When Alice asks what they will do when they have finally made a full circle, the March Hare prefers to change the subject and talk of more pleasant matters.

However, our planet is not a dinner table groaning under an abundance of food, nor can we force the annual additions to the population to emigrate to a Wonder Planet. The economic and social problems of our time, caused by the rapid population expansion, can and must be solved in a real world. Even as the way is being paved to mastering space, the problem remains with us.

That is why it must be constanly borne in mind that all the possibilities usually suggested for multiplying the earth's food output no matter how well founded on trustworthy calculations are actually only potential resources.

While quite correct in their calculations that the earth is capable of feeding billions of people, scientists often forget to mention what vast amounts of labor, knowledge and capital this requires and what other goals the human race has to sacrifice in order to attain this. The hope to create as soon as possible, and for all people without exception, the conditions which man truly deserves cannot be equated with the desire merely to "support" the largest possible number of people. The first is the motto of humanism and the goal of communism, the second just a survival of feudal morality, harking back to a time when rulers prided themselves on having more subjects than their neighbors.

The capital investments which any society can afford annually are not just a spontaneous magnitude: they are restricted by annual accumulation; and in all cases accumulation means a deduction from current consumption. Depending on what they are intended for, these capital investments may be used either for increasing the per capita national income (economic investments) or for providing the extra added annual population with the wherewithal of life at already established levels (demographic investments). Society must make the choice: either double the prosperity of a more or less static population every twenty years or so, or else double the population and maintain the living standards at the original level. One cannot [have] one's cake and [eat] it too.

Of course, in practice neither economic nor demographic investments can or must be excluded altogether. Putting a stop to all population growth would lead to extremely negative economic and social consequences for all of society. That is why in each and every society an optimum combination of these investments may be said to exist for any given country, depending on the level of the living standards already attained, the population's age structure, growth rate, etc.

The problem of capital investments looms particularly acute in the developing countries where a billion and a half people are no longer willing to put up with hunger, poverty and illiteracy and where the population increase is fifty million people annually. The governments of these countries are continuously confronted by a financial puzzle: whether to invest funds in the enlargement of crop areas so as to keep up the per capita food production or to develop machine building at an accelerated rate; whether to set up the largest possible gainful employment facilities, even if primitively equipped, or to be primarily concerned with raising the productivity of labor, and reconciling themselves to unemployment.

Even very small children soon learn that, when they are offered *either* a piece of chocolate *or* a ball, they can't have both. But alas, some economists both in our country and abroad refuse—or rather pretend not to— understand this. As soon as they come up against this distressing dilemma, they do as the March Hare did: they just change the subject.

As soon argue the question of how many billion people—whether 50 or 100—the earth will be able to sustain by the end of the next century, considering our rate of scientific and technical progress! . . . It is all very well to produce impeccable figures to prove that, as longevity increases and the proportion of old people to the total of population grows, the birth rate index shows a tendency to diminish. But this in no way reduces the annual population increase in terms of absolute numbers. . . .

Perhaps the most popular of all arguments among some Soviet economists is the thesis that the birth rate is bound to diminish in the course of economic and social progress, urbanization, emancipation of women, etc. What sense is there then to worrying now about the solution of the problems involved in the so-called population explosion, if they are bound to resolve themselves and fall away in the future?

However, demographic problems are not dealt with in a vacuum regardless of human actions. Between economic and demographic processes there exists both a direct and an inverse relationship.

The basic difference between Neo-Malthusians and Marxists is not in the fact that the former propose measures for birth control, while the latter reject such measures unconditionally. The question is, what importance do both sides attach to these birth control measures. . . . Marxists . . . [believe] that there neither are nor can be demographic solutions to the problems confronting mankind—that any solution of these problems presupposes, first and foremost, rapid economic development and profound social transformations. Demographic measures are no panacea against economic difficulties and social evil. At the same time a scientific population policy, which in some cases would encourage the birth rate growth and promote in others substantiated birth control, may serve as an auxiliary means for considerably enhancing social progress.

Is it, however, permissible in principle for the state to interfere in spontaneous demographic processes? This will obviously depend on the aims pursued and the means resorted to. We cannot but denounce, for instance, the measures practiced in Nazi Germany to increase the birth rate —measures dictated by aggressive aims and meant to produce as much "cannon fodder" as possible and populate lands pirated from other nations. We must also resolutely reject all compulsory measures, no matter how good the intentions that prompted them.

The state has certainly no right to decide for its citizens how many children they are to have. But it may, in the light of both the current and the long-range needs of society and based on a reasonable correlation of private and public interests, determine the optimum population growth rate; and in conformity with it, it has the right to encourage the people's desire for larger or smaller numbers of children and help them realize their objective interests or get rid of prejudices; it can also put at their disposal the most adequate and safest means of birth control so that the actual number of children in the family might coincide with the number wanted.

There is no doubt that implementation of a scientific population policy in the developing countries involves immense difficulties. These are not only of an objective nature, as for instance the extremely low living standards, but also of a purely subjective kind, such as all manner of traditions inherited from the distant past. In olden times some of them were justified by high infant mortality, while others were caused by the tendency of various religions and sects to ensure the largest possible number of adherents. By wiping out illiteracy, educating the masses on sanitation and medical questions, protecting the rights of women and children and striving to eliminate prejudice, it is possible to expect various demographic measures to be successful even now, so that there is no need to wait for the "prosperity factor" and the results of urbanization to do their job.

Malthus's notorious geometric progression cannot make us give way to pessimism. On the other hand, I must say that Academician Strumilin's formula concerning the inverse proportionality of birth rate to prosperity gives us rather doubtful grounds for optimism. True optimism rests on the certainty that mankind is capable of subordinating spontaneous processes, including demographic ones, and will ultimately be able to adjust the "production" of people just as, to paraphrase Engels, it will by then have adjusted the production of goods.

This goal will once and for all be attained in a communist society. "The people of the future, conscious of their goals and masters of their destinies, will be capable of regulating the size of the population in accordance with their potentialities and their needs. Far from any idea of reducing the birth rate for the sake of preserving the old hierarchy or pursuing a reactionary imperialist policy, they will consider birth control as a factor of equilibrium, for planning and progress." (Retranslated from the Russian.—Ed.) To this optimistic glimpse into the future offered by Jean Freville, the prominent French Marxist sociologist, we need only add that people can even now start struggling successfully to avert world wars, wipe out hunger and illiteracy, and strive for conscious control of demographic processes for the sake of the future of the human race.

5. Population Problems in Developing Countries. A Soviet View

V. GUZEVATY

The social and economic development of the young Asian and African states which have freed themselves from the yoke of colonialism encounters numerous difficulties, among which population problems are increasingly claiming attention. Besides causing serious national preoccupation, they are important factors which cannot be ignored in world politics.

Population growth is known to have accelerated sharply in modern times.[1] . . . This rapid growth in world population (often called the "population explosion") is caused by considerable changes in the population processes in Afro-Asian and Latin American countries. Now, as in the past, these countries have a high birth rate, double or even treble that of the developed industrial states.[2] This is quite natural when one takes into consideration the backward social structure which the emancipated countries inherited from the colonial epoch, a structure characterised by widespread survivals of feudal and primitive relations and an overwhelming majority of illiterate peasant population, often lacking in elementary culture, ossified in prejudices and superstitions.

In such conditions, large families are sanctified by long-standing tradition and are the fruit of early marriage, the active part taken by children in the family's economic life, woman's complete deprivation of social rights and, above all, the absense of any material or cultural stimuli to a conscious approach to family planning.

However, notwithstanding the high birth rate, the growth of the population in the colonial countries before their national liberation was comparatively moderate, since it was kept down by a high mortality rate. Hunger and unhygienic living conditions facilitated the spread among the

Condensed from *International Affairs,* September 1966, pp. 52-58. Reprinted by permission of the publisher.

[1] In 1965 alone the world population increased by 65 million, which is equivalent to a daily increase of 180 thousand.

[2] The birth rate is particularly high in West Africa, where, according to U.N. data, the average annual number of births per thousand of the population was: in Ghana 47-52 (1960), in Guinea 62 (1955), in Mali 61 (1960-1961). *Population and Vital Statistics Report, Statistical Papers,* Series A. Vol. XVIII, No. 1, United Nations, New York, 1966.

popular masses of all sorts of serious diseases such as smallpox, cholera, malaria, tuberculosis, and various forms of avitaminosis and helminthiasis. Under the colonial regime there was no serious fight against such diseases, and medical care for the population was practically non-existent. Infantile mortality was very high. In Togo, for instance, half the newborn children died before the age of one year.

With the appearance of effective anti-epidemic means, especially anti-biotics, a steady decrease in the death rate began. This was considerably accelerated after the liquidation of colonial and semi-colonial regimes, when in the course of state construction the national governments were able to implement measures for improving sanitation and the health services.[3]

If a high birth rate is maintained, it is obvious that even a small drop in the death rate leads to a rapid increase in the natural growth of the population.

Table 4. Natural Growth of Population in Asia and Africa
(Average Annual Percentage)

Continent	1930-1940	1950-1960
Africa	1.21	2.33
North Africa	1.5	2.39
Tropical and South Africa	1.1	2.3
Asia	1.31	2.11

Source: 1963 Report on the World Social Situation, United Nations, New York, 1963, p. 6.

The population of Asia rose in the first half of the 20th century by 370 million, and in the next 14 years by 500 million. The population of the Afro-Asian countries is still continuing to grow rapidly. . . .

The history of the industrial states has shown that the economic and cultural development of the liberated countries will gradually strengthen the material and psychological requisites for lowering the birth rate. These requisites are first and foremost the disintegration of the patriarchal system, especially as regards family relations, under the influences of agrarian trans-formations and industrialisation. The new opportunities that young people get as a result of the spread of education, greater participation by women in production, study, social and political life, have as one of their most im-portant consequences a rise in the marriage age and a lowering of the birth

[3] Thus, in the U.A.R. death rate per thousand of the population dropped from 27 in 1945 to 17 in 1960, i.e., by 40 per cent in 15 years. Correspondingly, the infantile mortality rate, or the number of deaths before the age of one year per thousand births, was reduced from 153 to 109. In some other liberated countries, the drop in the death rate was still more noticeable. A. E. Sarhan, *Mortality Trends in the United Arab Republic,* United Nations World Population Conference, Belgrade, Aug. 30-Sept. 10, 1965, A. 2/I/E/79, pp. 4-5.

rate. The desire for a reasonable limitation of the number of children is the result of increased demand for cultural and material values. Finally, the lowering of the birth rate is, in a way, a reaction to the drop in infant mortality, since a high birth rate is a sort of compensation for high infant mortality.

However, the inevitable changes in the way of life and family traditions during the revolutionary transformation of society constitute a slow process, and the tendency towards a lower birth rate associated with it is, therefore, not sudden, but spread over a long period. Moreover, an acceleration, not a slowing down of the population growth, is to be expected in the near future in many Afro-Asian countries. . . .

This rapid and accelerating growth of the population seriously complicates the already difficult economic and social problems facing young national states. . . .

In the conditions of a backward agrarian economy inherited from colonialism with conservative forms of land tenure and cultivation, primitive agricultural technology and above all lack of the capital and qualified labour indispensable for radically reorganising the economy, there is a "redundance" of manpower. . . .

The factors of overpopulation facing us are those which the Malthusians called manifestations of the "universal abstract law of nature," but in reality they are the results of the economic backwardness rising from completely concrete, historically transient socioeconomic conditions, and first and foremost the preservation in the Afro-Asian countries of widely developed survivals of feudal and primitive social relations. These backward, anachronistic social relations, which have persisted owing to the oppression of the colonial regimes, fetter the production forces of those countries, hinder technical progress and maintain agriculture in a state of stagnation and primitive routine. It is in such conditions that the population increase begins to outstrip the production of means of subsistence, and *for that reason the solution of the food problem in the liberated countries is possible only if the primitive and feudal survivals are eliminated through the abolition of colonialism and neo-colonialism and radical socio-economic transformations, in the first place sweeping agrarian reforms.*

But here again, the problem of capital is uppermost: without a definite minimum of capital investment it is impossible radically to reorganise the economy, to modernise agricultural technology, and so on. At the same time, the rapid population growth demands that the major part of the national income be used not for production, but to import food, to satisfy material and cultural requirements. The rapid growth of the population makes necessary increasingly high expenditures merely to maintain the former living standard, not to speak of raising it. There is growing demand for articles of primary necessity, for schools, educational equipment and teachers, hospitals, medicines, doctors and so forth. As a result, many countries postpone the liquidation of illiteracy among the adult population and the introduction of universal schooling for children. This is not so noticeable as long as the population leads a primitive way of life, but it becomes increasingly perceptible as national awareness develops and the material and cultural demands of the population grow.

Another economic problem resulting from specific population situation in the Afro-Asian countries is that owing to the high birth rate, the proportion of children under the age of fifteen to the total population is about 50 per cent higher than in the industrial states.[4] Hence there are more dependants per worker, and this leads to especially great economic difficulties in conditions of low labour productivity. The economic burden resulting from the considerable proportion of dependants among the population is accentuated by the acute employment problem in the Afro-Asian countries: the number of adolescents on the labour market increases, as a rule, at a greater rate than the number of working places.

The acute shortage of capital and food, increasing with the growth of the population, seriously hinders the strengthening of national independence in the liberated countries. Forced to turn to the imperialist states for credits, grain and other agricultural products, to meet the immediate needs of the population, these countries thereby throw open the door to foreign capital. This leads in a greater or lesser degree to their losing freedom of action in foreign politics. Besides, imperialist "aid" generally tends to consolidate the reactionary forces within the recipient country.

In the young national states which have chosen the non-capitalist path of development, the reactionary forces try to make use of the economic difficulties, especially food shortages, to discredit the ideas of Socialism and to fan dissatisfaction among the people. These counter-revolutionary schemes have more chance to succeed in countries where leaders of the national-liberation revolution underestimate the complexity of the economic tasks, and population problems in particular. There have been some who sincerely hoped that the liquidation of the colonial regime would by itself ensure national economic upsurge and prosperity.

These over-optimistic expectations have been mercilessly chastised by reality. . . .

Because of the "population explosion" from which the newly liberated countries are now suffering, *radical social and economic transformations are the chief and indispensable requisites for solving the population problems, but they will not necessarily solve those problems immediately.*

This is well seen in the case of the U.A.R., one of the few liberated countries where the tasks of the national-liberation revolution have, on the whole, been completed. . . .

The National Charter, proclaimed by President Nasser in May 1962

---

[4] Children under 15 constitute 24-32 per cent of the population in industrially developed countries compared with 40-45 per cent in the Afro-Asian countries.

as the revolutionary programme for the development of Egyptian society, noted the great difficulties raised in the way of a national production upsurge by population problems and justified the necessity for a family planning policy to make the problem less acute. At the same time, the Charter emphasised that irrespective of the results of birth control measures, the country must set to work as soon as possible to develop production so that the rate of increase of the national income would outstrip the rate of population growth and ensure the people a higher living standard.

In a speech on the Charter, President Nasser said: "The population increase constitutes the most dangerous obstacle that faces the Egyptian people in their drive towards raising the standards of production in their country in an effective and efficient way." He also stated that "attempts at family planning with the aim of facing the problem of increasing population deserve the most sincere efforts, supported by modern scientific methods."[5]

An increasing number of governments of young national states are now coming to similar conclusions and hope to diminish, by means of a birth control policy, the obstacles to eliminating their economic backwardness, that painful legacy of their colonial past. Besides the U.A.R., several other countries including India, Pakistan and Tunisia have proclaimed such a policy. A larger number of countries, including Ceylon, Malaysia, Thailand, Indonesia, Turkey and Nigeria are carrying out, with government help, limited birth control measures, frequently as yet experimental. . . .

A population policy is thus becoming an increasingly notable feature in the social life of the young national states. In principle this testifies to a more mature approach to problems of economic development. The overwhelming majority of newly liberated states are planning their economic development, but this cannot be achieved unless population factors are taken into account and efforts are made to influence them so as to ensure a better combination of population growth and economic progress.

But for this influence to be effective, it is of great importance that the place of demographic measures in the general system of state construction should be correctly determined. For example, it would be senseless to expect propaganda of family planning methods to be effective within the traditional stagnant social society, untouched by new ideas, bereft of prospects, insensible to real change in life and consequently unconscious of the need to change habits in the field of family relations. *Only in the course of a cultural revolution, relying on economic reforms and not supplanting them, can a population programme be effective.*

In state construction in some liberated countries there is, it is true, another approach to the solution of population problems. Birth control measures are considered *the chief means* of overcoming difficulties, and eco-

---

[5] Draft of the Charter (English version), Information Department. Cairo, May 1962, p. 53.

nomic and social transformations are given only a secondary, subordinate role. This approach coincides with the Malthusian assertion that the peculiarities of social development are determined first and foremost by population laws, and not by the nature of the relations of production, as is the case in reality. Such an assertion implies the conclusion that the economic and cultural backwardness of the African and Asian peoples bears a "natural," extra-historical and extra-class character. It is therefore an obstacle to correct determination of the ways for rapidly overcoming this backwardness. That is why a population programme which proceeds from Malthusian recommendations is necessarily doomed to failure and is capable only of worsening the economic situation of the liberated countries.

And, on the other hand, birth control measures can reduce the acuteness of population problems and favour economic development if they are based on profound socio-economic transformations and conform to the objective social processes which arise in the course of these transformations.

SUGGESTED READING

Annals of the American Academy of Political and Social Science, Vol. 369 (January 1967). Issue devoted to problems of world population.

Bogue, Donald J., "The End of the Population Explosion." *The Public Interest,* No. 7 (Spring 1967).

Chandrasekhar, S., "Marx, Malthus and Mao: China's Population Explosion." *Current Scene* (Hong Kong), No. 3 (February 28, 1967).

Ginzberg, Eli, "The Manpower Factor in Economic Development: East and West," *Population Review* (Madras, India), July 1963.

Guzevati, Ia., "Population and the Socio-Economic Problems of Developing Nations." *Problems of Economics,* Vol. IX, No. 2 (June 1966).

Kirk, D., and Nortman, D., "Population Policies in Developing Countries." *Economic Development and Cultural Change,* Vol. 15, No. 2, Part 1 (January 1967).

Mauldin, W. Parker, "Population Dynamics in Asia: A Research Focus on the Future—The Indian Subcontinent." *Asian Survey,* Vol. VI, No. 3 (March 1966).

Meade, J. E., "Population Explosion, The Standard of Living and Social Conflict." *The Economic Journal,* Vol. LXXVII, No. 306 (June 1967).

Mudd, Stuart (ed.), *The Population Crisis and the Use of World Resources.* Bloomington: Indiana University Press, 1967.

Samuel, T. J., "The Effect of Population Growth on Consumption and Labour Supply in Underdeveloped Countries." *Indian Journal of Economics,* April 1964.

The World Food and Population Crisis. OECD Development Assistance Committee Meeting at Washington. Statements by Secretary Rusk and Secretary Freeman; Remarks by Vice President Humphrey, and Text of Communiqué. *U.S. Department of State Bulletin,* Washington, D.C., August 8, 1966.

Thomlison, Ralph, *Population Dynamics: Causes and Consequences of World Demographic Change.* New York: Random House, 1965.

Thompson, Warren S., and Lewis, David T., *Population Problems.* New York: McGraw-Hill, 1965.

Chapter 2

From Underdevelopment to Affluence

WESTERN VIEWS

The Soviet Union or Communist China offers essentially a single pre-scription for the less developed countries, a single path for them to follow, a single, clearly-defined cure for all their age-old ills. But when the countries of the Third World turn their eyes toward the non-Marxist West in search of the most rapid way to proceed from underdevelopment to afflu-ence, they are told that there is no pat answer, no ready-made solution. Moreover, they find themselves faced with a wide variety of views, a num-ber of recipes—some of them differing merely in emphasis; others, confus-ingly contradictory. Marxists may ascribe the situation which today keeps almost two-thirds of the world's population in abject poverty to one funda-mental cause: exploitation by capitalist "monopolists," "imperialists," and "colonialists and neocolonialists." But from the West, no single answer emerges. Underdevelopment has been explained in terms of geography, of climate, of psychological, social, and cultural factors; and colonialism is seen by some (but certainly not by all) students of the subject as a growth-stifling, or at least growth-retarding, influence. Some scholars, as we have seen in the preceding chapter, conceive of the battle against underdevelop-ment primarily as a struggle to overcome the disproportion between popu-lation growth and the world's ability to feed the rapidly increasing number of mouths; others (e.g., Everett E. Hagen and David McClelland) seek the ingredient for economic development in personality factors; while yet others (such as W. W. Rostow) describe the preconditions necessary for the "take-off" stage after which economic development becomes self-generat-ing. There are balanced growth and unstable growth theories. Some Western scholars place primary emphasis on the export sector of the economy; others underline the need for the development of heavy industry; yet others stress the technical education without which neither industrialization nor improvement in agriculture is likely to proceed at a rapid pace. There are scholars like Karl de Schweinitz of Northwestern University who see foreign aid as the indispensable external factor in stimulating the internal transformation on which development of underdeveloped areas depends and who see the success of such aid as hinging "very specially on the willingness of the rich economies to create an international environment responsive to the needs of the poor economies."[1]

There are others such as Richard N. Gardner of Columbia University (formerly U.S. Deputy Assistant Secretary of State) who, while also advocating foreign aid, place faith in the United Nations and other international organizations, urging that they play the major role in bringing about increasing transference of capital from the developed to the underdeveloped countries in the world.[2] And there are yet others who emphasize that the underdeveloped countries themselves must assume the primary responsibility for the solution of their problems. "Economic development," writes the American economist Robert L. Heilbroner, "is essentially a bootstrap operation and the main pull on the boot must come from the developing nation itself. There is much that more fortunate nations can do to assist the less fortunate on their upward climb, but in a total perspective the help which one nation can give another is at best marginal."[3]

The prescriptions of some Western scholars contain a strong dose of free enterprise as an essential ingredient in any remedial medication. "No lesson for development policy emerges more clearly, . . ." states a recent study by the Committee for Economic Development, "than that a direct relationship exists between the climate for individual enterprise and the rate of economic growth";[4] and Aaron Scheinfeld pleads for government and business in the "free industrially-developed countries" to cooperate with their counterparts in the less developed countries, "weak as they may be" so as to create in the latter an "indigenous private capitalism."[5] Others, however, disagree, maintaining that "the free market and private invest-

[1] Karl de Schweinitz, "The Needs of Underdeveloped Economies," *Current History,* August 1966, pp. 72-77.

[2] Richard N. Gardner, "The Role of the United Nations in Trade and Development," *Review of International Affairs,* November 5, 1966, pp. 16-19.

[3] Robert L. Heilbroner, *This Growing World: Economic Development and the World Bank Group,* Public Affairs Pamphlet No. 237A, Public Affairs Committee Inc., New York, p. 9. Heilbroner, it should be pointed out, believes that the World Bank can and often does play a small but critical role in assisting underdeveloped countries in their efforts.

[4] *How Low Income Countries Can Advance Their Own Growth,* Committee for Economic Development (New York, September 1966), p. 23.

[5] Aaron Scheinfeld, *A Plan for Accelerating Private Investment in the Developing Countries,* Center for the Study of Democratic Institutions (Santa Barbara, Cal., June 1966), p. 6.

ments are often totally inadequate to solve the problems of development,"[6] that "Growth . . . is too important to be left to the realm of private conduct,"[7] and that the state must assume major responsibility for planning economic development.

Western scholars may disagree on all the points discussed above and on many more. They may disagree, for instance, on whether political democracy is a goal to be aimed for at the outset or to be postponed until a later date; they may even disagree on whether or not there is a basic formula for all societies. But there is at least one point on which there is rather widespread agreement, and that is that economic development is necessarily slow and painful: it is no overnight remedy. In the words of former U.S. Undersecretary of State George W. Ball, "Economic development is an intricate and difficult process. It has proved difficult for the industrialized countries who have gone through it in the past, and it will be so for the newer countries going through it now."[8]

The editors of this volume were faced with the difficult task of choosing selections for inclusion in this chapter from the vast literature in the field. No series of selections kept within the confining space limitations could possibly give the reader a thorough understanding of even the major theories and approaches. The editors can only aspire to present *some* of the views frequently found in Western literature. In the first selection, Robert L. Heilbroner paints a vivid picture of everyday life in the world's underdeveloped regions, outlines briefly the great awakening of the underdeveloped countries in recent times, and explains the appeal that collectivism and even communism hold for them.

One hundred fifty years ago, the per capita output in the economically advanced nations of Europe and of North America was two to three times that of the less developed regions of Asia, Africa, and Latin America. Today the per person output of the former is ten, fifteen, perhaps even twenty, times that of the latter;[9] and there are strong indications that the gap is widening. In the second selection, Gunnar Myrdal addresses himself to that widening gap, to the increasing awareness of the inhabitants of the underdeveloped countries that the rich are becoming richer while the poor are falling further and further behind, and to the resulting craving of the poor nations for economic development and national independence.

Irving Louis Horowitz, in the third selection, describes the Third World in terms of what he conceives of as common economic, political, and

[6] Alec Nove, "The Soviet Model and Underdeveloped Countries," *International Affairs* (London, January 1961), p. 33.

[7] Karl de Schweinitz, "The Role of the State in Underdeveloped Economies," Paper delivered at the meeting of the Association for Comparative Economics, November 1965.

[8] Address to the United Nations Conference on Trade and Development in Geneva in March 1964, as reported by UPI, March 25, 1965.

[9] Richard T. Gill, *Economic Development: Past and Present*, Foundations of Modern Economics Series (Englewood Cliffs, N.J., Prentice-Hall, 1963), p. 3.

ideological characteristics and ventures the prediction that in the near future the emerging countries will take a road paved with much social control and but limited amounts of "capitalism" and "democracy." No theory of economic growth is better known in the West than W. W. Rostow's stages of economic growth. His followers believe that his five stages of growth present a historically and analytically correct picture of economic development. His numerous critics, who find his presentation impressionistic rather than analytical, assert that his description in its entirety is not appropriate to any country; at best it applies in part to some countries or regions. They also charge that his emphasis on uniformity and rigidity of the stage pattern of growth is incorrect and a disservice to the poor countries. Whatever scientific validity this controversial present-day growth theory may or may not have, no student of the subject should fail to become acquainted with it. The fourth selection in this chapter is a summary by W. W. Rostow of his five stages of economic growth.

Robert E. Baldwin, in the fifth selection, outlines briefly some of the current approaches to underdevelopment, cautions that the cost of development in economic and social terms is necessarily high, and emphasizes that there is neither a single nor a simple policy prescription for successful growth. William McCord, in the final selection, presents the case for a combination of economic development and political freedom. Expressing his faith that the emerging nations can "end the tyranny of the stomach without resorting to the tyranny of the slave camp,"—without, even, "benevolent dictators"—he concludes that in spite of all the difficulties that may stand in the way, a pluralistic society can be achieved in the developing countries. Such a society "provides the surest defense of human dignity"; "totalitarian centralization offers no high road to abundance."

1. The Struggle for Economic Development in Our Time

ROBERT L. HEILBRONER

THE TABLEAU OF UNDERDEVELOPMENT

To begin to understand economic development we must have a picture of the problem with which it contends. We must conjure up in our mind's eye what underdevelopment means for the two billion human beings for whom it is not a statistic but a living experience of daily life. Unless we can see the Great Ascent from the vantage point of those who must make the climb, we cannot hope to understand the difficulties of the march.

It is not easy to make this mental jump. But let us attempt it by imagining how a typical American family, living in a small suburban house on an income of six or seven thousand dollars, could be transformed into an equally typical family of the underdeveloped world.

We begin by invading the house of our imaginary American family to strip it of its furniture. Everything goes: beds, chairs, tables, television set, lamps. We will leave the family with a few old blankets, a kitchen table, a wooden chair. Along with the bureaus go the clothes. Each member of the family may keep in his "wardrobe" his oldest suit or dress, a shirt or blouse. We will permit a pair of shoes to the head of the family, but none for the wife or children.

We move into the kitchen. The appliances have already been taken out, so we turn to the cupboards and larder. The box of matches may stay, a small bag of flour, some sugar and salt. A few moldy potatoes, already in the garbage can, must be hastily rescued, for they will provide much of tonight's meal. We will leave a handful of onions, and a dish of dried beans. All the rest we take away: the meat, the fresh vegetables, the canned goods, the crackers, the candy.

Now we have stripped the house: the bathroom has been dismantled, the running water shut off, the electric wires taken out. Next we take away the house. The family can move to the toolshed. It is crowded, but much better than the situation in Hong Kong, where (a United Nations report tells us) "it is not uncommon for a family of four or more to live in a bed-space, that is, on a bunk bed and the space it occupies—sometimes in two or three tiers—their only privacy provided by curtains."[1]

From pp. 33-37, 77-79, 157-164 THE GREAT ASCENT by Robert L. Heilbroner. Copyright © 1963 by Robert L. Heilbroner. Reprinted by permission of Harper & Row, Publishers, and the author.
[1] *Social Aspects of Urban Development*, Committee on Information from Non-Self-Governing Territories, March 10, 1961, p. 129.

But we have only begun. All the other houses in the neighborhood have also been removed; our suburb has become a shantytown. Still, our family is fortunate to have a shelter; 250,000 people in Calcutta have none at all and simply live in the streets. Our family is now about on a par with the city of Cali in Colombia, where, an official of the World Bank writes, "on one hillside alone, the slum population is estimated at 40,000—without water, sanitation, or electric light. And not all the poor of Cali are as fortunate as that. Others have built their shacks near the city on land which lies beneath the flood mark. To these people the immediate environment is the open sewer of the city, a sewer which flows through their huts when the river rises."[2]

And still we have not reduced our American family to the level at which life is lived in the greatest part of the globe. Communication must go next. No more newspapers, magazines, books—not that they are missed, since we must take away our family's literacy as well. Instead, in our shantytown we will allow one radio. In India the national average of radio ownership is one per 250 people, but since the majority of radios is owned by city dwellers, our allowance is fairly generous.

Now government services must go. No more postman, no more fireman. There is a school, but it is three miles away and consists of two classrooms. They are not too overcrowded since only half the children in the neighborhood go to school. There are, of course, no hospitals or doctors nearby. The nearest clinic is ten miles away and is tended by a midwife. It can be reached by bicycle, provided that the family has a bicycle, which is unlikely. Or one can go by bus—not always inside, but there is usually room on top.

Finally, money. We will allow our family a cash hoard of five dollars. This will prevent our breadwinner from experiencing the tragedy of an Iranian peasant who went blind because he could not raise the $3.94 which he mistakenly thought he needed to secure admission to a hospital where he could have been cured.[3]

Meanwhile the head of our family must earn his keep. As a peasant cultivator with three acres to tend, he may raise the equivalent of $100 to $300 worth of crops a year. If he is a tenant farmer, which is more than likely, a third or so of his crop will go to his landlord, and probably another 10 percent to the local moneylender. But there will be enough to eat. Or almost enough. The human body requires an input of at least 2,000 calories to replenish the energy consumed by its living cells. If our displaced American fares no better than an Indian peasant, he will average a replenishment of no more than 1,700-1,900 calories. His body, like any insufficiently fueled machine, will run down. That is one reason why life expectancy at birth in India today averages less than forty years.

[2] "The Cauca Valley," unpublished World Bank memo by George Young. (With the kind permission of the author.)

[3] *New York Times Magazine,* April 30, 1961.

But the children may help. If they are fortunate, they may find work and thus earn some cash to supplement the family's income. For example, they may be employed as are children in Hyderabad, Pakistan, sealing the ends of bangles over a small kerosene flame, a simple task which can be done at home. To be sure, the pay is small: eight annas—about ten cents—for sealing bangles. That is, eight annas per *gross* of bangles. And if they cannot find work? Well, they can scavenge, as do the children in Iran who in times of hunger search for the undigested oats in the droppings of horses.

And so we have brought our typical American family down to the very bottom of the human scale. It is, however, a bottom in which we can find, give or take a hundred million souls, at least a billion people.[*] Of the remaining billion in the backward areas, most are slightly better off, but not much so; a few are comfortable; a handful rich.

Of course, this is only an impression of life in the underdeveloped lands. It is not life itself. There is still lacking the things that underdevelopment gives as well as those it takes away: the urinous smell of poverty, the display of disease, the flies, the open sewers. And there is lacking, too, a softening sense of familiarity. Even in a charnel house life has its passions and pleasures. A tableau, shocking to American eyes, is less shocking to eyes that have never known any other. But it gives one a general idea. It begins to add pictures of reality to the statistics by which underdevelopment is ordinarily measured. When we are told that half the world's population enjoys a standard of living "less than $100 a year," this is what the figures mean. . . .

THE GREAT RESOLVE

A fact of which we can easily lose sight in studying economic development is how ancient is the condition with which it contends. If poverty is the basic measuring rod, then surely underdevelopment is as ancient as recorded civilization. Hobbes' famous characterization of life as "poor, nasty, brutish and short" is a fair generalization of the typical biography since time immemorial.

And yet underdevelopment as a "problem" is very recent. For into the traditional situation of the backward areas have come two radically new ingredients. The first is the availability of an industrial technology, now concentrated among a few advanced nations, which is capable of performing hitherto unimaginable feats of economic hydraulics. The second is an

[*] Such an estimate is, of necessity, highly conjectural. It takes in only 300 million of India's population and 50 million of Pakistan's, a charitable figure. It includes 50 million Arabs and 100 million Africans, a large underestimate. From South and Central America's poverty it adds in but another 50 millions. The remainder of the billion can be made up from mainland China alone. And we have kept as a statistical reserve the Afghans, Burmese, Indonesians, Koreans, Vietnamese—nearly 200 million in all, among whom is to be found some of the worst poverty on the face of the globe.

awakening, on the part of the peoples of the underdeveloped areas, to the remediable nature of their human condition. Together these forces have combined in a great resolve which underlies the development revolution. It is a commentary of some sort on human history that this resolve has only now emerged as a program for mankind, and that even now the very idea is regarded by some members of the favored quarter of humanity as premature.

Ideally, perhaps, a history of this idea should take as its starting point the web of causes by which that favored quarter began its own economic development in Europe in the sixteenth and seventeenth centuries. But that would take us beyond the confines of this small study. Instead, we can take as our point of departure the situation as it existed in the late nineteenth century, when the seeds of the present great resolve were first planted.

If we then spread out a map of the world in, say, 1900, we find a very interesting picture. Economically, the map looks much the same as it does today. But politically it is very different. From Egypt to the Union of South Africa, the continent of Africa was almost entirely white European real estate. Southeast Asia was dominated by Britain and Holland. China was a moribund society milked by various European concessionaire groups. Only South America appears as politically independent, and here, whatever the appearance, we do not have to look very deeply to discern the powerful influence of American, British, and European capital in its coffee and banana plantations, its meat-packing plants, its copper and tin mines, its chicle and sugar cane and sisal fields.

Thus what we see as the background for the present-day situation was the coexistence of two totally different, almost entirely separated, and yet dangerously interacting worlds. One was the dynamic, expansive, vigorous, self-assured world of capitalism in its heyday of imperialism. The other was the stagnant, passive, preindustrial world of the colonial or quasi-colonial nations and territories.

We need not here go into the complex history of imperialism and colonialism—a history which is only today drawing to its bitter end. But we must take note of the heritage of this history if we are to understand the course of economic development. Colonialism and imperialism are the schools in which most of the underdeveloped nations learned their lessons, and although the schooling was very different from colony to colony, a common distaste for their instructors is all too clearly apparent among all of the ex-students. . . .

THE LOGIC OF COLLECTIVISM

. . . Inherent to the process of economic development is the latent potential of revolutionary upheaval. As in all such unstable situations it is impossible to generalize as to when—or even whether—the latent forces will become active. Although development is the foe of apathy, history proves abundantly that the forces of inertia are vastly more powerful than those of upheaval, and it may yet be that some developing nations will manage to avoid the travails and bloodshed of violent social change—as did, for example, England during the miseries of the Industrial Revolution.

We should not entertain overly hopeful expectations in this regard, however. In nations which are beset by a desire to catch up, the tendencies for revolutionary change are apt to be much greater than in those which formed the vanguard of history. If social change is not rapid—if the progress of the Great Ascent lags or is purposely slowed down to avoid social stress—a new source of revolutionary disturbance is likely to originate in dissident political groups, whether communist or merely anti-*status quo.*

Hence, we must reckon with the likelihood that over the coming two or three decades, as the pressures grow and the difficulties assert themselves, the guidance of development will fall into the hands of dedicated revolutionary groups. Mild men will not ride the tigers of development. Neither will mild political or economic systems contain or impel it.

In most of the underdeveloped nations the choice for the command post of development is apt to lie between a military dictatorship and a left-wing civilian dictatorship. (The difference may not be very great, since many of the younger army officers have shown strong left-wing tendencies themselves.) In any event, as Professor Mason writes, the route chosen by the revolutionary developmental elites is not apt to be that of democratic capitalism. Given the inevitable slow pace of development, the heightening of social tensions, and the inescapable rigors of the Great Ascent, the logic of events points to the formation of economic systems and political regimes which will seek to *impose* development on their peoples.

But even the most rigorous governments can speed up development only by so much. The first great projects of social capital formation, with their brigades of labor, lend themselves easily to centralized dictatorship, and, given adequate foreign assistance, the creation of an effective industrial structure can be considerably accelerated by a ruthless concentration on strategic sectors. Yet the pace of over-all progress will still have to be hobbled to the sluggish pace of social change, especially in the recalcitrant peasant villages, and it will still have to cope with the population problem, which may prove intransigent even before totalitarian methods. Above all, the necessity to hold down the level of consumption—to force savings—in order to free resources for the capital-building process will make for a rising level of frustration even under the sternest discipline.

This frustration will almost surely have to be channeled into directions other than that of economic expectations. Hence a deliberately heightened nationalism, a carefully planned ideological fervor, even military adventures are a likely by-product of development. Indeed, in some nations only by marshaling sentiments for such ends may the energies of the peoples be contained and controlled. Thus China endlessly exercises the sentiments of anti-Americanism; Indonesia rattles the saber over the useless jungles of New Guinea; the African states eye each other suspiciously.

In a word, economic development has within it the potential, not alone of a revolutionary situation, but of heightened international friction. Much of this, no doubt, will be of a minor nature, comparable to the Indian march into Goa. Nevertheless economic development will continue to agitate the international scene, and will not, as is sometimes easily asserted, constitute a new force for world peace.

THE POSSIBILITIES FOR COMMUNISM

Everything that we have said brings us inevitably to the crucial relationship of communism to economic development—a relationship which, it must now be apparent, is a profoundly deep-rooted one.

It is clear that in the political turmoil of development conditions are often propitious for a communist coup. But if communism were a threat only because of its conspiratorial proclivities, the problem might not be so serious. What is much more important is that communism has a *functional* attractiveness to the underdeveloped lands—that it may be the political and economic system best adapted to the tasks of the backward areas.

There is no secret about the communist blueprint for development. It advocates doing only what every underdeveloped nation must do: reorganizing agriculture to achieve a surplus of food; transferring this surplus to workers who have been released from agriculture; relentlessly, continuously, single-mindedly using these workers to create capital. The difference is that communism, at least in theory, allows the job to be done with much less of the inertia and friction which hamper it in a non-communist society. Where land is needed, it is taken; where workers are needed, they are moved; where opposition occurs, it is liquidated; where dissent arises, it is suppressed. In place of entrepreneurs who may hesitate for fear of losses, it provides factory managers who are given orders to build. In lieu of a government which must accommodate the claims of the old order against those of the new, it establishes a government whose only orientation is to the future.

One need hardly point out that there is a long distance between theory and practice. Communist economic development has not been smooth or easy. We have seen many cases of partial communist failure, particularly in the reorganization of agriculture.* But these failures must be compared

---

* As a consequence of these failures we have increasingly witnessed the growth of diversity among communist economies. A considerable gulf today separates the economic system of Yugoslavia from that of Poland, Poland from Russia, Russia from China. Needless to say, this growing diversity of techniques enhances the relevance and attractiveness of communism to the underdeveloped nations.

against the greater failure which exists in the first instance—that is, the virtual absence of *any* development in many of the backward lands.

And here it is important to recognize that, with all its shortfalls, the communist record has been an impressive one. There is much talk in the West of the deceitfulness of communism—of its willingness to divert the attention of the masses from their hardships with wild promises and charges, of its propensity to falsify figures, to invent lies, to distort the intent and actions of the West. All this may be true enough. But when communism promises economic growth, it is on much stronger ground. China, at least until its recent agricultural catastrophe, was probably growing twice to three times as fast as India,[4] and if it can survive its food crisis, it is likely to do so again. Nor should we forget that Russia, now a contender for the industrial supremacy of the world, was, only two generations back, a nation at a stage of development no higher than, say, Brazil or Turkey today. Communism may well be the quickest possible way out of underdevelopment, and the desperate fact is that in many areas of the world the present non-communist effort looks like the slowest possible way.

We have already noted that there is nothing mysterious about the communist techniques for forcing growth. Rather, what is crucial is that communism, as an ideology and as a practical political movement, is prepared to undertake the revolutionary reorganization of society—a task before which the noncommunist governments shrink.

To the West, it is this very revolutionary ruthlessness which is the intolerable aspect of communism. And it is not alone the attack on vested interests which arouses Western antipathy. The contemptuous rejection of all noncommunist thought, the icy certitude of communist dogma, its machine-like methods, all repel the West, as do, too, the depressing standards of life so far achieved under communism.

But this is not necessarily the effect produced upon the peoples of the East and South. Never having known political freedom, the hungry peasant and city laborer do not regret its absence. Accustomed to brutality and indifference from the upper classes, the common man submits to the whip of new masters with resignation. Already bent under a heavy yoke, he will bear the still heavier burdens of communism (for communism will surely squeeze him harder and drive him faster than noncommunism), if he can see a chance of lifting the incubus of the past from the shoulders of his children and grandchildren. Even the economic realities of the present communist nations, with their drab living standards, are apt to appear more "real," much closer to imaginable achievement, even more psychologically appealing, to the common man of the backward areas than the gaudy and fantastically removed way of life of the West.

To set forth these considerations is not to prophesy that communism is the path which the developing lands must "inevitably" follow. Even

[4] Cf., e.g., A. Doak Barnett, *Communist Economic Strategy: The Rise of Mainland China* (National Planning Association, Washington, D.C., 1959), p. 11.

among the revolutionary leadership elites of the underdeveloped countries, few *wish* to follow the orthodox communist pattern. Other than the hard-core communist cadres, the radical leadership in the backward nations entertains no illusions as to the benefits of a junior partnership in the Sino-Soviet bloc. Hence it is at least possible—and, needless to say, desirable—that the extreme tasks of development may be carried through without subordinating the emerging nations to the ideological and political domination of the communist movement. This is a matter about which it is impossible to make blanket predictions; in the contest between the preferences of the developing elites and the pressures of the developmental situation, the decisive vote may be cast by many factors—the resistance of the Old Orders, the rise of an inspired political leader and his own ideological predilections, the success of noncommunist revolutionary groups in combining discipline with enthusiasm, the blunders—or successes—of the local communist organization.[5]

Whether or not the revolutionary regimes of development are finally pushed into the communist orbit, however, there is no doubt that these regimes will identify themselves as being within the *socialist* orbit. It must be noted that almost without exception every developing nation has dedicated itself to "socialism" from Cuba and China on one extreme, through Mexico and India, even to the recent right-wing government of Syria.

As these examples indicate, volumes could be written today on the variety of systems which pass themselves off as socialist. What is clear, however, is that everywhere in the underdeveloped world the word has a charismatic ring. And it is not merely the clarion syllables, with their overtones of social justice, which account for the ubiquity of the socialist term, but also a common functional idea—the superiority of a planned to an unplanned economy as a vehicle for providing rapid growth.

Thus the inner tensions of the development revolution promise the appearance of "socialism" on a world-wide scale, a fact which presents the capitalist West with a wholly new environment. That even the milder forms of this socialism will have to contend with powerful forces making for authoritarianism and collectivism is, as we have seen, a likely prospect for the future. Whether or not the trend will go "all the way," however, does not depend entirely on internal factors. In part it hinges on the response of the West to the challenge of development. . . .

[5] For an astute and balanced statement on the applicability and attractiveness of orthodox Soviet techniques to underdevelopment, see A. Nove, *The Soviet Economy* (New York, Frederick A. Praeger, 1961), pp. 303-6.

2. Rich Lands, Poor Lands, and the Widening Gap

GUNNAR MYRDAL

The facts of international economic inequalities in the present world, when viewed in the very broadest perspective, fall into a definite and simple pattern.[1]

A few countries are highly developed economically and have very high levels of average real income per head. Richest of all are those of the former British colonies which are located in the temperate zones and became populated mainly by European stock, i.e., the United States and Canada, Australia and New Zealand. The countries in northwestern and west central Europe also belong to this group. Together the inhabitants of these few countries make up about one-sixth of the total population in the non-Soviet world.

This is the economic upper class of nations in world society. The lower class of nations is far bigger: more than two-thirds of the people in the non-Soviet world live in countries where real income per head is only a very tiny fraction of what it is in the highly developed countries and, indeed, in most cases is much smaller than it was in those countries before they started to develop rapidly a century or more ago.[2]

To this majority group of very poor nations belong all the peoples of Africa except the white settlers in South Africa, entrenched behind their Apartheid legislation, and similar, though smaller, enclaves of white people in other parts of that continent which is still largely carved up into colonial possessions of West European powers. The whole of non-Soviet Asia belongs to this group of very poor countries, including the countries in the Middle and Near East. Finally, it includes the larger part of Latin America, which has, however, a few countries which have reached a "middle-class" position, like Argentina or Uruguay.

From pp. 3-5, 6-8 RICH LANDS AND POOR by Gunnar Myrdal. Copyright © 1957 by Gunnar Myrdal. Reprinted by permission of Harper & Row, Publishers. The same passages from the British edition entitled *Economic Theory and Underdeveloped Regions* are reprinted by permission of Gerald Duckworth & Co., Ltd.

[1] For verification of the broad survey of international economic inequalities in this section, I refer to the latest publications of the United Nations and the Secretariats of the three regional Economic Commissions.

[2] Cf. also Simon Kuznets, "Underdeveloped Countries and the Pre-industrial Phase in the Advanced Countries: An Attempt at Comparison." Paper to the *World Population Conference*, Rome, 1954 (to be published).

In the highly developed countries all indices point steadily upward. On the average and in the longer span there are no signs of a slackening of the momentum of economic development in those countries. Looking backward, business slumps and big depressions and even severe setbacks due to wars appear only as short-term waverings of the firmly rising long-term trend. In the period after the Second World War these countries have seen their labor and other productive resources constantly in work at full capacity. The general expectancy in these countries of a continued rapid economic development is part of the commonly shared assumptions on the basis of which national life evolves toward ever higher realization of democracy and national integration.

It is on the whole the industrialized countries which are industrializing further. By far the greater portion of the non-Soviet world's total savings originates in this smaller part of it where incomes are high. As new inventions are constantly raising the demand for capital, almost all of the available capital is invested there. If one counted as home investment also the expenditure made for building up the closely controlled enclaves for exploiting oil and mineral resources in the poorer countries, this would appear to be the case even more completely.

In the underdeveloped countries, on the other hand, where incomes are so very much lower, capital formation and investment tend generally to be smaller, even relative to their lower incomes. For equality in rate of development, they would instead need to be relatively bigger, as in the poorer countries the natural population increase is usually faster. The faster population increase is a result of a particular relation between fertility and mortality rates, where both are on a very high level, which, in addition, tends to make the age distribution of their populations relatively less advantageous. As a consequence of all this—and of the tradition of stagnation which has entrenched itself in their entire culture—their economic development usually proceeds more slowly. Many of these countries have during recent decades even moved backward in average income. . . .

The great differences between countries within both groups in actual economic levels, as well as in current development rates and development rates during different periods in the near past, do not invalidate the following broad generalizations:

That there is a small group of countries which are quite well off and a much larger group of extremely poor countries;

that the countries in the former group are on the whole firmly settled in a pattern of continuing economic development, while in the latter group average progress is slower, as many countries are in constant danger of not being able to lift themselves out of stagnation or even of losing ground so far as average income levels are concerned; and

that, therefore, on the whole, in recent decades the economic inequalities between developed and underdeveloped countries have been increasing.

This trend toward international economic inequality stands out in contrast to what is happening within the rich countries individually. There the trend has, in recent generations, been toward greater equality of opportunity, and this development has been an accelerating one which is still gaining momentum. The contrary development for the world as a whole should be related also to the fact that as yet there has been no real parallel within the poorer countries individually to the equalization process now going on in the rich countries. Most of the poorer countries have preserved as great internal inequalities among individuals, classes and regions as there have ever been; in many of them the inequalities are still growing.

In the highly developed countries there has been spectacular progress of which we, who live there, are acutely conscious. The poorer, underdeveloped countries, which on the average are developing more slowly, form, however, much the larger part of the world; again on the average, the population growth has been more rapid there than in the small group of rich countries. With these two facts in mind, it becomes very uncertain whether and in what sense it can be held that there has in recent decades been any economic progress at all for mankind as a whole. . . .

The peoples in the underdeveloped countries are becoming increasingly aware of these huge international inequalities and the danger that they will continue to grow; and these peoples and their spokesmen show an inclination to put part of the blame for their poverty on the rest of the world and, in particular, on the countries which are better off—or, rather, they see a cause of the inequalities in the world economic system which keeps them so poor while other nations are so rich and becoming richer.

The Second World War helped to release many checks and controls upholding the established power system in the world, and one of its results was the liberation on a vast scale of subject peoples from colonial rule. A very important characteristic of the new nationalism which was born in this process is, however, that the demand of the peoples is for equality of opportunity with other peoples as well as for liberty. All these very poor nations, as they are touched by the Great Awakening, crave economic development as well as national independence.

It is interesting to note in this connection that now we have all come to refer to this majority of very poor countries as "the underdeveloped countries." This dynamic term, which gained its present prevalence only after the Second World War, itself indicates the great change in the world political situation to which I have referred. The expression commonly used until quite recently was the static term "the backward countries."

Both terms—like all the fundamental concepts of the social sciences—are value-loaded,[3] and it is conducive to clarity in our thinking that we are aware of this fact. The use of the concept "the underdeveloped countries"

---

[3] This is not meant in a critical sense; see *An International Economy*, Appendix. "Methodological Note on the Concepts and the Value Premises," pp. 336 ff.

implies the value judgment that it is an accepted goal of public policy that the countries so designated should experience economic development. It is with this implication that people in the poorer countries use the term and press its usage upon people in the richer countries. When they, in their turn, accept this term and suppress the old one, "the backward countries," they also accept the implication.

The change from the static to the dynamic concept thus implies in the richer countries a registration of a positive attitude to the Great Awakening in the poorer countries and, therefore, an acknowledgment—given, naturally, only in a general and therefore necessarily vague form—that those countries are right in demanding higher standards of income, a bigger share in the good things of life, and greater equality of opportunity.

As part of the same intellectual realignment, the broad facts of international economic inequalities, referred to above, have begun to be disseminated ever more widely, not only in the underdeveloped countries, where they furnish part of the driving force in the political process I refer to as the Great Awakening, but also in the developed ones.

It can be seen that when ordinary people in our developed countries are for the first time made aware of these stern facts, this experience often has the character of a revelation to them; it can also be observed that the new knowledge is felt to be awkward. Their general concept of the world, as it is and as it ought to be, cannot easily be adjusted to a realization of all this abject poverty in most of the world and of the tendency for international inequalities to grow. . . .

3. What Is the Third World?

IRVING LOUIS HOROWITZ

In one of the most perceptive and imaginative sentences in *Das Kapital,* Marx wrote: "The country that is more developed industrially only shows to the less developed, the image of its own future."[1] It is amazing to note that what the mid-nineteenth century must have considered a wildly romantic thought is a commonplace today. Current events have become more complex than Marx could possibly have anticipated; more centered on facts than on images. The rise of a Third World, of a social universe in limbo and outside the power dyad of East and West, has generated new queries.

Assuming that the developed countries show to the underdeveloped the image of their own futures, the question arises, do these "expectant" nations accept this image? Are they prepared to accept modernism without qualifications? Does this include the exaggerated consequences of automated industrialism, of alienation and privatization? Will the antagonisms between the rich nations and the poor nations overwhelm potential commonalities of economy and culture? Do the less developed nations apply their energies to careful mending or to revolutionary smashing? Above all, does the developmental process change the terms of description and analysis, or provide them with a renewed urgency?

It is no exaggeration to say that the answers to these questions have been slow in coming. To some extent this is a consequence of the unevenness and lateness of development in some areas; cultural, ethnic, and racial apartness of other areas; and the ways in which resistance to social change has inhibited these areas from emulating the economic systems of advanced nations. The emergence of a Third World; the transformation of world relations from a dyadic to a triadic balance; the emergence on a mass scale of new nations; new economic systems; new cultural products; new political forms—all bound up with national traditions—not infrequently synonymous with national myths—have created a profusion of new issues for our times. Furthermore, the "image" of a developed nation has been fragmented into

[1] Karl Marx, *Das Kapital.* Chicago: Charles Kerr Publishers, 1905, Vol. I, p. 13.

"images" of developed nations. There is no question of rejecting development, except among those people overwhelmed with nostalgia; the only question is what direction such development is going to take. In the consciousness of a Third World lives the example of a Second World no less than of a First World—of the socialist Soviet Union no less than the capitalist United States. The *existence* of a development process is a social fact. The *recognition* of a need for development is a social value. What binds the Third World together is not just its being a geographic locale outside the main power centers, but a psychological unity built around a social value. The ideological accoutrements of these processes are responses and effects —which in turn stimulate a desire for accelerated industrialization and rapid modernization. But above all, the ideology of the Third World is a response to the pervasive problem of how to gain worldly pre-eminence. It is always a matter of "catching up" and perhaps ultimately "surpassing" those held to be most advanced. This in itself betrays the fact and shame of backwardness.

Put another way, the developed nations are "causes," not just because they are in the forefront of modernization and material wealth, but because they create the *conditions* for rebellion and revolution. The developed nations thus provide a chain of *effects*.[2] We might introduce the three *effects* as follows: (1) Developing nations define themselves as engaged in a mortal race with the most advanced sectors of the economic world. This is the *demonstration effect*. (2) Developing nations define themselves as economically and socially experimental and lean toward a "mix" rather than a "pure" system. The Third World believes in neither socialism nor capitalism, but also believes in them both. This is the *fusion effect*. (3) Developing nations are those which have the desire and the means to catch up to advanced forms of social and economic organization, and to do so in less time than it took the presently constituted advanced nations to reach their present levels. This is the *compression effect*. . . .

At one level, the designation Third World is a strategy for economic development rather than a type of economic or social structure. The "mix" in the Third World is ostensibly between *degrees of* (rather than *choices between*) capitalism and socialism at the economic level, and libertarianism and totalitarianism politically. It is not a new synthesis of political economy. One of the typical self-delusions of Third World nations is that they perceive themselves as developing new economic forms, when as a matter of fact this has not been the case thus far. There is little evidence that there will be any real new economic alternatives to either capitalist or socialist development in the immediate future. In the political sphere, however, the Third World seems to have added a new style if not a new structure.

The Third World is a mixture of different adaptations of capitalism

---

[2] See on this Gino Germani, *Politics and Society in Latin America,* edited by Irving L. Horowitz. Englewood Cliffs, N.J.: Prentice-Hall, 1966 (pending).

and socialism but not an option to either of them at the economic level. The Third World is transitional. It is in a state of movement from traditional to modern society. It is the forms of transition which therefore have to concern us.

The fact that the First and Second Worlds are always in competition within a relative balance of power makes possible the exercise of Third World strategies in determining the role of foreign capital and aid, and not being determined by such capital.[3] To be a member of the Third World, in short, is not to make a choice in favor of one political bloc or another. As a matter of fact, it is to be very conscious and deliberate about not making this decision for the present.

As might be expected, within the Third World there is a wide range of choices of economic methods. Thus it contains some very strange mixtures.

India and Brazil have more than 75 per cent of their productive industries in the capitalist sector, while Algeria and Egypt are more than 75 per cent nationalized. Yet all four nations belong to the emergent bloc. In other words, to be considered part of the Third World it is not necessary to limit the character of the national economic system. The political posture in relation to the main power blocs is central to defining conditions of "membership" in the Third World. . . .

Many Third World nations have achieved their sovereignty in the present century—and especially after World War Two. The Latin American states are exceptions in that they had at least their formal sovereignty for a longer period of time. They represent old states, and not simply new states evolved out of old nations. This formal sovereignty is primarily political and not economic. Thus the initial phase of entering the Third World bloc is the establishment of national state sovereignty. The swollen membership of the United Nations reflects this process. It has more than doubled its member states inside of fifteen years. This tendency does not foreshadow the breakup of the nation-state for the sake of international government, but rather the development of the nation-state as a prelude to, and the organizing force in, the economic development process.

An essential factor about the international status of Third World nations is that they hold no dependencies. The First World drew political prestige and economic wealth from its colonial holdings. The Second World did likewise with its satellites. But the Third World cannot develop in terms of colonial holdings, since as ex-colonial nations they have neither such possessions nor do they have the possibility of developing colonial ambitions. The development of the Third World nation-state is not tied to foreign colonial expansionism, although it can stimulate what is called "internal colonialism." Third World nations do not compete for membership

[3] See Albert O. Hirschman, *The Strategy of Economic Development.* New Haven: Yale University Press, 1958, pp. 202-8.

in the major power blocs. They generally form restricted regional organizations, such as the organization of Arab states, the organization of Pan-African unions, or the Latin American union. The policy of non-alignment militates against entry into such organizations as NATO or SEATO or the Warsaw Pact. Therefore treaty membership for Third World nations is considered undesirable and is avoided wherever possible.

In primary exchange economies, where raw materials are exported and finished commodities are imported, the gap between the Third World and the First and Second Worlds is widening, not narrowing. Therefore competition between the Third World and First and Second Worlds becomes increasingly keen. Preferential rates and prices between highly developed nations are established; and preferential prices for finished commodities over raw materials are set. As a consequence there is a curbing or unevenness of economic growth.[4]

Very few Third World nations have fully mobilized their industrial potential. As a general rule, when there is such a mobilization, it is of a sectoral nature, usually benefiting elite groups within the Third World nation-state, and it differs widely according to class interest. Thus the gap between classes keeps the level of development low and uneven. Judged by real income per person, 90 per cent of the Third World peoples are between the 400 and 500 U.S. dollar level and another 5 per cent are between the 500 dollar to 750 dollar level and another 4 per cent between the 750 dollar and 1000 dollar level. Not more than 1 per cent earns over $1000. This lag grows greater as the gap between falling prices for agricultural and mineral products confronts the rising costs of finished commodity production. This fact alone casts grave doubt on the theory that a "middle sector" will be the savior of the Third World, or at least, save it from social revolution. . . .

· In the main, the Third World is a low industrial, goods-producing area no less than a high commodity-cost area.[5] This affects the quality as well as the amount of foreign aid that they receive from the First and the Second Worlds. Disregarding the question of whether this aid is harmful or beneficent, with or without strings, the fact is that the Third World *receives* economic assistance, some kinds of funds, while the First and Second Worlds represent funding agencies for it. Thus national independence does not in itself guarantee an end to foreign domination. This distinction between nations receiving aid and nations rendering aid is central to a definition of the Third World.

The Third World supplies world markets with primary commodities, primary agricultural supplies, nonferrous base metals, etc. The First and Second Worlds basically export not primary commodities but manufactured

---

[4] See Raúl Prebisch, *Nueva Política Comercial para el Desarrollo.* Mexico-Buenos Aires: Fondo de Cultura Económica, 1964.

[5] The neglect of this correlation between low industrialization and high commodity costs in the Prebisch thesis has been called attention to by Ramón Ramírez Gómez. "El Informe Prebisch y la Realidad Latinoamericana," *Cuadernos Americanos,* Vol. CXXXI, No. 6 (Nov.-Dec., 1963), pp. 7-72.

goods. The Soviet Union has been more sensitive to the international imbalance between raw materials and finished products than has the United States. With the exception of wartime conditions, export of primary commodities is never as financially lucrative as export of manufactured goods. While it is true that without these primary commodities there can be no manufacture of goods, still the source of primary supplies is wider than imagined. Therefore, the First World has tended to maintain the imbalance between the fully advanced and the underdeveloped nations. Contrary to the rhetoric of foreign aid, the extent of First and Second World assistance to Third World development is not so much a question of direct fiscal support but rather of prices paid for raw materials, costs of importing goods, and control of international trade and money markets.

The question of setting market prices is generally allocated to the First and Second Worlds. That is, the Soviet Union can set the price on wool; the United States, along with its Western European cotton manufacturers, can set the price on cotton. This ability to set the price is a characteristic of monopolies in general, and this ability to monopolize prices is a characteristic of the First World. Monopolization is therefore a form for preventing price and wage fluctuation in the metropolitan areas. At the same time, by controlling the flow of vital parts, it is a way for preventing mass expropriation in the backward areas. Underdeveloped regions in the Third World suffer heavy price fluctuations and accentuated inflationary spirals, because they cannot control world markets, set or regulate prices, or expropriate property or resources when this is nationally desirable or feasible.

In the Third World the *formal* systems are nearly always and everywhere republican in character, while their *real* systems are nearly always authoritarian. They are neither monarchies nor total dictatorships. They are under the "rule of law"—that is, they have constitutions—but this lawfulness is deposited in the hands of the dynamic leader of the single party. They have an unchecked higher political directorate, a party charisma. There is neither a developed parliamentary system nor the kind of relatively stable multi-party groupings found in Western Europe and the United States. Where such parliamentary systems have been allowed to expand, they have been a conservative force which has served to fragment the political power of progressive social groups. Parliamentary rule is often present in older sectors of the Third World which already have achieved formal independence, as in Latin America. Here, for instance, the agricultural proletariat has been systematically excluded from effective participation, either directly through disenfranchisement, or indirectly through electoral frauds of various sorts. In such circumstances the legislative branch becomes the legal front for property ownership. In Africa, nations have avoided this situation by abandoning the multi-party system.[6] Thus, in Ghana, Algeria, Tunisia, Kenya, Egypt, and Guinea, there has been the gradual erosion of

[6] See Gwendolen M. Carter (ed.), *African One-Party States*. Ithaca, New York: Cornell University Press, 1962.

parliamentary norms in the name of mass participation. The Parliament has become an upper class forum, while the President has become the hope of the masses. This struggle is simply another way of describing the differences between formal and real political systems in emerging nations.

Given the great importance of this element, the revolutionary system is often identified in the minds of the mass with a particular party. Hence, Congress Party, however amorphous its organization may be, retains a virtual monopoly of the political apparatus in India. The same is true of the P.R.I. in Mexico. Thus, even in nations which are traditionally identified with Western values of democracy and libertarianism, parliamentary norms are more formal than real. To achieve even a minimum rate of growth, to enter the "take-off" period, the Third World nations have had to recognize the need for central planning. And such high level planning is in itself a political act, necessarily under the aegis of the state system. The politics of this system, while often "benevolent" in character, cannot be said to be particularly concerned with the observance of parliamentary norms.

A parliament is a forum of conflicting and contrasting interests and opinions. As such, its ability to serve the "whole people" is subject to ridicule and, ultimately, to disrepute. In the cases of the Congo and Pakistan parliamentary rifts prevented the normal functioning of society. And only with the passing of such nominally democratic forums was social order maintained.

Parliamentary development can be afforded as a splendid luxury when time and history allow. This was the case for the United States in the nineteenth century. Whether there is a margin for parliamentary developments in the Third World depends on the role that parliaments perform in these nations. The case histories presently available are hardly encouraging. In Latin America they have tended to preserve the *status quo* and to retard the development of central planning.[7] It is hard to imagine the new African states following such a model. Therefore, there is within the Third World a development of radical political orientations without many basic constitutional safeguards. This is one basic reason why Western social democratic ideology has found it extremely difficult to champion the Third World cause.[8]

The authoritarian nature of the Third World has resulted from the rapid growth and consolidation of the one-party state. Yet, this rarely spills over into totalitarianism, into the control of the total social system. Tech-

[7] See on this Irving Louis Horowitz, *Revolution in Brazil: Politics and Society in a Developing Nation.* New York: E. P. Dutton & Co., 1964, pp. 279-304; and for a more panoramic introduction, R. A. Gómez, *Government and Politics in Latin America* (revised edition). New York: Random House, 1963.

[8] For a sound introduction to this subject see Richard Harris, *Independence and After: Revolution in Underdeveloped Countries.* London: Oxford University Press, 1962.

nological advance and bureaucratic efficiency have not advanced to the point where this is possible. A verbal commitment to democratic values is retained. The democratic society remains a goal to be attained, while authoritarian solutions are considered temporary necessities. However, its governmental machinery is feared for its total control and the effect on the social system. Yet, almost every Third World nation has a written constitution and a formal legislative body. Oftentimes, these documents are tailored after those extant in the advanced countries. But generally these documents serve to legitimize bodies which act as rubber stamps. Actual political structures bear a much closer resemblance to the Second World of the Soviet orbit than to the First World. . . .

The Third World nations, as presently constituted, have attempted to develop military alternatives to the First and Second Worlds—not just political options to military power, but genuine large-scale military force.[9] The most powerful Third World nations are nations that had popular revolutions, which means revolutions which have either crushed or eliminated the old elites rather than just reshuffling power among them. It is no accident that nations such as Ghana, Algeria, Cuba, India, and Yugoslavia are leaders of the Third World; they represent the nations which have had this fully developed "revolution from below." For this reason Mexico can probably be considered a more fully developed member of the Third World than Venezuela, because in the 1910-20 Mexican Revolution the old military caste was crushed. The old military caste was tied up with the feudal aristocracy and the landed nobility. The new military was at the outset a popular peasant militia.

In the Third World, where revolutions have been successful, the traditional military has either been crushed or fully absorbed into revolutionary actions. There has not always been an armed struggle between military groupings. Nevertheless, the national liberation front has been the major stimulus to successful popular reform and revolutionary movements in the Third World nations. The development of these nations in large measure is connected to the outcomes of these internal military conflicts.[10] . . .

Ethnic and/or religious differences are exceedingly important in the Third World. With the exception of Latin America, religions of Asia and Africa are neither Roman Catholic, Protestant, Jewish, or Greek Orthodox. They are, basically, Moslem, Shinto, Taoist, Confucian, Buddhist, Hindu, primitive. Even Latin American Catholicism has always been special, often infused, as in Haiti and Brazil, with non-Christian sources of religious practice and ritual. Religious culture remains an element apart, as a cohesive

[9] See on this Morris Janowitz, *The Military in the Political Development of New Nations.* Chicago: University of Chicago Press, 1964.
[10] See J. K. Zawodny (ed.), "Unconventional Warfare," *The Annals of the American Academy of Political and Social Science,* Vol. 341, 1962.

factor for maintaining tradition in the Third World. The religious expression of the value of leisure over work, the sharp distinction between the sacred and the profane, and the separation between castes reinforces the fatalism often linked to ideas opposing development.

The Third World is an area where there are few competing religious institutions, since nationalism and patriotic fervor supercede linguistic and religious preferences. Whether Christian, Moslem, Hindu, or Hebrew, a national Church often accompanies the national State. Where different religions co-exist, there is usually strong conflict. The India-Pakistan partition was made inevitable by religious differences; and the Buddhist-Catholic rift in Vietnam is long-standing and severe. Many of the non-Christian religious organizations do not have established church hierarchies separate from the state bureaucracy. This is particularly true in the Middle East, and was true of pre-war Japan and China. Also, since leadership in the Third World is more tied to ethnic values than to religious values as such, the "secularization" process appears more accentuated than it is in fact. The parochial nature of religions in the Third World tends to force the individual to choose between religious belief and non-belief, rather than between competing religions. Socialist-atheist ideologies, rather than Western-Christian religions, compete with the established religions in Asia and Africa. And in a slightly modified sense, the same is true of Latin America—where Socialism is more tolerated than Methodism.

A large majority of the people in the Third World, prior to their independence, have very little, if any, primary or secondary school training. It is almost axiomatic that once the Third World nation passes through its first ordeal of development, the main push is toward cultivation of its people; at least the technical and primary training that a population needs in order to enter any socially developed world.[11] There is a modifying factor to be considered. Prior to the achievement of national independence, there is a heavy premium on ideological leadership. The new ruling class tends to be recruited from the political elite. In the second stage, once sovereignty and a level of primary education are also achieved, concern for technical proficiency promotes the demand for higher education for all, a new technical ideology replaces the conventional ideology of revolutionism. This took place in Russia. The first stage was experimentation and freedom followed by an emphasis on heavy industrial growth, which in turn slowly adapted revolutionary Marxism to technical needs—rather than developed a technological ideology as such. This same path seems to be pursued in such faraway places as Rumania and Cuba—where increasingly the political leadership is recruited from technical engineering sources.

[11] See on this Frederick Harbison and Charles A. Myers, *Education, Manpower, and Economic Growth: Strategies of Human Resource Development.* New York: McGraw-Hill, 1964, esp. pp. 49-130; also Adam Curle, *Educational Strategy for Developing Societies.* London: Tavistock Publications, 1963.

This changeover within the Third World, from a militant ideological point of view to a technological point of view, is accompanied by large-scale cultural reorientations. Hence, in all Third World nations, one finds a continuing struggle between humanistic traditions and growing technical predilections, between traditional values and scientific innovation. Each newly formed nation is working out the conflict between these "two cultures" that Charles P. Snow has described. As a general rule, the conventional revolutionary ideology lasts longer at the cultural level than at the economic level. Since Marxism, socialism, and the variants thereof represent a general way of life, an effort is made to rationalize technical change within the conventional ideology, rather than risk raising questions about the ideology. Hence, there is considerable disparity and lag between mass sentiments favoring the conventional ideology and technological demands for cultural innovation. This in itself can be an important factor in the emerging nations, as has been made plain in the cultural debates which have taken place in Cuba, almost without letup, since the Castro Revolution of 1959. Nonetheless, if the problem of two cultures is not quite resolved by the evolution of the Third World, thus far it has become a meaningful base for the reexamination of scientific and cultural integration.

"Natural" geographic and demographic factors also directly affect the structure of the Third World. For example, many of the Third World areas have unfavorable climate and/or soil resources. Extreme heat, bacteriological infiltration of the soil, heavy rainy seasons, etc., seriously impede sustained and rapid growth. There is no question that technological advancements such as air-conditioning and artificial irrigation can compensate for these natural deficits, but it would be foolish to deny the grave effects of geographical and ecological impediments in Third World areas.[12] Indeed, such a natural phenomenon as water supply has played an immense part in the political and economic development of China, determining the character of political control, no less than who shall rule at any given time.[13]

Complicating the tasks of development still further are the demographic imbalances that exist in the Third World. There is today a definite trend toward overpopulation in Asia, Africa, and, more recently, in Latin America. It is a vicious circle, in effect: an agricultural economy can sustain large populations, and large extended families are a requirement for the maintenance of an agricultural economy. The facts and figures on life expectancy rates, infant mortality, and per capita daily intake of calories are too well known to require elaboration. Yet, the demographic factor is complicated by the fact that medical and scientific innovation extends the life span, and in turn places a higher valuation on life. At the same time that

[12] See Wladimir S. Woytinsky and Emma S. Woytinsky, *World Population and Production*. New York: Twentieth Century Fund, 1963.
[13] See Karl Wittfogel, *Oriental Despotism: A Comparative Study of Total Power*. New Haven: Yale University Press, 1956.

mortality is steadily declining, there is no corresponding increase in family planning.[14]

The problems created by the transition from rural to urban life styles leaves no aspect of social life untouched. They affect everything from food tastes to cultural preferences. The impact of urban form—the first contact with foreigners and foreign ways—has profoundly shaped the attitudes of social classes in the Third World. People feel as strongly about mass leisure or political participation in Jakarta and Buenos Aires as they do in London or New York.[15] The transitional process is of a special nature. The Third World nations generally have a single metropolitan center, without either middle-sized cities or competing metropolitan centers within their boundaries. Thus they represent highly developed city-states, with a backward countryside surrounding them. This is particularly the case in Latin America. This promotes a great unbalance in migration patterns. Class and cultural dissonance becomes inevitable because of the gaps between country and city living, and the rapid and often difficult transition forced upon migrants who move to the city.[16] In addition, the large urban centers of the Third World are parasitic rather than promoters of development. They tend to exploit, through the domestic bourgeoisie, the labor and produce of the countryside. And in turn, this parasitism is extended to the international sphere. The cities are not favorably located with respect to further industrialization of the nation, but are evolved in terms of their uses as import-export centers. . . .

Three problems loom large in the decision to accelerate development: First, should the rate of national development be determined by the needs of the sovereign citizens, by other nations' rates of growth, or by general principles of planning? Second, are entrepreneurial or proletariat classes best suited to carry forth the developmental process, or, to state the issue another way, should elites or masses determine the tempo and themes of development? Third, what is the proper proportion of coercion and consensus in the developmental process?

At a more generic level, the solution would seem to hinge upon whether there is an economic basis to politics, as in the First World and Second World, or a political basis to economics, as in most of the Third

---

[14] See Ralph Thomlinson, *Population Dynamics: Causes and Consequences of World Demographic Change.* New York: Random House, 1965. Such problems are not unlike those faced by the poor in the developed nations. See, for example, Lee Rainwater, *And the Poor Get Children: Sex, Contraception, and Family Planning in the Working Class.* Chicago: Quadrangle Books, 1960.

[15] See Philip M. Hauser, *Population Perspectives.* New Brunswick, N.J.: Rutgers University Press, 1960.

[16] See Rodolpho Stavenhagen, "Classes, Colonialism, and Acculturation," *Studies in Comparative International Development,* Vol. I, No. 6 (1965), pp. 53–77; and for a theoretical exposition of the effects of the urban and industrial processes, see Herbert Blumer, "Early Industrialization and the Laboring Class," *The Sociological Quarterly,* Vol. I, No. 1 (January 1960), pp. 5–14.

World. In some measure this is an analytic problem of how the world is "carved up," and not exclusively a pragmatic one of how men shape their world. This combination of analytical, empirical, and practical may be untidy, but it is precisely the intellectual blend which we must ultimately come to terms with.

Putting the master issue in paradigm form, there is an economic continuum between capitalism and socialism and a political continuum extending from elite totalitarianism to mass democracy. The Third World mix is essentially unstable. What is at issue for the immediate future is the proportion of the "mix," that is, the particular combinations involving capitalism, socialism, democracy, and authoritarianism. The unstable mix is often taken to indicate the "transitional" character of the Third World. The problem is no longer traditionalism versus modernism, but rather the different political and economic arrangements covered by the word "modern."

Revolution is now being made in terms of socialism *plus* maximum social control. The alternative is not capitalism plus democracy, but rather capitalism and maximum social control. Third World revolutions have overthrown absolute tyrants, shiekdoms, petty militarists in the service of foreign rulers, and even some of the feudal "remnants." That these revolutions are not at the same time democratic is due to a multitude of factors—from the backwardness of the peoples involved to the political elitism bred by traditionalism. Modernization may be rapid, but development is still a slow and laborious process. The former is defined by industrialism while the latter must locate industrialism in an overall developmental scheme. One has to choose not simply between freedom and slavery, as free enterprise apologists maintain. The choice is really between socialism, with a minimum of conventional democratic safeguards, and colonialism, with little more conventional democracy than now obtains. To expect any more is simply asking for utopia. The Cuban Revolution of 1959 did not "crush" democracy, as there was precious little of it to crush. The Algerian Revolution did not abolish personal freedoms; under the French colonialists there were none to guarantee. The Egyptian Revolution did not deprive the bourgeoisie of the free trade it did not possess. . . .

4. Stages of Economic Growth

W. W. ROSTOW

It is possible to identify all societies, in their economic dimensions, as lying within one of five categories: the traditional society, the preconditions for take-off, the take-off, the drive to maturity, and the age of high mass-consumption.

THE TRADITIONAL SOCIETY

First, the traditional society. A traditional society is one whose structure is developed within limited production functions, based on pre-Newtonian science and technology, and on pre-Newtonian attitudes towards the physical world. Newton is here used as a symbol for that watershed in history when men came widely to believe that the external world was subject to a few knowable laws, and was systematically capable of productive manipulation.

The conception of the traditional society is, however, in no sense static; and it would not exclude increases in output. Acreage could be expanded; some *ad hoc* technical innovations, often highly productive innovations, could be introduced in trade, industry and agriculture; productivity could rise with, for example, the improvement of irrigation works or the discovery and diffusion of a new crop. But the central fact about the traditional society was that a ceiling existed on the level of attainable output per head. This ceiling resulted from the fact that the potentialities which flow from modern science and technology were either not available or not regularly and systematically applied.

Both in the longer past and in recent times the story of traditional societies was thus a story of endless change. The area and volume of trade within them and between them fluctuated, for example, with the degree of political and social turbulence, the efficiency of central rule, the upkeep of the roads. Population—and, within limits, the level of life—rose and fell not only with the sequence of the harvests, but with the incidence of war and of plague. Varying degrees of manufacture developed; but, as in agriculture,

From W. W. Rostow, *The Stages of Economic Growth* (Cambridge, Cambridge University Press, 1960), pp. 4-12. Reprinted by permission of the publisher.

the level of productivity was limited by the inaccessibility of modern science, its applications, and its frame of mind.

Generally speaking, these societies, because of the limitation on productivity, had to devote a very high proportion of their resources to agriculture; and flowing from the agricultural system there was an hierarchical social structure, with relatively narrow scope—but some scope—for vertical mobility. Family and clan connexions played a large role in social organization. The value system of these societies was generally geared to what might be called a long-run fatalism; that is, the assumption that the range of possibilities open to one's grandchildren would be just about what it had been for one's grandparents. But this long-run fatalism by no means excluded the short-run option that, within a considerable range, it was possible and legitimate for the individual to strive to improve his lot, within his lifetime. In Chinese villages, for example, there was an endless struggle to acquire or to avoid losing land, yielding a situation where land rarely remained within the same family for a century.

Although central political rule—in one form or another—often existed in traditional societies, transcending the relatively self-sufficient regions, the centre of gravity of political power generally lay in the regions, in the hands of those who owned or controlled the land. The landowner maintained fluctuating but usually profound influence over such central political power as existed, backed by its entourage of civil servants and soldiers, imbued with attitudes and controlled by interests transcending the regions.

In terms of history then, with the phrase "traditional society" we are grouping the whole pre-Newtonian world: the dynasties in China; the civilization of the Middle East and the Mediterranean; the world of medieval Europe. And to them we add the post-Newtonian societies which, for a time, remained untouched or unmoved by man's new capability for regularly manipulating his environment to his economic advantage.

To place these infinitely various, changing societies in a single category, on the ground that they all shared a ceiling on the productivity of their economic techniques, is to say very little indeed. But we are, after all, merely clearing the way in order to get at . . . the post-traditional societies, in which each of the major characteristics of the traditional society was altered in such ways as to permit regular growth: its politics, social structure, and (to a degree) its values, as well as its economy.

THE PRECONDITIONS FOR TAKE-OFF

The second stage of growth embraces societies in the process of transition; that is, the period when the preconditions for take-off are developed; for it takes time to transform a traditional society in the ways necessary for it to exploit the fruits of modern science, to fend off diminishing returns, and thus to enjoy the blessings and choices opened up by the march of compound interest.

The preconditions for take-off were initially developed, in a clearly marked way, in Western Europe of the late seventeenth and early eighteenth centuries as the insights of modern science began to be translated into new production functions in both agriculture and industry, in a setting given dynamism by the lateral expansion of world markets and the international competition for them. But all that lies behind the break-up of the Middle Ages is relevant to the creation of the preconditions for take-off in Western Europe. Among the Western European states, Britain, favoured by geography, natural resources, trading possibilities, social and political structure, was the first to develop fully the preconditions for take-off.

The more general case in modern history, however, saw the stage of preconditions arise not endogenously but from some external intrusion by more advanced societies. These invasions—literal or figurative—shocked the traditional society and began or hastened its undoing; but they also set in motion ideas and sentiments which initiated the process by which a modern alternative to the traditional society was constructed out of the old culture.

The idea spreads not merely that economic progress is possible, but that economic progress is a necessary condition for some other purpose, judged to be good: be it national dignity, private profit, the general welfare, or a better life for the children. Education, for some at least, broadens and changes to suit the needs of modern economic activity. New types of enterprising men come forward—in the private economy, in government, or both —willing to mobilize savings and to take risks in pursuit of profit or modernization. Banks and other institutions for mobilizing capital appear. Investment increases, notably in transport, communications, and in raw materials in which other nations may have an economic interest. The scope of commerce, internal and external, widens. And, here and there, modern manufacturing enterprise appears, using the new methods. But all this activity proceeds at a limited pace within an economy and a society still mainly characterized by traditional low-productivity methods, by the old social structure and values, and by the regionally based political institutions that developed in conjunction with them.

In many recent cases, for example, the traditional society persisted side by side with modern economic activities, conducted for limited economic purposes by a colonial or quasi-colonial power.

Although the period of transition—between the traditional society and the take-off—saw major changes in both the economy itself and in the balance of social values, a decisive feature was often political. Politically, the building of an effective centralized national state—on the basis of coalitions touched with a new nationalism, in opposition to the traditional landed regional interests, the colonial power, or both, was a decisive aspect of the preconditions period; and it was, almost universally, a necessary condition for take-off. . . .

THE TAKE-OFF

We come now to the great watershed in the life of modern societies: the third stage in this sequence, the take-off. The take-off is the interval when the old blocks and resistances to steady growth are finally overcome. The forces making for economic progress, which yielded limited bursts and enclaves of modern activity, expand and come to dominate the society. Growth becomes its normal condition. Compound interest becomes built, as it were, into its habits and institutional structure.

In Britain and the well-endowed parts of the world populated substantially from Britain (the United States, Canada, etc.) the proximate stimulus for take-off was mainly (but not wholly) technological. In the more general case, the take-off awaited not only the build-up of social overhead capital and a surge of technological development in industry and agriculture, but also the emergence to political power of a group prepared to regard the modernization of the economy as serious, high-order political business.

During the take-off, the rate of effective investment and savings may rise from, say, 5% of the national income to 10% or more; although where heavy social overhead capital investment was required to create the technical preconditions for take-off the investment rate in the preconditions period could be higher than 5%, as, for example, in Canada before the 1890's and Argentina before 1914. In such cases capital imports usually formed a high proportion of total investment in the preconditions period and sometimes even during the take-off itself, as in Russia and Canada during their pre-1914 railway booms.

During the take-off new industries expand rapidly, yielding profits a large proportion of which are reinvested in new plants; and these new industries, in turn, stimulate, through their rapidly expanding requirement for factory workers, the services to support them, and for other manufactured goods, a further expansion in urban areas and in other modern industrial plants. The whole process of expansion in the modern sector yields an increase of income in the hands of those who not only save at high rates but place their savings at the disposal of those engaged in modern sector activities. The new class of entrepreneurs expands; and it directs the enlarging flows of investment in the private sector. The economy exploits hitherto unused natural resources and methods of production.

New techniques spread in agriculture as well as industry, as agriculture is commercialized, and increasing numbers of farmers are prepared to accept the new methods and the deep changes they bring to ways of life. The revolutionary changes in agricultural productivity are an essential condition for successful take-off; for modernization of a society increases radically its bill for agricultural products. In a decade or two both the basic structure of the economy and the social and political structure of the society are transformed in such a way that a steady rate of growth can be, thereafter, regularly sustained.

. . . One can approximately allocate the take-off of Britain to the two decades after 1783; France and the United States to the several decades preceding 1860; Germany, the third quarter of the nineteenth century; Japan, the fourth quarter of the nineteenth century; Russia and Canada, the quarter-century or so preceding 1914; while during the 1950's India and China have, in quite different ways, launched their respective take-offs.

THE DRIVE TO MATURITY

After take-off there follows a long interval of sustained if fluctuating progress, as the now regularly growing economy drives to extend modern technology over the whole front of its economic activity. Some 10-20% of the national income is steadily invested, permitting output regularly to outstrip the increase in population. The make-up of the economy changes unceasingly as technique improves, new industries accelerate, older industries level off. The economy finds its place in the international economy: goods formerly imported are produced at home; new import requirements develop, and new export commodities to match them. The society makes such terms as it will with the requirements of modern efficient production, balancing off the new against the older values and institutions, or revising the latter in such ways as to support rather than to retard the growth process.

Some sixty years after take-off begins (say, forty years after the end of take-off) what may be called maturity is generally attained. The economy, focused during the take-off around a relatively narrow complex of industry and technology, has extended its range into more refined and technologically often more complex processes; for example, there may be a shift in focus from the coal, iron, and heavy engineering industries of the railway phase to machine-tools, chemicals, and electrical equipment. This, for example, was the transition through which Germany, Britain, France, and the United States had passed by the end of the nineteenth century or shortly thereafter. But there are other sectoral patterns which have been followed in the sequence from take-off to maturity. . . .

Formally, we can define maturity as the stage in which an economy demonstrates the capacity to move beyond the original industries which powered its take-off and to absorb and to apply efficiently over a very wide range of its resources—if not the whole range—the most advanced fruits of (then) modern technology. This is the stage in which an economy demonstrates that it has the technological and entrepreneurial skills to produce not everything, but anything that it chooses to produce. It may lack (like contemporary Sweden and Switzerland, for example) the raw materials or other supply conditions required to produce a given type of output economically; but its dependence is a matter of economic choice or political priority rather than a technological or institutional necessity.

Historically, it would appear that something like sixty years was required to move a society from the beginning of take-off to maturity. Analytically the explanation for some such interval may lie in the powerful arithmetic of compound interest applied to the capital stock, combined with the broader consequences for a society's ability to absorb modern technology of three successive generations living under a regime where growth is the normal condition. But, clearly, no dogmatism is justified about the exact length of the interval from take-off to maturity.

THE AGE OF HIGH MASS-CONSUMPTION

We come now to the age of high mass-consumption, where, in time, the leading sectors shift towards durable consumers' goods and services: a phase from which Americans are beginning to emerge; whose not unequivocal joys Western Europe and Japan are beginning energetically to probe; and with which Soviet society is engaged in an uneasy flirtation.

As societies achieved maturity in the twentieth century two things happened: real income per head rose to a point where a large number of persons gained a command over consumption which transcended basic food, shelter, and clothing; and the structure of the working force changed in ways which increased not only the proportion of urban to total population, but also the proportion of the population working in offices or in skilled factory jobs—aware of and anxious to acquire the consumption fruits of a mature economy.

In addition to these economic changes, the society ceased to accept the further extension of modern technology as an overriding objective. It is in this post-maturity stage, for example, that, through the political process, Western societies have chosen to allocate increased resources to social welfare and security. The emergence of the welfare state is one manifestation of a society's moving beyond technical maturity; but it is also at this stage that resources tend increasingly to be directed to the production of consumers' durables and to the diffusion of services on a mass basis, if consumers' sovereignty reigns. The sewing-machine, the bicycle, and then the various electric-powered household gadgets were gradually diffused. Historically, however, the decisive element has been the cheap mass automobile with its quite revolutionary effects—social as well as economic—on the life and expectations of society.

For the United States, the turning point was, perhaps, Henry Ford's moving assembly line of 1913-14; but it was in the 1920's, and again in the post-war decade, 1946-56, that this stage of growth was pressed to, virtually, its logical conclusion. In the 1950's Western Europe and Japan appear to have fully entered this phase, accounting substantially for a momentum in their economies quite unexpected in the immediate post-war years. The Soviet Union is technically ready for this stage, and, by every sign, its citizens hunger for it; but Communist leaders face difficult political and social problems of adjustment if this stage is launched.

BEYOND CONSUMPTION

Beyond, it is impossible to predict, except perhaps to observe that Americans, at least, have behaved in the past decade as if diminishing relative marginal utility sets in, after a point, for durable consumers' goods; and they have chosen, at the margin, larger families—behaviour in the pattern of Buddenbrooks dynamics.[*] Americans have behaved as if, having been born into a system that provided economic security and high mass-consumption, they placed a lower valuation on acquiring additional increments of real income in the conventional form as opposed to the advantages and values of an enlarged family. But even in this adventure in generalization it is a shade too soon to create—on the basis of one case—a new stage-of-growth, based on babies, in succession to the age of consumers' durables: as economists might say, the income-elasticity of demand for babies may well vary from society to society. But it is true that the implications of the baby boom along with the not wholly unrelated deficit in social overhead capital are likely to dominate the American economy over the next decade rather than the further diffusion of consumers' durables.

Here then, in an impressionistic rather than an analytic way, are the stages-of-growth which can be distinguished once a traditional society begins its modernization: the transitional period when the preconditions for take-off are created generally in response to the intrusion of a foreign power, converging with certain domestic forces making for modernization; the take-off itself; the sweep into maturity generally taking up the life of about two further generations; and then, finally, if the rise of income has matched the spread of technological virtuosity (which, as we shall see, it need not immediately do) the diversion of the fully mature economy to the provision of durable consumers' goods and services (as well as the welfare state) for its increasingly urban—and then suburban—population. Beyond lies the question of whether or not secular spiritual stagnation will arise, and, if it does, how man might fend it off. . . .

[*] In Thomas Mann's novel of three generations, the first sought money; the second, born to money, sought social and civic position; the third, born to comfort and family prestige, looked to the life of music. The phrase is designed to suggest, then, the changing aspirations of generations, as they place a low value on what they take for granted and seek new forms of satisfaction.

5. There Are No Simple Answers

ROBERT E. BALDWIN

Like so many modern problems, the urgency of economic development as a social question is all out of proportion to our knowledge about development as an economic process. Nevertheless, although we are still a long way from a general theory of development, significant advances have been made in the postwar period toward a better understanding of key factors and relationships in economic growth. Much of the analytical progress can best be characterized as a rejection of simple and extreme views concerning the nature of development patterns and a growing awareness of their complexity. At the same time, there is now greater confidence that we know enough about these processes to be able to make substantial contributions towards alleviating poverty in this generation.

One relationship being repeatedly verified in developing countries is that the great majority of the people respond positively to economic incentives. When cash market opportunities improve, the typical small farmer tends to respond by increasing production. Similarly, the supply curve of labor in less developed countries seems generally to be positively sloped. Since economic development via reliance upon the price system is the cheapest way for governments to carry out their development commitments, the mass of evidence indicating that most people respond favorably to economic incentives is a very hopeful sign. Those who believe that most individuals in developing countries possess limited wants and consequently work only to attain some "target" income either throw up their hands in despair about development prospects or argue that there is no hope until basic values and attitudes change. The latter course of action is at best very costly and time consuming and perhaps impossible to effectively carry out.

This does not mean that the cultural background of a country makes no difference. Quite clearly, the environment in which individuals are raised plays an important role in the development process, especially in determining the supply of entrepreneurial ability. However, there seems to be a broad spectrum of cultures where economic development by means of free-market methods can flourish and from which at least a minimum amount of entrepreneurial talent can spring. No longer do most economists

From Robert E. Baldwin, *Economic Growth and Development* (New York, John Wiley & Sons, Inc., 1966), pp. 112-116. Reprinted by permission of the publisher.

consider some particular culture as either essential for successful growth or a complete obstacle to such development.

At the same time, the accumulating evidence that most individuals respond favorably to economic incentive does not mean that merely providing economic opportunity is enough to achieve development. This is another simple view that is being discredited by recent experience. At one time many thought land reform to be the key to agricultural development. If a farmer owned his own land, it was thought that he would increase his market supplies of agricultural products. Now it is realized that land reform can be disastrous without concurrent programs to train farmers to direct their own agricultural operations, to provide credit facilities for new land owners, to furnish these farmers with appropriate market and technical information, etc. Likewise, juggling a few marketing board prices may be an important part of a rural development effort, but by no means should it be all there is to the program.

The rejection of some of the more extreme views about the nature of development carries over into the investment field. One widely held position has been that capital accumulation is the essence of development and that its pace can be increased more or less automatically by increasing the stock of material capital. A rather different, but similarly extreme notion is that, because of the complex interrelations among the detailed parts of the economy as well as the indivisibility of capital, a massive investment program covering all parts of the economy is needed for successful growth. Otherwise the economy will never break out of the vicious circle of poverty.

Postwar growth experience indicates that development is not as simple as the first position suggests or as difficult as the second view implies. Simple models based upon aggregate capital-output ratios or even the investment and saving schedules of the neoclassical writers are not very useful for understanding the growth process in developing countries. A more microscopic analysis of these economies is needed. In particular, the leading industries in terms of their direct and indirect development impact must be analyzed as well as the interactions among major sectors of the economy. In other words, a disaggregative approach is essential for an adequate analysis of the growth process in less developed nations.

A merit of the big-push approach to investment planning is that it points to the significance of the demand and supply interactions among various industries and sectors. However, this analysis overemphasizes the importance of these repercussions. Its policy implications are that investment must be pushed forward in unison in almost all productive lines because of the crucial nature of these interactions. This does not seem to be necessary, judging by recent development history. A pattern of uneven growth in which one sector stimulates development in other sectors and itself is pulled forward by other sectors has proved to result in successful overall development efforts. Of course, no one sector can get too far ahead, but balance among sectors is a flexible relationship that must be maintained for successful development. The proponents of the big-push approach also overstressed the limitations that the indivisibility of capital impose on a more gradual and selective approach to investment efforts.

The notion that the accumulation of physical capital is the essence of economic development has come to be less widely held in recent years. Currently, investment in human capital in the form of expenditures on general education, vocational training, and health is being stressed on an especially important requirement. This emphasis is partly because more and more developing countries are gradually breaking through the traditional barrier of very low rates of capital accumulation. As they do this, they are finding that a lack of trained personnel is what slows down their growth rates. Undoubtedly, as educational levels improve, new constraints such as poor natural resources, will come to the forefront. We have learned enough now, however, to know that no one factor is the answer to more rapid growth. At certain times, one economic variable is more important than others but, over the long run, all factors of production combine to produce growth. Consequently, theories based mainly upon changes in one particular productive factor are strictly limited in their usefulness. The same is true of analyses suggesting that development always follows in some particular pattern or occurs in definite stages.

The trend toward rejecting simple, easy solutions to development problems is evident in the policy field. Such policy gimmicks as painless development via inflation or utilizing surplus labor in agriculture to achieve costless growth are no longer taken very seriously. They usually contain the kernel of a good policy notion, but they need to be considerably modified to become relevant for the real world. Highly detailed and elaborate planning also has not as yet proved itself to be very useful in government efforts to accelerate growth. There may, some day, be a high payoff to these planning techniques but, as of now, development planning is still quite simple in the less developed, market economies.

Another encouraging trend in policy thinking within the developing countries is a growing awareness of the cost of development in economic and social terms. Too often in the past these countries viewed development as something that follows almost automatically from political independence and a moderate amount of foreign aid. They failed to appreciate that successful development at best is a relatively slow process and rests upon hard economic decisions at the domestic level and, even when successful, development brings a host of new problems. For example, the breaking-down of traditional attitudes and social organizations, which usually accompanies changes in productive structures, involves difficult personal readjustment problems. It is not enough for development leaders to think merely about steel mills and roads. They must also plan for new institutions and organizations to take over many of the social functions performed by the institu·

tional arrangements that development destroys. Fortunately, in recent years the price tags attached to development, as well as its benefits, are being better appreciated.

We are at the point in development economics where there appears to be no single or simple policy prescriptions for successful growth. Some generalities can be made with respect to such general topics as commercial policy and fiscal policy and also about development policies in such broad economic sectors as agriculture and manufacturing, but each country must be considered in detail in order to formulate appropriate specific development policies. What is important, however, is that we are acquiring the kind of general knowledge needed to take the complex economic conditions of any particular country and formulate a set of analytically sound development policies for each country.

6. Bread and Freedom: The Pluralistic Approach

WILLIAM McCORD

Our century will be chiefly remembered by future generations not as an era of political conflicts or technical inventions, but as an age in which human society dared to think of the welfare of the whole human race as a practical objective.

ARNOLD TOYNBEE

Over one hundred years ago, while deeply engaged in the battles of his own epoch, John Stuart Mill had the vision to foresee the issues confronting our generation. He observed that the basic dilemma of the future would be "how to unite the greatest individual liberty of action with common ownership in the raw materials of the globe, and an equal participation of all in the benefits of combined labor."[1] With an immensely greater store of resources at our disposal than there was in Mill's time, there is no technical reason why the problem cannot be solved. And, too, we have the advantage of historical perspective, for we know the results of the various social, political, and economic experiments which mankind has conducted during the last century.

It would be presumptuous to claim that this accumulated wisdom provides a map to utopia for leaders in emerging nations. The convulsions of modern times have outmoded the programs, plans, and prescriptions for progress which abounded in the nineteenth century. History does, however, offer certain broad guidelines—or perhaps, one might better say, warnings —to leaders in developing nations. Some appreciation of these general points may help in unweaving the skein of social, economic, and political problems which burden the "Third World."

RESPONDING TO THE SOCIAL CHALLENGE

The paramount requirement for the modernization of any society is that the people themselves must change.

MAX MILLIKAN and DONALD BLACKMER

From *The Springtime of Freedom* by William McCord. Copyright © 1965 by Oxford University Press, Inc. Reprinted by permission.
[1] John Stuart Mill, quoted in *The Age of Nationalism* by Hans Kohn (New York: Harper & Row, Publishers, 1962), p. 44.

Behind the abstractions with which we have dealt lie millions of hungry and often angry human beings, aware more than ever before of their misery. The social milieu of these *les misérables* of the globe has undergone profound alterations during the last decade. Colonialism, the impact of two world wars, the beginnings of a market economy, and the extension of transportation have, for good or ill, broken down the proud isolation of the traditional village community. The average man in developing societies has become aware, however dimly, of a larger world with its new horizons. Then, too, the usual hierarchical system of traditional societies—its respect for ancestors, or its caste ranks, or its reliance on the all-powerful patrons and priests—has haltingly given way to modern concepts of individuality and equality. Impelled by a belief in equality (sometimes conceived as the equal ranking of groups, sometimes as individual equality of opportunity), new political forces have been let loose which leaders everywhere find it difficult to trammel.

Perhaps of greatest significance, the fatalism characteristic of stagnant societies has been eroded by concepts of progress, by a vision that man's condition can be improved here and now, not in some hazy future. Platitudes and promises no longer serve to satisfy transitional men, nor do the usual metaphysical explanations continue to justify their lot in life. This emancipating, if often frustrating, belief in progress has worked its way down to even the most primitive villages. It has created a new type of man infected with "this-worldliness," as Barbara Ward has phrased it, an "immense interest in *this* world, in its processes, in its laws and construction, in the ways in which it can be set to work and made over according to human ends and purposes—in a word the world as an arena of work and effort where needs and dreams can be satisfied."[2]

To fulfill this hunger for progress requires that transitional men, already leavened with revolutionary ideas, need to undergo still further changes in their customs, habits, and values. By this, I do not mean that governments should set about dismantling the entire culture of their countries. Not only do such attempts usually fail, as Russia's early experiments indicate, but to mount an assault upon tradition *per se* unwarrantedly insults the past efforts of mankind. The old religions, social relationships, festivals and rites were built over centuries to give sense, dignity, and a measure of happiness to barren lives. It would take a foolhardy prophet to suggest that modernization, with all of its penalties as well as benefits, can repay a people for the conscious planned destruction of traditions which gave existence a meaning. Contrary to the gloomy, if currently fashionable, view, traditional cultures do not lack in entrepreneurs nor need they impede a thrust toward economic modernization. In periods such as those of Meiji Japan and nineteenth-century Denmark, a substantial part of the old society

[2] Barbara Ward, *The Rich Nations and the Poor Nations* (London: Hamish Hamilton, 1962), p. 19.

survived, or even gained in vigor, while a new economy emerged. Rational governments merged the ancient and the modern in a way which changed the economy but left the traditional culture with some integrity. This middle path should be the basic policy of governments today.[3]

Nonetheless, in almost every developing country, certain social reforms, sometimes of a far-reaching nature, will have to be enacted to produce the right climate for economic growth and individual liberty. In terms of specific policies, most emerging nations should envisage a social program embodying these elements:

The economic and political power of feudal ruling groups, firmly entrenched in the *status quo* and ideologically dedicated to its total preservation, has to be undermined.

In the economic realm, the need is obvious. The process of rural modernization, for example, must almost universally begin with land reform, and the old landlords will stringently oppose such change with any means available. The resistance of a feudal elite to progress may well extend into less obvious areas. It seems natural to suppose, as one instance, that everyone would favor the abolition of illiteracy and ignorance. Yet, in making this naïve assumption, as one American political scientist has correctly observed, "We forget that there are many countries in the world where the maintenance of illiteracy is one of the chief political weapons in defense of the status quo. . . . Even if *we* don't know it, the oligarchies in those countries know that education, the enlightenment of these oppressed masses, represents an implicit challenge to the status quo."[4] In one fashion or another, the grip of these oligarchs upon their societies must be loosened.

Sometimes, the required change in a feudal structure will occur in an evolutionary fashion, as the natural growth of Indian trade unions, "scheduled caste" organizations, and business groups has begun to balance the power of landlords. More often, a change in the structure of power needs to be made swiftly, although not necessarily violently, as Egypt rid herself of landlords, Bolivia took over the tin barons' fiefs, and India expropriated the princes. Particularly in Latin America, one cannot conceive of equitable economic development as long as the present rigid and reactionary social structures prevail. The required "structural" changes can be made, *if* the ruling government is sufficiently dedicated to the improvement of its society and *if* the emerging nation receives moral and economic support from advanced regions, particularly the United States.

As the old social groupings—communities based on language, religion, or ethnic considerations—tend to disappear, a developing nation should con-

---

[3] For evidence that ancient traditions can coexist with economic change in today's developing countries, see Reinhard Bendix, "Concepts and Generalizations in Comparative Sociological Studies," *Transactions of the Fifth World Congress of Sociology* (Louvain: International Sociological Association, 1963).

[4] Hans Morgenthau, "America and the World Revolution," *Commentary,* Oct. 1963.

sciously plan to replace them with newly articulated interest groups—unions, co-operatives, workers' or village councils. Without toleration of such interest groups, the elite can seldom gain accurate knowledge of the economic desires or negotiable interests that exist within their society; the people, on the other hand, do not possess agencies which would express their specific interests. The crushing of "modern" interest groups, as in Ghana and Indonesia, runs the risk of depriving the elite of information concerning the wants of the people and the degree to which they would tolerate a particular decision; the end result can be economic stagnation or retrogression.

India provides a prime example of a state which has not only allowed but encouraged the growth of interest groups. Thousands of voluntary agencies, caste groups, and unions have spontaneously emerged in India. Beyond this, however, the government has launched its boldly conceived Panchayat Raj program which will for the first time draw the mass of peasantry into the push and pull of politics. The new plan has two aspects: first, the government wishes to decentralize political power down to the village level, in the expectation that this will eventually give the numerically superior lower castes a genuine form of self-government; secondly, the new plan allots significantly greater power to village councils in allocating development funds—hopefully, this new economic influence will draw the peasant into the center of development, rather than treating him as a passive recipient of charity. The Panchayat Raj ambitions may well be frustrated in the foreseeable future: traditional elites will attempt to maintain their privileges and will, certainly for a time, win a majority of seats in the village councils.[5] Looking further ahead, however, one may expect that the peasantry will eventually exert their latent power and energies in the service of development.

In addition, new means of communication have to be opened between the elite who governs and the people who subsist and suffer. Somehow, the small governing class at the top of every developing nation must communicate its eventual goals, aspirations, and decisions to the people. By far the best manner in which to do this is through personal contact between the leaders and the governed. In this respect, certain nations could serve as models. China has poured millions of men into the rural areas in a more or less successful attempt to educate and indoctrinate the peasantry. India has hundreds of thousands of development officers at work in the often disappointing, but vitally necessary, task of convincing peasants to adopt new methods. An even more ambitious plan has been advanced by Asoka Mehta, head of India's Praja Socialists. He has argued for a draft system which would send perhaps two million university graduates into rural areas for two years of service. Such a corps could undertake projects of rural development, give the lead to modernization, help end the exodus to cities

---

[5] See "Public Authority in a Developing Community: The Case of India," by Reinhard Bendix, *Archives Européennes de Sociologie,* Vol. IV (1963).

and allow "the dialogue of development . . . to reach the people."[6] Without such efforts, developing nations who now adhere to democratic methods of persuasion will have to fall back on coercion to achieve their aims.

Education must, of course, receive strong emphasis. While exact calculations are difficult, some experts attribute 60 per cent of economic growth in the West during the last fifty years to the effects of education and research.[7] And, as we have seen, much of the success of Russia and Japan in achieving their exceptional economic progress should be traced to their unusually large investments in education. Bespangled universities must not, however, become the fetish of new nations; too much as well as too little can be spent on education. Not one of the newer nations can long afford the luxury of a system of education which would immediately produce both universal literacy *and* squadrons of university-trained men. Because of budgetary rigors, the leadership in developing countries must draw a delicate balance between concentrating its resources in building an "elitist pyramid" of university graduates, doctors, skilled personnel, mechanics, technicians, and other types of people who are immediately needed—and simultaneously, using cheap, informal means of mass education.

The proper mixture will differ for each region. Clearly, unconventional techniques will be tried: television as in Colombia, solar radios in former French Africa, teaching machines in Ghana, or the each-child-teach-an-adult method as in Cuba. The folkschools of nineteenth-century Denmark also deserve emulation in many contemporary countries.

Only a balanced combination of formal and informal approaches to education can produce a skilled elite necessary for economic growth, an informed public required for political sophistication—and a national budget which does not stagger under the burdens of school building and teacher training. A slim volume of technical, high-level education, built on a foundation of unconventional methods of mass information, has to be the aim of educational advance in the newer nations.

Attitudes toward human reproduction must alter, if economic advance is to occur. As of now, the breeding of babies exceeds or matches expansion of economic production in Latin America, Asia, and the Middle East. Only a well-financed program of birth control can reverse the pattern and save future generations from starvation. We know that the most illiterate peasant can accept these facts of life and will welcome methods which will enhance the chance of survival for his offspring. Experiments throughout the world—in Puerto Rico and Ceylon, Japan and India—have demonstrated that mankind everywhere can comprehend the need for birth control and learn effective techniques. If advanced regions contribute their knowledge, assistance, and moral force to the furthering of this cause, there can

[6] Asoka Mehta, "No Pre-ordained Path," *The Economic Weekly,* June 1960, pp. 855-9.

[7] Ward, *op. cit.,* p. 136.

be little doubt that the "human explosion" will be contained by the 1970's.

Most generally, the elite must look to the village as the foundation for its programs and must seek to reverse the flow of urbanization. There are many sound reasons why land reform, technical assistance, education, and other forms of aid to the peasantry should receive the highest priority: Planners in every nation must seek the modernization of village life in all its dimensions since, without a marked increase in rural productivity, no program of economic development can succeed; urbanization, at this point in history, has worsened the material welfare of city immigrants; in consequence, the anomic urbanite falls prey to extremist political appeals which threaten a democratic body politic; and after experiencing the city's frustrations, a majority of immigrants would choose voluntarily to return to their village, if they could be assured of economic opportunities. Even setting aside strictly economic concerns, a wise government should undertake measures to invigorate village life, decentralize industries in the countryside, transform agriculture, and avoid a concentration of industries in the already glutted cities. Egypt's experience and (until 1960) China's suggest that such an approach can achieve marked success. Well-planned programs can bring forth the immense constructive potentiality of the rural areas, where the great majority of transitional men live.

From the turmoil of the last decades, one clear, if obvious, lesson has appeared: social planning, based on persuasion rather than force, must go together with any move toward economic modernization or political liberation. If developing nations conceive sound attempts to alter the feudal structure, produce a skilled and literate population, control the birth rate, close the gap between the elite and the masses, and revolutionize village life, there can be a realistic hope that emerging peoples will build a world without want.

RESPONDING TO THE ECONOMIC CHALLENGE

So long as freedom from hunger is only half achieved, so long as two-thirds of the nations of the world have food deficits—no citizen, no nation can afford to feel satisfied or secure. We have the ability, we have the means, and we have the capacity to eliminate hunger from the face of the earth. We need only the will. . . .

JOHN F. KENNEDY

No battle on earth has greater importance than the striving to end poverty in all of its grim aspects. Yet while we possess the resources, as John F. Kennedy knew, we can have no certainty that victory will be won. The campaign to abolish poverty faces massive obstacles, for its path, to paraphrase economist Benjamin Higgins, is paved with vicious circles.

It is obvious, for example, that a change in one sector of an economy can precipitate motion in other sectors. An increase in rural productivity, for instance, issues a food surplus which can free men for industrial work; this, in turn, provides consumer goods which flow back to farmers. The obverse also holds true: stagnation in one critical area of an economy can retard development in other areas. Without an injection of capital, food production cannot improve; without a rural surplus, industrialization proceeds only fitfully, if at all; without industrialization, new sources of capital will not emerge—and, in consequence, agriculture will remain quiescent. Since progress seldom occurs simultaneously on every front, the essential problem which faces those who desire a more abundant life is how to enter this interlocking chain. It would be fruitless to try to pinpoint the exact place where continuous, self-sustaining growth can best be stimulated, for developing nations are at such different stages in their evolution. Only a specific and pragmatic evaluation of each country's potentialities can provide the answer to this problem. Any strategy of economic growth, however, has to take into consideration a few principles which apply with more or less validity throughout the "Third World":

The first commandment of development is that agriculture must be transformed. In every instance of "take-off," whether in the West, Russia, or Japan, an agricultural revolution preceded other forms of economic growth. Lacking virgin land and outlets for an expanding population, developing nations today must again look to the peasant for their economic salvation. Farm production has to increase, since the bulk of the emerging world's population lives on the land and provides the main source for capital accumulation. If a rural surplus can be obtained, some of it can be transferred to other parts of the economy—either in the form of food, raw commodities, or capital. Greater rural productivity is needed not only to feed urban industrial workers and to provide funds for development but simply to keep in step with an unprecedented population expansion. And clearly, if the countryside does not prosper, new industries will fail to find markets for their products.

That the transformation of farming presents a formidable challenge hardly requires restatement. Traditional landowners are not normally found in the front ranks of innovative entrepreneurs. And the peasant who lives within a step of starvation naturally hesitates to adopt new techniques or a market-oriented attitude. Further, the usual nostrums of the past do not apply today. The Soviet example (or the Chinese model after 1958) simply cannot be adopted by most emerging countries as a guide to rural development: unused land does not exist in most regions; mechanization could not solve the problem, since it would raise the demand for capital to an impossible level; the vast number of people thrown out of work by attempts at collectivization and mechanization could not be absorbed in an urban environment; and, above all, the attachment of peasants to their present holdings, however tiny, can be eradicated only by a violent suppression unmatched in history. "Such a terrific transformation would involve the destruction of many millions of men," a Socialist leader has commented about India, "and would raise such vast problems of adjustment that no dictatorship could solve them."[8]

While not susceptible to easy solutions, the cause of changing agriculture is by no means hopeless. Japan's experience in the cultivation of postage-stamp plots of land offers a great deal of promise to developing regions. And contemporary experiments in such diverse areas as Egypt, Kenya, Nigeria, and parts of India show that rural productivity can mount rapidly when certain conditions are met. Land reform, of one type or another, is almost always essential, and normally the government must take the initiative in changing the land-tenure pattern. The farmer must also receive guidance, tools, marketing outlets, and low-interest loans from an outside agency. In addition, the government has to assume responsibility for building the irrigation and transport systems to sustain rural advance. And most importantly, the peasants have to be taught the reasons for innovation, the methods to bring it about, and the rewards which they may expect. Taken together, these measures can modernize agriculture in developing nations and lay the base for all other forms of economic advance.

Clearly, the pace of saving and productive reinvestment has to be stepped up. Unless a society reaches a point where the people devote some 15 per cent of national income to capital formation, an economy cannot prosper. This simple, if crucial, fact places a major burden on poor countries, for it means that the propensity to consume has to be checked rather severely.

Domestically, only two sources of capital formation exist: the profits derived from private enterprise or the funds which come from government taxation. It is most difficult to provide a rule of thumb which would determine the proper balance between these two sources. Certainly, a private sector of some magnitude should be allowed to function, since the "self-correcting" mechanism of the profit motive can often work to a nation's advantage. By concentrating all major sources of capital in the government's hands, a country courts the economic disaster which has overtaken Indonesia. Such a policy scares away useful foreign enterprise; it can destroy the initiative and vigor which sometimes, as in India, characterizes the private sector; and it undermines the variegated economic foundation needed for political freedom. Nonetheless, governments must directly or indirectly play a much more prominent role in capital formation than they did in the West's early evolution. Only the government can undertake certain projects which confer indiscriminate benefits on the people; only the government can finance large-scale projects which would be unattractive to domestic investors; and only the government can promulgate measures

---

[8] Asoka Mehta, "Can Asia Industrialize Democratically?" *Voices of Dissent* (New York: Grove Press, 1958), p. 256.

which will persuade the private investor to place his funds in productive enterprises rather than luxury consumption.

Thus, much of the burden of capital accumulation in a developing country must fall on the state. Both to fill its own coffers and to stimulate useful private investment, a free state can venture a variety of policies: increased income taxes, taxes on unused land, restrictions on nonessential consumption, tax rebates for productive enterprises, the initiation of a moderate inflationary policy, and a reduction in consumer imports. At least some of these policies have to be implemented in every developing region for the nation to reach a point where capital formation exceeds the pace of population growth.

Light, decentralized, consumer-oriented industries should form the base of the industrial sector in most emerging nations. Japan has amply demonstrated that such small-scale enterprises, particularly when integrated with the development of complementary heavy industries, can set an economy solidly on the road of economic progress. Today, both the economic and the sociological reasons for giving preference to light industry are even more compelling than during the Meiji period: such a program conserves precious capital; it avoids the hidden costs which heavy industrialization and consequent urbanization entail; it draws upon the talents of idle labor; it provides the mass of people with the experience, attitudes, sense of self-sufficiency, and other motives necessary for modernization; it satisfies the immediate, limited demands of transitional man, thus relieving political tensions; and it allows the emerging nations to replace consumer imports with domestically produced items, thereby reducing the strain on foreign exchange reserves.

Unfortunately, developing countries have too often ignored these advantages.[9] The symbols of the 20th century have sometimes blinded them to their country's real needs for economic development. With his usual asperity, Hans Morgenthau has noted:

> Many underdeveloped nations want not economic development in the liberal economic sense; what they want rather, are the symbols of power—the symbols of having arrived in the 20th century. I have always been impressed with the statement which Nehru made to Chou En-lai . . . when Chou En-lai visited India, and Nehru showed him a hydroelectric dam and said, "here is where I pray." And in a less noble fashion, perhaps, you find underdeveloped nations wanting to have an airline of their own which they cannot produce, which they cannot run, and which they cannot maintain. . . . In the 50's a steel mill performed the same function. . . . The steel mill is now in the process of being supplanted by the atomic reactor. This has nothing to do with genuine economic development. . . .[10]

[9] See *Prospects for Indian Development* by Wilfred Malenbaum (London: George Allen & Unwin, 1962).
[10] Morgenthau, *op. cit.*

It is a good omen that in the 1960's, India and some other countries have demonstrated a new, firmer commitment to the encouragement of light industries, for it is in this area that the most meaningful advances can be made. As the costs become apparent, a government's infatuation with the symbols of modernity tends to wither.

Leaders in the new nations have often followed another will-o'-the-wisp: the nationalist goal of economic self-sufficiency. For most of the developing countries, this is an unattainable aim even at some ultimate stage of development. Except for rare exceptions, the emerging areas have neither the resources nor large enough markets to try to detach themselves from the world economy. And even the exceptional cases, like China, will need to import industrial goods and some commodities (such as oil) from abroad for the foreseeable future. Any plan for national development, then, depends on finding viable ways to fit a new nation's products into the international economy.

While it is impossible for developing nations to extricate themselves from the world market, it should also be confessed that global economic operations often work to the detriment of an emerging economy, particularly when a country depends upon a single export for its foreign revenue. A sensible government can find its way out of this puzzle, although the process of moderating the world market's impact on an economy may take many years. To the best of its ability, any emerging country should attempt to diversify its exports and thus reduce its dependence on fluctuations in the world price for a particular item. Specifically, such a policy would aim at diversifying commodity production, since exports of manufactured goods have little chance of competing with products from industrially advanced countries. In some areas, it should prove possible for developing countries to establish common markets among themselves and to reach agreements with advanced nations whereby the prices for commodities can be kept at a more stable level. Foreign private enterprise, when properly held in check, can also serve a useful purpose in providing skills, capital, and new industries for the home market. These measures, when buttressed by co-operation from industrially advanced regions—ideally, by the type of co-ordination which once existed between Russia and China—would allow developing regions to merge equitably into the world market.

National development plans should be encouraged. Without an overall strategy and a sense of the critical links in the economy where an impetus to growth might best be started, enormous waste can occur. Burma, for example, built a steel rolling-mill when no one had surveyed the availability of resources, workers, or managers; at great cost, outside technicians came to rescue the plant from total confusion. Now it produces a small range of products. Some foresight would have avoided the unnecessary strain the experiment caused to Burma's economy. In every growing country, knowledge of available resources and co-ordination between various sectors of the economy, as well as ministries within the government, constitute essential ingredients in economic growth. The power to decide where a dam should be placed or whether a school will be built instead of a rural industry should be put in the hands of a public authority. Such economic planning, as in India, must not be confused with government ownership or the use of force. All societies, including the United States, plan or "program" their economies. At the early stages of growth, such intelligent thinking ahead is particularly necessary for orderly and rapid economic growth.

These, then, constitute the necessary factors for breaking through the vicious circle of economic stagnation: encouragement of agriculture and small industries; higher taxes and higher savings; a sensible integration of a developing economy into the world market; economic planning for steady, efficient growth; and a set of social policies designed to encourage the development of attitudes and institutions receptive to modernization. Combined judiciously, these policies can ensure that the quest for bread will not end in a whimper.

RESPONDING TO THE POLITICAL CHALLENGE

No, I shall not believe that this human race . . . has become a bastardized flock of sheep . . . and that nothing remains but to deliver it . . . to a small number of shepherds who, after all, are not better animals than are we, the human sheep, and who indeed are often worse.

ALEXIS DE TOCQUEVILLE

In the drive for development, all signs point to the sovereignty of politics. At their core, attempts to change the wretched condition of transitional men rest on political choices. How to accumulate capital and yet resist the tempting path of compulsion? How to preserve traditional culture but still change a feudal social structure? How to build a growing economy and yet avoid the exploitation which accompanied the expansion of industry in the past? This is the apex of the problem, for political—or, if you will, ethical—decisions determine the answer to such questions.

In responding to the stresses which afflict their societies, leaders in developing countries have divided into two political camps. Ranged on one side stand the authoritarians who are willing to use any practical means, including force, to achieve their ends. Authoritarian ideologies, while presented in varied garbs, assert certain common goals:

The authoritarian wishes national independence, freedom for the State or People—but not for the individual. Sékou Touré of Guinea has stated this view with blunt openness, "We have chosen the freedom, the right, the power, the sovereignty of the people, and not of the individual."[11] The sur-

---

[11] Sékou Touré, quoted in *West Africa,* July 22, 1961, p. 799.

vival and power of the group comes first; no domain of the individual's life should remain—on principle or in fact—outside the purview of the state.

The authoritarian believes that only a single party can create a sense of nationhood and unity which he regards as necessary during a period of modernization. Autonomous organizations or political parties, each articulating its own goals, are dispensable. Through some mystic identification, the authoritarian contends, Leader, Party, and People can become one. The unified party supposedly serves as the vanguard of progress and discourages disunity, factionalism, and subversion during a time of great tensions.

The authoritarian demands that development should occur through "socialist" methods. He believes that only socialism, usually conceived as heavy industrialization, can eradicate the poverty, disease, and illiteracy characteristic of pauper nations.

For the authoritarian, all human resources must be mobilized in the service of Party and Productivity. While robed in new garments, the authoritarian of today can find ample, if unsavory, company in the past. His arguments have been advanced from the Pharaohs' epoch to that of Goebbels. Witness Frederick the Great, in his defense of a "modernizing" Germany: "At the moment when the State cries out that its very life is at stake, social selfishness must cease and party hatred be hushed. The individual must forget his egoism, and feel that he is a member of the whole body."[12]

The world has never lacked those who defend their own power, privileges, and perquisites in the name of a brave cause or those who have claimed that history will absolve them for any action they commit. The Cause, the Party, or God have almost always overridden the quiet cries of an unknown individual, caught in the movement of history.

Yet, with whatever effect—and sometimes it has been noble—a band of questioners have wondered whether the particular emperor wore any clothes. In the face of many temptations, these men still fight a battle for freedom in the developing countries. They can be found under a variety of labels: liberal, democratic socialist, even conservative. Yet, they share certain assumptions about the nature of man and society. This pluralistic political credo entails these commitments:

The pluralist affirms the potential creativity, rationality, and dignity of the individual. He rejects the supremacy of the State or People, as these abstractions are expressed in the arbitrary decisions of an uncontrollable leadership.

The pluralist views with suspicion any group which claims to have discovered "the true faith," for he believes that the road to progress is barred by dogma. He therefore rejects the pronouncements of those arrogant "shepherds" who assume that fate has elected them to herd the masses. He remembers Demosthenes' advice that "there is one safeguard known gen-

---

[12] Frederick the Great, quoted in "Africanism's Constitutional Malarkey," by Susan and Peter Ritner, *The New Leader,* June 10, 1963, p. 18.

erally to the wise, which is an advantage and security to all, but especially to democrats as against despots. What is it? Distrust!"

The pluralist wishes to create political and judicial institutions which will assure freedom from arbitrary arrest, freedom to criticize authority, freedom of movement, and freedom to organize a representative opposition to those in power. He rejects the fashionable argument that the social context of new nations alters the essential nature of these liberties, for he contends that freedom's defense, in today's West Africa as in ancient Greece, requires a vigilant watchfulness expressed in a network of institutions reinforced by the rule of law.

The pluralist finds unconvincing the argument that a one-party bureaucracy can somehow be cleansed by the vigilance of the people. He recognizes that, regardless of the historical situation, the victim feels the same when he fears an informer, when he knows that his judge is a political stooge, when he is kept in ignorance by a muzzled press, or when he languishes in jail for political crimes. The pluralist believes that no discourse about "new" forms of freedom can convince a political prisoner in Ghana, China, or Indonesia that he really has his liberty.

The pluralist knows well that a society cannot release itself from fear until the curse of starvation has ended. He adheres to Lord Acton's dictum that "the theory of liberty demands strong efforts to help the poor. Not merely for safety, for humanity, for religion, but for liberty."[13] The pluralist, therefore, wishes to abolish privilege, end economic serfdom, and extend equality of opportunity to all. He does not, however, necessarily identify human happiness with a growth in national income or the spread of industrialization. He understands that industrialization has not always extended the scope of individual freedom, and he knows that the most wealthy nations have the highest rates of mental disorder, alcoholism, and suicide —unmistakable signs that even a cornucopia of material goods cannot make up for a loss of personal dignity and security. In consequence, the pluralist believes that economic growth should be measured in terms of the degree to which it ends suffering, enhances individual dignity, and widens the possibility of free choice.

It is of vital importance to assert once again these principles of liberty and to recognize that men live not by bread alone. But for the embattled leaders in emerging nations—faced with the anarchy of the Congo, or the irresponsible union movement in Bolivia, or the reactionary power of a caste system—mere expostulation does not go far enough. In building a better society, as Africanist Immanuel Wallerstein has commented, "the only useful question to ask, in the old-fashioned American pragmatic tradition, is how you get from here to there."[14]

[13] Lord Acton, quoted in Kohn, *op. cit.*, p. 44.
[14] Immanuel Wallerstein, "An Africanist's Reply," *The New Leader*, June 10, 1963, p. 22.

Unlike the authoritarian, who has the propaganda advantage of claiming ready-made solutions to all problems, the pluralist has to content himself with accepting the uncertainties of responsibility. But the pluralist can depend on certain principles which history has validated:

The methods which leaders use affect them and their societies. If stampeded by cruel methods which destroy their dignity, self-reliance, and indigenous democratic institutions, the ruled lose their capacity for freedom and may, as in Indonesia, lose their prosperity, too. In particular, leaders must realize that an increase in wealth will not spontaneously produce a politically free society. History has yet to provide an example of a nation which, through the use of Draconian methods, achieved both literacy and prosperity, as well as liberty of conscience and a rule of law. As philosopher John Plamanetz has perceptively warned the new nations:

The recipe, *first* raise productivity and material well-being and abolish illiteracy, doing whatever needs to be done to these ends, and afterwards set about establishing freedom and democracy is bad . . . history gives us no example of a nation that first grew prosperous and acquired a strong centralized government and then afterwards became free and democratic. It is not true of the Greeks or the Romans or the Dutch or the English or the Swiss or the Americans; of any of the people who have cared most for freedom or democracy, or have enjoyed them the most securely.[15]

Those who desire both bread and freedom for their people should not be beguiled by the promise that authoritarian rule is merely a transitory stage.* From the beginning, leaders must use methods which are consonant with the goal of creating a free society.

To create a politically open society, the leadership must work to maintain or build a plural social structure—depositories of power independent of the group which controls the government. A rule of law, the right to criticize, the right of privacy—all the majestic liberties first created in the West —depend upon a complex, interdependent social structure which no government thinking of its own survival would dare to attack. Only a balance of economic power between various segments of a community can serve to preserve liberty. In particular terms, this means that the government should give all possible encouragement to trade unions and entrepreneurs, to rural co-operatives and village councils, to small industries and a free landholding peasantry. These independent units should be nourished both because

---

[15] John Plamanetz, *On Alien Rule and Self-Government* (London: Longmans, Green & Company, Ltd., 1960), pp. 139-40.

* There are, of course, exceptional periods in history where a free society has put extraordinary limits on the individual's liberty and yet eventually recovered these freedoms. American history—with its record of Lincoln's suspension of *habeas corpus,* the Palmer raids, and McCarthyism—serves as a case in point. Fortunately, liberal forces in America were able to overcome these indignities. The general pattern is nonetheless clear: once a nation starts down an authoritarian path, it becomes extremely difficult to retrace the steps.

of the economic reasons which we have previously discussed and because they serve as the surest defense of liberty.

A corollary of this position is, of course, that the central state should, as far as possible, avoid any movement toward total collectivization of property. History has issued a clear warning concerning the relationship of state authority and economic collectivization. As political scientist Massimo Salvadori has observed:

> Since the beginning of civilization there have been numerous collectivist societies. Not a single one has enjoyed free institutions. Miracles can happen; but it is wiser to believe in miracles (especially economic and political miracles) after they have happened and not before.[16]

In a developing country the government must play a very wide role indeed, not only in maintaining justice and order but also in planning and co-ordinating the economy, building an infra-structure, and breaking up concentrations of power in feudal hands. Nevertheless the government should try most of all to plan consciously for a devolution, rather than a concentration, of economic power.

A paradox which confronts pluralists in almost all countries is that, while seeking to encourage a diversity of pressure groups, they must also imbue their peoples with a "public philosophy" and a sense of nationhood. The leadership must encourage interest groups within their society to listen, negotiate, and compromise with each other in the name of the "national good." It would seem that only the vehicle of nationalism can transform warring tribes, castes, regions, economic or ethnic groups into united countries.[17] Yet, the dangers of narrowly conceived nationalism are all-too-obvious. The nationalist credo has served as an excuse for despotism, a hindrance to international economic co-operation, an incitement to wars large and small, and, in this era of global history, it carries the ultimate threat of atomic extermination.

The task is, therefore, a delicate one, calling for unusually talented and enlightened leadership. Despite all its troubles, India has managed an extraordinarily promising answer to this problem. While avoiding the dangers of chauvinism, the Indian leadership has created a fragile but still real sense of national identity in much of the population. The symbolic images of Gandhi and Nehru, public investments to strengthen national unity, institutional devices such as consultative committees to the government and public hearings on basic issues have been combined to make the people aware of themselves as Indians rather than solely as members of a particular subgroup. Too often, in viewing the give and take of Indian politics, observers see only the weakness of disunity—which, as we have noted, is

[16] Massimo Salvadori, *Liberal Democracy* (London: Pall Mall Press, 1958), p. 85.

[17] See *Expectant Peoples,* K. H. Silvert, ed. (New York: Random House, 1963), pp. 19 and 428.

quite apparent—while overlooking the achievements of the Indian leadership during the past fifteen years. In commenting upon India's accomplishments, Ambassador Chester Bowles has put the record in a more realistic perspective:

> If we should suddenly wake up to read that Europe had achieved unity comparable with that of India, with a single Prime Minister, a single Parliament, a single set of internal laws, with a common market and a common constitution, the event would be hailed as a modern political miracle. . . . Yet when the pessimists consider India they see not the remarkable unity of more than 450 million people in 15 states under a common government that provides a basis for growing political and economic strength, but the differences which it is assumed will at some point fragment the whole.[18]

While her problems are still vast, India's success—achieved with a minimum of compulsion and without the destruction of competing interest groups—gives reason to hope that unity amid diversity is not an impossible goal for developing societies.

Leaders in emerging nations must accept the fact that the maintenance of a free society sometimes exacts a cost in economic efficiency. Because of universal suffrage and the free play of political parties, a developing nation may have to divert some of its resources from productive enterprises to the satisfaction of popular demands, to fulfilling an increased wish for consumption, and to welfare services. Clearly, this has been the case in India: expenditures for consumption have been relatively high, and political considerations have sometimes forced the uneconomic placement of new industries. In Ghana, during the austerity budget crisis, a distinct choice had to be made between economic growth and political freedom. One observer commented at the time:

> The alternatives are clear-cut. The Government can revoke the system of compulsory savings; it can curtail less essential spending, spread the budget over a longer period of time, better prepare the people psychologically for new sacrifices, and be satisfied with a lower rate of economic development. Or the revolution can begin to consume its own children.[19]

In Ghana, the revolution "began to consume its own children," but even paying the devil's price did not bring the expected reward. Ghana has stagnated since 1960, while India, faced with similar alternatives, went a freer path and has maintained a steady, if modest, record of economic progress.

While admitting that freedom can carry a price tag, the leadership in developing nations must also come to understand a fact which it tends to ignore at this moment in history: that the imposition of an authoritarian

---

[18] Chester Bowles, *The New York Times,* Nov. 16, 1963, p. 7.
[19] Irving Markovitz, "Ghana: Background to Conflict," *Root and Branch,* No. 1 (1962), p. 68.

regime can also levy a heavy economic cost. Authoritarianism can decrease the flow of information from the people to the elite; it can destroy the individual's belief that he can change things; it can waste a nation's resources with greater largess than in a democracy; it can transform the social conflicts which always attend economic change into fatally violent battles. Indonesia's record serves as ample evidence, as do China's and Ghana's between 1960 and 1963. At times, a dictatorship can stimulate the rate of production; at times, it can decisively retard it—a simple lesson, repeatedly taught throughout history, but as yet unlearned by many.

The task of those who desire to create a free and abundant society in the "Third World" is by no means easy: they must decentralize power but maintain stability and a sense of nationhood; they must create a basic consensus without suppressing dissent; they must maintain a pluralistic social structure but undermine the power of traditionalist groups who seek to hold back progress; they must put their faith in the villagers and respect the peoples' potentiality, while realizing that tutelage from above may long be required; they must comprehend that now, as in Europe of 1848, the decisions taken by individual leaders at points of crisis will critically affect their nation's destiny—and they cannot fall back on the comforting sense that history is on their side. They find themselves involved in a series of paradoxes which inspire fear, if not despair, in the stoutest of hearts.

But regard the authoritarian alternative: a single party controlling all aspects of life; an elite arbitrarily and often mistakenly directing the economy; detentions without trial; a *Gleichschaltung* program of ranging everything from unions to the family under the guidance of a party bureaucracy; a "Redeemer" who promises, but often fails to deliver, economic welfare; a regime which treats men as part of an experiment in animal husbandry. Is this the way to a good life for mankind? Is this some new constitutional form, or merely tyranny adorned with different slogans? Those of good will, those of historical perspective, those who respect individuals rather than abstract masses will, I am convinced, choose the more ambiguous but eventually more rewarding path of building a plural society.

"ALL PEOPLES OF THE GLOBE TOGETHER SAIL"

To create a more equal allotment of property and of rights throughout the world is the greatest task which confronts those who lead human affairs.

ALEXIS DE TOCQUEVILLE

The fate of developing nations depends primarily on the courage and wisdom of their leaders—and on the responsiveness of the great peasant millions who are slowly awakening to the possibility of a better life. Yet, those of us lucky enough to have been born in an economically abundant region must also share the responsibility. For however Promethean the effort, it is clear that developing countries cannot bring the quest for bread and freedom to a successful ending without moral, economic, and political assistance from the rich nations.

On the economic level, the hard fact remains that only generous long-term aid from industrialized countries can provide the extra margin of capital and skills which emerging societies desperately need.

The world possesses abundant resources to fill the gap. War preparations alone gobble up $120 billion annually, a sum greater than two-thirds of the entire national income of all developing countries. If only a fraction of the capital now devoted to armaments were diverted to aiding developing nations, we would witness a real improvement in the material welfare of the majority of humanity. For example, to double the personal standard of living in the developing regions within the foreseeable future would use only 10 per cent of the capital saved from reducing armaments by one-half.

In those few instances where the rich nations have opened their purses to a poor country, the result has been an economic transformation of the region. Israel presents the best illustration. During the past fifteen years, the Israeli economy has grown enormously. While blessed with other fortunate attributes, Israel could not possibly have advanced so well without an unusually strong capital inflow. During her period of growth, Israel received the equivalent of some $2000 per person. Oscar Gass, an expert on the Israeli economy, has underlined the significance of this assistance:

> Israeli circumstances are somewhat special, the achievement in the case of Israel is greater than in other countries, the human material is different, the social situation is different. None of us working there, however, would have believed that anything remotely like what we achieved in Israel with a capital inflow of two thousand dollars per person could have been achieved with a capital inflow of five hundred dollars per person . . . we would probably have gone under, and the State of Israel would not have survived.[20]

In contrast to Israel's good fortune, Latin America—supposedly a major area of United States commitment—received an average of fifty cents per person between 1945 and 1960. Can one wonder, then, at the uneven performance of South American economies? The meager contribution in grants and loans from the United States could hardly have wrought an economic revolution even under the best conditions—and especially since the outflow of profits to North American companies greatly exceeded governmental aid.

In India, more substantial aid from the West, Japan, and Russia has led to steady progress, but this will continue only if advanced nations make a fully determined effort to aid India's experiment of combining economic development with freedom. In the third five-year plan, nearly 30 per cent

[20] Oscar Gass, "America and the World Revolution," *Commentary,* Oct. 1963.

of internal revenue will have to come from the equivalent of rupees from abroad. If this source of funds dried up, domestic austerities—already pushed to the boundary that persuasion allows—would have to be forcibly increased. But beyond this, India has to command an additional £2400 million in foreign funds to pay for vitally needed imports. Since exports cannot possibly rise enough to balance imports, at least £1950 million will be needed from abroad. If such aid is not forthcoming, the resulting chaos would doom India's attempt to create a prosperous, open, and plural society.

The facts are eminently clear: without massive sustained aid, there can be little, if any, economic progress in developing nations. And without such progress, the material welfare and even survival of the advanced nations themselves is endangered. On this issue, self-interest and morality dictate that advanced regions should have the vision to see beyond their own complacent horizons and accept the fact that they are members of the world family of man.

Politically, as Barbara Ward has rightly argued, "the need is to remove the work of world development from the subsidiary attention of the wealthy nations and to make it a central theme of their diplomacy, their international relations, their philosophy of world order. . . ."[21]

We must submerge nationalistic rivalries, as Russia and China did for a time, to establish a world common market which will give a margin of safety to the Third World's exports.

We must be willing to use our economic, moral, and, if necessary, military power to defend freely developing societies. This entails not only protecting India from further incursions by China but also the withdrawal of our support for petty dictatorships from Formosa to Saudi Arabia.

We must, of course, put our own house in order, for no society can proclaim its dedication to freedom while tolerating Little Rocks and *bidonvilles,* a Mississippi or a Notting Hill.

We must affirm, in words and actions, our belief that development can proceed without totally uprooting traditional culture; that a pluralistic society provides the surest defense of human dignity; and that totalitarian centralization offers no high road to abundance.

We must, when looking ahead to the grander sweep of history, press on for co-operation with Russia in the common task of consummating a world order. With a new philosophy of international relations and even a small degree of disarmament, the flow of aid to developing countries could be measurably increased.

All of this requires that we address ourselves with new seriousness to the encouragement of institutions which will protect freedom, feed the poor, and expand the scope of human dignity. To be sure, the task is grim

[21] Barbara Ward, *New Perspectives in Economic Development* (Oxford: Oxford Conference on Tensions in Development, 1961), p. 8.

and complicated. "But in such grave matters," Henry Kissinger has correctly observed, "the unforgivable sin is not to have failed but never to have tried."[22] If wisdom prevails, our grandchildren will live to see a world which fulfills Mill's prophecy: a more inhabitable planet, where the greatest sources of human degradation have been conquered by human care and effort.

[22] Henry Kissinger, *The Necessity for Choice* (Garden City, N.Y.: Doubleday & Company, Inc., 1962), p. 329.

APPENDIX TO CHAPTER 2

Selected Economic Data for the
*Less Developed Countries**

From *Selected Economic Data for the Less Developed Countries,* Statistics and Reports Division, Agency for International Development, June 1967.

Table 5. Latin America: Population, Area, and GNP

Country	Population (1966)			Area			GNP and Power			
	Total	Rate of growth	Density	Total	Agricultural land	Acres per capita	Gross National Product[a] (1965)			Power per capita
	Mill.	Percent	Per sq. mi.	1,000 sq. mi.	Percent of total area		Total $ Mill.	Per capita Dollars	Investment Percent of GNP	KWH per year
19 Republics total	236.9	2.9	31	7,710	25	5	88,286	385	17	400
Argentina	22.7	1.6	26	1,084	50	16	16,050	718	19	690
Bolivia	4.2	2.4	10	424	13	8	599	145	17	130
Brazil	84.0	3.0	26	3,280	15	4	21,970	270	15	410
Chile	9.0	2.4	30	286	17	3	4,257	485	13	690
Colombia	18.5	3.0	40	440	17	3	5,103	284	17	320
Costa Rica	1.6	3.8	80	20	30	2	593	395	21	430
Dominican Republic	3.7	3.6	200	.19	26	1	960	265	6	140

Ecuador	5.2	3.4	50	112	19	3	1,128	222	14	110
El Salvador	3.0	3.2	360	8	51	1	795	273	15	140
Guatemala	4.8	3.3	110	42	19	1	1,410	305	14	90
Haiti	4.8	2.3	450	11	31	0.4	327	70	n.a.	19
Honduras	2.3	3.1	50	43	38	4	504	223	14	80
Mexico	44.2	3.5	60	760	52	6	19,415	455	16	400
Nicaragua	1.7	3.5	30	57	13	3	588	355	17	190
Panama	1.3	3.2	40	29	18	3	617	495	20	400
Paraguay	2.1	2.6	13	157	27	14	443	221	15	60
Peru	12.0	3.1	23	514	16	4	4,281	367	21	330
Uruguay	2.8	1.4	40	72	86	14	1,555	573	10	640
Venezuela	9.0	3.4	26	352	22	5	7,691	882	24	920
Other										
British Honduras	0.1	3.1	12	9	2	1.1	39	370	n.a.	170
Guyana	0.7	2.8	8	83	13	10	193	298	n.a.	230
Jamaica	1.8	2.6	420	4	45	0.7	873	489	20	450
Surinam	0.4	2.9	7	55	0.3	0.3	139	392	n.a.	690
Trinidad and Tobago	1.0	3.0	500	2	35	0.4	630	646	27	930

n.a. Not available.
[a]GNP data unadjusted for inequalities in purchasing power among countries.

Table 6. Latin America: Exports, Transport, Education, and Health

Country	Export Trade		Transport		Literacy	Education			Health	
	Leading export	Percent 1963-65 exports	Miles improved roads	Motor vehicles		Primary school pupils	Secondary school pupils	Primary school teachers	Life expectancy	People per physician
	Item	-	Per 1,000 sq. mi.	Thousands	Percent	Thousands	Thousands	Thousands	Years	Number
19 Republics total	-	-	74	-	66	-	-	-	57	1,800
Argentina	Grains/Meat	51	27	1,265	91	3,252	177	164	66	670
Bolivia	Tin	72	30	25	32	527	78	18	50	3,830
Brazil	Coffee	50	104ᵃ	1,980	61	10,217	1,368	337	55	2,500
Chile	Copper	68	121	200	84	1,473	214	40	59	1,770
Colombia	Coffee	68	58	228	62	2,213	229	62	55	2,280
Costa Rica	Coffee	44	178	35	84	264	37	10	63	2,200
Dominican Republic	Sugar	53	236	25	64	558	59	10	58	1,620
Ecuador	Bananas	59ᵇ	64	43	68	752	57	20	53	2,990
El Salvador	Coffee	51	339	38	48	387	36	12	60	4,520
Guatemala	Coffee	49	169	45	38	405	36	12	49	4,190
Haiti	Coffee	47	40	14	10	274	19	6	40	14,980

Country	Product								
Honduras	Bananas	39	33	19	45	284	18	10	46	6,640
Mexico	Cotton/Cof	25	49	1,091	71	6,916	532	150[E]	60	2,020
Nicaragua	Cotton/Cof	62	34	24	50	199	16	5	54	2,370
Panama	Bananas/Oil	79	65	41	78	196	33	6	62	1,920
Paraguay	Meat/Lumber	45	11	12	68	349	20	13	55	1,660
Peru	Fishmeal/Cop	38	27	203	61	2,005	311	57	55	2,150
Uruguay	Wool/Meat	77	76	197	91	324	85	11	69	880
Venezuela	Petroleum	93	53	457	80	1,480	189	43	66	1,280
Other										
British Honduras	Wood/Citrus	37	93	3	89	27	2	1	60	3,700
Guyana	Sugar	34	11[a]	15	80	136	8	3	51	2,110
Jamaica	Bauxite/Alu	43	1,400	55	85	297	20	5	70	2,040
Surinam	Bauxite	78	14	9	80	63	9	2	n.a.	2,240
Trinidad and Tobago	Petroleum	81	2,086	72	80	207	34	6[c]	62	2,550

n.a. Not available.
[E] Estimate.
[a] All roads.
[b] 1962–1964.
[c] Public schools only.

Table 7. East Asia: Population, Area, and GNP

Country	Population (1966)			Area			GNP and Power			
	Total	Rate of growth	Density	Total	Agricultural land		Gross National Product[a] (1965)			Power per capita
					Percent of total area	Acres per capita	Total	Per capita	Invest-ment	
	Mill.	Percent	per sq. mi.	1,000 sq. mi.			$ Mill.	Dollars	Percent of GNP	KWH per year
East Asia										
Incl. Japan[b]	380.1	2.2	220	1,700	17	0.5	119,763	315	—	550
Excl. Japan[b]	281.2	2.7	180	1,560	17	0.6	35,203	125	—	90
Burma	25.2	2.1	100	262	13	0.9	1,760	71	16	24
Cambodia	6.2	2.1	90	70	16	1.2	830	136	n.a.	14
China (Taiwan)	13.3	2.8	960	14	25	0.2	2,828	221	22	490
Hong Kong	3.7	3.2	9,500	0.4	13	0.1	1,600	421	n.a.	650
Indonesia	106.9	2.3	190	576	12	0.4	10,450	100	n.a.	19
Japan	98.9	1.0	690	143	19	0.2	84,560	863	33	1,820
Korea, South	29.1	2.8	770	38	22	0.2	2,901	102	13	110
Laos	2.7	2.4	30	91	8	2.0	173	66	n.a.	7
Malaysia	9.7	3.0	80	128	17	1.4	2,866	305	19	210
Malaya, States of	8.3	3.1	160	51	19	0.8	2,517	315	18	240
Philippines	33.5	3.4	280	116	37	0.9	5,198	161	14	150
Singapore	1.9	2.7	9,500	0.2	22	.02	933	500	n.a.	500
Thailand	32.4	2.8	160	198	21	0.8	3,854	123	22	34
Vietnam, South	16.6	3.1	250	66	35	0.9	1,810	115	n.a.	39

[a] GNP data unadjusted for inequalities in purchasing power among countries.
[b] Totals for listed countries.

Table 8. East Asia: Export, Transport, Education, and Health

Country	Export Trade		Transport		Literacy	Education			Health	
	Leading export	Percent 1963-65 exports	Miles improved roads	Motor vehicles		Primary school pupils	Secondary school teachers	Primary school teachers	Life expect-ancy	People per physician
	Item		Per 1,000 sq. mi.	Thousands	Percent	Thousands	Thousands	Thousands	Years	Number
EAST ASIA										
Incl. Japan[a]	–	–	460	–	67	–	–	–	50	2,260
Excl. Japan[a]	–	–	100	–	55	–	–	–	43	5,150
Burma	Rice	63	60	65	60	1,804[b]	344[b]	37[b]	42	9,300
Cambodia	Rice/Rubber	83	40	20	31	691	82	15	44	24,700
China (Taiwan)	Sugar	23	590	36	78	2,189	593	52	63	1,500
Hong Kong	Clothing/Text.	42	1,470	82	71	605	167	20	67	2,800
Indonesia	Rubber/Oil	72	60	300	43	9,643	754	242	32	41,000
Japan	Manufactures	92	4,300	7,169	98	10,031	11,125	345	70	900
Korea, South	Fish/Plywood	22	400	47	71	4,941	1,005	79	52	2,600
Laos	Tin	57	20	11	15	144	4	4	30	49,000
Malaysia	Rubber/Tin	63	n.a.	n.a.	43	1,370	307	50	n.a.	6,500
Malaya, States of	Rubber/Tin	73	180	216	48	1,183	277	44	57	6,100
Philippines	Sugar/Copra	53	310	369	72	4,823	658	141	55	1,700
Singapore	Rubber/Oil	38	5,690	141	60	348	90	11	62	2,300
Thailand	Rice/Rubber	52	40	184	68	4,291	303	118	50	7,300
Vietnam, South	Rubber	58	110	67	40-50	1,623	351	31	35	16,600

[a] Totals for listed countries.
[b] Public schools only.

Table 9. Near East and South Asia: Population, Area and GNP

Country	Population (1966) Total	Population (1966) Rate of growth	Population (1966) Density	Area Total	Area Agricultural land Percent of total area	Area Agricultural land Acres per capita	GNP and Power Gross National Product[a] (1965) Total	GNP and Power Gross National Product[a] (1965) Per capita	GNP and Power Gross National Product[a] (1965) Investment	GNP and Power Power per capita
	Mill.	Percent	Per sq. mi.	1,000 sq. mi.	Percent of total area	Acres per capita	$ Mill.	Dollars	Percent of GNP	KWH per year
Near East total[b]	130.2	2.5	51	2,525	32	3.0	36,278	287	n.a.	210
Cyprus	.6	1.5	169	4	57	2.1	417	702	20	556
Greece	8.6	0.5	168	51	68	2.6	5,550	650	27	482
Iran	25.6	3.2	40	636	11	1.7	5,947	240	18	88
Iraq	8.4	3.2	48	173	35	4.6	1,909	233	15	138
Israel	2.7	2.6	332	8	53	1.0	3,397	1,325	28	1,575
Jordan	2.0	3.0	52	38	12	1.4	462	244	18	80
Kuwait	.5	12.0[c]	86	6	n.a.	n.a.	1,518	3,196	n.a.	1,223
Lebanon	2.6	2.5	635	4	27	0.3	1,120	450	n.a.	290
Saudi Arabia	6.9	1.7	9	772	43[d]	3.1	1,521	225	n.a.	n.a.
Syrian Arab Rep.	5.9	3.0	82	71	69	5.6	1,125	197	n.a.	65
Turkey	31.9	2.5	106	301	70	4.2	8,123	261	16	155
United Arab Rep.	30.4	2.7	79	386	3	0.2	4,700	160	n.a.	174
Yemen	4.1	n.a.	54	75	n.a.	n.a.	489	120	n.a.	n.a.
South Asia total[b]	653.3	2.4	333	1,961	43	0.8	63,991	100	n.a.	65
Afghanistan	15.4	2.0	60	254	19	1.9	1,250	83	n.a.	12
Ceylon	11.6	2.9	462	25	29	0.4	1,625	145	12	36
India	499.0	2.4	396	1,263	54	0.9	49,220	101	15	76
Nepal	10.3	2.0	191	54	13	0.4	736	73	n.a.	1
Pakistan	117.0	2.6	320	365	27	0.5	11,160	97	16	34

[a] GNP data unadjusted for inequalities in purchasing power among countries.
[b] Totals for countries listed.
[c] Reflects substantial immigration.
[d] Mostly grazing land.

Table 10. Near East and South Asia: Exports, Transport, Education, and Health

Country	Export Trade — Leading Export Item	Export Trade — Percent 1963-65 exports	Transport — Miles improved roads (Per 1,000 sq. mi.)	Transport — Motor vehicles (Thousands)	Literacy (Percent)	Education — Primary school pupils (Thousands)	Education — Secondary school pupils (Thousands)	Education — Primary school teachers (Thousands)	Health — Life expectancy (Years)	Health — People per physician (Number)
Near East total[a]	-	-	42	-	36	-	-	-	42	2,400
Cyprus	Minerals	34	1,409	42	76	70[b]	23[b]	2[b]	67	1,400
Greece	Tobacco	38	412	184	82	958	350	27	69	750
Iran	Oil	88	21	244	15-20	2,057	426	57	n.a.	3,200
Iraq	Oil	93	40	78	20	958	223	36	n.a.	4,800
Israel	Citrus	18	308	142	90	382[d]	62	20	72	430
Jordan	Vegt/Fruits	30	51	17	35-40	448	24	12[c]	n.a.	4,700
Kuwait	Oil	97	83	52	47	44	78	2	n.a.	800
Lebanon	Fruits	19	1,083	114	86	334	18[d]	14	n.a.	1,400
Saudi Arabia	Oil	98	4	78	5-15	219[d]		n.a.	30-40	12,700
Syrian Arab Rep.	Cotton	47	66	46	35	648	148	18	30-40	5,500
Turkey	Cotton	21	95	199	46	3,736	479	79	48	3,200
United Arab Rep.	Cotton	52	35	124	30	3,335	668	86	n.a.	2,500
Yemen	Coffee	30	5	n.a.	10	58	1	1	30-40	54,000
South Asia total	-	-	185	-	27			-	46	6,300
Afghanistan	Fruits	27	17	16	5-10	358[d]	34[d]	7[d]	n.a.	29,300
Ceylon	Tea	63	837	133	70-80	2,611[c]		94[c]	62	4,600
India	Jute Mfrs.	21	252	793	28	39,760	12,910	820	47	5,800
Nepal	Rice, Jute	Bulk	11	5	5-10	334	57	12	25-40	42,200
Pakistan	Jute & Mfrs.	50	52[e]	141	20	6,205	2,086	163	40-45	7,700

[a] Totals for countries listed.
[b] Greek schools only.
[c] Also includes preschool pupils and teachers.
[d] Public education only.
[e] National system only.

Table 11. Africa: Population, Area, and GNP

Country	Population (1966)			Area			GNP and Power			
	Total	Rate of growth	Density	Total	Agricultural land		Gross National Product[a] (1965)			Power per
							Total	Per capita	Invest-ment	
	Mill	Percent	Per sq. mi.	1,000 sq. mi.	Percent of total area	Acres per capita	Total $ Mill.	Dollars	Percent of GNP	KWH per year
Africa										
Incl. So. Africa[b]	270.6	2.4	24	11,295	31	8	40,637	154	-	192
Excl. So. Africa[b]	252.4	2.4	23	10,825	27	8	29,917	123	-	76
Algeria	12.1	2.9	13	920	19	9	2,630	225	n.a.	95
Angola	5.2	1.4	11	481	24	14	n.a.	n.a.	n.a.	43
Botswana	0.6	3.0	3	222	72	177	34	60	n.a.	n.a.
Burundi	2.9	2.5	267	11	71	2	140	50	n.a.	5
Cameroon	5.3	2.1	29	183	35	8	670	130	n.a.	212
Central African Rep.	1.4	2.0	6	238	10	11	122	90	n.a.	16
Chad	3.5	2.0	7	496	40	37	237	70	n.a.	5
Congo (Brazzaville)	1.0	2.5	8	132	2	2	138	140	n.a.	45
Congo (Kinshasa)	16.3	2.3	18	906	22	8	1,273	80	n.a.	160
Dahomey	2.4	2.9	56	43	18	8	165	70	n.a.	8
Ethiopia	20.5	1.4	45	457	66	10	1,171	58	12	12
Gabon	0.5	0.7	5	103	2	3	130	300	n.a.	84
Gambia	0.3	2.2	84	4	19	1	28	85	n.a.	22
Ghana	8.0	2.7	86	92	22	2	2,207	285	16	68
Guinea	3.6	3.0	38	95	n.a.	n.a.	257	73	n.a.	49
Ivory Coast	3.9	2.3	32	125	n.a.	n.a.	963	251	n.a.	57
Kenya	9.6	3.0	43	225	10	1	846	90	13[c]	55[d]
Lesotho	0.9	1.7	73	12	94	8	49	58	n.a.	n.a.
Liberia	1.1	1.6	25	43	37	9	213	199	n.a.	248

Libya	1.7	3.7	2	679	6	17	876	542	n.a.	83
Malagasy Republic	6.6	3.5	29	230	62	14	578	90	n.a.	21
Malawi	4.0	2.5	89	46	19	1	163	41	n.a.	13
Mali	4.7	2.1	10	465	n.a.	n.a.	297	65	n.a.	6
Mauritania	0.9	2.2	2	419	36	104	127	138	n.a.	6
Mauritius	0.8	2.8	1,086	1	66	3	176	231	11	139
Morocco	13.7	3.1	80	172	35	16	2,606	196	n.a.	96
Mozambique	7.0	1.3	23	302	59	13	n.a.	n.a.	n.a.	29
Niger	3.4	3.0	7	489	14	4	250	75	n.a.	6
Nigeria	43.6E	2.1E	122	357	24	1	4,852[e]	114[e]	15[c]	28
Rhodesia, Southern	4.4	3.2	29	150	17	1	1,022	240	14	966
Rwanda	3.2	3.1	315	10	71	4	155	50	n.a.	4
Senegal	3.6	2.3	47	76	28	6	680	195	n.a.	58
Sierra Leone	2.3	2.2	84	28	82	21	344	150	n.a.	38
Somali Republic	2.6	2.9	10	246	34	14	150	60	n.a.	4
South Africa, Rep.	18.3	2.3	39	471	84	6	10,720[f]	532	16	1,834
Sudan	13.9	2.9	14	967	12		1,387[g]	104[g]	n.a.	13
Swaziland	0.4	2.7	58	7	88	10	n.a.	n.a.	14[c]	n.a.
Tanzania	10.7	1.9	30	363	50[h]	11[h]	751	71	n.a.	22
Togo	1.7	2.7	77	22	42	3	156	95	n.a.	6
Tunisia	4.8	2.5	76	63	60[i]	5[i]	936	200	28	77
Uganda	7.7	2.5	85	91	16	1	658	87	14[c]	76
Upper Volta	5.0	2.0	47	106	18	2	257	53	n.a.	4
Zambia	3.8	2.9	13	288	41	20	842	227	26	798

n.a. Not available.

E Estimate.

[a] GNP data unadjusted for inequalities in purchasing power among countries.

[b] Excludes United Arab Republic but includes countries not listed.

[c] Fixed investment only.

[d] Includes imports of electricity.

[e] Fiscal year beginning April 1, 1965.

[f] Includes South West Africa, Botswana, Lesotho, and Swaziland.

[g] Fiscal year ending June 30, 1965.

[h] Over one-half is rough grazing land.

[i] Three-fourths is rough grazing land.

Table 12. Africa: Exports, Transport, Education, and Health

Country	Export Trade		Transport		Literacy	Education			Health	
	Leading export	Percent 1963-65 exports	Miles improved roads	Motor vehicles		Primary school pupils	Secondary school pupils	Primary school teachers	Daily Caloric intake	People per physician
	Item		Per 1,000 sq. mi.	Thousands	Percent	Thousands	Thousands	Thousands	Calories per capita	Number
Africa	–	–				–	–	–		
Incl. So. Africa[a]	–	–	43	–	18	–	–	–	2,380	11,400
Excl. So. Africa[a]	–	–	33	–	17	–	–	–	2,350	17,700
Algeria	Petroleum	54	41[b]	300	15	1,330	89	29.2	2,330	12,800
Angola	Coffee	45	46[b]	53	3	105	8	3.0	2,310	8,300
Botswana	Cattle & prod.	85[c]	12	3	20	63	1	1.4	n.a.	22,000
Burundi	Coffee	72[d]	382	n.a.	n.a.	147	4	2.8	n.a.	65,000
Cameroon	Coffee/Cocoa	48	22	39	10	693	25	5.9	2,470	26,900
Central African Rep	Diam./Cof/Cot	89	13	8	15	120	5	1.7	n.a.	40,000
Chad	Cotton	78	1	7	5	148	5	1.6	n.a.	81,900
Congo (Brazzaville)	Wood & prod.	71	51[b]	12	20-25	171	11	2.7	2,370	12,500
Congo (Kinshasa)	Copper	45	100[b]	53	30-40	1,995	92	53.3	2,460	30,100
Dahomey	Palm prod.	70	67	10	5	125	10	2.8	n.a.	20,100
Ethiopia	Coffee	61	8	35	5	317	33	7.7	2,090	61,400
Gabon	Wood/Mangan.	72	28	9	10-15	73	4	1.5	n.a.	5,700
Gambia	Peanuts	59	98	3	10	11	3	0.3	n.a.	18,200
Ghana	Cocoa	61	100	45	20-25	1,250	32	31.6	2,480	12,200
Guinea	Alumina	60[c]	32	22	10	178	14	3.9	2,400	28,400
Ivory Coast	Coffee/Cocoa	60	65	58	20	347	23	7.2	2,610	18,600
Kenya	Cof/Sisal/Tea	49[e]	28	84	20-25	1,011	48	30.6	2,380	9,700

Lesotho	Wool/Mohair	90[c]	77	5	35	154	2	2.5	n.a.	23,300
Liberia	Iron Ore/Rub.	89	33	11	10	79	6	2.4	2,430	11,700
Libya	Petroleum	98	6	53	30	176	23	5.9	2,360	4,000
Malagasy Republic	Coffee	29	24	55	35	684	55	9.5	2,480	10,300
Malawi	Tobacco/Tea	63	97	13	5-10	338	8	8.6	n.a.	43,100
Mali	Livestk/Peanuts	59	10	10	5	161	1	2.0	n.a.	40,000
Mauritania	Iron Ore	85[c]	1	4	1-5	19	1	0.9	n.a.	30,300
Mauritius	Sugar	95[c]	2	18	60	132	32	3.8	2,270	3,700
Morocco	Phosphates	26	84	219	10-15	1,160	212	26.7	2,170	10,800
Mozambique	Cot/Cashews	35	79[b]	55	2	416	5	4.4	n.a.	18,300
Niger	Peanuts	54	4	7	1-5	55	2	1.1	n.a.	64,700
Nigeria	Petrol/Peanuts	43[f]	21	105	30-35	2,896	212	94.2	2,450	26,500
Rhodesia, Southern	Tob/Asbestos	41[d]	148	142	20	680	41	15.7	n.a.	7,700
Rwanda	Tin Ore/Cof	90	n.a.	n.a.	5-10	330	6	4.9	n.a.	143,900
Senegal	Peanuts	77	35	46	5-10	206	21	4.9	2,600	15,200
Sierra Leone	Diam/Iron Ore	75	16	23	10	122	13	3.8	2,410	14,200
Somali Republic	Banan/Livestk	83	10	11	5	21	7	1.1	n.a.	31,900
South Africa, Rep.	Gold	42	257	1,572	35	2,267	367	69.7	2,720	1,900
Sudan	Cotton	51	1	38	10-15	550	26	9.5	2,190	29,500
Swaziland	Sugar/Asbestos	54	199	9	23	50	3	1.3	n.a.	9,200
Tanzania	Sisal/Cotton	46[e]	9	48	15-20	732	12	11.1	2,440	19,700
Togo	Phosp/Cof	55	53	11	5-10	156	11	1.9	2,570	23,100
Tunisia	Olive Oil/Phos	45	90	94	25-35	770	92	12.3	1,900	10,200
Uganda	Coffee/Cotton	75[e]	124	37	25	525	14	13.6	n.a.	12,600
Upper Volta	Livestock	60	35	8	5-10	86	6	1.7	n.a.	12,600
Zambia	Copper	90	37	65	15-20	454	17	6.2	n.a.	8,900

n.a. Not available

[a] Excludes United Arab Republic, but includes countries not listed.
[b] Includes unimproved road.
[c] 1962-1964.
[d] 1964-1965.
[e] Excludes trade among Kenya, Tanzania, and Uganda.
[f] 1966.

Table 13. Comparisons Between Developed and Less Developed Areas

Item	Unit	Developed Areas[a]		Less Developed Non-communist Areas[b]				
		Total	United States	Total[c]	Africa	East Asia	Latin America[b]	Near East and South Asia
Population								
Total (mid-1966)	Millions	635	197	1,600	250	280	240	780
Annual growth	Percent	1.2	1.4	2.5	2.4	2.7	2.9	2.5
Persons per square mile	Number	50	54	60	20	180	30	170
Land								
Total area	1,000 Sq. mi.	12,400	3,615	26,400	10,800	1,560	7,710	4,487
Agricultural land	% of Area	39	47	26	27	17	25	37
Acres per capita	Number	5	5	2.7	7.9	0.6	5.2	1.1
Gross National Product								
Total GNP (1965)	$ Billions	1,325	681	284	30	35	88	100
Annual growth (1957-58 to 1965-66[d])	Percent	4.8	4.3	4.7	3.7	4.6	4.6	4.9
GNP per capita (1965)	Dollars	2,110	3,500	180	125	125	385	130
Food Production								
Production index (1966)	1957-59 = 100	120	115	120	114	137	131	114
Per capita production Index (1966)	1957-59 = 100	109	102	98	95	112	104	94
Electric power per capita	KWH per Year	3,740	5,950	150	80	90	400	90
Foreign trade (value basis)								

Total exports, f.o.b. (1965)	$ Billions	129.6	30.4	34.9	7.2	6.4	10.4	9.8
Annual growth, 1960–1965	Percent	8.9	8.1	5.9	8.8	3.6	5.4	6.8
Total imports, c.i.f. (1965)	$ Billions	131.8	23.2	41.9	7.1	8.1	8.8	11.0
Annual growth, 1960–1965	Percent	8.6	7.2	5.9	4.1	4.8	2.7	6.6
Health								
Life expectancy	Years	70	70	48	39	43	57	46
Calories per day	Calories	2,920	3,090	2,250	2,350	2,160	2,560	2,145
People per physician	Number	780	690	3,900	17,700	5,150	1,800	4,900
Education								
Literacy	Percent	96	98	38	17	55	66	28
Pupils as percent of population[e]	Percent	19	23	12	8	14	16	11

[a]Generally the industrial countries of Western Europe, United States, Canada, Australia, New Zealand, Japan, and South Africa.
[b]For country composition of regional totals, see pp. 2–7; Latin America comprises the 19 Republics shown.
[c]Includes non-communist countries not specifically shown under listed areas.
[d]Based on data in constant 1965 prices.
[e]Primary and General Secondary students only.

General Note on Main Sources Used: POPULATION, LAND, FOREIGN TRADE AND EDUCATION— Publications of United Nations and its specialized agencies; AID reports. GNP— Official government reports and AID estimates. FOOD— Economic Research Service, USDA. HEALTH— UN, USDA, and official government publications. ELECTRIC POWER— Publications of UN, and US Federal Power Commission.

SUGGESTED READING

Alpert, Paul, *Economic Development: Objectives and Methods.* New York: Free Press, 1965.

Baldwin, David A., *Foreign Aid and American Foreign Policy: A Documentary Analysis.* New York: Praeger, 1966.

Balogh, Thomas, *The Economics of Poverty.* New York: Macmillan, 1966.

Crockett, J. P., "Tax Policy for Underdeveloped Countries," *National Tax Journal,* Vol. 19, No. 4 (December 1966).

De Benko, E., and Krishana, V. N., *Research Sources for South Asian Studies in Economic Development: A Select Bibliography for Serials Publications.* Asian Studies Center Occasional Papers No. 4, East Lansing: Michigan State University, 1966.

Gerschenkron, Alexander, *Economic Backwardness in Historical Perspective: A Book of Essays.* New York: Praeger, 1965.

Holt, Robert T., and Turner, John E., *The Political Basis of Economic Development: An Exploration in Comparative Analysis.* Princeton, N.J.: Van Nostrand, 1966.

Kurian, C. T., "Keynesian Economics and Underdeveloped Countries." *The Indian Economic Journal,* Vol. 14, No. 1 (July-September 1966).

Johnson, Harry G., *Economic Policies Toward Less Developed Countries.* New York: Praeger, 1967.

Kamarck, Andrew, *The Economics of African Development.* New York: Praeger, 1967.

Meier, Gerald M., *Leading Issues in Development Economics: Selected Materials and Commentary.* New York: Oxford, 1964.

Mountjoy, Alan B., *Industrialization and Under-Developed Countries.* Chicago: Aldine, 1967.

Myers, C. A., "Human Resources and World Economic Development: Frontiers for Research and Action." *International Labour Review,* Vol. 94, No. 5 (November 1966).

Patel, S. J., "Asia in the Changing World Economy." *The Journal of Development Studies,* Vol. 3, No. 2 (January 1967).

Paulsen, A., "Real Capital and Human Capital in Economic Development." *The German Economic Review,* Vol. 4, No. 4 (1966).

Schatz, S. P., and Zielinski, J., "Forced Savings and Investment Opportunities in the Less Developed Economies." *Economia Internazionale,* Vol. 15, No. 2, Part 1 (January 1967).

Waterston, Albert, *Development Planning: Lessons of Experience.* Baltimore: Johns Hopkins, 1965.

Chapter *3*

From Underdevelopment
to Affluence

SOVIET VIEWS

In Western Europe, and in the New World as well, industrialization came about under an economic system in which private individuals owned the means of production, hired wage laborers, and produced goods according to the dictates of the market and under the guidance of the profit motive. Utopians may have dreamed of more perfect societies, but no Utopian ever came up with a practical method other than that of capitalism to lead a country out of an agricultural system and into a higher stage of economic development.

Karl Marx may have talked about "exploitation of labor," about "surplus value" that remained in the hands of the bourgeoisie, and about the ever-present "class struggle"; yet his model of economic development included an unavoidable stage of "capitalist industrialization." A "bourgeois" revolution would have to dislodge the landowning class that ruled in the pre-capitalist era. Tearing asunder all the previously existing economic relationships and ways of producing and distributing goods, the bourgeoisie would become the ruling class during the era of industrialization. Only when capitalism had reached its highest stage of development would its "inherent contradictions" lead to its "inevitable" downfall, enabling the working class, under the leadership of the Communist Party, to take over and carry on where the capitalists had left off. This model of development was accepted by all the early followers of Marx.

Vladimir Ilyich Lenin, in his younger years, also appeared convinced that the sensible thing for Russia's peasants and workers to do was to support a bourgeois revolution, then go into opposition and prepare for the eventual proletarian revolution that was to usher in the eras of socialism and communism. As late as February, 1917, the Mensheviks and most of the Bolsheviks were apparently convinced of the necessity of a bourgeois era. But Lenin, by that time, was already strongly inclined to agree with Leon Trotsky that both the bourgeois and the proletarian revolutions could be carried out simultaneously. They based their hopes on a successful revolution in at least one of the capitalist countries—Germany—which, they expected, would help the new society in Russia to industrialize, thus obviating the necessity of going through a stage of capitalism.

The Russian Revolution succeeded; and the Bolsheviks, under Lenin's leadership, took over the reins of government. But the revolution in Germany failed, and Lenin was faced with the choice either of abdicating the working classes' power to the bourgeoisie or of finding an explanation for the phenomenon of workers and peasants, triumphant in revolution, taking over and holding on to state power not in an economically advanced, but in a fairly backward, country.[1] Lenin chose the latter course. He argued that the economically backward parts of the world had been split up among the major powerful capitalist nations, that these were intent on keeping the underdeveloped countries as sources of raw materials and markets for their finished products, and that as long as this situation persisted the latter would not be permitted by the former to go through a stage of industrialized capitalism at all. With no hope for a bourgeois revolution in these countries, and with but few immediate prospects for a successful revolution in the advanced countries (now that it had failed in Germany), Lenin advanced the theory that the socialist revolution (a) must be carried out by workers and peasants together, probably under the leadership of members of the middle-class intelligentsia, and (b) would not necessarily take place in the most advanced capitalist country, but in the "weakest link in the capitalist chain."

"Only when the country has been electrified," said Lenin after the Bolsheviks came to power in Russia, "when industry, agriculture, and transportation have been placed on the technical basis of modern large-scale industry, only then shall we be victorious."[2] The Soviets have taken Lenin's words seriously. In the half century since they came to power they have proved that, whatever else may be "good" or "bad" about them, their system provides a means of industrializing a relatively backward country. Surely, this success must have an effect on less developed countries.

In the economically backward regions of the world, hungry, illiterate people with strong nationalistic feelings, people who have come to hate colonialism and to associate it with the West, are looking for the fastest way to political independence and economic progress. To these people, Marxists

---

[1] Although Russia was, at the time, the fifth most industrialized country in the world, she was far behind the other four—England, France, Germany, and the United States—with about three-fourths of her population still engaged in agricultural pursuits.

[2] Lenin, *Selected Works* (New York, International Publishers), Vol. III, p. 556.

carry the message of common ownership of the means of production and centrally planned economic development. When in 1928 the Soviet Union embarked on her first five-year plan, no other country in the world was systematically planning its economic development. Today, as one Western expert recently phrased it, "the plan appears to have joined the national anthem and the national flag as a symbol of sovereignty and modernity,"[3] and practically every country in Asia and in Africa has a development plan. Moreover, nationalization of existing industries and state ownership of new enterprises is widespread among the nations which have gained their independence since the end of World War II.

And yet, in spite of economic planning and a certain (and in some cases preponderant) degree of social ownership of the means of production, the overwhelming majority of the underdeveloped countries have not chosen the communist path. Just as they may vilify capitalism and "imperialism" while eagerly seeking aid from and trade with the West, so do they often welcome Soviet aid and trade while imprisoning or even executing local communists. Under these circumstances what should the Soviet Union's approach be?

An orthodox Marxist-Leninist might demand that the Soviet Union support only countries that are willing to overthrow the "exploiters" and embark forthwith on a Marxist-Leninist course. But this would be a highly unrealistic approach from the point of view of power politics, for it would exclude from Soviet influence most of the new countries in the world today. Hence the Soviets no longer insist that their developmental path be followed. They are quite satisfied with a "non-capitalist" path, confident that the emerging nations will eventually wind up in the socialist camp. How the Soviets view the Third World—and more precisely what model of development Soviet policy encourages—this is the topic of this chapter.

The first two selections are by American non-Marxist authors. Donald S. Carlisle, first, traces the changing pattern of Soviet-proposed models and Soviet approaches to the underdeveloped countries from the early post-World War II days to 1964. He distinguishes three phases: the first characterized by a rigid orthodox line with full support to local communist parties, bypassing any opportunity to establish political and economic ties with the new states of the Third World; the second, starting around mid-1951, an era of transition in which local communist parties were advised to follow a less militant line while the Soviets began to suggest that the U.S.S.R. could replace the West as a market for the products of less developed countries, and as a source for industrial goods and machinery; and the third, the post-Stalin era, when trade, aid, and the "magnetic appeal of the Soviet industrialization model" were to take the place of the previous militant, revolutionary strategy. Carlisle concentrates his discussion on So-

[3] Albert Waterson, "What do we know about planning," *International Development Review,* December 1965, p. 20.

viet policies as they apply to the less developed countries in Africa and Asia, and reaches the conclusion that "Moscow still aspires to a monistic future—an aspiration hardly compatible with the political and economic expectations of the nationalists in the new Afro-Asian states."

Roger E. Kanet, in the second Western analysis of Soviet approaches to the new countries of the Third World, examines changes in the political structures and international alignments of these countries which have taken place since the mid-1960's, and the revision of Soviet attitudes toward non-communist, one-party regimes. He emphasizes Soviet reassessment of class structures and of leadership in these countries, and the shift of Soviet attitudes toward the nationalist versions of socialism which have been expounded in recent years throughout Asia and Africa. This reassessment, Kanet shows, has gone so far that even countries in which local communist organizations are banned can be considered truly progressive under the new Soviet approach. Kanet then proceeds to a discussion of Soviet aid and trade with the developing countries. Pointing out that in recent years the Soviets have established economic relations with even the less radical countries of the Third World in an effort to wean them from their dependence on and ideological orientation toward the West, Kanet concludes that, since Stalin's death, Soviet "policy has been one of constant reassessment and revision."

The Soviet selections, representing the current Soviet position, have been compiled from a variety of sources. K. Brutents, first, comments on the disintegration of the colonial system in the post-World War II era—a twenty-year period during which the leading colonial powers have lost most of their colonial empires. Konstantin Ivanov and Boris Batsanov, next, describe the abject poverty under which most of the peoples in Asia, Africa, and Latin America live and the efforts of the new countries to "eradicate the grave aftermath of colonial oppression." They point to the Soviet example, which, they assert, has won admiration and aroused interest throughout the Third World; and they make a plea for general disarmament and the diversion of arms expenditures to peaceful uses for the industrial development of the new nations. Next, Kuusinen and others, in the Soviet manual *Fundamentals of Marxism-Leninism,* argue that the young, independent states cannot take the capitalist path of development since they have no colonies to "exploit," and since working sections of their own people will not tolerate the "bitter suffering" that is associated with the "classical capitalist course." V. Yegorov and I. Pronichev, in the next Soviet selection, describe briefly the "non-capitalist way of development," which they see as a stepping stone on the road to socialism. R. Avakov and others, next, elaborate at length on the initial steps leading up to the non-capitalist stage of development; and they analyze various aspects of this stage and the problems connected with it. They perceive many of these problems as resulting from the lingering influence and power of "bourgeois" forces, although some elements among the bourgeoisie often play an important role in the "anti-imperialist struggle" and in the introduction of agrarian reforms. In the next selection, taken again from the writings of Pronichev and Avakov, the "transition to socialism" is examined in greater detail. The non-capitalist path, so the argument goes, will gradually bring about the predominance of the state sector with its adjuncts of government ownership of the means of production and centralized economic planning. In conjunction with wider public participation in national affairs, the road will thus be open to full socialism. In the final selection, A. Tkachenko takes up the issue of aid and assistance from the socialist camp, emphasizing that the developing countries can count on such aid and assistance and contending that it is given unselfishly, without any strings attached.

1. The Changing Soviet Perception of the Development Process in Underdeveloped Countries. A Western Non-Marxist Analysis

DONALD S. CARLISLE

MOSCOW AND THE UNDERDEVELOPED COUNTRIES

Revolutionary change in the Afro-Asian world since the end of the Second World War has offered the Soviet Union manifold opportunities to play on anti-Western feeling and to associate itself with a vibrant and vocal anti-colonial nationalism. Moscow had been disillusioned by its earlier attempt in the 1920's to manipulate Afro-Asian nationalism; after 1945 it was offered a chance to replay the hand and to devise a new design for driving these revolutions in an anti-Western direction. The Soviet leadership, however, faced a new issue that both created enticing openings and yet placed special obstacles in the way of an effective response: the policy problem revolved around the nature and direction of the economic development programs that the newly emergent states would embark upon once political independence was won. The new Afro-Asian elites have been confronted with an immense and pressing task: how to transform their countries from a backward, underdeveloped status to a modernized, industrialized stage. They have sought to avoid the pitfalls of the nineteenth-century European development ventures and have adopted variants of a "socialist" or planned modernization model. The conscious planned efforts to jump economic centuries has posed a series of unusual problems for the nationalist leaders of the new states. Although the socioeconomic structure expected to emerge from development has not been clear, there has been little question regarding their commitment to a non-capitalist economic model; large-scale transformation called for intensive capital investment, and in view of the lingering suspicion of foreign and private capital, such investment has usually been considered the prerogative of the state or public sector.

One might have expected the Soviet Union to have a special attraction for the development-minded ruling elites in these newly independent states.

Reprinted from "The Changing Soviet Perception of the Development in the Afro-Asian World," *Midwest Journal of Political Science,* Vol. VIII (1964), pp. 385-407, by Donald S. Carlisle, by permission of the Wayne State University Press and the author. © 1964 by Wayne State University Press.

One might have assumed the basis for a common alliance, or at least a certain affinity, since Communists and ex-colonials shared hostility towards the West. A second source of affinity might have been discerned in their common rejection of the capitalist or unplanned economic order. Thus the USSR appeared to enjoy special advantages denied the West in any post-war effort to court these new states: an anti-imperialist, anti-Western doctrinal framework, succinctly expressed in Lenin's theory of imperialism, and a successful industrialization experience, undertaken at rapid tempo and in non-capitalist fashion. It is strange then that until Stalin's death Soviet post-war policy toward colonial nationalist movements and ex-colonial states consisted mainly of missed opportunities and repeated failures to use these advantages effectively; after 1953, the Soviets embarked on an almost frantic effort to catch up with events that had bypassed them and to court the nationalist leaders. Paradoxically, it is these post-Stalinist ideological and policy innovations that have had a feedback effect on the cohesion and stability of the Communist camp, breeding dissatisfaction among Communist militants and playing a special role in the Sino-Soviet conflict. This paper will trace the changing Soviet perception of underdeveloped countries and analyze Moscow's new ideological schema for evaluating development prospects in non-Communist underdeveloped countries; it will also treat the disintegrative forces unleashed within the world Communist movement by Moscow's efforts to come to terms more realistically with political and economic forces in the non-Western world.

The Soviet post-1945 response to development problems in non-Communist Afro-Asian states has passed through three phases. The appearance after the war of such states as India, Pakistan, Burma, Ceylon, and Indonesia elicited the response that initiated the first phase. The Soviet leaders were equipped with both a doctrinal schema and practical experience in dealing with colonial nationalism. The Leninist framework assured them that these new states would be "objectively" anti-imperialist, while the experience of the 1920's raised serious doubts as to the "subjective" inclinations and reliability of the nationalists. Between 1947 and 1951 Moscow bypassed any effort to establish political and economic ties with the new states or to recognize their development aspirations.[1] Instead, support was given to local Communist parties' efforts to seize power. The Leninist framework on imperialism was married to a militant action program demanding immediate Communist revolution; a dogmatic analysis emerged that claimed industrialization was the prerogative of Marxist-Leninist parties. The Soviet line paralyzed any potential anti-Western alliance between nationalists and Soviet-inspired Communists. The anticipated anti-imperial-

---

[1] See Max Beloff, *Soviet Foreign Policy in the Far East, 1944-1951* (London, 1953). For a discussion of the impact of the Communist victory in China on Soviet views and the emergence of what the author has termed "Neo-Maoism," see John Kautsky, *Moscow and the Communist Party of India* (New York, 1956).

ist harmony was undermined by a Soviet refusal to recognize the new states' political independence, let alone their commitment to modernization.

Soviet participation in United Nations' bodies dealing with economic development highlighted the interaction between the rigid Stalinist analysis and the demands of the underdeveloped countries.[2] Moscow's spokesmen had an explanation for economic backwardness and they did not hesitate to articulate it. Continued colonial dependence was the root cause, and they cautioned against mistaking political forms for real economic independence; they advised the underdeveloped countries to cut their economic ties with the West. At times the Soviet analysis found a receptive audience among Asian spokesmen. They wanted to develop a national economy, and heavy industry served as the symbol of their search for power and political prestige. They were acutely conscious of the trade dilemma: the low import prices, their year-to-year fluctuation and the consequent instability of trade income. Although not pointing to a conscious, malevolent Western design, their demands and grievances made the Soviet analysis enticing and plausible. But the Leninist-Stalinist analysis proved a two-edged sword. Soviet spokesmen did not simply underline the past evils of imperialism or stress the present burdens of backwardness. They pushed on indiscriminately to undermine much of the anti-Western propaganda advantage already won; for Soviet representatives linked the "bourgeois nationalist" leaders with the West in a continuing conspiracy to exploit their own countries. There were repeated and indiscriminate attacks on the governments of the new states for accepting aid from the West, the International Bank, and the United Nations. The Russian performance offered repeated instances of clumsy and inept responses when economic development was discussed. In their efforts to embarrass the West, they engaged in a self-defeating tactic that antagonized Asian representatives and betrayed a lack of interest in practical solutions to development problems.

However, in mid-1951 there was a crucial shift in Soviet policy, that, although not recognized at the time, provides the essential background and sets the stage for the more dramatic post-Stalinist about-face in Moscow's appraisal of Afro-Asian nationalists. This second or transitional phase in Soviet policy brought recognition of the possibility of manipulating economic trends so as to drive a wedge between Asia and the West.[3] The Korean War stimulated a rise in export prices paid for Asian raw materials; however, by the spring of 1951, the export boom had collapsed. Asia's temporary trade advantage was replaced by the familiar situation of low fluctuating export prices and high import costs. Beginning in late 1951 one could discern a subtle shift in Soviet efforts to play on the economic

[2] See the unpublished study, Donald S. Carlisle, "Soviet Policy in the United Nations and the Problem of Economic Development, 1946-1956" (Doctoral dissertation, Harvard University, 1962).

[3] *Ibid.*, Chapter 4.

"contradictions" within the colonial system. Communist parties were advised to move away from a narrow militant line.[4] Moscow singled out the trade issue for special emphasis. During 1951 and 1952 Soviet spokesmen focused on the West's exploitation of Asia through non-equivalent trade. Trade as a source of revenue and channel for obtaining consumer and capital goods was of central importance if economic development was to move forward. The Russians had clearly seized on a sore point in Asia's relations with the West. For the first time Soviet representatives suggested that the USSR might replace the West as a market for Asian exports and as a source of industrial goods and machinery.[5] Little attention was paid to the trade offers and no one took them seriously, for the Russians continued to use heavy-handed arguments in debate and to attack Afro-Asian nationalists as "lackeys" of imperialism.

A third sharply delineated phase in the changing Soviet perception of economic development in non-Communist underdeveloped countries followed Stalin's death. The new Soviet leadership embarked on a flexible search for influence in the Afro-Asian world; no longer was there an insistence on direct Communist control, nor was there a demand for rigid domestic development patterns. After 1953 there was an unmistakable shift in Soviet policy from the strategy and tactics of revolution-making to reliance on trade, aid and the magnetic appeal of the Soviet industrialization model as the entering wedge for enhanced influence and prestige.

Moscow's concession that non-Communist nationalists, the "national bourgeoisie," could achieve industrialization, with Soviet assistance, marked a dramatic about-face in the Communist appraisal of development prospects in backward countries. Perhaps the most startling innovation was the expectation, never fully elaborated but present, that the attraction of the Soviet model would lead non-Communist elites to pattern their development ventures on the Russian experience. One consequence of the recent Sino-Soviet conflict has been to prod Moscow to articulate more clearly and to elaborate more fully this belief in the magnetic pull of the "socialist" model: the expectation that by indirection or by proxy domestic economic process

---

[4] In 1951 Moscow began to urge the discarding of "liberation armies" and violence as proper tactics. This had been an integral part of "Maoism" or the "Chinese way" that John Kautsky has analysed. The discarding of this feature seems to me to have been of special significance. Although, as Kautsky contends, the question of the use of violence by Communist Parties is in the realm of *tactics,* in the Asian context, its use or non-use had profound implications for the effectiveness of the anti-imperialist *strategy.* Moscow's rejection of violent tactics as universally binding on Asian Communist Parties was, to use Marxist jargon, a *qualitative* not simply a *quantitative* change: it opened up the possibility of Communists linking themselves with the nationalist movement in areas where the rather unique forces operative in China were not present.

[5] Beginning with the Singapore Trade Conference held in 1951 under UN auspices, there were a number of Soviet offers to barter Russian industrial goods for Asian raw materials. It was this type of barter, with added credit provisions, that after 1954 became the core of the Soviet foreign aid program.

could be set in motion that would overwhelm the nationalist leaders and force their replacement by more radical or "progressive" Soviet-oriented elites.

IDEOLOGY AND POLICY IN FLUX

.Stalin and his successors had identical strategic aims in Asia—to deny the West this area with its immense political significance and economic potential and, ultimately, to draw it into the Soviet orbit. Between 1953 and 1956 there emerged a more realistic appraisal of indigenous forces and a more flexible time schedule for achieving this goal than previously operative under the Stalinist rubric. During 1954 and 1955 there was a growing recognition of the positive role neutralism could play in denying Asia to the West and simultaneously opening the way for Soviet influence. Endorsement of non-alignment reflected the first objective, while trade and aid was to serve the latter purpose. The immediate goal in Asia was to forestall the creation of a military alliance around China and along USSR's Asian periphery. Broadly speaking, Moscow had to concoct its own non-military version of "containment" while shaping a more realistic and flexible policy than that pursued by Stalin. A rapid growth of trade with underdeveloped countries unfolded during this new phase of Soviet foreign policy.[6] Superimposed on the trade offensive was a dramatically new economic strategy —the extension of credits and technical assistance to Afro-Asian non-Communist states as a contribution to their economic development. The assistance strategy reinforced long-term economic ties with the "socialist world market," for aid was both theoretically and operationally linked to increased and continuing trade with the Soviet bloc. The Soviet aid program was based on the extension of long-term credits at low interest rates for the purchase of machinery and equipment in the USSR. These credits were to be repaid by the export of traditional primary products, or by repayment in local currencies, which presumably would be used by the Soviet Union to purchase goods in the assisted country. The scheme was breathtakingly simple; however, focusing on its surface character obscured its multi-dimensional impact. One might refer to its dual impact: its short term psychological and propaganda function and its long-term political and economic implications. The assistance strategy engaged the USSR in contributing in some measure to the economic development of non-Communist regimes. It helped undermine the negative image generated by Stalinist reliance on political exclusivism and economic autarky. Moreover, it served a more im-

---

[6] By 1957, Soviet trade with underdeveloped countries was three times that of 1953. At the end of 1953, the Soviet bloc had nine trade and payments agreements with non-Communist Asia; by August 1956, the total had zoomed to 37. For a thorough treatment of this early period in the Soviet trade and aid offensives, see the Department of State study, *The Sino–Soviet Economic Offensive in the Less Developed Countries* (Washington, 1957).

mediate foreign policy objective: it made neutralism an economically rewarding stance. Nor did the program involve large grants as was American practice. By tying aid to long-term trade, Moscow was assured of a continuing influence on the future economic status of the assisted country while reaping the immediate propaganda benefit of "disinterested" aid. The new program was shaped to manipulate, and seemingly to cope with, the endemic trade crisis that confronted exporters of primary products. Bypassing the self-defeating Stalinist techniques, yet just as surely directed at driving a wedge between Asia and the West, these economic weapons played subtly on the problems bred by the West's exit and Asia's demand for rapid modernization.

The revised Soviet appraisal of non-Communist Asia had two dimensions: approval of neutralism as a foreign policy position, and re-evaluation of the domestic "correlation of class forces" within underdeveloped countries. Soviet commentators waxed enthusiastic over the Bandung Conference of Asian and African states, and by mid-1955 non-alignment between the socialist and imperialist camps was fully acknowledged.[7] There was more difficulty reconciling the recognized superiority of the "hegemony of the proletariat" and its vanguard, the Communist Party, with the new thesis that the "national bourgeoisie" could also accomplish successfully national liberation. The new ideological line stressed the "contradictions" between the interests of the national bourgeoisie and the imperialists: the bourgeoisie's urge to lead their countries to independent capitalist development collided with the imperialists' need to retain underdeveloped areas as sources of raw materials and cheap labor. Soviet theorists began to comment favorably on the planned character of Afro-Asian development programs, particularly with regard to the growth of the "state sector"; its expansion played a progressive role, since it narrowed the sphere for foreign and domestic private capital.[8] These limited concessions to the reality of economic independence among underdeveloped countries raised a series of sticky problems. The central thesis of the dichotomic Stalinist analysis had been that the formal grant of political sovereignty had been vitiated by continued economic dependence on the colonial Powers. Communist theorists now set about constructing a revised ideological framework, both embracing the newly emergent states and their non-capitalist economic program, and yet containing clear norms for differentiating "bourgeois" modernization efforts from those undertaken by Communist-directed regimes. Between 1956 and 1960 the adjusted framework emerged; the proposition was advanced that these new states, although "state capitalist" and part of

---

[7] A new Russian journal—*Sovetskoe Vostokovedenie*—devoted to Asian and African studies began publication significantly in the month of the Bandung Conference, April 1955; see "Konferentsia Stran Azii i Afriki v Bandunge," *Sovetskoe Vostokovedenie*, No. 3, 1955, pp. 36-45.

[8] For the new Soviet analysis see B. Semyonov, "Raspad Kolonial'noi Sistemy Imperializma i Voprosy Mezhdunarodnykh Otnoshenii," *Kommunist*, No. 18, December 1956.

the world capitalist system, occupied a special place within that system, reflected in their neutralist foreign policy and their desire for economic independence. Thus they had a special status, marking a progressive stage on the road to socialism.

This new phase of Soviet policy, perhaps originally embarked upon to shore up and expand the neutralist "zone of peace," had ideological implications, raised embarrassing questions, and had a feedback effect on the unity and cohesion of the international Communist movement. Mounting Russian aid, the moderation demanded of Asian Communists, the nationalists' claims that they were building socialism, and Moscow's failure to develop clear theoretical norms, raised the basic ideological question: how necessary was Communist hegemony in the "transition to socialism"? Communist hegemony during the transition period in economically backward countries was an article of faith; it was the core dogma that, if tampered with, would undermine Marxist-Leninist doctrine on the bourgeoisie, socialism, and more decisively, the role of the Communist Party. In 1956, Khrushchev, while stressing the positive character of neutralism and the possibility of a "peaceful transition" to socialism, had stated:

Whatever the forms of transition to socialism, the decisive and indispensable factor is the political leadership of the working class headed by its vanguard. Without this there can be no transition to socialism.[9]

No Soviet theorist could envisage dispensing with the need for Communist direction in the transition period; a fundamental revision would call in question the usefulness of Leninist class analysis and the significance of the Soviet experience. However, the decision to court the new states and to contribute to their economic development still left unanswered the question of their role in the inevitable transition to socialism. Although the question was left open and ideological norms remained vague, there were recurrent hints as to the USSR influencing the future through trade, aid and the "demonstration effect" of its industrialization experience. A prominent Soviet analyst expressed this expectation when he observed:

The great successes of the socialist countries exert a great influence on the peoples of the underdeveloped countries, strengthen the ideas on the authority of socialism among different progressive factors of the population, which have decisively declared themselves against capitalism. In connection with this, in many underdeveloped countries there is manifest a striving for the predominant development of state-owned industry as the basis of economic development. . . . The active intervention of the state in economic life creates the prerequisites for a planned economy in the state-owned sector.[10]

[9] N. S. Khrushchev, *Report of the Central Committee, 20th Congress of the Communist Party of the Soviet Union, February 14, 1956* (London, 1956), p. 14.

[10] Y. Osirov, "Ekonomicheskoe Sotrudnichestvo Stran Sotsialisticheskov Lagerya so Slaborazvitymi Stranami Azii i Vostoka," *Finansy SSSR,* No. 8, August 1957.

As to what might emerge from such state-directed development patterns, another Soviet theorist ambiguously observed:

Where will the further development of state ownership of the most important means of production lead—this will depend upon the correlation and struggle of class forces. In certain conditions, this may become the material basis for the peaceful transformation to socialism.[11]

Although the question remained open as to what these conditions were, it was abundantly clear that Moscow felt that neutralism and the economic aspirations of the national bourgeoisie had an anti-Western impact. While this Soviet perspective seemed to open new foreign policy alternatives and served as one avenue for the escape from the Stalinist legacy, it also spawned unexpected dissension within the international Communist movement. It brought to the fore once again the old and recurrent policy dilemma of reconciling the "exclusive" and "inclusive" impulses of the Communist perspective in a concrete action program. Moscow's failure to develop clear and acceptable norms to suit the Chinese and other Communist militants has proved to be one of the main issues in the Sino-Soviet conflict—a dispute that pushed Communist policy toward underdeveloped countries to a new stage.

CONFLICT AND COHESION WITHIN THE COMMUNIST CAMP

In general, Communist attitudes toward the Afro-Asian world have been shaped by two related yet contradictory impulses. There has been, on the one hand, a tendency to regard the colonial peoples as potential allies in the anti-Western, anti-imperialist struggle. But there has also been active a second equally strong impulse to mistrust all non-Communists, to expect them to betray the movement, to regard all alliances as *ad hoc,* and to have confidence only in fronts controlled by the proletariat's vanguard, the Communist Party. The militant, "exclusivist" impulse finds expression in Lenin's elite "party of a new type"; but Leninism also spawns a concomitant and conflicting urge to link the elite with the masses, to draw in a broad following, and to search out allies in order to give the movement a wider inclusive character.[12] Each impulse gives birth to distinctive political perspectives and serves contradictory functional purposes in enhancing Communist confidence and in preparing the path to power. The elitist urge, the exclusivist impulse, breeds suspicion and hostility to all outside the charmed circle of party affiliation; it stimulates cohesiveness by stressing the elite's

[11] M. Rubinshtein, "Nekotorye Voprosy Ekonomiki Slaborazcitykh Stran," Mirovaya Ekonomiki i Mezhdunarodnye Otnosheniya, No. 3, September 1957.

[12] For a similar analysis stressing the dual character of the Leninist action program, see Alfred G. Meyer, *Leninism* (Cambridge, 1957), Chapter 4.

select character and by stimulating a militant stance to all "out groups." Turning in on itself and ignoring the search for allies, the elite is prepared for adventure and steeled to adversity. The distinction between "we" and "they" is clear-cut, sharply focused and admits no compromise. It is this political orientation and psychic tendency that at times has been labeled by Communist and non-Communist alike as "leftism," "dogmatism," and "sectarianism."

Anticipating an anti-imperialist orientation from the colonial and ex-colonial peoples, Communists have been driven also by the impulse to draw these "exploited" to the movement as allies and sympathizers. However, the strategy and tactic enhancing the Communist movement's cohesiveness and breeding the elitest frame of mind has repeatedly collided with the forces favoring increased inclusiveness and a broader mass base. The persistent tension between these two impulses has plagued the development of international Communist strategy and is by no means a problem peculiar to policy in colonial or underdeveloped areas. The policy pendulum has swung through the political spectrum, alternating between phases of "rightism"—a reaching out to make the movement more inclusive, by creating broad support and a wide mass base—and "leftism"—a turning inward with a sharp ideological distinction between elect and reject. In colonial areas the tension has been acutely felt and sharply focused on the issue of Communist attitudes toward emerging nationalism and the national bourgeoisie, the class expected to lead these movements. The persistent and seemingly intractable problem has been how to relate Communists and nationalists for anti-imperialist purposes while retaining distinct ideological and operational identities for the subsequent revolutionary transformation that would pit proletariat against bourgeoisie. The policy problem has revolved around finding the right "mix" between inclusive and exclusive impulses thus establishing a "general line" for the international Communist movement. Historically, it has been the Soviet leadership that has determined this general line which is binding on all Communist parties and which has shifted in turn with Moscow's changing perception of its foreign policy needs.

The post-Stalinist effort to mobilize an international anti-imperialist alliance of socialist and neutralist states meant that Moscow had opted in the direction of an "inclusive," united front strategy; the response demanded of Asian Communists contrasted sharply with the earlier post-war general line, and had a direct impact on their attitudes toward the nationalist regimes and on their prospects for coming to power. It is unlikely that this about-face was an entirely painless process for these Parties. Earlier post-war united fronts had been directed as much against the nationalist governments as against the imperialist powers. Communists in newly independent states had not been deprived of the "internal enemy" since opposition to the domestic policies of the nationalists had given class analysis a continuing relevance and sustained the expectation of taking power. As long as friend and foe had been clearly differentiated on the domestic scene, Communist Parties' elan could be sustained and their cohesion maintained. The new Soviet diplomatic and economic line, from the militant Communist's perspective, paralyzed activism and sanctioned a blurred and dangerous class analysis.[13] However reasonable the Soviet argument that economic aid shored up neutralist regimes against imperialism, it was equally clear to militant Communists that these nationalist governments were being simultaneously strengthened against domestic difficulties; Soviet foreign aid thus cut against both the West and local Communists.[14]

Although some discern a resemblance between the Khrushchevian approach and Moscow's collaboration with the national bourgeoisie in the 1920's, there is a new and significant dimension in the most recent post-Stalinist collaboration phase; Moscow is now dispensing more than moral and diplomatic support—it is doling out economic aid. The recent challenge that the Chinese Communists threw down to the Soviet comrades provides the dissatisfied militants with a champion within the international Communist movement. In an earlier phase, they might have been silenced by Russian power and prestige; now they can rally around an independent Communist regime that is jealous of its own prestige, confident of its analysis and anxious to prod history along its determined path. The Sino-Soviet conflict revolved around divergent appraisals of how the interests of the international Communist movement might be advanced in a period of potential nuclear war and the "disintegration of the colonial system." One of the chief charges brought against the Russian position was that Communists in underdeveloped countries were being sacrificed to the needs of Soviet foreign policy. Visions of 1927 and Chiang Kai-shek apparently haunted Peking while the success of the Maoist formula reinforced its confidence. The Chinese contended that "proletarian hegemony" and Communist Party direction of economic development was essential if domestic progress

---

[13] Moscow made clear what is expected of these Communists. Consider the implicit guidance in E. Zhukov's reference to Lenin's warnings that a proletarian party would be committing a grave error if it expected "only fully consistent, straight-line, anti-imperialist actions"; he went on to contend that such action:

". . . might be led by parties and groups very far removed not only from the working class, but even from the working population in general. These parties and groupings might set themselves, and actually do set themselves, as history shows, very limited aims. At times they tend to compromise with the imperialists. And yet, for the Marxist-Leninist what is important is not so much the subjective tendency of the anti-imperialist action of this or that political grouping, party, or even individual, as the objective consequences of those actions and their real historical importance."

E. Zhukov, "The October Revolution and the Rise of the National-Liberation Movement," *International Affairs,* No. 9, September 1957, p. 41.

[14] Between 1954 and 1962, total Soviet credits and grants to non-Communist underdeveloped countries amounted to $3.5 billion; Department of State, Bureau of Intelligence and Research, *Research Memorandum, RSB-173,* November 14, 1962, pp. 17-18. Also see Klaus Billerbeck, *Soviet Bloc Foreign Aid to the Underdeveloped Countries* (Hamburg, 1960).

was to be achieved; they warned Moscow that the national bourgeoisie were unreliable allies.[15] The challenge of the "dogmatists" focused on the least elaborated and doctrinally-grounded feature of the Khrushchevian design: the role of state-directed development ventures in non-Communist underdeveloped countries.

Between 1955 and 1960 there had been a conspicuous Soviet silence on how these neutralist states would make the necessary "transition to socialism." The reluctance to elaborate was logical; there were good reasons to avoid antagonizing the nationalists by too explicit a juxtaposition of Communist-directed industrialization to their "state capitalist" planning. Moscow preferred to side-step the issue since a more systematic analysis entailed either deepening the commitment to the neutralists or alienating them by stressing the superiority of Communist economic patterns. The former course leaned too close to "revisionism" and would have further confused the already blurred distinction between nationalist and Communist; the latter alternative would have undermined the search for anti-imperialist allies. The precarious balance between exclusive and inclusive tendencies in the post-Stalinist strategy could be maintained only as long as the question of the next historical phase—the transition to socialism—was not raised. The Chinese challenge forced the issue into the open with the demand for ideological clarity, a demand that from Moscow's perspective entailed a premature and politically inopportune elaboration. The Soviet response was the new ideological category of "national democracy."

THE "NATIONAL DEMOCRATIC STATE" AS A TRANSITIONAL REGIME

Authoritative reference to a "national democratic state" first appeared in the 1960 Moscow Statement of the 81 Communist and Workers' Parties. The Moscow Conference was called to reconcile the differences between the

---

[15] For a study of the early dialogue and resultant conflict see, Donald S. Zagoria, *The Sino-Soviet Conflict, 1956-1961* (Princeton, 1962), especially Chapter 10. Consider the following analysis by a Chinese ideologist:

"The victory of the Chinese revolution is a typical example of the transition from new-democratic revolution to socialist revolution in an originally semi-colonial and semi-feudal country. The basic condition for ensuring this transition is that the proletariat should take the leadership of the revolution firmly in its hands during the democratic revolution. This is the case of the Chinese revolution. . . .
. . . In certain Asian and African countries where the bourgeoisie is in power it counts on developing the economy by taking the road of capitalism or state-capitalism, which it euphemistically styles as the 'democratic' road. The fact is, by following this road these countries will not be able to rid themselves of the exploitation and oppression by imperialism and feudalism. . . ."
Wang Chia-hsiang, "The International Significance of the Chinese People's Victory," *Ten Glorious Years* (Peking, 1960), pp. 276-9.

Chinese and Soviet Parties; as subsequent events were to demonstrate, the differences were not resolved but merely papered over. The Moscow Statement defined national democracy as a state which:

. . . consistently upholds its political and economic independence, fights against imperialism and its military blocs, against military bases on its territory; a state which fights against the new forms of colonialism and the penetration of imperialist capital; a state which rejects dictatorial and despotic methods of government; a state in which the people are ensured broad democratic rights and freedoms (freedom of speech, press, assembly, demonstrations, establishment of political parties and social organizations), the opportunity to work for the enactment of an agrarian reform and other domestic and social changes, and for the participation in shaping government policy.[16]

Although Soviet attention to the national liberation movement increased after the Moscow Conference, it was difficult to determine just what this new category signified. Did it presage a change in attitudes, or was it an attempt to paper over the Sino-Soviet differences without forcing the Russians to abandon their previous views? Soviet commentators weaved around the question of how to differentiate a national democratic state from other neutralist regimes. They intimated that several states approximated it, but refused to attach the label specifically.[17] If national democracy represented a more progressive way station on the road to socialism, and a concession to the militants, it remained uncertain as to what unique features distinguished it from state capitalist regimes. To complicate matters, the 1961 draft program of the CPSU announced that the possibility existed for non-Communist states to embark on the "non-capitalist" development path;[18] the national democratic state was apparently Moscow's chosen vehicle for such a journey. Since Moscow did not set proletarian hegemony as a prerequisite for national democracy, one might suppose that the new theo-

[16] For the text of the programmatic statement of the Moscow Conference see, *The China Quarterly,* No. 5, January-March 1961, p. 42.

[17] See the article by a leading Soviet ideologue, B. Ponomarev, "Concerning the National Democratic State," *Kommunist,* No. 8, May 1961, as translated in the *Current Digest of the Soviet Press,* Vol. 13, No. 22.

[18] See the text of the 1961 Draft Program of the Communist Party of the Soviet Union, *New York Times,* August 1, 1961, p. 15. At the 22nd Party Congress, Khrushchev observed:

"After accomplishing their national-liberation, anti-imperialist revolution, the seething underdeveloped states of Asia, Africa, and Latin America will be able to effect the transition to socialism. Today practically any country irrespective of its level of development, can enter on the road leading to socialism. . . .
. . . The peoples of the underdeveloped countries do not wish to remain tied to imperialism. They can see the example set by socialism. It is not from books alone that the peoples now judge socialism, but first and foremost by its actual achievements. The peoples see that it has not taken centuries but the lifetime of one generation for Soviet power to do away with age-old backwardness, and for the Soviet Union to become a mighty world power."
N. S. Khrushchev, *Report on the Program of the Communist Party of the Soviet Union* (New York, 1961), pp. 136, 139-140.

retical innovations did little to quiet Chinese apprehensions regarding "revisionism" in the Kremlin.

Moscow's intention may be set in perspective if we view these developments as an effort to continue the basic policy of courting neutrals essentially unadjusted while taking into account some of the complaints from within the international Communist movement. The Soviets were out to rebuild the fractured unity of the movement by expressing a willingness to sanction more militant perspectives; in these terms, one ought to focus on the emphasis on "democracy" in a progressive national democratic state. Moscow was voicing its displeasure at the persecution of Communists in underdeveloped countries such as Egypt and Iraq: in the projected national democratic state Communists were to have the right to operate legally. Also a preference was simultaneously expressed for regimes which offered Communists the opportunity to play an active role in governmental decision-making. The outlines were sketched for a more advanced stage beyond the Indian and Egyptian "state capitalist" phase—Indonesia perhaps serving as a model—while not accepting the radical Chinese view that only Communist-led regimes could take "progressive" steps towards socialism.

The new Soviet posture sanctioned activism for Communist Parties in the struggle for "national democracy." But it was an activism that did not correspond to any previous Communist strategy, nor did it necessarily anticipate early proletarian hegemony. Domestic "progressive forces" were being urged to bring pressure to bear on their governments to follow a consistent anti-imperialist line and to initiate more radical internal reforms.[19] There was, however, abundant evidence that no stamp of approval was given to a militant, exclusivist line.[20] To bring about radicalization of

[19] "The people can thwart the intrigues of imperialism and domestic reaction only by opposing to them a broad combination of all the patriotic and democratic forces carrying out an anti-imperialist policy. The national front is a major weapon in the struggle for general democratic transformations. The united national forces can exert considerable influence on the government, driving it to conduct needed reforms. . . ."
G. Starushchenko, "Through Democratic Transformations to Socialist Transformation," *Kommunist,* No. 13, September 1962, as translated in the *Current Digest of the Soviet Press,* Vol. XIV, No. 41, p. 15.

[20] "In our time, when the socialist and general democratic tasks are very tightly interwoven, the struggle for general democratic transformations broadens the socialist base of the revolution, prepares the masses for the solution of socialist tasks and raises the authority of socialism. Conversely, neglecting the general democratic tasks and spurting forward will narrow the mass base of the socialist revolution and compromise the noble idea of socialism in the eyes of the people. That is why Communist and Workers' Parties warn the masses and individual political figures against groundless infatuation with socialist slogans. The Indonesian Communist Party, for example, while approving the endeavor to follow the socialist path as expressed in the official Political Manifesto of the Republic of Indonesia *as a long-range aim* considers the task of the nation *in the present day* to be the completion of the anti-imperialist democratic revolution."
Starushchenko, *op. cit.,* p. 25.

government policy, Communists were to build and participate in a broad national patriotic front; the united front was to "embrace all the patriotic forces of the nation" that were willing to strive for:

. . . the consolidation of political independence, the carrying out of agrarian reforms in the interests of the peasantry, elimination of the survivals of feudalism, the uprooting of imperialist economic domination, the restriction of foreign monopolies and their expulsion from the national economy, the creation and development of a national industry, improvement of the standard of living, the democratization of social life, the pursuance of an independent and peaceful foreign policy, and the development of economic and cultural cooperation with the socialist and other friendly countries.[21]

Subsequent exposition made clear that although a new stage was being introduced as the first step on the "non-capitalist development" route, it was still far removed from people's democracy and proletarian hegemony. There were repeated references to Moscow's belief that in underdeveloped countries socialism's irresistible appeal and capitalism's rejection was the opening wedge for Soviet influence and the rallying point for construction of a national front.[22] It was also abundantly clear that the "non-capitalist path" could be embarked upon without Communist control.[23] By introducing this new possibility, Moscow thus proved its willingness to espouse a stage more acceptable to the militants while simultaneously avoiding the alienation of the nationalists; such an alienation was likely if the Chinese position had triumphed. "National democracy," explained a Soviet ideologist, "does not pose as its immediate goal the liquidation of all exploiting classes or the construction of socialism."[24]

Moscow was also willing to sketch the outlines of the process by which "progressive forces" would move to a more independent position within the national front as less advanced social elements proved unable to solve the complex problems of economic transformation:

As a country enters the stage of general democratic transformations, the class struggle cannot cease. . . . The consequence of this struggle is a class differentiation of forces in the national front. The most conservative elements, rejecting the democratic transformations, place themselves outside the front, lose the

[21] The 1960 Moscow Statement, *The China Quarterly, op. cit.,* p. 41.

[22] Ye. Bragina, "Planning as a Method of Developing the National Economy," and V. Kondratyev, "Industrialization Upon the Example of the Countries of Socialism," *Kommunist,* No. 13, September 1962, as translated in the *Current Digest of the Soviet Press,* Vol. XIV, No. 41 pp. 12-14.

[23] "A feature of national democracy, and one that lends it its transitional character," writes a Soviet theorist, "is that it is not a state of a single class, or even of two classes. It will be a state representing the interests of the patriotic section of the nation vis-a-vis the deposed reactionary classes."
A. Sobolev, "National Democracy—the Way to Social Progress," *World Marxist Review,* February, 1963.

[24] Starushchenko, *op. cit.,* p. 14.

confidence of the people and are therefore eliminated from the leadership of the state.

The polarization of forces in the national front is made inevitable also by the changes in the class struggle of a society carrying out a general democratic program. Here, the feudal lords are liquidated as a class and the power and influence of the big bourgeoisie are curtailed. Owing to the purposeful activity of the national state in the development of the state sector, the working class grows quickly in size and in degree of organization; moreover, this is not attended by the growth of the bourgeoisie. The realization of agrarian reform, the establishment of government domains and cooperatives in agriculture, stirs the awareness of the peasants and makes them reliable allies of the proletariat.[25]

Thus in the context of a functioning political democracy, the bourgeoisie and other non-Communist elements could be induced to commit political suicide through introduction of economic measures that would breed mass discontent susceptible to Communist manipulation. The "inevitability of the class struggle" would clear the way for the next stage and would:

. . . determine the character of the transition from the general democratic to the socialist stage of the liberation movement. Such a transition is possible only as a result of revolutionary socialist transformations effected in the course of the class struggle under the leadership of the working class, headed by a genuinely revolutionary party armed with a proletarian ideology. By virtue of substantial transformations of the society at the general democratic stage, the transition from national democracy to the socialist state will be shorter and easier than from the most liberal bourgeois democracy. As a rule, it will be peaceful in nature and will consist of a series of radical revolutionary transformations.[26]

However, this author made clear that national democracy was not obligatory and that the tempo might be speeded up or the stage bypassed; he noted that "the Cuban revolution from its very first days carried out all the major social transformations with a view to the evolution of the antiimperialist and anti-latifundist revolution into the socialist revolution."[27]

THE ROLE OF THE INTELLIGENTSIA IN NEW STATES

The recent Soviet elaboration of long-term development prospects has also been accompanied by the shaping of a flexible set of analytical tools for dealing with intermediate-range trends in underdeveloped countries. Stalinist analysis had delineated sharp and rigid categories for characterizing the relations between bourgeoisie and proletariat. The early post-Stalinist revision had blurred these distinctions. Now Soviet theorists contend that class relations are even more confused and complicated; it is impossible to give a clear and consistent appraisal of the national bourgeoisie

---

[25] *Ibid.*, p. 15.
[26] *Ibid.*, p. 15, p. 25.
[27] *Ibid.*, p. 25.

that is independent of a particular national context.[28] It has also become clear that the category of "national bourgeoisie" is inadequate to encompass the complicated political reality that Moscow feels is in prospect for the immediate future. More attention is being paid to a new phenomenon that portends the radicalization of the national liberation movement. The notion of the "intelligentsia" has emerged as a more accurate characterization of the leading elements in national movements and parties. Consider the following analysis of a Soviet writer:

The intelligentsia of the underdeveloped countries deserves special attention. Since the general level of political development of both the proletariat and bourgeoisie under colonial rule always was considerably lower than in the industrially developed countries, the intelligentsia, basically bourgeois-feudal in origins, played a leading role in the national-liberation movement from its beginnings. In a majority of cases, the activist cadres of political parties come from the ranks of the free professionals and employees. Lawyers, doctors, teachers, engineers, municipal employees, students—these are the people who along with the small businessmen form the backbone of nationalist parties and groups. To them ought to be added the military officers, who in most underdeveloped countries, are recruited from petty-bourgeois strata. And it is precisely the rather widespread political thinking of this category of people that has become the vehicle of nationalist ideology. Part of them pass over to the defense of the working peoples' interests, joining in the nucleus of Marxist parties. The majority of the representatives of the intelligentsia express the interests of the emerging class of national bourgeoisie.[29]

The Soviet leadership apparently envisages widening prospects for influencing a ruling intelligentsia, witness the strange class mutation suggested in this use of the Cuban experience as a model:

In the contemporary epoch, the possibility of a transition from one social developmental form to another, from one stage to another, is not direct, but through a series of intermediate stages. There is a real possibility—in conjunction with definite circumstances—for the transition of the most far-sighted representatives of non-proletarian elements to the position of the working class. The experience of the development of the Cuban revolution shows that representatives of the radical petty bourgeoisie, in the course of development of a genuine people's revolution are able to pass over to the position of the working class and to stand in the ranks of active fighters for a socialist transformation of society.[30]

[28] R. Avakov and G. Mirsky, "Klassovoi Strukture v Slaborazitykh Stranakh," *Mirovaya Ekonomika i Mezhdunarodnye Otnoshenia* (No. 4, April 1962). Although the new schema included a less optimistic appraisal of the bourgeoisie's ability to "consistently" carry forward the revolution, it was still argued that, as a class, it had not outlived its usefulness. There were indications, however, that in some countries—India in particular—the national bourgeoisie was splitting into a reactionary and progressive section. *Ibid.,* pp. 74-75, 79-81.

[29] *Ibid.,* pp. 73-74.

[30] V. Tyagnenko, "Tendentsii Obshchestvennogo Pazvitia Osvobodivshikhsya Stran v Sovremennuyu Epokhy," *Mirovaya Ekonomika i Mezhdanarodnye Otnoshenia,* No. 3, May 1962, p. 33.

It was evident that an analytical advance had to be made beyond the notion of the national bourgeoisie; the Soviets envisage the possibility of a "non-capitalist development" that will not necessarily be directed by the proletariat alone. Who then were to be the allies that would move the transformation beyond capitalism? It would have made Marxist-Leninist class analysis completely irrelevant to concede that the national bourgeoisie could initiate a "non-capitalist" phase; what substance would be left in the notions of the bourgeoisie and capitalism if such a possibility were conceded? But apparently some group, in alliance with the proletariat, would embark on the non-capitalist journey and the most likely recruit is the "intelligentsia" which has suddenly been discovered as a leading political force.[31]

This search for more discriminating analytical tools is also reflected in a new set of categories to capture differences among underdeveloped countries. Stalinism had recognized only the distinction between people's democracies under proletarian hegemony and Western controlled colonies and semi-colonies. The post-Stalin reorientation added a new category: ex-colonial states ruled by the national bourgeoisie, politically neutral, and struggling for economic independence. The present schema includes six categories to characterize underdeveloped countries outside the Communist camp:[32]

1. The first group includes the Philippines, Turkey, Thailand, Pakistan and "many Latin-American states." The ruling coalition consists of the proimperialist bourgeoisie and feudal landowners; Moscow contends that these states have little prospect for real economic development.

2. Another group is made up of Nepal, Yemen, Saudi Arabia, Ethiopia, Afghanistan, and some others; here there is a small proletariat and virtually no bourgeoisie. The feudal class rules, but carries out a neutralist foreign policy.

3. In this category are states with the most developed capitalist structure and a strong ruling national bourgeoisie. Soviet writers cite as examples: India, Burma, Ceylon, Syria, Lebanon, Tunisia, Brazil and Mexico.

4. Another set of states is distinguished in which capitalist relations are less developed and the national bourgeoisie is weak. Reference is made specifically to: Iraq, Morocco, Nigeria, Somali, Sudan, and Cambodia.

5. In the last two categories one finds most of the new African states. A "special group of countries" including "Ghana, Guinea and Mali" is singled out for attention. Soviet analysts contend that their class structure is peculiar: there is hardly any bourgoisie or feudal class, and the proletariat is just in the process

---

[31] "National democracy can be established under the leadership of any democratic class—the working class, the peasantry, or the small urban bourgeoisie. In some countries the leading force may be the intelligentsia, including the revolutionary army officers."
Sobolev, *op. cit.,* p. 46.

[32] For the outline and analysis of these categories see the article by Avakov and Mirsky, *op. cit.,* pp. 76-78.

of formation. Indonesia is also admitted to this "special group" whose prospects for the future are particularly good.

6. The final category includes most of the former French colonies in West and Equatorial Africa, the Malagasy Republic, and the Congo. Excluding the Congo, Tanganyika and Senegal, "the proletariat is very weak and is just being formed as a class." These states are differentiated from Guinea, Ghana and Mali because the imperialists continue to have a strong influence on the new rulers.

Soviet commentators are somewhat equivocal about prospects in Egypt and India, although, in general, the analysis of the nationalist leadership is favorable. The possibility of a "non-capitalist" path appears to be most likely in the African countries, but the process is not excluded for the other countries. Both economic structure—less developed capitalism and a weak bourgeoisie—and foreign policy alignment converge to determine Moscow's optimism for a particular country. The domestic political dimension is highlighted in the case of Indonesia where the enhanced position of the Communist Party is repeatedly noted.[33] The inclination to distinguish between the ruling nationalists and the national bourgeoisie, and the expectation of Soviet influence on the intelligentsia, will very likely become integral features of future analyses of underdeveloped countries. A sample of what can be expected follows:

One cannot directly identify the ruling groups in the UAR, and in Iraq, Indonesia and many African states, with the interests of one class. Naturally, the Indian Government is forced to consider the interests, not only of the Indian bourgeoisie but of other classes. On the other hand, the Indian bourgeoisie has an incomparably greater possibility of exerting influence on its government than the Egyptian or Indonesian bourgeoisie.

. . . in Ghana, Guinea and Mali, the government consists of the radical, antiimperialist intelligentsia. In ordinary conditions, this intelligentsia would necessarily have become the spokesman for the interests of a rising bourgeoisie. In today's world conditions are not ordinary but unprecedented, a quite new situation, engendered by the struggle of the two systems. The socialist camp proves to be a powerful continuously growing influence on the course of events, and in those countries situated in a transitional phase, the petty bourgeois intelligentsia does not necessarily have to become the champion of the capitalist development path.[34]

[33] "In a series of countries, the national bourgeoisie rules and directs the state apparatus. But in Indonesia the bourgeoisie never was as strong and influential as in India, and was not able to monopolize state power. A powerful Communist Party, nearly two-million strong, using its huge authority with the masses, unquestionably influences government policy . . . in contemporary Indonesia there is no one class that has full power in its hands. The country is going through a transitional period; as noted by Comrade Aidit, liberal democracy (i.e., bourgeois democracy) has outlived itself, but the conditions are not yet ripe for people's democracy."
Ibid., pp. 78-79.

[34] *Ibid.*, p. 79.

DEVELOPMENT THEORIES AND SOVIET COMMUNISM'S WORLD VIEW

The early post-Stalinist perspective on short-range prospects in non-Communist underdeveloped countries had been deliberately ambiguous; it had to remain so as long as Moscow was convinced that "socialism" was in vogue, local Communists were weak, and the chances of influencing nationalists by trade and aid were good. The Chinese challenge forced more attention to imminent development patterns; but the Russians intend to continue to court the neutralists and therefore want to keep several alternatives open. Forced to elaborate the new ideological schema, they have found a substitute for the previous ambiguity by increasing new categories, hedging on predictions, attaching conditions, and, in general, laying out multiple alternatives. Thus the Khrushchevian design remained essentially unchanged even after the attack of the Chinese comrades. Moscow apparently felt it had covered all its bets: Soviet aid and support for neutralism would divorce the new nations from the West, while Soviet economic experience would gradually shape domestic development, thus setting in motion economic processes that would eventually draw these states into the Communist orbit. And the Khrushchevian design for local Communists—building a mass following by playing on the mistakes of the nationalist rulers—correlated with the foreign policy strategy: the Communist parties would be waiting in the wings, prepared to manipulate whatever domestic crises the nationalists could not master as they moved, with Soviet advice and guidance, to a more radical internal transformation.

One of the most striking characteristics of the Khrushchevian style has been a preoccupation with keeping alternatives open, with maximizing Soviet flexibility so as to maneuver and jockey for position as new and unexpected openings appeared. This predilection was clear in Soviet policy in underdeveloped countries both before and after the Chinese challenge. The Soviet Union has arrived at that historical juncture when it must inescapably play several roles simultaneously, appeal to manifold audiences and consider many publics. Authoritative center of the world Communist movement, leader of the Soviet bloc, friend, ally and mentor of the uncommitted, underdeveloped world, supporter of the peace and disarmament movement, protagonist of the capitalist states—the Sino-Soviet conflict vividly illustrated the difficulty Moscow faced in integrating these diverse roles and divergent interests. The adjustments in the Marxist-Leninist schema for analysing change in the underdeveloped countries brought Soviet perception in closer touch with reality: the introduction of the notion of the "intelligentsia" to supplement the inadequate class category of the "national bourgeoisie" was a striking illustration of this process. But the story of Moscow's coming to terms with empirical reality is also a tale of increasing dissension within the international Communist movement. It highlights the dual function of ideology as description and prescription. Moscow's adjustment of the ideology to fit its foreign policy needs produced a new description of class relations in underdeveloped countries that had clear prescriptive implications for Communist Parties in these areas: Moscow was thus setting the "general line" for the world Communist movement, and from the point of view of the militants, the new ideological schema appeared to subordinate their interests to the needs of Soviet foreign policy. Communist ideology is monistic and claims a monopoly of truth. However much recent adjustments in Moscow's perception of development in non-Communist ex-colonial states brought the ideology closer to reality, it threatened to relativize its universal significance; further, the Soviet general line paralyzed the activism of Communist Parties. The Chinese challenge was a reminder that preoccupation with a transitory anti-imperialist alliance with neutralists posed the danger of taking the future for granted. Insight into the future, the Chinese contended, imposed the Leninist obligation of shaping emergent patterns and not allowing optimism to undermine militancy and activism. It was precisely as conscience of the international Communist movement that the Chinese challenged Russian policy, reminding the Soviet comrades that the ultimate design for a Socialist world order demanded a militant action program, a husbanding of scarce economic resources, and a sharper differentiation of friend and foe in the transition period.

There is a basic flaw in the Soviet design. The Communist world-view allows only conditional support for "national democracy" and a temporary commitment to the proliferation of neutral nation-states in former colonial areas. Moscow's short-range commitment to pluralism is no more deep-seated in underdeveloped countries than it is in Eastern Europe. Fragmentation of the colonial system serves an immediate anti-imperialist function; it is, however, a long way from ultimate socialist aspirations and expectations. For all expression of sympathy for non-Communist development efforts, the Soviets concede no intrinsic value to neutralism; on the questions of nationalism and neutralism, the interests of Moscow and the Afro-Asian states diverge. There is no place to be allotted to neutralists in the future Communist structuring of international society. Moscow's support in the present phase plays an instrumental role, taking on positive meaning as a tactical footnote to the more fundamental Communist dichotomic perception of contending world forces. Having adjusted to the complexity of development in the ex-colonial states, Moscow still aspires to a monistic future—an aspiration hardly compatible with the political and economic expectations of the nationalists in the new Afro-Asian states.

2. The Recent Soviet Reassessment of Developments in the Third World. A Western Non-Marxist Analysis

ROGER E. KANET*

In the past three years a number of very important changes have occurred in the countries of the Third World. Ben Bella, Nkrumah, and Sukarno—all of whom had been praised by the Soviets—have been overthrown; military regimes have come to power in much of Africa; Pakistan's relations with the United States have cooled appreciably; a number of African and Asian governments have nationalized large portions of their economies. All of these developments have had their repercussions on Soviet attitudes toward the Third World. The Soviets have expanded their contacts with developing countries to include such conservative African regimes as those of Senegal and Ivory Coast and members of the Western alliance system, such as Turkey, Iran, and Pakistan. The Soviets have also recognized that the national revolutionary movement has not progressed as smoothly and rapidly as they had hoped it would. One writer, for example, has emphasized the difficulties encountered in attempting to explain developments in the Third World:

The only general conclusion that can be drawn is that there is no peace in the Third World, nor political stability, nor smooth political, economic and social development. . . .

All the storm and stress in the Third World is but a manifestation of social and other antagonisms which inevitably become more acute as the national liberation movement spreads and develops.[1]

However, all is not bleak for, even though there might be temporary setbacks in the movement, in the long run things will work out well.[2]

This article was written especially for inclusion in this book.

* I am grateful for financial support from The University of Kansas and the Social Science Foundation of International Studies of the University of Denver.

[1] Lev Stepanov, "Troubled Year in the Third World," *New Times,* No. 1 (1967), p. 13. See, also, the earlier admission of G. Mirskii, at a discussion held in Moscow, that there may be a swing to the right in some developing countries. "Metropolii bez kolonii," *Mirovaia ekonomika i mezhdunarodnye otnosheniia,* No. 10 (1965), p. 107.

[2] See O. Tuganova, "Co-operation for Peace and Progress," *International Affairs* (Moscow), No. 9 (1966), p. 38.

During the first years of the present decade, Soviet theoreticians developed a model for the newly independent countries to follow in order to make the transition from the stage of underdeveloped, agricultural ex-colonies to that of socialist states. This model of a state of "national democracy" represented an interim goal, the completion of the tasks of the nationalist stage of the colonial revolution, which was still necessary because most of the former colonial countries had achieved independence without acquiring the prerequisites for the socialist stage of the revolution.[3] The major characteristics of this new type of state, according to the Soviet writers, included: (1) the refusal to join military blocs or to permit foreign military bases on its territory, (2) a major effort to decrease Western economic influence in its economy, (3) the granting of democratic rights and freedoms to progressive political parties, including the Communist Party, to labor unions, and to other social organizations, and (4) the introduction of major social changes, especially agrarian reforms, in the interests of the people.[4] The national democratic state was not viewed as a state of one class, but as one of the whole patriotic section of the nation which was to eliminate the reactionary elements which still existed.[5] The progressive forces, which were to come to power, were composed of a united front of workers, peasants, the democratic intelligentsia, and a segment of the national bourgeoisie. However, in the state of national democracy it was not necessary for the proletariat to play the leading role, according to Soviet theory, for any progressive class could initiate the necessary reforms. Actually the whole doctrine represented an attempt to pave the way for the gradual development of the necessary prerequisites for a socialist society in countries in which the working class was extremely weak. Although any class could fulfill the tasks of national liberation and begin the work of the state of national democracy, only the proletariat was considered capable of completing the tasks and bringing the country to full socialism.[6]

Although the Soviets were willing to proclaim that a number of countries—especially Ghana, Guinea, and Mali—were approaching the goal of a state of national democracy, none of these countries was willing to permit the development of local communist parties in accordance with one of the requirements of the state of national democracy. In all three of these "progressive" countries, single-party systems were established which precluded the existence of independent communist parties or independent labor

---

[3] The most complete and detailed study of the national democracy doctrine has been written by Leland G. Stauber, "Recent Soviet Policy in the Underdeveloped Countries: The Significance of the 'National Democracy' Doctrine," unpublished doctoral dissertation, Harvard University, 1964.

[4] B. Ponomarev, "O gosudarstve natsional'noi demokratii," *Kommunist,* No. 8 (1961), pp. 43-45. See, also, G. Skorov, "Krushenie kolonial'noi sistemy," *Mirovaia ekonomika i mezhdunarodnye otnosheniia,* No. 3 (1961), pp. 17-18.

[5] Ponomarev, "O gosudarstve natsional'noi demokratii," p. 41.

[6] See N. S. Khrushchev, "For New Victories for the World Communist Movement," *World Marxist Review,* Vol. IV, No. 1 (1961), p. 21.

unions, youth organizations, and so forth. In the United Arab Republic, Algeria, and other "progressive" countries, local communists were arrested and thrown into jail. With the sole exception of Indonesia, none of the revolutionary states of the Third World permitted the development of strong communist parties. The policy of national democracy seemed to be a failure.[7]

Beginning in 1963, the Soviets revised their attitudes toward non-communist, one-party regimes in the Third World, as well as toward the socialism advocated by the nationalist leaders of Africa and Asia. In an article published in 1962, Professor Ivan Potekhin, the dean of Soviet African scholars until his death two years later, had condemned the negative aspects of attempts on the part of African and Asian leaders to seek a "third way." According to him, "African Socialism," although it contained "sincere efforts of progressive individuals to find the transition to socialism which fits in with the special conditions of African reality," was also "used as a means to deceive the working masses in the interests of capitalist development."[8] Another Soviet specialist on developing countries was more blunt in his denunciation of ideas of a "third way": "There is not and cannot be any 'third path' and experience shows that the African peoples are not looking for one."[9] In this period, although the Soviets were willing to develop economic and political ties with one-party regimes, they were extremely critical of their political and ideological positions.[10] More

---

[7] John Kautsky argues that the doctrine of national democracy represented merely a verbal change and that even during the early 1960's the Soviets made no efforts to encourage independent action on the part of local communists. During this period, he maintains, the Soviets continued to support all types of regimes, including those which did not permit the development of local communist parties. John H. Kautsky, "Soviet Policy in the Underdeveloped Countries: Changing Behavior and Persistent Symbols," in Adam Bromke and Philip E. Uren, eds., *The Communist States and the West,* (New York, 1967), pp. 19-20, especially footnote 5.

[8] Ivan I. Potekhin, "Nekotorye problemy Afrikanistiki v svete reshenii XXII s"ezda KPSS," *Narody Azii i Afriki,* No. 1 (1962), p. 15.

[9] G. Mirskii, "Whither the Newly Independent Countries," *International Affairs* (Moscow), No. 12 (1962), p. 25.

[10] See, for example, Khrushchev's statement at the Twenty-first CPSU congress in 1959. In Leo Gruliow, ed., *Current Soviet Policies III: The Documentary Record of the Extraordinary 21st Communist Party Congress,* (New York, 1960), p. 60. Three years later Khrushchev voiced a strong Soviet complaint about the treatment of communists in developing countries:

> Unfortunately, truths which are fully obvious to us Communists are not always acceptable to many leaders of the national-liberation movement. . . . Under contemporary conditions the national bourgeoisie has not yet exhausted its progressive role. However, as contradictions between the workers and other classes accumulate, it reveals more and more an inclination for agreement with reaction.

> Leaders who really hold dear the interests of the people and of the toiling masses will have to understand sooner or later that only by relying on the working class . . . can victory be achieved. . . . Either they will understand this, or other people will come after them who will understand better the demands of life.

Pravda, May 19, 1962, pp. 2-3.

recently, however, they have been much more lenient in their evaluation of these regimes. The reasons for this change in attitude seem to be easy to find. According to the national democracy doctrine, only the working class and its vanguard were considered capable of initiating the social revolution which was required for the development of truly independent states. However, some of the very regimes which banned the activities of local communist parties also initiated radical measures of nationalization of "both domestic and foreign capital and were willing to rely on the support of the Soviet bloc in any ensuing conflict with the Western powers."[11] The question which the Soviet leadership must have asked itself was: "Why wait for the development of strong local communist parties, if non-communist nationalist governments were willing to carry out much of the program advocated by the Soviets?"

In an article published in *Kommunist,* the theoretical organ of the CPSU, R. Ul'ianovskii has outlined the new policy which is to be followed by local communist parties. Rather than calling for the formation of strong communist organizations, the Soviets now argue that "the most consistent and best trained Marxist–Leninist elements should play the role of friend and assistant" of the nationalist leaders:

Upholding the principles of Marxist–Leninist doctrine, Marxists must be flexible and shrewd, in order not to antagonize the masses. They must constantly seek to find their allies among those social strata and groups which at the moment do not fully accept the theory of scientific socialism, but who today make partial use of it and may fully arm themselves with it tomorrow.

Ul'ianovskii adds that the question concerns the initial approach to the building of socialism and not its detailed construction or completion:

If the working people of an economically undeveloped country, without a formed working class, had to wait for the possibility of forming a national proletarian dictatorship in order to begin the transition to socialist development, this would mean that it was necessary to develop capitalism rapidly, in order that a working class might be created on the basis of capitalist industrialization and subsequently, a Marxist-Leninist party might be formed on this base.[12]

Actually, before the shift in Soviet attitudes and policies toward the nationalist, one-party regimes in Africa and Asia had occurred, Soviet scholars were already questioning the foundations of the national democracy doctrine. First of all, the question of class structure in the developing countries was raised. Already in 1958 and again in the early sixties, Professor Potekhin admitted that classes, as defined in Marxism–Leninism, did

---

[11] Richard Lowenthal, "Russia, The One-Party Systems, and the Third World," *Survey,* No. 58 (January 1966), pp. 46-47. In this article Lowenthal gives an excellent analysis of the recent shifts in Soviet doctrine.

[12] R. Ul'ianovskii, "Nekotorye voprosy nekapitalisticheskogo razvitiia osvobodivshikhsia stran," *Kommunist,* No. 1 (1966), pp. 113-114.

not exist in Africa.[13] Two young Soviet economists, Gordon and Fridman, published studies of the class structure in the Middle East and North Africa in which they argued:

An underestimation of the depths of the real socio-political differences between the modern proletariat, which is connected with large-scale capitalistic ownership on the one hand, and the majority of agricultural and artisan-handcraft workers on the other, will lead to an oversimplified understanding of the problems of the formation of the working class in Asia and Africa. An unconditional unification of all elements of the army of hired labor into an entity embracing almost one-half of the gainfully employed population would in reality be an admission that the proletariat has already become the most numerous class of society. Such an approach could produce an incorrect evaluation of the degree of capitalist development and arrangement of the class forces.[14]

Besides reevaluating the position of the workers, Soviet writers began to take a closer look at the role of the military and the intellectuals in the developing countries. Georgii Mirskii, a scholar at the Institute of World Economics and International Relations, called for more detailed study of the intelligentsia and the army, from whose ranks have come the "revolutionary and national democrats" in the developing areas. Mirskii argued that the group of revolutionary leaders who were ruling in such countries as the U.A.R., Ghana, Guinea, and Mali could not be called members of the bourgeoisie, but was composed of progressive elements of the intelligentsia and the army; and the men who make up the class were truly striving to build the foundations for future socialism.[15]

In addition to reconsidering their views of the class structure and

[13] See, for example, I. I. Potekhin, *Afrika smotrit v budushchee*, (Moscow, 1960), pp. 18-19. For a discussion of Soviet views of the class structure in Africa see Roger E. Kanet, "The Soviet Union and Sub-Saharan Africa: Communist Policy Toward Africa, 1917-1965," unpublished doctoral dissertation, Princeton University, 1966, pp. 247ff.

[14] L. Gordon and L. Fridman, "Osobennosti sostava i struktury rabochego klassa v ekonomicheski slaborazvitykh stran Azii i Afriki (na primere Indii i OAR)," *Narody Azii i Afriki*, No. 2 (1963), pp. 3-22. Translated in Thomas Thorton, ed., *The Third World in Soviet Perspective: Studies by Soviet Writers on Developing Areas* (Princeton, 1964), pp. 180-181. For a later study by the same authors see "Rabochii klass osvobodivshikhsia stran," *Mirovaia ekonomika i mezhdunarodnye otnosheniia*, No. 12 (1965), pp. 75-87 and No. 1 (1966), pp. 27-39.

[15] G. I. Mirskii, "Tvorcheskii marksizm i problemy natsional'no-osvoboditel'nykh revoliutsii," *Mirovaia ekonomika i mezhdunarodnye otnosheniia*, No. 2 (1963), p. 65. More recent communist writings have reemphasized the potentially progressive nature of the military in developing countries. See, for example, A. Iskenderov, "Problems and Judgments: The Army, Politics, and the People," *Izvestiia*, January 17, 1967, p. 2. Translated in *Current Digest of the Soviet Press*, Vol. XIX, No. 3 (February 6, 1967), pp. 9-10. Tigani Babiker, a Sudanese journalist on the staff of *Problems of Peace and Socialism*, has argued that the new generation of African military officers is drawn from the petty bourgeoisie and workers and peasants, has fought against colonialism and is, therefore, "more likely to be imbued with hatred of imperialism, to find friends among the younger people, presently active in the revolutionary struggle, and to be more amenable to revolutionary ideas." "At the Cairo Seminar," *World Marxist Review*, Vol. X, No. 1 (1967), p. 54.

leadership of the nationalist regimes in the Third World, Soviet theoreticians began to analyze the economic policies of these leaders. According to the national democracy doctrine, only the active influence of the communists would lead to the introduction of socialist programs in the developing countries. Domestic "progressive" forces were urged to bring pressure on their governments to initiate radical internal reforms. However, even without the existence of legal communist parties, a number of African and Asian regimes did decide to select the non-capitalist path of development. For example, in discussions held in Moscow by the Institute of World Economics and International Affairs and published in its journal in 1964, Soviet scholars admitted that some developing countries had begun economic reforms which were aimed at both foreign and domestic capital. In these countries—especially Burma, the U.A.R., and some African countries —the state sector was growing at the expense of the private sector of the economy. According to G. Akopian, one of the participants at the discussion, "in a number of liberated countries of Asia and Africa not only have the principles of socialism been proclaimed, but the first practical steps to the realization of these principles have been made."[16] One Soviet writer went so far as to say: "If the conditions for proletarian leadership have not yet matured, the historic mission of breaking with capitalism can be carried out by elements close to the working class."[17]

Not only did the Soviets reassess the class structures of the developing countries and the role of the nationalist leaders in economic and political development, but they also shifted their attitudes toward the nationalist versions of socialism which have been expounded throughout Africa and Asia. As noted above, as late as 1962, Professor Ivan Potekhin had strongly condemned those who proposed a "third path" for the new states. However, more recent Soviet writing on the non-capitalist path of development has emphasized the progressive influence of such doctrines. After speaking of the great differences between scientific socialism and the various forms of national socialism, R. Avakov noted:

However, all this cannot hide the fact that in the socialist doctrines of a nationalist type there are definite revolutionary and progressive beginnings. The existence of principles found at the heart of these doctrines can assist national progress, the development of revolutions of liberation, and their transition to the stage of national democracy.[18]

Another Soviet writer argued that the ideologies of the developing states are not the most important factor in evaluating their progressive nature.

[16] "Sotsializm, Kapitalizm, slaborazvitye strany," *Mirovaia ekonomika i mezhdunarodnye otnosheniia,* No. 4 (1964), pp. 117, 119 and No. 6 (1966), p. 75. See, also, K. Ivanov, "National-Liberation Movement and Non-Capitalist Path of Development," *International Affairs* (Moscow), No. 5 (1965), p. 61.
[17] G. Mirskii, "The Proletariat and National Liberation," *New Times,* No. 18 (1964), pp. 8-9.
[18] "Sotsializm, Kapitalizm, slaborazvitye strany," No. 6, p. 66.

"Actually the real content of any revolution is determined . . . solely by the objective socio-economic content of the changes (chiefly in settling the question of ownership of the means of production) which the revolution brings about."[19] Revolutionary practice in such countries as the U.A.R., Burma, and Mali is said to be ahead of the development of ideological doctrine. "Social and economic reforms in these countries are often deeper and more radical than the theories 'elucidating' them. . . ."[20]

Since the Soviet reassessment of the nationalist regimes has led to the conclusion that these regimes are truly progressive, even though they have banned local communist organizations, the Soviets have decided that their interests would be better served by not calling for independent communist movements, but rather by having local communists operate inside the single-party regimes. In late 1963 and early 1964, even before the new doctrines had been fully enunciated, the Algerian communists supported the establishment of a non-communist, one-party state in Algeria. Ben Bella was declared a "hero of the Soviet Union" and the local communists accepted positions within the nationalist government.[21] In April, 1965, the Egyptian Communist Party officially dissolved itself and declared that Nasser's single party was the only organization capable of carrying out the revolution in the U.A.R.[22] Obviously the communist leaders in Moscow had decided that the best means to maintain and increase Soviet influence in the Third World—at least in the "revolutionary" countries—was by infiltrating nationalist parties with individual communists. This course has been followed in Algeria and the U.A.R., as well as in Mali, Guinea, and Ghana (until the 1966 overthrow of Nkrumah). European and African communists have been sent to man training schools for party and labor leaders which have been constructed with Soviet aid. Soviet and East European economic and technical advisors have played important roles in economic planning in these countries.

However, even though the Soviets have been relatively successful in implementing this new program, they have found that the instability of the domestic political situation in many developing countries is a threat to the continued success of their policy. In the past two years three of the leaders to whom the Soviets had given the most economic and political support were overthrown by military coups—Ben Bella, Nkrumah, and Sukarno. The Soviets now realize the weakness of a policy which is based largely on favorable relations with a single charismatic leader and are now encourag-

[19] Ivanov, "National-Liberation Movement," p. 65.

[20] V. Tiagunenko, "Sotsialisticheskie doktriny obshchestvennogo razvitiia osvobodivshikhsia stran," *Mirovaia ekonomika i mezhdunarodnye otnosheniia,* No. 8 (1965), p. 85. See, also, Iskenderov, "Problems and Judgments," p. 9.

[21] See Lowenthal, "Russia," pp. 50-52 and V. Kaboshkin and Iu. Shchepovskii, "Alzhir: ot natsional'nogo osvobozhdeniia k sotsial'nomy," *Kommunist,* No. 16 (1963), pp. 115-119.

[22] "Party Dissolved by Reds in Cairo," *The New York Times,* April 26, 1965, p. 16.

ing the development of "vanguard" parties which would be able to institutionalize the revolutionary policies of individual leaders, even if the leader himself were to disappear. The communist interpretation of Nkrumah's overthrow emphasizes the "absence of a well-organized vanguard party capable of rallying the masses to the defense of their gains."[23] Georgii Mirskii has written of the necessity for the Egyptian leaders "to train a new cadre of officials and extend the political education of the masses." He argues that a mass party like the Arab Socialist Union, although it has played a positive role in Egyptian life, "cannot act as a politically conscious vanguard. Socialist development is inconceivable without a party, without ideological work among the masses. That is precisely what the Egyptian revolution lacks, for from the very outset its leaders came from the middle strata, which had no social platform, and were inspired solely by the ideals of 'pure' nationalism."[24]

Since the proletariat is extremely weak in most African and Asian countries, "socialist consciousness" must be stimulated from the outside, with the cooperation of the international proletariat—i.e., of the Soviet Union and other communist countries. Developing countries should look to the example of other backward regions which have made the transition from feudalism to socialism, such as Soviet Central Asia and Mongolia.[25] The major thrust of Soviet policy in the "progressive" states of the Third World is now support for revolutionary regimes. No longer do the Soviets call for freedom for Communist Party activities as a sign of a progressive regime, as they did when the doctrine of national democracy was in vogue.[26] According to the more recent view, the only political prerequisites for progressive regimes are internal democracy for progressive elements, not necessarily communists, and a strengthening of ties with the socialist countries.[27]

The Soviets have implemented their policy by granting large amounts of economic and military assistance to such countries as Algeria and the U.A.R. Through 1965, Soviet economic aid to Algeria totaled $230 million and the U.A.R. had received more than $1 billion in assistance. Indonesia

---

[23] Thierno Amath, "Some Problems of Tropical Africa," *World Marxist Review,* Vol. IX, No. 8 (1966), p. 33. One Soviet writer points to the examples of Mali and the U.A.R., which are attempting to create vanguard parties inside the mass parties that have existed for a number of years. N. Gavrilov, "Africa: Classes, Parties and Politics," *International Affairs* (Moscow), No. 7 (1966), pp. 43-44.

[24] Georgii Mirskii, "United Arab Republic: New Stage," *New Times,* No. 48 (1965), p. 4.

[25] G. F. Kim and P. Shastiko, "Proletarskii internatsionalizm i natsional'no-osvoboditel'nye revoliutsii," *Pravda,* September 14, 1966, p. 4.

[26] See Khrushchev, "For New Victories," p. 21; and A. Sobolev, "National Democracy—The Way to Social Progress," *World Marxist Review,* Vol. VI, No. 2 (1963), p. 45.

[27] I. Pronichev, "Nekapitalisticheskii put' razvitiia i ego mesto v istoricheskom protsessa," *Mirovaia ekonomika i mezhdunarodnye otnosheniia,* No. 12 (1966), pp. 7-8.

was also a major recipient of Soviet largesse before the recent turmoil there removed Sukarno from power—approximately $740 million in aid was sent by the Soviet Union.[28] Recent (June 1967) developments in the Middle East, however, indicate that the Soviets, although they speak of undying support for the Arabs in their struggle with Israel, are not willing to take any action which might bring them into military conflict with the United States. They are willing to supply arms and grant diplomatic support, as they are doing at the United Nations, but they are not willing to risk a military confrontation with the West. Such an attitude has also been evident in Africa, where they refused to take concrete measures to return Nkrumah to power.[29] Whether the Soviets will be able to regain the prestige which they have lost by their refusal to take concrete steps to support the Arabs in their war with Israel is a question which only future developments can answer. What is clear, however, is that the Soviet leadership has been extremely successful, up until the present time, in increasing its influence among the leaders of the revolutionary states of the Third World. On most international issues of importance to the Soviets, such as the war in Vietnam, they have had the diplomatic support of these countries. In domestic developments, these nationalist regimes are carrying out much of the program that the Soviets have proposed.

So far we have spoken only of Soviet views toward the "revolutionary" regimes in the developing world. What of their attitude toward the much larger number of countries whose leaders must be classified as moderate or conservative? In 1962 two Soviet writers presented a classification of developing countries based on the class or classes in power, the type of foreign policy pursued, and the nature of the domestic policies implemented in these countries. According to them, the developing countries could be divided into six different categories of states:

1. National bourgeois regimes, seeking independent economic development and nonaligned foreign policies;
2. Alliances of the national bourgeoisie with feudal elements, seeking independent economic development and nonaligned foreign policies;

[28] U.S. Department of State, Bureau of Intelligence and Research, *Communist Governments and Developing Nations: Aid and Trade in 1965.* Research Memorandum, RSB-50 (June 17, 1966), p. 2.

[29] In a *Pravda* editorial of October 1965, it was argued that the best assistance which the Soviet Union could render the new states was the strengthening of its own economy: "In building socialism and Communism, the socialist countries make the most important and decisive contribution to the world revolutionary movement. This is what determines their vanguard role in the contemporary revolutionary struggle." The primary role in ending all forms of colonialism and neocolonialism must be taken by the peoples of Asia and Africa. The Soviet Union and the other socialist countries "cannot take the place of the peoples of the young national states in the solution of the tasks of the national liberation movement," for this would result in forcing one's own will on these peoples. Besides, such assistance might lead to the unleashing of a worldwide nuclear war. "Vyshnii internatsional'nyi dolg stran sotsializma," *Pravda,* October 27, 1965, pp. 3, 4.

3. Regimes composed of pro-imperialist bourgeoisie, either alone or in alliance with feudal landowners, which do not seek real political or economic independence;

4. Regimes in which neither the national bourgeoisie nor the feudal class is strong enough to dominate and which favor a non-capitalist path of development and nonalignment;

5. Regimes in which the class structure is similar to that in the fourth category, but which are strongly influenced by the imperialists; and

6. Feudal regimes which follow a neutralist policy in foreign affairs.[30]

The countries about which we have spoken so far have been mainly those which are in the fourth group. The Soviets have maintained friendly relations with countries which were listed in some of the other groups: India, Mexico, Syria (group 1); Somalia, Nigeria (group 2); and Ethiopia, Afghanistan, and Nepal (group 6). However, it has only been recently that they have developed contacts with countries in the other two categories —pro-imperialist bourgeois regimes and countries, mainly in Africa, which are still strongly influenced by the West. Now Turkey, Iran, and Pakistan, which were classified as countries ruled by the pro-imperialist bourgeoisie, receive large amounts of Soviet economic and military aid.[31] Senegal, the Ivory Coast, and Cameroon, which were strongly condemned by Soviet writers in the early sixties, now have diplomatic relations with the Soviet government and have received Soviet economic and technical assistance.[32] The Soviets have even continued to maintain diplomatic relations with the new anti-communist governments of Ghana and Indonesia, although they have strongly criticized developments in these two countries.

Whereas the Soviet goal in the more radical countries is aimed at support for anti-Western policies and the promotion of the transition to socialism, even if this is not scientific socialism, the goal in less revolutionary countries is one of denial of these areas to the West or intrusion into areas of Western control. In some areas of Latin America, and in Turkey and Iran, the Soviets are attempting to weaken the ties to the West and dependence on it. By offering alternative markets for the products of these countries, as well as new sources of economic and military assistance, the Soviets hope to be able to break the monopoly of contacts which the West has

[30] R. Avakov and G. Mirskii, "O klassovoi strukture v slaborazvitykh stranakh," *Mirovaia ekonomika i mezhdunarodnye otnosheniia,* No. 4 (1962), pp. 76-77.

[31] For a recent Soviet evaluation of developments in Turkey see I. Shatalov, "Ankara: New Climate," *International Affairs* (Moscow), No. 3 (1967), pp. 71-75.

[32] The government of Cameroon was called a group of marionettes; the politicians of the moderate African countries were termed propagandists for imperialism; Khrushchev himself spoke of those African leaders whose "skin is the same color as that of their countrymen, but [whose] morals and habits have been acquired in the service of the colonialists." See V. G. Trukhanovskii, *Istoriia mezhdunarodnykh otnosheniia i vneshnei politiki SSSR 1917-1963,* Vol. III (Moscow, 1964), p. 639; S. Volk, "Sudileshche v Senegale," *Aziia i Afrika segodnia,* No. 8 (1961), p. 54; N. S. Khrushchev at a meeting of the Mali-Soviet Friendship Association in Moscow, *Pravda,* June 1, 1962, p. 2.

been able to maintain ever since World War II.[33] Rather than relying on military threats and subversion, as they did for many years, the Soviets have renounced all territorial claims on their neighbors and have offered, instead, the means for economic development.

If one were to characterize the policy of the Soviet Union in the Third World during the fourteen years since Stalin's death, one would have to say that this policy has been one of constant reassessment and revision. When it became clear that a policy of isolation was unsuccessful, the Soviets developed economic and political contacts with the Third World; when it became evident that neutralism was the basis of the foreign relations of many of the new states, Soviet leaders came out in favor of non-alignment; when the weakness of the proletariat and local Communist parties was recognized, the Soviets introduced the doctrine of national democracy. Most recently, they have once again revamped their doctrine in order to fit it more closely to reality. The goal of scientific socialism and workers' states has been pushed far into the future. The major immediate task is the increase of Soviet influence in the developing countries. This, it is felt, can best be accomplished by supporting the existing nationalist governments, by granting military and economic assistance, and by developing political, economic and cultural ties with the peoples of these countries.

[33] See Shatalov, "Ankara," pp. 72-75.

3. The Breakup of the Colonial System

K. BRUTENTS

The disintegration of the colonial system is a stormy revolutionary process which began less than a quarter of a century ago. As a matter of fact, up to the Second World War this disgraceful system of oppressing and exploiting the majority of mankind was still almost intact.

. . . The mortal disease which struck the colonial system as a result of the Great October Socialist Revolution had been ominously heralded by the national and social emancipation of the colonial borderlands of tsarist Russia, by the Mongolian people's achievement of their right to decide their own future, the failure of the imperialist intrigues with regard to Turkey, Afghanistan and Iran and the unrest which gripped ever wider sections of the people in the enslaved countries.

Nevertheless, in 1939 more than two-thirds of mankind languished in colonial and semi-colonial bondage, which still prevailed in the greater part of Asia and practically the whole of Africa and Latin America.

British jingoists could still boast that the sun never set over the British empire. This prison of the peoples covered over 14 million square kilometres in five continents, and their 450 million inhabitants constituted a quarter of the world's population. France's colonial empire extended to almost 12 million square kilometres with a population of 70 million; that of the United States to 1.85 million square kilometres and 15.7 million people; of Japan to 298,000 square kilometres and more than 30 million; of Belgium to 2.4 million square kilometres and 14.5 million people.

It is not easy for the younger generation to imagine the world at that time. There were only 12 independent Afro-Asian states; the map of the world did not have the republics of Guinea and Mali, Kenya and Tansania, or the Democratic Republic of Viet-Nam. On the other hand, there were French West Africa, British East Africa and French Indochina. The imperial Powers had no idea that the end of colonial rule was near. Even during the war years, Winston Churchill, as incidentally the other leaders of colonialism, categorically rejected the possibility of losing their empires.

But history ruled otherwise. The colonial empires began to break up

From K. Brutents, "Developing Countries and the Break-up of the Colonial System," *International Affairs,* No. 1 (1966), pp. 62-71. Parts here reprinted are from pp. 62-63, by permission of the publisher.

during the war, and after its termination this process spread like wildfire. During the first 12 post-war years, 17 countries—almost the whole of Asia —shook off their chains. In the following ten years Africa became the centre of the liberation process: from 1956 to 1965, 34 countries in that continent won their state sovereignty. The flames of the struggle have also spread to the Western Hemisphere. Heroic Cuba, having won national independence, became the first country in the Americas to take the Socialist road. The flags of the colonialists were struck in three Central American and one European country. More than 1,500 million people, or over nine-tenths of the population in the enslaved countries, broke free from colonial and semi-colonial bondage. This was brought about by the dissolution of colonial regimes and fundamental changes in the position of dependent countries in conditions of the break-up of the colonial system and the rise of the community of Socialist states.

The British empire took more than 350 years to build, but 20 years were enough to reduce it to ruins. So far it has lost 96.8 per cent of its population and almost 87 per cent of its territory. By January 1, 1966, France had lost 98.8 per cent of the territory and 98 per cent of the population of her empire, the Netherlands 93 and 94.4 per cent respectively, the United States 99 and 82.9 per cent. Belgium, Japan and Italy have lost all their colonial possessions. . . .

4. *What Disarmament Will Give to Developing Countries*

K. IVANOV

B. BATSANOV

TWO FIFTHS OF THE WORLD'S POPULATION LIVE IN ABJECT POVERTY

It is said that the dead clutch at the living and that the horrors of past generations prey like a nightmare on the minds of the living. Today the overwhelming majority of the peoples in Asia, Africa and Latin America have won through struggle their national liberation and have put an end to hated colonial slavery. However, the politically liberated peoples have found on the shores of national independence not manna falling from the skies as a reward for past sufferings, but want, poverty, backwardness of production, a shortage of skilled personnel and the highest child mortality in the world. This is what the peoples gripped with the fire of national enthusiasm have to face in their countries.

Here are United Nations statistics on per capita national income of some countries (in American dollars, 1960):

Table 14.

United States	2,288	Paraguay	102
Britain	1,085	India	62.5
West Germany	967	Indonesia	60.7
France	962	Tanganyika	56
United Arab Republic	109	Pakistan	52
		Burma	50

Per capita national income in the developing countries is only one-tenth or one-twentieth of that in the industrial capitalist states. This gap has even widened in the last ten years. The difference here is qualitative; it

From Konstantin Ivanov and Boris Batsanov, *What Disarmament Will Give to Developing Countries* (Moscow, Novosti Press Agency Publishing House, 1965), pp. 30-40. Reprinted by permission of the Novosti Press Agency (London correspondent).

reveals the division of nations into oppressing and oppressed, characteristic of imperialism.

Table 15.

	Developing countries	Developed capitalist countries
Food consumption	1,850 calories a day	3,140 calories a day
Number of literates per each thousand of population	135	985
Number of doctors per 100 thousand of population	8	102
Average life-span	35	65

In Asia, Africa, and Latin America we enter a world of the direst poverty and a world of patriotic self-sacrifice, proud awareness of their national and human dignity. About two-fifths of the world's population, that is about 1,300 million people, live in these states, many of which were formed only recently on the ruins of colonial empires. The arms expenditure of these states, and to a large degree also the military spending of the Western powers, constitute a direct deduction from the wealth created by the population in the developing countries which could be employed for the advance of their peaceful economy.[1]

Imperialist powers rob the countries of Asia, Africa and Latin America of *about 20,000 million* dollars annually by way of unequivalent exchange and profit on the invested capital. This comprises approximately one-sixth of their gross national product.

The past colonial regime robbed the countries and suppressed everything independent and individual in their peoples. Torture, imprisonment for life, execution without investigation or trial were the answer to the striving for national freedom, and, as is the case now in Angola, even to learning the ABC. The fiendish regimes still prevailing in Angola, Southern Rhodesia, Mozambique or the South African slave republic—this is the horrible picture of *yesterday* in India, Indonesia, Algeria or Ghana.

All these countries had suffered the ruthless and tyrannical rule of colonialism. Deprivation of rights and racial discrimination of the indig-

---

[1] The idea that the military expenditure of the United States, for example, is covered fully by the American taxpayers or Britain by the British taxpayers, and so on, obscures the real picture. A considerable part of the military budgets of the Western powers is closely linked with the incomes of the big monopolies which are exploiting and robbing the population of the developing countries (remittance of foreign companies' profits, unequivalent exchange, machinations with monopoly prices —these are some of the means used by them).

enous population, almost complete illiteracy, widespread diseases and high mortality, primitive machinery and implements, a one-crop economy, the absence of the rudiments of a national industry, control of foreign monopolies and their agencies over all foreign trade and to a large extent of home trade, finances, currency and banking—all this is the result of the deliberate policy of imperialists, who regarded the colonies and dependencies only as areas for the extraction of profit, for swift and easy enrichment. It is not surprising that these countries, possessing exceptionally favourable natural conditions, are even now unable to provide their population with the necessary food, clothing and shelter. Robbed and poor now too they are actually compelled to subsidize the economic development of the industrial Western countries.

The young countries feel their economic backwardness in all spheres of life. . . . [However, not only] the peoples of these countries suffer from this backwardness and the preservation of colonialism (whether in old or new forms), but also all the other peoples, the entire world economy. . . . If colonial oppression and inequality in relations between states and peoples is not eliminated, if the millstone of militarism and the arms race is not lifted from society, it is impossible to dream of a lasting peace and a truly swift economic advance of the African, Asian, or Latin American countries.

The young sovereign states have been freed politically, but political freedom alone does not feed or clothe the people.

These states are confronted with a new, more intricate, but truly decisive historical task—to overtake the advanced countries economically. Undoubtedly, this task will to a great extent determine the course of development of these states in the next decades and its solution will largely determine also the face of world history in the immediate future.

The hierarchic pyramid of nations, peoples and tribes, in which the rich imperialist countries sit on the top while the poor peoples and states oppressed by them suffer on the bottom, has so far been preserved in the world. . . .

This system of exploitation is backed up by the entire might of NATO, CENTO, and SEATO. The new colonialists want now also to use the state machine, court and the troops of the young states to protect the property of the foreign monopolies. But the peoples are able already at this stage to prove *in practice* that they themselves, and not colonialism as formerly, decide the destinies of their development.

The countries liberated from the colonial yoke are now exerting efforts to eradicate the legacy of economic backwardness. Gross output in these countries has increased at an annual rate of four per cent in the last ten years as against one per cent prior to the Second World War. However with such growth rates the developing countries will need 17-18 years to double gross production and not less than 80-100 years to attain the present level of output in the developed capitalist countries. We refer to the

gross output and not per capita productions. To achieve the present level
. . . [of per capita production of the developed countries,] they would need
several centuries.

The economic task . . . is promptly to eradicate the grave aftermath of
colonial oppression and to overtake the highly developed countries of the
world in a brief historical period. The development level of modern science
and technology enables the developing countries to accomplish this primary
task in the lifetime of one generation in conditions of peace, abolition of
colonialism, general and complete disarmament. . . . Such a task might
seem fantastic: the abyss separating the imperialist states and the Asian,
African and Latin American countries is so deep. But if we ponder over
the present situation in the world and take into account the achieved level
and the possibilities for the development of industry, agriculture, science
and technology, it will become clear that the task of eliminating the economic backwardness of the liberated countries can be fully accomplished
in the lifetime of this generation.

THE SOVIET EXAMPLE

. . . The experience of the Soviet Union and other socialist countries
is of immense significance for the young developing states. The imperialist
countries developed at the expense of the colonies and at present . . . continue largely to live at the expense of the developing non-socialist countries.
On the other hand, the socialist countries, having overthrown the yoke of imperialism and inspired by the Leninist ideas of national and social liberation, were the first to demonstrate what a free people having done away
with imperialist bondage and exploitation, both internal and international,
can achieve by their own labour.

Adlai Stevenson (. . . [former] US representative to the United Nations) wrote at one time about the situation in the Asian countries that the
basic problem of most underdeveloped areas which had gained their independence only recently was how to implement the slogans of their revolutions, how to raise the rate of literacy and improve the organisation of the
public health services; how to utilise their natural resources and develop
idle lands; how to increase the output of farm produce and consumer
goods—in brief, how to carry out the delayed industrial revolution and improve the living conditions of the people and, moreover, do it swiftly possessing only meagre capital of their own and limited national resources.

Stevenson noted that this was a very difficult task, to say the least,
and that it was hardly surprising that the amazing successes achieved by
the Soviet Union under similar conditions were winning admiration and
arousing interest.

The young sovereign states of Asia, Africa and also the states of

Latin America which have taken the road of industrialisation have before them the rich experience of peaceful economic construction in the Soviet Union and the other socialist countries. After the Great October Revolution in 1917 the Soviet people built a number of large industrial centres in the Urals, Kazakhstan, Siberia and Central Asia, elevating thereby the extremely backward borderlands of Russia to the level of the advanced areas. The Soviet state introduced modern industry and technology everywhere, undaunted by outlays, difficulties and privation, at times developing at the same time national personnel of skilled workers, engineers, technicians and other specialists.

Practical experience has proved that society can turn to its advantage that which is entirely disadvantageous for narrow groups of capitalists guided by the profit motive.

If we exclude the years of war and restoration of war damage imposed on the USSR, we find that the Soviet Union has been able in 20–25 years, *in the lifetime of one generation,* to overtake developed capitalist countries in total output and to become the second industrial power in the world.

What was decisive in the amazingly rapid economic advance of the Soviet Union? In the final count, the main thing has been the widest, vigorous, constructive and decisive participation of the masses in the reconstruction of their country and in laying the new basis of its economy. It is neither foreign loans nor outside help, nor reliance on a generous uncle that have translated into reality the Soviet plans. Moreover, the entire imperialist world, so powerful at that time, set out to crush the young Soviet republic, employing its worldwide economic and financial blockades, wars, intervention, sabotage and other subversive measures. And what happened? The Soviet people have reduced all these exertions to dust. Today they are already overtaking the most industrially developed country of the capitalist world, the United States, and have surpassed it in a number of important branches.

ECONOMIC ASSISTANCE INSTEAD OF GUNS!

The peoples increasingly realise that industry is the instrument with the help of which the backward and less developed areas can be reconstructed. And agriculture, in which three-fourths of the world's population are engaged, is a basis for the development of industry, a market for its output, a supplier of raw material and foodstuffs, a source of a country's export reserves needed for economic advance. The crux of the economic problem can be formulated as follows: simultaneously with advancing industry to provide a new scientific and technical basis for agriculture as well, supplying it with modern machinery. This, in turn, again calls for the rapid progress of industry both in the industrially less developed and highly developed countries. True, large resources and forces are necessary which the present age could give it if . . . oh, *this if!*

"Before you stands Africa," Kwame Nkrumah of Ghana stated in the United Nations. "You behold the striving and aspirations of millions of Africans, who received only the crumbs of civilisation falling from the rich tables of the Western world. Present-day Africans stand only at the beginning of their risky road. They are in need of education. They are in need of progress. They are in need of capital without which it is impossible to move ahead to higher living standards. But what do we Africans see when we look beyond the boundaries of our countries? We see wealthy states squandering their huge resources on stockpiling mountains of weapons. We see mighty nations engaged in the futile and ruinous arms race. We see how precious capital which could promote the advance of Africa and Asia is squandered on weapons of potential destruction. What has this in common with the Christian charity proclaimed by the West?" . . .

A "Declaration Concerning the Conversion to Peaceful Needs of the Resources Released by Disarmament" . . . was submitted to the 17th session of the UN General Assembly. Here are some excerpts from the draft which reveal the essence of the concept of overcoming economic backwardness by the young developing countries as a result of disarmament.

"If, for example, one fifth of the resources spent for military purposes by States belonging to military-political groups was used to promote the economic development of the under-developed countries, it would make available $20,000 million a year for that purpose, or $500,000 million in twenty-five years. According to existing estimates, the use of that sum, in conjunction with their domestic efforts and resources, would suffice to enable all the economically under-developed countries of the world to overcome their economic backwardness and closely to approach the current level of industrial output in such developed countries as the United Kingdom and France within the lifetime of the present generation—that is, within the next twenty to twenty-five years.

"With these resources it would be possible to set up from thirty to forty power-based industrial centres of world significance in the under-developed countries of Asia, Africa and Latin America. To do so it would be necessary to harness and make extensive use of the rich resources of those countries in water power, petroleum, gas, ferrous and non-ferrous metal ores and other natural wealth. Industrial development would make it possible to exploit the surrounding agricultural areas on a modern technical basis. Many such projects exist. It is for the States concerned to decide which of them are essential, and in what order of priority. It is possible forthwith, however, to envisage the general outline of a programme of measures aimed at transforming . . . entire continents.

"Disarmament and the conversion of immense resources to peaceful needs would give ample scope for the development of peaceful co-operation between States, on the basis of equality and in the interests of all concerned. The expansion of international trade and mutual assistance would redound to the benefit of all countries, great and small, economically developed and under-developed; would ensure the growth of production; and would provide employment for additional millions of people."

The creation in the Asian, African, and Latin American countries of several dozens of power-based industrial centres of world importance would lay a firm foundation of industrialization of the developing countries, would enable them to overcome the narrowness of the agrarian and raw-material structure of their economy, and would radically change the present division of states into highly or less developed industrially.

The Soviet draft Declaration outlined the main contours of such a general programme for transforming the face of these continents.

"These projects," it is noted in the draft Declaration, "are not idle fancies, but realistic estimates. They have been worked out by eminent scientists on the basis of the most recent achievements of science and technology. Their realisation would radically change the economic and cultural situation in the still under-developed areas of the world in a very short time. In those areas new centres of culture would be formed, educational establishments and scientific and research institutes would be built, and each country would have its own national cadres of engineers, technicians, skilled workers, economists, agronomists, land-reclamation specialists, physicians and teachers." . . .

5. *They Will Not Choose the Capitalist Path*

O. V. KUUSINEN
AND OTHERS

One of the basic problems today is that of the paths and prospects of historical development of the countries liberated from the colonial yoke. It affects the fate of many large and small peoples comprising a considerable section of mankind. The question of the direction in which they are going is of vital importance both for these peoples themselves and for the progress of the world as a whole.

The young independent states . . . belong neither to the system of imperialist states, nor to that of socialist states. But the overwhelming majority of them have not yet broken loose from the network of world capitalist economy although they occupy a special place in it. They are a part of the world that is still exploited by the imperialist monopolies. So long as these countries do not put an end to economic dependence on imperialism they will play the part of the "world countryside" and remain an object of semi-colonial exploitation.

Clearly, the liberated states cannot simply repeat the usual course of capitalist development that was passed through by the old European states.

Such a repetition cannot happen in our day because both the internal and external conditions for it are absent. It is well known that in the Western countries capitalist industrialisation was carried out largely by means of the exploitation of the colonies and other weak states. National capital in the young states of Asia and Africa does not have this possibility; it is not only unable to "conquer" foreign markets and sources of raw materials, it is still forced to wage a hard struggle for existence against the old imperialist plunderers.

The prospect of a "leap" from backwardness by super-exploitation of the working class and ruination of the peasantry, as happened in the countries of "classical" capitalism, is also unreal. The mass of the people will now certainly not tolerate the "classical" capitalist course with its painful primitive accumulation and bitter suffering of the working sections of the people. A certain part is also played by such factors as the general discredit of capitalism in the eyes of the peoples and the growing influence of the example and experience of the socialist countries. . . .

From O. V. Kuusinen and others, *Fundamentals of Marxism-Leninism,* 2nd rev. ed. (Moscow, Foreign Languages Publishing House, 1963), pp. 417-418.

6. The Non-Capitalist Way of Development

V. YEGOROV

I. PRONICHEV

What then is the most effective and advantageous way of development for the young sovereign countries?

The Programme of the Communist Party of the Soviet Union says: "It is for the peoples themselves to decide which road they will choose. In view of the present balance of the world forces and the actual feasibility of powerful support from the world socialist system, the peoples of the former colonies can decide this question in their own interest. Their choice will depend on the balance of the class forces. The non-capitalist road of development is ensured by the struggle of the working class and the masses of the people, by the general democratic movement, and meets the interests of the absolute majority of the nation."

Many young countries are still following the capitalist way of development, remaining a part of the international capitalist division of labour. These states remain as agrarian and raw material appendages of the imperialist powers, who find it more advantageous to leave the colonial structure of the economy of the developing countries untouched.

However there does exist another way, which is already being followed by a large number of young sovereign countries. The way of non-capitalist development was formed when imperialism's colonial system crashed under the blows of the national-liberation movement, and the peoples, who were formerly deprived of legal rights, finally awakened to a new life and began to search for ways of social development, excluding all forms of exploitation. They have convinced themselves that the shortest way to eliminate age-long backwardness and to improve their living conditions lies in the non-capitalist way of development. . . .

In the economic [sphere] the non-capitalist way is characterised by

The first four paragraphs of this section have been taken from V. Yegorov, *The Neocolonialists' Barbed Weapon* (Moscow, Novosti Press Agency Publishing House, 1966), pp. 40-41 (distributed by Soviet Booklets, London). The rest of this section has been taken from I. Pronichev, "The Non-Capitalist Path of Development and Its Place in the Historical Progress," *Mirovaya Ekonomika i Mezdhunarodnye Otnosheniya,* No. 12 (December 1966) (distributed in English translation for the Novosti Press Agency by the Soviet Embassy in Washington). The passages reprinted here have been taken from pp. 6-8 of the English translation. Reprinted here by permission, respectively, of the Novosti Press Agency (London correspondent) and the Soviet Embassy in Washington.

government control and restriction and, in the future, by the stopping of the activities of foreign monopolies; by the nationalisation of the basic means of production and setting up of a state sector—the material foundation of revolutionary-democratic power; by the gradual elimination of big national capital, and in the future also of middle national capital, from all the spheres of production and from the non-productive sphere; by the restriction of capitalist profits by fixing stable prices and introducing a system of progressive taxation; by carrying out radical land reforms designed at abolishing pre-capitalist relations—setting up state farms, encouraging and financing by the state producers' cooperatives; by the tendency at decolonialising the economy by diversifying agricultural production and industrialising the country, chiefly within the framework of the state sector; by introducing current and long-term economic planning; by establishing government monopoly of foreign trade and government control (and in the future goverment monopoly) of internal trade. The economy of almost all developing countries following the non-capitalist path is characterised by a diverse property structure. There is the state sector, a mixed or state-capitalist sector, a cooperative sector (mostly in the countryside) and the private sector in town and countryside. Of all these, it is the state and cooperative sectors that form the economic foundation for non-capitalist development.

In the political sphere, non-capitalist development manifests itself in two aspects: internal and external. The former involves, first and foremost, the nature of state power, for the problem of ways of development is ultimately always a problem of state power. All the countries developing along non-capitalist lines have revolutionary-democratic regimes which are characterised by strong personal authority, the steadily growing participation of working masses in political life, as well as the rallying of the country's progressive forces and the gradual political isolation of reactionary elements. The consolidation of government and party relations with socialist countries is a common feature of these countries' foreign policy.

In the social . . . [sphere], non-capitalist development is characterised by the gradual restriction, and in the future by the elimination of all exploitation, by government regulation of the legal relations between workers and private enterprise owners in the interests of the former; by the gradual modification of society's class structure as the working class and cooperative peasantry increase in numbers and by legislative restriction of the exploiting strata of the urban and rural population; by raising the living and cultural standards of the working people, and by other measures both within bourgeois-democratic boundaries and beyond these.

In the sphere of ideology, non-capitalist development has not acquired stable features, complete theoretical substantiation and an integral pattern yet. We observe the intertwining of various ideological trends, including petty-bourgeois conceptions of socialism, too. . . .

Even without resorting to additional comparisons, the non-capitalist path . . . differs . . . radically from capitalism, the development of which it either breaks off (the UAR, Algeria, Burma and Syria) or actually averts (Mali, Guinea and the Congo/Brazzaville/). But there remain certain and sometimes quite significant distinctions from socialism, too. These countries have neither become socialist yet, nor are they capitalist countries any more.

Though it differs from capitalism and from socialism, the non-capitalist way of development is, of course, not some kind of another, "third" socio-economic formation or a special version of socialism. It is not a new form of society, but a trend along which society is developing, a transitional state, an intermediate stage to socialism. The non-capitalist path is a path of progress towards socialism, averting the stage of complete capitalist development or breaking off this development and implying the gradual development of socialist elements and reproduction and the transformation of former relations into socialist relations. In other words, the non-capitalist path of development is a phase of the transition of liberated economically weakly developed countries to socialism.

7. Vital Problems of Non-Capitalist Development

R. AVAKOV
AND OTHERS

THE TRANSITION TO NON-CAPITALIST DEVELOPMENT

Today the problem for most ex-colonies is to begin the transition to non-capitalist development when the . . . socio-political and economic situation is not yet stable and imperialism is out to hold these countries in the orbit of capitalism.

These countries face an important theoretical and practical problem . . . to find the *intermediate links or stages* from backwardness to progress. . . . The best way of eliminating age-old backwardness and improving the living conditions is non-capitalist development.

Of course, it is the nation itself that must choose the path of its development. The choice will result from the correlation of class forces and the struggle between them. However, it is already clear that the factors favouring the young countries' non-capitalist development begin to prevail over the opposing trends. Highly favourable international conditions have emerged in our epoch for the transition to non-capitalist development.

The peoples' struggle for economic independence and the choice of socio-economic development unfolds when there exist and compete two international social systems. The prevalence of the forces of socialism and peace over those of imperialism and war becomes internationally ever more conspicuous. The socialist system has become a reliable shield of the peoples' independent national development. The events of recent years in several countries of Asia, Africa and Latin America demonstrate that the imperialist powers cannot any longer resort to large-scale colonial ventures without a decisive rebuff from the joint forces of socialism and the world national-liberation movement. Peaceful coexistence reduces the possibility of imperialist aggression against the young states, furnishes favourable premises for the further progress of the national-liberation movement and facilitates the struggle for the most progressive way of socio-economic development.

From "Vital Problems of Non-Capitalist Development," in R. Avakov and others, *National Liberation Movement, Vital Problems,* Moscow, Novosti Press Agency Publishing House, (1965), pp. 56-76. Reprinted by permission of the Novosti Press Agency (London correspondent.)

In the struggle for independence the economically less developed countries may rely on the socialist system's all-round assistance in the establishment of their own independent national economies and the development of productive forces. This radically changes the prospects for their economic progress. The socialist countries' economic aid to these countries has ended the imperialist powers' monopoly for the delivery of industrial equipment, loans and technical experience. Monopoly capital cannot any longer dictate its own terms to the young countries. . . . Economic cooperation [on the basis of equality][1] between the socialist and newly independent countries is a major factor strengthening the latter's position in their relations with imperialism. The socialist countries' generous aid contributes to the young nations' realisation of the advantages of socialism over capitalism. They can grasp the meaning of socialism by comparing socialist aid and the "aid" from the leading imperialist countries. The prestige of capitalism in these countries is steadily declining, while that of socialism is mounting. The socialist countries' friendly economic aid paves the way for the final elimination of the ignoble system of enslavement and exploitation of some countries by others. The collapse of this system accelerates the debacle of imperialism on the world scale and the peoples' free choice of the progressive way of development.

Imperialism remains the main obstacle in the ex-colonies' solution of urgent historical problems and attainment of political independence. Imperialism uses every means to arrest these countries' independent economic development and preserve them in the world capitalist economy as exploited appendages supplying farm products and raw materials to the imperialist states. Therefore genuine independence and elimination of economic backwardness are impossible without opposing imperialism.

Along with the external conditions, there are favourable home conditions for the economically less developed countries' transition to non-capitalist development. In the mentality of the population of the developing countries colonialism and imperialism, the policy of wars, plunder, exploitation, enslavement and poverty are associated with the capitalist social system. The people of the ex-colonies and ex-dependencies know to their own cost the seamy side of capitalist pseudo-civilisation.

The lessons of some young countries' capitalist development indicate that the basic nation-wide aims cannot be attained along these lines. Wide sections of population get more and more convinced, that once in power the bourgeoisie tends to shift the hardships of economic progress onto the shoulders of working people, and the radical socio-economic reforms it promised are impeded and sabotaged by bourgeois governments. These governments often make concessions to those anxious to arrest a steady national development. Private capital is still predominant and is growing at the expense of the population. The concentration of wealth within the con-

[1] The original translation reads: "Equal economic cooperation between . . ." [Editors' note]

trol of a relatively small section of the population continues to increase. Despite the growth of efficiency and of profit, real wages fail to rise and in many cases they go down. Unemployment and the spiral of prices mean new hardships.

Farming which accounts for half of these countries' national income or more is stagnant. Rich landowners, usurers and profiteers retain control over farming and the pauperisation of wide sections of farmers and farm labourers proceeds apace.

It is not for the sake of suffering for many years yet from capitalist exploitation and poverty that the people of these countries rose in arms. They do not want to follow the western countries along the road of "free enterprise," which inevitably leads to the amassment of weath at one pole and impoverishment at the other. The working people of the developing countries are in a state of social motion. They want to get rid of backwardness and poverty within the shortest time possible and they struggle for the democratic goals of national-liberation revolutions, and this develops the civic mentality of wide sections of population.

They insist on their participation in the government of their countries and they want to interpret and utilise the experience of the socialist countries' economic and cultural development. The revolutionisation of wide sections of population deepens in the economically less developed countries, their organisation improves and the influence of democratic forces increases. Hence the possibility for the young countries' non-capitalist development is inherent in the objective conditions of these countries themselves.

It would be wrong, however, to assume that the young countries' awareness that their vital problems cannot be solved by capitalist development would automatically channel these countries into socialist development. There is ample historical evidence that quite often a country's problems remain unsolved though the objective premises for the transition to a new social system have long been ripe.

The transition to non-capitalist development cannot be spontaneous. It requires deliberate purposeful activity on the part of all progressive democratic forces of each country. Non-capitalist development is ensured by the struggle of the working class, of the masses, of the general democratic movement, and it corresponds to the interests of an absolute majority of each nation.

An acute class struggle is raging in the young countries around the problems of further development. Essentially, the statesmen of young states which relied on the support of wide sections of the population during the liberation struggle period are now facing this dilemma: either private capital will have laissez-faire and then no vital demand of the population will be met, or the national-democratic revolution will develop towards a social revolution.

In many young countries the current situation does not permit as yet the transition to the building of socialism, while capitalist development does not solve any of their problems. The leaders of these countries realise that progress is impossible unless they lead their peoples along the lines of non-capitalist development.

The realistic possibility for the ex-colonies' transition to non-capitalist development has arisen:

a. when the colonial system of imperialism has collapsed under the blows of the national-liberation movement and the once oppressed and downtrodden peoples have awakened to new life and become active participants in the historical process of today;

b. when the peoples who have gained national independence are searching for the ways and means of social development without any form of exploitation;

c. when the newly-free peoples witness the competition of the two socio-economic systems—socialism and capitalism—and thus realise that the best way of eliminating age-old backwardness and improving living conditions is non-capitalist development;

d. when world socialism is becoming the decisive factor of the development of human society and the prevalence of the forces of socialism over those of imperialism is ever more conspicuous internationally.

Under these conditions the young countries can well embark on the path of non-capitalist development.

NATIONAL-DEMOCRATIC AIMS

In most ex-colonies the national-liberation democratic revolution is not yet over. Its further development is aimed at major targets, such as the consolidation of political independence and elimination of imperialist exploitation; radical solution of the agrarian problem in the interests of peasantry and removal of the parasitic class of landlords; accelerated industrial development with the state directly engaged and controlling it; strict state supervision over foreign property and the property of big local capitalists; and extensive democratisation of social and political life.

The solution of these problems does not yet bar capitalist development. On the contrary, the elimination of foreign oppression and feudal survivals, removes the obstacles in the way of home capital. Supported by international firms the bourgeois elements seize the opportunities thus created in order to strengthen and expand their sphere of activity. In several ex-colonies (India, the Philippines, Pakistan, Nigeria and some other African countries, let alone Latin America) the political liberation from imperialism stimulated the development of capitalist relations. . . .

At the same time an opposite trend is at work in many countries: restriction of capitalist relations already during general-democratic reforms.

One of the urgent and perfectly feasible problems for the young countries is the elimination of their direct exploitation by the imperialist monopolies. New forms and methods of restricting capitalism are formed and new social relations created as this problem is solved. The legislative restriction of foreign capital has been widely practised. The key branches are proclaimed to be the state's exclusive sphere. Privileges for national capitalists are granted. The transfer of profit abroad is restricted and part of it is required to be reinvested into the branches indicated by the government: repatriation of capital is forbidden. Profit is paid not in cash but in deliveries of raw materials and finished products.

In many young countries the government's share in the profit from the exploitation of their natural resources has been increasing appreciably. Restrictions are imposed on the activity of foreign firms in foreign trade and finances. Measures are taken to completely liberate the country from foreign capital in the future. For example, it is made binding of foreign firms to train within certain limits an adequate number of local specialists and skilled workers; foreign specialists are debarred from some posts in administration and management. The establishment of the workers' and government's control over the activity of foreign specialists is an important means for restricting and ousting foreign firms. Apart from sharply limiting the imperialists' exploitation this control may become an important *transitional* form for the subsequent nationalisation of these companies.

Though the measures restricting foreign firms' activity have effect they do not eliminate the imperialist exploitation of the young countries. However, if consistent, these measures may restrict the imperialists' activity and even force them to retreat.

The most radical means to which young states resort more and more often is the nationalisation of foreign property, especially in the key branches of the economy. The former foreign enterprises are controlled by the state, whose economic positions are thereby strengthened. Though compensation is usually paid to the ex-owners, nationalisation ends the unchallenged domination of foreign capital in this or that branch or in the economy as a whole.

The best results in the struggle for economic independence have been achieved where nationalisation has become a consistent policy.

The advance against foreign firms, nationalisation of their property and expulsion from the country are an effective means of developing the national-liberation revolution, furnishing economic premises for non-capitalist development.

Without consolidating the positions of democratic forces the domination of foreign capital in the economy cannot be eliminated.

Nationalisation of foreign property requires adequate economic, social and political preparations taking into account both international and home situation. On the other hand, to postpone the nationalisation when all the necessary conditions are in evidence means to arrest the progress of the revolution and give the right-wingers another chance for consolidating their positions.

Most young countries simply have to apply [for assistance] to the more developed countries since they have no national industry or any modern productive forces, or well-trained engineering and managerial personnel. At a certain stage this measure is indeed inevitable.

Today the developing countries may obtain technical aid without considerable economic concessions to imperialist firms. The existence of a powerful socialist system enables them to reduce to a minimum the imperialist firms' exploitation and get favourable terms from monopoly capital.

The countries of Asia, Africa and Latin America cannot, of course, count that the socialist countries are able to satisfy all their needs for capital, equipment and technical aid. They have to meet part of their demand through imperialist countries. However, owing to the support of the international system of socialism they can act as an independent and equal partner. Permitting imperialist firms' investment in their economies the young countries may now insist on their own terms and use the means thus obtained for accelerating their development.

The progressive forces tend to reduce to a minimum the negative consequences of the activity of foreign capital. The use of foreign capital is not accepted unless any encroachment on the country's sovereignty is ruled out. The young countries' independent development shows that the most acceptable form in this respect is loans to the government allocated at its discretion to the key branches of the economy. Foreign capital is used increasingly often under contracts according to which a foreign firm is to build an enterprise, start its production and hand it over to the state. Imperialist firms bargain for some shares and managerial posts at the enterprises built. However, the socialist countries' aid to the young states compels imperialist firms to make concessions more and more often. The attraction of foreign capital on "production sharing" terms (a foreign firm delivering the capital and specifications for the construction of an enterprise and receiving the remuneration in the form of its products) has been used more and more extensively.

Wherever a revolutionary-democratic government is in power the elimination of foreign firms' positions also strikes (as is evidenced by Algeria, Burma, the UAR, Mali and some other countries) at the *local* bourgeoisie—at first at its upper crust linked with these firms and then at other capitalists as well. However, the revolutionary-democratic leadership does not encroach upon the interests of the local petty bourgeoisie and the local middle bourgeoisie loyal to the government. In these countries nationalisation covers not only the branches or enterprises which yield low profits from the point of view of private capital, but also the spheres of investment which are the most profitable for the bourgeoisie, such as banking, insurance, foreign and wholesale trade, etc.

An important national-democratic problem facing the countries of Asia, Africa and Latin America is the elimination of pre-capitalist relations and the radical solution of the agrarian problem. The main claim of the broad masses of peasantry—distribution of the land owned by landlords and feudals—has not yet been satisfied. The revolutionary potentiality of peasantry which constitutes the bulk of the former colonies' and semi-colonies' population is tremendous. The solution of the agrarian problem is quite vital for the general-democratic non-capitalist stage of the revolution. Without radical agrarian reforms the development of productive forces cannot be essentially accelerated, nor can the food problem so urgent in these countries be solved.

As there is no uniform pattern of agrarian relations, there can be no uniform method of solving the agrarian problem. In some countries or areas the land is owned mostly by big landlords and tilled by small holders, while in others the patriarchal-feudal relations based on communal ownership of land may predominate. In some countries problem No. 1 is the elimination of feudal and semi-feudal exploitation, while in others the expulsion of imperialist monopolies firmly ensconced in farming takes priority. Sometimes different methods of exploitation combine. Therefore the development of the agrarian revolution in the young countries assumes different forms. An elaborate programme for agrarian reforms can only be worked out taking into account each country's specific background, social pattern, and economic development.

The agrarian problem was solved in the Soviet Union by nationalising all land and handing it over free of charge to farmers for unlimited use. In the other socialist countries there has been no nationalisation of land and the agrarian problem was solved gradually by establishing a maximum allotment, confiscating all extras and distributing them free of charge among farmers on the principle: "Land belongs to its tillers." The formulation and consistent realisation of these propositions eliminated completely landlords' latifundia[2] and exploitation of farmers, satisfied the latter's demand and consolidated the alliance of workers and farmers.

The agrarian reforms carried out in some form or other nearly throughout Asia and Africa have not yet been completed. The agrarian reforms do not satisfy the peasantry wherever the bourgeoisie and landlords are in power. They merely restrict the size of large holdings and reduce somewhat the rent. Considerable compensation is paid out when the extras are confiscated. Payments for land are so high that only the most prosperous strata of rural population can afford them. The exploiting

[2] Large landed estates [Editors' note].

classes' policy of this kind is warmly supported by the imperialists. In many countries of Asia and, more even, Africa they implant private ownership of land and even divide part of their latifundia among the peasants to create a new social basis.

To stave off the agrarian revolution, the imperialists and rich landowners set forth their own programmes opposed to the platforms advocated by democratic forces.

In those countries where latifundia are widespread the progressive forces, expressing the vital needs of wide sections of peasantry, demand that the landlords' land be confiscated and handed over to its tillers. In some areas, especially in East Africa and Latin America, the main landholders are large imperialist firms, and hence the solution of the agrarian problem assumes above all the nationalisation of foreign firms, property and organisation of large-scale state or cooperative farms on its basis.

The nationalisation of *all* land proclaimed in Indonesia soon after World War II did not reflect the aspirations of the bulk of peasantry who would not therefore welcome this measure. The response changed when the confiscation of landlords' and feudals' land and its transfer to peasantry were demanded. It is not always that wide sections of peasantry support a government's attempt to give up the idea of dividing land as if to avoid the deterioration of production. The latter is a weighty economic argument, but at the first stage of the agrarian revolution it must not overshadow the need to satisfy the peasants' age-long yearning for land.

It would be wrong, however, to extend this proposition to all countries and areas. In some cases it proves most inexpedient to divide all land, especially if the land hunger is acute. For example, fellahs in the UAR are obliged to join a cooperative as they receive land from the state which has expropriated it from the feudals or has reclaimed new areas. In some areas the agrarian reform is not carried out and fellahs are put under no obligation to join the cooperatives which are being organised.

The division of land is also unnecessary if a large farm produces export goods and is an important source of state revenue. The nationalisation of this farm and its conversion into a state or cooperative farm may become the most expedient measure in this case. The ex-French Company "Office du Niger" has been converted into a state company in the Republic of Mali. Land is nationalised in Zanzibar.

In the countries where revolutionary-democratic forces expressing the interests of wide sections of peasantry are in power and where traditional communal land ownership still exists cooperation is the principal method of the agrarian reforms.

Agrarian reforms in the young countries are essentially general-democratic and not socialist. They do not prevent the development of capitalism, but on the contrary, remove the greatest obstacle in its path: pre-capitalist relations. At the same time the elimination of pre-capitalist relations as well as feudal and semi-feudal forms of exploitation furnishes important premises for the transition to socialist reforms.

Encouraged by the state and organised on a democratic footing, the cooperative movement may become, along with the state sector, a material basis for the non-capitalist development of ex-colonies.

The radical solution of the agrarian problem in the interests and with participation of farmers relieves them from feudal oppression, eliminates landlords' landownership and allocates the long-awaited land to its tillers. To satisfy the main demand of a large section of peasantry means to rev-olutionise the most numerous stratum of the population of ex-colonies, draw them into the revolution and thus raise it to a higher stage.

The historical experience of the development of the People's Republic of Mongolia shows that under certain specific historical conditions the solution of the dual problem—the elimination of pre-capitalist social rela-tions and the creation of socialist elements—is not ruled out at the general-democratic stage of the revolution.

An important constituent of the national democratic revolution is the democratisation of social and political life, including the attraction of wide sections of population to the participation in social reforms and administra-tive activity. This problem follows from the very nature of the national-democratic revolution which is a set of radical social changes.

The revolution is to develop the initiative of the masses, the architects of history, and put an end to the control of narrow groups of external and home exploiters. Radical socio-economic reforms may only be carried out if the masses—the main force which wants the elimination of age-long backwardness without any compromises—are deeply involved.

The democratisation of socio-political life assumes above all the break-up of the old bureaucratic machinery created by colonialists, di-vorced from the people and opposed to them; education and promotion in all fields of economic and social activity, of new leaders who have emerged from the thick of the people, who know the people's needs and defend their interests; development of the activity of the political parties which share the united-front platform; activisation of trade unions and other mass or-ganisations and the recognition of their rights and important political role in the state; emancipation and attraction of women into active socio-po-litical life; all-out activisation of peasantry, their direct enlistment for the participation in the agrarian reforms and their political education; replace-ment of the pseudo-democracy implanted by the colonialists to promote the obedient elite to power by genuine democracy ensuring the freedom of speech and press, establishment of election from top to bottom in the ad-ministrative and political agencies; drawing of working people into running and controlling production and distribution; the possibility for the people to enjoy all benefits of civilisation, including health protection and public education.

A sharp struggle is afoot in the young countries around the programme of general-democratic reforms. Supported by imperialism, the Right-wingers oppose this programme, while revolutionary, democratic forces are working for its realisation. This struggle leads to the differentiation of class and political forces.

UNITED NATIONAL-DEMOCRATIC FRONT

The further development of the national-democratic revolution, including the solution of vital national problems, calls for the unity of all patriotic forces. Confronted by imperialism, all basic social strata and classes suffering from imperialist exploitation and economic backwardness are interested in this unity. It is the anti-imperialist orientation of the national-liberation movement, the trend to eliminate the young countries' economic backwardness that furnish objective premises for the establishment of a united national front.

The struggle for the general-democratic programme does not require a new revolution. This struggle is waged in the course of the anti-imperialist, anti-colonial revolution, i.e., the revolution which made the country independent. The demand to eliminate the colonial regime and gain state independence served as a platform uniting all national patriotic forces at the stage of the struggle for political independence. At the current stage of development, the programme of general-democratic reforms serves as this platform.

The establishment of a united national-democratic front is a complex process. The united front can be established for both long and short periods for major national goals and for particular targets. A stable and militant front cannot result from provisional top-leadership agreements. It can only emerge in the course of mass activity from *below,* joint efforts of various classes and social groups. This front is set up in the course of the daily struggle for the working people's specific, economic, social and political rights.

The consolidation of different social forces in a united front may be stable if a well-substantiated programme has been worked out, defining national targets over a considerable historical period and taking into account the vital interests of the forces united by the front.

The composition of the front differs from country to country and from stage to stage of the revolution. It depends on factors like the nature of contradictions between imperialism and feudalism, on the one hand, and the democratic forces, on the other, the sharpness of class contradictions, the social composition of population, political maturity and organisation of the working class and other social forces. The composition of the front may change in the course of the struggle for concrete aims as well as general national goals. Usually the composition changes at each stage of the struggle. Some social groups, parties and public organisations or individuals believe that their demands have been satisfied and withdraw from active political life. However, new forces join the movement. As the mass struggle develops the nucleus rallying all democrats takes shape.

The establishment of the front and non-capitalist progress is possible under the leadership of any democratic class: workers, peasants, or urban petty bourgeoisie. In some cases progressive intellectuals, including revolutionary officers, become the leaders of the front. Changes in the correlation of class forces are inevitable during the struggle.

The selfless struggle of the working class, the most consistent revolutionary class of today, wins over more and more peasants, urban petty bourgeoisie and other social groups that believe it to be the leading force of the movement. The working class's leadership is ensured not by decrees, but by the daily struggle for the consolidation of its influence on wide sections of population. It is only on this basis that the proletariat can take over the leadership of the united front.

The proletariat is the vanguard of the national-democratic front, and the workers-peasants alliance is its nucleus. Peasantry is the working class's most reliable ally in the struggle against imperialism, and for the solution of general-democratic problems. The working class cannot lead farmers unless it fights for the satisfaction of their demands and the completion of the agrarian revolution and attracts them for active participation in the revolutionary process. The workers-peasants alliance strengthens the basis of the democratic revolution. It is on the stability of this alliance that the participation of other classes and social groups in the national democratic revolution ultimately depends. These classes and social strata are themselves interested in the working class's support.

The establishment of the world system of socialism multiplied the chances of the victory of peasant revolutions in some countries. National revolutions extended their framework as they coalesced with socialist revolutions. The peasant movement (especially if headed by revolutionary democrats) has opened fresh prospects for the victory over imperialism and for further non-capitalist development.

Now that the national-liberation revolutions have triumphed in many economically developing countries where there is scarcely any working class, the development largely depends on whether these countries will be led by pro-imperialist, pro-feudal or revolutionary, democratic forces and on whether these forces will rely on the imperialist powers or the international system of socialism. The socialist countries' support makes it possible to accelerate socially and economically non-capitalist development, which inevitably leads to the growth and consolidation of the national working class and development of the democratic revolution into socialist under the direct leadership of the proletariat in close alliance with the peasantry.

Urban petty bourgeoisie has considerable revolutionary potentialities. Holding an intermediate position between the proletariat and the middle bourgeoisie, this section is an especially active force at the initial stages of the revolution. The representatives of this section try to shape their own policy in the revolution and create their own parties and national groupings. This is not a homogeneous section: some of its layers are anarchic, subject to vacillations, inevitably slipping towards the middle bourgeoisie and becoming counter-revolutionary, while others are closer to the proletariat in their position, join it during the revolution and become a genuine revolutionary element under the proletariat's leadership.

The young countries' independent development shows that having come to power some petty-bourgeois leaders degenerate into a reactionary force (e. g. the leaders of the Baath Party in Iraq). They are subject to corruption, they enrich themselves using their official position, they break away from the masses, implant red tape and treat the working people's needs with scorn. At the same time the enlistment of the urban petty bourgeoisie into the united front augments the revolutionary forces considerably.

Strengthening its alliance with the peasantry, the working class develops in every way possible the agrarian movement and at the same time supports the demands of the petty urban bourgeoisie, protecting the inviolability of its earned property and helping its struggle against usury.

Petty-bourgeois intellectuals, students and revolutionary officers are very active in the national-democratic revolutions of many countries. Sometimes they act as exponents of the interests of the peasantry though quite often they come from the families of rich landowners. A rapid development of the revolution may also draw them into the working-class movement, to which they bring their petty-bourgeois ideology. The more far-sighted intellectuals realise in the course of the revolution the aims of the proletariat's class struggle and become active advocates of its interests. An intermediate force, the intelligentsia follows the historically most promising class at a given moment. At the same time its democratic section usually leads the movement since it can see farther than the majority of the usually illiterate population.

The drawing into the revolutionary struggle of all the social strata extends the basis of the united front and strengthens the progressive forces in their struggle for general-democratic reforms. In those countries where the proletariat is small and has not yet realised its historical mission, revolutionary-democratic intellectuals lead the movement and implement radical socio-economic reforms.

In many former colonies and semi-colonies there are considerable sections of city paupers, declassé elements whose position objectively prompts them towards the revolution. However, they are extremely unstable, easily succumb to outside influences and can be carried away by pseudo-revolutionary demagogy. Some of these modern lumpen-proletarians may be bribed by reactionaries. Others may join the revolution. The lumpen-proletariat[3] cannot play an independent role in the revolution, but it can be used by both counter-revolutionary and progressive forces and at crucial moments it can become the reserve which may tip the scale of the revolution.

The revolutionary movement does not develop uniformly in different countries of Asia, Africa and Latin America. The united national front—its purposes, nature, composition and leadership—vary from country to country. What is common for all these countries is the need for pooling the efforts of the working class and nonproletarian elements and strengthening political work among peasantry, petty urban bourgeoisie and intelligentsia to draw them into the active struggle for the solution of general national problems.

The establishment of the united democratic front does not end the class struggle. Representatives of each class defend its own interests and are working for the leadership in the movement. While joining the front with other classes and social strata, the working class does not get dissolved in this alliance but defends its vital interests for the sake of attaining the ultimate goal: culmination of the democratic revolution and its development into the socialist revolution.

The correct attitude towards the united national front is of primary importance at all the stages of the national-liberation revolution. Underestimation or neglect of the role of the proletariat's allies, and especially the role of the national bourgeoisie, intermediate class groups and democratic intelligentsia, leads to failures.

Sectarian, dogmatic misconceptions prevent the alliance between the working class and its possible and necessary allies. The working class's and its Communist Party's policy with respect to the national bourgeoisie is not always correct. The working class's interests require not the break-away from the anti-imperialist national bourgeoisie, but cooperation in the struggle against imperialism and home reactionaries anxious to attract the bourgeoisie. Imperialism cannot satisfy the national bourgeoisie, no matter how many concessions it can make. The national bourgeoisie wants independent management and equal status among international capitalism. Imperialism opposes this trend. Hence the contradiction between imperialism and the national bourgeoisie and the possibility for the latter's participation in the anti-imperialist front.

The bourgeoisie is heterogeneous as a class. The rich bourgeoisie

[3] Literally the "proletariat in rags," it refers to the poorest section of the proletariat: to the unemployed, the lazy, the shifty, the beggars, the tramps [Editors' note].

makes up as a rule the right wing inclined most of all to agreement with imperialism and feudalism and openly advocating capitalist development. Politically close to this stratum in the more developed young countries is the trade bourgeoisie of the developing young countries for which cooperation with western firms is a paying proposition. The middle national bourgeoisie is more sensitive to the pressures of foreign capital, it plays an active role in the anti-imperialist struggle and supports the programme of agrarian reforms.

The participation of the national bourgeoisie in the struggle for general-democratic reforms does not make the national bourgeoisie consistent. Their narrow class interests drag them towards the cooperation with imperialism. However, the desire to get rid of foreign firms' oppression and patronage and to win a "place under the sun" in the capitalist world prompts their struggle for economic independence and against imperialism.

Despite its duality and unreliability the national bourgeoisie cannot be ignored as a part of the united front. A split of the united national front would mean the alignment of forces in favour of imperialism and home reaction. This does not mean, however, that the bourgeoisie should be given complete control over the revolutionary movement. The national unity of today is not the unity around the bourgeoisie, but the unity with a possible participation of the bourgeoisie.

The revolution in most young countries is a national, general-democratic event. The interests of the population as a whole clash with the aims of imperialism and home reaction. These interests have deep roots in the contemporary socio-economic system and reflect the needs of the main social forces of each country as a whole.

STATE OF NATIONAL DEMOCRACY

There is no doubt that the methods of solving vital national problems must vary taking into account the vast variety of specific conditions in the countries which have risen to make their own history. Therefore, Marxist theoretic thought has put forward a new form of uniting all healthy forces of each nation: *the state of national democracy*.

The state of national democracy is to make the masses realise that there is no unbridgeable gap between the general-democratic demands and the socialist transformation of society, but on the contrary, there is a direct connection between the two phases. As the state of national democracy attains the targets set by the anti-imperialist national-democratic revolution, it brings the country to socialism through non-capitalist development.

By its origin and main character the state of national democracy is an agency of the united national front, and by its purpose it is an instrument of solving general-democratic problems, completing the national-democratic revolution and furnishing conditions for the country's general transfer to socialist development.

The establishment of the state of national democracy logically follows from the development of the national-liberation revolution today. A profound popular movement, this revolution cannot be confined to the solution of problems set by the national liberation and the bourgeois-democratic revolution. National independence does not lead automatically to a radical and democratic solution of the agrarian problem or the elimination of deep economic and social backwardness. Yet it is for these purposes and not only for the removal of foreign political oppression that the national-liberation revolutions have been accomplished.

The problems facing national-liberation revolutions can be solved successfully if consistent anti-imperialist forces representing wide sections of population come to power. In other words, the establishment of the state of national democracy implies the re-arrangement of class forces. The working class, peasantry and democratic intellectuals give their leadership to the united front of patriotic forces, including the anti-imperialist section of the national bourgeoisie.

The democratic stage of the national-liberation revolution when the masses become the masters of their country is a sign that the national revolution is developing into the social revolution. The coalescence of the goals set by the national-democratic and social revolutions is one of the most characteristic features of the world revolutionary process of today. No national-liberation revolution can attain its ultimate goals in our epoch without profound social reforms.

The state of national democracy may become instrumental in these reforms. It is not impossible, however, that the revolutionary élan of the masses will put forward other state forms of the transitional period. No doubt, however, that it is only the preparation for the building of socialist society that can be the meaning of the state of national democracy as well as any other possible state form of the young countries' current social development. Socialism is the logical sequence of the entire process of development of the national-liberation revolution.

Consequently, the state of national democracy is a transitional form of administration. The mission of this state is to pave the way for transition from pre-capitalist relations to socialism by-passing the stage of capitalist development. Its political groundwork is the united national-democratic front comprising all national-patriotic and progressive forces.

The structure of the state of national democracy is determined by its class basis. This state is not purely bourgeois-democratic. Essentially and objectively, this state is from the very beginning the democratic dictatorship of the revolutionary bloc of the proletariat, peasantry and urban petty bourgeoisie. The state of national democracy cannot fulfill its mission without transcending the framework of bourgeois democracy. A revolutionary anti-imperialist, anti-feudal state of working people, it is to accomplish the transition to non-capitalist development and the transfer of the revolution via several stages to socialist revolution.

It is impossible to describe all the variety of the development of the revolution from stage to stage in each country. Specific conditions will inevitably develop at each stage of the revolution and these will determine in the last analysis the trend of development and the alignment of class forces. Nor is it possible to define once and for all the social basis of the state of national democracy even for one country since this is a *transitional* (as was stressed before) and not static settled form. The meaning and message of its existence is the development of the revolution along the non-capitalist path towards socialism. Fresh problems will arise in the course of this progress. The alignment of class forces will change accordingly at each such turn. Those social groups which have exhausted their revolutionary potentialities will leave active revolutionary struggle and some of them will probably go over to the counter-revolutionary camp, while fresh forces will join the movement.

All these readjustments occur, of course, within the bloc of revolutionary forces in the course of class struggle. As the revolution enters a new phase, the bourgeoisie will realise that the anti-imperialist struggle led by the proletariat slips their control and objectively threatens their interests and will fight for the leadership in order to crush the revolution. It is at such crucial moments that the bourgeoisie can venture upon the most desperate acts, up to the physical destruction of the leaders of the revolutionary wing: in many countries there are numerous examples of assassinations, subversion. At the same time the bourgeoisie intensifies its attempts to influence the revolutionary movement by the ideology of bourgeois nationalism and anti-communism spearheaded against the ideology of class struggle.

This pattern of the development of the revolutionary struggle and the realignment of social forces may be characteristic of some young countries of today too. However, the movement may also take different forms, especially in those countries where there is scarcely any working class and the national bourgeoisie is weak. In these countries the development of the revolution from stage to stage may be accompanied by the removal of leaders who have become steeped in bourgeois mentality and succumbed to disintegrating influences and the emergence of the most staunch forces loyal to the cause of the revolution. At the same time vacillating elements dissatisfied with the growing revolutionary orientation of the movement will withdraw their support and the movement will develop by relying on the initiative of the masses. In this case the realignment in the government in favour of the revolutionary forces may initiate a new stage.

It is quite possible that revolutionary élan will lead to a political realignment of forces before the social and economic reforms corresponding to the current stage have been completed. Far from holding back the development of the revolution, this may accelerate the transition of the movement to the next stage at which what was left undone will be completed.

The national-liberation revolution following the path of non-capitalist development is inevitably accompanied by the creation and consolidation of the economic basis of the new social system. The transitional nature of the state corresponds to transitional economic relations. Cooperation of different classes and social groups in the state of social democracy arises due to the existence of different socio-economic formations. As was emphasised above, the development becomes non-capitalist not because socialist production relations are introduced immediately and the channels for the development of capitalism are closed completely, but because advantages are created for such economic forms which are likely to become socialist in the future or which are restricting the growth of capitalism. The meaning of non-capitalist development is that the foundations of socialism are being laid down and consolidated in its course.

The economic system based on the constantly growing state and co-operative sectors, i. e., on the social mode of production, corresponds best of all to the political and social structure of the state of national democracy.

8. *The Transition to Socialism*

R. AVAKOV
I. PRONICHEV
AND OTHERS

The transition from this form of non-capitalist development to socialism presupposes, naturally, a much more radical remaking of socio-economic relations. The difficulty and the possibly long duration of this process
are not only due to economic complications which remain partly under
socialism, too, but also to the slow formation of new leading ideological
conceptions—up to the moment scientific socialism is established as the
official ideology and practice of socialist construction. . . .

Breaking off or averting the development of capitalism, the non-
capitalist path is a socio-economic and ideological negation of the latter.
Moreover, it does not only and simply mean the negation thereof, but it is
also the socio-economic, political and ideological opposite of capitalism, as
we have seen when examining its essence. In all these aspects, non-capitalist
reality is characterised by the formation and development of new elements
which are contrary to the socio-economic basis and ideological superstructure of capitalist society.

The obvious unfeasibility of obtaining economic liberation and the
rapid development of the national economy and of eliminating the backwardness and poverty of young Asian and African countries on the capitalist path of development is a feature of the general crisis of capitalism.
The choice of the non-capitalist path by a number of newly independent
countries is a most vivid manifestation thereof.

The non-capitalist path of development forms the material elements
of socialism. Among them, there is the state sector of the economy, first
and foremost. In the countries where revolutionary-democratic regimes are
in power, there is no exploitation of man by man in this sector through the
object and right of property, and conditions are being created for its serving
the interests of the working people. In the UAR, for instance, 25 per cent
of the enterprises' and companies' profits are used for the benefit of workers and office employees. They get 10 per cent thereof in money, which

From Pronichev, *op. cit.* The passages here reproduced are from pp. 10-14 of **the**
English translation. The last paragraph of this section has been taken from Avakov
and others, *op. cit.,* p. 79. By permission, as *op. cit.*

means higher earnings, and 15 per cent go into public funds of consumption (5 per cent are used for housing construction and special services and 10 per cent for other social needs of wage and salary earners, thus increasing their real wages). In Algeria, a third of the enterprises' net profits is distributed among their workers or used for the needs of the latter. The public funds of consumption are used to improve the social insurance system, to introduce free medical service, etc.

The government-owned means of production functioning in the various sectors of the national economy cannot be appropriated either by individuals or groups of people and are nation-wide property. The state sector has become an immense economic force in all the countries developing on non-capitalist lines. In the UAR, the government either owns or controls about 90 per cent of all production capacities in the country, and the share of the state in the sum total of capital investments is approaching 95 per cent. In Mali, the state controls 80 per cent of the national economy. In Syria, 80 per cent of all industrial production is accounted for by state-owned enterprises. The measures taken to extend and consolidate the state sector involve the restriction of private capital within the country and the elimination of prospects for its future existence. Revolutionary-democratic regimes have put the activity of the private capitalist sector under government control and restricted its structural framework by national economic development plans. The government is interfering directly or indirectly into the reproduction process in the private sector, more and more often, which shows a tendency for turning it into a state-capitalist and in the future into a nation-wide sector.

The producers' cooperatives of the higher and transitional type for the joint tilling of land are another element of socialism, which originates in non-capitalist development. The material forms of socialism, both in the state sector and in the cooperative sector of some countries, lean upon quite an effective principle of the economic and political reconstruction of the economy—the principle of self-government.

Current and long-term planning by the government, which includes an ever increasing range of the national economy, is another material element of socialism in countries developing along the non-capitalist path. Economic development plans are discussed at plants and factories, at cooperative organisations and educational institutions. They are widely popularised because, as UAR President Nasser pointed out, everyone must have a clear idea of what is going on in his country. In 1965, the UAR fulfilled successfully its five-year economic development plan. Among the main targets of the second long-term plan there is that of developing the heavy industry, for which 874 million Egyptian pounds are to be appropriated. As of July 1963, Guinea has been carrying out its seven-year economic development plan. Parallel with expanding industrial output (it is planned to build 26 new state-owned enterprises) provisions are made for organising the profitable operation of the functioning factories and plants and for completing production cooperation. In Burma's seven-year plan (1963-1970) stress is laid upon enlarging the output of agriculture and upon cooperation in agriculture. The country also has and is implementing a 10-year plan for the mechanisation of farming in Burma and a 4-year programme for developing fallow lands in Lower Burma. The Republic of Mali will complete its first five-year plan this year.

Speaking about the material elements of socialism we must bear in mind the revival of social, political and cultural life in the non-capitalist developing countries. The nature and functions of the supreme bodies of state administration reflect the immense revolutionary transformations already carried out or in progress. In the UAR, 198 out of 350 elected deputies to the national assembly are workers and fellahs. The persons who fall under the law of the land reform, nationalisation or whose property is under sequester cannot be nominated. Similar measures have been carried out or are mapped in Algeria, Mali, Guinea and some other countries. They introduce free education which paves the way to creating a truly national stratum of intellectuals. The army's officer corps is formed of workers and peasants. The social composition on all the levels of the political and government machinery is gradually changing, and the political significance, influence and functions of the toiling masses are steadily growing.

And, last but not least, the evolutionising socialist doctrines and the growing democratisation of public and political life are also elements of socialism. The development of the material elements of socialism will be limiting the sphere of operation for the economic laws of capitalism. Basically new economic laws, regulating an ever increasing share of production, distribution, exchange and consumption, are originating within the framework of the state and cooperative sector.

The elimination of the social heterogeneity of the economy, the predominance of the non-capitalist sector over the other sectors and the gradual ousting of the forms of economy which are alien to socialism—all this will lead to the prevalence of new economic laws over the economic laws of capitalism, thus stepping up the outcome of class struggle in favour of socialism. This will promote the ripening of the non-capitalist form of development and eradicate to a considerable measure the distinctions between this form and socialism.

The ultimate transition from non-capitalist development to socialism will acquire a definite pattern when the now originating elements of the socio-economic basis of socialism gain absolute prevalence and the lagging ideological superstructure turns from a transitional one into a clearly defined and fully socialist superstructure.

Each step along the path weakens imperialism and brings closer man's age-long dream: the final eradication of the ignominious system of enslavement of country by country and exploitation of man by man, and then the world-scale building of communism, the most progressive social system.

9. The Developing Countries Can Count on Aid and Assistance From the Socialist Camp

A. TKACHENKO

Every day ships carrying the most diverse cargoes leave the ports of the socialist countries; every day hundreds of ships return from long voyages. The merchant fleets of the socialist countries perform great and lofty international tasks by delivering vitally necessary cargoes to the young states of Asia, Africa and Latin America that are waging a struggle to strengthen their economy, to free it from capitalist domination and the encroachments of the predatory monopolies.

In recent years Soviet seamen have opened up new trans-oceanic routes. From the Black Sea, Baltic and northern ports a bridge has been thrown across the Atlantic to the shores of Cuba. From the Black Sea a line has been opened through six seas and the Indian Ocean to the ports of India, from the shores of the Baltic ships sail to the shores of distant Africa. Routes have been opened to Brazil and other Latin American countries.

There is no sea which the ships of the socialist countries do not sail. In 1964 Soviet ships alone called at over 700 foreign ports in 80 some odd countries, covering tens of millions of miles on the sea lanes of Europe, Asia, Africa and Latin America. If to this is added the distance covered by the ships of Poland, Bulgaria, Roumania, Yugoslavia and the other fraternal countries, the figure will be greatly increased.

In their holds the ships of the socialist countries carry industrial goods of all kinds: machine tools, motor vehicles, agricultural machinery, industrial and geological equipment, excavators, bulldozers, building machinery, measuring instruments; they carry timber, iron ore, coal, rolled steel, apatite. . . .

The socialist countries' air and rail transport systems are closely coordinated with the merchant fleets. At the big transport junctions millions of tons of freight are reloaded from goods wagons to ships and vice versa. The fraternal countries' aircraft today fly to the most distant parts of the globe.

At the dawn of Soviet rule, when Asia and Africa were shackled in

From A. Tkachenko, *Community of Fraternal People* (Moscow, Novosti Press Publishing House, 1966), pp. 56-65. Reprinted by permission of Novosti Press Agency (London correspondent).

the chains of savage colonial slavery, Lenin said that the peoples of those continents were requesting Soviet assistance openly or covertly, consciously or unconsciously—that they were beginning to realize the economic necessity of alliance with Soviet Russia against international imperialism. (Lenin, Coll. Works, V. 31, p. 446, Russ. Ed.)

The formation of the world socialist system and the elimination of the colonial regimes in the majority of the Afro-Asian countries have created a new basis for establishing and extending economic cooperation between the young national states and the socialist countries. The equitable and selfless character of this cooperation is the most important and most distinctive feature of socialist assistance to the liberated countries.

The socialist countries do not attach political demands of any kind to the economic and technical assistance rendered other countries, as is done by the imperialists, who violate sovereignty and insult the dignity of nations. The socialist countries seek no advantages for themselves in the countries to whom they give assistance. They need no military bases, no shares or concessions, no profits or high interest on credit extended. The projects built with the socialist countries' assistance, as well as all products put out from the moment projects are commissioned, are the complete and unconditional property of the country where they are erected.

In all this one sees a vivid manifestation of the new type of relations between countries which are free from the fetters of imperialism and colonialism. Peoples who for many years experienced the most abhorrent features of capitalist "civilization" clearly see from the assistance rendered by the socialist countries the indisputable advantages of this new type of relations between countries; they see for themselves that the selfless assistance of friendly countries promotes the prosperity of the independent states.

By the middle of 1962 the socialist countries had granted the young states credit to the sum of over 3.5 thousand million roubles;[1] this included about 3 thousand million roubles from the USSR, almost 300 million roubles from Czechoslovakia and 160 million from Poland. Total credits increased considerably in 1964. Credits extended by the COMECON[2] countries have become an important factor for independent economic development. In Indonesia, for example, Soviet credits constitute 15 per cent of state capital investments during 1961-1968; in India they amount to approximately 12 per cent of state capital investments under the third Five-Year Plan covering 1961-1966; in Afghanistan Soviet assistance financed

[1] At the official rate of exchange, one rouble (also spelled ruble or rubel) equals $1.11 [Editors' note].

[2] Council for Mutual Economic Assistance, sometimes referred to as CMEA or CEMA. All European Communist countries are full participants, and so is Mongolia. North Korea, Yugoslavia, and Cuba send observers; China withdrew from her observer status in 1961. Albania no longer attends COMECON sessions [Editors' note].

more than one-third of capital investments under the first Five-Year Plan covering 1956-1961.

The Soviet Union and the other socialist countries grant credit on easy terms. Credit is extended at low interest and is advantageous to both sides. The Soviet Union supplies the Afro-Asian countries with machinery and complete plant and gives scientific and technical assistance, receiving in exchange traditional export staples which are used to satisfy the needs of the Soviet people.

The socialist countries' economic, scientific and technical assistance is a substantial contribution to the development of the liberated countries' national economy. In 1963 the number of important projects that had been built with the assistance of the COMECON countries in countries of Asia, Africa and Latin America, together with those under construction or planned exceeded 1,100; this included 166 projects in India, 50 in Indonesia, 178 in the United Arab Republic, 48 in Syria, 17 in Mali, 6 in Morocco, 9 in Argentina, 10 in Brazil and so on.

Of these 1,100 projects, 480 industrial enterprises and other projects of paramount importance for the independent economic development of the countries involved had been built or were being built with Soviet assistance. Among them there were 34 steel plants, nonferrous metal smelters and the like; 30 odd engineering plants; 20 odd chemical plants and oil-processing plants; 20 enterprises producing building materials; 20 electric stations; 43 factories for the light and food industries. The many projects already in operation included the Bhilai Iron and Steel Works and the Ankleshwar oil-field in India; a motor repair plant, river port and mechanized bakery in Afghanistan; a cotton spinning mill in the United Arab Republic; a sea port in the Yemen; a technological institute and hospital in Burma; a radio station in Guinea.

The following example is significant: the capacity of electric stations being built in the newly independent states with the assistance of the COMECON countries will come to 5.2 million kilowatts or one-third of the capacity of the stations now operating in those states.

Plants and other projects built with Soviet assistance are equipped with the most up-to-date machinery and apparatus. They will serve as the foundation for the technical reconstruction of the young states' national economy.

A feature of Soviet assistance to the liberated countries is the fact that it ensures the development of the leading industries. In India, for instance, Soviet assistance is aimed at developing the steel and heavy engineering industries; at finding, producing and processing oil; at developing the production of mineral fertilizers. In the United Arab Republic, the Aswan High Dam and a 2.1 million kilowatt hydroelectric station are being constructed. The dam will increase the area under cultivation by one-third (2 million acres) and will increase agricultural production by 50 per cent.

One of the most important and most difficult problems confronting the liberated countries is the training of their own scientific and technical personnel. The colonialists spread the myth that the peoples of Asia, Africa and Latin America were incapable of independently managing their own economy without scientific and technical guidance on the part of the "developed" powers. The actual development of events has exploded this "theory." Today young specialists of the independent countries, trained in the colleges and schools of the socialist countries and in local educational institutions, are successfully managing different sectors of production, and are in the front ranks of the fighters in the cultural revolution.

The developing countries' national personnel are continuing to increase in number. The USSR and other socialist countries are rendering assistance in their training. Twenty-one thousand young foreign students from 119 countries are studying in Soviet universities and colleges.

The USSR is likewise selflessly assisting the young Afro-Asian states in training national personnel on the spot. Twenty educational institutions have been built with Soviet assistance or are under construction in Afghanistan, India, Burma, Cambodia, Ethiopia, Algeria, Tunisia, Guinea, Mali and Kenya. Every year the Soviet Union supplies a large amount of equipment, instruments, machines and installations necessary for educational purposes and research work.

On the basis of realistic possibilities, Soviet economists have come to the conclusion that the Soviet Union's trade with the developing countries will increase by approximately 150 per cent by 1970 as compared with 1963 and about eightfold by 1980, when it should exceed 11 thousand million dollars. Such prospects have awakened lively interest among the peoples of Asia, Africa and Latin America.

Speaking at the Geneva Palace of Nations at the United Nations Trade and Development Conference, Mr. Manharial Mansukhlal Shah, the Indian delegate, Minister of Commerce and Industry, said on behalf of the young national states that he most heartily congratulated the governments and delegations of the USSR and the other socialist countries, who had rendered the developing countries enormous support and had promised to increase trade with them several times over. He added that he hoped the other developed countries of the world would follow this historic example.

Here is what representatives of the newly independent states have to say about the socialist countries' assistance. We first quote from a letter addressed to the editors of *Komsomolskaya Pravda,* the Soviet youth paper, by Mr. Gausu Diavara, a student from Mali. He writes:

"It was only quite recently that the people of Mali freed themselves of colonial oppression. The selfless friendship of the countries of the socialist community and especially the Soviet Union supported the young republic and now she is confidently advancing along the road of independence.

"There is much we must learn, but from whom? We have before us the example of the USSR—the country which was the first to realize mankind's age-old dream of creating a genuinely free society.

"Soviet specialists are assisting us, sharing their experience with us, and soon we shall have our own doctors, teachers, geologists, architects, engineers and economists. Our people are studying and they will show the whole world that they can wisely and correctly order their own destiny."

Similar sentiments are expressed in a letter from Mr. Mohammed Elias, Secretary General of the Indian National Federation of Metal and Engineering Workers. It contains these lines:

"The Soviet Union assisted India in building the main branches of heavy industry and strengthening the foundation of our national economy. Our Federation remembers that every time the question rose of carrying out strategically important national projects in the newly independent states, the Soviet Union offered them selfless assistance and the services of specialists. It was that way in the case of the Aswan High Dam, in the construction of which the Western imperialist countries refused to help the United Arab Republic.

"Our country had the same sad experience with the steel plant at Bokaro. After negotiating with American departments for many years our government withdrew its request for assistance. Consequently our workers cannot but contrast the real intentions of the imperialists who offer to assist us in words, and the real assistance given us by the socialist countries, including the Soviet Union, in developing our basic industries in the state sector."

Expressing the thoughts and feelings of many Africans, Bashir Haj Ali, prominent public leader in the Algerian People's Democratic Republic, said this:

"The Great October Socialist Revolution, which signified the beginning of a new era in mankind's history—the era of the victory of socialism —opened a new and decisive stage in the colonial peoples' struggle for liberation. After the Great October Socialist Revolution the national-liberation movement assumed immense proportions. The victory of the colonial peoples would have been impossible without the socialist countries' political and material assistance."

SUGGESTED READING

I

Brutents, K., "The National-Liberation Movement Today." *Pravda*, February 1, 1967. Condensed text in *The Current Digest of the Soviet Press*, Vol. XIX, No. 5 (February 22, 1967).

———, "African Revolution: Gains and Problems." *International Affairs* (Moscow), No. 1 (January 1967).

Fedoseyev, P. N., "Great Threshold in the History of Mankind" [Worldwide Significance of the October Revolution]. *Izvestia*, April 30, 1967. Condensed text in *The Current Digest of the Soviet Press*, Vol. XIX, No. 17 (May 17, 1967).

Iordansky, Vl., "Problems and Judgments: Difficult Coming of Age" [Africa's Growing Pains]. *Izvestia*, February 24, 1967. Condensed text in *The Current Digest of the Soviet Press*, Vol. XIX, No. 8 (March 15, 1967).

Iskenderov, A., "The Army, Politics and the People" [The Army and Politics in the Former Colonies]. *Izvestia*, January 17, 1967. Complete text in *The Current Digest of the Soviet Press*, Vol. XIX, No. 3 (February 1967).

Keuneman, P., "New Features of the National-Liberation Movement." *World Marxist Review*, Vol. VII, No. 12 (1964).

Kodachenko, A., "Economic Cooperation Between Developing Countries." *International Affairs*, December 1966.

Krasin, Yu., "Experience of Lasting Significance" [Strategy and Tactics of the October Revolution as Models]. *Pravda*, January 11, 1967. Condensed text in *The Current Digest of the Soviet Press*, Vol. XIX, No. 2 (February 1, 1967).

Kudrayavtsev, V., "Unity of Purpose" ["Arab" and "African" Socialism Criticized]. *Izvestia*, March 12, 1967. Condensed text in *The Current Digest of the Soviet Press*, Vol. XIX, No. 10 (March 29, 1967).

Maslennikov, V., "Neo-Colonialism: Its Forms and Methods." *International Affairs*, December 1966.

Mirskiy, G., "Developing Countries at the Crossroads." *New Times* (Moscow), No. 48 (November 30, 1966).

Olsevich, Iu., "Problems of Reproduction in the Developing Countries and the Structural Crisis of the World Capitalist Economy." *Problems of Economics*, Vol. IX, No. 4 (August 1966).

Russia and Africa. Moscow: Nauka, 1966.

Stalin, Joseph, *Marxism and the National and Colonial Question.* New York: International Publishers, n.d.

Toltsikov, V., "The World Revolutionary Movement and Contemporary International Relations." *International Affairs*, May 1967.

II

Fallenbuch, Z. M., "Collectivization and Economic Development." *The Canadian Journal of Economics and Political Science,* No. 1 (February 1967).

Goldman, Marshall I., *Soviet Foreign Aid.* New York: Praeger, 1966.

Ingram, David, *The Communist Economic Challenge.* New York: Praeger, 1965, Chapters IV, V, XI.

Moseley, Philip E., "Communist Policy and the Third World." *Review of Politics,* April 1966.

Nove, A., and Newth, J. A., *The Soviet Middle East: A Communist Model for Development.* New York: Praeger, 1966.

Prybyla, Jan S., "Soviet and Chinese Economic Aid to North Vietnam." *The China Quarterly,* No. 27 (July-September 1966).

Ranan, Uri., "Moscow and the 'Third World.' " *Problems of Communism,* Vol. XIV, No. 1 (1965).

Sawyer, Carole A., *Communist Trade with Developing Countries, 1955-1965.* New York: Praeger, 1966.

Stokke, Baard Richard, *Soviet and East European Trade and Aid in Africa.* New York: Praeger, 1967.

Thornton, Thomas P., "Communist Attitudes Toward Asia, Africa, and Latin America," in *Communism and Revolution,* edited by Cyril E. Black and Thomas P. Thornton. Princeton, N.J.: Princeton University Press, 1964.

Thornton, Thomas P. (Ed.), *The Third World in Soviet Perspective: Studies by Soviet Writers on the Developing Areas.* Princeton, N.J.: Princeton University Press, 1964.

Chapter *4*

From Underdevelopment
to Affluence

CHINESE VIEWS

*1. China's Prescription for Economic Growth**

JAN S. PRYBYLA

China's advice to the underdeveloped countries is to follow China's way. There are in this attitude shades of the old Middle Kingdom, the ways and manners of which stood as a civilizing example which other, less fortunate peoples were expected to emulate, if they could. In the selections included here, there is little direct preaching and exhortation; they are more an invitation to study China's performance and then to get on with the job by relying on one's own resources. The inspiration, the thought, and the general method can, and should, come from China; but the effort, the raw muscle of revolutionary transformation, must be furnished by each country alone. Foreign aid is at best secondary to self-reliance; at worst it is subversive of the people's cause. The call to practise the ascetic virtue of hard work without expectation of outside help or immediate reward echoes the Chinese communists' two decades of revolutionary guerrilla struggles and almost twenty years of economic and political nation-building on the Marx-

* This article serves both as an introduction to the chapter and a Western, non-Marxist, introductory description, evaluation, and analysis of the Chinese position. For further clarification, brief editors' comments precede each subdivision of the chapter.

183

ian Maoist pattern. It also evokes memories of China's equivocal experience with Soviet aid.

Yet the invitation to study and then follow China's revolutionary path is not a take it or leave it proposition. In the view of the Marxists in Peking, it is a historical necessity revealed by a scientific analysis of contradictions in the contemporary world. Those who reject the invitation or turn a deaf ear to it, do so at their own peril, out of ideological immaturity or worse.

This triple emphasis on China's example, self-reliance, and the need to follow in China's footsteps at the risk of falling into moral error pervades the policy and theory statements coming out of Peking. It is explicitly recognized in the selections which follow, especially in the sections entitled "The Chinese Revolution Points the Way to the Emancipation of Other Asian as well as African and Latin American Countries," "Self-Reliance Based on Correct Thought is the Way to National Liberation and Socialist Development," "Underdeveloped Countries and Foreign Economic Aid," and finally "Those Who Oppose China's Prescription for National Liberation and Socialist Development are Lackeys of Imperialism.

One thing should be borne in mind. The various statements quoted in the pages which follow sound monolithic, as indeed they are, for they are the pronouncements of those in the political saddle, and little else. But China is not monolithic. As the turmoil and bloodshed of 1966 and 1967 have shown, there are in China strong dissenting views which exist and manifest themselves in action even though they are denied the opportunity of appearing in print. Occasionally in the past, such dissenting opinions have been published here and there, but always in the form of apparent agreement with and loyalty to the ruling thesis. It is the Aesopian way of saying no in a totalitarian setting. The existence of an intellectual protest against the official theory and policy line should be noted, however, both because of its apparent diffusion and because it may well herald the wave of the future. In so far as can be determined, the dissenting opinion is more pragmatic and less violent than the official line. Moderation in making revolutions and building socialism seems to be the underlying theme.[1] This is a significant point which should be remembered while reading the official literature.

The "revisionist" line of the silent but not silenced opposition has at times infiltrated the ruling thesis. This was especially so in the period following the collapse of the Great Leap Forward. It is a reasonable hypothesis that after 1960 and until the outburst of Mao's Great Proletarian Cultural

[1] A glimpse of what is involved may be gained by reading the two extremely virulent attacks on the economist Sun Yeh-fang in the *Peking Review* of October 21 and 28, 1966, and the condemnation of the one-time editor of *Frontline*, Teng To. The attack on Teng To was published in Shanghai's *Jie-fang Jih-pao* and *Wenhui Pao* on May 10, 1966. It is available in English in *The Great Socialist Cultural Revolution*, No. 1 (Peking, Foreign Languages Press, 1966), pp. 26-69. It followed an article published in the *Liberation Army Daily* (an organ of Lin Piao, Defense Minister and Mao's heir apparent as of 1967) of May 8, 1966. It is available in English in *ibid.*, No. 2, pp. 12-49.

Revolution[2] in the latter part of 1965, much of the opposition's pragmatic thinking was embodied in the official Maoist line, especially, it may be presumed, at the operational level. The section entitled "The Peasant Question and Agricultural Development are Basic to Socialist Construction Once the National Democratic Revolution is Completed" is a good sample of the revisionist approach to questions of economic policy. The ranking of agriculture first, light industry second, and heavy industry third is not orthodox Marxism-Stalinism-Maoism, but it is prudently ascribed to Mao. It smacks of out and out revisionism served up by the Party's dialecticians as pure orthodoxy. It was certainly not the line followed in China from 1953 to 1960, and its belated attribution to Mao must surely have irked the Maoists. Yet, in so far as can be determined, it is still the policy line, even though challenged, besieged, and stalled. It is embodied in the third Five-Year-Plan outline. However, because of other matters at hand, the plan is in abeyance.

China's domestic wrangling has tended to lessen the impact of China's official teaching on the underdeveloped world, communist and non-communist alike. The People's Communes, for example, have not been adopted by other underdeveloped communist countries, and wisely so. In spite of all the political and economic advantages ascribed to them even today, they were a rash creation that did not work. In the 1961-1965 period the experiment was abandoned in practice, if not in theory. The phenomenon is described in the section entitled "The People's Communes are China's Contribution to the Question of Transition from Collective Ownership to Ownership by the Whole People—An Important Step in the Direction of Full Communism."

It is an old law that doubtful truths are those most vocally asserted.[3] A rigidity has set into the Chinese position on economic development, an atrophy which manifests itself in the loud and endless repetition of formulas which once worked in China and are presumed to work everywhere else. Moreover, the contested leader and his intellectual constructs have become canonized to the point where a contrary reaction is produced in those not within the reach of the ruler's strong arm. The excessiveness of the personality cult in China verges on the pathetic and the tragi-comic. It beats anything that ever happened in the Russia of Stalin. Since the end of 1965 the praises heaped on Mao Tse-tung's thinking by the official press and other media have displaced most down-to-earth discussions of the means and methods to be employed to bring China out of her present poverty. An

---

[2] The "Great Proletarian Cultural Revolution" was unleashed in Mao's name at the end of 1965. It was intended to check alleged "revisionist" trends in the Party and Government, and led to attacks on some of the top leaders, including Liu Shao-ch'i (the Head of State) and Teng Hsiao-p'ing (the Party's General Secretary). It resulted in bloody factional clashes and a turmoil verging on civil war which had not subsided by mid-1968.

[3] See Bertrand Russell, *The Will to Doubt* (New York, The Wisdom Library, A Division of the Philosophical Library, 1958), p. 40.

idea of what is involved is given by the paragraphs headed "Correct Leadership is Important at All Stages of the Revolution." It is quite typical of the writing of that period—the upper hand, official writing, that is. The thought of Mao Tse-tung has been vested with infallibility on all matters of national liberation and socialist construction. There is no room here for the thinking of a Bourguiba or anyone else. There is only one path leading from "feudal" exploitation to full communism. That path has been charted by Mao once and for all.

Notice the gradual transition from basically Marxist–Leninist theorizing about the world (the sections on "contradictions") to what may perhaps be termed "romantic socialism" found in the passages dealing with "Politics Must be Put in Command of Economics and All Other Work." The importance of the political will and of "correct" ideological postures has been a constant of the Maoist interpretation of Marx and Lenin. But with time it has come to dominate every sphere of activity to the almost total exclusion of rational, extra-ideological, calculation. Maoist Marxism-Leninism has undergone a curious metamorphosis, not out of tune with China's intellectual history. It has turned into a vast, unending revival meeting in which preoccupation with the form of words obliterated the logic and the meaning of words. Even the old political will, the resolve to do things according to some more or less rational scheme, has turned into pure exultation. Such plans for economic development as at one time existed have been de-emphasized, swamped by calls to pure revolutionary exhilaration. The spirit of revolutionary transformation has come to overshadow the day-to-day means of such a transformation. Forms of conduct which served the Maoists well in the process of seizing power have been grafted onto the very different process of socialist construction. It is an interesting comment on China's prescription for planned economic development that in the eighteen years of communist rule, there were in fact and in actual practice only three years of economic planning (1955-1957). The first Five Year Plan (1953-1957) was not finally elaborated till 1955. The second Five Year Plan (1958-1962) was disrupted and relegated to the dust heap of history by the Great Leap Forward and the Sino-Soviet quarrel. The third Five Year Plan (1965-1969) has not been published; and, in any event, even if it does exist on paper, it has no chance at all in the setting of Mao's Cultural Revolution.

Hence, it is not a blueprint for economic planning and development that the Maoist Chinese offer the underdeveloped countries, but advice on how to make violent revolutions. The counsel runs like this:

1. According to Marx there exist antagonistic forces in the world, the clash of which moves history forward. These "contradictions" are of different kinds. (See "What Are the Fundamental Contradictions in the Contemporary World?")

2. The various types of contradictions in the contemporary world are concentrated in the vast stretches of Asia, Africa, and Latin America.

These are "imperialism's" most vulnerable areas. In Maoist terms, imperialism's colonial rear has been turned into the anti-imperialist front. The revolutionary struggles of the peoples of Asia, Africa, and Latin America are of the utmost significance for the success of world revolution, for the transition from "feudal" backwardness to socialism and communism. Put that way, the theory makes rural, underdeveloped China the spokesman for the revolutionary cause of the world's countryside. (See "Contradictions in the Contemporary World are Concentrated in Asia, Africa, and Latin America: the Storm Centers of World Revolution.")

3. The first task of the people in these key areas is to overthrow colonialism and, if already independent, rid themselves of all vestiges of colonialism. This process is called the "national democratic" or "new democratic" revolution, and it is the stepping stone to the next stage: socialism. The new democratic revolution must be carried out by a united front of communists and other strata of society (especially the poor, lower-middle, and middle peasants) under the firm leadership of the Communist Party. The united front, led and managed by the communists, is a temporary alliance against colonialism, imperialism, comprador capitalists, lackeys, and puppets. The rallying call is nationalism and patriotism. (See "First Task for the Peoples of Asia, Africa, and Latin America: National Democratic Struggle Against Imperialism, Colonialism, and Neocolonialism.")

4. The blueprint for this type of struggle is provided by China's revolutionary experience (1928-1949) and by the theory of "New Democracy" elaborated by Chairman Mao. China's new democratic revolution is an example for all colonial and semi-colonial peoples. (See, "The Chinese Revolution Points the Way to the Emancipation of Other Asian as well as African and Latin American Countries.")

5. The national democratic (new democratic) revolution takes on a violent, guerrilla form and is waged in the countryside by the peasants led by the communists. In his military writings, Chairman Mao has described in detail the strategy and tactics of such a revolutionary rural upheaval. His theories, elaborated long ago, are applicable today. Today, the countries of Asia, Africa, and Latin America are the world's countryside surrounding and pounding at the world's cities—the industrialized, developed (capitalist) countries. (See "Liberation from Colonialism—National Democratic Revolution—on the Chinese Model Means People's Liberation Wars Waged in the Countryside by Peasant Guerrilla Armies under the Leadership of the Communists.")

6. The economic program of the new democratic revolution must lay the groundwork for transition to socialism. It is important to note that whereas orthodox Marxism envisaged the "bourgeois democratic" revolution (the revolution which destroys feudalism) as resulting in capitalism and "bourgeois democracy" (parliamentarianism), Mao's "new democratic" revolution leads out of feudalism into a sort of pre-socialism in

which the communists already have the deciding voice in government, and the economic system is not capitalist but semi-socialist. (See "The Economic Program of the National Democratic—New Democratic—Revolution.")

7. New democracy of the Maoist type evolves into socialism through relentless struggle against capitalist and neocolonialist elements, its dictatorial form of government, and its specific economic policy. This transition occurred in China between 1949 and 1952. As in new democracy, the peasant question and the development of agriculture remain important policy planks of socialism. (See "The Peasant Question and Agricultural Development are Basic to Socialist Construction once the National Democratic Revolution is Completed.") Agricultural collectivization of an advanced type must be pushed through. Attention should be paid to the development of industry.

8. At some stage in the proceedings the cooperative form of ownership in the countryside should be changed into ownership "by the whole people" through the establishment of the People's Communes. Although the People's Communes represent only a progressive change in forms of ownership, they move society toward full communism. (See "The People's Communes are China's Contribution to the Question of Transition from Collective Ownership to Ownership by the Whole People—An Important Step in the Direction of Full Communism.")

9. Both the new democratic revolution against imperialism, feudalism, and colonialism and the socialist revolution against neocolonialism, external aggression, and revisionism have to be accomplished by the people themselves relying on their own efforts and resources and correctly led by a Marxist–Leninist Party. Foreign aid is subsidiary and must at all times be examined with care, for the old system as well as revisionism are often imported into the lands of true revolution in this guise. Reliance on foreign aid leads to subservience and loss of revolutionary élan. (See "Self-Reliance based on Correct Thought is the Way to National Liberation and Socialist Development," and "Underdeveloped Countries and Foreign Economic Aid.")

10. The fact that socialism has been implanted in a country does not mean that all revolutionary struggles are over. On the contrary, a prolonged period of sharp struggles begins with the laying of the foundations of socialism and continues right through the socialist stage. Externally, these struggles take the form of opposition to the aggressive schemes of capitalist-imperialism. Internally, the fight is against degenerate elements both within and outside the Party which at all times try to bring back the old system. Contradictions do not disappear with the attainment of socialism. The revolution is permanent. (See "Even During the Period of Socialist Construction Class Struggles Continue.") The dictatorship of the proletariat (that is, the dictatorial rule of the Communist Party) must continue until the final

achievement of full communism. There is to be no lessening of tensions, no liberalization of any kind. Successive generations of revolutionaries, steeled in struggle against imperialism, colonialism, neocolonialism, revisionism, and all domestic demons and monsters, all running dogs and lackeys, must be formed by a tough, self-reliant, ever watchful Party.

11. That is why correct politics must at all times be placed in command of all endeavors. Purity and correctness of thought is the essence. (See "Politics must be Put in Command of Economics and All other Work.")

12. This correct thought is the thought of Mao. (See "Correct Leadership is Important at All Stages of the Revolution.")

13. And those who do not believe it, shall perish. (See "Those Who oppose China's Prescription for National Liberation and Socialist Development are Lackeys of Imperialism And All Opposition Must Be Silenced.

That, in brief, is the thesis, the official thesis, the thesis of Mao and his lieutenants. It may appear crude and repetitious, but it has made its mark on history. Like the Marxism from which it springs, it is emphatic and exclusive. But it has also become Sinified and agrarianized, militarized beyond even the wildest dreams of Lenin. Its emphasis is on revolutionary upheaval, on the destruction of "the old and evil things." It has little to say about the complexities of economic construction, perhaps because it is still seeking the right formula; and what with the struggle against incorrect political thinking, there is little time left for economic calculation. Yet, in spite of its surface crudeness and its deep suspicion of all things intellectual, it has shown itself to be a powerful weapon of social transformation. Perhaps the reason is that it speaks the language of the unlettered poor and voices the impatience and anger of the destitute. It puts Marxian dialectics to work to seek out the positive side of poverty: the patience, courage, dogged determination, and persistence of the very poor. It minimizes or tries to "remold" the negative features of poverty: apathy, resignation, and sloth. The selections in this chapter will enable the reader to appreciate the power of the message.

An appendix has been added to this chapter consisting of two articles published in the West. The first of these, taken from the London journal *Mizan,* tries to show that internal difficulties and political setbacks abroad have not prevented China from continuing to expound to the peoples of Asia and Africa her revolutionary thesis. The second selection in the appendix has been taken from an American "independent socialist" periodical, *Monthly Review,* edited by Leo Huberman and Paul M. Sweezy. It presents a Western Marxist evaluation of the Chinese position which is sympathetic towards the Chinese approach. In this sense, it is not typical of the majority Marxist view in the West.

2. What Are the Fundamental Contradictions in the Contemporary World?

The "contradictions" referred to are the antagonistic forces which, accord-
ing to Marx, move history forward through its clashes and syntheses. More than
any other Marxist thinker, Mao Tse-tung sees the progress of humanity in terms
of a continuing clash of contradictory forces. The history of societies is, to him,
the resolution through violent confrontation of societies' opposing tendencies.
The precise and "correct" identification of these conflicting forces is, in Mao's
view, basic to the proper formulation of policy in a changing world [Editors'
note].

. . . What are the fundamental contradictions in the contemporary
world? Marxist-Leninists consistently hold that they are:

the contradiction between the socialist camp and the imperialist camp;

the contradiction between the proletariat and the bourgeoisie in the
capitalist countries;

the contradiction between the oppressed nations and imperialism; and

the contradictions among imperialist countries and among monopoly
capitalist groups.

The contradiction between the socialist camp and the imperialist camp
is a contradiction between two fundamentally different social systems, socialism and capitalism. It is undoubtedly very sharp. But Marxist-Leninists
must not regard the contradictions in the world as consisting solely and
simply of the contradiction between the socialist camp and the imperialist
camp.

The international balance of forces has changed and has become increasingly favourable to socialism and to all the oppressed peoples and
nations of the world, and most unfavourable to imperialism and the reactionaries of all countries. Nevertheless, the contradictions enumerated
above still objectively exist.

These contradictions and the struggles to which they give rise are interrelated and influence each other. Nobody can obliterate any of these
fundamental contradictions or subjectively substitute one for all the rest.

From "A Proposal Concerning the General Line of the International Communist
Movement," Letter of the CC of the CPC to the CC of the CPSU, March 30, 1963,
Peking Review, June 21, 1963, pp. 7-8.

It is inevitable that these contradictions will give rise to popular revolutions, which alone can resolve them.

The following erroneous views should be repudiated on the question of the fundamental contradictions in the contemporary world:

a. the view which blots out the class content of the contradiction between the socialist and the imperialist camps and fails to see this contradiction as one between states under the dictatorship of the proletariat and states under the dictatorship of the monopoly capitalists;

b. the view which recognizes only the contradiction between the socialist and the imperialist camps, while neglecting or underestimating the contradictions between the proletariat and the bourgeoisie in the capitalist world, between the oppressed nations and imperialism, among the imperialist countries and among the monopoly capitalist groups, and the struggles to which these contradictions give rise;

c. the view which maintains with regard to the capitalist world that the contradiction between the proletariat and the bourgeoisie can be resolved without a proletarian revolution in each country and that the contradiction between the oppressed nations and imperialism can be resolved without revolution by the oppressed nations;

d. the view which denies that the development of the inherent contradictions in the contemporary capitalist world inevitably leads to a new situation in which the imperialist countries are locked in an intense struggle, and asserts that the contradictions among the imperialist countries can be reconciled, or even eliminated, by "international agreements among the big monopolies"; and

e. the view which maintains that the contradictions between the two world systems of socialism and capitalism will automatically disappear in the course of "economic competition," that the other fundamental world contradictions will automatically do so with the disappearance of the contradiction between the two systems, and that a "world without wars," a new world of "all-round cooperation," will appear.

It is obvious that these erroneous views inevitably lead to erroneous and harmful policies and hence to setbacks and losses of one kind or another to the cause of the people and of socialism.

3. *Contradictions in the Contemporary World Are Concentrated in Asia, Africa, and Latin America: The Storm Centers of World Revolution*

This is the area in which China's experience and influence are most relevant—especially with regard to Asia. The thesis was formulated in 1963 at the very time that Sino–Soviet relations hit a new low [Editors' note].

. . . The various types of contradictions in the contemporary world are concentrated in the vast areas of Asia, Africa and Latin America; these are the most vulnerable areas under imperialist rule and the storm-centers of world revolution dealing direct blows at imperialism.

The national democratic revolutionary movement in these areas and the international socialist revolutionary movement are the two great historical currents of our time.

The national democratic revolution in these areas is an important component of the contemporary proletarian world revolution.

The anti-imperialist revolutionary struggles of the people in Asia, Africa and Latin America are pounding and undermining the foundations of the rule of imperialism and colonialism, old and new, and are now a mighty force in defense of world peace.

In a sense, therefore, the whole cause of the international proletarian revolution hinges on the outcome of the revolutionary struggles of the people of these areas, who constitute the overwhelming majority of the world's population.

Therefore, the anti-imperialist revolutionary struggle of the people in Asia, Africa and Latin America is definitely not merely a matter of regional significance but one of overall importance for the whole cause of proletarian world revolution.

Certain persons[1] now go so far as to deny the great international significance of the anti-imperialist revolutionary struggles of the Asian, African and Latin American peoples and, on the pretext of breaking down

From: "A Proposal Concerning the General Line of the International Communist Movement," *loc. cit.*, pp. 9-11. The second selection, headed "Two Main Currents in Modern Asia," is from Lu Ta-nien, "How to Appraise the History of Asia?" *Peking Review*, November 5, 1965, pp. 24-25. The author was Deputy Director of the Institute of Modern History under the Chinese Academy of Sciences.
[1] This refers to the Soviets [Editors' note].

the barriers of nationality, colour and geographical location, are trying their best to efface the line of demarcation between oppressed and oppressor nations and between oppressed and oppressor countries and to hold down the revolutionary struggles of the peoples in these areas. In fact, they cater to the needs of imperialism and create a new "theory" to justify the rule of imperialism in these areas and the promotion of its policies of old and new colonialism. Actually, this "theory" seeks not to break down the barriers of nationality, colour and geographical location but to maintain the rule of the "superior nations" over the oppressed nations. It is only natural that this fraudulent "theory" is rejected by the people in these areas.

The working class in every socialist country and in every capitalist country must truly put into effect the fighting slogans, "Workers of all countries, unite!" and "Workers and oppressed nations of the world, unite!"; it must study the revolutionary experience of the peoples of Asia, Africa and Latin America, firmly support their revolutionary actions and regard the cause of their liberation as a most dependable support for itself and as directly in accord with its own interests. This is the only effective way to break down the barriers of nationality, colour and geographical location and this is the only genuine proletarian internationalism.

It is impossible for the working class in the European and American capitalist countries to liberate itself unless it unites with the oppressed nations and unless those nations are liberated. Lenin rightly said:

The revolutionary movement in the advanced countries would actually be a sheer fraud if, in their struggle against capital, the workers of Europe and America were not closely and completely united with the hundreds upon hundreds of millions of "colonial" slaves who are oppressed by capital.[2]

Certain persons in the international communist movement are now taking a passive or scornful or negative attitude towards the struggles of the oppressed nations for liberation. They are in fact protecting the interests of monopoly capital, betraying those of the proletariat, and degenerating into social democrats.

The attitude taken towards the revolutionary struggles of the people in the Asian, African and Latin American countries is an important criterion for differentiating those who want revolution from those who do not and those who are truly defending world peace from those who are abetting the forces of aggression and war.

If the proletariat becomes the tail of the landlords and bourgeoisie in the revolution, no real or thorough victory in the national democratic revolution is possible, and even if victory of a kind is gained, it will be impossible to consolidate it.

[2] Lenin, "The Second Congress of the Communist International," *Selected Works* (Moscow, Foreign Languages Publishing House, 1952), Vol. II, Part 2, pp. 472-73.

In the course of the revolutionary struggles of the oppressed nations and peoples, the proletarian party must put forward a programme of its own which is thoroughly against imperialism and domestic reaction and for national independence and people's democracy, and it must work independently among the masses, constantly expand the progressive forces, win over the middle forces and isolate the reactionary forces; only thus can it carry the national democratic revolution through to the end and guide the revolution on to the road of socialism. . . .

TWO MAIN CURRENTS IN MODERN ASIA

. . . Two major historical currents of the world meet together in modern Asia.

Since World War II, there have been great developments in the history of the people's revolutionary struggles in Asia, Africa and Latin America. These areas have become the focus of various types of contradictions in the world. Imperialist rule in these areas has steadily weakened and one after another great movements of the people's revolutionary struggles have emerged and developed vigorously. The national democratic revolutionary movement in Asia, Africa and Latin America together with the international socialist revolutionary movement form the two major historical currents of the present-day world.

With these two massive forces of world history come together in Asia, no force on earth can now prevent Asia from advancing with giant strides. Since World War II, more than 50 countries in Asia and Africa have declared their independence. In Asia, independence was declared by some ten countries, including Indonesia, India and Pakistan—countries with large territories and populations, which were subject to colonial rule for several centuries. Since World War II, the People's Republic of China, the Democratic Republic of Viet Nam and the Democratic People's Republic of Korea have embarked on the road of socialism. These are changes of epoch-making significance in the history of Asia as well as in the history of the world. . . .

4. First Task for Peoples of Asia, Africa, and Latin America: National-Democratic Struggle Against Imperialism, Colonialism, and Neocolonialism

This struggle implies the formation of a united front of communists and broad social strata of each society. The leadership of this front must, however, rest with the Communist Party. This is the process of "national democratic" or "new democratic" revolution, which may involve the use of armed struggle [Editors' note].

. . . The oppressed nations and peoples of Asia, Africa and Latin America are faced with the urgent task of fighting imperialism and its lackeys.

History has entrusted to the proletarian parties in these areas the glorious mission of holding high the banner of struggle against imperialism, against old and new colonialism and for national independence and people's democracy, of standing in the forefront of the national democratic revolutionary movement and striving for a socialist future.

In these areas, extremely broad sections of the population refuse to be slaves of imperialism. They include not only the workers, peasants, intellectuals and petty bourgeoisie, but also the patriotic national bourgeoisie and even certain kings, princes and aristocrats, who are patriotic.

The proletariat and its party must have confidence in the strength of the masses and, above all, must unite with the peasants and establish a solid worker-peasant alliance. It is of primary importance for advanced members of the proletariat to work in the rural areas, help the peasants to get organized, and raise their class consciousness and their national self-respect and self-confidence.

On the basis of the worker-peasant alliance the proletariat and its party must unite all the strata that can be united and organize a broad united front against imperialism and its lackeys. In order to consolidate and expand this united front it is necessary that the proletarian party should maintain its ideological, political and organizational independence and insist on the leadership of the revolution.

The proletarian party and the revolutionary people must learn to master all forms of struggle, including armed struggle. They must defeat

From "A Proposal Concerning the General Line of the International Communist Movement," *loc. cit.,* p. 10.

counter-revolutionary armed force with revolutionary armed force whenever imperialism and its lackeys resort to armed suppression.

The nationalist countries which have recently gained political independence are still confronted with the arduous tasks of consolidating it, liquidating the forces of imperialism and domestic reaction, carrying out agrarian and other social reforms and developing their national economy and culture. It is of practical and vital importance for these countries to guard and fight against the neo-colonialist policies which the old colonialists adopt to preserve their interests, and especially against the neo-colonialism of U.S. imperialism.

In some of these countries, the patriotic national bourgeoisie continue to stand with the masses in the struggle against imperialism and colonialism and introduce certain measures of social progress. This requires the proletarian party to make a full appraisal of the progressive role of the patriotic national bourgeoisie and strengthen unity with them.

As the internal social contradictions and the international class struggle sharpen, the bourgeoisie, and particularly the big bourgeoisie, in some newly independent countries increasingly tend to become retainers of imperialism and to pursue anti-popular, anti-communist and counter-revolutionary policies. It is necessary for the proletarian party resolutely to oppose these reactionary policies.

Generally speaking, the bourgeoisie in these countries have a dual character. When a united front is formed with the bourgeoisie, the policy of the proletarian party should be one of both unity and struggle. The policy should be to unite with the bourgeoisie, in so far as they tend to be progressive, anti-imperialist and anti-feudal but to struggle against their reactionary tendencies to compromise and collaborate with imperialism and the forces of feudalism.

On the national question the world outlook of the proletarian party is internationalism, and not nationalism. In the revolutionary struggle it supports progressive nationalism and opposes reactionary nationalism. It must always draw a clear line of demarcation between itself and bourgeois nationalism, to which it must never fall captive. . . .

5. The Chinese Revolution Points the Way to the Emancipation of Other Asian as Well as African and Latin American Countries

As models for underdeveloped colonial and semi-colonial countries, China holds out her own national democratic revolution and subsequent socialist construction, rather than the Bolshevik revolution of 1917 [Editors' note].

SIGNIFICANCE OF CHINESE REVOLUTION

Among the changes which have taken place in Asia since World War II, the victory of the Chinese people in their democratic revolution and the start of the socialist era in Chinese history are historical events of the first magnitude. They have not only influenced Asia but have deeply influenced the whole world. The Chinese revolution has, in the first place, fundamentally changed the world's balance of forces between revolution and counter-revolution, between the socialist camp and the imperialist camp. The victory of the Chinese revolution delivered a crushing blow to imperialist domination. Yesterday's great rear of imperialism has been turned into a base area, into a forefront of the anti-imperialist struggle. Everything is turning into its opposite. China's area is approximately the same as that of Europe. China's population is larger than that of Europe. The forces of the world's revolutionary camp obviously exceed those of the world's counter-revolutionary camp.

In the second place, the victory of the Chinese democratic revolution and the advent of socialism in Chinese history have set a brilliant example for the colonial and semi-colonial countries of the world. The victory of the Chinese people over imperialism and its lackeys and the founding of the People's Republic of China have greatly inspired the people of many colonial and semi-colonial countries in their struggle for national independence and the complete victory of their people's democratic revolution. The Russian October Socialist Revolution served as an example for revolution in the oppressor nations, that is, for revolution in the imperialist countries; while the Chinese revolution set an example for revolution in the oppressed nations, that is, the colonial or semi-colonial countries. In

The first five paragraphs of this selection are from Lu Ta-Nien, *loc. cit.*, p. 26. The section headed "China's Revolution is the Key" is from Lin Piao, *loc. cit.*, pp. 22, 24, 25. The last selection, "The Chinese Revolution is part of the World Revolution," is from Mao Tse-tung, "On New Democracy" (January 1940). *Selected Works* (Peking, Foreign Languages Press, 1965), Vol. II, pp. 342-347.

studying the changes in Asian history since World War II, we need to make an adequate appraisal of the path as well as the influence of the Chinese revolution. For it is of significance for the whole world far beyond the East or Asia.

While the Asian people are attacking the imperialists and carrying history forward, the imperialists and reactionaries are not sitting back with folded arms. Since World War II, far from abandoning colonialism in Asia, Africa and Latin America, the imperialists are hanging on wherever they can. In this regard, U.S. imperialism is the most cunning and desperate. In face of the powerful struggles of the people of the world the U.S. and other imperialists and colonialists have been compelled to change some of the old methods of direct colonial rule and introduce the "new" methods of neo-colonialism. They foster puppet regimes and practice various subtler methods of colonial control; organize military blocs and build up military bases, and plunder the wealth of countries by means of economic "aid" and various other forms of economic "exploitation." They engage in "spiritual" infiltration and cultural aggression; organize subversion and engineer military coups d'état; they engage in direct armed intervention and launch large-scale armed aggression. U.S. armed aggression against Korea and the current U.S. armed aggression against Viet Nam and Laos are only two of these examples.

In brief, imperialism has not perished, the anti-imperialist struggle of the Asian people is not over. Asia has been and still is a stormy battlefront of the anti-imperialist struggle.

The modern history of Asia today appears at once more complicated and simpler than ever before. On the one hand, it has witnessed the impact of the two great historical currents of the national democratic revolutionary movement and the international socialist revolutionary movement; on the other, it is seeing the death-bed struggles and desperate attacks put up by U.S. imperialism and all the old and new colonialists. . . .

CHINA'S REVOLUTION IS THE KEY

. . . The Chinese revolution is a continuation of the Great October Revolution. The road of the October Revolution is the common road for all people's revolutions. The Chinese revolution and the October Revolution have in common the following basic characteristics: (1) Both were led by the working class with a Marxist-Leninist party as its nucleus. (2) Both were based on the worker peasant alliance. (3) In both cases state power was seized through violent revolution and the dictatorship of the proletariat was established. (4) In both cases the socialist system was built after victory in the revolution. (5) Both were component parts of the proletarian world revolution.

Naturally, the Chinese revolution had its own peculiar characteristics.

The October Revolution took place in imperialist Russia, but the Chinese revolution broke out in a semi-colonial and semi-feudal country. The former was a proletarian socialist revolution while the latter developed into a socialist revolution after the complete victory of the new-democratic revolution. The October Revolution began with armed uprisings in the cities and then spread to the countryside, while the Chinese revolution won nation-wide victory through the encirclement of the cities from the rural areas and the final capture of the cities.

Comrade Mao Tse-tung's great merit lies in the fact that he succeeded in integrating the universal truth of Marxism-Leninism with the concrete practice of the Chinese revolution and has enriched and developed Marxism-Leninism by his masterly generalization and summation of the experience gained during the Chinese people's protracted revolutionary struggle. . . .

The October Revolution opened up a new era in the revolution of the oppressed nations. The victory of the October Revolution built a bridge between the socialist revolution of the proletariat of the West and the national-democratic revolution of the colonial and semi-colonial countries of the East. The Chinese revolution has successfully solved the problem of how to link up the national democratic revolution with the socialist revolution in the colonial and semicolonial countries.

Comrade Mao Tse-tung has pointed out that, in the epoch since the October Revolution, anti-imperialist revolution in any colonial or semi-colonial country is no longer part of the old bourgeois, or capitalist world revolution, but is part of the new world revolution, the proletarian-socialist world revolution. . . .

The Chinese revolution provides a successful lesson for making a thorough-going national-democratic revolution under the leadership of the proletariat; it likewise provides a successful lesson for the timely transition from the national-democratic revolution to the socialist revolution under the leadership of the proletariat. . . . The new experience gained in the people's revolutionary struggles in various countries since World War II has provided continuous evidence that Mao Tse-tung's thought is a common asset of the revolutionary people of the whole world. This is the great international significance of the thought of Mao Tse-tung. . . .

THE CHINESE REVOLUTION IS PART
OF THE WORLD REVOLUTION

The historical characteristic of the Chinese revolution lies in its division into the two stages, democracy and socialism, the first being no longer democracy in general, but democracy of the Chinese type, a new and special type, namely, New Democracy. . . .

. . . It follows from the colonial, semi-colonial and semi-feudal character of present-day Chinese society that the Chinese revolution must be divided into two stages. The first step is to change the colonial, semi-colonial and semi-feudal form of society into an independent, democratic society. The second is to carry the revolution forward and build a socialist society. . . .

A change . . . occurred in China's bourgeois-democratic revolution after the outbreak of the first imperialist world war in 1914 and the founding of a socialist state on one-sixth of the globe as a result of the Russian October Revolution of 1917.

Before these events, the Chinese bourgeois-democratic revolution came within the old category of the bourgeois-democratic world revolution, of which it was a part.

Since these events, the Chinese bourgeois-democratic revolution has changed, it has come within the new category of bourgeois-democratic revolutions and, as far as the alignment of revolutionary forces is concerned, forms part of the proletarian-socialist world revolution.

Why? Because the first imperialist world war and the first victorious socialist revolution, the October Revolution, have changed the whole course of world history and ushered in a new era.

It is an era in which the world capitalist front has collapsed in one part of the globe (one-sixth of the world) and has fully revealed its decadence everywhere else, in which the remaining capitalist parts cannot survive without relying more than ever on the colonies and semi-colonies, in which a socialist state has been established and has proclaimed its readiness to give active support to the liberation movement of all colonies and semi-colonies, and in which the proletariat of the capitalist countries is steadily freeing itself from the social-imperialist influence of the social-democratic parties and has proclaimed its support for the liberation movement in the colonies and semi-colonies. In this era, any revolution in a colony or semi-colony that is directed against imperialism, i.e., against the international bourgeoisie or international capitalism, no longer comes within the old category of the bourgeois-democratic world revolution, but within the new category. It is no longer part of the old bourgeois, or capitalist, world revolution, but is part of the new world revolution, the proletarian-socialist world revolution. Such revolutionary colonies and semi-colonies can no longer be regarded as allies of the counter-revolutionary front of world capitalism; they have become allies of the revolutionary front of world socialism.

Although such a revolution in a colonial and semi-colonial country is still fundamentally bourgeois-democratic in its social character during its first stage or first step, and although its objective mission is to clear the path for the development of capitalism, it is no longer a revolution of the old type led by the bourgeoisie with the aim of establishing a capitalist society and a state under bourgeois dictatorship. It belongs to the new type of revolution led by the proletariat with the aim, in the first stage, of establishing a new-democratic society and a state under the joint dictatorship of all the revolutionary classes. Thus this revolution actually serves the purpose of clearing a still wider path for the development of socialism. In the course of its progress, there may be a number of further sub-stages, because of changes on the enemy's side and within the ranks of our allies, but the fundamental character of the revolution remains unchanged.

Such a revolution attacks imperialism at its very roots, and is therefore not tolerated but opposed by imperialism. However, it is favoured by socialism and supported by the land of socialism and the socialist international proletariat.

Therefore, such a revolution inevitably becomes part of the proletarian-socialist world revolution.

The correct thesis that "the Chinese revolution is part of the world revolution" was put forward as early as 1924-27 during the period of China's First Great Revolution. It was put forward by the Chinese Communists and endorsed by all those taking part in the anti-imperialist and anti-feudal struggle of the time. However, the significance of this thesis was not fully expounded in those days, and consequently it was only vaguely understood.

The "world revolution" no longer refers to the old world revolution, for the old bourgeois world revolution has long been a thing of the past; it refers to the new world revolution, the socialist world revolution. Similarly, to form "part of" means to form part not of the old bourgeois but of the new socialist revolution. This is a tremendous change unparalled in the history of China and of the world . . .

From this it can be seen that there are two kinds of world revolution, the first belonging to the bourgois or capitalist category. The era of this kind of world revolution is long past, having come to an end as far back as 1914 when the first imperialist world war broke out, and more particularly in 1917 when the October Revolution took place. The second kind, namely, the proletarian-socialist world revolution, thereupon began. This revolution has the proletariat of the capitalist countries as its main force and the oppressed peoples of the colonies and semi-colonies as its allies. No matter what classes, parties or individuals in an oppressed nation join the revolution, and no matter whether they themselves are conscious of the point or understand it, so long as they oppose imperialism, their revolution becomes part of the proletarian-socialist world revolution and they become its allies . . .

The first step or stage in our revolution is definitely not, and cannot be, the establishment of a capitalist society under the dictatorship of the Chinese bourgeoisie, but will result in the establishment of a new-democratic society under the joint dictatorship of all the revolutionary classes of China headed by the Chinese proletariat. The revolution will then be carried forward to the second stage, in which a socialist society will be established in China. . . .

6. Liberation From Colonialism (National Democratic Revolution) on the Chinese Model Means People's Liberation Wars Waged in the Countryside by Peasant Guerrilla Armies Under the Leaderships of the Communists

According to Maoist interpretation, the form taken by the national democratic (or new democratic) revolution is primarily that of peasant violence led by the Communist Party. The peasants are the basic force of the new democratic revolutions against colonialism and neocolonialism; the countryside is the stage. This reasoning can be applied to the world as a whole. The advanced industrial countries of North America and Western Europe, the Maoist view holds, are the cities of the world which are to be surrounded by the world's countryside (the underdeveloped countries of Asia, Africa, and Latin America) in arms [Editors' note].

1. THE IMPORTANCE OF VIOLENCE

War is the highest form of struggle for resolving contradictions when they have developed to a certain stage, between classes, nations, states, or political groups, and it has existed ever since the emergence of private property and of classes . . . War, this monster of mutual slaughter among mankind, will finally be eliminated through the progress of human society, and in no distant future too. But there is only one way of eliminating it and that is to oppose war with war . . . Revolutions and revolutionary wars are inevitable in class society and without them, it is impossible to accomplish any leap in social development and to overthrow the reactionary ruling classes and therefore impossible for the people to win political power.

* * *

We believe in the absolute correctness of Lenin's thinking: War is an inevitable outcome of systems of exploitation and the source of modern wars is the imperialist system. Until the imperialist system and the exploiting classes come to an end, wars of one kind or another will always occur . . . Marxist-Leninists absolutely must not sink into the mire of bourgeois pacifism . . . It would be in the best interests of the people if the pro-

The first paragraph is from Mao Tse-tung, "Problems of Strategy in China's Revolutionary War" (December 1936), and from "On Contradiction" (August 1937), *Selected Works* (Peking, Foreign Languages Press, 1964), Vol. I, pp. 180, 182, 344. The second paragraph is from "Long Live Leninism!" *Hung Chi*, No. 8 (1960).

letariat could attain power and carry out the transition to socialism by peaceful means. It would be wrong not to make use of such a possibility when it occurs. Whenever an opportunity for 'peaceful development of the revolution' presents itself, Communists must seize it, as Lenin did, so as to realize the ultimate aim of a socialist revolution. However, this sort of opportunity is always, in Lenin's words, 'an extraordinarily rare opportunity in the history of revolutions' . . . But even then, the peaceful development of the revolution should never be regarded as the only possibility and it is therefore necessary to be prepared at the same time for the other possibility, i.e., non-peaceful development of the revolution . . . The question is not whether the proletariat is willing to carry out peaceful transformation; it is rather whether the bourgeoisie will accept such a peaceful transformation. This is the only possible way in which followers of Lenin can approach this question. . . .

* * *

VIOLENT REVOLUTION IS A UNIVERSAL LAW OF PROLETARIAN REVOLUTION[1]

The entire history of the working-class movement tells us that the acknowledgment or non-acknowledgment of violent revolution as a universal law of proletarian revolution, of the necessity of smashing the old state machine, and of the necessity of replacing the dictatorship of the bourgeoisie by the dictatorship of the proletariat has always been the watershed between Marxism and all brands of opportunism and revisionism, between proletarian revolutionaries and all renegades from the proletariat.

According to the basic teachings of Marxism-Leninism, the key question in every revolution is that of state power. And the key question in the proletarian revolution is that of the seizure of state power and the smashing of the bourgeois state machine by violence, the establishment of the dictatorship of the proletariat and the replacement of the bourgeois state by the proletarian state.

Marxism has always proclaimed the inevitability of violent revolution. It points out that violent revolution is the midwife to socialist society, the only road to the replacement of the dictatorship of the bourgeoisie by the dictatorship of the proletariat, and a universal law of proletarian revolution.

[1] The section titled "Violent Revolution is a Universal Law of Proletarian Revolution" is from "The Proletarian Revolution and Khrushchov's Revisionism," Eighth Comment on the Open Letter of the Central Committee of the CPSU by the Editorial Departments of *Jen-min Jih-pao and Hung Chi* (March 31, 1964), in *The Polemic* . . . , *op. cit.,* pp. 366-369. The section headed "Rely on the Peasants and Establish Rural Base Areas" is from Lin Piao, *loc. cit.,* pp. 14-16, 24-27.

Marxism teaches us that the state itself is a form of violence. The main components of the state machine are the army and the police. History shows that all ruling classes depend upon violence to maintain their rule.

The proletariat would, of course, prefer to gain power by peaceful means. But abundant historical evidence indicates that the reactionary classes never give up power voluntarily and that they are always the first to use violence to repress the revolutionary mass movement and to provoke civil war, thus placing armed struggle on the agenda.

Lenin has spoken of "civil war, without which not a single great revolution in history has yet been able to get along, and without which not a single serious Marxist has conceived of the transition from capitalism to socialism."

The great revolutions in history referred to by Lenin include the bourgeois revolution. The bourgeois revolution is one in which one exploiting class overthrows another, and yet it cannot be made without a civil war. Still more is this the case with the proletarian revolution, which is a revolution to abolish all exploiting classes and systems.

Regarding the fact that violent revolution is a universal law of proletarian revolution, Lenin repeatedly pointed out that "between capitalism and socialism there lies a long period of 'birth pains'—that violence is always the midwife of the old society," that the bourgeois state *"cannot* be superseded by the proletarian state (the dictatorship of the proletariat) through the process of 'withering away,' but, as a general rule, only through a violent revolution," and that "the necessity of systematically imbuing the masses with *this* and precisely this view of violent revolution lies at the root of *all* the teachings of Marx and Engels."

Stalin, too, said that a violent revolution of the proletariat, the dictatorship of the proletariat, is "an inevitable and indispensable condition for the advance towards socialism" in all countries ruled by capital.

Can a radical transformation of the bourgeois order be achieved without violent revolution, without the dictatorship of the proletariat? Stalin answered:

Obviously not. To think that such a revolution can be carried out peacefully, within the framework of bourgeois democracy, which is adapted to the rule of the bourgeoisie, means that one has either gone out of one's mind and lost normal human understanding, or has grossly and openly repudiated the proletarian revolution.

Basing himself on the Marxist-Leninist theory of violent revolution and the new experience of the proletarian revolution and the people's democratic revolution led by the proletariat [i.e., the national democratic or new democratic revolution], Comrade Mao Tse-tung advanced the celebrated dictum that "political power grows out of the barrel of a gun." Comrade Mao Tse-tung said:

. . . revolutions and revolutionary wars are inevitable in class society and that without them, it is impossible to accomplish any leap in social development and to overthrow the reactionary ruling classes and therefore impossible for the people to win political power.

He stated:

The seizure of power by armed force, the settlement of the issue by war, is the central task and the highest form of revolution. This Marxist-Leninist principle of revolution holds good universally, for China and for all other countries.

He stated further:

Experience in the class struggle in the era of imperialism teaches us that it is only by the power of the gun that the working class and the labouring masses can defeat the armed bourgeoisie and landlords; in this sense we may say that only with guns can the whole world be transformed.

To sum up, violent revolution is a universal law of proletarian revolution. This is a fundamental tenet of Marxism-Leninism. . . .

* * *

A PEASANT-BASED WAR LED BY THE COMMUNISTS RELY ON THE PEASANTS AND ESTABLISH RURAL BASE AREAS

The peasantry constituted more than 80 per cent of the entire population of semi-colonial and semi-feudal China. They were subjected to three-fold oppression and exploitation by imperialism, feudalism and bureaucrat-capitalism, and they were eager for resistance against Japan and for revolution. It was essential to rely mainly on the peasants if the people's war was to be won.

But at the outset not all comrades in our Party saw this point. The history of our Party shows that in the period of the First Revolutionary Civil War, one of the major errors of the Right opportunists, represented by Chen Tu-hsiu, was their failure to recognize the importance of the peasant question and their opposition to arousing and arming the peasants. In the period of the Second Revolutionary Civil War, one of the major errors of the "Left" opportunists, represented by Wang Ming, was likewise their failure to recognize the importance of the peasant question. They did not realize that it was essential to undertake long-term and painstaking work among the peasants and establish revolutionary base areas in the countryside; they were under the illusion that they could rapidly seize the big cities and quickly win nation-wide victory in the revolution. The errors of both the Right and the "Left" opportunists brought serious setbacks and defeats to the Chinese revolution.

As far back as the period of the First Revolutionary Civil War, Comrade Mao Tse-tung had pointed out that the peasant question occupied an extremely important position in the Chinese revolution, that the bourgeois-democratic revolution against imperialism and feudalism was in essence a peasant revolution and that the basic task of the Chinese proletariat in the bourgeois-democratic revolution was to give leadership to the peasants' struggle.

In the period of the War of Resistance Against Japan, Comrade Mao Tse Tung again stressed that the peasants were the most reliable and the most numerous ally of the proletariat and constituted the main force in the War of Resistance. The peasants were the main source of manpower for China's armies. The funds and the supplies needed for a protracted war came chiefly from the peasants. In the anti-Japanese war it was imperative to rely mainly on the peasants and to arouse them to participate in the war on the broadest scale.

The War of Resistance Against Japan was in essence a peasant revolutionary war led by our Party. By arousing and organizing the peasant masses and integrating them with the proletariat, our Party created a powerful force capable of defeating the strongest enemy.

To rely on the peasants, build rural base areas and use the countryside to encircle and finally capture the cities—such was the way to victory in the Chinese revolution.

Basing himself on the characteristic of the Chinese revolution, Comrade Mao Tse-tung pointed out the importance of building rural revolutionary base areas.

Since China's key cities have long been occupied by the powerful imperialists and their reactionary Chinese allies, it is imperative for the revolutionary ranks to turn the backward villages into advanced, consolidated base areas, into great military, political, economic and cultural bastions of the revolution from which to fight their vicious enemies who are using the cities for attacks on the rural districts, and in this way gradually to achieve the complete victory of the revolution through protracted fighting; it is imperative for them to do so if they do not wish to compromise with imperialism and its lackeys but are determined to fight on, and if they intend to build up and temper their forces, and avoid decisive battles with a powerful enemy while their own strength is inadequate.

Experience in the period of the Second Revolutionary Civil War showed that, when this strategic concept of Comrade Mao Tse-tung's was applied, there was an immense growth in the revolutionary forces and one Red base area after another was built. Conversely, when it was violated and the nonsense of the "Left" opportunists was applied, the revolutionary forces suffered severe damage, with losses of nearly 100 per cent in the cities and 90 per cent in the rural areas.

During the War of Resistance Against Japan, the Japanese imperialist forces occupied many of China's big cities and the main lines of communication, but owing to the shortage of troops they were unable to occupy the vast countryside, which remained the vulnerable sector of the enemy's rule. Consequently, the possibility of building rural base areas became even greater. Shortly after the beginning of the War of Resistance, when the Japanese forces surged into China's hinterland and the Kuomintang forces crumbled and fled in one defeat after another, the Eighth Route and New Fourth Armies led by our Party followed the wise policy laid down by Comrade Mao Tse-tung and boldly drove into the areas behind the enemy lines in small contingents and established base areas throughout the countryside. During the eight years of the war, we established nineteen anti-Japanese base areas in northern, central and southern China. With the exception of the big cities and the main lines of communication, the vast territory in the enemy's rear was in the hands of the people.

In the anti-Japanese base areas, we carried out democratic reforms, improved the livelihood of the people, and mobilized and organized the peasant masses. Organs of anti-Japanese democratic political power were established on an extensive scale and the masses of the people enjoyed the democratic right to run their own affairs; at the same time we carried out the policies of "a reasonable burden" and "the reduction of rent and interest," which weakened the feudal system of exploitation and improved the people's livelihood. As a result the enthusiasm of the peasant masses was deeply aroused, while the various anti-Japanese strata were given due consideration and were thus united. In formulating our policies for the base areas, we also took care that these policies should facilitate our work in the enemy-occupied areas.

In the enemy-occupied cities and villages, we combined legal with illegal struggle, united the basic masses and all patriots, and divided and disintegrated the political power of the enemy and his puppets so as to prepare ourselves to attack the enemy from within in co-ordination with operations from without when conditions were ripe.

The base areas established by our Party became the centre of gravity in the Chinese people's struggle to resist Japan and save the country. Relying on these bases, our Party expanded and strengthened the people's revolutionary forces, persevered in the protracted war and eventually won the War of Resistance Against Japan. . . .

Taking the entire course of the Chinese revolution into account, our revolutionary base areas went through even more ups and downs, and they weathered a great many tests before the small, separate base areas, expanding in a series of waves, gradually developed into extensive and contiguous base areas.

At the same time, the work of building the revolutionary base areas was a grand rehearsal in preparation for nation-wide victory. In these base areas, we built the Party, ran the organs of state power, built the people's armed forces and set up mass organizations; we engaged in industry and agriculture and operated cultural, educational and all other undertakings necessary for the independent existence of a separate region. Our base areas were in fact a state in miniature. And with the steady expansion of our work in the base areas, our Party established a powerful people's army, trained cadres for various kinds of work, accumulated experience in many fields and built up both the material and the moral strength that provided favourable conditions for nation-wide victory.

The revolutionary base areas established in the War of Resistance later became the spring-boards for the People's War of Liberation, in which the Chinese people defeated the Kuomintang reactionaries. In the War of Liberation we continued the policy of first encircling the cities from the countryside and then capturing the cities, and thus won nation-wide victory. . . .

It must be emphasized that Comrade Mao Tse-tung's theory of the establishment of rural revolutionary base areas and the encirclement of the cities from the countryside is of outstanding and universal practical importance for the present revolutionary struggles of all the oppressed nations and peoples, and particularly for the revolutionary struggles of the oppressed nations and peoples in Asia, Africa and Latin America against imperialism and its lackeys.

Many countries and peoples in Asia, Africa and Latin America are now being subjected to aggression and enslavement on a serious scale by the imperialists headed by the United States and their lackeys. The basic political and economic conditions in many of these countries have many similarities to those that prevailed in old China. As in China, the peasant question is extremely important in these regions. The peasants constitute the main force of the national-democratic revolution against the imperialists and their lackeys. In committing aggression against these countries, the imperialists usually begin by seizing the big cities and the main lines of communication, but they are unable to bring the vast countryside completely under their control. The countryside, and the countryside alone, can provide the broad areas in which the revolutionaries can manoeuvre freely. The countryside, and the countryside alone, can provide the revolutionary bases from which the revolutionaries can go forward to final victory. Precisely for this reason, Comrade Mao Tse-tung's theory of establishing revolutionary base areas in the rural districts and encircling the cities from the countryside is attracting more and more attention among the people in these regions.

Taking the entire globe, if North America and Western Europe can be called "the cities of the world," then Asia, Africa and Latin America constitute "the rural areas of the world." Since World War II, the proletarian revolutionary movement has for various reasons been temporarily held back in the North American and West European capitalist countries, while the people's revolutionary movement in Asia, Africa and Latin America has been growing vigorously. In a sense, the contemporary world revolution also presents a picture of the encirclement of cities by the rural areas. In the final analysis, the whole cause of world revolution hinges on the revolutionary struggles of the Asian, African and Latin American peoples who make up the overwhelming majority of the world's population. The socialist countries should regard it as their internationalist duty to support the people's revolutionary struggles in Asia, Africa and Latin America. . . .

At present, the main battlefield of the fierce struggle between the people of the world on the one side and U.S. imperialism and its lackeys on the other is the vast area of Asia, Africa and Latin America. In the world as a whole, this is the area where the people suffer worst from imperialist oppression and where imperialist rule is most vulnerable. Since World War II, revolutionary storms have been rising in this area, and today they have become the most important force directly pounding U. S. imperialism. The contradiction between the revolutionary peoples of Asia, Africa and Latin America and the imperialists headed by the United States is the principal contradiction in the contemporary world. The development of this contradiction is promoting the struggle of the people of the whole world against U.S. imperialism and its lackeys.

Since World War II, people's war has increasingly demonstrated its power in Asia, Africa and Latin America. The peoples of China, Korea, Viet Nam, Laos, Cuba, Indonesia, Algeria and other countries have waged people's wars against the imperialists and their lackeys and won great victories. The classes leading these people's wars may vary, and so may the breadth and depth of mass mobilization and the extent of victory, but the victories in these people's wars have very much weakened and pinned down the forces of imperialism, upset the U. S. imperialist plan to launch a world war, and become mighty factors defending world peace.

Today, the conditions are more favourable than ever before for the waging of people's wars by the revolutionary peoples of Asia, Africa and Latin America against U.S. imperialism and its lackeys. . . .

Everything is divisible. And so is this colossus of U.S. imperialism. It can be split up and defeated. The peoples of Asia, Africa, Latin America and other regions can destroy it piece by piece, some striking at its head and others at its feet. That is why the greatest fear of U.S. imperialism is that people's wars will be launched in different parts of the world, and particularly in Asia, Africa and Latin America, and why it regards people's war as a mortal danger.

U.S. imperialism relies solely on its nuclear weapons to intimidate people. But these weapons cannot save U.S. imperialism from its doom. Nuclear weapons cannot be used lightly. U.S. imperialism has been condemned by the people of the whole world for its towering crime of dropping two atom bombs on Japan. If it uses nuclear weapons again, it will become isolated in the extreme. Moreover, the U.S. monopoly of nuclear weapons has long been broken; U.S. imperialism has these weapons, but others have them too. If it threatens other countries with nuclear weapons, U.S. imperialism will expose its own country to the same threat. For this reason, it will meet with strong opposition not only from the people elsewhere but also inevitably from the people in its own country. Even if U.S. imperialism brazenly uses nuclear weapons, it cannot conquer the people, who are indomitable.

History has proved and will go on proving that people's war is the most effective weapon against U.S. imperialism and its lackeys. All revolutionary people will learn to wage people's war against U.S. imperialism and its lackeys. They will take up arms, learn to fight battles and become skilled in waging people's war, though they have not done so before. U.S. imperialism like a mad bull dashing from place to place, will finally be burned to ashes in the blazing fires of the people's wars it has provoked by its own actions. . . .

7. The Economic Program of the National Democratic (*New Democratic*) Revolution

After the seizure of power by the "United Front" of Communists and others, Mao Tse-tung urges, economic reforms must be instituted at once. These should be such as to lay the groundwork for the revolution's next social-ist stage. Nationalization of main industries and distribution of land to the peas-ants are the key [Editors' note].

THE ECONOMY OF NEW DEMOCRACY

If such a republic is to be established in China it must be new-dem-ocratic not only in its politics but also in its economy.

It will own the big banks and the big industrial and commercial en-terprises.

Enterprises, such as banks, railways and airlines . . . which are either monop-olistic in character or too big for private management, shall be operated and administered by the state, so that private capital cannot dominate the livelihood of the people: this is the main principle of the regulation of capital.

. . . In the new-democratic republic under the leadership of the pro-letariat, the state enterprises will be of a socialist character and will con-stitute the leading force in the whole national economy, but the republic will neither confiscate capitalist private property in general nor forbid the development of such capitalist production as does not "dominate the liveli-hood of the people," for China's economy is still very backward.

The republic will take certain necessary steps to confiscate the land of the landlords and distribute it to those peasants having little or no land . . . , abolish feudal relations in the rural areas, and turn the land over to the private ownership of the peasants. A rich peasant economy will be al-lowed in the rural areas. Such is the policy of "equalization of landowner-ship." "Land to the tiller" is the correct slogan for this policy. In general, socialist agriculture will not be established at this stage, though various types of co-operative enterprises developed on the basis of "land to the tiller" will contain elements of socialism.

China's economy must develop along the path of the "regulation of capital" and the "equalization of landownership," and must never be "privately owned by the few"; we must never permit the few capitalists and

From Mao Tse-tung "On New Democracy," *op. cit.*, pp. 353-354.

landlords to "dominate the livelihood of the people"; we must never establish a capitalist society of the European-American type or allow the old semi-feudal society to survive. Whoever dares to go counter to this line of advance will certainly not succeed but will run into a brick wall. . . .

Such is the economy of New Democracy.

And the politics of New Democracy are the concentrated expression of the economy of New Democracy.

8. The Peasant Question and Agricultural Development Are Basic to Socialist Construction Once the National Democratic Revolution Is Completed

At the end of 1960 China's communists launched the slogan "agriculture as the foundation and industry as the basic link of socialist development." Prior to that time the Chinese, following the Soviets, had emphasized heavy industry as the foundation of socialist construction. However, since 1960, the "agriculture as foundation" theory has been offered as the "correct" model for all underdeveloped countries which have completed the national democratic revolution and are beginning "socialist construction" [Editors' note].

ON THE QUESTION OF THE PEASANTS' PLACE IN SOCIALIST REVOLUTION AND CONSTRUCTION

Comrade Mao Tse-tung has always attached the greatest importance to the peasant question. As early as the beginning of the democratic revolution led by our Party, he pointed out more than once that the peasant question was the basic question of the Chinese revolution and that the strength of the peasantry made up the main force of the Chinese revolution; he went on to note that the Chinese democratic revolution was in essence a peasant revolution and that the Chinese revolutionary war was essentially a peasant war. However, the Right opportunists within the Party turned a blind eye to the broad masses of the peasants and regarded the democratic revolution as mainly a matter of the bourgeoisie. In another way the "Left" opportunists neglected the special role of the peasants in the Chinese revolution, they stressed work in the cities as the centre of gravity and made the middle-of-the-road forces the main direction of attack, thus pushing the peasants into the arms of the bourgeoisie.

In the course of the Chinese democratic revolution Comrade Mao Tse-tung thoroughly refuted these erroneous views and defined a Marxist-Leninist line for the Chinese revolution; i.e., that under the leadership of the proletariat we should give full play to the revolutionary enthusiasm of the peasants, shift the centre of gravity of the Party's work to the countryside, give a free hand to the development of peasant guerrilla warfare, build revolutionary base areas in the countryside, encircle the cities from the countryside, lead the revolution to victory step by step, and finally seize

From Tao Chu "A Guide for 500 Million Peasants Advancing Along the Socialist Road" *Hung Chi,* No. 8 (1965) in *Peking Review,* August 20, 1965, pp. 8-9.

state power throughout the country. By carrying out the correct line of Comrade Mao Tse-tung, the Chinese Communist Party finally won the great victory of the people's revolution in China with its more than 600 million people. This is a great achievement unprecedented in the revolutionary movement of the world's proletariat.

In the period of socialism, Comrade Mao Tse-tung has continued to view the peasant question as an extremely important one. He said: "We have a farm population of over five hundred million, so the situation of our peasants has a very important bearing on the development of our economy and the consolidation of our state power." The scale of our socialist revolution and socialist construction and the speed of their development depend on the policy we adopt to solve the peasant question and the agricultural question.

Comrade Mao Tse-tung correctly solved the relationship between the socialist transformation of agriculture and the socialist transformation of capitalist industry and commerce in the cities. He views the socialist transformation of agriculture as the key link in the whole chain of the socialist revolution because, with the socialist transformation of agriculture, the ties between the bourgeoisie and the peasants are cut, the source generating capitalism on a mass scale is eliminated, and urban capitalist influences are thus isolated. In our country where small-peasant economy held the upper hand, this thesis is particularly important.

Comrade Mao Tse-tung negated the view that cooperation should develop slowly and stressed that the advance of socialist transformation in agriculture should be quickened. In this way, we would not only be able to solve the question of agriculture more quickly but greatly promote the socialist transformation of urban individual handicrafts and capitalist industry and commerce, thereby developing the socialist revolution more smoothly, more extensively and more thoroughly. Subsequent facts have fully proved the correctness of this policy. It was under the impact of the movement for agricultural co-operation that the upsurge in the transformation of individual handicrafts and capitalist industry and commerce took place in 1956.

One of the most fundamental questions in socialist construction is how to handle the relationships between the workers and peasants and between industry and agriculture. Some people held that in building socialism it was sufficient to pay attention only to the development of industry. Comrade Mao Tse-tung refuted this harmful viewpoint. He said: "We must on no account look at industry and agriculture, socialist industrialization and the socialist transformation of agriculture as two things which can be separated and isolated from each other, nor must we on any account emphasize the one and underrate the other."

Industry is closely interrelated with agriculture. In socialist construction, it is, of course, extremely important to develop industry, especially heavy industry. But that development must take agriculture as the foundation and the problem of food, clothing and other consumer goods must be solved first. Food grains and other foodstuffs come from agriculture; light industry which provides people with clothings and other consumer goods gets most of its raw materials from agriculture too. Moreover, the funds used in the building of heavy industry are mainly accumulated from agriculture and light industry; the labour power necessary for the development of industry has to be furnished by the countryside; and only by taking the countryside as its main market, can industry have broad prospects of development. Agriculture is the foundation of the national economy. Therefore, only by combining the industrialization of the country with the socialist transformation of agriculture, and the rapid development of industry with the rapid development of agriculture can there be a firm and sure guarantee for the development of our national economy as a whole.

AGRICULTURE, HEAVY AND LIGHT INDUSTRIES

The development of our industry according to the policy of taking agriculture as the foundation of the national economy involves two requirements. One is that the size of the labour force needed for industrial development must be basically proportioned to the amount of marketable grains and other means of subsistence that can be provided by agriculture. The other is that in serving all branches of the national economy, industry must concentrate mainly on serving agriculture. All industry, whether light or heavy, must make the countryside its principal market. Heavy industry in particular must regard supporting the technical reform of agriculture as its foremost task, and must see to it that socialist industrialization and the modernization of agriculture are closely integrated and help each other forward. Practical experience has taught us that our industrialization can advance in the right direction and enjoy unlimited prospects only when it advances along the line of taking agriculture as the foundation of the national economy and adapts itself to the two above-mentioned requirements.

Our stress on developing industry according to the policy of taking agriculture as the foundation of the national economy and the carrying out of socialist economic construction centering on heavy industry is not contradictory; the two are a unity. Taking agriculture as the foundation of the national economy does not in the least imply the weakening of the growth of heavy industry; it actually creates even better conditions for heavy industrial development.

The carrying out of socialist industrialization directly entails the gradual building of a powerful industry, the leading branch of the national economy, and, first and foremost, the building of heavy industry which is the principal productive branch of the means of production. This is because only when heavy industry is developed and priority is given to growth of the means of production can social expanded reproduction be realized, can advanced technical equipment be provided for the technical transformation of the entire national economy, including agriculture, and for the strengthening of the national defence. Only under these circumstances can the leading role of industry in the national economy be brought into full play. Unless we make big efforts to build up the machine-building, metallurgical and chemical industries and other heavy industries, we will not be able to obtain the various kinds of machines and the steel products and building materials, electricity and fuel which are needed; we will not be able to equip our agriculture, light industry and transport; our national economy will remain backward for a long time and we will not be able to build up modern national defence. . . .

In industrial construction during the past two five-year plans, we concentrated our main strength on heavy industry. A considerable number of our major construction projects were heavy industrial enterprises. This was absolutely necessary. This is precisely the reason why we succeeded in building the foundations of socialist industrialization in such a relatively short time. It is either a big misunderstanding or a distortion to say that our opposition to one-sided development of heavy industry means neglect of such industry.

Practice has brought it home to us that energetic promotion and not limitation of the development of light industry in accordance with the possibilities of supplies of raw materials and funds as well as the market demand, is not detrimental but beneficial to socialist industrialization.

As is well known, industry shoulders the task of providing not only the means of labour, but also consumer goods. This is a very heavy task for industry in our country with its large population and economic backwardness. Energetic development of light industry will keep the market brisk, maintain commodity prices stable, satisfy appropriately the needs of the people's livelihood, and link socialist industrialization more closely with the vital interests of the people. This conforms completely with the aims of socialist production.

Moreover, light industry, as an important link, is closely connected with agriculture and heavy industry. The growth of light industry means the production of more and more light industrial goods to exchange for products of agriculture and farm side-occupations, thus promoting agricultural production and supporting industrial construction. Light industry is also an important source of accumulating funds for construction, because its factories are easier to build, need smaller investments, give quicker results and earn larger profits. At the same time, the growth of light industry also demands huge amounts of raw materials, machinery and equipment from the various branches of heavy industry, and this, in turn, promotes the development of heavy industry.

Our experience of industrialization has proved that there is no sound basis to views separating light industry from heavy industry and even opposing one to the other and regarding the energetic and appropriate development of light industry as being detrimental, rather than helpful, to the growth of heavy industry.

The question of our country's road to industrialization also involves the simultaneous development of national and local industries and of large enterprises as well as small and medium-sized enterprises under the conditions of centralized leadership, overall planning and division of labour and co-operation. . . .

9. The People's Communes Are China's Contribution to the Question of Transition From Collective Ownership to Ownership by the Whole People— An Important Step in the Direction of Full Communism

Although the people's communes collapsed for all practical purposes in 1959-1960 (i.e., operationally as production and accounting units), theoretically they are still being offered as a particularly felicitous organizational form of transition from a "lower" (collective) to a "higher" (people's) socialist ownership. The ideological framework of the communes has not been abandoned [Editors' note].

In 1958 a new social organization appeared, fresh as the morning sun, above the broad horizon of East Asia. This was the large-scale people's commune in the rural areas of our country which combines industry, agriculture, trade, education and military affairs and in which government administration and commune management are integrated. Since their first appearance the people's communes with their immense vitality have attracted widespread attention.

The movement to set up people's communes has grown very rapidly. Within a few months starting in the summer of 1958, all of the more than 740,000 agricultural producers' co-operatives in the country, in response to the enthusiastic demand of the mass of peasants, reorganized themselves into over 26,000 people's communes. Over 120 million households, or more than 99 per cent of all China's peasant households of various nationalities, have joined the people's communes. . . .

Although the rural people's communes were established only a short while ago, the mass of peasants are already conscious of the obvious benefits they have brought them. Labour power and the means of production can, on a larger scale than before, be managed and deployed in a unified way to ensure that they are used still more rationally and effectively, and consequently the development of production will be further facilitated. Under the unified leadership of the commune, industry, agriculture (including farming, forestry, animal husbandry, side-occupations and fish-

From "Resolution on Some Questions Concerning the People's Communes" (Adopted by the Eighth Central Committee of the Communist Party of China at its Sixth Plenary session on December 10, 1958) (Peking, Foreign Languages Press, 1958), pp. 12, 13-14, 15, 16, 17-18, 20-21, 24-26.

eries), trade, education and military affairs have been closely co-ordinated and developed rapidly.

In particular, thousands and tens of thousands of small factories have mushroomed in the rural areas. To meet the pressing demands of the masses, the communes have set up large numbers of community dining-rooms, nurseries, kindergartens, "homes of respect for the aged" and other institutions for collective welfare, which have, in particular, completely emancipated women from thousands of years of kitchen drudgery and brought broad smiles to their faces. As the result of the bumper crops[1] many communes have instituted a system of distribution that combines the wage system with the free supply system; the mass of peasants, both men and women, have begun to receive their wages and those families which in the past constantly worried about their daily meals and about their firewood, rice, oil, salt, soya sauce, vinegar and vegetables are now able to "eat without paying." In other words they have the most important and most reliable kind of social insurance. For the peasants, all this is epoch-making news. The living standards of the peasants have been improved and they know from practical experience and the prospects of the development of the communes that they will live much better in the future.

The development of the system of rural people's communes has an even more profound and far-reaching significance. It has shown the people of our country the way to the gradual industrialization of the rural areas, the way to the gradual transition from collective ownership to ownership by the whole people in agriculture, the way to the gradual transition from the socialist principle of "to each according to his work" to the communist principle of "to each according to his needs," the way gradually to lessen and finally to eliminate the differences between town and country, between worker and peasant and between mental and manual labour, and the way gradually to lessen and finally to eliminate the internal function of the state. . . .

People's communes have now become the general rule in all rural areas inhabited by our people of various nationalities (except in Tibet and in certain other areas). Some experiments have also begun in the cities. In the future urban people's communes, in a form suited to the specific features of cities, will also become instruments for the transformation of old cities and the construction of new socialist cities; they will become the unified organizers of production, exchange and distribution and of the livelihood and well-being of the people; they will become social organizations which combine industry, agriculture, trade, education and military affairs, organizations in which government administration and commune management are integrated.[2] . . .

[1] Crop failures were reported from China in 1959, 1960, and 1961 [Editors' note].

[2] The project was dropped in 1960 but revived in the midst of the Cultural Revolution in 1966 [Editors' note].

The people's commune is the basic unit of the socialist social structure of our country, combining industry, agriculture, trade, education and military affairs; at the same time it is the basic organization of the socialist state power. Marxist-Leninist theory and the initial experience of the people's communes in our country enable us to foresee now that the people's communes will quicken the tempo of our socialist construction and constitute the best form for realizing in our country the following two transitions.

Firstly, the transition from collective ownership to ownership by the whole people in the countryside; and,

Secondly, the transition from socialist to communist society. It can also be foreseen that in the future communist society, the people's commune will remain the basic unit of our social structure.

From now on, the task . . . is: through such a form of social organization as the people's commune . . . to develop the social productive forces at high speed, to advance the industrialization of the country, the industrialization of the communes, and the mechanization and electrification of agriculture; and to effect the gradual transition from socialist collective ownership to socialist ownership by the whole people, thus fully realizing ownership by the whole people in the socialist economy of our country and gradually building our country into a great socialist land with a highly developed modern industry, agriculture, science and culture. During this process, the elements of communism are bound to increase gradually and these will lay the foundation of material and spiritual conditions for the transition from socialism to communism.

This is a gigantic and extremely complex task. In the light of experience already gained, as the concrete conditions now stand in our country, it is possible that socialist ownership by the whole people may be fully realized at a somewhat earlier date but this will not be very soon. Though the pace at which we are advancing is fairly rapid, it will still take a fairly long time to realize, on a large scale, the industrialization of our country, the industrialization of the communes, the mechanization and electrification of agriculture and the building up of a socialist country with a highly developed modern industry, agriculture, science and culture. This whole process will take fifteen, twenty or more years to complete, counting from now.

The imperialists and those who parrot them[3] say that this is too short a time for us to build a highly developed modern industry, agriculture and science and culture, and that we won't be able to achieve our aim. We've got used to such tunes; we needn't pay any attention to them; the facts are bound to batter these people down time and time again. But there will be other people who will say that this time is too long. They are good-hearted people in our own ranks, but they are over-eager. . . .

To gradually promote the transition from collective ownership to ownership by the whole people, every county should set up its federation of

[3] This is a reference to the Soviets [Editors' note].

communes.[4] In coming years, on the basis of the energetic development of production and the raising of the people's political understanding, such federations should take suitable steps gradually to increase the proportion of their means of production that is owned by the whole people and the proportion of their products that is subject to unified distribution by the state, and, when conditions mature, should change collective ownership into ownership by the whole people. If timely steps are not taken to promote and complete this change and if the existing collective ownership is kept intact indefinitely with the result that commune members confine their attention to the relatively narrow scope of the interests of their collective, the continuous development of social productive forces and the continuous raising of the people's political understanding will be impeded. This is not appropriate. However, it must be pointed out that collective ownership still plays a positive role today in developing production in the rural people's communes. How soon the transition from collective ownership to ownership by the whole people will be effected will be determined by the objective factors —the level of development of production and the level of the people's political understanding—and not by mere wishful thinking that it can be done at any time we want it. Thus this transition will be realized, by stages and by groups, on a national scale only after a considerable time. Those who, because they fail to understand this, confuse the establishment of people's communes with the realization of ownership by the whole people, making impetuous attempts to abolish collective ownership in the countryside prematurely, and trying hastily to change over to ownership by the whole people, will not be doing the right thing and therefore cannot succeed.

Furthermore, the change from socialist collective ownership to socialist ownership by the whole people is not the same thing as the going-over from socialism to communism. Still less is the change from agricultural producers' co-operatives to people's communes the same thing as the change from socialism to communism. The change from socialism to communism will require much more time than the change from socialist collective ownership to socialist ownership by the whole people. . . .

On the question of transition from socialism to communism, we must not mark time at the socialist stage, nor should we drop into the Utopian dream of skipping the socialist stage and jumping over to the communist stage. We are advocates of the Marxist-Leninist theory of uninterrupted revolution; we hold that no "Great Wall" exists or can be allowed to exist between the democratic revolution and the socialist revolution and between socialism and communism. We are at the same time advocates of the Marxist-Leninist theory of the development of revolution by stages; we hold that different stages of development reflect qualitative changes and that these stages, different in quality, should not be confused. The Political

[4] The project was dropped after the collapse of the Great Leap in 1960. It is still, however, on the books [Editors' note].

Bureau of the Central Committee has pointed out clearly in its August Resolution on the Establishment of People's Communes in the Rural Areas: in the case of the people's communes, "the transition from collective ownership to ownership by the whole people is a process, the completion of which may take less time—three or four years—in some places, and longer—five or six years or even more—elsewhere. Even with the completion of this transition, people's communes, like state-owned industry, are still socialist in character, i.e. the principle of 'from each according to his ability and to each according to his work' prevails. Some years after that the social product will become very abundant; the communist consciousness and morality of the entire people will be elevated to a much higher degree; universal education will be achieved and the level raised; the differences between worker and peasant, between town and country, between mental and manual labour—the legacies of the old society that have inevitably been carried over into the socialist period—and the remnants of unequal bourgeois rights which are the reflection of these differences will gradually vanish; and the function of the state will be limited to protecting the country from external aggression; and it will play no role internally. At that time Chinese society will enter the era of communism in which the principle of 'from each according to his ability and to each according to his needs' will be practised. . . ."

10. Self-Reliance Based on Correct Thought Is the Way to National Liberation and Socialist Development

Throughout their history, but especially after their break with the Soviet Union in 1958-1960 the Chinese Communists have stressed the constructive virtues of relying on one's own resources [Editors' note].

We stand for self-reliance. We hope for foreign aid but cannot be dependent on it; we depend on our own efforts on the creative power of the whole army and the entire people. . . .

*   *   *

In the fight for complete liberation the oppressed people rely first of all on their own struggle and then, and only then, on international assistance. The people who have triumphed in their own revolution should help those still struggling for liberation. This is our internationalist duty. . . .

*   *   *

The superiority of the socialist system and the achievements of the socialist countries in construction play an exemplary role and are an inspiration to the oppressed peoples and the oppressed nations.

But this exemplary role and inspiration can never replace the revolutionary struggles of the oppressed peoples and nations. No oppressed people or nation can win liberation except through its own staunch revolutionary struggle. . . .

*   *   *

The liberation of the masses is accomplished by the masses themselves—this is the basic principle of Marxism-Leninism. Revolution or people's war in any country is the business of the masses in that country and

The first paragraph is taken from Mao Tse-tung, "We Must Learn to Do Economic Work" (January 10, 1945), *Selected Works* (Peking, Foreign Languages Press, 1965), Vol. III, p. 241. The second paragraph is from Mao Tse-tung, "Talk with African Friends" (August 8, 1963), in *Quotations from Chairman Mao Tse-tung* (Peking, Foreign Languages Press, 1966), pp. 177-178. The third and fourth paragraphs are from "A Proposal Concerning the General Line of the International Communist Movement," *Peking Review*, June 21, 1963, p. 13. The fifth paragraph is taken from Lin Piao, "Long Live the Victory of People's War!" *Peking Review*, September 3, 1965, pp. 19-20.

should be carried out primarily by their own efforts; there is no other way. During the War of Resistance Against Japan, our Party maintained that China should rely mainly on her own strength while at the same time trying to get as much foreign assistance as possible. We firmly opposed the Kuomintang ruling clique's policy of exclusive reliance on foreign aid. In the eyes of the Kuomintang and Chiang Kai-shek, China's industry and agriculture were no good, her weapons and equipment were no good, nothing in China was any good, so that if she wanted to defeat Japan, she had to depend on other countries, and particularly on the U. S.-British imperialists. This was completely slavish thinking. . . . Difficulties are not invincible monsters. If everyone cooperates and fights them, they will be overcome. . . . The peoples of the world invariably support each other in their struggles against imperialism and its lackeys. Those countries which have won victory are duty bound to support and aid the peoples who have not yet done so. Nevertheless, foreign aid can only play a supplementary role. In order to make a revolution and to fight a people's war and be victorious, it is imperative to adhere to the policy of self-reliance, rely on the strength of the masses of one's own country and prepare to carry on the fight independently even when all material aid from outside is cut off. If one does not operate by one's own efforts, does not independently ponder and solve the problems of the revolution in one's own country and does not rely on the strength of the masses but leans wholly on foreign aid —even this be aid from socialist countries which persist in revolution—no victory can be won, or be consolidated even if it is won.

11. Underdeveloped Countries and Foreign Economic Aid From Capitalist Countries

In the view of China's communists, foreign economic assistance must at all times be screened for political and other attached conditions. Even aid from socialist countries should be carefully scrutinized and never allowed to take the place of domestic revolutionary efforts [Editors' note].

Recently, a cabinet minister of a certain country told me that some newly independent countries could not openly denounce U. S. imperialism at the African-Asian Conference because of their need for U. S. aid to solve the bread question. On the other hand, some other Afro-Asian countries hold that the first and foremost task of the African-Asian Conference is to denounce U. S. imperialism, otherwise there will be no sense in convening the conference. These two tendencies are now engaged in a struggle. China firmly sides with those that stand for condemnation of U. S. imperialism. This position of China's will never change. For without adopting resolutions condemning U. S. imperialism, the African-Asian Conference will disappoint the people of Asia, Africa and Latin America. To hold such a conference would be a waste. As for the bread question, it is my view that if one relies on U. S. aid one will get less and less bread, while by relying on one's own efforts one will get more and more. So far as certain countries are concerned, the more they denounce U. S. imperialism, the more bread they will probably get from it, otherwise they will not get any. Such is the character of U. S. imperialism—bullying the weak-kneed and fearing the strong.

I have told the leaders of some Afro-Asian countries: since many Afro-Asian countries are receiving aid and loans from the United States and other countries, thus incurring ever-increasing burdens, it may be advisable to adopt a resolution at the African-Asian Conference declaring the cancellation of all debts which Afro-Asian countries owe to the United States. If this can be done, the debts owed to China may also be cancelled. They said this was a very good idea and could be considered. . . .

The more foreign aid with conditions attached a country receives, the more difficult will it be for her to stand up. This is like drinking poison to quench one's thirst.

Before liberation, China was wholly controlled by the United States,

From the Press Conference of Vice-Premier and Foreign Minister Chen Yi, *Peking Review*, October 8, 1965, pp. 10-11.

and it was with political, economic and military aid from the United States that Chiang Kai-shek collapsed. And the situation in New China has become still better after she thoroughly embarked on a path of self-reliance upon the stoppage of all aid by Khrushchov. A country's economy will gain vigour in a few years' time, if she makes up her mind to stop relying on foreign aid, carries on construction with her own efforts and resources and turns out the products she needs. So long as this path is followed with determination, all Afro-Asian countries can solve their own economic problems, because they have all got a certain foundation for economic development.

Of course, on the above basis, Afro-Asian countries need to help supply each other's wants and aid each other on the principle of equality and mutual benefit. Such aid is not harmful but helpful. However, it is only of secondary importance. The point of primary importance is to rely on one's own efforts in national construction instead of being dependent on others. . . .

FOOD FOR CONTROL[1]

In his . . . *Neo-Colonialism: The Last Stage of Imperialism,* President Nkrumah [formerly of Ghana] wrote that the U. S. Central Intelligence Agency and the "Peace Corps" were engaged in subversive activities, that U. S. monopoly groups had plundered the Congo and that U. S. missionaries and Hollywood films were instruments of U. S. spiritual aggression. Such neo-colonialist aggression, he said, was more dangerous than old colonialism. . . . Together with the C. I. A., "Peace Corps," American missionaries and Hollywood films, the "Food for Peace" programme is an instrument used in the U. S. policy of aggression, control, intervention, and bullying.

AID FROM SOCIALIST COUNTRIES[2]

The leaders of the CPSU [Communist Party of the Soviet Union] boast of the role played by their economic aid to the newly independent countries. Comrade Khrushchov has said that such aid can enable these countries "to avoid the danger of a new enslavement," and that "it stimulates their progress and contributes to the normal development and even acceleration of

[1] From the *Peking Review,* December 3, 1965, p. 29.
[2] The first two paragraphs are from "Apologists of Neo-Colonialism," Fourth Comment on the Open Letter of the Central Committee of the CPSU by the Editorial Departments of *Jen-min Jih-pao* and *Hung Chi* in: *The Polemic on the General Line of the International Communist Movement* (Peking, Foreign Languages Press, 1965), p. 194.

those internal processes which may take these countries onto the highway leading to socialism". . . .

It is necessary and important for the socialist countries to give the newly independent countries economic aid on the basis of internationalism. But in no case can it be said that their national independence and social progress are due solely to the economic aid they receive from the socialist countries and not mainly to the revolutionary struggles of their own people.

*　*　*

12. Even During the Period of Socialist Construction Class Struggles Continue

The Maoist thesis of historical stages proclaims that after the completion of the national democratic revolution, during the period of socialism, there remains the danger of imperialist aggression and of domestic deviation and revisionism. Hence the need for all countries which have entered the stage of socialism via new democracy to continually purge themselves of hostile elements. Hence, also, the continued need for a truly proletarian party like that of China, and the state of the dictatorship of the proletariat. Mao and his followers insist that the revolution must be permanent, that is, until the final stage of communism has been reached [Editors' note].

Historically, when the bourgeoisie overthrew the feudal system by revolutionary means, its advanced elements did carry out ruthless criticism of feudalism. As Engels noted, "They recognized no external authority of any kind whatever. Religion, natural science, society, political institutions—everything was subjected to the most unsparing criticism: everything must justify its existence before the judgment seat of reason or give up existence."

Of course, the revolutionary spirit of the bourgeoisie can in no way be compared with that of the proletariat. For the bourgeoisie, the winning of state power signifies the end of their revolution. For the proletariat, it is the beginning of the revolution, the starting point for the work of creating a new social system. Hence, the proletariat must raise the banner of criticism still higher, and make a complete break with all out-moded ideas, concepts, habits, and traditions, because only thus can the establishment and consolidation of a brand-new social system be ensured.

As the socialist revolution and socialist construction advance further, it is imperative that these ideological criticisms be intensified still further.

Guided by Mao Tse-tung's thought and the Marxist-Leninist line of the Chinese Communist Party, the Chinese people have gained tremendous successes in the socialist revolution and socialist construction. The old social system has been basically destroyed in our country. Great changes

From "Using the Proletarian World Outlook to Create Our New World," *Hung Chi* Editorial, October 1, 1965, in *Peking Review*, October 1, 1965, pp. 11-12. The extract headed "A Fifteen-Point Program for Socialism" is from "On Khrushchov's Phoney Communism and its Historical Lessons for the World," Ninth Comment on the Open Letter of the Central Committee of the CPSU by the editorial departments of *Jen-min Jih-pao* and *Hung Chi* (July 14, 1964), in *The Polemic, loc. cit.*, pp. 470-476.

have taken place in men's ideology. Nevertheless we must take note of the fact that class struggle remains and sometimes is very sharp. The various kinds of out-moded ideas and concepts which reflect the old system will not easily retire from the stage of history. The spectres of feudal and capitalist ideas, traditions of a semi-colonial and semi-feudal society and many other old forces of habit still more or less haunt the minds of many people.

The question facing us now is that under the powerful dictatorship of the proletariat, old ideas often will not reveal themselves in undisguised forms; they always try to hold on and disseminate their influences by taking cover behind socialist and Marxist-Leninist phraseology and slogans.

Everybody knows that new ideas may be expressed in old forms, but not many of us take into account sufficiently the fact that old ideas may also employ new forms. Old ideas in disguised forms often sneak their way into new things, corrode men's minds bit by bit and change the colour of new things, thus paving the way for the restoration of the old system. We must pay serious attention to this.

Old ideas, concepts, habits and traditions are very stubborn things. It is a long-time task for us to battle against them. What has been criticized today will crop up again sometime later and so the struggle will have to be carried on again. The advance of revolution and construction imposes on revolutionaries the need to have a firm grasp of the proletarian world outlook and to master proletarian ideology and make criticism and self-criticism constantly. It is necessary to discern and eliminate the out-moded ideas which have been expressed in various forms. All those old things which are not in the interests of the people and socialism must be uprooted without the slightest compromise. . . .

In the course of our revolution and construction, all those who have the courage to smash the fetters of out-moded ideas and traditions and can adopt the proletarian world outlook and Mao Tse-tung's thought to observe and deal with questions will be able to make new discoveries and inventions, and go on creating and advancing.

A FIFTEEN-POINT PROGRAM FOR SOCIALISM

The struggle in the socialist countries between the road of socialism and the road of capitalism—between the forces of capitalism attempting a comeback and the forces opposing it—is unavoidable. But the restoration of capitalism in the socialist countries and their degeneration into capitalist countries are certainly not unavoidable. We can prevent the restoration of capitalism so long as there is a correct leadership and a correct understanding of the problem, so long as we adhere to the revolutionary Marxist-Leninist line, take the appropriate measures and wage a prolonged, unremitting struggle. The struggle between the socialist and capitalist roads can become a driving force for social advance.

How can the restoration of capitalism be prevented? On this question Comrade Mao Tse-tung has formulated a set of theories and policies, after summing up the practical experience of the dictatorship of the proletariat in China and studying the positive and negative experience of other countries, mainly of the Soviet Union, in accordance with the basic principles of Marxism-Leninism, and has thus enriched and developed the Marxist-Leninist theory of the dictatorship of the proletariat.

The main contents of the theories and policies advanced by Comrade Mao Tse-tung in this connection are as follows:

FIRST, it is necessary to apply the Marxist-Leninist law of the unity of opposites to the study of socialist society. The law of contradiction in all things, i.e., the law of the unity of opposites, is the fundamental law of materialist dialectics. It operates everywhere, whether in the natural world, in human society, or in human thought. The opposites in a contradiction both unite and struggle with each other, and it is this that forces things to move and change. Socialist society is no exception. In socialist society there are two kinds of social contradictions, namely, the contradictions among the people and those between ourselves and the enemy. These two kinds of social contradictions are entirely different in their essence, and the methods for handling them should be different, too. Their correct handling will result in the increasing consolidation of the dictatorship of the proletariat and the further strengthening and development of socialist society. Many people acknowledge the law of the unity of opposites but are unable to apply it in studying and handling questions in socialist society. They refuse to admit that there are contradictions in socialist society—that there are not only contradictions between ourselves and the enemy but also contradictions among the people—and they do not know how to distinguish between these two kinds of social contradictions and how to handle them correctly, and are therefore unable to deal correctly with the question of the dictatorship of the proletariat.

SECOND, socialist society covers a very long historical period. Classes and class struggle continue to exist in this society, and the struggle still goes on between the road of socialism and the road of capitalism. The socialist revolution on the economic front (in the ownership of the means of production) is insufficient by itself and cannot be consolidated. There must also be a thorough socialist revolution on the political and ideological fronts. Here a very long period of time is needed to decide "who will win" in the struggle between socialism and capitalism. Several decades won't do it; success requires anywhere from one to several centuries. On the question of duration, it is better to prepare for a longer rather than a shorter period of time. On the question of effort, it is better to regard the task as difficult rather than easy. It will be more advantageous and less harmful to think and act in this way. Anyone who fails to see this or to appreciate it fully will make tremendous mistakes. During the historical period of socialism it is necessary to maintain the dictatorship of the pro-letariat and carry the socialist revolution through to the end if the restoration of capitalism is to be prevented, socialist construction carried forward and the conditions created for the transition to communism.

THIRD, the dictatorship of the proletariat is led by the working class, with the worker-peasant alliance as its basis. This means the exercise of dictatorship by the working class and by the people under its leadership over the reactionary classes and individuals and those elements who oppose socialist transformation and socialist construction. Within the ranks of the people democratic centralism is practised. Ours is the broadest democracy beyond the bounds of possibility for any bourgeois state.

FOURTH, in both socialist revolution and socialist construction it is necessary to adhere to the mass line, boldly to arouse the masses and to unfold mass movements on a large scale. The mass line of "from the masses, to the masses" is the basic line in all the work of our Party. It is necessary to have firm confidence in the majority of the people and, above all, in the majority of the worker-peasant masses. We must be good at consulting the masses in our work and under no circumstances alienate ourselves from them. Both commandism and the attitude of one dispensing favours have to be fought. The full and frank expression of views and great debates are important forms of revolutionary struggle which have been created by the people of our country in the course of their long revolutionary fight, forms of struggle which rely on the masses for resolving contradictions among the people and contradictions between ourselves and the enemy.

FIFTH, whether in socialist revolution or in socialist construction, it is necessary to solve the question of whom to rely on, whom to win over and whom to oppose. The proletariat and its vanguard must make a class analysis of socialist society, rely on the truly dependable forces that firmly take the socialist road, win over all allies that can be won over, and unite with the masses of the people, who constitute more than 95 per cent of the population, in a common struggle against the enemies of socialism. In the rural areas, after the collectivization of agriculture it is necessary to rely on the poor and lower middle peasants in order to consolidate the dictatorship of the proletariat and the worker-peasant alliance, defeat the spontaneous capitalist tendencies and constantly strengthen and extend the positions of socialism.

SIXTH, it is necessary to conduct extensive socialist education movements repeatedly in the cities and the countryside. In these continuous movements for educating the people we must be good at organizing the revolutionary class forces, enhancing their class consciousness, correctly handling contradictions among the people and uniting all those who can be united. In these movements it is necessary to wage a sharp, tit-for-tat struggle against the anti-socialist, capitalist and feudal forces—the landlords, rich peasants, counter-revolutionaries and bourgeois rightists, and the embezzlers, grafters and degenerates—in order to smash the attacks they unleash against socialism and to remould the majority of them into new men.

SEVENTH, one of the basic tasks of the dictatorship of the proletariat is actively to expand the socialist economy. It is necessary to achieve the modernization of industry, agriculture, science and technology, and national defence step by step under the guidance of the general policy of developing the national economy with agriculture as the foundation and industry as the leading factor. On the basis of the growth of production it is necessary to raise the living standards of the people gradually and on a broad scale.

EIGHTH, ownership by the whole people and collective ownership are the two forms of socialist economy. The transition from collective ownership to ownership by the whole people, from two kinds of ownership to a unitary ownership by the whole people, is a rather long process. Collective ownership itself develops from lower to higher levels and from smaller to larger scale. The people's commune which the Chinese people have created is a suitable form of organization for the solution of the question of this transition.

NINTH, "Let a hundred flowers blossom and a hundred schools of thought contend" is a policy for stimulating the growth of the arts and the progress of science and for promoting a flourishing socialist culture. Education must serve proletarian politics and must be combined with productive labour. The manual workers should at the same time be intellectuals and the intellectuals manual workers. Among those engaged in science, culture, the arts and education, the struggle to promote proletarian ideology and destroy bourgeois ideology is a protracted and fierce class struggle. It is necessary to build up a large detachment of working-class intellectuals who serve socialism and who are both "red and expert", i.e., who are both politically conscious and professionally competent, by means of the cultural revolution, and revolutionary practice in class struggle, the struggle for production and scientific experiment.

TENTH, it is necessary to maintain the system of cadre participation in collective productive labour. The cadres of our Party and state are ordinary workers and not overlords sitting on the backs of the people. By taking part in collective productive labour, the cadres maintain extensive, constant and close ties with the working people. This is a major measure of fundamental importance for a socialist system; it helps to overcome bureaucracy and to prevent revisionism and dogmatism.

ELEVENTH, the system of high salaries for a small number of people should never be applied. The gap between the incomes of the working personnel of the Party, the government, the enterprises and the people's communes, on the one hand, and the incomes of the mass of the people, on the other, should be rationally and gradually narrowed and not widened. All working personnel must be prevented from abusing their power and enjoying special privileges.

TWELFTH, it is always necessary for the people's armed forces of a socialist country to be under the leadership of the Party of the proletariat and under the supervision of the masses, and they must always maintain the glorious tradition of a people's army, with unity between the army and the people and between officers and men. It is necessary to keep the system under which officers serve as common soldiers at regular intervals. It is necessary to practise military democracy, political democracy and economic democracy. Moreover, militia units should be organized and trained all over the country, so as to make everybody a soldier. The guns must for ever be in the hands of the Party and the people and must never be allowed to become the instruments of careerists.

THIRTEENTH, the people's public security organs must always be under the leadership of the Party of the proletariat and under the supervision of the mass of the people. In the struggle to defend the fruits of socialism and the people's interests, the policy must be applied of relying on the combined efforts of the broad masses and the security organs, so that not a single bad person escapes or a single good person is wronged. Counter-revolutionaries must be suppressed whenever found, and mistakes must be corrected whenever discovered.

FOURTEENTH, in foreign policy, it is necessary to uphold proletarian internationalism and oppose great-power chauvinism and national egoism. The socialist camp is the product of the struggle of the international proletariat and working people. It belongs to the proletariat and the working people of the whole world as well as to the people of the socialist countries. We must truly put into effect the fighting slogans, "Workers of all countries, unite!" and "Workers and oppressed nations of the world, unite!", resolutely combat the anti-Communist, anti-popular and counter-revolutionary policies of imperialism and reaction and support the revolutionary struggles of all the oppressed classes and oppressed nations. Relations among socialist countries should be based on the principles of independence, complete equality and the proletarian internationalist principle of mutual support and mutual assistance. Every socialist country should rely mainly on itself for its construction. If any socialist country practises national egoism in its foreign policy, or, worse yet, eagerly works in partnership with imperialism for the partition of the world, such conduct is degenerate and a betrayal of proletarian internationalism.

FIFTEENTH, as the vanguard of the proletariat, the Communist Party must exist as long as the dictatorship of the proletariat exists. The Communist Party is the highest form of organization of the proletariat. The leading role of the proletariat is realized through the leadership of the Communist Party. The system of Party committees exercising leadership must be put into effect in all departments. During the period of the dictatorship of the proletariat, the proletarian party must maintain and strengthen its close ties with the proletariat and the broad masses of the working people, maintain and develop its vigorous revolutionary style, uphold the principle of integrating the universal truth of Marxism-Leninism with the concrete practice of its own country, and persist in the struggle against revisionism, dogmatism and opportunism of every kind. . . .

13. Politics Must Be Put in Command of Economics and All Other Work

Although the socialist revolution has been won on the economic front, so the argument goes, the class enemy has not yet been eliminated. Hence politics, based on the class struggle, must take precedence over economics, must clear the road for and protect the economic system of socialism, or Chinese society will revert to capitalism [Editors' note].

Whether or not we put proletarian politics first is a question that concerns which direction we will go: whether we will keep steadfastly to the socialist road or not; whether our society will advance to communism or revert to capitalism.

It is some time now since our country entered the stage of socialism but many comrades are still very unclear about this question. Some have given it no serious thought; others still have reservations. Some comrades think that since the revolution has succeeded and our country has already entered the stage of socialist construction, construction under the socialist system naturally means developing socialism, so how can there be any question of which direction we are going? Actually, these comrades do not understand that, in a socialist country, construction depends primarily on politics. Without proletarian politics we may lose our bearings and get nothing done well.

RELATIONSHIP BETWEEN POLITICS AND ECONOMICS

To clarify this question, let us first get a clear idea of the relationship between politics and economics.

Comrade Mao Tse-tung teaches us: "Politics, whether revolutionary or counter-revolutionary, is the struggle of class against class." He also points out: "Economics is the base and politics the concentrated expression of economics."

Class struggle is the motive force in the development of class society. The relations of men to each other in the process of production, that is, the relations of production, are the basis of classes and class struggle. Land-

From "Putting Politics First is Fundamental to all Work," *Peking Review,* April 22, 1966, pp. 15-18.

lords own land, and use it to exploit the peasants; the bourgeoisie owns factories, mines and other means of production, and use them to exploit the proletariat. The class struggle between the ruling classes and the classes under their rule is a concentrated expression of the relationship between exploitation and anti-exploitation in the economic sphere. In order to consolidate the economic system of exploitation of man by man, the ruling classes employ the state machine to suppress the resistance of the exploited classes. In order to overthrow the system of exploitation and establish an economic system which conforms to their own class interests, the classes that are ruled must carry out a violent revolution and seize state power, and, relying on their state power, establish, consolidate and develop their new economic system. Feudal economy was born in slave society, but it was consolidated and developed only after the feudal class overthrew the slave system. Capitalist economy was born in feudal society, but it, too, became consolidated and developed only after the bourgeoisie had overthrown the feudal system. Socialist economy is different to the economies of the slave system, of feudalism and capitalism. It is an economy that has eliminated private ownership of the means of production. It cannot be born within capitalist society; it can only emerge and grow when the proletarian revolution has destroyed the bourgeois state machine and the proletarian dictatorship has been set up.

Lenin said: ". . . without a proper political approach to the subject the given class cannot maintain its rule, and consequently cannot solve its own production problems." "Politics cannot but have precedence over economics."

That is to say, all class societies put politics first, the politics of one class or another. The economic system depends on politics to clear the road for it, protect it and develop it. Politics serve the economic base.

In a socialist society, it is all the more imperative that politics be put in first place. . . .

In a socialist society, the question of "who will win in the political and ideological spheres, socialism or capitalism?" will be resolved in protracted and intense class struggle. This is because once the socialist revolution on the economic front is in the main completed, the class enemy in its attempt to restore capitalism has to gain the upper hand first of all on the political and ideological fronts. Bourgeois and feudal ideas still command considerable influence in the political, and in particular in the ideological, realm —in the fields of art and literature, history, philosophy, economics, education, journalism and so on—since there are still bourgeois elements and bourgeois intellectuals who have not been reformed or not been sufficiently reformed, and the spontaneous tendency to capitalism still exists. Some places or departments are even still dominated by these bourgeois and feudal ideas. The class enemy tries to take advantage of these factors to effect a "peaceful evolution" within socialism. Unless proletarian politics is put first, unless attention is paid to the class struggle on the political and ideological fronts, bourgeois politics will certainly come to the fore and the poisonous stream of bourgeois and other non-proletarian ideas will rise unhindered to a flood.

The proletariat wants to transform the world in line with its own world outlook, and so does the bourgeoisie. If proletarian ideas do not take hold of people's minds, they will certainly be taken hold of by bourgeois ideas. Therefore, we must persist in the socialist revolution on the political and ideological fronts to consolidate the proletarian dictatorship—vigorously develop proletarian ideas and thoroughly eliminate bourgeois ideas, defeat the attacks of the bourgeoisie against socialism in the political and ideological realms, and ceaselessly consolidate and expand proletarian positions there. Only so can we transform the people's subjective world while transforming the objective world. Only so can we overcome and eventually eradicate bourgeois and other non-proletarian ideas, give a great forward thrust to the communist consciousness and moral qualities of the entire people, develop the initiative of the masses in socialist construction, consolidate and develop the socialist system, cultivate a new generation for the cause of communism, and thus guarantee the future transition to communism.

Communism is our ultimate goal. In the course of building socialism, while greatly developing the forces of production we must gradually narrow the gaps between worker and peasant, town and country and manual and mental labour. This is a long-term historical task. If we do not take effective revolutionary measures in the course of building socialism and widen rather than narrow these gaps, we will not be able to advance to communism but will certainly slip back to capitalism. In order to narrow these gaps, it is above all necessary to put proletarian politics first and, under the command of proletarian politics, greatly develop the forces of production. . . .

In 1963, Comrade Mao Tse-tung pointed out to the whole Party: "Class struggle, the struggle for production and scientific experiment are the three great revolutionary movements for building a mighty socialist country. These movements are a sure guarantee that Communists will be free from bureaucracy and immune against revisionism and dogmatism, and will for ever remain invincible. They are a reliable guarantee that the proletariat will be able to unite with the broad working masses and realize a democratic dictatorship. If, in the absence of these movements, the landlords, rich peasants, counter-revolutionaries, bad elements and ogres of all kinds were allowed to crawl out, while our cadres were to shut their eyes to all this and in many cases fail even to differentiate between the enemy and ourselves but were to collaborate with the enemy and become corrupted and demoralized, if our cadres were thus dragged into the enemy camp or the enemy were able to sneak into our ranks, and if many of our workers, peasants, and intellectuals were left defenceless against both the soft and the hard tactics of the enemy, then it would not take long, perhaps only several years or a decade, or several decades at most, before a counter-revolutionary restoration on a national scale inevitably occurred, the Marxist-Leninist Party would undoubtedly become a revisionist party or a fascist party, and the whole of China would change its colour." We should always bear in mind this warning from Comrade Mao Tse-tung.

Guided by Mao Tse-tung's thinking, the Chinese Communist Party has built up a fine tradition of putting politics first. When our Party formed the first detachment of the Workers' and Peasants' Red Army and established the first revolutionary base more than 30 years ago, Comrade Mao Tse-tung already pointed out the importance of political work, criticized a purely military viewpoint, and clearly pointed out that politics must be in command of military affairs. Since then, Comrade Mao Tse-tung has always emphasized that politics must be in command, that it is the very soul of all our work. This was true in the period of the democratic revolution, and it is even more true in the period of the socialist revolution. Precisely because of this, our Party has led the Chinese people from one great victory to another. Today, a new upsurge is shaping up throughout the country in industry and agriculture and in the study of Comrade Mao Tse-tung's writings, and this, too, is precisely a result of putting proletarian politics first.

14. Correct Leadership Is Important at All Stages of the Revolution

This means "correct" thinking, which is the universally applicable thinking of Mao Tse-tung [Editors' note].

China today is a China that works energetically to achieve the complete ascendancy of Mao Tse-tung's thought.

The world today is a world in which Mao Tse-tung's thought shines in all its spendour.

The great, unparalleled proletarian cultural revolution is a great revolution to vigorously achieve the complete ascendancy of Mao Tse-tung's thought. . . .

A new era of energetically establishing the complete ascendancy of Mao Tse-tung's thought has begun!

ONLY WITH MAO TSE-TUNG'S THOUGHT CAN THERE BE A NEW WORLD

In these world-shaking months which have just gone by, our most, most respected and beloved great leader Chairman Mao personally initiated and led the great proletarian cultural revolution. It came with an irresistible swiftness and force. Its achievements are immortal. Never has a revolution on such a scale and of such profound depth been seen in history.

In a little over three months, Chairman Mao received the revolutionary masses eight times. Such unity of heart between the leader and the people, too, has never before been witnessed in revolutionary history.

Each review shows the triumph of the vigorous efforts to establish the complete ascendancy of Mao Tse-tung's thought.

Each review is a solemn pledge to strive vigorously to establish the complete ascendancy of Mao Tse-tung's thought.

Comrade Lin Piao, Chairman Mao's close comrade-in-arms, said of the great proletarian cultural revolution: "In a word, we will work with great energy so that Mao Tse-tung's thought achieves complete ascendancy."

From "A New Era of Vigorously Establishing the Complete Ascendancy of Mao Tse-tung's Thought," *Peking Review,* December 9, 1966, pp. 12, 13, 15.

Today, the Chinese people and the people of the world see more and more clearly the profound and far-reaching significance of this great revolution to vigorously establish the complete ascendancy of Mao Tse-tung's thought.

It is a great revolution affecting the success or failure of the proletarian revolution! It is a great revolution that affects what road a socialist country takes! Only by vigorously working to achieve the complete ascendancy of Mao Tse-tung's thought, by carrying through to the end the socialist revolution on the ideological and cultural fronts, can we build our great motherland into an impregnable proletarian state that will never change colour.

To energetically establish the complete ascendancy of Mao Tse-tung's thought is the greatest need of our people and the urgent demand of the world's revolutionary people.

Revolutionary teachers and students from the old revolutionary base area of northern Shensi Province came to Peking and to the Tien An Men Square exultantly singing *The east is red, the sun rises; Mao Tse-tung appears in China.* . . . Over twenty years ago, the old poor peasant Li Yu-yuan in northern Shensi first sang this ode. Since then, the song—*The East Is Red*—has spread throughout China, throughout the Asian, African and Latin American continents and throughout the whole world. As the teachers and students sing the song today, their hearts swell. They say with feeling, "In the past, we relied on Mao Tse-tung's thought to turn all China red in a very short time. Today, by working together with the world's peoples to achieve the complete ascendancy of Mao Tse-tung's thought, a red world will swiftly come into being!"

Fighters from the anti-revisionist front, as they stood on the reviewing stands or walked past the Tien An Men gate, looked up to Chairman Mao with tears in their eyes. They exclaimed: "Long live Chairman Mao! Long, long life to him!" These included the children of poor herdsmen who had dwelt by the side of the Ili River for generations, and Chinese students who had been compelled by the leading group of the Soviet revisionists to leave the Soviet Union recently. They saw most clearly that, with this great cultural revolution personally initiated and led by Chairman Mao, China will never become revisionist like the Soviet Union and that the Chinese land will never change colour. The great proletarian cultural revolution is the greatest revolutionary mass movement in history. Only Chairman Mao, the greatest proletarian revolutionary, has the tremendous courage and determination to mobilize the revolutionary masses to completely uproot revisionism. They could not help singing from the depths of their being: With the reddest of all red suns in our hearts, we march on the broad road of the cultural revolution. May socialism and communism flourish through the ages. . . .

In all corners of the globe, all revolutionary people warmly praise the great proletarian cultural revolution in China as a great creation in human history. They hail Chairman Mao for revealing to the hundreds of millions of revolutionary people this inevitable law of historical development.

China's great proletarian cultural revolution proclaims to the world: Victory belongs to the revolutionary people who vigorously establish the complete ascendancy of Mao Tse-tung's thought. A new world without imperialism, without capitalism and without the exploitation system will be born! . . .

LEARN, LEARN AND LEARN FROM CHAIRMAN MAO

The East is Red sounds out loudest and clearest,
The greatest leader is Mao Tse-tung!
This is the voice of the young revolutionary fighters when they are being reviewed, the voice of the Chinese people and the voice of the revolutionary people all over the world!

Oh Chairman Mao, Chairman Mao! In the great proletarian cultural revolution personally initiated and led by you, you have received us many times, and again and again pointed out for us the road of advance, cleared away the obstacles and given us more strength.

You have summed up the experience and lessons of the international communist movement and led 700 million people to a completely new stage of socialist revolution. . . .

You . . . turned the great proletarian cultural revolution into a prairie fire.

You presided over the charting of the proletarian revolutionary line and thereby declared the bankruptcy of the bourgeois reactionary line.

You put on a red arm band and became the supreme commander of the Red Guards, a revolutionary organization that shakes the whole globe.

You gave us the instruction: "You should pay attention to state affairs and carry the great proletarian cultural revolution through to the end!"

You told us: "I give you my firm support!"

You highly appraised our revolutionary actions: "This is a movement of a momentous scale. It has indeed mobilized the masses. It is of very great significance to the revolutionization of the thinking of the people throughout the country."

You taught us: "You should put politics in command, go to the masses and be one with them and carry on the great proletarian cultural revolution even better."

You grasped the newborn thing of exchanging revolutionary experience on a big scale and pushed the great cultural revolution forward to a new high tide.

Where is the greatest proletarian revolutionary of the present era? He stands by our side and before our eyes, and he is our most respected and beloved great leader Chairman Mao!

Chairman Mao is always with us the revolutionary masses, showing full confidence in the masses, sharing the same fate and breathing the same air as the masses, and giving wholehearted support to the revolutionary mass movement. The great revolutionary practice of Chairman Mao sets the most brilliant example for all the comrades in the Party, all the Chinese people and the young generation.

To learn from Chairman Mao, study his great theory and learn from his brilliant practice—this is the common determination of the millions upon millions of revolutionary teachers and students being reviewed. They say: Chairman Mao's teachings are embodied in his great works, and we should study and apply them throughout our lives and always act according to Chairman Mao's instructions; at the same time, there is much of Chairman Mao's "works" not published in the books—his brilliant practice, from which we should learn still more. We shall take Chairman Mao's great teachings as our guide and his brilliant practice as our example, and we will do whatever Chairman Mao tells us to do; we will do things the way he does them!

15. *Those Who Oppose China's Prescription for National Liberation and Socialist Development Are Lackeys of Imperialism. All Opposition Must Be Silenced*

With political success and a modicum of economic achievement came self-assurance and the conviction that all who dissent from the official Chinese view of the world are monsters and devils in deep moral error. Some could be "re-molded"; others (the "die-hards"), could not [Editors' note].

PRESIDENT BOURGUIBA OF TUNISIA

. . . Tunisian President Habib Bourguiba pours out groundless abuses and with great zest joins in the anti-China chorus. Since the beginning of this year, Bourguiba has let loose a flow of anti-China statements . . . He scurrilously described China as a "madman" who unleashed wars and is filled with "inordinate strategic ambitions" and who wants to "plunge our continent into anarchy and subversion," and "create racism" and so on and so forth. He even abused the Chinese leaders in a most unwarranted manner. Thus the Tunisian President did not miss a single weapon in the imperialists' anti-China arsenal. And from this it is not difficult to see in whose service Bourguiba has placed himself. . . . He has even said that "the inordinate strategic ambitions of the biggest Asian power" was the true cause of the Viet Nam trouble and that "wars are brought about by such a 'madman' ". . . . Bourguiba alleges that " 'imperialism' and 'colonialism' no longer exist," but that China "infiltrates everywhere, creates difficulties, aggravates existing contradictions" and wants to "plunge our continent into anarchy and subversion." . . . The language used by him in attacking China as well as lauding the United States is the language of Washington . . .

From "Whom Does Bourguiba Serve?" by *Jen-min Jih-pao* Commentator, in *Peking Review,* November 26, 1965, pp. 25-26. The reference is to an interview granted by President Bourguiba to the French magazine *Réalités* on September 11, 1965. The second paragraph is from "U.N. has no Right to Discuss Korean Question," an article which appeared in *Jen-min Jih-pao* on December 1, 1965, and was reprinted in an abridged form in the *Peking Review* of December 3, 1965, pp. 10-11. The third paragraph is from "The United Nations—Instrument for U.S. Aggression," *Peking Review,* October 15, 1965, pp. 10-11. The paragraph on the United Nations' Tibet resolution is from "Another Entry in Shameful U.N. Record," a *Jen-min Jih-pao* editorial of December 21, 1965, in *Peking Review,* December 24, 1965, pp. 16-17. The last selection (on Soviet revisionism) is from "A Comment on the March Moscow Meeting," *Peking Review,* March 26, 1965, pp. 7-13.

It is by no means fortuitous that Bourguiba has danced more and more closely to Washington's tune. In the last year [1964-65] U.S. "aid" to Tunisia has increased sharply. Tunisia is one of the African countries that have received the most U.S. "aid" per capita . . . It is precisely with the inundation of a flood of dollars that a so-called "Bourguiba doctrine" has sprouted. In Bourguiba's own words, the essence of this doctrine, commonly known as Bourguibaism, is "to keep sacrifice, suffering, tears and rancour to the minimum" and "the tactical means to achieve this aim is through moderation, and temporary compromise." In fact, Bourguiba shed no tears at all; nor has he any hatred for U.S. imperialism. He is grateful and renders willing service to U.S. imperialism. Last spring he openly beat the drum for "coexistence" between Arab countries and Israel, a U.S. tool of aggression. This was an evidence of his efforts to help U.S. imperialism out of its predicament in the Arab region and to serve it. . . . Imperialism has tried more than once to stir up an anti-China campaign in Africa, but failed each time. It has only succeeded in getting a few theatrical hams to perform for it on an empty stage. We would like to warn those anti-China knights that their performances only serve to further reveal their own ugly nature.

THE UNITED NATIONS ORGANIZATION

The United Nations is again ready to begin its illegal discussion of the "Korean question" at its 20th General Assembly. As usual, the so-called "United Nations Commission on the Unification and Rehabilitation of Korea" has published an "annual report" in defence of the U.S. imperialist policy of aggression against Korea. The "report" which is full of fabrications gives a false picture of the present situation in south Korea from beginning to end and tries to turn things upside down. Under the fascist tyranny of the U.S. occupation army and the Pak-Jung Hi clique, south Korea has now been turned into an absolute colonial prison . . . But the report says that the "representative government" in south Korea has developed. As a result of greedy plunder by U.S. monopoly capital and insatiable extortions from the people by the puppet regime, the national industry in south Korea has been ruined, while its rural economy has been severely damaged and unemployment and starving people stalk the land. The "report," however, says that the economy in south Korea has made improvements and has been stabilized. It is by such clumsy means that the "United Nations Commission on the Unification and Rehabilitation of Korea" tries to hoodwink world opinion and serve U.S. imperialism . . . The "report" . . . has completely suppressed [the] obvious facts and has shifted the responsibility for the failure of Korea's unification on to the Democratic People's Republic of Korea [i.e., North Korea]. From this, people can see once again to what depths the United Nations controlled by U.S. imperialism has sunk as well as the criminal designs of U.S. imperialism which uses this organization for its aggressive activities . . . The "United Nations Commission on the Unification and Rehabilitation of Korea," which is an American tool, is constantly calling for "U.N. supervised elections" with a view to extending the criminal rule of the south Korean puppet regime to north Korea under the signboard of the United Nations so that the whole of Korea may be turned into a U.S. colony and military base . . . We always hold that the United Nations, as an aggressor and belligerent party, has no right whatever to discuss the Korean question. Any resolution on this question adopted by the United Nations which is a tool used by U. S. imperialism for aggression, is illegal and therefore null and void.

* * *

No one can cover up the criminal record of this organization which is dominated by the U.S. imperialists and their partners. Following a joint U.S.-U.S.S.R. conspiracy the U.N. Security Council on September 20 [1965] adopted a resolution which brought pressure to bear on Pakistan to effect a ceasefire with the Indian aggressor. This is only the latest example showing how the United States employs the U.N. to bully other nations and carry out its policy of war and aggression . . . The Vietnamese question has nothing to do with the U.N. and the organization has absolutely no right to intervene . . . The United Nations itself is used by the United States and other imperialist countries to fashion tools of aggression to threaten the Afro-Asian countries . . . The United Nations has done more than enough wrongs in the 20 years since its founding. Now there are only two alternatives: Either the organization rids itself of U.S. domination, corrects its mistakes and gets thoroughly reorganized, or a revolutionary United Nations will be set up to replace it.

* * *

As a result of U.S. machinations and manipulation, the 20th session of the U.N. General Assembly discussed the so-called Tibet question and adopted a resolution slandering the People's Republic of China. This has added another page to the shameful U.N. record of serving as a U.S. imperialist tool against China. . . . The latest resolution, like all previous resolutions on the same subject, is a flagrant interference in China's domestic affairs and a vicious slander against the Chinese people. It is completely illegal and null and void. . . . U.S. imperialism's cries and curses cannot save rotten feudal serfdom from extinction. They only serve to expose it as an enemy of the genuine freedom and liberation of the people of Tibet and all other nationalities of China and as defender of the worst cannibal system in the world. . . . It should be pointed out that Britain, the Netherlands and Norway, which maintain either full or partial diplomatic relations with China, submitted to U.S. pressure and voted in the U.N. General Assembly for the resolution on the "Tibet question." This is a very unfriendly act towards the Chinese people. . . . Let U.S. imperialism and its faithful running dogs lament and curse the extinction of the feudal serfdom and the reactionary serf-owner class in Tibet. The buzzing by these few flies cannot harm but will only benefit the people of Tibet and the entire Chinese people. While building their happy life, the emancipated one million serfs in Tibet and the people of the whole country will not forget that there are still a handful of monsters and freaks who are always trying to drag them back into the dark inferno. This can only stiffen our determination to carry the struggle against U.S. imperialism and its lackeys through to the end.

THE SOVIET REVISIONISTS

It is now possible for people to see more clearly that these new leaders of the CPSU [Brezhnev and Kosygin] had to oust Khrushchev, not because Khrushchev had become too odious and had been too stupid in some of his practices but because Khrushchev himself had become a serious obstacle to the carrying out of Khrushchev revisionism. In replacing Khrushchev, they simply changed the signboard and employed more cunning methods and subterfuges in order the better to push through and develop Khrushchevism and to carry out the general line of revisionism, great-power chauvinism, and splittism which Khrushchev had forged at the 20th Congress of the CPSU, systematized at its 22nd Congress and embodied in the Program of the CPSU . . . The leaders of the CPSU and the U.S. imperialists have joined in a love feast exchanging information and working in common against communism, against the people, against revolution, and against the national liberation movement for the purpose of maintaining imperialism, revisionism, and reaction everywhere against all revolutionaries. . . . Unless [the revisionists] openly announce the withdrawal of . . . anti-Chinese resolutions, statements, and articles, and publicly admit their mistakes, it will be absolutely impossible to silence us. Can the whole affair be reckoned as ended when Your Lordships go off, shrugging your shoulders, after abusing others? . . . If we need to make self-criticism, we should say that, in comparison with the support given by the leaders of the CPSU to the revisionist groups in many countries, we have not given enough support to the revolutionary left in some countries, and henceforth must greatly intensify our endeavours in this respect. . . .

APPENDIX TO CHAPTER 4

1. China: A Revolution for Export.

Chinese setbacks in African and Asian countries in 1966, and the concentration of Chinese mass communications media on propagating the cultural revolution within China, have led some to suppose that, despairing of revolution abroad and absorbed in revolution at home, China no longer has a revolutionary message for the peoples of Africa and Asia. In fact, the contrary is the case. The following notes are intended to provide documentation on some relevant Chinese views and activities which have been reported by the New China News Agency during the period of the cultural revolution, up to 15th March 1967. . . .

LESSONS OF THE SETBACKS

In January 1966 the *People's Daily* said that the actions of Dahomey and the Central African Republic in ending diplomatic relations with China were imperialist-inspired "anti-China instigations." Imperialism headed by the USA was "trying to bring about a breach in the normal relations between China and African countries", and to bring about an "adverse anti-China current." But this could not in any way impair China's prestige: it could only damage the international reputation of the African countries concerned.[1]

In April 1966 "Africa Freedom Day" was the occasion for an NCNA dispatch which put the Ghana coup into Chinese revolutionary perspective:

From *Mizan:* U.S.S.R., China, Africa, Asia (London, Central Asian Research Centre, March-April 1966), pp. 80-85. Reprinted by permission of the publisher.
[1] NCNA 9.1.66.

It is too early for the imperialists and their lackeys to be overjoyed. Their counter-offensive and the temporary adverse current it represents cannot possibly beat back the main current—the African people's anti-imperialist revolutionary struggle—or alter the excellent revolutionary situation on this continent.

The counter-offensive is helpful in that it teaches the African people a lesson and brings about a new awakening among them . . . The military coup d'état in Ghana . . . caused a wave of strong reaction and is precipitating new anti-imperialist storms . . . When all is said and done, the imperialist counter-offensive only pours fuel on the fire of the African people's hatred and heightens the anti-imperialist revolutionary spirit.[2]

On 5th May 1966 half of the *People's Daily* international page was devoted to Africa. The colonialists, said the paper, were "desperately manoeuvring to stage a comeback" in Africa. "On the surface these counter-attacks appear weighty, but in actuality they represent the impotent deathbed struggles of the imperialists and colonialists . . . From Angola to 'Portuguese' Guinea, from Zimbabwe to Equatorial Guinea, the African people are raising high the banner of armed struggle. From Guinea in the West to Tanzania in the East, the people are rallying more closely to defend their independence."[3]

MESSAGE OF THE CULTURAL REVOLUTION

During the summer, reflections of the cultural revolution began to appear in Chinese reports of individual Africans' and Asians' devotion to the works of Mao Tse-tung. The following is typical:

A freedom fighter from Azania (South Africa) was very happy to have obtained a volume of selected works of Mao Tse-tung. Pressing it to his breast, he told NCNA with deep emotion: "This book is more valuable to me than anything else. With it I feel confident in the ultimate victory of my country's struggle."[4]

The Chinese Foreign Minister Chen Yi, who has been present at many African or Asian receptions and other functions in Peking in recent months, has recently made a point of referring in his speeches to the cultural revolution—as in his speech at a reception to mark the Algerian revolution anniversary on 1st November.[5]

Earlier, an NCNA dispatch from Dar es Salaam on 10th September said that "African freedom fighters here acclaimed the great proletarian cultural revolution and the young Chinese Red Guards" as "shock brigades of a revolution without parallel in the history of the progressive world."

[2] NCNA 14.4.66.
[3] NCNA 5.5.66.
[4] NCNA 16.8.66.
[5] NCNA 1.11.66.

NCNA quoted statements to this effect made by Peking representatives of the Pan-African Congress of South Africa and the South West African National Union. Albert Lounda, a party leader in Congo (Brazzaville), said in Shanghai that the people in his country "are looking to great China as the revolutionary bulwark of the world anti-imperialist fight"; "this great cultural revolution has struck terror in the Western countries." Congo (Brazzaville) and countries like it could easily refute Western "rumours that China is isolated."[6] A Yemeni, the Deputy Director of San'a radio, said during his first visit to the CPR that what most impressed him was "the proletarian cultural revolution led by Chairman Mao."[7]

To date, the most highly placed African visitor to express his admiration for the cultural revolution is Birane Mamadou Wane, Minister of External Affairs and Planning of Mauritania who led a government delegation to China in February this year. At a farewell reception in Peking he said: "We must follow the example of the valiant Chinese people in daring to struggle and daring to win." The Chinese people had proved that man's courage and will were irresistible: "And of all their victories the most brilliant one is unfolding before our very eyes—I mean the great proletarian cultural revolution." Chen Yi thanked him for his "positive appraisal" of the cultural revolution and his resolute support for the people of Vietnam, Palestine, etc. "You dare to speak out the truth which certain so-called big nations dare not."[8]

ARMED STRUGGLE

At a Ceylon Independence Day reception in Peking on 4th February, Chen Yi, after speaking of the "excellent situation" throughout China with the progress of the cultural revolution, said that the "slanders" of the imperialists and modern revisionists would only recoil on themselves: "A socialist China which will never change its colour will wage even more resolute struggle against US-led imperialism and its lackeys, give even more powerful support to the revolutionary people of Asia, Africa, Latin America and the rest of the world, and fulfil even better our international duty." US imperialism had made "repeated military provocations against China" in an attempt to extend the Vietnam war to China. "We have long been prepared. China's great proletarian cultural revolution is itself the most extensive and best preparation against war."[9]

Chinese commentators particularly pick on Africa as a region for the application of Mao's thought on people's war. The following are some recent examples.

[6] NCNA 11.10.66.
[7] NCNA 19.10.66.
[8] NCNA 15.2.67.
[9] NCNA 4.2.67.

From an NCNA correspondent's article, Peking 27.12.66:

Following the extensive dissemination of the invincible thought of Mao Tse-tung on the African continent, the revolutionary people of Africa have become still more awakened in 1966 and their national liberation struggles have developed in depth, winning one victory after another . . . After innumerable trials and through a path full of twists and turns an increasing number of [the African people] have at last found this revolutionary truth—the great thought of Mao Tse-tung. Mao Tse-tung's thought is the beacon light for the African revolution . . . The patriotic armed forces of the Congo (Leopoldville) . . . make a point of studying Chairman Mao's works in the course of intense fighting, especially his theory of people's war . . . Chairman Mao's brilliant ideas of people's war have also circulated widely in other African countries and regions where patriotic armed struggles are going on [Angola, Portuguese Guinea, Mozambique, Equatorial Guinea, Zimbabwe (Rhodesia) and South West Africa are cited].

Chairman Mao has said: "Make trouble, fail, make trouble again, fail again . . . till their doom—that is the logic of the imperialists . . . in dealing with the people's cause . . . The development of the African situation in the past year has provided added proof of the correctness of this brilliant thesis . . . The imperialists' counter-revolutionary activities have brought on a new awakening among the African people . . . Following the series of military coups . . . and in particular the counter-revolutionary coup in Ghana, the African people rose into action and waged a massive campaign against subversion [anti-government plots defeated in Uganda, Guinea, Tanzania and Congo (Brazzaville)].

From a *People's Daily* commentary, summarized by NCNA 25.1.67:

"The enemy will not perish of himself," Chairman Mao has said . . . Like a wounded beast [the imperialists and colonialists] are still making frantic preparations to launch counter-attacks at any time and regain their lost positions . . . This counter-attack shows that it is impossible for the African people to win easy victories in their anti-imperialist struggle and that even some reversals are unavoidable. The African people therefore require to maintain at all times high vigilance . . . Chairman Mao has said: ". . . Whoever relaxes vigilance will disarm himself politically and land himself in a passive position."

From a *People's Daily* editorial, summarized by NCNA 16.2.67:

The scientific thesis "A single spark can start a prairie fire," advanced by Chairman Mao more than 30 years ago on the then revolutionary situation in China, is perfectly valid in describing the present revolutionary situation in the various countries of Asia, Africa and Latin America . . . [Their peoples] have grasped the truth that "political power grows out of the barrel of a gun." . . . Chairman Mao has said: "Revolutionary parties and forces at their very outset are invariably in the minority, but it is they, nevertheless, who have the best prospects." Although the patriotic guerrilla forces in Asia, Africa and Latin America may be weak and small and may face a multitude of difficulties today, they will assuredly be able to grow in strength and size, win major victories after winning minor ones, and establish with guns a land of the people, provided they rely on the people and persist in struggle."

The Arab World is regarded as another promising theatre of revolutionary struggle, inspired by Mao's teachings:

The year 1966 saw the 100-million Arab people . . . carrying their struggle against imperialism to a higher stage. The struggle against US imperialism, the common enemy of world people, was especially fierce . . . Israel is a dagger thrust into the heart of the Arab world by US imperialism . . . In defiance of the violent opposition of the Arab people, the USA has been arming Israel in increasing tempo . . . On 13th November Israel went further by mounting a massive aggression . . . mainly against the Palestinians. This . . . stirred up a gigantic storm of protests and demonstrations . . . In their anti-imperialist struggles, the revolutionary Arab people have come to see that Mao Tse-tung's thought is the only correct guidance with which to achieve national liberation, and that the Chinese people are dependable friends in their just cause. Palestinian Arabs are firmly convinced that the Palestine issue can be settled, not at the forum of the UN, but by armed struggle alone, as Chairman Mao Tse-tung has pointed out. Arab people in South Yemen under British occupation . . . have won one victory after another . . . Nationalist fighters there have begun to study and apply Mao Tse-tung's theory about guerrilla warfare . . . Popular armed struggle is also going on in Oman . . .

The Arab countries and people waged in the past year a bitter and ceaseless struggle against US imperialism . . . particularly in the field of oil . . . Syria's struggle to win back its legitimate oil rights . . . has won general support from the Arab countries.[10]

Another year-end review dealt with the Asian peoples' struggle, guided by the thought of Mao:

The peoples of the Asian continent, where the invincible thought of Mao Tse-tung is widely spread, have scored great new victories in their struggle against US imperialism, Soviet modern revisionism, and reactionaries of various countries during the outgoing year . . . In Vietnam, the focal point of the anti-US struggle of the world's people, the past year has witnessed brilliant victories for the heroic Vietnamese people . . . In Laos, Thailand and other countries the people's armed forces have been dealing heavy blows at the enemies . . . The Thailand people's armed forces have grown steadily and developed rapidly in the struggle . . . At present they are active not only in the north-eastern part of Thailand but have spread their activities to the southern part of the country . . . In the Philippines the outgoing year saw unabated armed struggle coupled with anti-imperialist demonstrations . . . In India sweeping mass actions against the foreign and domestic policies of the Congress government broke out in one place after another . . . this mass movement, which swept India like a hurricane, has drawn into its ranks a total of some 12,000,000 people . . . In Indonesia hundreds of thousands of people have fallen . . . But the Indonesian people have lived up to their glorious militant tradition by waging

[10] NCNA 6.1.67.

a sustained struggle against the fascist régime. They are now reorganizing their ranks and beginning to meet counter-revolutionary arms with revolutionary arms . . . Chairman Mao has said: "The imperialist wolves should remember that the days when they could manipulate the fate of humanity and carve up the Asian and African countries as they liked have gone for ever." The course of events in the past year shows that the Asian people, guided by the thought of Mao Tse-tung, are advancing with gigantic strides to shatter once and for all the old Asia where the imperialists and reactionaries have ridden roughshod.[11]

REVISIONISM AND COUNTER REVOLUTION

Chen Yi, addressing on 29th December a Peking rally to welcome 41 Overseas Chinese returned from Indonesia, said:

The Soviet revisionist clique is intensifying its collusion with US imperialism . . . They are flinging off their masks and openly standing under the White banner of counter-revolution held by US imperialism. Now throughout the world the demarcation line between revolution and counter-revolution is getting clearer and clearer. For the revolutionary people of the whole world, this is a very good thing.[12]

Soviet emphasis on social and economic aspects of the national liberation movement is adduced as evidence of Soviet anxiety to stop the liberation revolution, in the interests of accord with the West:

To break up the anti-imperialist revolutionary movement in Africa, the Khrushchev revisionists try their best to spread the illusion that imperialism has become "sensible," that it will "get out of the colonies" of its own accord, and that "the national liberation movement has entered the final phase of the abolition of colonial rule" and that "in the new stage of the national liberation revolution the socio-economic question becomes the key question" . . . These views . . . are intended to lead the African people astray and render service to imperialism . . . What they mean is that the African countries should give up their struggle against imperialism and stop their national democratic revolution half-way. What after all is the reality in Africa? . . . Imperialism, far from having withdrawn from Africa, is still frenziedly launching one counter-offensive after another.[13]

Chinese efforts to get Asian and (particularly) African nationalist and liberation organizations to express support for the Chinese line, and if possible to take sides with China in this dispute, now have the inspiration of the cultural revolution's anti-revisionism behind them. The Afro-Asian Peoples' Solidarity Organization is the most internationally public arena of the resulting squabbles. The Chinese are still reporting demands made by

[11] NCNA 29.12.66.
[12] NCNA 29.12.66.
[13] NCNA 15.4.66.

members of the organization, in this and that country, that its fifth conference should be held in Peking this year, as was agreed at its fourth conference. The Chinese view is that the AAPSO Council meeting in Nicosia in February, which decided to change to Algiers the venue of the 1967 conference, was "illegally convened" and "manipulated by the Soviet clique."[14] According to NCNA, the Malian delegate "protested on three occasions against such undemocratic practice," and the delegates of North Vietnam, the South Vietnam NFL and Palestine wanted the 1967 conference held in Peking as originally decided. Five African delegations left the meeting in protest—those of the South West African National Union, Bechuanaland People's Party, Basutoland Congress Party, Swaziland Progressive Party and Pan-African Congress of Azania (South Africa). Their statement even declared that "the people of the Soviet Union and some Eastern European countries under the rule of modern revisionism must be liberated," and the delegations made their exit from Nicosia in Red Guard style:

On the eve of their departure from Nicosia . . . they gathered in a room and jubilantly played the Chinese records they had brought with them, especially the songs "The East is Red" and "Sailing the Seas Depends on the Man at the Helm" . . . As they drove to the airport they waved from the bus windows with the red-covered booklets "Quotations from Chairman Mao" in their hands . . . Inspired by the all-conquering thought of Mao Tse-tung, these African freedom fighters resolutely combated the Soviet revisionists and came out with flying colours.[15]

Of African liberation organizations, apart from SWANU and PAC who figure above, only ZANU (Rhodesia) seems openly to have taken sides with the Chinese. It will be noted that each of these three organizations disputes the field with a rival organization—SWANU with SWAPO, PAC with ANC, and ZANU with ZAPU.

The quintet of pro-Chinese African organizations which figures at Nicosia also figured in July in a statement by their delegations attending the "emergency conference of Afro-Asian writers" in Peking (this itself was a rival of a parallel Soviet-supported conference). The statement condemned as "bogus revolutionary organizations" and "tools of the counter-revolutionary foreign policy of the Soviet government" the following organizations: SWAPO (South West Africa), FRELIMO (Mozambique), MPLA (Angola), IPGE (Equatorial Guinea), ANC (South Africa) and ZAPU (Rhodesia).[16]

The Afro-Asian Journalists' Association and the Afro-Asian Writers' Bureau having now split into rival pro-Soviet and pro-Chinese organizations, Chinese-sponsored delegations claiming to represent the AAJA and

[14] NCNA 20.2.67.
[15] NCNA 20.2.67.
[16] NCNA 10.7.66.

the AAWB were touring Middle East and African countries last year to rally support.

Meanwhile, as regards Communist verbal support for the rebels in the Congo, the Chinese seem now to have the field to themselves. NCNA claims that "the Soviet revisionists have sunk so low as . . . to hold 'secret negotiations' with the Mobutu régime on establishing 'diplomatic relations' with this US puppet." An NCNA dispatch from Brazzaville quotes a rebel statement as declaring: "If we close our ranks to achieve unity in revolutionary action, we will surely smash the double encirclement of the imperialists and modern revisionists."[17]

[17] NCNA 28.11.66.

2. War and Revolution

PAUL M. SWEEZY

LEO HUBERMAN

September 3rd [1965] was celebrated in China as the 20th anniversary of the victory of the Chinese People's War of Resistance against Japan. To commemorate the occasion, Lin Piao, Vice Premier, Minister of Defense, and Vice Chairman of the Central Committee of the Communist Party of China, published a long article entitled "Long Live the Victory of the People's War!" (English translation in *Peking Review*, September 3, pp. 9-30). This article has been widely, and no doubt correctly, interpreted as an authoritative statement of the official Chinese position on the state of the world and what can and should be done about it. Since the bourgeois press is not particularly reliable in matters affecting the socialist countries, and since not everyone has access to the text of Lin Piao's article, it seems desirable to combine a discussion of the Chinese position with a condensed summary of what the article actually says.

Lin Piao begins by stating two theses which probably few would deny: that the Chinese achieved victory in the war against Japan and subsequently against the Kuomintang reactionaries because it was a genuine people's war under inspired leadership; and that this victory "breached the imperialist front in the East, wrought a great change in the world balance of forces, and accelerated the revolutionary movement among the people of all countries." He then spells out why the Chinese believe that this experience from their recent past has the greatest importance for the world today:

Today, the U.S. imperialists are repeating on a world-wide scale the past actions of the Japanese imperialists in China and other parts of Asia. It has become an urgent necessity of the people in many countries to master and use people's war as a weapon against U.S. imperialism and its lackeys. In every conceivable way U.S. imperialism and its lackeys are trying to extinguish the revolutionary flames of people's war.

The rest of the article follows logically from this beginning. First comes a lengthy review and analysis of the strategy and tactics of the Chinese struggle against the Japanese and the Kuomintang, and then an assessment of the relevance of this experience for the present-day struggle against United States imperialism.

From Paul M. Sweezy and Leo Huberman, "War and Revolution," *Monthly Review*, November 1965, pp. 1-11. Reprinted by permission of the editors.

STRATEGY AND TACTICS OF THE CHINESE STRUGGLE

Politically, the central problem faced by the Communist Party (CPC) was how to unite all classes and groups willing to resist the Japanese, without surrendering control and leadership to those who for one reason or another could not be relied upon to carry through to the end a principled struggle for genuine national independence. At this stage, as Lin Piao makes quite clear, social reform was looked upon not as an end in itself but rather as a means to mobilize the maximum possible strength against the Japanese and later against the American-backed Kuomintang. What was required was *both* a united national front—excluding only "a handful of pro-Japanese traitors among the big landlords and the big bourgeoisie"—*and at the same time* a policy within the united front of independence, initiative, and struggle against any vacillation or backsliding. The success of the Chinese Communists depended upon correctly applying this political strategy, avoiding on the one hand the error of refusing temporary alliances with potential enemies (including even anti-Japanese imperialisms), and on the other hand the error of handing over control to potential enemies. Either error could have been fatal, and it was Mao Tse-tung's genius to know how to steer the narrow course between them, not in abstract theoretical terms but in the concrete historical conditions of China in the 1930's, 1940's, and 1950's.

Militarily, the grand strategy of the CPC is summed up by Lin Piao: "To rely on the peasants, build rural base areas, and use the countryside to encircle and finally capture the cities—such was the way to victory in the Chinese Revolution."

Relying on the peasants and building rural base areas were two sides of the same coin. In Lin Piao's words:

Building the revolutionary base areas was a grand rehearsal in preparation for nation-wide victory. In these base areas we built the Party, ran the organs of state power, built the people's armed forces, and set up mass organizations; we engaged in industry and agriculture and operated cultural, educational, and all other undertakings necessary for the independent existence of a separate region. Our base areas were in fact a state in miniature. And with the steady expansion of our work in the base areas, our Party established a powerful people's army, trained cadres for various kinds of work, accumulated experience in many fields, and built up both the material and the moral strength that provided favorable conditions for nation-wide victory.

The keystone of the arch was the people's army which had to be "of a new type" and had to apply tactics at every stage of the struggle appropriate to its nature and resources. The special characteristic of the army was that it "must first and foremost be built on a political base."

Politics is the commander, politics is the soul of everything. Political work is the lifeline of our army. True, a people's army must pay attention to the constant improvement of its weapons and equipment and its military technique, but in its fighting it does not rely purely on weapons and technique; it relies mainly on politics, on the proletarian revolutionary consciousness and courage of the commanders and fighters, on the support and backing of the masses.

Tactically, the people's army must master the art of guerrilla warfare and stick to it until conditions are ripe for a transition to mobile warfare.

Lin Piao puts much stress on the principle of "adhering to the policy of self-reliance." He recognizes that the Chinese struggle was a part of the world-wide Anti-Fascist War and that many forces contributed to the common victory. He also affirms the duty of revolutionary and progressive forces to aid and support each other in their struggles. Nevertheless:

The liberation of the masses is accomplished by the masses themselves—this is a basic principle of Marxism-Leninism. Revolution or people's war in any country is the business of the masses in that country and should be carried out primarily by their own efforts; there is no other way. . . . If one does not operate by one's own efforts, does not independently ponder and solve the problems of the revolution in one's own country and does not rely on the strength of the masses, but leans wholly on foreign aid—even though this be aid from socialist countries which persist in revolution—no victory can be won, or be consolidated even if it is won.

THE LESSONS OF THE CHINESE EXPERIENCE FOR THE WORLD TODAY

Lin Piao opens this part of his article with a comparison between the Russian and Chinese Revolutions. First he emphasizes continuity and similarities:

(1) Both were led by the working class with a Marxist-Leninist party as its nucleus. (2) Both were based on the worker-peasant alliance. (3) In both cases state power was seized through violent revolution and the dictatorship of the proletariat was established. (4) In both cases the socialist system was built after victory in the revolution. (5) Both were component parts of the proletarian world revolution.

Next come differences:

The October revolution took place in imperialist Russia, but the Chinese Revolution broke out in a semi-colonial and semi-feudal country. The former was a proletarian socialist revolution, while the latter developed into a socialist revolution after the complete victory of the new-democratic revolution. The October revolution began with armed uprisings in the cities and then spread to the countryside, while the Chinese Revolution won nation-wide victory through the encirclement of the cities from the rural areas and the final capture of the cities.

The point of this comparison is not immediately apparent since, having made it, Lin Piao turns his attention to more general problems of war and revolution, including the meaning of Mao's dictum that "imperialists and all reactionaries are paper tigers." And yet if we understand him correctly, the comparison is crucial to the whole Chinese position.* They are in effect saying that the world of today has given us two models of the revolutionary process. The first, exemplified by the Russian Revolution, applies to imperialist countries; the second, exemplified by the Chinese Revolution, applies to the colonial countries (using the term "colonial" in its broadest sense). The first type of revolution is socialist from the outset, starts in the cities and spreads to the countryside; the second aims initially at national liberation, starts in the countryside and spreads to the cities, and becomes socialist after the conquest of power.

Which of these models is relevant to the present world situation? The Chinese evidently believe that for the vast majority of mankind the second, or "Chinese," model is the only relevant one. In Lin Piao's words:

> It must be emphasized that Comrade Mao Tse-tung's theory of the establishment of rural revolutionary base areas and the encirclement of the cities from the countryside is of outstanding and universal practical importance for the present revolutionary struggles of the oppressed nations and peoples in Asia, Africa, and Latin America against imperialism and its lackeys.

> Many countries and peoples in Asia, Africa, and Latin America are now being subjected to aggression and enslavement on a serious scale by the imperialists headed by the United States and their lackeys. The basic political and economic conditions in many of these countries have many similarities to those that prevailed in old China. As in China, the peasant question is extremely important in these regions. . . . The countryside, and the countryside alone, can provide the broad areas in which the revolutionaries can maneuver freely. The countryside, and the countryside alone, can provide the revolutionary bases from which the revolutionaries can go forward to final victory.

Does this mean that in the eyes of the Chinese the "Russian" model has lost all relevance? No clear answer is possible on the basis of Lin Piao's article. There is one somewhat enigmatic statement which might be interpreted as suggesting that the "Chinese" model is applicable to the entire world:

> Taking the entire globe, if North America and Western Europe can be called "the cities of the world," then Asia, Africa, and Latin America constitute

---

* To avoid misunderstanding: we are not concerned in the present context with the extent to which the Chinese analysis agrees or disagrees with classical Marxian theory, nor do we ask whether their characterizations of the Russian and Chinese Revolutions are historically accurate. These are obviously important questions which deserve separate and detailed treatment.

"the rural areas of the world." Since World War II, the proletarian revolutionary movement has for various reasons been temporarily held back in the North American and West European capitalist countries, while the people's revolutionary movement in Asia, Africa, and Latin America has been growing vigorously. In a sense, the contemporary world revolution also presents a picture of the encirclement of cities by the rural areas. In the final analysis, the whole cause of world revolution hinges on the revolutionary struggle of the Asian, African, and Latin American peoples who make up the overwhelming majority of the world's population.

This passage has been gleefully pounced upon by the bourgeois press as evidence of Chinese "aggressiveness," the imputed meaning being that the Chinese want the revolutionaries of Asia, Africa, and Latin America, after they conquer power in their own lands, to attack North America and Western Europe. Such an interpretation is almost certainly wrong. By comparing the advanced capitalist countries to the cities and the colonies to the rural areas, Lin Piao is using a figure of speech to stress that at the present stage of development the former are strongholds of reaction and the latter breeding grounds of revolution. But there is no justification for pushing the analogy further. The fact that Lin Piao speaks of the revolutionary movement in the advanced countries being *temporarily* held back shows that the Chinese have by no means written it off. Presumably they believe that it will come back to life again in due course and play its appointed role in overthrowing the world capitalist order. And more than likely they believe that the ever-sharpening contradictions within the imperialist countries resulting from their vain efforts to contain the revolution in the world's "rural areas" will be a decisive factor in reviving the now moribund revolutionary forces in North America and Western Europe. If this interpretation is correct, it would be perfectly consistent for the Chinese to hold that while the "Russian" model has no relevance to the *present* stage of the world revolution, it will regain its full relevance in the *final* stage of this great historical drama.

The concluding pages of Lin Pao's article are largely devoted to (1) Mao's theory of the relation between the "national-democratic" (also called "new-democratic") and socialist revolutions in the "Chinese" model, (2) the necessity for the colonial peoples to wage revolutionary wars and the reasons why their chances of winning are good, (3) denunciation of "Khrushchev revisionists" as "betrayers of people's war," and (4) a confident prediction that if the United States chooses to follow in Japan's footsteps by invading China, she will suffer the same fate. For the most part what is said on these themes is reasonably familiar, and we can confine comment here to a few remarks on the first of them.

What is crucially important is *not* to confuse the Maoist conception of the national-democratic revolution with the traditional theory of the bourgeois revolution against feudalism. True, both bring together very similar class coalitions: proletariat, peasantry, petty bourgeoisie, and national (anti-imperialist) bourgeoisie. But there the similarity ends. The bourgeois revolution is led by the bourgeoisie and results in the establishment (or consolidation) of capitalism. The national democratic revolution is led by workers (or a worker-peasant alliance), results in national independence, and clears the way for the immediately following socialist revolution. To quote Lin Piao:

> Comrade Mao Tse-tung's theory of the new-democratic revolution is the Marxist-Leninist theory of revolution by stages as well as the Marxist-Leninist theory of uninterrupted revolution.
>
> Comrade Mao Tse-tung made a correct distinction between the two revolutionary stages, i.e. the national-democratic and the socialist revolutions; at the same time he correctly and closely linked the two. The national-democratic revolution is the necessary preparation for the socialist revolution, and the socialist revolution is the inevitable sequel to the national-democratic revolution. There is no Great Wall between the two revolutionary stages. But the socialist revolution is only possible after the completion of the national-democratic revolution. The more thorough the national-democratic revolution, the better the conditions for the socialist revolution.

In summary, the Chinese position, as we interpret it, is approximately as follows: The non-socialist world is divided into a handful of advanced capitalist-imperialist nations on the one hand and a large number of exploited and underdeveloped countries on the other. In the present stage of development, revolutionary forces are weak and ineffective in the advanced countries and are rapidly gaining strength in the underdeveloped countries. In these circumstances it is the "Chinese," not the "Russian," model of revolution which is relevant. The "Chinese" model comprises two stages: a national-democratic revolution, led by the working classes and supported by elements of the bourgeoisie; and an immediately following socialist revolution, also led by the working classes and resulting in the complete overthrow of capitalism and the beginnings of socialist construction. The tasks facing the underdeveloped countries now are to carry through the national-democratic revolution. This requires building a united front under worker leadership to fight a people's war against imperialism and its local allies. Politically, the leadership must aim to unite as large a proportion of the population as possible while carrying on an unremitting struggle against vacillation and backsliding. Militarily, people's war requires building revolutionary bases in the rural areas, forging a politically highly conscious army, employing guerrilla tactics until the relation of forces permits going over to mobile warfare, surrounding and eventually capturing the cities. The success of the Chinese revolutionaries against the Japanese and the American-backed Kuomintang proves that these tasks can be accomplished. "Victory will certainly go to the peoples of the world! Long live the victory of people's war!"

HOW VALID IS THE CHINESE POSITION?

We do not see how any Marxist, or for that matter any informed person with a sense of history, can fail to agree with the underlying postulates of the Chinese position. The nonsocialist world *is* divided into a handful of exploiting nations and a large number of exploited colonies or semi-colonies. The United States as the leading imperialist country has announced a thousand times, beginning with the Truman Doctrine in 1947, that it means to do everything in its power to prevent any change in this situation. To this end it has built up the most formidable military machine in history and has already demonstrated—in Asia (Vietnam), in Africa (the Congo), and in Latin America (the Dominican Republic)—that it will use this machine without the slightest regard for international law, treaty obligations, or moral scruples. The idea, once so hopefully entertained, that economic development in the dependent countries can be successfully promoted by reforms within the existing framework plus aid from the advanced countries, can now, after two decades of bitter experience, be seen for what it is: ideological eyewash. The disparity between the advanced and backward countries grows year by year; many of the latter are losing ground absolutely as well as relatively; with world population due to double within the next half century, the continuation of present trends can only bring social and biological disaster. Clearly, the choice before the masses in the exploited countries is to starve or fight. And who can doubt that, given the inevitably increasing understanding of the potential plenty made possible by modern science and technology, the masses will sooner or later elect to fight to take control of their own destiny rather than starve to death for the benefit of others? (This is of course not to say that there is any guarantee of victory. Revolutionaries have often in the past been defeated, and doubtless will suffer many setbacks in the future too. What now seems impossible is that starving people will forever continue to bear their fate in passivity.)

Whether the revolutionary struggles of the period ahead will conform as closely to the "Chinese" model as the Chinese leaders now appear to think, is another matter. Latin American experience, the latest phase of which is dealt with in three articles in this issue of MR,* suggests that important variations are not only possible but probable. Let us attempt a tentative identification of the main points of similarity and difference.

First, the Chinese thesis that it is necessary to rely on the peasantry,

---

* "A Guerrilla Wind," by Adolfo Gilly, pp. 41-45; "The Peruvian Revolution: Concepts and Perspectives," by Luis F. de la Puente Uceda, pp. 12-28; and "Venezuela and the FALN Since Leoni," by James D. Cockcroft and Eduardo Vicente, pp. 29-40.

build rural base areas, forge a politically conscious army, and wage guerrilla warfare, seems to be fully confirmed by recent developments in Guatemala and several of the South American countries. On the other hand, the Dominican uprising indicates that a different pattern is possible. There a split in the armed forces led to the arming of the people in Santo Domingo and the rapid defeat of the old apparatus of repression. But for prompt imperialist intervention, the revolution would have triumphed in the capital city and spread to the countryside, in the manner of the "Russian" model. It is of course true that imperialism cannot be treated as some sort of "outside" force; it is the main variable in the equation to be solved. And it may well be that from now on the Dominican struggle will conform to the "Chinese" pattern. Nevertheless, one can imagine that in some bigger country—Brazil, for example—a revolution beginning as the Dominican revolution began might follow a different course. A revolutionary government might be formed and the main cities brought under control *before* imperialist intervention could be organized. In that case the next stage might be a classical revolutionary war directed primarily against the foreign invader. Here the "Russian" model would be very relevant indeed.

There is no intention here, of course, to downgrade the military importance of the "Chinese" model. What has been happening in large parts of Latin America requires greater emphasis than ever on this aspect of Chinese experience. But at the same time one should not close one's mind to the possibility that the "Russian" model may also have relevance for the underdeveloped countries, or even that some combination of the "Chinese" and "Russian" models may throw more light on some situations than either by itself. Generals are always being accused of dogmatically planning the next war as though it were a mere continuation of the last; revolutionaries should not make the same mistake.

Politically, too, Latin American experience throws doubt on the universal validity of the "Chinese" model. No one questions the desirability of forming as broad a united front as possible to fight against imperialism and for national independence, but what Latin American experience does call in question is the possibility, at least in the conditions of the Western Hemisphere at the present time, of devising a program which will unite not only workers and peasants but also a significant section of the bourgeoisie. The workers and peasants have seen so many well-meaning reformers stymied and then thrown out by the military watchdogs of the old oligarchies that they are not likely in the future to trust any state that they do not directly control through their own people's army. But no considerable section of the bourgeoisie, especially after the experience of the Cuban Revolution, is going to support, still less fight for, the establishment of such a state. With the (very important) exception of those—mostly students and intellectuals—who are ready to throw in their lot with the workers and peasants, the Latin American bourgeoisies are not interested in any kind of a revolution: they prefer to throw in *their* lot with the imperialist defenders of the status quo. Under these circumstances, Latin American revolutionaries are finding that it is vastly preferable to rouse the morale and enthusiasm of workers and peasants by boldly proclaiming a full-fledged socialist program than to seek vainly to enlist the backing of a largely nonexistent anti-imperialist bourgeoisie. What this means is not that carrying through the national democratic revolution as a preliminary to the construction of socialism has lost any of its importance, but rather that in Latin American conditions the national democratic and socialist revolutions are apparently going to be carried out under a single unified program and in this sense are being telescoped into one.

Whether or not this is considered to be a real departure from the "Chinese" model and Mao Tse-tung's theory of revolutionary strategy is perhaps a matter of terminology. It might be more accurate simply to say that some things which were necessary and right in China in the 30's and 40's are neither necessary nor right in Latin America in the 60's: both the composition and the program of the united front have to be worked out in accordance with the specific conditions of time and place. But the aims, national independence and socialism, remain the same.

These aims are indeed universally valid in the second half of the 20th century, and by boldly holding them up and calling on the peoples of the whole world to struggle for them against any and all enemies, the Chinese do great credit to themselves and deserve the gratitude of all socialists and revolutionaries.

SUGGESTED READING

I

"Arab People, Unite, Make Sustained Efforts, and Fight Imperialism to the End!" *Peking Review,* June 16, 1967.

Huang, Chang-pen, " 'Underdeveloped Economy': A Neo-Colonialist 'Theory.' " *Peking Review,* November 1, 1963.

Ide, Junichiro, "China's Great Cultural Revolution Has Opened a New Era in World History." *Peking Review,* May 1967.

"Let U.S. Stooge Mobutu Fool No One." *Peking Review,* April 28, 1967.

Study and Propagate Mao Tse-tung's Thought to Promote the Revolutionary Cause of Asia and Africa. General Resolution on the Current International Situation Adopted at the Fifth Plenary Meeting of the Secretariat of the Afro-Asian Journalists' Association in Peking, from June 15 to 17, 1967. *Peking Review,* June 23, 1967.

II

Adie, W. A. C., "China, Russia, and the Third World." *The China Quarterly,* No. 11 (1962).

Eckstein, Alexander, *Communist China's Economic Growth and Foreign Trade: Implications for U. S. Policy,* New York: McGraw-Hill, 1966.

Gelman, Harry, "Russia, China, and Underdeveloped Areas." *Annals of the American Academy of Political and Social Science,* Vol. 369 (1963).

Kovner, Milton, "Communist China's Foreign Aid to Less Developed Countries," in *An Economic Profile of Mainland China,* Joint Economic Committee, Congress of the United States, Vol. 1, Washington, D.C.: U.S. Government Printing Office, 1967.

Lee, Joseph L., "Communist China's Latin American Policy." *Asian Survey,* Vol. IV, No. 11 (November 1964).

Prybyla, Jan S., "Soviet and Chinese Economic Competition Within The Communist World." *Soviet Studies,* Vol. XV, No. 4 (April 1964).

———, "Communist China's Economic Relations with Africa, 1960-1964." *Asian Survey,* Vol. IV, No. 11 (November 1964).

———, "Communist China's Economic Relations with Cuba." *Business and Society,* Vol. 6, No. 1 (Autumn 1965).

———, "Soviet and Chinese Economic Aid to North Vietnam." *The China Quarterly,* No. 27 (July-September 1966).

Yu, George T., "China's Failure in Africa." *Asian Survey,* Vol. VI, No. 8 (August 1966).

Appendix

Case Studies of
Five Developing Countries

In their endeavor to move from a state of poverty and underdevelopment to a condition of material affluence, the backward countries and regions of the world must choose from among a variety of possible developmental strategies and tactics which broadly fall into "Marxist" and "non-Marxist" groups. These, to repeat, are very broad and rather loose classifications since there exists a wide spectrum of "Marxist" routes to development and affluence and an even broader range of "non-Marxist" paths: the reader has had occasion to examine some of the Western (non-Marxist) prescriptions in Chapter 2 and to compare them with Soviet and Chinese Communist (Marxist) views (Chapters 3 and 4).

There is one feature common to the prescriptions contained in the preceding pages: they all issue from countries whose own actual experiences have, on the whole, been successful. At the present stage, China's effectiveness in building a prosperous economy is the most difficult to evaluate, not only because Chinese endeavors are still in their early stages but also because the Chinese Communist government has published few meaningful statistics since 1960. In any case, as can be seen from the selections in Chapter 4, what the Chinese Maoists advocate is primarily a method of seizing state power rather than a blueprint for economic construction.

Neither the Soviets nor the West propose models that are exact replicas of their own past; only the followers of Mao urge the underdeveloped countries to follow to the letter the path onto which Mao led the Chinese people (a point elaborated on by the editors in the preface of this book). Yet all prescriptions, Marxist as well as non-Marxist, bear the imprint of some of the experiences of the advocates' homelands. But the overwhelming majority of social scientists, East and West, who are concerned with problems of economic growth and development are in agreement on one point: any assumption that the same methods which proved successful in one part of the world during a specific time in history are equally workable in other countries, on other continents, and at different times is of questionable validity.

Quite obviously, the circumstances of countries emerging from political dependence and economic stagnation today are, in many fundamental respects, different from the situations which prevailed in the West more than a hundred years ago, in Russia at the beginning of this century, or in China some two or three decades ago. The fact that capitalism and parliamentary democracy have been visibly successful in Western Europe and on the North American continent does not in and of itself ensure that they would work as successfully elsewhere in the world. The same applies to the Soviet experience with a highly centralized economy and an authoritarian form of government, and to China's guerrilla, and increasingly romanticized, socialism. The acclimatization of Soviet-type socialism in Cuba and Eastern Europe has been accompanied by changes and mutations that over time have given rise to new varieties, more suited to local conditions and temperament. The transplantation of market systems of the European and American type to Latin America and parts of Asia and Africa has resulted in the emergence of systems which only vaguely resemble, and sometimes caricature, the parent model. In short, each country has to find by trial and error the way appropriate to itself, with the experience of the more advanced countries serving as a useful backdrop to its effort, but not as a detailed and infallible blueprint.

To stop with Chapter 4 would have meant omitting one of the most interesting parts of the survey of development; it would have meant turning a deaf ear to the experiences and the counsel of those countries which in the last decade or two have taken to the long road from underdevelopment to affluence. The rationale of this Appendix is to introduce the reader to the views, policies, and actual experiences of at least some of the nations which are currently embarked on the painful process of development. Their opinions, their strategies, their accomplishments, and their failures will surely gain additional pertinence in years to come as new paths are explored, rejected, or proven successful.

The five countries chosen for inclusion in this Appendix are illustrations of non-capitalist, non-Soviet, and non-Chinese paths which to a greater or lesser degree still bear the imprints of experiences of countries which have traveled the road before them. The economic systems of these five countries range from the joint private and public efforts of Japan, through the state-private approach of India, the curious case of Israel, the Arab "socialism" of Egypt, to the planned-market socialism of Yugoslavia. Politically, the five span forms ranging from parliamentarism that closely resembles the Western conception and style to manners of ruling which are more akin to Moscow. More important, they give an idea of the wide spectrum of possibilities, the relevance of local circumstances, the pervasiveness of specific cultural traits, and the evolution of ideas. Perhaps the most salutary lesson to be drawn from this survey is that to those involved, the immediacy of local problems is of overriding import. Foreign offers of socioeconomic systems and foreign advocacy of political philosophies are to the less developed countries interesting phenomena but quite often irrelevant to the problems at hand. Frequently, these unsolicited blueprints are seen as a threat to efforts aimed at national consolidation and the evolution of an indigenous style in politics as in economics. Hence the sensitivity and the apparent "ingratitude" of the less developed nations of which one hears so much.

JAPAN

By almost every economic measuring rod, Japan is today the richest country in Asia; in per capita income she is surpassed on that vast continent only by Israel. Yet, a hundred years ago Japan was an underdeveloped, tradition-bound country like all the others: poor except in her ambition and the latent industriousness of her people. Japan is not a large continental power like the United States, the Soviet Union, or China; her natural resources have at all times been relatively limited; until recently, the rate of population increase was comparable to that typical of most of the other Asian, African, and Latin American underdeveloped countries. Surely her strategy of economic development, conscious or not, merits the closest scrutiny.

There are many lessons to be learned from the Japanese experience, many pitfalls to be avoided. The lesson is all the more salutary since Japan has not adhered to any one specific prescription for moving from poverty to affluence; rather, she has combined many ways and assimilated numerous influences without losing her identity. Not without friction and travail, Japan has succeeded in combining an ardent nationalism with selective technological and other borrowing from abroad. The restrictive practices of an oligarchy and the inbred conservatism of its elites were merged with a revolutionary spirit of enterprise, a willingness to experiment and a boldness that, until recently, were unique in Asia. Japan's economic and social system defies facile classification because it was arrived at in a tortuous way, before the concepts of "socialism" and "capitalism" had had time to harden. Perhaps the most interesting aspect of Japan's example (as also of Israel's from which it differs in many fundamental respects) is her success in combining an adequate and rising standard of living with democratic forms of political behavior.

The first two selections trace this development from the early years to the present time. The problems now facing Japan are those which arise in all advanced industrial societies; they are problems of affluence threatening the more graceful qualities of the old Japan. The last selection, taken from a Japanese source, examines Japan's role in stimulating the development of her Asian neighbors. This question is acquiring increasing urgency if only because of the rapidly emerging challenge of Communist China. In the midst of their full enjoyment of the good life, the Japanese are uneasily conscious of this disturbing influence on their insular affairs. Try as she may, Japan cannot shut herself off from the outside world; geographically small, she is economically too big.

1. The Economic Development of Japan

WILLIAM W. LOCKWOOD

ROLE OF THE STATE

Clearly the course of Japan's economic development after the Restoration was powerfully influenced by the militaristic and mercantilistic cast of her political institutions. Her heritage of feudalism, the ambitions of her new leaders, the kind of world she now entered—all combined to project the State into a prominent role and endow it with broad responsibilities in creating the framework of industrialization.

. . . The authority of the government was freely invoked in the early years to stimulate new investment and technological change, and to guide economic development in accordance with national interests as conceived by those in power. Conceptions of national interest were intermingled and identified with personal and group interest of course, as they were in the Navigation Laws of seventeenth century England or the Bonapartist reforms of nineteenth century France. A rapid succession of measures established a milieu of law and administration and finance within which the gestation of capitalism took place. Beyond this the government itself actively shared the initiative in building systems of transport and communication, establishing credit institutions, and even launching new factory enterprise. After the turn of the century, as it receded more into the background, it still kept its grip on certain levers of economic power. It used them to underwrite the established order and to move its economic center of gravity increasingly toward industrialism. Particularly it employed them to encourage those industries and activities which were strategic to Japan's war potential. . . .

The more difficult problem is to evaluate the importance of political factors in the real substance and dynamics of Japan's economic growth over half a century. Particularly, what part did social action through political mechanisms play in the crucial process of innovation by which Japan moved from the old to the new? If industrialization multiplied the nation's productive powers four- or fivefold, through what propelling force and by what instrumentalities was this achieved? The basic tools were modern

From THE ECONOMIC DEVELOPMENT OF JAPAN: GROWTH AND STRUCTURAL CHANGE, 1868-1938 by William W. Lockwood, 1954, pp. 571-592, except p. 583 and omitted phrases. Reprinted by permission of Princeton University Press and Oxford University Press.

science and machinery. The opportunity for rapid economic advance was provided by opening the door to foreign trade and cultural contact. But the task itself required sweeping changes in the organization of national life. It called for increasing specialization of functions, new forms of social cooperation—above all, a new spirit of enterprise in large sectors of the economy.

In interpreting this process, the historian can be misled by the fact that its political features are more readily observed and recorded. Public decisions like the enactment of a statute or an investment by a State bank inevitably attract more attention than bits of power machinery adopted by thousands of small weavers, whatever their real significance. The vigorous initiative of the Meiji oligarchy, and the pervasive influence of the State in subsequent times, make it easy to exaggerate their substantive importance for the process of economic growth. From some accounts one might conclude that Japanese industrialization from 1868 to 1938 was largely the creation of a quasi-totalitarian state. The political authorities are pictured as bending their energies to the task with far-seeing unity of purpose and an almost unlimited grant of authority from a docile people. If great strides were made in assimilating machine technology, if capital accumulated rapidly, if output and markets grew apace, this is attributed in large measure to the driving political leadership of the State and the disciplined obedience of its population. In particular, war and armament are sometimes said to have given the chief impetus, and to have swallowed up most of the fruits.

Any such picture of Japan's economic development greatly oversimplifies and distorts the reality of events. For one thing, the Japanese State was by no means so monolithic or single-minded in its leadership as this would imply. Within the oligarchy no such unity of interest and outlook existed, except on the broad fundamentals of internal stability and overseas expansion. On the contrary, in many particulars of economic policy one finds sharp conflicts and rivalries among various factions of the military, the civilian bureaucracy, and business interests. Commonly decisions regarding a budget, a tariff, or a banking statute were reached by a process of political logrolling and compromise which was consistent with no single, calculated philosophy of national interest. Hesitation, indecision, stalemate are no less a part of the record.

Especially was this true after the turn of the century, with the gradual disappearance of the elder statesmen who had piloted Japan through the Restoration period. As the commercial classes grew in influence, and with them the political parties, the emphasis in national economic policy shifted increasingly from national power to wealth and well-being, at least for the propertied class. Perhaps it would be more accurate to say that elements of self-interest, always present in the Mercantilist policies of the clan oligarchs, became more confused and more contradictory as wider groups in the population came to share increasingly in political power. The military counterrevolution of the thirties reversed this trend for the time being. But even when it involved the nation in total war, it never succeeded in fashioning an all-powerful party ideology, apparatus, and discipline such as Hitler fastened upon Germany. Considering Japan's authoritarian traditions, one cannot fail to be impressed with the bitter divisions and deadlocks which persisted throughout the war crisis among elements of the armed forces, the career bureaucrats, and the industrialists. Still less is there reason to believe that Japanese political leadership in economic affairs was particularly coherent or far-seeing through much of the period after 1900.

What is more relevant here, a study of the whole process of economic growth in modern Japan leads to the conviction that the real drive and momentum lay in large measure outside the realm of national political ambition and State activity. At most the latter only accelerated a process of industrialization which was latent in the whole conjuncture of forces at work. The underlying motivations were doubtless complex, joining personal aspirations for economic betterment, nationalist sentiment, and other values which facilitated common action toward socially approved goals. At home were latent resources, both human and material, which only awaited development through the growth of knowledge and widening of personal opportunity. Abroad, the Japanese had the good fortune to enter the world economy at a time when they were able to gain relatively free access to the industrial technology and the materials in which they were deficient. In this setting they proceeded to build a new structure of industrial and commercial enterprise on the foundations already laid in Tokugawa times.

T. S. Ashton speaks of "those spontaneous forces of growth in society that arise from ordinary men and women and find expression in voluntary association, as well as in the State."[1] If we bear in mind the context of Japanese tradition, with its stress upon leadership, imitation, and teamwork, this is more suggestive of the process by which the modern Japanese economy was built than those formulations which put the emphasis on coercion and repression. Except in a few respects, some important and others quite marginal, it did not grow in response to the plans or dictates of the government. Political forces helped to create a favorable psychic milieu; the political mechanism was employed to provide certain important stimuli; and direct controls were applied at various points to serve political ends. But if economic expansion turned almost at once toward industrialization it was basically because Japan's resources, aptitudes, and opportunities drove her in this direction. If it was an orderly, organized process, it reflected less the coercive drive of the State than the Japanese capacity for consensus and cooperation. If it had real substance, it was because of the enterprise and energy of millions of small businessmen, farmers, and workers.

[1] "Economic History and Theory," *Economica,* Vol. XIII, No. 5, May 1946, p. 84.

To be sure, the more advanced techniques of finance and industrial organization were pioneered by the big concerns in close association with the government. They developed new sources of fuel and power. They created a network of long-distance transport. They provided a large share of industrial capital formation. No less important, they built up an overhead structure of commercial and credit organization which enabled myriads of small traders and industrialists to be linked together in coordinated but highly specialized patterns of activity geared to expanding markets. Nevertheless, without the exercise of personal initiative and entrepreneurial responsibility in increasingly pervasive fashion, and not merely at the top, the imperial ambitions of Japan's rulers would never have achieved any material foundation. They would have remained little more than the dreams voiced by Motoori Norinaga in the eighteenth century.

The sphere of actual State ownership was closely circumscribed after the experimental ventures of the early years. Aside from routine government services, indeed, State undertakings provided only a negligible share of the national product. Furthermore, the real economic growth of Japan took place chiefly in those areas of private activity which owed least to political subsidy and support. Vast sums were spent on conquering and developing the colonies, it is true, but this effort returned only a modest yield in trading or job opportunities. Particularly as a source of food the colonies were important; yet Japan's primary economic interests abroad lay outside the Empire. They were only placed in jeopardy by military expansionism.

Meanwhile, at home, those industries for which the government was always most solicitous, and where the *zaibatsu* were preeminent—the strategic industries—furnished only a small part of the growth in Japanese national income before 1935. Probably they served as an actual drag insofar as they were expanded after 1920 by political protection which attracted capital and skills from more productive employment. However this may be, they remained a small segment of the Japanese economy, despite their sheltered position. By way of illustration, the entire complex of mining, metallurgy, and machinery industries furnished no more than 8% of Japan's national product in 1930, and still less of her gainful employment.

Various exceptions may be made to this general argument, of course. Money values of production and trade are a poor guide to the importance of particular lines of enterprise, some of which are fundamental to a whole array of activities. The Japanese railways and electrical communications were of this character. They were either built by the government or soon nationalized. On the other hand, two other basic industries, coal and electric power, were developed mainly through private investment and enterprise, profiting of course from political favors whenever they could be secured. The rapid rise of the merchant marine owed much to the assistance lavishly given by the State. Yet even the shipping industry grew even-

Japanese economic life. In the neighborhood and the village, no doubt, few

tually to large proportions chiefly because underlying economic circumstances were favorable. (See above.)

Still more was this true of the broader fields of consumer industry, agriculture, and miscellaneous services which made up the great bulk of Japanese economic life. In the neighborhood and the village, no doubt, few major innovations in such trades were ever attempted without the consent and support of the local elders, who also controlled political life. Similarly in larger affairs the degree of informal control exercised by politically dominant groups went well beyond the laws on the statute books and the formal regulations of government ministries. By and large, however, through a wide range of small-scale industry, local commodity-handling trades, and personal services, even in a good deal of large-scale enterprise, one gets the impression of governmental indifference, certainly of inaction, so far as positive intervention through the formal mechanisms of the State is concerned.

One aspect of economic growth, associated as cause and effect with many others, was the secular expansion of market demands. This had two characteristics worth recalling in the present context. First, it occurred predominantly in the home market. Foreign and colonial markets at their prewar peak (1927-36) took no more than 25 to 35% of Japan's manufacturing output, and no more than 20% of her entire national product of all types. Nor—contrary to a widespread impression—did the overseas market for all goods and services, or even for manufactures alone, increase much more rapidly than the domestic market after 1910. Second, the national demand represented mainly the growing requirements of the civilian economy, expressed through private expenditures for goods and services. Private consumer outlay certainly accounted for at least 65% of gross national product, and private capital formation for most of the remainder. . . . Notwithstanding the catalytic effect of certain State expenditures this was true of the Meiji years; equally from 1911 to 1936.[2] In this realm of civilian enterprise occurred the great expansion of Japan's productive powers which carried the more marginal, strategic industries, as well as the whole cost of Japanese armament. Here was produced the real wealth which enabled the country, in addition, to support a growing population at a slowly rising standard of living.

The factor of war, with which State economic policy was so closely identified, has often been exaggerated as the mainspring of Japan's industrialization. The constructive achievement of Japanese militarism was to preserve the nation's independence, particularly in the early years. There-

[2] . . . It might be added that State activities of many kinds—e.g., the tax reform of 1873, the building of railways, the creation of a uniform currency, the promotion of exports—were especially important during the early years in fostering an increasing commercialization of the market and enlargement of its geographic scope. Nothing said above is intended to deny these strategic contributions, to which much space has already been devoted.

after military expenditures in the limited conflicts with China and Russia gave a fillip to economic expansion through the multiplied effects of State borrowing and spending on the whole economy. They reinforced the bias toward easy money and a high level of investment which was a marked characteristic of this period. In this respect they may actually have paid for themselves in good part, by stimulating fuller employment and technical progress even in civilian production.

Against these gains must be set the continual drain of armaments on Japan's limited capital resources, on her advanced machine skills, and especially on the government budget itself. From 1895 to 1935 some 40 to 50% of the national revenue was regularly spent on the Army and Navy, or on servicing loans incurred for military purposes. . . . This cut heavily into the governmental resources available for public works. It crippled education, farm relief, and other welfare expenditures which only a government could undertake. The dearth of public funds for such purposes was a persistent feature of the whole period. Moreover, the taxes which supported the military establishment probably came increasingly out of private income which would otherwise have been saved and invested. Even the foreign borrowings of the national government, which climbed 1,200 million yen in one decade, 1904-13 . . . were devoted in large measure to military use, either directly or indirectly. So, too, was a large share of the 360 million yen indemnity secured from China just previously. A small fraction of these sums spent on reducing disease and accident rates in urban industry, for example, would have increased production efficiency as well as human well-being.

The drain of empire building went far to nullify the more constructive use of State power to mobilize savings for investment in productive enterprise. Fiscal and monetary measures employed for this latter purpose were especially important in the early years. At that time the private capital market was undeveloped. The problem in considerable degree was one of mobilizing surplus income from agriculture for industrial and commercial investment. Then, too, armament building could be justified much more easily as a measure of defense. After the turn of the century, however, Japan's economic advance owed little to her military expansion, unless we are to assume that otherwise the Japanese islands would have been placed under foreign subjection. Rather, the debt was the other way.

Significantly, the war which profited Japan the most was World War I, when she remained neutral in all but name. Had she again stayed on the side lines in World War II, she might once more have reaped fabulous gains. Instead, she wrecked her own economy and laid waste that very part of the world on which her prosperity depended. Professor Ashton, to quote him again, once suggested that the misery and unrest which attended the Industrial Revolution in England during the early nineteenth century were not so much the product of the factory system as of the Napoleonic wars.

Under more peaceful conditions it would have been far easier to raise living standards as productivity advanced, to mitigate the evils of slums, and to reduce the insecurities to which industrialism exposed both the farm and city worker. Certainly this has been true of Japan.

The foregoing remarks . . . all cast doubt on the thesis even in the case of Japan that the State was "the chief element in economic development" or the statesmen "the chief actors." Much the same opinion may be ventured with regard to the *zaibatsu,* especially in those undertakings which required continued patronage from the government because they were never able to stand on their own feet. The energies, the skills, and the ambitions which provided the real motor force of Japanese industrialization were much too pervasive and too diverse to be compressed into any such formula. They found expression through the activities of millions of small industrialists, tradesmen, technicians, farmers, and workers, as well as in the superstructure of big business. The economic modernization of Japan cannot be explained by "laws" of economic determinism, in which new modes of production follow one another in an inexorable sequence. But equally it went far beyond the activities of a few bold pioneers and organizers, whether statesmen, industrial magnates, or scientists. Also involved were myriads of small, unknown entrepreneurs who introduced and spread the new learning, and still larger numbers of humble workers who provided the growing pool of modern technological skills. This, too, called for initiative and adaptability.

INNOVATION AND ENTERPRISE

It would be interesting to know more about the social and technical processes by which such innovations were introduced and spread through Japanese economic life. They included new goods and new materials; new markets, modes of production, and organization; new wants, as well. Some were massive innovations like steam power, modern metallurgy, and the joint-stock company. Others were modest adaptations and improvements in old ways, no less significant in their cumulative effect. The actual dynamics of change and growth are an elusive subject, as remarked above, but a few observations made here and there in preceding chapters may be brought together at this point.

One cannot escape the conviction, first of all, that the comparative speed of Japan's economic modernization owed much to the fact that both her geographic position and her particular complement of resources fitted her for the role of an industrial power with extensive maritime trade.

Already by 1868 Japan was densely settled, with a population of 2,000 per square mile of cultivated land. This is almost as many as in the United Kingdom today. If she was to develop she had to industrialize; her primary industries offered only limited opportunities for expansion. And if she was to industrialize, she had to trade, especially as she lacked so many essential materials. Fortunately the Japanese islands lay athwart what were destined to become the main trade routes of the western Pacific. They were well situated for extensive contacts with both Asia and the West. Overseas commerce, particularly with the United States and Europe, served as a broad highway for the introduction of new stimuli and new techniques. These in turn pushed the nation still further along the road to industrialization.

A related geographic factor of hardly less importance was the confi uration of the country. Japan is smaller than Sweden or Siam. Most of tl land area is within 100 miles of a port city which has also tended to gro into an industrial center. Short land distances and interior communicatioi by sea were a great advantage in achieving political order and unity; al in fostering the easy movement of goods and people within the framewoi of a growing national market. They partly explain the remarkable sur of the population to the cities which was such a conspicuous and essenti feature of industrialization. They also encouraged the dispersion of man industries through the countryside, even industries heavily dependent o imported materials and export markets. In such ways they favored th diffusion of new wants and new knowledge far more readily than is apt t be the case in a massive continental area like India or China. And the spared Japan part of the immense capital outlays required by such coun tries for land transport and water control. For example, coal at tidewate and localized water supply for irrigation were great advantages.

Finally, if the practices of industrial monopoly did not exert a mor baneful effect on Japanese economic development than they did, this wa due in part to competitive safeguards imposed by this necessary depend ence on foreign trade. At home there existed no raw material base com parable to the Ruhr on which to build powerful and restrictive monopolies in large-scale industry. Most Japanese industries had to rely in increasing degree on foreign materials if they were to grow. Moreover, the big com bines were apt to find themselves on both sides of the fence, as importers as well as producers. A further restraint on market monopoly was the per sisting need to import a good deal of machinery and equipment from West ern manufacturers; also the importance for many industries of a highly competitive export business, which in turn handicapped efforts to control the domestic market.

After World War I the competitive stimulus of imports was weakened by the rise of Japan's tariff duties and the growing technical maturity of her industry. A number of large-scale trades, particularly those sheltered from foreign competition, were characterized by what was described earlier as a blend of jealous rivalry and mutual solidarity, of rugged independence and collusive agreement. Still, the continuing necessity of foreign trade, and its competitive character, operated as a check on the traditional Japanese propensity toward combination and group action. Otherwise the latter might have had more stifling influence on technological progress.

Smallness and poverty in resources are hardly unmixed blessings, to be sure. Yet with nations as with individuals they may contribute powerfully to the dynamics of development. Japan's small size, her insular position off the coast of Asia, and her meager endowment in natural wealth per capita are often said to have created a national sense of inferiority and insufficiency which has made her people historically receptive to new ideas from abroad. However this may be, as a practical matter they aided the Japanese materially during the nineteenth century—first, in avoiding the full force of Western imperialism and preserving their political independence, and, second, in launching a program of rapid modernization. Among various patterns of economic development, circumstance directed them almost from the outset toward industrialization, urbanization, and trade, if in fact any far-reaching expansion of productive powers was to take place. This pattern is not without its disadvantages, and Japan has certainly not escaped the ills which attend it. It did serve, however, to maximize the inflow and permeation of science and industrial arts from the West at a rate not yet experienced by any other Asiatic nation.[3]

Physical factors alone, of course, do not explain the dynamics of growth. Many nations bear witness today to the fact that modern technology does not necessarily seed itself and take root in a backward, tradition-bound economy even where outside contacts bring it within easy reach.

It is true that Japan's industrialization was more largely a matter of transplanting and adapting to Japanese conditions the techniques already developed in the West than of making primary contributions to the world's stock of knowledge. Yet borrowing of this sort calls for more than rotelike absorption. It involves purpose, criticism, and a creative synthesis. It entails persistent trial and error, and the risking of fortunes both large and small, in a setting which offers rewards for success. New modes of production are apt to encounter subtle and powerful resistance. And this may take the form not only of political disorder, or indifference to material

---

[3] England, too, in an earlier day and a quite different setting, reaped the advantages of island security and political unity; of easy access to a continent and the New World; of limited wars fought with the aid of subsidies and the balance of power; of tidewater coal; of a climate salubrious for the cotton textile industry, the pioneer of the Industrial Revolution; and of a long succession of technical borrowings through the migration of technical skills from Germany, France, and the Low Countries. These circumstances help to explain the paradox, which is no less applicable to Japan, described by Barbara Ward as follows: "Knowing what we know today about the advantages to industrialization of large internal markets . . . and of secure access to raw materials, we should not have picked an island off the coast of Europe as the most favorable spot for beginning the industrial experiment. Geography would always set limits to the growth of a large internal market . . . [and] few of the raw materials necessary to modern industry can be found within Britain's frontiers." *The West at Bay,* New York, 1948, p. 23.

progress, but a deeper hostility to the habits of mind and social arrangements which these modes require. Even within a single country the degree of assimilation may be uneven among various regions and occupations. The case of Japan herself well illustrates this fact.

Like the other great societies of the East, Japan resisted certain aspects of Western culture, with its emphasis on individual self-assertion, competitive striving, and democratic expression. Inner values of the spirit have been tenaciously shielded from the disruptive penetration of Western ideals. But in the realm of the industrial arts, at least, too much has been made of the docility and conservatism of the Japanese. Here, within the limits of his environment and the opportunities which have come to hand, he appears to have displayed a ready willingness to abandon old ways, particularly where the acknowledged leaders of society pointed out the new. One recalls Sir George Sansom's remark, with reference to an earlier historical period in Japan, that the nation of the "unchanging East" is "a very dubious dictum." . . .

. . . This willingness to venture and to learn, if not to pioneer at least to imitate, in a climate of opportunity which makes it pay, is certainly an essential condition of economic development. That it appeared first at the top of Japanese society is not surprising. What impresses one is the degree to which it spread subsequently through a broad stratum of the population.

It was of great importance, of course, that a considerable segment of Japan's ruling class manifested a spirit of enterprise and adaptability at an early stage of her contact with the West. In contrast to the gentry and aristocracies of most other Asiatic nations, and many of their own compatriots, numerous young *samurai* grasped eagerly at the potentialities of Western learning. They were already restive in the chaotic state of affairs under the Shogunate. Already a good many had virtually been declassed and driven into farming and trade. Despite the antimercantile tradition of their class, it was they who began to display a spirit of capitalistic enterprise in manufacturing and commerce long before the overthrow of the old regime. In this they were joined by the many rich peasants of the central and western regions, and the new merchant class emerging in the port cities. From these elements were recruited the new bureaucrats, businessmen, and technicians who led the way in exploiting the new technology, in economic life as well as government. The common class roots of many leaders in the two fields facilitated the close interrelationships stressed earlier in this chapter.[4]

[4] "The section of the *samurai* class that did not take an active part in politics entered the business world. Many of these failed miserably in their new ventures, but the capitalist spirit which they displayed in trying their hands at company enterprises did much to arouse public interest in such enterprises. The general sentiment among the *samurai* in those days was that if new occupations must be chosen, they should turn to novel industries and undertakings not yet tried by *chōnin* or farmers. Prince

Only later, as experience accumulated and knowledge became more widely diffused, did increasing numbers of commoner families begin to respond to the new forces in such a way as to give breadth and depth to the process of modernization. Certain economic gains followed quickly and almost automatically from the new freedom of occupation, the extension of cultivation, the reforms in currency and taxation, the improvement in transport, etc. However, beyond the façade of State-sponsored industries hastily erected in the early years, it took time for the process of innovation and imitation to reach back into traditional Japanese society. One great retarding factor was the quick response of population increase, which so discouraged advances in productivity by more capitalistic methods. Many traditional occupations seemed unaltered in their essentials even after fifty years. In particular, Japanese farming as a way of life changed very little, despite scientific improvements in agriculture which the experts have described as "a chemical and botanical revolution."

Throughout this whole process of growth emphasis must be placed on what seem today very modest improvements: the ricksha and the bicycle; the rodent-proof warehouse; elementary sanitation; better seeds and more fertilizer; the kerosene and then the electric lamp; a simple power loom; the gas engine in the fishing boat; the divorce of personal from business accounts; the principle of limited liability. Big and dramatic innovations like railways and great banks and holding companies might provide the scaffolding. But the structure itself was built, brick upon brick, by myriads of individual experiments and commitments. Inevitably this was a slow process, as it will be throughout Asia.

The system of enterprise through which Japanese development was organized and directed has been referred to above as predominantly one of private ownership and market competition. There are many qualifications to this statement, of course. Yet in the actual conduct of business operations little capital was invested in new undertakings except on the basis of private profit expectations. Losses were mainly a private responsibility, except in comparatively few trades. The innumerable decisions regarding what to produce, how to produce it, where and how to sell it, were left primarily to private initiative, subject only to various political inducements and controls.

Iwakura was quite right when he declared that the *samurai* class alone had the capitalist spirit." Yasuzo Horie, "An Outline of the Rise of Modern Capitalism in Japan," *Kyoto University Economic Review,* Vol. xi, No. 1, July 1936, p. 112.

It has often been remarked, on the other hand, that the leading *chōnin* of the Tokugawa era failed as a rule to make a successful transition to positions of prominence in the new order. Their generally conservative outlook and their close ties with the old nobility stood in the way. This exemplifies what is perhaps almost a law of economic evolution. The leading industrialists of nineteenth century England, too, were not in the main the successors of the merchant manufacturers of the eighteenth century. For example, the woolen masters of Norfolk and Devonshire were unable to change their ways. So it was very largely throughout Europe.

Within this system it is significant that as late as the year 1930 one in every three persons gainfully employed in Japan was still in some sense an entrepreneur, carrying some risk and responsibility for business enterprise. . . . Even in manufacturing, plants of less than 100 workers, most of them separately owned, still accounted for at least one half of total output and two thirds of total employment. . . . Despite all the limitations upon the independence and the resources of the small businessman which prevailed, this meant a vast number of establishments within which new products and new ways of getting things done might be tried out. It put to work a strong incentive to save, which everywhere tends to be more powerful among small businessmen than among wage earners or large capitalists. It divided the risks in tiny parcels, with a cumulative gain from successful innovations. Much of the most productive investment and modernization of techniques took place in these medium- and small-scale sectors of the economy.

To speak of private enterprise and competition as characteristic of the prewar Japanese economy is not to deny the inward differences between the system as it developed here and its prototypes in the West. If competition was keen, its forms were influenced by age-old traditions of hierarchy and group solidarity. If enterprise was privately owned, the individual entrepreneur yet conducted his affairs in a context of Japanese ideals and institutions, with its own set of family obligations, paternalistic controls, and other social incentives and restraints. No people have ever organized economic life on the basis of unrestrained individualism, and certainly not the Japanese.

The small industrialist or trader, as well as the farmer, continued to operate essentially a family enterprise, utilizing family labor and drawing little distinction between family and business affairs. His independence in external relations was closely limited by mental horizon as well as meager financial resources. Where he was integrated into a larger framework of production and trade, he was apt to be heavily dependent on a larger merchant, factory, or bank. These circumstances are not peculiar to small-scale enterprise in Japan, of course. What is striking about the Japanese case is the amount of growth and technical improvement which nevertheless took place in many such trades. Perhaps the outstanding reason is the one already remarked upon. The Japanese were peculiarly successful in organizing and extending complex systems of production and marketing within which numerous small establishments came to perform highly specialized functions and were yet linked together in a flexible and far-reaching pattern of social cooperation. Geography favored such arrangements through providing good interior communications and easy contacts between the port cities and much of the countryside. But the Japanese themselves would appear to have inherited a flair for such patterns of group action.

The financiers and executives who built Japan's large-scale industries displayed marked capacity in performing the classic functions of capitalistic innovation. Yet here as well, it may be remarked that Japanese business-men often seemed cautious in asserting the spirit of self-reliant venture. The corporation manager, like the political bureaucrat, was prone to take shelter in group responsibility. There were few rugged "captains of indus-try" even in the early days; corporate action came naturally to the Japa-nese. The great combines employed all the latest financial devices for con-centrating business power, but their prominence in modern Japan was itself an expression of old traditions of authority and teamwork. So, too, were their close and mutually dependent relations with the government.

The opportunities of industrialization enabled successful enterprises to reap handsome, quasi-monopolistic rewards, for private capital would venture into new and risky fields only where large profits could be antici-pated. Even then, the tendency was to insure against risks wherever possible by restraining competition and securing the patronage of the State in one form or another. A British observer of Japanese business at the close of the Meiji era had this to say: "Men look to the Government for aid, and hav-ing received it try to stifle competition. Success depends more on manoeu-vering for privilege than on a steady persevering struggle against obstacles. As a natural sequence the supply of active, resourceful, self-reliant men of affairs does not keep pace with the demand, hence the timidity of capital and the cry for more and still more Government assistance."[5]

All this is not surprising, in view of Japan's authoritarian background, her intense nationalism and the difficulty which any people face in moving out of a static, traditional economy into new and untried fields. More sur-prising is the speed with which the Japanese moved to take over the organ-ization and the skills necessary to modern industrialism. For example, while other peoples in Asia have shown no less aptitude for mechanical skills, the Japanese, aided by geographic circumstance, accomplished with unu-sual facility the great occupational and regional shifts in population which were no less important for industrialization. . . . Considering the age-old emphasis on status and conformity, and the attachment of the peasant family to the soil, one might have looked for much more inertia, if not active re-sistance, when it came to new modes of activity which put a premium on per-sonal initiative and dynamic change.

It appears, too, that the Japanese experienced less difficulty than most Oriental peoples in building and operating large-scale administrative struc-tures which would make effective use of the new skills and energies in modern business and government. Elsewhere in Asia, such structures have degenerated all too often into nightmares of nepotism, corruption, and ad-ministrative disorder. Japanese society, like Chinese society, was tradition-ally oriented on a family basis in considerable degree. But not in the same

[5] Charles V. Sale, "Some Statistics of Japan," *Journal of the Royal Statistical Society,* Vol. LXXIV, No. 5, April 1911, p. 472.

exclusive, atomistic fashion. The family obligation was qualified by, and ideally subordinate to, higher loyalties to one's overlord, and ultimately to the emperor. This helped not only to forge a new political unity after 1868, with the almost bloodless surrender by the feudal nobility of its traditional prerogatives, but also to create other new forms of social cooperation which functioned fairly efficiently.[6]

In the military realm, most vividly perhaps, one sees how Japan's feudal heritage helped her to take over modern patterns of large-scale administration. The modern Japanese Army has had its cliques and internal political intrigues. Yet it is interesting how quickly the Japanese created a centralized structure of command and general staff, based on German models, a modern system of technical training, and a practice of assigning new young officers on the basis of merit to responsible posts of command and administration. Their success in this regard, and the utter failure of the Chinese mandarinate under Li Hung-chang, gave Japan an easy victory over China in 1894-95. The same traits applied in the business world, in more qualified fashion, contributed greatly to the growth and efficiency of large financial and industrial organizations. They facilitated the adoption of joint-stock enterprise and the factory system. And they gave a degree of cohesion and order to the whole process of political and economic development which is one of the most striking features of modern Japan.

Yet respect for hierarchy, group discipline, and teamwork will not alone create modern industrialism. They may serve only to stifle it. One should beware of exaggerating this feature of Japanese modernization. It was an asset only insofar as it was accompanied by, and did not stultify, the ambition to advance through adopting new ways, and the willingness to adventure along new paths pioneered by leaders. Since it is so commonly stressed in accounts of Japanese industrialization, I have chosen rather to emphasize the factors of innovation and enterprise. Only slowly and unevenly did new value standards and technical capacities mature, of course. And they remained heavily qualified among the great mass of the people, especially in the more remote rural areas, away from the urban centers of change. Yet it was this process, advancing bit by bit through a wide range of occupations, which gave mass and momentum to Japan's economic advance.

THE STATE AND ECONOMIC GROWTH: CONCLUSIONS

The dynamics of Japan's economic development thus involved numerous elements of social organization, geographic circumstance, and histori-

[6] See Marion J. Levy, "Contrasting Factors in the Modernization of China and Japan," *Economic Development and Cultural Change,* Vol. II, No. 3, October 1953, pp. 161-97.

cal setting. Many of them are not difficult to observe in operation. But to evaluate and integrate all of them in a comprehensive theory of economic growth which really gets at the root of the matter is hardly to be attempted in the present state of knowledge. Perhaps, to quote Lionel Robbins again, it is better left to poets and metaphysicians.

One aspect of the matter in particular, the role of political forces operating through agencies of the State, has been examined in this chapter. The outlook, the energies, and the authority of the Meiji leaders were clearly of immense significance, leaving a deep imprint on the subsequent course of economic development.

Yet the picture which emerges does not show the State in the central planning and directing role often ascribed to it, so far as the principal areas of economic growth are concerned. Especially is this true of the period after 1890, when the great expansion took place. Certainly no sufficient explanation of Japan's industrial development can be found merely in the thesis that her political tradition endowed her with an authoritarian military caste which engineered the modernization and industrialization of their country as the means to national power.[7] The existence of a strong central government infused with imperial ambitions served in some respects to stimulate and facilitate the process; in other respects it operated as a decided drag; in still other respects it had little direct influence on what took place.

The truly signal contributions to economic growth which were made through the political mechanism were, first, to ward off foreign subjection and assure the nation's political unity and order; second, to clear away the whole complex of political obstacles to freedom of ownership, occupation, and movement; and third, to carry through a series of architectural reforms in law, education, taxation, currency, etc. which created a setting favorable to the emergence of new forms of productive enterprise. In the realm of industrial development, particularly, the government furnished more direct encouragements and even actual entrepreneurship during the earlier years. Yet its influences exerted here through the prewar decades were inconsistent and discriminatory in their total effect, so far as real economic growth was concerned.

While the Meiji State was absolutist in politics, it was not totalitarian. Its policies widened steadily the range of personal freedom and opportunity in economic life. Such opportunity remained closely circumscribed for most people, and freedom was all too often the freedom to be exploited by the moneylender and the landlord. On the other hand, the State never substituted political rewards and punishments for private incentives to material

[7] Nevertheless, for an interesting comparison between Japan and China in this respect see Hu Shih, "The Modernization of China and Japan: A Comparative Study in Cultural Conflict," *China Quarterly,* Vol. 5, No. 4, winter number, supplement, 1940, pp. 773-80.

gain. It enlarged the sphere of private ownership rather than government collectivization. It replaced a harsh and oppressive rule by feudal aristocrats with something which approached increasingly the modern standards of constitutional rule by law. The Japanese adopted Western technology much more readily than ideas of personal freedom; the latter remain heavily qualified to this day. Probably, too, the dependence of one on the other is less unconditional in the twentieth century than in the pioneering days before 1850. Yet it is significant that the Industrial Revolution in Japan, as in most of the West, was generated by such innovations as the abolition of heritable servitude, legal equality before the law, free choice of occupation and residence, and the construction of a new framework of security and opportunity within which private enterprise could develop.

Notwithstanding other, less constructive aspects of State policy, this framework made possible the building of a new national market for goods and capital, linked with the outside world through expanding trade. It encouraged that internal mobility of people among jobs and places which was so essential to economic growth and structural change. It provided a climate favorable to the cumulative advance of new investment and technical change. Other features of State encouragement and regulation reviewed earlier in this chapter were important in their respective spheres, of course. No one would say of Japan, as of nineteenth century Britain, that her industrial development "owed practically nothing to State aid."[8] But where State action contributed to the expansion of Japan's productive powers, and did not merely warp it in particular directions, or redistribute its benefits among classes, it served mainly to hasten and facilitate a process the chief motive force of which lay elsewhere.

The case of Japan is nevertheless significant, perhaps unique in Asia, in that political and social leadership throughout this period of transition was exercised by certain dominant groups who remained firmly in the saddle and were technologically progressive on the whole. These groups maintained their ascendency, accommodated their differences, and pursued their aims through a variety of social institutions and controls. Of these the political hierarchy was only one, although perhaps the most important.

Here, paradoxically, we may have the reason why direct State intervention in economic life was rather limited through most of the prewar period, judged by modern standards. Given the temper of Japan's leaders, their control over wealth, and the strength of the Japanese social fabric, it was unnecessary to rely on State coercion extensively to mobilize resources for industrialization. Moreover, while different elements of the ruling coalition—for example, the military and the *zaibatsu*—often had divergent interests, they found it possible for a long time to harmonize their differences in a political regime with limited economic responsibilities; and no popular

---

[8] L. C. A. Knowles, *The Industrial and Commercial Revolutions in Great Britain during the Nineteenth Century*, London, 1921, p. 171.

movement arose with sufficient power to wrest control and impose a different pattern.

Commenting on this point, Robert E. Ward raises more explicitly "the question whether or not reasonably effective national economic planning and the satisfactory implementation of large-scale developmental programs require the same degree of overt positive State participation in Japan—or perhaps in any major Oriental society—that the achievement of comparable results would necessitate in a Western society." He continues: "Making due allowance for the imperfection of the following categories, is it still not possible, in a Japanese cultural context characterized by a relatively homogeneous and continuous ruling class, a tradition of collective action and responsibility and some general pragmatic agreement that industrialization and economic development are desirable, that such informal oligarchic solidarity would of itself prove capable of achieving many of the results reflected by Japan's present stage of economic development? Such societies perhaps have more 'built-in social controls' than do more individualistically-structured ones. If so, this may somewhat explain the surprising moderation of the Japanese government in terms of formal participation in or the imposition of extensive controls on the national economy prior to the 1930's."[9]

It may well have been these circumstances which made Japan as responsive as she was to the liberal principles of economic organization current in the nineteenth century West, and enabled the system of private enterprise to prevail in such large degree for half a century. Significantly, it was only as internal tensions mounted after 1925, and as international tensions gathered throughout the world, that the State moved increasingly to take over direct control and management of the Japanese economy.

How far these circumstances prevail elsewhere today in Asia—or in postwar Japan itself—is less clear. As regards capital formation, for example, it may be doubted whether private initiative can do the job, or will be allowed to do it, in anything like the same degree. Many of the peoples of Asia are developing a set of social expectations and immediate demands such that they will probably be unwilling to tolerate the great inequalities of private property and income so patiently borne by the Japanese. Equally important, where income continues to be as unequally distributed as it is in, say, the Philippines, there is little evidence that the well-to-do class is disposed so largely as it was in prewar Japan to save and invest its money in creating new capital assets for productive enterprise.

A greater spirit of egalitarianism among the people, and a lack of entrepreneurial spirit among the owning class, where they prevail, will impel greater reliance on the State to mobilize capital and assume the risks

[9] Comments on this chapter submitted to the Conference on Economic Growth in Selected Countries, April 25-27, 1952, sponsored by the Social Science Research Council.

and responsibilities of economic development, if it is to take place on any scale. Also, the tradition of private enterprise is greatly weakened, where it has not been discarded altogether, in the West. Moreover, the internal cleavage and balance of forces in most countries of Asia are such as to create a more violent struggle for political power than in pre-1931 Japan. These factors accentuate still further the tendency to State intervention in economic life as a weapon for enforcing the will of the group which manages to seize control of the apparatus of government. Finally, international tension and insecurity in the East, no less than the West, work in the same direction.

So far as this holds true, the pattern of organization and entrepreneurship which produced such rapid economic growth in Japan can hardly be duplicated elsewhere in Asia. Whether this is for better or worse remains to be seen. From the standpoint of democracy and well-being, one would hope that some of the human costs and social injustices of the Japanese experience could be avoided. The dilemma appears to lie in the urgent demands being made on new, untried governments to produce large and impressive results, when these governments are so lacking in the very skills and standards of large-scale, responsible administration which the job requires. Perhaps, as in Japan, once a pattern of order and growth is established, an initial period of State leadership and control will give way later to a larger measure of private enterprise, with some dependable demarcation of their respective spheres. The tasks required of the State are crucial in all these countries. Yet it is hard to see how their economic development can be either rapid or sustained without the release of the spring of private initiative.

In any case the lessons of Japan are worth pondering. In two respects they are a warning. Unless population growth can be held in check, the mere increase in numbers will absorb much of the gain of development. And unless political institutions can be created to harness productive power to welfare goals, still more of the gain may be dissipated in war and conquest.

But there is also a more constructive lesson in Japan's experience. It testifies to the potential of one Asiatic people at least for assimilating the skills necessary to economic progress, once a framework and atmosphere are provided to give full play to their productive energies. If the history of modern Japan argues for vigorous leadership in economic development, it is a tribute no less to the capacities of the common people.

2. Japan's Economic Expansion: Achievements and Prospects

G. C. ALLEN

. . . Japan, having successfully overcome the difficulties caused by her immense material losses and the post-war disorganization of her economy, came within a few years to rank with the leading industrial countries of the world. Her 'recovery' may be said to have been accomplished by the middle 1950s. By then she had restored financial stability, rebuilt in large part her industrial and commercial organization, increased manufacturing output to twice that of the middle 1930s, and raised income a head above the pre-war level. An achievement of this magnitude was remarkable when viewed against the adversities with which the post-war world had afflicted her. Her traditionally intimate economic relations with North East Asia had been destroyed by territorial changes and political upheaval. Her former specialization in textiles proved to be ill suited to the demands of post-war markets. Her technology had been cut off from the sources of invention just when they were gushing copiously in the outside world. Meanwhile, her old centres of initiative had been dissolved, and resources for re-equipment were scarcer than ever at a moment when they were most urgently required.

There can be little wonder that the outlook was considered bleak. The rehabilitation of the economy called for qualities of resilience and energy which the Japanese, in their exhaustion and despair at the end of the war, seemed unlikely to command. Foreign opinion about Japan's capacity to find a successful issue from her troubles was for some years deeply pessimistic, largely because attention in the outside world was focused on the persistent weakness of the export trade. Up to 1955 the Japanese themselves shared this opinion. At that time they still spoke of themselves as 'marginal suppliers' of manufactures for international trade, and they feared that such recovery as had occurred was insecurely based on American 'special procurement' and on temporary shortages of capacity in competitor-countries.

From G. C. Allen, *Japan's Economic Expansion,* published by the Oxford University Press under the auspices of the Royal Institute of International Affairs (London, New York, Toronto, 1965), pp. 247-262. Reprinted by permission of the publisher.

The contrast in temper between that period and the early 1960s is striking. Pessimism and diffidence have given place to an easy self-confidence. The present mood can find ample justification. Since 1950 Japan has achieved a rate of growth which is the marvel and envy of the rest of the world.[1] She cannot claim to have enjoyed 'stable growth,' but at least she has been skilful in coping with the recurrent balance-of-payments crises which her rapid development has provoked, and she has so far avoided serious inflation.

In manufacturing industry, where her major successes have been won, she has found a new dimension. Her accomplishment is demonstrated not merely by the growth of industrial output as a whole but also in the wide extension of her range of products. Trades that went unremarked during the pre-war decade now rank among her largest industries, and several entirely new branches of manufacture have grown to great size. Many of her leading industries still rest on her resources of skilled and assiduous labour, but the most notable developments of the last seven or eight years have occurred in industries that depend on advanced technology. The result is that her industrial activities are now centred upon the production of metal, engineering, and chemical goods, including the latest innovations among them, and Japan has joined the company of the half a dozen countries which are responsible for the bulk of these products. Among the leaders her position has constantly improved. For instance, in the non-Communist world she has lately come to occupy the second place in steel production; she is the largest producer of ships and of some kinds of electrical apparatus; she is second only to the United States as a manufacturer of synthetic fibres. In the generation of electric power and the production of finished textiles, machinery (including machine tools), motor vehicles, plastics, and certain kinds of chemicals, she holds rank with the four or five largest producing countries.

It has been claimed that in the recovery of the economy during its initial stages Japan owed a heavy debt to fortune. No one can deny that the Korean War and the sustained 'special procurement' demand gave an immense stimulus to industry, especially to the heavy trades, and that they presented Japan with exceptionally favourable opportunities for acquiring foreign exchange essential for reconstruction. Indeed, the American demand for Japan's goods and services that was called into being by the political situation in the Far East may be said to have offset the damaging effects of the loss of trade with North East Asia, itself the consequence of the same train of events. Then in the middle 1950s, a further stimulus was administered by the world investment boom, and as this was accompanied

---

[1] Between 1950 and 1960 the annual rate of growth of GNP (in real terms) is estimated to have been 9.5 per cent for Japan, 7.6 per cent for West Germany, 5.9 per cent for Italy, 4.3 per cent for France, 3.3 per cent for the US, and 2.7 per cent for the UK (UN, *Yb. of National Accounts Statist., 1962*).

by a large demand for ships, especially tankers, it brought expansion to a sector of industry in which Japan's competitive position had hitherto been undistinguished. Finally, at the end of 1956, the Suez crisis for a short period conferred considerable advantages on Japan in her competition with Western producers in Asian markets.

Fortune has certainly shown Japan her engaging and amiable aspect. Yet even in the early post-war period her favours would have availed little without good management, and for the accelerated development of the last seven or eight years other explanations must be sought. They have been discussed in earlier chapters, and at this point the factors mainly responsible need only be listed. They are:

1. The closing of the technical gap by the import of new technology.
2. An exceptionally high rate of investment buttressed by a very high rate of saving, both institutional and personal.
3. The direction of investment into uses which yielded quick returns and the absence of wasteful investment in armaments.
4. The large reserve army of workers at the beginning of the period of growth and the successful transference of huge numbers from low-productivity to high productivity occupations.
5. The reconstruction of the *Zaibatsu* and the creation of other business groups capable of organizing development.
6. A monetary system and policy which were successful both in providing industries with the finance needed for expansion and also in cutting back credit quickly whenever the economy became 'overheated.'
7. A taxation system which kept clear of measures likely to curb industrial investment and damage personal incentives.
8. The effective use of official controls over foreign trade and payments.

The outside world may wonder whether the convergence of so many factors favourable to growth is likely to persist, and this question must certainly be examined. Before embarking on such speculation, however, some other comments on Japan's economic experience are necessary. First, it should be emphasized that Japan today possesses one of the most highly competitive economies in the world. This characteristic is revealed most obviously by the conduct of small and medium-sized firms in manufacturing industry and distribution, but it is also present among large-scale enterprises. Indeed, the fierce rivalry among oligopolists has undoubtedly been responsible for much of the breathless innovation and lavish investment in new equipment during the last few years. The progress of Japan, the flexibility of her costs and prices, and her quick adaptation to economic change owe much to these conditions. Yet keen competition and the boisterous struggles of free enterprise are not there associated with *laissez-faire*. On the contrary the government in regulating, guiding, and directing the economy, during the post-war period as in the past, has made an essential contribution to the achievement. The public sector itself is small by modern standards. Many industries which in the majority of Western countries are under State ownership, in Japan are in private hands. Nevertheless, the government has made constant use of a number of powerful instruments in shaping the economy, e.g. the official banks which direct capital resources into the preferred fields, fiscal devices, foreign trade controls, and 'indicative planning.'

This combination of free enterprise and government control imposed at key points in the economy has been a familiar feature of Japan since early Meiji. Throughout the modern era up to the Second World War responsibility for development and innovation had been shared between the State and the *Zaibatsu*. During the war economic authority became more highly centralized in the government, and the eclipse of the *Zaibatsu* after 1945 and the circumstances of the Occupation confirmed this concentration. For a time private entrepreneurial initiative seemed to have lost direction and purpose. After 1952, however, the broad pattern of leadership in industry and commerce was redrawn. While the government, aided by a highly competent bureaucracy, steadily gained assurance and skill in its administration of economic policy, some of the economic empires of the past were reorganized and other powerful centres of initiative arose. In this way the forms of economic direction were restored and its efficiency augmented.

Responsibility for reconstruction was, of course, shared with the Americans. For over six years after the end of the war the Occupation authorities were in control of policy, and even after 1952 the United States government exerted a powerful influence upon it. In certain respects, the effect of the intervention, at any rate in the early post-war period, may have been to retard recovery; but on balance there can be no doubt that the American association with Japan's affairs during the Occupation period conferred signal benefits upon her. Without the aid so abundantly provided between 1945 and 1951, Japan would almost certainly have sunk deeper into economic chaos. The same conclusion applies to the subsequent period when, although her trading enterprise was handicapped by limitations imposed by the United States on her dealings with China, she enjoyed the advantage of a vast dollar expenditure at a critical stage of her reconstruction. Then in 1960 the flow of private American capital began.

Of the reforms introduced by the Americans, and of their continuing influence on the economy, it is more difficult to make a just appraisal. SCAP has been accused of impercipience in its effort to impose American ideals on a society where they were little esteemed, and of obtuse benevolence in trying by administrative measures to remove blemishes in social arrangements which were the manifestations of deep-rooted economic disabilities. Yet whatever may have been the immediate effect of the reforms in thwarting recovery and provoking social tensions, the enduring consequences were by no means deleterious. The reforms which were out of tune with Japan's purposes could not, and did not, long survive the end of the Occupation. This does not mean that any of the social and economic institutions or relationships were restored to precisely their old form. The American impress was nowhere completely obliterated, nor did the Japanese themselves wish that it should be. But we have shown how in several spheres of national life (notably in industrial and financial organization) the reforms soon yielded to the policy of the 'reverse course.' On the other hand, not all of them were equally fragile. Some were acceptable to the Japanese and could readily be assimilated, even though they might not have been undertaken on native initiative. The Land Reform can be quoted as an outstanding example. It is true that the conditions of tenure that it created are now proving detrimental to agricultural progress. But in the early post-war years the Reform certainly made some contribution to efficiency besides exerting a stabilizing social influence at a critical time. Again, many of the innovations in labour relations have survived intact. Here the result was to bring into existence, by edict, a code of industrial relations and a trade union movement which might otherwise have taken many years to evolve.

The initiative came from without, but even during the Occupation success in formulating and administering the reforms depended closely on the co-operation of the Japanese authorities and individuals. Where this co-operation was accorded, the reforms endured. Where there was opposition, they were fugitive. As in earlier times the Japanese showed themselves ready to tread new paths once they were convinced that the route led towards national well-being, as they conceived it. They certainly did not offer a sullen resistance to the zeal of the reformers merely because the latter were foreigners in occupation of Japanese territory.

The Occupation period during which the foundations of future growth were laid can now be viewed in perspective. Even the most censorious foreign commentator must pay tribute to the generosity of the Americans in providing resources for rebuilding Japan's economy, and to their enthusiasm, if not their tact, in reshaping her institutions. And when Americans themselves are reflecting glumly on the great stream of dollar aid which maladministration or corruption, in one recipient country after another, has allowed to run to waste, they can perhaps find some solace in recalling one Asian protégé who has used their benefactions to good effect. For their part in these transactions the Japanese also deserve credit. They showed a sure political instinct in their readiness to co-operate in the institutional innovations imposed by the victors. A people less opportunist in temper and less adroitly governed might well have rejected the chance of testing the merits of what the Americans had devised for them. Since on balance the innovations were instrumental in promoting both economic and social progress, the Japanese were rewarded for their inspired empiricism.

No one acquainted with their history is likely to be surprised at their acquiescence on this occasion. The Japanese have never hesitated to use foreign models when they have been devising institutional constructions apt for some new national purpose. They have always welcomed novelties and have then proceeded to adapt them to their needs. This process can be seen at work throughout the post-war period. On the other hand, identities with the past are more numerous than is sometimes supposed. We have observed these in our examination of financial organization and monetary policy. It was shown in Chapter IV that throughout the modern era Japan has been inclined to follow a boldly expansionist policy. The result was that for long periods she found herself on the verge of inflation, with her balance of payments frequently precarious. But the situation was never allowed to get out of hand, at any rate up to the outbreak of the Second World War. Short periods of ruthless deflation punctuated the general expansionist tendency.

The post-war period reproduced these experiences. We have described how the violent inflation of the late 1940s was brought to an abrupt end by the Dodge deflation. This measure was, of course, imposed by the Occupation. But the Japanese authorities themselves were responsible for the successful policies of 1954 and 1958. On both these occasions the deflationary measures prepared the way for the forward surge in production that followed. The more limited success that attended similar measures in 1962 may foreshadow a time when different methods of monetary control will have to be employed. It is ironical that at a moment when Europeans are ready to do obeisance to Japan's skill in handling her monetary problems, the Japanese (or at least the financial authorities) profess themselves increasingly dissatisfied with their own methods and are inclining towards what in this country are regarded as the conventional instruments of monetary policy.

The dissatisfaction has its roots in the fundamental changes to which the economy has been subjected. The success of the existing policy has depended in large measure on two conditions, first the flexibility of Japan's costs in response to financial pressure, and secondly the powerful official controls over foreign transactions. The first of these conditions is threatened by the growing shortage of labour and the approximation of employment conditions in large-scale and small-scale industry. The second can hardly survive the policy of liberalizing trade. The consequences of the change may be momentous. Japan has not hitherto felt nervous at times of extraordinarily rapid growth because she has had at hand effective weapons for dealing with a crisis. Should these weapons become blunted the whole policy of rapid economic growth might have to be reconsidered, especially as it may not be easy for Japan to operate the conventional measures of continuous monetary control if the existing measures of spasmodic control should fail her.

Yet the problem itself is largely the consequence of her success in carrying development to the point at which the barriers between the two parts of the dual economy have crumbled. Up to the middle 1950s Japan inhabited two worlds. To the Asian she appeared as a modern state masquerading as undeveloped; to the Westerner, and to many Japanese themselves, it was the vestigial remains of a pre-industrial society that were most prominent. Peasant agriculture, though far more efficient than elsewhere in Asia and yielding higher financial returns than before the war, was still over-stocked with labour. The same was true of the great mass of very small units in manufacturing industry and the service trades where (though by no means universally) productivity, incomes, and conditions of work compared unfavourably with those of large modern establishments. In manufacturing industry these contrasts are fast disappearing, with consequences already described. In other sectors also the dichotomy is becoming less and less obvious. It was once usual to contrast the efficient and up-to-date railway and shipping services with the ill-developed system of motor transport, handicapped as it was (and still is) by the primitive roads. The proposed heavy investment in both urban and trunk roads may well remove this contrast by the end of the present decade. In distribution the most casual observer was impressed by the coexistence in the great cities of the huge departmental stores and the multitude of family shops with a minute turnover. The distributive trade as a whole is now on the eve of a transformation brought about by the introduction of supermarkets, and many of the small shops are likely to disappear in the years ahead. Again, the premises occupied by large industrial, financial, and commercial concerns are indistinguishable from their counterparts in the West, and the most recently built are impressively well-equipped. Yet throughout the country the standard of housing accommodation remains exceedingly low.[2] This contrast may persist for many years, but the present Income Doubling Plan, which looks forward to a substantial increase in housing investment, should gradually make it less glaring. Thus throughout all branches of the economy there is a trend towards uniformity.

In the past Japanese economists were much preoccupied with the problem of 'disguised unemployment' or 'underemployment' in the small-scale sectors of industry, agriculture, and the service trades. This condition had been associated with the insufficiency and biased distribution of capital in a society in which the labour supply was rapidly increasing. Throughout the modern era a high proportion of new fixed investment was directed into a narrow range of industries, mainly those concerned with capital and intermediate goods, where for technical reasons factor-propor-

[2] The Japanese point out that people who are comfortable at work but uncomfortable at home have every inclination to 'keep at it.'

tions were rigid. The result was that agriculture and most of the consumption-goods industries and service trades, where factor proportions were elastic, attracted comparatively little investment, and they were left to absorb, in low-productivity occupations, a large share of the increasing labour supply.[3] Such a distribution of capital was probably justified in a period when rapid development depended on the establishment of basic industries, especially those concerned with power and transport. It has been argued, however, that in the early 1950s an excessively high proportion of the new investment was directed by the government and its financial agencies towards a few large-scale undertakings. The productivity of Japanese industry as a whole might have benefited if the smaller establishments had been able to obtain improved equipment and to gain readier access to new techniques. However this may be, it is evident that as soon as the demands by large-scale industry for labour became of such a magnitude as to absorb the bulk of the recruits to the labour market and also to draw off the surplus workers from agriculture, the problem of underemployment was on the way to solution. Once the small firms were forced to pay rates of wages as high as those in the large firms, they could survive only by modernizing their methods and so raising their productivity. The same forces at work in agriculture have led to a substitution of capital for labour to an extent unimaginable only a few years ago. It is true that Japan by the standards of industrial Western countries still retains a high proportion of its occupied population in the primary industries and in small-scale industry and trade. For some years to come she will have reserves to draw upon (more particularly, reserves of female labour), and they will help to sustain her rate of growth. But the time when massive and apparently inexhaustible reserves were available has gone.

With this discussion as a background, we can now return to the question posed earlier in this chapter. Are the factors which produced the rapid development of the last decade likely to operate during the rest of the 1960s as powerfully as in the past? The short answer is that the effect of some of these factors is weakening and that further success depends upon the solution of hitherto familiar problems. Let us consider the list of factors on page 289 from this point of view.

First, the great technological advance through the assimilation of foreign inventions and processes is virtually complete and Japan must henceforth rely increasingly, though not, of course, exclusively, on her own innovations. Secondly, so far as investment is concerned, we have seen that its direction is now changing. Whereas in the 1950s most of it went into industrial equipment, in the present decade a high proportion is being turned into the infrastructure. The latter kind of investment will add much

---

[3] Cf. K. Ohkawa, 'Economic Growth and Agriculture,' Ann. Hatotzubashi Acad., Oct. 1956, pp. 56-60.

to the efficiency of the economy[4] as well as to social amenity, but most of it will not yield returns as quickly as investment in industrial machinery. Up to the present it has been possible to maintain a high rate of investment without the risk of inflation because of the high rate of savings. With the recently awakened desire of the people to acquire such goods as refrigerators, television sets, and motor vehicles, which are now heavily advertised in the home market, the propensity to save may possibly decline to an extent that more than counter-balances the rise in personal incomes.[5] The combination of an increased propensity to consume together with a reduction in the rate of investment in industrial plant may affect the rate of growth during the next few years. On the other hand, some Japanese economists are of the opinion that during the present decade a high rate of growth can be sustained only by a great expansion of expenditure on consumers' capital goods, since otherwise the volume of effective demand will be inadequate. They may be right. But if such expenditure must be relied on increasingly as the agent of rapid growth, then the adverse effect on savings may release the danger of inflation.[6] Of this the rapid rise in prices during the last two years may be a symptom. In other words, the rate of growth that can be contemplated without excessive risk may be lower than in the immediate past.

We have already emphasized certain significant changes in the third factor (the supply of underemployed workers available for transference to high-productivity occupations). The transformation in the labour market lies, indeed, at the foundation of the new order that is now emerging. The labour shortage is likely to affect profits and private investment by closing the gap between the growth of productivity and the rise of wages that was a prominent feature of the 1950s. The narrowing wage-differentials foreshadow the demise of the dual economy. The decline in wage plasticity may well reduce economic resilience and complicate the process of correcting disequilibrium. Hitherto, as we have seen, inflation has been effectively controlled by restraints on demand. If the problem of 'cost-push' should present itself for solution, Japan may not be so well equipped to deal with it. When wage settlements are local and particular, and when earnings differ widely for the same occupation, the introduction of a national wages or incomes policy encounters peculiar difficulties. For these and other reasons, the new conditions in the labour market are likely to

---

[4] For example, investment in improved means of transport will not only reduce the direct costs of distribution but will also lead to economies by making it possible for manufacturers and merchants to hold smaller stocks; hitherto the investment in stocks has been very high.

[5] Within recent years a slight decline in saving habits has in fact been detected (EPA, *Econ. Survey, 1963-4,* pp. 274-7).

[6] The monetary authorities will probably find greater difficulty in controlling this type of expenditure than they have hitherto found in controlling investment.

provoke a resolute attack on some of the most cherished features of Japanese industrial relations, namely, the 'lifelong engagement' system and the method of payment by seniority. Such an attack (and already it is being mounted), might have serious social repercussions. It is also probable that many of the self-employed (e.g. farmers, small manufacturers, and shopkeepers) who find difficulty in adapting themselves to economic change may react vigorously against it. Pressure from these quarters might well retard the redistribution of labour unless the government were ready to provide compensation payments or subsidies to assist migration to other occupations. A solution of this problem may become more difficult because of other changes which are now only just beyond the horizon of Japan's experience. The age of automation is now treading on the heels of the full-employment era with social consequences that may be as momentous for Japan as for other countries. It is, however, a matter of speculation whether automation in the course of the next decade will reverse the present trends in the labour market to the detriment of all those not already installed in the comfortable security of the great concerns.

Finally, we must refer to the controls until recently exercised over foreign trade and payments. The controls made it easier for the Japanese authorities to drive their economy ahead in the knowledge that powerful weapons were in their hands for dealing with any disequilibrium in the balance of payments that might accompany very rapid growth. Now, with the controls abandoned, the authorities must watch any oscillations in the balance of payments with apprehension, and they must adopt a more cautious attitude towards the 'overheating' of the economy. Their anxiety will not be relieved by the growing deficit in the balance of invisible payments. Another aspect of liberalization deserves comment. The control over imports meant that certain new industries, despite fierce inter-firm rivalries, were not exposed to foreign competition. Hence their methods of production and forms of organization have sometimes been inefficient from an international standpoint. One of the chief defects has been the lack of plant specialization. The liberalization of trade is now enforcing reorganization on the most vulnerable industries, and it is reasonable to suppose that the problem will soon be solved. Rationalization may sometimes be impeded by inter-group rivalries, but in some industries these are being overcome by the growth of *Kombinats*.

It is clear that in many respects Japan has entered upon a new phase in her economic development. While it seems that she will easily achieve the goals set by the Income Doubling Plan, some of the factors which contributed most powerfully to growth are weakening or are changing their form, and certain industrial and social relationships intimately associated with Japanese enterprise are now being modified. The revolution in agriculture, the disappearance of the dual economy, the change in the nature of investment and personal expenditure, the liberalization of trade, the new financial and monetary problems, all these are calling into being a new kind of economy. The time is in sight when some of the most familiar contrasts between Japan and the West will have faded, and as the changes described gather strength Japan is likely to meet with difficulties of choice in the field of social as well as of economic policy similar to those that have long perplexed Western countries.

Neither her recent successes nor her capacity for dealing with the problems that lie ahead can be assessed solely in economic terms. The proximate forces responsible for the high felicity of her economic achievement are not difficult to identify and to analyse. But observers of the process of development are tempted to extend their curiosity towards the deeper springs of this unique accomplishment. It may perhaps be rewarding to refer briefly to the social and political conditions that made possible the emergence of Japan as a modern State in early Meiji, and underlay her subsequent achievement, and then to consider how far those conditions have persisted into the present era. The causes of the early development may be summarized as, first, a political and social system that presented opportunities for the exercise of leadership to persons (private individuals or bureaucrats) whose interests lay in promoting economic change; secondly, an inheritance of organizing capacity and skill; and finally, institutional arrangements conducive to the rapid accumulation of capital. The society that satisfied these conditions was hierarchical, drawing its leaders mainly from a privileged class constantly invigorated by the entry of men of talent from outside its ranks. When, by a conjunction of political and social changes, the leaders were enlisted on the side of modernization and economic development, they found in the mass of the people, long trained in obedience to authority, a ready instrument to their hand. There was a fine legacy of skill in textiles and metal manufactures, and certain family businesses had a long experience of large-scale organization. The capital accumulation required for development was a function of the unequal distribution of income characteristic of that type of society and of the propensity of the wealthy to apply their savings to industrial and commercial development. The taxation system which succeeded the old feudal arrangements was very regressive, pressing lightly on high personal and corporate incomes and harshly on the peasants. These conditions persisted with comparatively little modification up to the Second World War.

The war, the inflation, and the post-war reforms destroyed powerful sections of the oligarchy, chiefly the military cliques and the rural landlords. These formed, however, the most conservative or reactionary element in society, elements which in Japanese opinion were largely responsible for the catastrophe of 1945. The dismissal of the chief 'architects of ruin' still left power highly concentrated and, in spite of the growth of parliamentary institutions, the leadership of the official and business oligarchies has not yet been seriously disturbed. Labour organizations have arisen and their economic foundations, once weak, have been strengthened by the changes in the labour market. But the political side of the movement has not yet acquired the power that it has long enjoyed in Britain and other European countries. On the other hand the mood of the people has changed. They now breathe the air of freedom. They are less pliable than in the past and more concerned with enjoying the amenities of life which prosperity has presented to them. The release of energy by the social and political reforms immediately after the Second World War probably deserves a high place among the causes of growth.

It will be generally conceded that the progress that began in the Meiji era cannot be explained solely in terms of economic calculation. As in all great movements in human affairs, in the material no less than in other aspects of national life, an element of grandeur was present, a touch of the idealism which, as Alfred Marshall said, 'can generally be detected at the root of any great outburst of practical energy.' In Japan it was patriotic fervour that supplied the impulse to achievement and at the same time made it possible for her to undergo massive material changes without the disruption of social unity. In the end this sentiment was polluted and drove the country to a disastrous indulgence in military aggression. Present-day Japanese have been deeply affected by this experience and have displayed new powers of self-criticism. Yet self-criticism is more likely to chill the ardour of ambition than to inspire practical endeavour. It cannot furnish a clue to the enterprise and self-confident leadership of recent years. Where, then, is an explanation to be found? Japanese writers, teachers, and politicians lament that their country has failed to discover a new source of inspiration or a strong unifying purpose. One may suggest to them that a certain ideological scepticism is to be expected of the victims of an age of faith, and it may be that material progress itself has proved to be a sufficiently absorbing pursuit. Perhaps the explanation is that the challenge presented to Japan after her defeat was of a kind that called forth the full energies of her people and concentrated them on economic achievement. The disaster that had overtaken her former policy was so complete that she was impelled to set out on a new course undistracted by regrets for past ambitions. She may have been fortunate in being left with only a single rational choice in 1945, the acceptance of temporary political subordination and co-operation with her victors in economic rehabilitation. Once she had crossed that threshold she seems to have allowed no regret for the past to haunt her journey into the new world. In this she may be contrasted with Britain, where to a large extent the challenge presented to the nation by post-war problems went unremarked in the confusion of voices, where economically progressive courses received conventional deference rather than the assent of conviction, and where the imperialist past, though outgrown, was still remembered with pleasure.

It cannot be claimed that Japan has entirely escaped internal conflict.

She has suffered from numerous and occasionally prolonged industrial disputes. There have been a few occasions of civic disorder. Political stability, although never so far seriously threatened, is not invulnerable to the struggles of factions over Japan's foreign policy in regard to the United States and China, or to the propaganda of new right-wing parties such as that supported by the *Soka Gakkai,* a movement representing those who have failed to share in the benefits of recent progress. As elsewhere, the war interposed a screen between old ways and the new, between the conventions of the middle-aged and the aspirations of the young, and this screen has become more opaque with the years. In academic circles Marxist ideas have enjoyed a vogue and the Communist Party, though small, has been assertive. The history of modern Japan suggests, however, that the ready acceptance of intellectual and political fashions does not necessarily have much effect on conduct among a people who are inclined to esteem administrative efficiency more highly than political principles. Nevertheless it would be rash to predict that extremist movements on the left or the right would not enlist considerable support in the event of any deterioration in economic conditions or of a rebuff from outside. But so far, despite the crumbling of many institutions and conventions once regarded as part of the essential fabric of Japanese life, social unity has been maintained unimpaired.

Japan today moves with assurance among the most progressive nations of the world. But the problems which are now emerging out of the revolutionary economic changes of the last decade are different in kind from those which have previously confronted her. Their solution will make heavy demands on her resources of administrative ingenuity, political wisdom, and social tact. The problems, economic and political, are for the most part those with which advanced industrial societies have long been familiar. Japan has taken her place with them and now shares their perplexities. It is yet another question to ask how far the transformation in her economic life will permit the survival of the more graceful qualities of the old Japan—the fine manners, the etiquette that relieves the acerbities of personal relations in a materialistic society, the aesthetic traditions, the strong sense of reciprocal obligation among individuals that corresponds to the recognition of public duty in the West. To such a question, which is similar to that posed in all countries during periods of rapid economic progress, no easy answer can be found. There are Japanese who turn a cold eye on the past and view ancestral institutions and conventions with indifference or distaste. But others have been able to combine a liberal and modern outlook with respect for aesthetic and social traditions. One can at least hope that their influence will prevail.

3. *Japan's Economic Cooperation With the Developing Countries*

SHIGEO HORIE

. . . Although Japan may be an "advanced" nation, in not a few aspects, such as her agriculture and her medium and small enterprises, she might also be styled a "semi-advanced" nation. She accordingly finds it difficult to fall in with the demands of the developing nations where questions such as primary products and preferential treatment are concerned. Moreover, co-operation in the provision of funds also raises serious difficulties, both because of the still considerable gap between the level of income in Japan and in the West and because of the scanty accumulation of capital in Japan. For reasons such as these, the current international calls for co-operation put the Japanese economy in something of a tight spot.

At the same time, the favorable turn in Japan's trade balance which occurred in late 1965 and early 1966—which will be taken as an indicator of the increasing ability of the Japanese economy to compete on the international scene—will almost certainly serve to step up demands for aid from abroad, and make it difficult for Japan to cite the special factors mentioned above as justification for her receiving exceptional treatment.

It also goes without saying that successful economic development of the developing countries and their achievement of economic independence would obviously further the harmonious development of the world economy as a whole, and that any excessive gap in economic development between the advanced and developing nations would, equally obviously, be detrimental to the political and economic stability of the world, so that economic co-operation given by the advanced nations to the developing nations can be considered essential. Such being the case, while the developing nations themselves must also be required to make the basic effort to help themselves, it is clear that the advanced nations, acting in close collaboration, must press ahead steadily with co-operation, and that exceptions cannot be allowed.

In Japan's case in particular, her position as the only advanced nation in Asia, and her experience in having achieved economic development at

Condensed from Shigeo Horie, "Economic Co-operation with the Developing Countries," *Japan Quarterly*, April-June 1966, pp. 172-179. Reprinted by permission of the author and the publisher.

a great speed from a previous state of under-development, make it natural that she should assume a leading role where economic co-operation with Asia is concerned.

Recently . . . international interest in the development of Asia has been rising. The Asian zone is not merely crowded and underdeveloped, with a generally low economic level, but political differences hinder the development of any sense of regional solidarity. With such a state of affairs in Asia, it is a matter of rejoicing for Japan, too, that such international interest should be shown in promoting the development of the area. She herself must extend the scope of her economic co-operation, particularly in the Asian area, and work for the development of trade and the economy on both sides.

The improvement, both qualitatively and quantitatively, of Japan's economic co-operation should mean, not merely going along subserviently with the world trend, but positive and unmistakably Japanese economic co-operation such as can bring about an improvement in quality and quantity.

SUGGESTIONS FOR ECONOMIC CO-OPERATION

By now, the Japanese are already fully aware of the need for economic co-operation with the developing countries. The question facing the country now is, rather, how to expand and put into practice this co-operation as effectively as possible. At the same time, the very fact that this stage has been reached makes it all the more necessary, I feel, to reconsider those ways of co-operation which have already become obsolete.

In the first place, the criticism has often been heard abroad that Japanese economic co-operation is too commercial and calculating, aiming at promoting Japanese exports and reaping commercial profits without including any real "aid" at all. And it is true, indeed, that apart from reparations it has consisted largely of deferred payment credit for Japanese exports. However, this is closely bound up with the fact that Japanese co-operation is inspired largely by purely economic motives, and not by military or even political considerations.

In Japan's case it is, basically, nongovernmental businessmen and exporters who have been responsible for promoting economic co-operation. The only areas in which the Government could make its own policy aims felt were pure gifts such as reparations and technological co-operation, and direct loans. In other areas, nongovernmental initiative was essential in getting things going, and government organizations merely encouraged and complemented it.

Thus the assurance that something would pay commercially was an essential prerequisite: however desirable the Government might think certain measures to be in the light of political and economic relations with the other countries, they were unlikely to win the support necessary from business circles so long as there was any doubt as to their profitability.

Now, however, developments in the international situation have made it impossible to remain satisfied with the way co-operation is being carried on at the moment simply on the grounds that Japan is a free country. What is more, Japanese trade depends heavily on markets in these countries, and the expansion of trade with them—especially the import of primary products—is in this sense an important question which also links up with the maintenance of Japan's export markets.

More specifically, there is the question of the present one-way trade with Africa and the Near and Middle East, to remedy which Japan has received strong requests from the countries concerned that she should purchase their primary products. The need for some solution is becoming pressing, and, particularly when one considers the international pressure on Japan already discussed above, constitutes one of the greatest problems she has to deal with at the moment.

Admittedly, co-operation in the form of aid and co-operation as part of a policy for promoting exports stand in a mutually interdependent international relationship, nor is it always possible clearly to distinguish between the two sets of motives. Nevertheless, it is still necessary to make a clear distinction between them where basic policy is concerned. To do so would accord with the general trend in the world today, and also serve to resolve international misunderstanding of Japan's behavior.

What is still more basic, however, is the need for Japan to establish some consistent policy on economic co-operation. In so far as one-way trade with the developing countries is not confined to the present, but is quite likely to develop in the future also, this need should speak for itself. . . .

SUGGESTED READING

Allen, C. G., *Japan's Economic Expansion.* New York: Oxford, 1965.

Beardsley, Richard K. (ed.), *Studies on Economic Life in Japan.* Ann Arbor: University of Michigan Press, 1964.

De Vos, George A., "Achievement Orientation, Social Self-Identity, and Japanese Growth." *Asian Survey,* Vol. V, No. 12 (December 1965).

Fairbank, John K., Reischauer, Edwin O., Craig, Albert M., *East Asia: The Modern Transformation.* Tokyo: Charles E. Tuttle; Boston: Houghton Mifflin, 1965.

Horie, Y., "The Role of the *IE* (House) in the Economic Modernization of Japan." *Kyoto University Economic Review* (April 1966).

Hoshii, Iwao, *The Economic Challenge to Japan.* Tokyo and Philadelphia: Orient/West Inc., 1964.

Ike, Nobutaka, "Japan, Twenty Years After Surrender." *Asian Survey,* Vol. VI, No. 1 (January 1966).

Jacobs, Norman, "The Institutional Approach to Japanese Economic Development." *Asian Survey,* Vol. V, No. 9 (September 1965).

Jansen, Marius (ed.), *Changing Japanese Attitudes Toward Modernization.* Studies in the Modernization of Japan, No. 1, Association for Asian Studies, Princeton, N.J.: Princeton University Press, 1965.

Japan: For A Better Understanding of Her Economy. Tokyo: Japan Economic Research Institute, 1966.

Japan's Growing Role in Development Assistance. Washington, D.C.: United States–Japan Trade Council, 1967.

Johnston, B. F., "Agriculture and Economic Development: The Relevance of the Japanese Experience." *Food Research Institute Studies,* Vol. 6, No. 3 (1966).

Lockwood, W. W. (ed.), *The State and Economic Enterprise in Japan.* Studies in the Modernization of Japan, No. 2, Association for Asian Studies, Princeton, N.J.: Princeton University Press, 1966.

McDiarmid, O. J., "The Rapid Economic Growth of Japan and Israel." *Population Review,* Vol. 10, No. 2 (July 1966).

Silberman, Bernard S., "The Bureaucracy and Economic Development in Japan." *Asian Survey,* Vol. V, No. 11 (November 1965).

Taira, K., "Participation by Workers' and Employers' Organizations in Economic Planning in Japan." *International Labour Review,* Vol. 94, No. 6 (December 1966).

Takane, Masaaki, "Economic Growth and the 'End of Ideology' in Japan." *Asian Survey,* Vol. V, No. 6 (June 1965).

Tsuneishi, Warren M., *Japanese Political Style: An Introduction to the Government and Politics of Modern Japan.* New York: Harper & Row, 1966.

Yamamura, Kozo, *Economic Policy in Postwar Japan: Growth versus Economic Democracy.* Berkeley: University of California Press, 1968.

INDIA

India is trying to combine what many observers believe to be the two great incompatibles: political democracy and take-off from poverty. The result to date has been mixed. There has been considerable if unspectacular progress in many areas, notably in education and public health. Output of agriculture has risen significantly, spurred by rising productivity; and industrial production has doubled in the last decade. There has been an important broadening of the industrial structure with notable successes in the transportation sector. A brave attempt has been made to promote exports in order to pay for the imports needed for industrialization. Most important, there seems to be a willingness on the part of those responsible for economic policy to learn from past mistakes. One of the major lessons taken to heart is the urgent need for greater self-reliance, implying a more intensive utilization of the economy's latent resources. But there have also been serious failures and disappointments: in planning and in the conflict between principles and practice. Political instability, commodity shortages, continuing poverty, and a growing backlog of unemployment have been India's constant companions since independence.

Both the achievements and the many failures are examined in Dilip Mukerjee's essay on "India's Painful Experiment." Mukerjee's insistence on the shortcomings of Indian planning, with all the cultural, political, and bureaucratic implications, is developed in the second selection, Wayne Wilcox's study of "Politicians, Bureaucrats, and Development in India." Sidney Klein and Wilfred Malenbaum clash, in the last two selections, on a somewhat different issue: the comparison between the performance of India and her political, ideological, and military antagonist, Communist China. Klein's thesis is that India's performance in this respect is probably as creditable as China's. This proposition is challenged by Malenbaum who, moreover, concludes that China's prospects for the future are more favorable than those of India.

1. India's Painful Experiment

DILIP MUKERJEE

Just about everything has gone wrong in India. Agriculture has suffered a severe setback as a result of the worst drought in 70 years. Industries are grinding to a halt for want of materials and components; many of
them have had no import licences for the past 12 months. The upswing in
exports has petered out, while imports have risen sharply with more food
and fertiliser being brought in to avert disaster. As a consequence, the payments deficit has widened alarmingly and put the *rupee* under heavy
pressure.

The crisis has hit the man in the street with shortages and high prices.
Rationing and "fair price" shops touch only the fringe of the problem; their
coverage is too small. What is more, the Government is having a hard time
keeping them supplied with stocks of anything other than PL 480 wheat
from the US. The great bulk of the consumers are at the mercy of the free
market on which a kilogram of rice costs more than a labourer's daily wage
in the deficit areas. There are other shortages too (kerosene for instance).
It was a students' procession demanding kerosene (so that they might get
on with preparations for year-end examinations) that touched off the rioting and violence which engulfed the Calcutta area for several days in
March.

The dimensions of the rioting were something new. Gone for good is
the fear of authority ingrained in the national consciousness during 150
years of colonial rule. In many urban areas these days, the policeman with
his baton no longer strikes awe. He is more often the object of derision to
young men who are becoming increasingly adept at building barricades,
uprooting rail and telephone lines, and more ominously, at matching hand-
made bombs against police rifles.

On top of this general unrest has come an upsurge of self-assertive-
ness among several minority groups. The Nagas, who have been up in arms
for over ten years, constitute something of a special case. Their separatism
reflects the fears of an isolated religious and cultural minority. But the

From Dilip Mukerjee, "India's Painful Experiment," *Far Eastern Economic
Review,* May 5, 1966, pp. 248-253. Reprinted by permission of the publisher.

uprising of the neighbouring Mizos, the outbreak among the tribal population of the Bastar district, the urge of the Sikhs for a separate State of their
own, the anti-Hindi demonstrations in South India are all instances of economic discontent masquerading as something else. The country's halting
progress has prevented India from giving special attention to the needs of
backward areas and peoples. They have perhaps not even had their fair
share out of the national cake. The distribution of development expenditure
is influenced, as in any other country, by the voting power commanded by
the beneficiaries.

Similar heart-burning over the sharing of the national cake accounts
for the present bickering among the States, and between the States and New
Delhi. The resulting tensions often reduce the effectiveness of nation-wide
planning. Food provides a particularly glaring example of the failure: rice
in a surplus State sells for only half the price it may fetch in a deficit area
less than 100 miles away because of arbitrary restrictions placed on inter-
State movement of grains. Jealousies are equally intense in the industrial
sphere as a result of which important decisions get delayed at times, or
worse still economic common sense has to be sacrificed to political expe-
diency. A more dangerous development is the willfulness displayed by some
States in pushing ahead with pet projects regardless of overall national
priorities. One State, for instance, has been taking soundings in a foreign
country on the prospects for obtaining supplier's credit for an industrial
venture to which the local Government feels committed. On the face of it,
this kind of enthusiasm may seem quite harmless, but the concept of nation-
wide planning may well be jeopardised unless such individual initiatives are
kept strictly within bounds.

Thoughtful persons in India and elsewhere are asking themselves
where the current difficulties may be leading. Addressing a public meeting
shortly after the violence in West Bengal and Punjab, the President of the
ruling Congress party warned that people might at this rate soon decide that
they have had enough of democracy, or the military might on its own conclude that the time had come to put paid to the present Parliamentary
system. Others express even graver fears: will Indian unity survive the increasingly unquiet crisis? The question is too hypothetical to attempt an
answer, but it is plain that the present political difficulties are bound to
deepen unless the country regains the economic momentum which sustained
its hope and faith in the 'fifties.

DIMENSIONS OF FAILURE

Before the latest agricultural crisis, it was expected that the Third
Five-Year Plan would end in 1966 with a 20% increase in national income
at constant prices, falling a third short of the 30% target. The fortuitous

result of an exceptionally poor harvest may be disregarded in discussing long-term trends. The point really is that, even if there had not been the ruinous drought, *per capita* income would have risen by just about 7% or 8% over the whole five-year period, against a promised increment of 17%.

In other words, Indian development is failing to offer any relief from the grinding poverty which is the lot of millions. In rural areas, two-thirds of the population has to subsist on less than *Rs* 20 ($4.2) per head per month while the richest 5% have no more than *Rs* 61 ($12) to spend. The position is only slightly better in the urban areas. So that in India as a whole, all but the top crust (constituting less than 5% of the population) live on less than *Rs* 2 ($0.42) per day—a measure of the depth of India's persisting poverty. Dr. P. V. Sukhatme, Director of FAO's Statistics division, estimates that at least one in every four Indians lives in hunger while one in two is suffering from malnutrition (the latter implying a qualitative deficiency in the diet).

It was hardly to be expected that planning over a brief 15-year period would wipe out this enormous backlog of hunger accumulated over decades, but one may certainly ask why the supply of home-grown foodgrains per head should have shown scarcely any improvement. The immediate answer is that a population explosion is obliging India to run merely to stand still; but this does not alter the fact that agricultural shortfalls are negating the whole planning effort. The consumption of the great bulk of the people is sustained by agriculture, which means shortages prevent improvement in living standards and thus undermine the hope and faith needed to sustain planning.

UNEMPLOYMENT

Another major cause of popular dissatisfaction is the growing backlog of unemployment. In every Plan period, the number of new job opportunities has fallen short of the increase in the labour force. The Second Plan began with an estimated 5.3 million out of jobs and ended with 8 million unemployed. The Third Plan may have pushed up the figure to 12 million, which will go up to 14 million by 1971 by the planners' own admission.

Both the major shortcomings—the scarcity of food and the lack of enough jobs to go round—are the predictable result of an inadequate growth rate. The inadequacy cannot however be blamed on any shortfall in investment. Net domestic saving has now risen to 13% against a target of 11% set at the start of the Third Plan. Net investment, including the proportion supplied by foreign aid, has gone up to 16% against 14% originally envisaged. Judging from this, it seems that resources have yielded a poorer return than the planners had hoped for, either because expectations were set too high, or because the resources have been inefficiently used.

The shortfalls in production have directly contributed to the alarming increase in trade deficits. Dependence upon PL 480 wheat has already been mentioned, while lags in the industrial sector explain the still substantial imports of intermediate goods which India should have been producing for itself by now. For example, imports of steel have continued at the level of a million tons a year, accounting last year for 5% of the import bill. Import deficits have been financed by aid, the total rising from Rs 8,900 million ($1,780 million) in the Second Plan to Rs 20,900 million ($41,80C million) in the Third (the latter figure includes a quarter absorbed by debt service against less than one-seventh in the previous Plan period).

Another aspect of failure is that the severe inequality of wealth, characteristic of a semi-feudal economy, has increased despite the Socialist professions of the Government. An official study confirms that direct taxes have not affected the pattern of personal incomes to any significant extent. As for land reform, the abolition of feudal estates has had no appreciable impact on the distribution of land ownership. In 1960-61, the top 10% of the cultivators operated 56% of the cultivated acreage while the bottom 50% accounted for less than 3%.

Even with all this inequality, the rich are numerically so few. The number paying income tax—with assessable incomes of Rs 4,000 ($800) a year or more—is less than a million. It is possible to argue therefore that conspicuous consumption by the rich has no great economic significance but this is to miss the psychological impact of sharp contrasts on morale. A plea for austerity often evokes from the masses nothing but derision—a dangerous reaction in a country where austerity is and will remain a pre condition of growth.

THE ACHIEVEMENTS

India has indeed fared badly; but to draw up a true balance sheet credit must be given to the achievements of the past 15 years.

The biggest achievement of all is the human transformation that i taking place as education reaches out to the remotest villages. In 1955 only two out of five children in the 6-13 age group were at school. Ten years later, the proportion has changed to two out of three. Implicit in this is both hope and despair; schooling will make the children better farmer and better factory hands but what happens if society fails to fulfill their enhanced aspirations.

The number of secondary schools and the scholars enrolled in them has increased by 250% over the past decade. Enrolment in higher educational institutions—universities, professional colleges and the like—is now over a million. One out of every five college students is a girl, indicative of the change in women's status that has taken place. Over 10,000 graduat engineers and over 17,000 qualifying at the diploma level are entering the job market every year against only 4,000 in each category ten years ago.

Broadly speaking, India has now the manpower and skills required to sustain rapid industrial growth. Experience gained over the past decade has equipped Indian personnel to take operating responsibility in practically every branch of manufacture. A particularly heartening development is the capacity now built up for the design and engineering of large, new projects—among them power plants, steel mills and fertiliser factories. But there is still a shortage of talent, notably in agriculture. A country in which seven-tenths live by farming turns out far fewer agricultural graduates than mechanical engineers.

Striking achievements can also be claimed in the field of public health. This is at once evident from the increase in the average expectation of life at birth, which was only 32 in 1951, 41 in 1961 and is now in the neighbourhood of 50. The great scourge of malaria has been virtually eliminated, and other killers like cholera are being gradually dealt with. The number of hospital beds has doubled in the past ten years, and there are a great many more doctors, nurses and midwives in position. But for some half a million villages and 2,000-odd urban centres, there are still only 6,800 family planning clinics.

For all the gloom over performance on the farm front, the fact remains that agricultural output was rising in the 'fifties at 3.2% a year while growth in food production was 2.6% against 4.4% in the case of cash crops. The bulk of increase in food came from higher productivity. The yield per acre of rice went up by 16% over the decade while the increase in wheat was smaller because of a less favourable market environment as a result of massive PL 480 imports. In six out of the 16 States, growth rates were higher than the national average: Punjab and Madras were for instance going ahead at almost 5% a year. Progress in the past five years has been more halting, but mostly on account of a succession of poor monsoons. Last year when the rain gods were less unkind, output shot up by 10% over the previous year's level, indicating the considerable productive capacity that has been built up through investments of the past five years.

In industry, the last ten years have witnessed a 75% increase in total production. This understates the growth and diversification achieved, the reckoning being based on an index of industrial production in which old industries—cotton and jute textiles—carry a weight of almost 40 out of 100. According to one analysis, growth in the "old" sector has been as little as 2.5% a year while the output of the new industries has gone up from 7.5% year before 1956 to 11% in the subsequent period.

The most impressive aspect of growth has been the broadening of the industrial structure. As much as 63% of the outlay for industry in the second Plan went into heavy industry, the proportion rising to 73% in the Third Plan. Steel output, although still short of needs, has increased three-fold, with another big rise due within the next few months. The larger availability of steel has spurred the growth of a large number of steel-using capital goods industries. For instance, India is now in a position to produce machinery and equipment for all the major consumer industries, among them cotton textiles, paper and pulp, sugar, food processing, and plastic extrusion and moulding.

In transport equipment, self-sufficiency is now not too far away. India is in fact in a position to export railway track material and wagons. Within the next five years, adequate capacity will have been built up to produce diesel and electric locomotives with some surplus to spare for export. Automobile plants are turning out trucks in several sizes, with manufacture coming to depend less and less upon imported components as ancillary units develop. Two units are progressively manufacturing aircraft, and a third is now being built. None of these is particularly relevant to civilian needs but the know-how and skills being built up in this technically challenging field cannot but be of benefit to many industries. The next five years should be even more rewarding in terms of diversification. There will be three plants, for instance, making heavy electrical machinery—generating equipment for both hydro and thermal power of up to 100 kW, transmission equipment, traction and other types of motors including those needed for working very large steel mills. One of the three plants is already in operation, while the other two are nearly complete. A heavy foundry-forge and an associated machine-building complex is coming up at Ranchi, some 200 miles due north west of Calcutta, which should be producing steel plant equipment, oil drilling rigs, heavy cranes, excavators and the like. Tooling up is now in progress at this plant for the fabrication of a 2,000 ton-a-day blast furnace, while a pig casting machine has already been delivered.

These plants have unfortunately taken long to build, perhaps because they have been designed from the start for a very large volume of output. The Ranchi machine-building plant is for example intended to produce each year enough equipment to set up a million-ton steel plant. Even after the units are complete, it will take several years to build up production to the full rated capacity. There are production skills to be acquired, design know-how to be brought or developed, and ancillary production to be organised. But by 1970-1, it is safe to assume that the units will be in full production permitting India to add, for instance, a million tons of new steel capacity or 2 million kW of power every year out of her own resources.

Thus the investments already made in heavy industry at considerable sacrifice provide a reasonable degree of assurance that growth in almost all consumer industries and over very large areas of basic industry and infrastructure can be self-sustaining in another five years. It will undoubtedly be necessary to make large maintenance imports to work this industrial capacity fully since India can not possibly produce enough non-ferrous metals (excepting aluminium), nor would it be possible, or even desirable, to produce all components within the country (as for instance electronic instrumentation) because the scale of output may be quite uneconomic. But these import requirements need cause no worry—it has never been India's objective to build a closed and entirely self-contained economy—as long as adequate effort is made to build up export capacity.

To say this is really begging the question. To make exports of manufactured goods in competition simultaneously with the developed economies (which despite high wage costs retain their competitiveness in many light engineering products because of much superior productivity) and with other developing economies (which are just as keen to expand their foreign exchange earnings) is perhaps the most challenging problem facing India today. Over the past five years, India's export earnings have been pushed up by 38%, but this is nothing compared to the increases needed to meet the mounting maintenance needs of a diversifying economy and to service the debt obligations incurred in the current phase of development.

Critics are right in blaming India for not having got to grips with this problem sooner, but they should not fail to note the change wrought in the nation's entire approach to the problem by the severe difficulties of the past twelve months. After an agonising reappraisal, Indian policy-makers have taken a series of steps to narrow the balance of payments gap. Import duties have been sharply raised to make *rupee* prices reflect the true scarcity value of foreign exchange—this more than anything else should hasten import substitution wherever economically feasible. Secondly, some fiscal incentives have been offered, and others are clearly in the offing, to give exports a big boost. More may have been attempted immediately but there is not much point in whipping up export promotion until the current short-term difficulties arising out of the food shortage and the aftermath of last year's war have been overcome.

ANATOMY OF FAILURE

Notwithstanding the many shortfalls and some pretty serious mistakes, India has certainly managed to give its stagnant, colonial economy a new orientation over the past decade. This makes the present crisis in the country's affairs the more unfortunate.

Diagnosing the crisis is none too easy, not least because we stand too near the events to be able to look at them in perspective. Besides, failure (like success) is cumulative, making it difficult to pinpoint what went wrong in a particular situation. But basically failure has occurred in three main spheres: in planning, in policy and in execution.

In the sphere of planning, a particularly unfortunate failure was the assumption that defence could be combined with development without any serious difficulty. This assumption made on the basis of rather irrelevant analogies was widely shared by officials, businessmen and many economists; but experience was soon to prove them wrong. The super-imposition of a sharp increase in defence expenditure—going up from *Rs* 3,000 million ($600 million) to the present level of *Rs* 9,000 million ($1,800 million) on the rising curve of development spending gave inflation a big push. Money supply increased by 14% in 1963-64 and by 9% in the two subsequent years, racing far ahead of the real product. Prices which were already under pressure because of the agricultural shortfalls defied all attempts at regulation through the use of monetary and fiscal instruments. Measured by the official wholesale price index which may be understating the rise, prices have gone up by 9% in each of the last three years. Food prices have gone up by much more—by something like 50%—although in their case an upward adjustment had even otherwise become necessary to correct the terms of trade between town and country.

The second major failure in planning was an inability to identify the real requirements of agricultural growth. It was fondly believed that agricultural and industrial development could proceed independently of each other, the theory being that "the scarce inputs they need are largely dissimilar." In other words, the linkage of agriculture with industry was played down, which may go to explain the shortfalls in the supply of key industrial inputs needed for achieving a breakthrough in productivity. It is now widely agreed that failures on the farm front should be blamed in fact on the industrial sector's inability to provide enough cement, power, fertilisers and pesticides.

The third failure was an inability to plan in depth. The lack of expertise to undertake detailed project studies may have been an extenuating circumstance in the early years of planning, but this explanation cannot be accepted for persisting failure. Projects taken up on the basis of wholly inadequate homework were bound to run into difficulties, causing delays and additional expenditure. For instance, it has taken between 52 and 71 months to build fertiliser plants in India against 26-28 months usual in advanced countries. Part of the delay can no doubt be explained by the difficulties of organising construction in an underdeveloped country, and also by reference to purely administrative defaults. But the planners must take a fairly large share of the blame for failing to insist upon sufficiently-detailed preparatory work on projects before including them in a plan. In this important sense, planning has been incomplete and perfunctory despite the sophistication displayed by the planners in constructing highly detailed models.

Indian planning has fallen down elsewhere in failing to provide built-in checks against defaults and deviations. Some manufacturers have failed to adhere to the schedule agreed with government whereby they promised to substitute domestically produced supplies for imported items. The automobile industry was given protection in 1965, and only those units which undertook to reduce the import content were allowed to continue. Some units shut down, but those left in the field would seem to have taken their obligations rather lightly. Their defaults were highlighted by two subsequent enquiries in 1956 and 1960, but little seems to have been done to make them live up to their promises. It should have been relatively simple to link import licensing to an agreed schedule for local manufacture, but this powerful weapon does not seem to have been effectively used. This might also be viewed as merely an administrative failure, but planning is incomplete unless it does two things: locate defaults and bottlenecks as they occur, and allow for flexibility in year-to-year planning to remedy them. This India's planners have by and large failed to do.

As for the failures at the policy-making level, a major source of difficulty seems to have been the constant temporising between the Socialist values professed by the ruling party, and the realities of Indian political life which do not seem to permit much Socialism. It is possible to argue that this conflict between principles and practice is inescapable in India's circumstances but the fact remains that a series of half-way houses cannot give the economy the sense of direction and purposefulness which Japan and China, each in its own way, display.

For instance, the whole paraphernalia of controls over price and distribution were maintained by India until pressure from the World Bank and from the Indian private sector obliged New Delhi to agree to a change of course. The Government was fully aware that controls were holding up new investment in such key industries as cement and fertilisers. It had a choice—either to allow prices to rise sufficiently to make investment more attractive, or to offset the shortfalls in the private sector through State initiative. It did a bit of both—but not vigorously enough to make much impact, with the result that a stalemate continued. The reason for this was not a misjudgment about the size of the problem but political pusillanimity. It did not have the courage to write off the private sector (neither the domestic situation nor such external constraints as the need to keep on the right side of the World Bank permitted it to do so). Nor did it have the courage to sanction large price increases to big business for fear of ruining its public image. The dilemma has now been resolved in the only way possible—by an abolition of control altogether in the case of most of the key industries.

While discussing price policy, it is necessary to recall two other errors mentioned earlier in a different context. In deference to the vocal urban consumer, agricultural prices were unwisely held down to an extent that the farmer had little incentive to invest in modernisation. Similarly, too much reliance was placed on administrative controls to shut out unnecessary imports and too little on the price mechanism. The result was that import substitution was hindered by the cheapness of imports in terms of *rupee* prices. Theoretically, this could hardly have happened with the kind of screening of imports undertaken every six months by the Government but the fact is that it did happen. This is demonstrated by the potential for import substitution discovered over the past year when India found itself up against the wall by the US embargo on non-project aid.

One more policy failure calls for mention. While extensive use has been made of negative measures to discourage investment in areas of low priority, it is only in the last two years that attention has been given to the alternative of inducing the right kinds of investment by offering fiscal incentives. The failure in this regard was the result, it seems, of a belief that assured markets and the undoubted growth potential (as for instance in fertilisers) would automatically attract capital into such priority areas. Admittedly, there was some warrant for the belief while the investment boom between 1958 and 1962 lasted, but it is a sad commentary on the policy-making machine's responsiveness to changing situations that it took two years to decide that positive encouragement had become necessary.

As for administrative failures, two extenuating circumstances should be noted. When India began its experiment in modernisation, there was no opportunity to learn from others' mistakes, because in many ways it was the first among the poor countries to undertake large-scale planning within a democratic framework. Secondly, India began with a great shortage of skills and expertise. It had inherited from the British an administrative framework which was wholly unsuitable for coping with the challenges of development. However the problem was certainly aggravated by the proliferation of detailed administrative controls which threw an intolerable burden on an already overstretched civil service.

A more intractable difficulty was presented by the novelty of many new administrative services. For instance, unfamiliarity with the very idea of an agricultural extension service meant that the farmers themselves failed to insist on satisfaction from village-level officials. In services of this nature, vigilance from above could scarcely be expected to ensure efficiency, which is why the performance of the administrative machine was often indifferent. The delays, the lack of co-ordination, the inability to see a problem as a whole are evident in the record of Indian planning over the last decade.

Nevertheless, despite everything, the outlook is far more hopeful than the present situation may suggest. This optimism rests on two basic premises. First, there is a willingness to learn from past mistakes. The severe disappointments of this Third Plan have led to much anxious heart-searching, as a result of which many far-reaching changes in relation to both planning and policy are under way. It is safe to assume that there will be less temporising on such key issues as prices and incomes. This should make for greater purposefulness.

Secondly, difficulties of the past year, sharply aggravated by the India-Pakistan conflict, have taught India some salutory lessons. "Self-reliance" has acquired a compelling urgency, making for a vigorous utilisation of the economy's latent resources. A period of consolidation is now inescapable, while India tries to correct some of the imbalances that have developed in the economy. But this pause is likely to leave India stronger and better equipped to cope with the challenges of the future.

2. Politicians, Bureaucrats, and Development in India

WAYNE WILCOX

India occupies an important place in the study of political development chiefly because of the immensity of its problems and the democratic framework of development planning. While India serves many observers as the representative model of an underdeveloped country, its political development has been quite unique.

Few countries have been as explicitly prepared for independent democratic development as India. The institutions and practice of representative government had steadily evolved for over a century, and the civil and military services were experienced and professional.[1] A body of fundamental law, an independent Bar and Bench, and a considerable public understanding of civil rights were established facts in Indian life in 1947. And in the last four decades of British rule, Indians in the public services came to play an increasingly important role in the public policy process.

Popular political organization was also well developed, the Congress party having been founded in 1885. In the sixty-two years between its inception and its triumph, the nationalist movement had given experience in party politics to three generations of Indians. From the outset of the twentieth century, politicians and a progressively larger segment of the population had experienced the drama and the hard work of the hustings. The public men of the subcontinent also learned a bitter lesson about the violence of a militant opposition which could not find a place in the program of the majority.

The leadership of independent India was thus well tempered. Leaving aside the vague qualities of charisma and the mystique of nationalism, the

From Wayne Wilcox, "Politicians, Bureaucrats, and Development in India," *Annals* of the American Academy of Political and Social Science, Vol. 358 (March 1965), pp. 115-122. Reprinted by permission of the author and the publisher.

[1] Paul Appleby has written that India was one of the dozen best administered states in the world. *Public Administration in India* (Delhi, 1953), pp. 8-9. Praise for the army is summarized in Lord Birdwood's *India and Pakistan* (New York: Frederick A. Praeger, 1954), pp. 82-98.

party men of the Indian National Congress and the Indians in the public services represented an unusually competent and cohesive leadership. To the British who were giving up the jewel of their empire, the Indian elite seemed to be an embodiment of the 1835 desiderata of Macauley, "a class of persons Indian in blood and colour, but English in taste, in opinions, in morals and in intellect."[2]

The British took a grudging pride in this class, which had its beginnings in the enhanced opportunities for social mobility in British India, opportunities for promotion by merit which set the standard for the new India. The class had grown from direct recruitment through the educational process at the completion of which better graduates either took appointments in the imperial *apparat* or in the restrained opposition to it.[3] Other opportunities for profitable achievement lay in the new commerce of the port cities, in the British law which was displacing older norms, and in Western medicine. Regardless of vocation, the new recruits to the British Indian subculture had to know the English language and to be able to manipulate a set of ideas and practices indigenous to the West.

The "modern" Indians who inherited the urban civilization of British India in 1947 were therefore in reality an extremely small "Westernized" professional middle class: a class molded by a nineteenth-century English educational system, sustained in cities requiring a high degree of specialization of labor, and employed in managerial and professional occupations. In general, they had weak links to real property, were drawn from higher caste backgrounds, and inherited a radical and alien social perspective based largely on the European experience in the twentieth century.[4]

The impressive political consensus on the eve of independence can be explained not only with reference to nationalist loyalties but as well by the common heritage and predicament of the managers of the new state. For them, the industrial *Weltanschauung* was not only a credo for the future, but a rationale for the continuation of systems of education, wealth, status and authority in which they were dominant. Gandhi's vision of *gram raj,* the rule of the villages, was fundamentally hostile to the heirs of British rule because it would have undermined the interests and ideals not only of the governmental elite, but of functional elites created in the cities as well. The Gandhian program was politically impotent in 1947, therefore, because there were no visible alternative elites to whom authority could be transferred.

---

[2] T. B. Macauley, "The Minute on Education," reprinted in W. T. de Bary (ed.), *Sources of Indian Tradition* (New York: Columbia University Press, 1958), pp. 596-601.

[3] Jawaharlal Nehru's choice of the law and politics rather than the civil service seems to have been dictated by his preference for a settled place of residence. See M. Brecher, *Nehru, A Political Biography* (London, 1961 [abr. ed.]), p. 31.

[4] For a less generalized statement, see B. B. Misra, *The Indian Middle Classes: Their Growth in Modern Times* (New York: Oxford University Press, 1961).

In general, therefore, independent India possessed the first requirement of political development, a stable government resting on elite unity and a viable state machinery.

THE CONTEXT OF POLITICAL DEVELOPMENT IN INDIA

Indian nationalism developed as a result of the diffusion of the methods and products of Western scientific and social organization. In a sense, it was so completely a creature of its British origins that an intellectual could dedicate his memorable autobiography.

To the memory of the British Empire in India which conferred subjecthood on us but withheld citizenship; to which yet everyone of us threw out the challenge: "Civis Britannicus Sum" because all that was good and living within us was made, shaped, and quickened by the same British rule.[5]

While this might seem to be an unrepresentative minority position, it can be argued that the Gandhian *via media* has been overemphasized. Gandhi's contribution enriched and empowered Indian nationalism by exploiting great strengths in the indigenous culture,[6] but his ideas seem to have been neither the product of an intellectual revolution nor a stimulus to one. In fact, Gandhi's mark upon Indian life is notable only by its near absence in contrast to the continuing unusual receptivity of Indian society to external influences.[7]

The enormity of the problems of development in India are also unique. In brief, the economic problem is one of a large and exceedingly poor population expanding somewhat faster than production.[8] Economic development is inhibited by various social obstructions, some of them embedded in custom and others in circumstance. Basically the Indians have a severe communications problem, evident in the lack of community between elite and mass, city and hinterland, literate and unschooled. It is complicated by the presence of multiple linguistic communities and the "vertical" divisions of the class-caste system which inhibit intergroup contact and often act as a barrier to mutual confidence and identification.

The character of the society suggests its correspondence to Rapoport's model of "Praetorian society"[9] in which rule is simple but government is

[5] Nirad C. Chaudhuri, *The Autobiography of an Unknown Indian* (London: Macmillan and Company, 1951).

[6] See Joan Bondurant's sensitive study, *The Gandhian Conquest of Violence* (Princeton, N.J.: Princeton University Press, 1959).

[7] The absence of an indigenous modern intellectual tradition independent of the colonial rule and a foreign language is an unexplored and yet obviously crucial characteristic of Indian nationalism.

[8] A detailed study of the problem is Wilfred Malenbaum's *Prospects for Indian Development* (New York: Free Press of Glencoe, 1962).

[9] David Rapoport, "A Comparative Theory of Military and Political Types," in *Changing Patterns of Military Politics,* ed. Samuel P. Huntington (New York: Free Press of Glencoe, 1962), pp. 71-100.

almost impossible; in which the coercive mechanism of the state is not linked to fixed political factors in the general society. Before accepting this description of the Indian situation, however, it is essential to study the political structure and practices of the modern Indian state.

THE POLITICAL DEMANDS OF
DEMOCRATIC DEVELOPMENT

Indian political development was predicated on the existence of a voluntaristic society in which the mandate of leadership was valid only with the continuing consent of the people, and productive only with their participation. Parliamentary government was adopted, and the protagonist system of party life was accepted as a concomitant to political liberty. Many Indians recognized that this form of political organization is basically an equilibrium system, and hence more conducive to stability than to radical change.

The dilemma facing Indian leadership after the adoption of the constitution was clear; their political mechanism was most effective in accommodating the demands of a changing society rather than in programming and administering change.

The first requirement for democratic change, therefore, was effective and purposive policy which "trains, educates people, makes them think in a particular way and drives all of them forward in a particular direction."[10]

Nehru's conception of the role of leadership and of the true requirements of public policy in a democracy seems to have been based on his notion that it was impossible "for the mass of the people to be taken away, far away, from their mooring"[11] but perhaps more importantly on his understanding that "command and discipline, furthermore, can eventually be no more than symbols of something deeper and more real than themselves."[12]

The first task of leadership was to develop and direct patterns of identification between the rulers and the ruled. The importance of a sense of national community is evident in most developing countries as they seek to minimize parochial loyalties and establish common goals for the future.[13] The long history of Indian nationalism and the continuity dramatized in Nehru's pivotal role in both the nationalist and the independence periods

[10] Jawaharlal Nehru, quoted in Brecher, *op. cit.*, p. 248.
[11] *Idem.*
[12] Harry H. Turney-High, quoted by Rapoport, *op. cit.*, p. 79.
[13] For more lengthy treatment of this theme, see Lucian Pye, *Politics, Personality and Nation-Building* (New Haven: Yale University Press, 1962) and my "Nation-Building: The Problem in Pakistan," *Asia*, Vol. I, No. 1 (Spring 1964), pp. 75-92.

were strengths in building a national outlook, but subordinate community loyalties were unusually strong.[14]

The second dimension of the task of leadership was to develop a policy consensus which included most of the centers of effective social power. Inasmuch as extragovernmental interest groups were considered part of a democratic society, the Indian government had to bring them together in a policy consensus. This proved to be a troublesome problem, as it is in most countries, because the articulated interests are often competitive. In the immediate postindependence period, for example, the prime minister acceded to the demands of the commercial community to remove price controls in spite of heavy inflationary pressures. The same general problems have been faced with the other organized groups in the country, and have generally been resolved at the expense of the abstract or ideological "public interest."[15]

While it is frequently charged that India has not followed a radical policy of planned change because vested interests have used democratic institutions and practices to frustrate it, the critics rarely consider the value and strength of the broad national policy consensus forged in the first decade of Indian independence. The few bills passed to assuage the ideological conscience of various "ginger groups" in the Congress or the social ideals incorporated in the constitution have been notable neither in conception nor in effect, especially if they ran counter to the interests of "modern" elites.

It is difficult not to agree with Taya Zinkin's praise for the Indian leadership which "has gone at the pace which the people could follow, always taking time to explain, to convince, and to wait until enough people had been won over to give him their support."[16]

The other broad need of democratic leadership is to ensure adequate public policies and the discipline of public administration in fulfilling them. It is not enough in a developing country to act as the "broker" in minimizing social conflict and ensuring stability; the state also must create an environment in which development and change can take place, and in which unarticulated future interests of the country are put forward by imaginative public leaders.

The Indians, like many other newly independent peoples, conceived

[14] Even in the Indian army, for example, it has been suggested that "caste loyalty evokes greater emotional appeal than national loyalty." M. S. A. Rao, "Caste and the Indian Army," *The Economic Weekly,* Vol. XVI, (35), August 29, 1964, p. 1441.

[15] For a full discussion of articulated interests in India, see Myron Weiner, *The Politics of Scarcity* (Chicago: University of Chicago Press, 1963). An interesting study of the absence of midsystem voluntary social organizations is Allen Grimshaw, "The Impact of National Disaster on Governmental Bureaucracies in Three Cultural Settings" (Unpublished paper, 1964).

[16] Taya Zinkin, *India* (New York: Oxford University Press, 1964), p. 96.

of development primarily as an economic process. Planning commissions, they argued, are task forces concerned with technical problems such as steel mills and the gross national product. This technical bias was especially pronounced in India because of the nature of the bureaucratic elite and its dominance of the policy-making process. The first five-year plan was successful in the main, but it was based on an extension of capital investment rather than intrinsic changes in the mode and structure of production. This was especially true in agriculture, the dominant sector of the economy, and its most stagnant one.

One of the perverse effects of Nehru's great stature was that he held the confidence of both a rapidly changing political system and an ultra-stable administrative machinery. This had the effect of separating felt needs from abstract planning, and produced a minimum social input in Indian development. Representative institutions were mirroring their constituencies which were rural, ignorant of English, unevenly schooled, and hungry. Bureaucratic institutions were mirroring their elitist backgrounds inherited from the colonial urban setting.

The struggle was joined as the central government adopted an *Etatist* economic policy which established a public sector economy dominated by the public services. This tended to insulate the professional middle classes from the increasingly strident demands of the new enterpreneurial middle class and from the politicians who wanted more authority at the local level at the expense of the local administration. The linguistic states' agitation and the second general elections of 1957 were dominated by this struggle, although it was obscured by the verbal fog of ideological postures.[17]

Each elite group struggling for power in India had a different base and different assumptions. The civil servant was highly educated and trained, and held a "pure" and technical view of development in which he was dominant. The demands of politicians looked venal and selfish, and the siege on elitist education seemed to be a demand for lower standards. The politician considered his constituency the source of all true authority in India, and its felt needs were superior to bureaucratic models and "gigantism." The entrepreneur knew the value of his daring and wealth, his role as the prime mover in development, a role frustrated by red tape and his lack of political power. The intelligentsia's role was little more than as camp follower of the professional middle classes or a more radical *Etatist* pattern in which they would be subsumed under government service.

Whatever the form, the real struggle for power between the elites in independent India by-passed the legislatures and was focused on the administrative nexus. In part this was a continuation of the nationalist struggle for more participation in colonial rule, a rule which after independence had

[17] On this general point, see W. H. Morris-Jones, "India's Political Idioms," *Politics and Society in India,* ed. C. H. Philips (New York: Frederick A. Praeger, 1963), pp. 133-154.

continued to be concentrated in the *apparat*. This produced bureaucratic factions and lowered efficiency, a process hastened by the ministerial penchant for using government agencies to further their political claims. On the local level, the stuff of politics often took the form of administrative sabotage, legal obfuscation, or judicious inaction on the part of officials.

In the process of the democratization of public administration, standards have shifted, and there is considerable concern about "corruption, indiscipline and falling standards." In the aftermath of the Chinese border war of 1962, the prime minister remarked with disgust that "the real thing that's out of joint is our whole mentality, our whole government, the way government is run here."[18]

The fact is that with the end of the Nehru era Indian political development has begun to threaten the continued dominance of the "modern" urban professional middle class. There is little to suggest that this will be contraproductive of economic development,[19] and, in fact, expert opinion is on record as having argued:

Until they [India's elites, especially those in the public services] break the traditional pull toward the ways and solutions of other, more well-to-do nations, or until they are replaced by leaders more attuned to specific Indian problems and developments, the prospect is for more plans like the second and the draft third —plans which give little promise of initiating a process of dynamic growth.[20]

The primary problem of Indian development, therefore, seems to lie in the connection between representative institutions and the implementation of public policy. In the main, and in places to a very high degree, the political system has operated in an environment of rapid change and has held it within the national consensus. The operational side of politics, the "output" of the system in terms of development, has been weak. The question is, therefore, whether the free operation of the representative system has inhibited development, or whether higher levels of compulsion are necessary for growth.

The Consent-Coercion Continuum. The heritage of British rule in India was not solely democratic and parliamentary; it included a well-developed coercive machinery. The All-India Civil Liberties Council once wrote that "India is, we believe, the only democratic country in the world whose fundamental law sanctions detention without trial in time of peace and in a situation which is not in the nature of an emergency."[21] Preventive detention legislation was promulgated to control incipient rebellion, to confine would-be rebels before their agitation threatened the fabric of the state.

[18] Prime Minister Nehru quoted by the *New York Times,* November 12, 1962.
[19] This point is persuasively argued by Myron Weiner in "India's Two Political Cultures," *Political Change in South Asia* (Calcutta, 1963), pp. 115-152.
[20] Malenbaum, *op. cit.,* p. 323.
[21] Cited in David H. Bayley's unique book, *Preventive Detention in India* (Calcutta, 1962), p. 1.

This was in addition to the normal devices of social control exercised by all organized political communities in the interests of their own survival and stability.

While this is a unique aspect of Indian authority, it is merely an extension of the limited and passive role of law enforcement agencies in maintaining a given set of social norms. The coercive dimension of the dictatorial model of political development goes well beyond the stabilizing function of law. In theory and in practice of some socialist states, force can be used to modify a society as well as maintain one. Therefore, development planning by governments not willing to use force suffers from an inadequate exploitation of governmental prerogatives, and is inefficient because it empowers vested interests in the society against rational state policy, or so it is argued.

While the general dimensions of the alternative advantages of democratic and authoritarian systems have been spelled out since the *Federalist* papers and before, the dialogue in the Afro-Asian world is still relevant. The growth of one-party states, the appeal of the Bolshevik model, and the demise of democratic forms in many of the new states testifies to the glamor of "controlled development."

On one point, the alternative models of development agree: that traditional subsistence economies must be set into motion to free the human spirit for more creative work, especially work in cities leading to higher standards of living and a more intensive use of intellect. Leadership is therefore necessary, in the form either of popular and purposive democratic leadership or of powerful and efficient dictatorship.

The greatest contrast in the system lies in communication patterns, the one resting on voluntary participation and mobilization by autonomous social and political agencies, and the latter controlled and programmed participation corresponding to an intellectual framework. This in turn assumes either a relativist or a positivist attitude toward the process of development. Compulsion in development, to be justified, must be established to be more productive than systems allowing a wider range of alternatives resting on pragmatic and multicentric decisions.

Leaving aside the broad outlines of the rival development theories, the pertinent question in the Indian context is which of these alternatives would tend to maximize development. Two assessments are necessary. (1) Are the primary problems of development in India those of inertia or those of obstruction and (2) is the Indian government capable of using higher levels of coercion in support of well-articulated policy?

If the analysis of India's past as a "Praetorian" society is correct, the impediments to development are the lack of linkages between the masses and the elite, and the lack of a dialogue in their co-operative urge for achievement. The "mai-bap" syndrome, the traditional way of viewing government as authority-bounty or authority-privation, is completely unsuited to stimulating new patterns of co-operative undertakings, especially in the rural sector. The alternative of an authoritarian government, if it is an alternative in India, would be a return to externally directed social action. Only a romantic could think that this could lead to agricultural progress.

While it is no doubt true that various groups inhibit the implementation of state policy, and that various elites compete for control and power in democratic systems, so too would these conditions apply under any other social arrangement. They can be either mobilized or excluded, but the latter posture assumes high levels of coercion, which in turn require strong administrative discipline and ideological commitment. The November 1964 debate on food rationing in India was turned down by every chief minister on the ground that their state administrations could not administer such a far-reaching policy. Paul Appleby, resurveying the public administration in India after his 1953 report, found

The great achievements of recent years have been beyond the capacity of the Indian administration system. . . . It puts too much reliance on a very small number of individuals, whereas for a much larger achievement reliance must be on a greatly improved organizational performance of systematic character.[22]

Assuming that this group could be expanded, and that it could hold and exercise coercive power, the question is whether its alien orientation and technical background would allow its members to plan effective national development for India. Few observers would see this change as revolutionary or successful. Misra harshly argues that the civil servants "traditionally recruited from the literary classes, with no business acumen . . . are most unsuited to accelerate production in Indian conditions, especially within the framework of law and legislative authority."[23] The fact is that the technical elites in India are more conservative than the new strata of political leadership. The revolution is being generated outside the formally "modern" class which, because of its background and vulnerability to economic change, is cautious.

CONCLUSION

It may be, as Mackenzie once argued, that "there is no country in the world where modern democratic notions find a less congenial society than India, or where they may, if pushed to extremes, afford more dangerous mischief."[24] But nothing in the political development of India would support the notion that an *Etatist* or totalitarian system would be any less mischievous. Nehru's leadership, the consensus-building policies of the

---

[22] Quoted in Norman D. Palmer, *The Indian Political System* (Boston: Houghton Mifflin, 1961), p. 133.

[23] Misra, *op. cit.*, p. 340.

[24] *Ibid.*, quoting the Lieutenant-Governor of Bengal in 1895, p. 344.

Congress party, and the thrust of public policy resting on general consent has begun to lead to a widespread popular participation in Indian public life which is unique in history. The nationalist credo and the modern communications media have made it possible for India to develop as a nation-state, and its political system has been successful in forwarding this goal.

Governmental leadership has been less responsive to currents within Indian life, and has been particularly concerned with international models of economic and social development. The elitist, technical bias has not helped it to mobilize political and social inputs in economic development, nor has it made a dialogue on national goals significant. Mistakes in planning have been uncorrected by a broad public awareness of the process of economic development, although deepening crises in agricultural production have led to a reappraisal.

The success of India in development ultimately lies in the growth of patterns of common loyalty and work toward common goals. There is no reason to believe that the democratic system is not the most useful framework in nation-building because of its flexibility, its sensitivity, and its dynamism. But all systems require leadership and a definition of alternatives for future growth.

3. Recent Economic Experience in India and Communist China: Another Interpretation

SIDNEY KLEIN

With Excerpts From a Discussion by

WILFRED MALENBAUM

I. INTRODUCTION

For the past fifteen years, comparisons of the economic organization and development of India and Communist China have had a strong fascination for analysts in many parts of the world. The similarities of the economic structures of and problems faced by the two most populous nations

From Sidney Klein, "Recent Economic Experience in India and Communist China: Another Interpretation," with excerpts from a discussion by Wilfred Malenbaum, *American Economic Review: Papers and Proceedings,* May 1965, pp. 31-45. Reprinted by permission of the authors and the publisher.

on earth and the sharp contrast offered by their economic doctrines have been grist for numerous articles in many languages. Perhaps the best known and most influential in the English language has been that by Wilfred Malenbaum published in the June, 1959, *A.E.R.* In it, Malenbaum concluded that in the years immediately preceding and in the years of each of their First Five Year Plans (FFYP), 1950-56 for India and 1950-57 for China, China's performance dwarfed that of India's by a considerable margin. Many other economists, writing at the same time, came to similar conclusions. I could not, on the basis of the data available, agree with them then, nor, on the basis of somewhat more data and a little more hindsight, can I agree with them now. The functions of my paper today are to: briefly review the years 1950-57 so as to take into account recent scholarship by others; evaluate selected major developments since 1957; and offer some conclusions on the subject of Indian vis-à-vis Mainland Chinese economic progress since 1950.

II. DEVELOPMENTS 1950-57

As all students of the subject agree, the statistical data issued by both governments have left and still leave much to be desired quantitatively and qualitatively. Particularly relevant to the question of their respective growth rates are the accuracy of the data in the base years and the relative strengths of the upward and downward biases in the data for subsequent years. In the case of China, studies completed since 1959 almost uniformly point to sharp upward biases in the official data and cast serious doubt on the accuracy of the large increases in gross national product, investment, and physical output reported for the years 1950-57. In one study of the statistical system, it was found that in predominantly agricultural China, up until 1958, regular statistical services to cover the agricultural sector had never reached down to the county much less the town and village level; and in late 1957, the director of the State Statistical Bureau had been forced to admit that they were not even clear about such basic agricultural data as the size of the territorial area of and the amount of cultivated land in China. In the study, the conclusion was reached that for the first five years, i.e., from 1949 to 1954, the official statistics are poor estimates, with the exception of those for state and joint industrial enterprises, which had higher but widely varying degrees of reliability.

Another study which dealt exclusively with industrial enterprises found upward biases due to the concept of the gross value of output used, pricing practices, and changing coverage. While unable to determine the exact magnitude of the identified biases for any one year, the researcher was able to state that their impact on the official indexes operated throughout the whole period and, becoming more pronounced after 1958, exerted a greater upward influence on the official data thereafter. Still other studies of China's national income completed since 1959 have yielded estimates for one or more of the years between 1952 and 1959 which, to varying degrees, have been below those claimed in the official data.

On the Indian side, it has been observed by students of that nation's statistics that, similarly to China's, they have required and still require invocation of the doctrine of *caveat emptor*. It is apparent that neither the absolute data nor the index numbers issued by the Indian government warrant confidence with respect to their accuracy for a wide variety of reasons, including, in a number of cases, being strikingly mutually incompatible. In the late 1950's and in the early 1960's, in predominantly agricultural India, the Ministry of Food and Agriculture cautioned against overreliance on its absolute data, because variations in coverage and changes in the method of estimation had made many of the years noncomparable. Further, for lack of sufficient detailed information as to what specific techniques had been used to create a number of its index numbers, it has not been possible for outsiders to verify the calculations which lead to them. Other Indian ministries issued roughly similar caveats about their data and raised similar doubts in the minds of outsiders. The reticence of the Indian government to make technical information known which a priori one would expect to be innocuous, by the early 1960's led one close observer to the suspicion that a drastic downward revision in the government's assessment of India's progress over the past ten years was in process, and that it was being carried out under the guise of a correction for noncomparability. Still more recently, a study published in August, 1964, dealing with food grains production from 1949-50 to 1960-61, indicates that actual production may have been only two-thirds to three-fourths that shown in the official data, even after adjustments for variations in coverage and statistical methods employed.

The most significant point which emerges from these studies of the statistics of India and Mainland China is that we have been hasty in rendering judgment on the issue of their relative rates of growth through 1957; and as we shall see below, should not duplicate this error by hastily rendering a strong official-data-oriented judgment on the issue of their relative rates of growth since then. Perhaps the most conclusive proof of the inadequacies of the official data for this purpose and the folly of accepting any more than their general tenor, if indeed even that, are the major developments which have occurred since 1957.

III. DEVELOPMENT SINCE 1957

According to the official data, between 1957 and 1962, national income and per capita income in India increased by 22.8 percent and 10.3

percent, respectively, or, on the average, by 3.8 percent and 1.7 percent per annum, respectively. While not unrespectable, these performance data seem to be dwarfed by estimates of China's performance based on official data over the same period. In the Middle Kingdom, between 1957 and 1959 national income and per capita income increased by 31.1 percent and 27.0 percent, respectively, or by 15.6 percent and 13.5 percent annually, respectively. The performance gap in the macroeconomic data seems to be reflected in and supported by the individual production data issued by both nations. However, the tenor of these data is not supported by developments in these two nations not subject to complete statistical control by their governments. This is particularly true of China. In at least three major categories, common problems have been encountered and deficiencies have been registered which indicate to this observer that the development of their economies has been and the structures of their economies are more nearly alike than has been generally believed; and that the sharp contrasts in performance alluded to by earlier writers overstates whatever differences in development and structure may actually exist. The common problems are:

1. *Major Failures in Their Industrialization Efforts.* The year 1959 is the last one for which the Chinese Communist Party (C.C.P.) has issued a relatively full set of economic statistics. From 1960 to the present, in accordance with its explicitly stated policy of issuing only data which reflect favorably on them, they have issued very few statistics of any sort. However, in spite of the data blackout, it is known that even in 1959, to say nothing of later years, grave inefficiencies and dislocations due to lack of coordination among the various sectors of the economy and within the branches of industry occurred. In the years 1959 through 1962, machinery and equipment in a number of industries had to lie idle for long periods because the industries had so expanded that they were able to produce more output than the inputs required for them which were available. In various industries, wide-spread attempts to economize on the use of critically important raw materials (e.g., coke and silicon in the production of steel) resulted in large quantities of substandard output. Continued misuse of and failure to maintain adequately machinery and equipment in 1959 and subsequent years resulted in increasingly numerous reports of breakdowns of industrial equipment and transportation facilities; and their continued inoperability for long periods of time. The few data available indicate that in 1960, 1961, and 1962, industrial production declined by at least 10 percent in each year and more probably closer to 15 percent. In September, 1962, the C.C.P. was forced to recognize its inability to continue its industrialization drive and it directed that henceforth, for an unstated period of time, the limited resources at its disposal were to be invested in agriculture rather than heavy industry. For 1963 and 1964, the C.C.P. claimed substantial improvements in percentage or qualitative terms

in the output of agriculture-related industries, such as chemical fertilizer and simple agricultural machinery, and only modest increases in others.

In statistically more "open" India, roughly comparable industrial failures took place. Between 1956 and 1961, serious production failures occurred in thirteen industrial lines, some of which warrant description as being of crucial importance to India's industrialization efforts. The outright failures in these lines and failure to maximize production in others were due to a wide variety of specific reasons similar to those which operated as development drags in China. Essentially, these drags were technical and administrative inexperience or incompetence in the construction and operation of the plants. The inexperience and incompetence resulted in not only lower production levels but considerably higher production costs than originally anticipated. Indicative of how poorly executed the industrial effort was is that in spite of a monetary investment approximately 30 percent above the Plan estimates, the physical targets attained in industry were only 85 percent to 90 percent of Plan.

2. *Major Failures in Agriculture.* In China, despite grain production having increased from 108 million metric tons to reportedly successive all-time highs of 250 and 270 million metric tons in 1958 and 1959, respectively, in the years 1959 through 1963 there were numerous widespread reports of severe food shortages. In 1960 and 1961, sharp increases in the incidence of illness caused by malnutrition were reported. Still other evidence of food shortages in this period were occasional pillaging of rice stores, increased flaunting of authority in remote places, and the development of illegal markets. The food situation was reportedly so critical in China that between December, 1960, and the end of 1963, it was necessary to import 16 million metric tons of grain; and, as of mid-1964, an additional 5.45 million metric tons were scheduled for delivery prior to the end of this year. Thus, by December 31, 1964, China will have imported nearly 21½ million tons of grain over a forty-nine month period, or about 5.3 million metric tons per year on the average. While the agricultural crisis in China did not necessitate large-scale imports of industrial raw materials of agricultural origin, it did require sharp reductions in the exports of these goods.

In India, the agricultural situation was roughly the same despite the tenor of many of the official data. Despite increases in aggregate and per capita food production between 1957 and 1962, it was necessary for India to import 23.2 million metric tons of food grains or an average of 3.9 million metric tons per year. Assuming an average population of 432 million for India during the period and an average population for China of 714 million for the years 1961 through 1964, inclusive, then grain imports per capita on the average for each of the years in these different but partially overlapping periods were .00895 metric tons for India and .00736 metric tons for China. Although—or perhaps because—larger grain imports per capita occurred in India than in China, there were not the same reports of desperate acts or desperate situations within India that emanated from China. Also, although it was necessary for India to import more food per capita than China, unlike China it was both necessary and possible for India to import relatively larger quantities of capital goods and industrial raw materials as well. This will be discussed in greater detail below. Suffice to note now that as in China, the food imports required consumed some foreign exchange which otherwise would have been used to underwrite India's industrial efforts. Were it not for US PL 480 which permitted successively larger food purchases by India from 1956 on with Indian currency, the foreign exchange drain attributable to food and other agricultural products would have been considerably larger. Aid from the U.S. and other friendly nations permitted and sustained industrial growth in India which otherwise would have been severely inhibited, as in fact it was inhibited in China for lack of the same external assistance. This brings us to what may be the crux of the question of Indian vis-à-vis Chinese economic growth since 1950.

3. *Major Dependence on Foreign Aid.* Both before and after 1957, India and China were extremely dependent on foreign aid in connection with their industrialization efforts; and without this foreign aid the efforts of both would have ended in failure. With respect to China, during the years 1950-57, inclusive, the total value of Russian exports was U.S. $4.9 billion, while the total value of the loans extended was U.S. $2.8 billion plus the costs incurred in sending up to 10,800 Russian technicians to work in China, 1949-57, and the cost of transporting and maintaining 13,600 Chinese students and workers in Russia, 1951-57. If one arbitrarily assumes an average cost of U.S. $1,200 per person per year, then the entire cost of the technical services and training involved was no more than U.S. $230 million.

The Russian exports consisted of equipment vital to China's industrialization program. In 1957, for example, 50 percent of the Soviet exports consisted of industrial machinery and equipment, with the remainder being fuels, lubricants, and related products, ferrous and nonferrous metals, and miscellaneous other items relatively scarce in China, such as chemical fertilizer and drugs. In return for such critically scarce capital goods and related items, China exported hair nets, knitted goods, and a whole host of other innocuous consumer-type goods plus industrial raw materials relatively more abundant in China. Especially significant is that the Russians shipped to China not only machinery and equipment per se but complete plants. In most of the years of the FFYP, the ratio of the value of complete plants to the total value of machinery and equipment imported from Russia was 60 percent or higher; in 1957 it was 77 percent. By the end of 1957, about 57 percent of China's steel production and 50 percent of her coal production were coming from Soviet-constructed enterprises—this despite the fact that the Russians had built only 3 of the 15 iron and steel plants planned for the period and only 27 of the 194 installations planned for the coal industry. The conclusion is inescapable that the Russian plants were the larger, more efficient production units as compared to the plants built by the Chinese and that without such significant external aid, as a minimum, the industrial aspects of the FFYP would have been a failure. This conclusion is reinforced by consideration of the role of the East European satellite nations. To the 156 "above-norm" (i.e., large-scale) industrial projects designed and constructed by the U.S.S.R., they contributed an additional 68 plants and mines plus the services of 1,500 technicians.

In 1958 and 1959, Soviet exports to China were sharply higher than in 1957, and as in 1957, consisted of complete industrial plants, individual pieces of machinery, transportation equipment, and varied other capital goods. The year 1959 represents the high point of Soviet aid to China's economy with total exports reaching U.S. $955 million, of which machinery and equipment were valued at nearly $600 million, with two-thirds of this latter figure representing complete plants. Because of the Sino-Soviet rift which developed in mid-1960, 1960, 1961, 1962, and 1963, Soviet exports to China were 84.8, 38.1, 24.1, and 19.6 percent, respectively, of the 1959 level. In 1960, 1961, 1962, and 1963, Russia shipped U.S. $500, $100, $27, and $42 million worth of machinery, respectively, to China. It is not mere *post hoc propter hoc* reasoning to say that as Russian aid to China flowed and ebbed, so did the rate of industrialization in China. Indisputably in the FFYP and the first half of the SFYP, China received capital goods which she did not have and could not have made in so short a period of time. Without Russian assistance, the FFYP would have failed and there could not have been an SFYP. Without substantial assistance from Russia up to the break in mid-1960, the SFYP would have been more of a failure than it was and economic conditions would have been even more serious from 1960 on than they were.

In India the situation was roughly the same. For the relatively small-scale FFYP, external financial assistance accounted for only 10 percent of total outlay on the Plan; however, for the industrially more ambitious and financially far more costly SFYP, it was budgeted at 24 percent and in fact was actually a good deal higher. This was due to classification of large loans to the government by the State Bank involving US PL 480 deposits as internal rather than external financing. For the Third Plan, foreign financial assistance was budgeted at 29 percent of the total outlay on the Plan including such use of PL 480 funds. For the years 1950-57, the comparison with China seems close, for in this period the direct aid extended by the U.S.S.R. to China amounted to 12 percent of the amount reported invested in capital construction. For 1958 and 1959, the Russian aid apparently amounted to only 4 percent. However, this observer attributes the unusually low proportion to an upward bias in the capital construction data and would hazard the guess that the actual proportion was at least 6 percent.

In India as in China, these percentages based on the official data do not impart a sense of the full value of the foreign assistance extended to the industrialization program undertaken. Between 1950-51 and 1960-61 India's imports of capital goods increased in irregular fashion from U.S. $227 million in absolute terms and 20 percent of total imports to U.S. $686 million in absolute terms and 31 percent of total imports. Concurrently, in irregular fashion, imports of intermediate goods and consumer goods also rose sharply in absolute terms. However, while the proportion of iron and steel, nonferrous metals, fertilizers, and other intermediate goods tended to remain relatively stable at about half of total imports, the proportion represented by consumer goods fell in irregular fashion from about 24 percent to 19 percent. The increase in the proportion accounted for by capital goods and the decrease in the proportion accounted for by consumer goods was made possible as noted previously by US PL 480 exports to India. For the years 1957 through 1961, such imports by India for local currency amounted to U.S. $1.1 billion and permitted the allocation of scarce foreign exchange to the capital goods imports cited above. Clearly, aid from the U.S. and other friendly nations was to India during the SFYP what aid from the U.S.S.R. and the Eastern Bloc of nations was to China during both the FFYP and the first half of the SFYP. For the even more financially expensive and industrially more ambitious Third Plan, the role of the friendly nations was expanded. In June, 1961, a Consortium of nations agreed to provide U.S. $3.2 billion to meet India's immediate balance-of-payments problem and import orders to be placed through 1962-63. Interestingly enough, the U.S.S.R., Czechoslovakia, and Poland—nations not members of the Consortium and former major contributors to the economic development of China—agreed to contribute credits of over U.S. $500 million in addition. Thus, insofar as the period of the Third Plan is concerned, the foreign aid dependence pattern is being continued.

IV. SUMMARY AND CONCLUSIONS

The performance of China's economy—and particularly her industrial growth rate vis-à-vis that of India since 1950—has been grossly exaggerated. This is as true of 1957 and earlier years as it is of "The Great Leap Forward" and the subsequent period of distress. The extent of the exaggeration over the last fourteen years and the extent of whatever differences in performance may actually exist are impossible to determine, at present, given the statistical impasse which prevails. What can be substantiated now, directly or indirectly, is that in both nations the industrialization plans formulated depended to a considerable extent on external financial and material assistance; and that with the passage of time and the accumulation of experience, this dependence increased rather than decreased.

In both cases, the statistical association between the amount and kind of foreign aid received on one hand and the industrial progress registered on the other was self-evidently very high. Moreover, this writer would suggest that we may have cases of concealed classification and downward biases in the correlation coefficients with respect to the statistical problems being considered. Actually, what was compared in the late 1950's by various writers was the progress of the FFYP for India as executed by India alone with the progress of the FFYP for China as executed by China, the U.S.S.R., and the East European satellites jointly. What this paper on recent economic experience has compared to a large extent is the progress of the SFYP for India as executed by India and friendly nations jointly with the SFYP for China as executed by China, the U.S.S.R., and their East European allies jointly for the first half and executed by China alone for the second half. From an analytical rather than a chronological point of view, the comparisons should have been India's FFYP and the last half of China's SFYP; and China's FFYP and the first half of the SFYP on one hand and India's SFYP and the first half of the Third Plan on the other. Undoubtedly, such comparisons would add further support to the position that the development and structure of their economies have been and are still more nearly alike than has been generally believed. For obvious reasons such comparisons and thesis validation (or invalidation) must wait for another occasion. In the meanwhile, let us apply the caveat of that long-forgotten confidence man who said that the best way to get an education is to doubt. With respect to comparative growth rates in India and China, let us be more skeptical in the future than we have been in the past.

WILFRED MALENBAUM: Economists study the record of economic growth in nations pushing their expansion because economists desperately need new insights into this elusive process. India and China are of special interest. India is the perfect case: statistics, models, and procedures are more or less public. There is no obvious bias in official presentations. China is a challenging case: official data are limited and what are available are held to be systematically biased. Models must be inferred; important procedures are not known. But China's economic philosophy has fascinating parallels in the Soviet Union, which has been extensively and effectively analyzed by foreigners without special access to official materials. Moreover, India and China offer such strong parallels and contrasts that there is a marked gain from joint study with focus on the marginal influence of specified differences. Needless to emphasize—as a further reason for our interest—is the importance of development in these lands to operating officials in third governments like ours in the U.S.

Given the limitations of accepted growth doctrine and the inadequacies of even good data in poor lands, analysis of India and China challenges the economist and social scientist, All his skills are tested, his perseverance tried. What is the correct record? How do you explain the pattern it reveals? What are the "true" technological and behavioral relationships for the short run? Klein's paper in no way reflects this challenge—nor this opportunity for discovery. He neither poses the economist's problem nor applies any of his tools. He offers one basic theme: the records available exaggerate the reality for the two countries and we therefore can make no valid inference about relative progress. . . .

[Thus] Klein's paper throws no relevant light on the relative achievements of China's and India's development efforts. What he says bears neither on what was nor on what is likely to be with this comparison.

Again, this is a great pity, since the subject is of importance from both an analytic and operational viewpoint, and since there is so much that the economist's tools permit him to say about it. May I therefore try to rectify this inadequacy by indicating in a few minutes what might now be said about these two countries? While these are my own statements, I use the abundant material now available (1963, 1964) from serious scholars on China.

China experienced major expansions in industrial and overall product in the 1950's until sometime in 1959; the peak agricultural output may have been in 1957 (1958?) but there was an adverse crop in 1959. The years 1959-62 were crisis years, including three very poor harvests. Industrial production may also have fallen absolutely after 1960, especially in the modern sector. Very rough estimates of national product in 1961 and 1962 place it below its 1957 level. By 1961 the rate of decline of modern industry had certainly slackened off; by 1962 an upward movement occurred in agriculture and national product. Expansion has continued to date, with some evidence of a marked growth during 1964. With agricultural output currently at the 1957 or 1958 level, it is probable that China in 1964 has at least attained its national product of the early-leap period, 1957-59.

If we now accept the official output data for India, there has been an expansion of about 40 percent in national product since 1952. One answer as to which nation has done better between 1952 and 1964 thus depends upon the quantitative increase between 1952 and 1957-59 in China, since 1964 output may not have exceeded the latter level. Even the most conservative estimates place this increase above 40 percent. Thus, progress as measured by total income is of the same order of magnitude in the two countries, if we take the official figures for India, if we prorate over the entire period the serious reversals in China over the 1959-62 years and if we discount heavily (by one-third or one-fourth) the official data on Chinese overall growth from 1952 through 1959.

In the context of present interest in these two countries, much more significant observations need to be made. For both the development of theory over the past five to ten years and careful study of the experience of labor-abundant countries have given us new insight for hypotheses on the growth process. There cannot be a self-reinforcing growth process in these economies without sustained increases in output per man in the populous labor intensive, more traditional parts of the economy. Progress in the modern industrial sector, whatever the levels of foreign assistance, cannot substitute for progress in the more traditional parts, at least over the early period (first decade or two) of a program for accelerating or initiating growth. This seems to be a basic characteristic of the dynamics of growth in countries like India and China. Whatever the inadequacies of their industrial effort, whatever the extent and duration of foreign assistance to them, their overall performance responds, with appropriate multipliers, to the trend in output per man in agriculture, say. Unless the action program is geared directly to generate this (not as a substitute for, but in addition to, the much easier program for modern industry), the nation will not move toward self-sustaining growth.

There are important differences between Indian and Chinese growth efforts in this reward. The course of economic policy in India has persistently, over the past decade, disregarded this requirement of the more traditional sectors. With what must be termed ideological rigidity, the program for growth has not dealt with these sectors (except in words); the Indian ("Western") model has focused on modernization and industrialization, and these, in proper turn, were to spark change in the more backward sectors. India pays a high price for this rigidity: the rates of overall growth have been lower relative to plan in each successive plan. In a fundamental sense India is farther from being able to grow on its own momentum than India was a decade ago. Without policy changes (which are as yet in no way evident), the outlook for a successful growth effort in India is a bleak one indeed.

The situation in China is different. Economic growth policy has undergone basic shifts. During the period through 1957 (perhaps into 1958) policy was essentially consistent with what, according to the argument above, the Chinese (and Indian) situation needed. The industrial sector was favored, but a major effort was put upon agricultural and small industry development, with the conscious aim of expanding the use of manpower. Rural-urban migration was discouraged. The "great leap forward" reflected a shift to a more familiar pattern of investment and development priority. Push the modern sector and its effects will spread throughout the economy. The hard years, 1958-62, cannot be analyzed here. But it seems to be true that present policy (since late 1962) is essentially back to that of the early years. Perhaps, as this brief account suggests, "eleven years of planned development, including five years of economic trials, have driven home some valuable lessons" (to quote Professor Choh-Ming Li). The prospects for steady improvement may thus be favorable—although there is of course no guarantee that Chinese leaders, once the nation is again on the move economically, will not again seek what they originally wanted from the "great leap."

In the light of the "facts" and the research results currently available for India and China, one must conclude that the Chinese prospect is the more favorable. China is seeking an effective program for its Communist society. India's intellectual commitments to inappropriate models continue to defy the evidence of India's own experience and to thwart the real opportunities for India's economic expansion.

SUGGESTED READING

Aiyar, S. P., and Srinivasan, R. (Eds.), *Studies in Indian Democracy*. Bombay: Allied Publishers Private Ltd., 1965.

Arokiasamy, M., *India and Mixed Economy*. Gorkhale Endowment Lectures, 1964-1965. Tiruchirapalli: The author, 1966.

Chandrasekhar, S., "Should We Legalize Abortion in India?" *Population Review*, Vol. 10, No. 2 (July 1966).

Das, A. B., and Chatterji, M. N., *The Indian Economy: Its Growth and Problems*. Calcutta: Bookland, 1963.

Das, Nabagopal, *The Public Sector in India*, 3rd ed. New York: Asia Publishing House, 1966.

Fourth Five Year Plan—A Draft Outline. New Delhi: Planning Commission, Government of India, 1966.

Gandhi, Mohandas Karamchand, *Socialism of My Conception*. Edited by Anand T. Hingorani. Bombay: Nharatiya Vidya Bhavan, 1966.

Ghoshal S. N., and Sharma, M. D., *Economic Growth and Commercial Banking in a Developing Economy: India, A Case Study*. Calcutta: Scientific Book Agency, 1965.

Gupta, R. C., *Socialism, Democracy and India*. Agra: Ram Prasad, 1965.

Hidatatullah, M., *Democracy in India and the Judicial Process*. Bombay: Asia Publishing House, 1966.

India News. Information Service, Embassy of India, Washington, D.C.

Kyn, Petwas, "India: Problems of Socio-Economic Development." *World Marxist Review*, September 1966.

Mann, J. S., "The Impact of Public Law 480 Imports on Prices and Domestic Supply of Cereals in India." *Journal of Farm Economics*, Vol. 49, No. 1 (February 1967), Part I.

National Council, Communist Party of India, *The Present Political Situation*. New Delhi, 1966.

Neale, Walter C., *India: The Search for Unity—Democracy and Progress*. Princeton: N.J.: Van Nostrand, 1965.

Rosen, George, *Democracy and Economic Change in India*. Berkeley, Calif.: University of California Press, 1966.

Sharma, B. M., *The Republic of India: Constitution and Government*. New York: Asia Publishing House, 1966.

ISRAEL

In many respects, the experience of Israel stands apart. It is an isolated country, surrounded by hostile neighbors vowed to its destruction, yet one which in the course of its short nation-state history has relied heavily on foreign contacts and external aid. Outside grants, loans, and reparations payments, however, do not explain Israel's economic performance. Against seemingly overwhelming natural and political odds, Israel in the short space of twenty years has raised itself from underdevelopment to the affluent levels of Holland or Finland. Israel's road from poverty to relative comfort, even though in many respects unique, presents useful lessons for, and parallels with, other countries. The Israel way is of special interest in answering the question whether political freedom and economic development can be compatible in the early stages of the long pull out of poverty. Israel has elected a path which seems to avoid the excesses of early industrial capitalism as well as the absolute political uniformity and the surrender to a deified leader which have characterized the non-capitalist path of development in many countries.

Israel has so far managed to strike the delicate and elusive balance between political democracy and economic coercion, between individual initiative and state intervention, and between a binding ideology and the freedom of every man to follow the dictates of his own conscience. Bitter personal experience need not, the Israeli experience says, lead to a philosophy of hate: private, class, national, or otherwise. Rather than project past sufferings, degradation, and legitimate grievance into the future, instead of raising resentment to a national goal, the Israelis have elected to tackle the problems at hand in a spirit of pioneering pragmatism in which each obstacle and each potential advantage is weighed separately and in accordance with its own merits. It has been a hard road, but one which so far, in spite of all pressures and temptations, has paid off handsomely in terms of human dignity and material comfort.

1. The Israeli Road From Underdevelopment
to Affluence

LEONARD J. FEIN

Fein, in the selection below, discusses what he considers the uniqueness of Israel's position, her relationship with her Arab neighbors, her economic development, her basic ideology, her political institutions, and, briefly, her hopes and prospects for the future [Editors' note].

All countries are unique, set apart by some special blend of geography, tradition, economic and political organization, ethnic composition, ideology, and culture. But some are more unique than others, and it is among these that Israel must be numbered. There are, no doubt, other nations which experience one or more of the conditions which make Israel, first of all, an isolated country. But no other confronts them all: land borders shared entirely with unfriendly neighbors, across which no airplanes can fly, no letters be sent, no roads be built; a language spoken by no other People; a past, both within and outside the nation's borders, devoid of special ties to any other people; located in a region culturally alien as well as politically hostile. To these must be added the size of the country, for Israel's smallness—eight thousand square miles, one-third the size of Lake Michigan, smaller than all but six of America's fifty states—reinforces, intractably, its isolation.

Nor is this splendid isolation Israel's only distinguishing quality. Alone among the nations of the world, most of its adult citizens were born elsewhere, and have come to the country with some part of their diverse native cultures still intact. Like its people, Israel's political institutions trace their roots to another time, and, in some measure, another place. The result is that Israel's quest for national identity must follow a lonely and pitted path; no trail has been blazed by others, no partners share the journey's perils.

Israel is, as well, a nation of sharply dramatic contrasts. Some of these are trivial, though picturesque, deriving from peculiar juxtaposition: the tallest building in Jewish Jerusalem is the Young Men's Christian Association, ancient Caesaria is now the site of an elegant golf course, the neon lights of Tel Aviv beckon in the language of the Bible. Others are of greater import, and as the conflicts they represent and generate are the stuff of Israel's political life, we shall confront them again and again as we proceed. The most intriguing contrast, however, is the least obvious, and requires special emphasis at the outset.

That contrast is implied by the inclusion of sections on Israel in studies of both the "modern nations" as well as the "emerging nations."[1] The case for the former is impressive: Israel is one of the most urban countries in the world, has more doctors per patient than any other country, and, in literacy, unionization, agricultural development, basic scientific research, primary school enrollment, economic planning, or number of people per newspaper, resembles the modern Western nation far more than it does the newer societies.[2] Yet there is also a compelling case for classifying Israel among the developing nations: large numbers of its adult population have immigrated from the less developed regions, such as Yemen, North Africa, or Kurdistan, and many of these are socially and psychically more akin to the peoples of their birthplace than to their new compatriots; most of the country's 250,000 Arabs (12 per cent of the population) are rural traditionals; a small but significant minority of the Jewish population are ultra-orthodox Jews, whose commitments are to past rather than future, to faith rather than science; ascription still vies with achievement as the primary basis for recruitment to significant social roles, and the agrarian, peasant-oriented ideology of old continues to impede a total commitment to science and technology. Finally, the political system itself has yet to reach and pass that critical transition when the reins of leadership are handed from the preindependence founding fathers to a new and younger generation, as it has yet to find a way to satisfy its preindependence goals with its postindependence resources.

Yet it will not do to say merely that from the economic standpoint, Israel has "achieved" modernity, while its sociopolitical life is still in an early phase of transition. The spheres of national existence are not so easily separable, even for analytic purposes; the very fact that tradition still impinges more heavily on one area than on another alters each, as it alters the context and the substance of politics. For this reason, among others, models of transitional politics developed in somewhat more conventional settings will be of only sometime utility in understanding politics in Israel.

Emphasis on Israel's uniqueness may, however, be overstated. Were Israel so idiosyncratic that no useful parallels might be drawn, in either

[1] See, for example, the chapter on Israel by S. N. Eisenstadt in Arnold Rose (ed.), *The Institutions of Advanced Societies* (Minneapolis, 1958), and data on Israel in Gabriel Almond and James Coleman, *The Politics of the Developing Areas* (Princeton, 1960), unnumbered appendix.

[2] See Almond and Coleman, *op. cit.*, and Bruce Russett, *et al., World Handbook of Political and Social Indicators* (New Haven, 1965).

direction, between it and other countries, one could hardly justify the effort required to explore its political system. But the bits and pieces which, combined in a specific way, define Israel and no other country, themselves have precedents and analogs. Moreover, some facets of the Israeli experience are prototypical, and may offer useful insight into political change and development in other states. Thus, to argue that Israel's total experience is "more unique than others" is not to contend that students of comparative politics have nothing to learn from it nor anything to contribute to its understanding.

The American reader with no special knowledge of Israel may be perplexed by these opening paragraphs. For most Americans, awareness of Israel has centered on the drama of what has come to be known as its "rebirth," as well as on its involvement in the continuing Middle East crisis. Israel's image as an embattled young nation, peopled by a tough and resilient breed, was given initial impetus by the struggle for independence, encouraged by subsequent history and by press release, and derived final confirmation, however simplistically, from the best-seller and motion picture, *Exodus*. The international politics of the Middle East have also shaped American consciousness of Israel. The Sinai Campaign, the Arab refugee problem, the Gaza Strip—these and many more have taken their place in that growing and confusing lexicon which the responsible citizen feels compelled to master. . . .

Israel's . . . agenda of political concern is overwhelmingly dominated by three major questions: war and peace, economic viability, and social integration. The policy options available in these three problem areas, especially the first and last, are not matters for independent governmental determination. No Government, no matter how resourceful, can "solve" these problems, as a Government might "solve" the "problem" of the electoral system. No amount of tinkering or manipulation can remove these problems from the agenda. The issue of war and peace will remain an issue as long as other nations threaten Israel's existence. The issue of economic viability will remain an issue so long as military needs and mass immigration drain the economy, and so long as Israel must remain dependent on infusion of foreign capital. The issue of integration will remain an issue so long as images of personal identity are not amenable to legislation or directly responsive to Government intervention.

Yet, that is not the end of the matter. Though options may be limited, and though problems may not be wholly soluble, there are options, and there are proximate solutions. If Israel cannot unilaterally proclaim peace, it can help stave off war; if it cannot find resources that are not there, it can inventively exploit the ones it has; if it cannot legislate equality, it can compensate for inequality. And so we shall find some reward in entering fleetingly into a consideration of these and other problems which are the staples of Israel's political agenda.

ISRAEL AND THE ARAB NATIONS

Israel has fought two wars with the Arab states, one for survival, in 1948, and one for security, in 1956. Many Israelis, perhaps even most, expect that there will be a third round. And few are sanguine about Israel's prospects should that come to pass. That public concern is widespread is confirmed by the Cantril survey, which shows that almost 50 per cent of the Israelis mention war with the Arabs as one of their "fears for the nation," that 30 per cent mention war in general, and that 9 per cent fear an end to national independence. War is by far the most pervasive fear, and this is true for every subgroup within the population, whether defined by class, ethnicity, time of immigration, political affiliation, sex, educational attainment, region, religion, age, or occupation. Similarly, peace with the Arabs is the chief hope for the nation, for the population as a whole, and for all but two subgroups within it.[3] Even when asked to express personal fears and hopes, many Israelis mention war and peace.

Everything that happens in Israel happens against the background of the threat of war, against the realization that Israel's destiny, in the most fundamental sense, is not in its own control. More than 57,000,000 people live in the seven nations which declared war on Israel in 1948, and which have yet to make peace with her. They outnumber the Israelis by better than twenty to one. Together, these seven nations contain an area about the size of India, well over 1,000,000 square miles; Israel is about the size of New Jersey, less than 8,000 square miles. Israel has altogether 613 miles of land borders, and across each and every one of those miles is a hostile neighbor.

The relative advantage the Arabs enjoy in manpower and territory may mean less and less in an era of pushbutton war, when technology rather than manpower determines victory. Yet, quite apart from the greater economic resources which the Arabs can bring to bear on the military balance, their massiveness has a marked psychological effect. The Israelis know that the Arab stake in any war is minimal. After the bullets—or missiles—have stopped flying, the worst the Arabs can fear, in hard military fact, is a minor loss of territory and a high number of casualties. Israel's stake, however, is total; it could be permanently crippled, even destroyed. It lacks entirely a fall-back position, both because its territory is so small and so vulnerable, and because the Arabs have repeatedly asserted that their goal is its annihilation. In their own view, Israelis have few negotiable

[3] The two exceptions are white-collar workers, for whom peace is a close second to technological advancement, and members of Herut, Israel's most militantly aggressive political party, for whom war is again behind—though not by much—technological advance.

assets, for the outstanding issues between Arabs and Israelis which might be bargained over, such as the repatriation of Arab refugees or a return to the boundaries set by the United Nations, are matters of vital national concern.

Israelis are fond of saying that two secret weapons have enabled them to survive—their own realization that there is no alternative, and Arab disunity. The knowledge that the only alternative to staving off the Arab threat is total destruction provides them, no doubt, with an important resource. It impels the nation to make greater sacrifices, and its army to be more tenacious, than they might were the issues less compelling than life and death. But again, human will seems decreasingly relevant as a national military resource as war itself becomes increasingly impersonal. And Arab disunity, except in the most tangential ways, is not a matter which Israel can affect. Hence Israel's active response to the Arab threat has not rested merely on such "secret weapons," but instead has been directed to developing both military and political deterrent strength.

Military Deterrence. The military deterrent is enormously expensive. It involves a commitment to maintaining the Israel Defense Forces at a level which will cause any potential aggressor serious pause, no mean feat when the potential aggressor involved has both income and manpower far in excess of the prospective defender. Estimates of Israel's actual defense expenditures vary widely, ranging from about 200 to almost 400 million dollars a year; even a relatively low estimate suggests that at least 7 per cent of Israel's gross national product goes directly for defense needs.[4] And the 7 per cent figure excludes (1) classified expenditures and (2) the vast supportive contributions made to the defense effort by other sectors of the economy. Thus the location of new agricultural settlements is generally more a response to military exigencies than to economic planning. A proper accounting system would charge the losses to the economy generated by introducing such noneconomic considerations into economic planning against the account of the defense establishment, thereby considerably increasing the size of that account. And, after these several calculations were made, the cost of taking large numbers of people out of the economy, perhaps the most significant, however indirect, would still have to be added.

The standing army in Israel is usually thought to be relatively small, numbering as it does only 70,000 men. That is a small number, however, only in relation to the total strength available after mobilization, which stands at over 250,000 men. It is not small as a *percentage* of the total population; indeed, it is the highest proportion of men in uniform in the

[4] Estimates are available from various sources, including the official Israeli figures as they appear in the UN *Statistical Yearbook* as well as reports published regularly by the Institute for Strategic Services in London. A figure of $385 million was cited by *The New York Times* of December 24, 1963. Several sources give 9 or 10 per cent of GNP as a best estimate.

Near East, it is higher than in the United States, the United Kingdom, Cuba, and most other countries. The strength of the defense forces is based on universal military training, lasting 26 months for men and 20 months for women. (The figure of 70,000 for the standing army includes conscripts. The professional military numbers only about 12,000.) Moreover, men are liable for reserve duty through the age of 49, and women until they are 34; such duty involves up to one day per month plus one month per year of active service.

The combination of relatively many people in uniform and the small size of the country make the military presence highly conspicuous. Even were it more hidden, however, Israelis would hardly be able to escape the awareness of danger. Hardly a week goes by without some new border incident, and the press reports fully on relevant developments in the Arab countries. Tel Aviv, the center of Israel's largest concentration of population, is 12 miles from the Jordanian border; no place in Israel is more than 70 miles from a hostile nation. There is, in short, an immediacy and a constancy to the threat of war which few nations experience so totally.

One learns to live with it. Jerusalem, divided close to its downtown center by a wall which marks the national boundary, joined to the rest of the country by a narrow land corridor, scene of occasional exchanges of gunfire, does not seem, to the casual visitor, an abnormal city. One needs to have the source of tension pointed out; it is by no means palpable. So, too, for its residents. Their brows are no more furrowed, their walk no more furtive, than those of people in more normal climes. They work, and play, and buy, and learn, much as they might elsewhere. This equanimity bespeaks no superhuman stamina, no extraordinary character. Around the world, there are many people who have come to terms with hazard, whether natural or of man conceived. Perhaps an as yet unexecuted psychoanalytic study might reveal the human costs of such adjustment; they are not manifest. It is no small matter to be threatened with extinction from nearby year-in year-out. But people have a wondrous capacity for learning to walk with danger, for adapting and repressing and surviving. It is possible, of course, that in making peace with the threat of war one must attach to the threat an inevitability which in turn sustains it; this we do not really know. It is clear, at the same time, that one major source of strength is the presence of a defender marked by competence and invested with confidence.

Thus the defense forces, quite apart from their deterrent impact on the Arab states, are a source of high morale to the Israelis. The army is not only taken for granted, it is honored. However much the earlier tradition of the Jew eschewed the military, Israelis have come to know the armed forces as their lifeline. No subtle reasoning is required for this knowledge, no complex extrapolation about what might happen if there were no Israeli army. The alternative is clear and present, as is the danger.

The army does more than reassure Israelis. It undertakes explicit responsibilities in education and integration, and it implicitly provides the most manifest symbol of Israel's nationhood, undiluted by political debate, unencumbered by ideological baggage, unblemished by scandal. There is no question that the army is seen as the most "pure" of Israel's institutions.

Yet with all the respect that is accorded it, with all the homage it receives, with all the purity of purpose and command that is imputed to it, the principle of civilian control is unquestioned. Its sharpest tests came in the protracted period of haggling after Sinai, when the army was visibly disconcerted by being forced to sacrifice its military gains under United Nations pressure. The Government, however reluctantly, acceded to that pressure, and, despite massive misgivings among many leading military figures, there was neither hesitation nor public expression of disapproval. This, no doubt, bewilders many who have imputed a special character to "the military mind." However bewildering, Israel has managed to maintain its military forces as a citizens' army. Although some Israelis believe that in the early years of statehood, there was a minor possibility of military putsch, it is hardly likely that anyone in Israel today is seriously concerned with such a possibility. It is so far from likely, so almost literally inconceivable, that it is totally discounted.

One puzzles over this, and wonders why it should be so. The reasons are at best unclear; most likely, they depend upon an interplay of factors ideological, institutional, and cultural. The antimilitary tradition, though generally overcome, provides a residue of concern, and hence of security. The nature of reserve service, and the small size of the professional army, militates against a sharp cleavage between citizen and soldier. The policy of early retirement of staff officers, prevents, in part, a full-blown professionalism. Finally, the army has a present job to do, and it is fully supported in that job by the organs of the State. It is not frustrated by inactivity, nor at odds with Government policy. There is, after all, little room for option in that policy. Israel cannot hope to "conquer" its neighbors, nor does it have any reason to want to. Its policy of containment—a containment, be it noted, defended within its own territory—has room for innovation only at the margins. Hence there is little ground for the emergence of a radical cleavage between civil and military wings.

Diplomatic Perspectives. Though Israelis take great pride in the competence of the military, and Israel takes great pains to preserve and expand that competence, it is quite clear to all that military proficiency is not a sufficient deterrent, at least over the long run. Strategic estimates vary widely, but it is commonly believed in Israel that there is a natural limit to Israel's capacity to compete with the Arab nations in armed might. Some gloomily predict that the limit will be reached several years hence; others expansively maintain that at least a decade will pass before the Arabs can hope to overpower Israel. In either case, much sustenance must be derived from faith—faith in continued Arab disunity, faith in a major international détente which will encompass the Near East, faith even in a turn of heart among the Arabs, and chiefly in Egypt. Again, these are matters beyond Israel's control, and the faith may be a wishful thinking bred by desperation. It is a strange juxtaposition, this—a new State, still somewhat surprised to find itself taken seriously, proud, intensely proud of its successes, and yet, on the crucial question of survival, at the mercy of others, save for the passing might of its own armies.

There is, however, more to it than this. For aside from its investment in military power, Israel has sought to increase its international political capital. The development of a political deterrent has been less costly, but hardly less taxing, than maintaining a military edge. Israel has never been enthusiastic about relying on major power guarantees, and has grown less enthusiastic with increased Egyptian capacity to deal a severe first blow before any guarantee could become operative. Since the Sinai Campaign of 1956, when England and France were unwilling to follow through the initial victory, Israel's policy planners have become still more reluctant to take any guarantee seriously. It is evident to Israel that the nation would enjoy support from the major powers only if and as their needs were to coincide with her own, and that her own tactic ought therefore to be a persistent effort at persuading those powers of the coincidence of interests.

This task has been greatly complicated by what Israel perceives as American overcommitment to Nasser. In the Israeli view, America is deluded in its apparent persuasion that Nasser is the chief bulwark against Communist penetration of the Near East. Israelis argue, to the contrary, that Nasser is the key destabilizing element in the region, and that withdrawal of American support from Nasser might well lead to a significant reduction of tensions in the area. They reject, at least for the record, the view that only the continued American relationship with Nasser provides the Near East with what stability it does enjoy.

Whatever the "facts" of the matter, the difference in view has limited Israel's readiness to place great trust on repeated American pronouncements of support, or on such guarantees of territorial integrity as are sometimes proposed. All such efforts and proclamations alter the tactical conditions of a prospective confrontation. They force the recognition that no protracted land war will be fought between Israel and the Arabs, for intervention would surely come in a matter of days at most. But the strategic question is left untouched, for what Israel fears is what it must assume to be a growing Arab capacity to deliver a swift, crippling, and irretrievable blow. And even the strength of Israel's armies is little protection against such a possibility.

In addition to concerning itself with both defensive measures against sudden and massive devastation and—perhaps—with the development of second strike capacity, Israel has sought to overcome that early isolation which, it was felt, might lead the Arabs to believe that no one would much regret Israel's demise. The policy of developing international ties, of making allies and influencing nations, has obviously been more than a response to the Arab-Israel dispute alone. It has been, in at least as great a measure, a way of overcoming the anxieties of isolation, the insecurity that issues from finding that no one takes you seriously. The isolation is geographic: Israel's land borders are virtually sealed; it is diplomatic: Israel is systematically excluded from the regional councils of Afro-Asian states, and is effectively barred from participating in numerous international conferences whose sponsors are forced to choose between Israel and the Arabs; it is, to some degree, economic: the Arab states maintain a boycott, which enjoys only limited success, and bar all direct trade with Israel, an economic fact of some importance. The psychological impact of these several forms of isolation is heightened also by Israel's own sense of difference, based on such things as its Jewishness, with all the uniqueness that implies, its language, unspoken elsewhere, and its peculiar position in a land to which it feels such deep attachment in a region where it feels so very alien.

A partial remedy to the ensuing loneliness has been the systematic development of ties to other countries, and especially to the new nations of Africa and Asia. The policy of pursuing such ties was first seen as a way of "leap-frogging" the Arab encirclement, and every success was greeted with high enthusiasm and not a little surprise. The new relationships are now viewed more realistically and more naturally, and have resulted in more than a rebuff to the hostile Arab states. Israel sends large numbers of its citizens to other nations on foreign aid projects of one kind or another, and plays host each year to thousands of visitors from developing nations, come primarily to study in her institutions. Out of this has come quite meaningful political benefit—Egypt is no longer able to find widespread endorsement for its hostile statements from the new nations—and also, perhaps more significant, another kind of reward, less tangible but more durable—a sense of relevance, the security of acceptance and friendship.

These paragraphs suggest a kind of permanence about Arab-Israel hostilities which may mislead. Some observers, perhaps too rational in their view, assert the increasingly difficult burden of the Near Eastern arms race, and conclude that the time is not far off when lack of resources will put an end to what has been a steady escalation, leading the parties to welcome plans for regional arms control. Others profess to find good omens elsewhere, in political developments inside the Arab world. In Israel, however, no sense of imminent relief is present, no sighting of an end, or even of a beginning to an end, of hostility. The continuing tension, the occasional aggravation, and the ever present possibility of major conflict, are accepted as part of the environment, to be protested against, to be prepared for, to try to circumvent, but neither to forget nor to wish away.

Inevitably, such massive preoccupation affects the society, both directly and indirectly. The military threat diverts, as we have seen, much of the nation's resources. It places Israel in a rather uncomfortable position in its international relations, for it can never be viewed solely in its own right, but must always be juxtaposed against the Arab world. It provides, in limited measure, an issue for political debate within the country, although the basic format of Israel's policy—more properly, Israel's response—is generally taken for granted. Less directly, and more beneficently, it provides to Israel an undoubted source of unity, an issue so preeminent and so undisputed as to make all other cleavages seem trivial. The "ifs" of history are frustrating questions, because unanswerable. But one may speculate that if there had been no massive threat to Israel's existence, the several social conflicts which have thus far been contained might well have proved uncontainable. Against the urge to give domestic ideological conflict its head, there has always been the looming foreboding that beyond a certain point lay disaster, doom doers ready and waiting to exploit the first immobilizing crisis. No one can know, but it may well be that Israel's is an example of a nonworking multiparty system which works, which works because of factors extraneous to the system itself. And no one can know, but it may well be that the degree of social integration which has been achieved, the capacity Israel has demonstrated to handle the vast immigration, has owed much to the unifying symbol of the army, and to the integrative experience of the army itself, to the always evident fact that, in this most important institution, in this one institution which may make the difference between national—and personal—life and death, there is neither East nor West. On the contrary. Westerners may feel more easy and more comfortable with others of similar background, with tourists and visitors of "their own kind" —but they know, as do the Easterners, that it is the massive immigration since 1948 which has provided the manpower Israel requires for her survival, and that all the good wishes and sympathies of other more congenial guests are as nothing against the gift of blood of young Israelis, whatever their complexion and whatever their cultural sophistication. In Israel, as far as we can see into the future, that gift remains an operative distinction, and quite probably a useful one.

The larger questions, the question of war and peace itself, lie beyond the scope of this discussion. There are no easy answers to these questions, ranging, as they do, from nuclear development to refugee policy to water resources to initiatives for peace. They have been, and continue to be, amply discussed elsewhere. Their bearing on domestic politics is not wholly clear, for, once again, they have generally been excluded, or dealt with only casually, in political debate, reflecting Israel's self-perception as an unwilling victim of others' policies. Here and there, political leaders have vied with one another to appear more "activist," more militant, and from time to time, minor issues have been disputed publicly. Such cases have been unusual. The Israeli view is that independent initiatives on her part are difficult to come by, because she has so few resources with which to bargain and such obdurate hostility to overcome. Similarly, a more expansive policy is generally viewed as self-defeating, for no one seriously believes that Israel either would be permitted to occupy Arab territory or that such occupation would serve any useful purpose.

At the same time, the apparently endless conflict exacerbates Israel's quest for identity, for it raises once again, and now in the most direct way, the issue of what Israel is to be. Is this country a European enclave at the Afro-Asian crossroad, or shall it be, in some still uncertain way, a part of the Near East? Neither view is easy, nor is any other, but so long as the essential abnormality of Israel's position among its neighbors remains, no honest selection is possible. Instead, and Israelis are most sensitive to this, the land which embraced the eternal stranger has itself now become stranger to its region; the walls of hostility which bar passage from Israel to Lebanon and Syria and Jordan and Egypt are no less barriers to national normalcy than the ghetto walls of Europe in their day.

THE ECONOMY

There is a peculiar analogy between Israel's search for identity in the sociopolitical arena and the country's economic character. The economy is hardly more coherent, more clearly defined in purpose and direction, or less beset by problems than the society. The structural similarity between the two is, in part, mere coincidence. It is, however, also the result of interplay between them: the nature of the human resources available to exploit the natural resources, the ideological and political environment which gives direction to the economy, and Israel's relations with other countries.

On the surface, Israel's record of economic development is extraordinarily impressive. Since independence, the gross national product has increased at an average of better than 11 per cent per year, and the per capita GNP has risen by about 5 per cent per year. This means that at one and the same time, Israel has managed to absorb hundreds of thousands of immigrants, maintain a modern defense establishment, and still raise the standard of living for the whole society quite significantly. The value of agricultural production has risen from under $15 million a year in 1949 to over $400 million in 1963 (in stable dollars); irrigated land has increased five-hundred fold. Expansion has been no less dramatic in the industrial sector. Unemployment, at over 11 per cent in 1953, has been replaced by a mild labor shortage. Income tax revenues were $3 million in 1949-1950, rose to over $100 million by 1960-1961, and are by now over $300 million.

There are other measures of the expansion, more intuitive but no less real. In 1953, Israel was in the midst of an official regimen of austerity, including food rationing and a black market to go with it. There was little private traffic on the highways, and there were none of the conventional amenities of an upper middle class. Housing was scarce, as were recreational facilities, as were refrigerators, good restaurants, or what have you. By the mid-1960's, the change was quite visible. Israelis were criticizing each other for inflated private consumption, new cars were clogging the highways, almost all homes had gas stoves, more than a quarter of Israeli families owned washing machines, housing advertisements now cited luxury features, the growing number of fine restaurants now insisted upon reservations well in advance.

How had all this come to pass? Not a few early prognoses painted a far gloomier future, one at best never far from collapse. Analysts did not tire of citing Israel's economic liabilities, and they were many:

1. Natural resources are limited. They include, most prominently, a climate favorable to citrus fruits, some mineral deposits in the Dead Sea area, enough oil for perhaps 10 per cent of the country's needs.

2. Water is a perennial problem. The largest water resource is the Sea of Galilee, less than one one-hundredth the size of the smallest of the Great Lakes. The smallest, the eight mile long Kishon River, is large enough to be included in the list of Israel's principal rivers.

3. Half the country is arid, a third of its acreage nonirrigable.

4. New immigrants are, at least for their first year, a net cost to the economy, even though the cost may be viewed as an investment.

5. The prevailing ideology of welfare and social services involves some diversion of investment capital.

6. The standard of living to which some Israelis were accustomed, either in their countries of origin or in preindependence Palestine, and to which most aspire, again limits savings, and thereby investment.

7. Military needs siphon additional sums out of productive enterprise.

Indeed, any of these problems would have been sufficiently troublesome by itself. When joined to all the others, Israel's economic success appears all the more remarkable.

The necessary, though by itself not sufficient, condition for that success has been the availability to the economy of large amounts of foreign capital, especially of unilateral (i.e., non-repayable) receipts. Total foreign capital has averaged, over the years, between 15 and 20 per cent of GNP, a figure probably unique among the nations of the world. It has included grants-in-aid from the United States, moneys collected by Jewish charities, and especially by the United Jewish Appeal, reparations and personal restitution payments by West Germany, as well as government bonds sold abroad. Not quite coincidentally, the rate of net investment between 1950 and 1960 was about 15 to 20 per cent of available economic resources— that is, it was about the same as capital inflow. In other words, it is as if all of Israel's capital investment has been subsidized, leaving the country able to spend all of its domestic income on private consumption and governmental expenditure.[5] Or, to use a different measure: in 1960, capital inflow to the government was about $210 million—or roughly the same amount as Israel's defense expenditures in that year. We might, then, take the view that Israel's defense needs rather than its investments, have, in effect, been subsidized.

This vast quantity of assistance does not itself explain the entire growth in the economy. The investment rate has accounted, over the years, for no more than 2 or 3 per cent of the annual growth in GNP. In addition, it has made possible the full utilization of manpower, and the added labor input has accounted for half the rise in GNP. Another 2 to 3 per cent, however, owes to increased productivity. At the same time, the unprecedented inflow of foreign capital has had other kinds of effects. It has reinforced certain patterns of planning, and generated special problems for the economy.

Most capital inflow has been to the Government of Israel, enabling the Government to manage much of the national investment. In fact, about 60 per cent of investment in Israel since 1950 has been made, directly or indirectly, by the Government. This contrasts quite sharply with such investment in most other countries. Yet it is not simply an expression of socialist doctrine; witness the fact that over two-thirds of Government investments are in the form of loans to private and public corporations. It is, instead, a response to the availability of large amounts of capital to the Government, which itself reinforces a marked propensity for central planning. That propensity owes something to socialist doctrine, and something more to the Yishuv tradition, when the Histadrut rushed in where others feared to tread. The combined defense and immigration needs further encourage this tradition, leaving the Government in a position of massive predominance in the economy.

But at the same time as the Government's hand has been so markedly strengthened, the Government's problems have multiplied. The reason is basically very simple: capital inflow has made possible a dramatic rise in the standard of living at the same time as other major costs have been absorbed. Capital inflow cannot be counted upon indefinitely. Indeed, American grants-in-aid have all but halted, and German reparations have come to an end. If the extra burdens of immigration and defense must still be met, then it follows that the rate of growth of personal income will have to decline. In other words, insofar as massive investment is still required, private (and public) consumption will have to slow down. Yet, no matter how simple this reasoning and how unassailable, no Government has yet found a way to persuade its people that a steady path of upward progress now a decade old must level off. Instead, inflation remains a most serious obstacle to stability.

[5] This point is well made, as are others, by Avner Hovne in *The Economy of Israel* (Jerusalem, 1963).

Moreover, without the surplus flow of foreign funds, the problem of financing imports will grow more difficult. This has been the constant problem of the Israeli economy, and it remains the central problem today, despite a thirteen-fold increase in net exports since 1949, a period during which net imports only tripled. The problem is that in 1949, exports totaled 11 per cent of imports; the vast expansion that has since taken place has brought the 11 per cent figure up to about 45 per cent; but the absolute quantity of the deficit has increased, because of the difference in percentage bases. Thus the $200 million plus deficit of 1949 had grown, by 1964, into a $450 million deficit.

When a country buys so much more than it sells, it must make up the difference somewhere. Israel has large capital reserves, but they are not unlimited. And, if capital inflow declines, then either imports (i.e., purchases) must be curbed, or exports (i.e., sales) must be increased. In the long run, it is better to increase exports, since that bespeaks a healthier economy. It is also politically more feasible. For if a healthier balance depends upon curtailing desired foreign commodities, as happens when the economy does not grow rapidly enough to redress the trade deficit "naturally," then the political problem becomes quite sharp.

By and large, Israel's planners have emphasized increased exports as the best way to economic stability. But it is fairly clear that that is insufficient. At the very best, it leaves untouched the question of sufficient investment capital, which can be generated only by increasing domestic saving. Yet such saving cannot come out of reduced spending, since it is hardly likely that such a move would be politically acceptable. Instead, if there is to be adequate saving, it must come from a reduction in the rate of increase of consumption, which has been growing at a per capita rate of about 6 per cent a year. Such a reduction is a major object of Government economic policy, and has been for some time, but has yet to be attained. The difficulty of achieving it may be easily seen if we look only at the governmental sector, where the reduction must compete with increasing expenditures for defense and a growing commitment to free and compulsory secondary education. It is hardly easier in the private sector, where reducing consumption would mean either that the 25 per cent of Israeli families who, in 1964, did not have refrigerators would have to content themselves with ice-boxes for the time being, or that a major redistribution of income, with severe limits on spending by the well-to-do, would be required.

It is a rather peculiar condition that an economy in which the Government, by circumstance and by design, plays so important a role, has no single planning authority. Economic decision making is quite decentralized within the Government, with various ministries, as well as the Histadrut, to a lesser degree, operating somewhat autonomously. This situation has begun to change, especially as a result of growing reliance on professional economic advice. But there remains, even now, amateuristic bias, a readiness by senior ministers to depend upon their own instincts. This bias quite naturally developed during the pre-State years when these same ministers were successfully refuting expert advice in almost every sphere. It was abetted by Ben Gurion, who preferred not to involve himself in economic planning, leaving the Government without firm leadership in this regard. Ministers were thereby encouraged to go their own way. The shift towards professionalism and centralization began with Eshkol's accession to power, but has yet to overcome the inertia of earlier years.

The lack of a central authority may, in the long run, prove to have been functional to economic development, as well as to political stability. From the economic standpoint, it has prevented, in large measure, the sorts of catastrophic errors which have been fairly common in developing countries. No one economic bet has ever been so large as to involve fatal risks. The country has been able to experiment with various approaches, instead of prematurely opting for an economic destiny based on one or another untested axiom. From the political standpoint, decentralization has meant that various ideological perspectives could be accommodated simultaneously. The right hand, supporting private enterprise, could claim ignorance of the left hand, busily investing in cooperative enterprise. Concessions to the kibbutz movement could be balanced against concessions to foreign investors. Different parties, and different factions within the same party, could all have their ideological predilections subsidized, which has doubtless made all of them happy.

The happiness depends upon continued growth. All economic decisions are made against a background of scarce resources, but Israel's resources have been, thus far, less scarce than they may be in the near future. The sensitive question is, therefore, whether the principle of central economic planning, with two decades of trial and error to guide it, will become sufficiently acceptable before time, in the form of money to subsidize political stability, runs out. And how will people grown accustomed to rapid progress accept a coordinated plan which seeks to force a public belt-tightening that has until now proved merely slogan?

These questions cannot be isolated from Israel's international position. Economic viability will continue to depend, for some time to come, on Israel's special relationship with the Jewish People, and on the responsiveness of Jews, especially in the United States, to Israel's needs. Tourism, a mainstay of economic growth, depends upon reasonable stability in Arab-Israel relations. (The steady upward sweep of tourism was sharply interrupted only in 1956 and 1957, partly because of the Sinai Campaign.) Israel's association with the Common Market, a near necessity for her citrus industry, depends to some degree on the special sympathy of European nations. In general, as in the military sphere, Israel is highly sensitive to decisions made elsewhere and by others. Once again, if we accept the paucity of resources, the policies of others, and the basic ideological commitments of the system as inevitable, the relevant options for economic planning are severely curtailed. The economy may be more or less mixed, planning may be more or less central, the standard of living may rise more or less rapidly —but the essential directions are relatively fixed. Being fixed, they are not much debated. Instead, political debate centers on the "mores and lesses," albeit in inflated style which makes the stakes seem more compelling than they are.

HUMAN AND IDEOLOGICAL RESOURCES

Economic development and military security problems may be the most pressing which face Israel, but they are not, at least in this context, among the most interesting. To the degree to which it is true that they fundamentally depend upon decisions made outside the Israeli political system, it follows that little can be said about them here. Moreover, early Zionist theory was never particularly interested in technical economic problems, much less in military strategy, whereas the most intriguing aspect of contemporary Israel is the manner in which the early vision has adjusted— or failed to adjust—to the present reality.

Zionist theory was oriented chiefly to the shape and purpose of the future society, to an eschatalogical emphasis on ends rather than means. The substance of the orientation rested on certain assumptions about the nature of man, and, more particularly, about the nature of the prospective Jewish settler. These assumptions had been derived almost exclusively from the Eastern European setting, now long since reduced in relevance. The human resources with which Israel's founding fathers have in fact had to go about building their new society have borne little resemblance to the early expectation. Had that expectation been fulfilled, it would have been immediately apparent that it provided an insufficient basis for social revolution. The idyllic image of a nation of educated pioneers, plow in one hand, book in the other, could hardly sustain a modern, differentiated economy. The doctrinaire aversion to the "middleman" neglected the hard requirements of complex societies. The naive egalitarianism was uninformed by a sophisticated psychology. And the image of nation as solidary unit neglected the intractable fact of human difference.

In the best of all possible worlds, in a world in which the country were left alone to manage its own affairs and determine its own destiny, it is doubtful that the pioneering vision could have been sustained. The shift from cooperative commonwealth to social service state, from poetry to textbook prose, was probably inevitable. But older Israelis are sometimes resentful, sometimes nostalgic, for they do not feel the poetry was given a fair reading. The world of Israel is not the best of all possible worlds. It matters not that no world ever is; theirs did not have its fair chance. It has changed in many ways, of course, in its context and in its necessary agenda. Not the least of the changes has been in the human resources on which it now depends, those same resources which were the key to erstwhile hopes.

In 1948, on the eve of independence, Israel was probably the best educated country in the world, at least as education is conventionally measured. The vast influx of immigrants cut sharply into the pre-State levels. Educational attainment appears, today, on superficial examination, relatively high still, but the average now masks a disparity between the very high levels of the Europeans and the very low levels of the Easterners. These conditions are not irrelevant to the economy; the availability of professionals in abundance has helped in development, and the relative absence of a skilled laborer class, somewhere between the Easterner and the European in educational attainment, has hindered it. But they are of still greater significance to the nation's self-image. At the very least, they force a drastic revision in the utopian timetable. More often, they, together with the other differences of which we have already spoken and which they bespeak, force a revision of the utopian commitment.

It has now become manifest, despite massive reluctance to confess it, that people are not quite so instantly malleable as was once believed. Neither the Mediterranean climate, nor the country's historicity, nor even the carefully nurtured cooperative institutions, brought with them rapid transformation. Whether the fault lies with the nature of the universe, or simply with the overburdening problems which Israel has had to face, is an issue of fading interest; almost everyone has now acknowledged that what chance there was is gone, gone and increasingly forgotten.

Herein lies the chief difficulty of telling Israel's story, for there has yet to come a new dream to replace the old. It will no doubt be said that dreams are of little significance in the dispassionate analysis of politics. But neither the older generation, still somewhat bewildered by what events have made of its hopes, nor the younger, still searching for an authentic replacement of the old, can well be understood without them. The temporary compromise is the social service state, the thorough consensus on the propriety of welfare and of investment in human resources. Perhaps the technical dimensions of these commitments are sufficient to capture the imagination, at least of those who have not known more expansive visions. It is too soon to say.

Yet, despite the pain and the confusion, the kernel of the old commitment is still visible, and is still viable. The dream spoke not only of personal redemption, but also of community behavior. And if it is permissible to take state action as a partial substitute for the more amorphous concept of community behavior, then it is apparent that something still remains of the faded dream. For Israel is, at least in firm principle, a welfare state. Despite the drain on its resources, it has expanded the scope of its educational program by 500 per cent since 1948; it has compulsory and comprehensive old age insurance, maternity insurance, workman's compensation; special benefits are provided large families; 82 per cent of the population is covered by health insurance, and 60 per cent of the work force benefits from pension programs. The penal system, rehabilitation programs, cultural institutions—all these and more are matters of imaginative attention and action by the State. The system is still inefficient, and there are gaps. Slums exist, and poverty has yet to be eliminated. But goals are not debated; the society is unquestioningly committed to a full-scale welfare system, closest to the Scandinavian model. Given the costs involved, and the sense that welfare is only an intimation of social justice, the fact of the commitment is significant. It is based, fundamentally, on a non-economic understanding of social responsibility, which, incidentally, makes demonstrable good sense as investment policy.

IDEOLOGY AND DEVELOPMENT

It is somewhat unconventional to speak of ideology as a resource, even though its role as resource is often implicitly assumed in discussing economic development. It is no longer surprising to hear economists talk about the ways in which certain Weltanschauungen impede development, whereas others facilitate it. And, of course, the intellectual tradition of concern with the facilitative function of ideology in development goes back at least as far as Max Weber. Such discussions, whether the relationships they assert are made explicit or not, have in common their view of ideology as means. Ideologies are seen as appropriate or inappropriate for certain ends, usually the end of economic modernization. Yet that is precisely the point at issue in Israel.

The Israeli case is one in which a very explicit ideology was seen as end, and economic goals were appraised according to the ideology. Violating conventional Western assumptions, at least of current vintage, Zionist theoreticians did not accept either the fixedness of human motivation or the autonomy of economic development. Both people and institutions could, it was believed, be shaped to the form specified by ideological conviction. That, of course, is a utopian understanding, an understanding not open to test if only because the convictions themselves are not always commonly understood and are never universally shared.

The preindependence success of Zionism "spoiled" many of its adherents, led them to believe that Herzl's "If you will it, it is no legend," knew no boundaries. Hence the shock and the disillusionment, and, for some, the tenacity, in the face of the present inability to make dreams real. The Western observer, and even the younger Israeli, is likely to evince an impatient astigmatism in appraising ideology's role in Israel. He is likely to conclude that the older ideology is now impediment, marking its bearers as conservative, anachronistic, unsympathetic to the hard facts of economic development. But that is not the issue at all, except as economic development is assigned priority. The issue is, instead, whether economic development *ought* to be assigned priority, whether it is, in fact, the given it is so widely assumed to be. Increasingly imprisoned by events, the older ideology now gives way, reluctantly, to the new. Unable to provide even for themselves convincing proof that one can stand against history any longer, and even divert history's course to channels of one's own choosing, the older Zionists now accept, with varying enthusiasm, the new dispensation. But much of the system's inertia, and many of its conflicts, derive from precisely this differential understanding of what ideology is all about, of whether the proper course for man is to fit his understanding to the universe or to twist the universe to fit his understanding.

Such differences become operational, as we have seen, especially in the battles between the generations. They lap over also into the economic sphere, where policy decisions at times reflect one view, at times the other. They affect also the perspectives of the parties, for it is the clear brunt of left-wing criticism of Mapai that it has sold out too early to the empiricists. That criticism, presumably, is more easily made by those who do not bear the primary burden of decision making. But one would do the nature of the discussion, whether as history or as contemporary analysis, great injustice to dismiss it casually as either wasteful from the standpoint of development or futile from the standpoint of possibility. Whether it is wasteful, whether economic development deserves the absolute priority it is now widely accorded, whether it is futile—these are the questions debated, and dismissing them as insignificant distorts a dominant theme of the system.

IDEOLOGY AND EQUALITY

It may be of some value to provide an illustration of the ways in which the general ideological predispositions work themselves out in substantive policy debates. One such debate is on the question of wage policy. Israel has, even now, one of the most egalitarian wage structures of any country with a wage economy. This is in keeping both with the socialist orientation of the pioneering ideology and with economic circumstances such as the large amount of investment handled by public institutions and the youth of the economy. But since independence, the gaps between income groups have grown apace, and other differences have also become more marked. For example:

1. In 1950, the poorest half of Israel's urban wage and salary earners received 37 per cent of the income earned by such workers; by 1957-1958, their share had fallen to 26 per cent. In 1950, the wealthiest 10 per cent

earned 18 per cent of the income; by 1957-1958, their share had grown to 24 per cent.

2. Between 1950 and 1956, real average income rose by 29 per cent; the average real income of the poorest fifth rose by 4 per cent, while the average real income of the wealthiest fifth rose by 47 per cent.[6]

Because of tax and welfare policies, the gap in disposable income was not quite so large. But the steady increase in the gap reflects a direct confrontation between the older egalitarianism and the new economics. It must be borne in mind that the proportion of all salaries paid by either the Government or the Histadrut is extremely high, so that any shifts in income distribution are partly the results of public policy decisions. And the decisions made during the past decade have frequently been in response to demands, not that income ought to be raised absolutely, but that there ought to be more differentiation between the wages of skilled and unskilled laborers, or between the wages of professionals and those of clerks. The first debates on this principle were most intense—a cardinal socialist tenet was at stake. Since that time, the new doctrine has been tacitly accepted, and, to the extent to which Government still wishes to direct wage policy, it has chosen the more conventional means of income redistribution through taxation.

It is interesting that the over-all share of income earned by Easterners has suffered a steady proportional decline. In 1951, Easterners earned 61 per cent as much as Europeans, on a per capita basis; by 1956-1957, they earned 47 per cent as much; by 1960, 45 per cent as much. (In 1956-1957, Israel-born children of Eastern parents earned 68 per cent as much as Israel-born children of European parents.) This is due, in part, to the vast increase in the proportion of Easterners in the population. But the decline is marked even when the group size, and family size as well, are controlled. Herein lies one major source of tension within the system, for with all the progress that Easterners have enjoyed, they are quite correct in their assessment that they are today earning less, in relation to others, than they were a decade and a half ago. And herein lies, again, a major confrontation with the ideology of equality.

IDEOLOGY AND PUBLIC OPINION

Few issues have engaged so much attention in recent Western criticism as the purported end of ideology. In general, discussants have either lamented the passing of ideological orientations, or rejoiced in the end of the

[6] Data in this section are from a most interesting essay by Giora Hanoch, "Income Differentials in Israel," published as part of the *Fifth Report* of the Falk Project for Economic Research in Israel (Jerusalem, 1961).

dogmatism that has seemed a necessary concomitant of ideology. The pages of *Dissent* reflect the former view, *The True Believer* implies the latter. In our own discussion, we are less concerned with the value judgment than with an exposition of the role of ideology in Israel's political system. Yet, whatever one's tastes in the matter, it is necessary to point out that one apparent consequence of Israel's intense ideological tradition is a relative insensitivity on the part of the Government to public opinion. Though the hard data that might confirm this description are lacking, the impression that the public pulse of Israelis is not regarded as an especially relevant piece of political information is both widely shared and strongly held.

It is not that the ideology itself is antidemocratic in substance. On the contrary, it speaks of radical democracy. But ideological commitment leads the committed to believe that they know better. Its common consequence is an elitist view, in which the committed see themselves as the enlightened. In Israel, this view receives significant support from other aspects of the system. The electoral system is relatively insensitive to minor shifts in public opinion; members of the Knesset have only weak ties to the heterogeneous constituencies which might alert them to public feelings, nor is their political future dependent on their accord with the mass public; there are, in Israel, so many publics, so sharply demarcated, that "representing" public opinion is either a hopeless task or a danger to the fragile national consensus.

It may well be that even without ideology the system would not develop formal channels for communicating the public will. But it is more likely that one of the central impediments to institutional change is the lack of any powerful pressure to create such channels, a lack which derives in the first instance from the elitist consequences of ideological commitment. If that is true, then we are warranted in supposing that one likely effect of the waning of ideology in Israel will be the first appearance of organized pressures to reform the system's institutions in a direction which would link them more closely to the publics they serve.

POLITICAL INSTITUTIONS

Proposals for institutional reform are not unknown in Israel, but they are both disorganized and desultory. Yet the question of institutional change cannot be ignored; in Israel, as in many other new nations, political structures have not yet come to be taken for granted. Their form and their function remain, to some degree, open questions, even when the questions are not presently debated. They may, if debated, be the most explosive policy questions of all. It was this potential hazard which caused the Knesset to shelve the question of a written constitution. Of course, Israel's institutions go back in some sense well beyond the eighteen years of independence, and therefore have about them an authenticity that is less likely to be questioned. Yet here again, the issue is one of continuity and timing: will social tensions, as they are translated into political terms, come to be seen as soluble through institutional change, hence making the debate over such change a symbol for more far-reaching goals, or will the institutions, by the time effective challenges might otherwise be mounted, have moved beyond the pale of easy questioning? Specifically, will aggrieved Easterners come to identify redress of their grievances with reform of their Government; if they do, will the Government still be, as to some degree it is today, vulnerable to their attacks?

These kinds of questions cannot now be answered, nor are they on Israel's political agenda yet. Most proposals for institutional change, for obvious reasons, have thus far focused on Israel's electoral system. The assumption is, with good reason, that adoption of a constituency election system, or even of some compromise between such a method and proportional representation, would probably put an end to coalition Government, and hence bring about fundamental change in almost every other area. Unfortunately, from the perspective of the would-be reformers, the political system has borne the consequences of PR with remarkable equanimity. It has experienced very little of that instability which is presumed to be the normal consequence of party fragmentation, itself assumed to be the outcome of PR. The effects of the electoral system, pervasive though they may be, are indirect, neither immediately evident nor obviously dysfunctional. Indeed, the image of stability derives not only from the relative absence of protracted governmental crises, but even from the electorate's behavior, a phenomenon so unexpected that it deserves some special comment. It would hardly have surprised any observer, confronting a system of many parties and an electorate more than doubled in size and multiplied still more in diversity, to find great volatility in party support. Instead, however, one finds, as can be seen in Table [16], that aggregate voting behavior has not changed very much at all over eighteen years and six elections.

Mapai's proportion of the total vote has varied by no more than 6 per cent, the NRP's by less than 2 per cent. Yet the 400,000 voters of 1949 had, by 1965, grown to 1,250,000. Can it be that all the new voters have conveniently disturbed themselves in roughly the same proportions that had existed all along?

Several explanations have been proffered, but none is wholly satisfying. Some have suggested that assigning care for immigrants according to a "party key" has helped preserve the prevailing distribution. No doubt it has, but such assignment was neither so universal nor so successful as to account for more than a small part of the regularity. Others have proposed

Table 16. Results of Parliamentary Elections in Israel (Percentage of Seats Won and Number of Seats)

Knesset

	First	Second	Third	Fourth	Fifth	Sixth
Mapai	35.7% / 46	37.3% / 45	32.2% / 40	38.2% / 47	34.7% / 42	Rafi 7.9% / 10 → Alignment 36.7% / 45
Ahduth Avodah			8.2% / 10 →	6.0% / 7	6.5% / 8 →	
Mapam	14.7% / 19	12.5% / 15 →	7.3% / 9	7.2% / 9	7.6% / 9	6.6% / 8
Arab Parties	3.0% / 2	4.7% / 5	4.9% / 6	3.5% / 5	3.5% / 4	3.3% / 4
Herut	11.5% / 14	6.6% / 8	12.6% / 15	13.6% / 17	13.7% / 17	Gahal 21.3% / 26
GZ	5.2% / 7	18.9% / 23	10.2% / 13	6.1% / 8 → Liberals 13.6% / 17	Ind. Liberals 3.7% / 5	
Prog.	4.1% / 5	3.2% / 4	4.4% / 5	4.6% / 6 →		
Communists	3.5% / 4	4.0% / 5	4.5% / 6	2.8% / 3	4.1% / 5	Arab Comm. 2.3% / 3, Jewish Comm. 1.3% / 1
Religious Bloc / NRP	Religious Bloc 12.2% →	NRP 8.3% / 10	NRP 9.1% / 11	NRP 9.9% / 12	NRP 9.8% / 12	NRP 8.9% / 11
Agudah & Agudah Workers	16 →	Agudah & Agudah Workers 3.6% / 5	Agudah & Agudah Workers 4.7% / 6	Agudah & Agudah Workers 4.7% / 6	Agudah 3.7% / 4, Agudah Workers 1.9% / 2	Agudah 3.2% / 4, Agudah Workers 1.8% / 2
Other Parties	10.1% / 7	0.7% / -	0.7% / -	3.4% / -	0.7% / -	2.9% / 1

360

that the system is in some way in harmony with "nature," and that any random assortment of immigrants would probably have recreated roughly the same parties with roughly the same strengths, just as some scientists have contended that the normal curve is a natural phenomenon. Yet what little evidence there is shows quite decisively that the curves of distribution of political opinions differ quite sharply from group to group.[7]

Perhaps the most useful explanation, though still not a comprehensive one, combines organizational and structural elements. From the organizational point of view one may argue that parties of given strengths have the resources to recruit new voters in rough proportion to their strength; a party which begins with 5 per cent of the vote is hardly likely to find the means to make converts of 20 per cent of the new voters. From the structural point of view one can account for the varying support given Mapai, Herut, and the General Zionists by arguing that many voters disregard ideological differences and vote instead either for or against the Government. Mapai, of course, is perceived as the Government; the General Zionists were seen as the opposition in the elections to the Second Knesset, but then, because they shared in the coalition, lost their opposition status in the elections to the Third, at which time Herut replaced them as the party of opposition. That many voters do, in fact, see things in just this way is evident from the results of the most recent Histadrut elections, when many voters switched from Mapam to Herut, ideologically sharp antagonists. Herut was competing in Histadrut elections for the first time; the support hitherto given Mapam was not so much ideological as oppositional. Hence the availability of a party nationally known as the primary party of opposition was much more important than ideological consistency.

These explanations point in quite different directions. For if the differences among the parties mirror real ideological differences within the population, then replacing the present electoral system by one more aggregative might not do justice to those differences. If, on the other hand, the real explanation for the system's operation is inertia, it may well be that it exaggerates trivial differences. Nor is the fact of differences, if differences there be, necessarily to be lamented. Political systems require consensus to survive, not unanimity. The important question is whether the differences overwhelm the consensus, whether they immobilize the system. And that is a function of the strength of the system, and of the sharpness of the differences, and of the extent to which the system is seen as the arbiter of difference. Some differences in Israel defy aggregation; the dispute over the proper role of religion in the State is one example. There are others, such as the question of how much autonomy the Histadrut should have, which can more easily be compromised. There are others still, which have not yet ripened into political maturity—e.g., the ethnic divide—which could

[7] In this regard, Matras, *Social Change in Israel* (Chicago, 1965), pp. 86-130, is most useful.

develop into insoluble crises, but whose fate depends upon the system's capacity to defuse them before they do.

Whether the electoral system as presently managed sharpens or weakens differences is an open question. The conventional literature on multiparty systems and coalition governments argues most persuasively that they necessarily encourage difference and increase rigidity, for they force the parties to distinguish themselves sharply from each other in order to retain support. Yet coalition government also forces a choice between compromise and immobility, a choice easily settled in Israel for fear of what immobility might bring. Coalition government introduces a measure of ambiguity into the system; it is never wholly clear who is responsible for what. Yet perhaps some ambiguity is useful in a system still feeling its way into the task of governing a society so marked by rapid change. The availability of many parties, to which voters may respond with ideological sophistication or with political naiveté, is a problem for the analyst, and may be thought a source of confusion to the voter. Yet in a time of rapid change and rapid growth, the implicit anarchy of such a system may be congenial to the facts of national life—given, at any rate, the experience of the parties in getting along with each other somehow and the pressures from without which act as a constant reminder of the consequences of not getting along.

In short, the propriety of an electoral system is not an issue which can be settled in the abstract, without considering the nature of the society the system serves. Once such considerations are introduced in the case of Israel, the arguments go both ways. For that reason, among others, one of the more intriguing proposals for institutional reform would have half of the Knesset elected in the current manner, and half elected from geographic districts, as in England or the United States. Such a method would, presumably, still permit small parties some parliamentary representation, but would at the same time confer special advantage upon the larger parties, thereby bringing more coherence to both Government and opposition. Politically, such an alternative is more likely to be adopted than one involving total rejection of the present electoral system. Some see it as temporary compromise, some as a way of having the best of both worlds. Many are quite taken with the prospect of a system in which one party can control exclusively the machinery of government, providing a politics that is more orderly and more simple than is now possible. Yet it is precisely that prospect which raises quite dramatically the special problem of electoral reform. The social sphere in Israel is so thoroughly penetrated by the political that political control carries with it unusually extensive opportunities for social management. Israel's Government is no metronome, dutifully keeping time as others play the tune; it is orchestrator and conductor, intimately involved in every way with Israel's developing melody. This is basic to the system and to its future, and is the subject of our concluding section.

POLITY AND SOCIETY

We have already reviewed, in passing, several reasons why Israel's Government is so intensively and extensively involved with Israel's society. Utopian ideology justifies the involvement; Yishuv history provides the precedent; circumstances, ranging from the need to handle large numbers of immigrants to the Arab threat to the availability to the Government of abundant investment capital, support it. There are other things as well; the country is small and its communications well developed; there is no hiding place from politics. The relative weakness of local government inflates still further the importance of the national. Amidst all the heterogeneity, the Government and its symbols seem a natural focus of attention, and the drama of rebirth a natural source of affection. Welfare policies again make more intimate the tie between society and polity.

In fact, the relationship between the two is so close that it is hardly possible to distinguish between a social and a political sphere. It is entirely unclear where Caesar ends and the people begin. Looking back over the preceding pages, we see much that confirms this view. The Government exerts massive control over the economy, the Histadrut is the nation's largest employer, parties sponsor enterprises that have little direct relationship to politics, military problems loom large, new immigrants are cared for by the Government, the location of new settlements is decided by the Government, integration is a subject of policy decision. There is no insulation from the world of politics and Government.

Students of political theory commonly hail the emergence of a radical distinction between state and society as one of the great landmarks of political development. The Rousseauan alternative, in which government is simply an articulation of the general will, is typically seen as totalitarian. In the United States, especially, the desirability of a clear demarcation between society and government is taken very seriously, and the "size of government" has been a major source of political debate throughout American history.

Students trained in such traditions find the Israel system most discomfiting. Very little discussion is addressed to the abstract question of the size of Government or its justifiable responsibilities. For the most part, it is assumed that the society's shape and Government's policies are inseparable, and that any social problems are naturally the concern of Government. At the same time, there is no real issue of totalitarianism in Israel. It is not a threat which is discussed, because there is nothing in the present or past disposition of the governors to indicate that it is a threat at all.

That this should be so may follow from the restraint of the governors, or from the structural limitations imposed by coalition government. Were any one party to have available the entire machinery of government, it might find it difficult to refrain from imposing its ideological vision on the society—although it must be added that Mapai, the only party presently a candidate for such exclusive power, is so far from being sure of its own ideology that the threat is hardly imminent.

Quite apart, however, from the threat of totalism, the state-society of Israel raises other problems. Of all the reasons that explain its being, the most important is that there has not yet been time to develop a reasonably stable and articulated social order. In that sense, political development in Israel, with its roots reaching well back into the Yishuv, is more complete than societal development. The kinds of problems that have needed solving, therefore, have not had any address other than that of the Government to which they might be sent for handling. That, together with a justifying ideology for Government involvement, imposes enormous burdens on a Government itself still learning how to govern. The most impressive fact of Israeli political life is that Government has managed to survive at all amidst awesome burdens. That it has not only survived, but managed to do reasonably well in the business of social management, is an achievement of heroic proportion.

If, in time, the society "settles down," is given a chance to stabilize and normalize, then in time we may expect that in Israel, too, there will be an issue of "how much" government is proper. Since, by then, the ideological convictions of old will have passed, there will be less support for the pervasive politics of Israel's first two decades. By then, Israel's Government may find the problems of economic growth and peripheral social engineering sufficient as a challenge. Today, its visions are still larger, more radical in content and in scope. Perhaps such visions have no place in politics. Perhaps the good life, if it can be had, must come in other ways. Perhaps, in any case, the shift to the more conventional differentiation between state and society is inevitable. Perhaps, even, dreams and visions are dysfunctional. Yet withal: it was the dreamers and the visionaries who made the State, and who have managed it, against all odds, 'til now.

SUGGESTED READING

Chenery, H. B., and M. Bruno, "Development Alternatives in an Open Economy: The Case of Israel." *The Economic Journal,* Vol. LXXII, No. 285 (March 1962).

Drajr, Yehezkel Benjamin, *Israel: High Pressure Planning.* North Planning Series, Syracuse, N.Y.: Syracuse University Press, 1966.

Eban, Abba Solomon, *Israel in the World.* Two television interviews with Abba Eban. South Brunswick, N.J.: T. Yoseloff, 1966.

Gersh, G., "Israel's Aid to Africa." *Commonweal,* November 25, 1966.

Heth, Meir, *The Legal Framework of Economic Activity in Israel.* New York: Praeger, 1967.

Hovne, Avner, "The Economic Scene in Israel." *Midstream,* May 1967.

Kanovsky, Eliyahu, *The Economy of the Israeli Kibbutz.* Harvard Middle Eastern Monograph No. 13, Cambridge, Mass.: Harvard University Press, 1966.

Kreinin, Mordechai Elihau, *Israel and Africa: A Study in Technical Cooperation.* New York: Praeger, 1964.

Prittie, Terence C. F., *Israel: Miracle in the Desert.* New York: Praeger, 1967.

Safran, Nadav, *Israel Today: A Profile.* New York: Foreign Policy Association, 1965.

Weingrod, Alex, *Israel: Group Relations in a New Society.* New York: Praeger, 1965.

Winch, Kevin, "National Policy and Economic Decisions in Israel." *Social and Economic Studies,* Vol. II, No. 2 (1965).

EGYPT

The socioeconomic and political orientation of post-1952 Egypt has to a considerable extent been determined by a combination of external events and President Nasser's perceptive reading of the nationalist temper and ambitions of his countrymen. As in Cuba, the pre-Nasser regimes had failed to provide the country with a leadership whose policies and goals could give vent to the nation's accumulated frustrations. As in China, repressed nationalism was the driving force, a history of foreign domination and early power the spur, and a rather loose and vague rendering of "socialism" the means of rising from underdevelopment and humiliation to affluence and national recognition.

As in many other underdeveloped countries, economic development and capabilities have been inadequate to back international political ambitions and aspirations to world greatness. The result has been a series of resounding defeats—in 1948, 1956, and 1967—smoothed out and turned into moral victories, in so far as the domestic political market was concerned, by a recourse to national pride and old remembrances of evil schemings by outside powers. Like Cuba and China, Nasser's Egypt has held the international stage for longer and in a more important role than would normally be expected in the case of a country at so low a level of economic development. Even Egypt's official international name, the United Arab Republic, is a fiction since Syria's secession from the brief union in 1961. Egypt's worldwide great power ambitions—whatever their historical justification—are ultimately conditioned by what Egypt can do in Egypt, rather than what it can do in Israel or Yemen. World powers are built at home, on the cruel logic of economic development. To expand, there must first be something to defend; to expand effectively, there must first be a domestic base capable of sustaining the goals of the nation's international commitment. To proceed otherwise, is to put the cart before the camel.

In the first selection below, Peter Mansfield traces Egypt's development under Nasser and its gradual evolution toward socialism. Mansfield's discussion, centering on Egypt's domestic scene, is intended to show that economic conditions—although still far from satisfactory—made much progress between 1952 and 1965 in alleviating some of the worst economic ills of the pre-Nasser era. Mansfield was fairly optimistic as to Egypt's future when he wrote the passages below in 1965. Whether in light of the effects of the June, 1967 war with Israel he would still hold the same view (at least as regards the immediate future) is uncertain.

Willy Linder, in the second selection, is much more critical of Nasser's policies than Mansfield. He paints a rather grim picture of Egypt's present condition, considers austerity a necessity, and concludes that "the future does not look very bright, the less so as the basic structure of the economy and the principles underlying the social and political conditions are greatly to be blamed for the development."

1. Egypt: The Way Out of Poverty

PETER MANSFIELD

. . . The economic policies of Nasser's Egypt have evolved over the past twelve years, with external circumstances deciding the pace but not the direction in which they have moved. Nasser's reading of Egyptian history and his basic political aim of a renascent, self-reliant Egypt, freed from all forms of foreign domination and playing a key role in the Arab world and Africa, made it virtually inevitable that sooner or later he would seek solutions in a crash programme of industrialization and a highly centralized, nationalistic socialism. Suez gave a sharp impetus to the process of removing foreign economic influence and also turned Egypt away from its traditional trading partners in the West towards the Eastern bloc. Syria's secession from the U.A.R. in 1961 gave Nasser a jerk to the left because he believed that it had been engineered by the capitalist classes in Syria, with sympathetic support from their Egyptian counterparts, against the ex-

From *Nasser's Egypt* by Peter Mansfield (Baltimore, Penguin Books, 1965), pp. 129-69, 170-71, 173-83, 186, and 189-91. Reprinted by permission of Penguin Books Ltd., London.

tension of U.A.R. socialism. But without Suez or the secession, the trend would have been the same.

In the early years after the Revolution Nasser's thoughts and energies were heavily absorbed by foreign affairs. Between 1958 and 1961 it was the problems of union with Syria which took up most of his time. The secession therefore gave him the opportunity to think out his ideas on Egypt's social, political and economic structure and the result is contained in the National Charter, a 30,000-word document which he presented to the National Congress of Popular Powers on 21 May 1962. Much of this consists of his explanations of the need for fundamental social revolution in Egypt and, as might be expected, it is coloured throughout with his sense of Egypt's own history. Most of the practical proposals have already been put into effect, and it seems likely that as long as Nasser's authority inside Egypt remains without serious challenge, the system he has evolved will survive with only minor changes.

The essence of his economic argument can be found in a passage where he considers the reasons for the failure of Saad Zaghloul's 1919 revolution.

The leaders of the 1919 revolution could not see clearly that a revolution cannot achieve its aims for the people unless it goes beyond the mere political goal of independence and tackles the roots of economic and social problems. The most that could be done at that time was to demand that some financial activities be Egyptianized whereas there was a more pressing need for a radical redistribution of wealth.

This failure to carry through a social revolution in the 1920s enabled imperialism to maintain its influence after independence.

'It paved the way for a batch of capitalists, who in fact inherited the role of the nineteenth-century foreign adventurers who made only a superficial impression and failed to develop the country.' These capitalists, like the politicians and intellectuals, 'all fell into the arms of the palace at one time and of imperialism at another.'

From this he concludes that

in the countries forced to remain under-developed, a free capitalist system is no longer able to lead the economic drive at a time when the great capitalist monopolies in the advanced developed countries can rely on the exploitation of the sources of wealth in the colonies. Local capitalism can only survive either by tariff protection, which is paid for by the mass of the people, or by making itself an appendage to world monopolies and dooming the country to subservience.

The race to catch up with the developed countries cannot be left to 'desultory individual efforts motivated by private profit.'

Three steps must accordingly be taken: mobilization of national savings; the use of modern scientific techniques to exploit these savings; and the drafting of a complete plan for production.

The absence of a social revolution, runs Nasser's argument, also meant that Egyptian parliamentary democracy before the revolution was a sham.

Political democracy cannot be separated from social democracy. No citizen can be regarded as free to vote unless he is given the following three guarantees: (a) he should be free from exploitation in all its forms; (b) he should enjoy an equal opportunity with his fellow citizens to enjoy a fair share of the national wealth; (c) his mind should be free from all anxiety likely to undermine his future security.

Thus, in Nasser's view, neither national independence, nor true democracy, nor the status of an economically developed country can be achieved without socialism. He summarizes the economic aspect of socialism in Egypt as:

First—That the economic infrastructure including railways, roads, ports, airports, power supplies, dams, sea, land and air transport, and other public services should all come under public ownership.

Second—The majority of heavy, medium, and mining industries should be publicly owned. Although it is possible to allow private ownership in this field, it should be controlled by the public sector owned by the people. Light industries must be free from monopoly, and though this field is open to private enterprise it must be guided by the public sector.

Third—Foreign trade must be under the people's full control. All the import trade must be within the public sector, and although private capital has a part to play in the export trade, the public sector must possess the main share so as to prevent all possibilities of fraudulence. If the proportion is to be fixed exactly, the public sector must control three-quarters of exports while the private sector is responsible for the rest. The public sector must within the coming eight years take charge of at least one quarter of domestic trade to prevent monopoly, and expand the range of internal trade before private and cooperative activities.

Fourth—Banks and insurance companies should come under the public sector to ensure that capital is not left a purely speculative role, to protect national savings and to ensure against their misdirection.

Fifth—There must be a clear distinction between the exploiting and non-exploiting ownership of land. Agricultural land is limited to one hundred *feddans* per family. The ownership of buildings is controlled by taxation and rent restriction. Constant supervision is still essential to prevent exploitation, but the increase in public and cooperative housing will assist in this matter.

As the basis of an economic programme this gives the State a bigger role than merely 'occupying the commanding heights of the economy,' as the British Labour Party phrases the socialist objective today, but it leaves more to the private sector than Marxism. The Marxist influence on Nasser's historical analysis of Egypt's 'failed revolutions' in the 1880s and 1919 is obvious. There is also a strong element of Titoism in his views on the structure of the Egyptian State. But whatever the outside influences he has absorbed, his conclusions have a strongly Egyptian flavour which is wholly to be expected from such a devoted nationalist. As he remarks: 'The real solutions to the problems of the people cannot be derived from the experiences of another.'

Several important differences from orthodox Marxism in his political creed have been emphasized by Nasser himself. He rejects, for instance, such ideas as the atheistic State and the dictatorship of the proletariat. In the economic sphere, he proclaims that the production of consumer goods should not be neglected through the concentration on heavy industry.

Heavy industry no doubt provides the solid foundation for any large-scale industrial framework . . . but the masses of our people have been long deprived; to mobilize all of them for the building of heavy industry and overlook their needs as consumers is incompatible with their right to make up for their long deprivation and delays. . . .

This idea that the mass of the Egyptian people deserve to be compensated for their past sufferings colours all Nasser's thinking. It is the reason for the continuation of subsidies for basic necessities despite Egypt's present acute economic difficulties, which are partly due to a massive rise in consumption in the towns and cities. Nasser would passionately discard any scheme that allowed prices to rise as a means of reducing consumption.

As has been said above, the economic principles of the regime took several years to evolve. In fact the policies of the early years after the Revolution were more liberal and orthodox than before. When the Free Officers took over, the country was tottering into bankruptcy as a result of the irresponsible actions of the last Wafd government; there were heavy deficits in the budget and the balance of payments in both 1951 and 1952. The new Finance Minister, Dr Abdel Galil al-Emary, pushed through a drastic policy of deflation and austerity through import and currency restrictions and severe cuts in government expenditures. Imports were reduced from £E. 210.5 million to £E. 150.7 million in 1954, and the balance of payments actually showed a surplus of £E. 3.3 million in 1954.

Similarly, the budget deficit was turned into a surplus of £E. 6.7 million in 1953-4. There was no attempt at central planning but two new bodies were created, the Permanent Council for Social Services and the Permanent Council for the Development of National Production, composed of technicians and economists with the task of studying and reporting on all schemes presented by the various Ministries. As research and advisory bodies these did valuable work, but their scope was necessarily limited. The Finance Ministry set out to attract private Egyptian and foreign capital into investment in Egyptian industry and other socially profitable enterprises. Hopes that after the agrarian reform the large landowners would invest their capital in industry were soon disappointed, however, for they diverted it into real estate. Attempts to attract foreign capital were equally unsuccessful. In an effort to reassure foreign investors, some pre-revolutionary legislation of nationalist character was amended; Law No. 138 of 1947, which required all foreign limited companies in Egypt to have at least fifty-one per cent of Egyptian capital, was amended so as to reduce the minimum to forty-nine per cent. But the part of Law 147 stipulating that ninety per cent of the workers in foreign companies should be Egyptian and receive eighty per cent of the salaries, was retained. Foreign capital remained extremely wary of the young military regime.

By the end of 1954 the government had come to realize that it would have to increase expenditure even if it meant deficit financing. There was an urgent need to step up the pace of development because production was failing to keep up with the growth of population. Although even reasonably accurate estimates for *per capita* income are unavailable, it seems virtually certain that this was falling between 1952 and 1954. At the same time the new military regime wished to increase expenditure on defence and on health, education, and other social services to satisfy the popular hopes that had been raised by the Revolution. Public expenditure increased from £E. 233 million in 1953-4 to £E. 358.1 million in 1956-7. Of this only about five per cent was government investment in development, and the rest was current expenditure. A separate Development Budget was created which was financed mainly through public loans and the banks and by foreign loans and aid; it is estimated that the proportion of outstanding public debt to national income rose from 22.4 per cent in 1954 to 28.6 per cent in 1957.

Orthodox conservative economic policies had been thrown out of the window, but Egypt was still a long way from socialism. Even by 1959-60 only eighteen per cent of the Gross Domestic Product originated in the public sector, compared with sixteen per cent at the Revolution, and only twelve per cent of the labour force was employed by the government. Subsidies for basic necessities were used to keep down the cost of living for the mass of the people, but at the same time the government kept much stricter control over the trade-unions than before the Revolution and strikes were prohibited. Any European socialist would probably have described the system as 'State-controlled capitalism.'

The Suez war in 1956 had several important effects on the economic scene. Domestic prices rose sharply, and there was a drastic fall in the price of the Egyptian pound abroad; an economic boycott by the West (including the U.S.A.) and the consequent loss of export markets caused a severe strain on the balance of payments. Net holdings of foreign assets were reduced from £E. 214 million in 1954 to £E. 110.6 million in 1957. The Egyptian economy was saved from disaster by the Communist bloc countries, several of which concluded bilateral trade agreements with

Egypt; but these did not altogether compensate for the loss of Western markets, especially because the Eastern European countries resold some of the cotton they had taken from Egypt in Western Europe at a discount.

The Egyptian Government's immediate response to the Anglo-French invasion was to sequester all British and French property. A series of laws issued in January 1957 obliged all foreign banks and insurance companies to Egyptianize themselves, and British and French banks, such as Barclay's and Crédit Lyonnais, were sold to Egyptian banks. Together with the nationalization of the Suez Canal company, this meant that the greater part of the foreign share in the Egyptian economy had been liquidated. Much of this share was transferred to the Egyptian Government, and between 1957 and 1960 a number of public economic organizations were created, while others already in existence were expanded, to look after the government's interests and to fill the vacuum left by Egyptian private capital; these included the Economic Development Organization, the Bank Misr, the General Organization for Maritime Transportation, the al-Nasr Organization, and the Suez Canal Authority. At the end of 1959 the total assets of the various companies affiliated to the Economic Development Organization amounted to some £E. 506 million, of which more than half was in banking and one quarter in industry, mining, and agriculture.

The State's actual share in the economy was growing, and a trend had begun which ensured that it would continue to do so. The 1956 republican constitution stated that 'development must be planned.' A State National Planning Committee was established which absorbed the semi-private Permanent Council for the Development of National Production, and in 1958 a Five-Year Plan for Industry was launched in which the State was to provide sixty-one per cent of the finance—mainly for the heavy industry programme. Thus although only eighteen per cent of the Gross Domestic Product originated in the public sector by 1959-60, seventy-four per cent of total investment was undertaken by the government compared with only thirty-one per cent in 1952-8. If the trend continued, the industrial sector of the Egyptian economy would inevitably become socialized, although it would be a long time before the State actually held a majority share. Towards the end of 1957 Nasser first spoke of a 'socialist, democratic, cooperative system' as Egypt's goal. But the State's role was still strictly limited. On 5 December 1957 he told the Cooperatives Conference at Cairo University:

In dealing with feudalism our aim was to transform tenants into owners. Thus we shall have a socialist, democratic, cooperative society. When the State intervenes in industry it does not mean at all that it is the only capitalist. We believe that national capitalism is essential to strengthen and expand our economy and to achieve our country's economic independence.

In February 1958 Egypt entered into the union with Syria which called for a period of adjustment. Egypt was already far ahead in building a socialist pattern of a planned economy with a land reform, a large public sector, an industrial five-year plan and highly progressive taxation. Syria had a private enterprise mercantile economy with minimum controls on imports and foreign exchange. (National Bank of Egypt, Economic Bulletin, Vol. XVII, No. 1.)

Throughout 1958 and most of 1959 Nasser was deeply involved in trying to create a workable political structure for the union and had in addition to deal with urgent problems of foreign policy raised by the anti-government insurrection in Lebanon, the Iraqi revolution followed by the landing of American troops in Lebanon and British troops in Jordan, and in early 1959 by his breach with General Kassem and his near-break with the Soviet Union. Except for one or two occasions such as the inauguration of the Iron and Steel Plant at Helwan, Nasser's speeches were devoted exclusively to foreign affairs and Arab nationalism. For the time being the 'socialist, democratic, cooperative society' was scarcely mentioned.

By the end of 1959 Egypt, Nasser, and his able Finance Minister, Dr Abdul Moneim el-Kaissouny, were ready for a new move towards socialism, but this time they were going to take a deeply reluctant Syria at least part of the way with them. In Egypt the move began in February 1960 with the nationalization of the Bank Misr and the National Bank of Egypt.

The step was significant because the previous 1956 nationalizations had been concerned with foreign-owned firms while this was concerned with firms owned or mainly owned by nationals. (National Bank of Egypt, Economic Bulletin, Vol. XVII, No. 1.)

In June 1960 the Press was nationalized, and the Cairo bus services were municipalized. But the really big step was taken in June and July 1961. In a series of decrees the government took over the entire import trade of the country and a large part of the export trade including cotton, which is much the biggest item in Egypt's exports. All banks and insurance companies were nationalized, and about 300 industrial and trading establishments were taken over either wholly or partly by the State. A highly progressive taxation system was introduced with the declared objective of making £E. 5,000 a year the maximum income in Egypt. Individual shareholdings in companies affected by the July nationalization decrees were limited to £E. 10,000. The working day in industry was limited to seven hours (as a means of increasing employment), and a quarter of all profits made by companies was to be distributed to the workers.

In July 1960 a comprehensive Five-Year Plan for 1960-5 was launched. This was to be followed by a second Five-Year Plan for 1965-70 with the target of doubling the national income by 1970. The 1958 Five-Year Plan for Industry, which had already had considerable success in speeding up industrialization, especially in light industry, was absorbed into the new Five-Year Plan, which now covered the agricultural sector as well. This time eighty per cent of the £E. 1,634 million to be invested would be undertaken by the public sector. About forty per cent would be allocated to industry and twenty-five per cent to increasing the agricultural potential.

Some of the socialist decrees were also applied to the Syrian region. The Five-Year Plan for Syria put the government's share of the total investment at fifty-six per cent, which was not as high as Egypt's eighty per cent but still a substantial increase on the nineteen per cent provided by the Syrian public sector as the proportion of total investment in 1954-6. Before the union with Egypt, the Syrian economic system had been predominantly *laissez-faire* capitalist, and there was a powerful and experienced business and merchant class that bitterly opposed the progress towards socialism. When part of the Syrian army rebelled against the union in August 1961, this class immediately supported the secession.

It was a terrible blow to Nasser's prestige which many thought might be mortal. In his bitter self-criticism after the secession, he declared:

We fell victims to a dangerous illusion. . . . We always refused to make peace with imperialism, but we made the mistake of making peace with reaction. . . . Closely connected with this illusion is another illusion, that it is possible to reach a compromise with reaction on national grounds. . . . We have seen how Syria, capitalism, feudalism and opportunism joined forces with imperialism to wipe out the gains of the masses and to strike at the socialist revolution.

His conclusion was that the capitalist and land-owning classes had taken their revenge. They had managed to infiltrate into the National Union, the U.A.R.'s single political organization created after the union, and now that they had had their way in Syria there was a grave danger that they would try to do the same in Egypt. There was a story going around Cairo that a toast had been drunk to Syria's secession at the bar of the Gezira Club, still a focal point for the unreconciled old regime.

The precautionary counter-offensive took place in Egypt between October 1961 and February 1962. Six hundred of Egypt's wealthiest families, a high proportion of them Copts and Jews, had their property sequestered by the State. About forty were arrested, and although they were released three or four months later, all of them and those affected by the sequestration were politically 'isolated,' forbidden to vote or take part in the political life of the State.

These sequestrations hardly added up to the 'liquidation of the Egyptian kulaks' as they were described in the Beirut Press. Compared with the nationalizations and the July decrees, they were of minor political or economic importance. But they received very bad publicity abroad, because it looked as if the regime in its rage at not being able to harm the Syrian bourgeoisie had turned on its own. Some of the best known figures among those who had been sequestered, such as the multimillionaire industrialists Ahmed Abboud and Francois Tagher, were known to have been encouraged by the regime until very recently to expand their investments, on the understanding that they were regarded as patriotic national capitalists and would not be touched. The large number of non-Muslims among the sequestered also gave the impression of religious discrimination; certainly it would be difficult to deny that some bias was shown against the minorities, but it is also true that any comprehensive list of Egyptian millionaires would have included a high proportion of Copts, Jews and Levantines.

In August 1963 there was a further series of nationalizations covering some firms which had already been partly nationalized, some companies in part privately owned under sequestration, and private companies. About 300 concerns were affected including the Dutch-British Lever Brothers, fourteen partly nationalized shipping companies, and twenty-nine land transport companies. At the same time under Republican Decree 73 all contracts for quarrying and mining issued to private concerns were ended.

The model for the economic structure of the country presented by President Nasser in the National Charter was now virtually complete, and private enterprise had been relegated to a relatively minor role. In the phrase of the Egyptian Marxist Anwar Abdul Malek the 'dismantling of the Old Bourgeoisie' had been achieved. Private property had not been abolished, but as a result of the land reform and nationalizations there had been a redistribution of the national wealth; as Mr Aly Sabry, the Minister of Presidential Affairs, said after the issuing of the July decrees: 'The public sector is not for us a means of liquidating property but of spreading it wider.' On the other hand, large-scale investment by private Egyptian *entrepreneurs* had been effectively discouraged. None of the capitalists who had been left at large could be sure that his concerns would not suddenly be taken over by the State, however well regarded by the regime he might feel he was at present. There was therefore good reason to believe that even the minor twenty per cent share of investment in the first Five-Year Plan that had been allocated to private enterprise was too optimistic.

After the 1963 nationalizations Mr Aly Sabry more than once gave assurances that private buildings were not going to be nationalized, and in March 1964 when the new provisional constitution was introduced it was announced that all sequestrations were to be wound up. Each sequestered person would be allowed to keep property or shares up to a value of £ E. 30,000 in addition to all furniture or jewels or other valuables that had been kept at home.

In 1964 it seemed unlikely that the government intended to sequester or nationalize any further on a substantial scale, although efforts to rationalize the structure of industry might involve taking over small firms to merge them into larger groups. This in fact was done in March 1964 to 119 contracting companies—already fifty per cent nationalized by the 1961 decrees—which were fully nationalized and merged into thirty-five companies.

But the attitude of private investors both outside and inside the country remained cautious and suspicious with good reason. In April 1964 there was a laconic government announcement that Shell-BP interests in the U.A.R. had been nationalized. Since Esso and Mobiloil were not touched it seemed likely that there was a political motive behind the move; Anglo-Egyptian relations were at a low ebb because of the situation in South Arabia. In 1963 two U.S. companies had entered into partnership arrangements with the Egyptian Petroleum Organization for oil exploration in the country, and at the time the Minister of Industry Dr Aziz Sidqi had said, in an interview published in *Petroleum Intelligence Weekly* on 25 November, that among the advantages to foreign concessionaires of signing agreements with Egypt were: the political stability of the government; the 100 per cent certainty that the contract would be respected; and the clear definition of policy by the Egyptian Government which left the concessionaire in no doubt where he stood. There was some truth in these claims, and it certainly seemed highly improbable that Egypt would break any new contract entered into after the nationalization decrees. But the Shell nationalization (like the sequestration of Belgian property in Egypt during the Congo crisis of 1960) emphasized the fact that Egypt's economic policies were influenced by political events. It was always conceivable that a sudden deterioration in the relations between Egypt and the U.S. would cause the Egyptian Government to revise its attitude towards American interests in the country.

There was also the problem of compensation. In 1938, when the Mexican Government nationalized all the oil companies in Mexico, the U.S. Government publicly acknowledged the right of a sovereign State to nationalize foreign-owned interests on its territory provided that adequate compensation was paid. Egypt had earned some international credit by completing the payment of compensation to the Suez Canal Company shareholders one year early; but for British, French, Belgian, Swiss, Lebanese and other interests which had been sequestered or nationalized, compensation arrangements were long delayed by lashings of red tape. In September 1964 the President of the International Bank for Reconstruction and Development, George Woods, publicly stated that the Bank would not make loans 'to countries where there had been sequestration of property without compensation within reasonable time.' There was good reason to believe that the statement was provoked by an article in *al-Ahram* on 7 August by Muhammad Hassanein Heykal in which he argued that Egypt was not morally bound to pay compensation to foreigners who had looted its wealth and that if anything the compensation should go to the Egyptian people who had been exploited. In particular he protested against an agreement which was about to be signed with the Lebanese Government and which would include the payment of nearly £E. 1 million to Francois Tagher—a man, he said, who had come penniless to Egypt at the beginning of the Second World War and had made more than £E. 4 million on the cotton market within a few years. Heykal quoted Egypt's former Finance Minister Abdul Galil al-Emary as comparing the Egyptian economy with a huge cow that grazed on Egyptian pastures but had its udders outside being milked in foreign lands.

There was much force in Heykal's argument that Egypt had been exploited in the past. But his suggestion that this freed Egypt from the moral obligation to pay adequate compensation was certain to provoke reactions like that of Mr Woods at a time when the country needed all the foreign loans it could get. On the other hand, a little-publicized agreement concluded between the United States and Egyptian Governments in 1963 whereby the U.S. Government became the ultimate guarantor of all private investments in Egypt did much to make the country more attractive to U.S. investors.

Many of the same considerations apply to Egyptian investors who have been demoralized by the series of nationalizations and sequestrations since 1960. In 1964 it would have required courage to the point of rashness for any of the remaining private companies to undertake any important new investment. Indeed the share of the private sector in total annual investment fell from 17.3 per cent in 1961-2 to 9.7 per cent in 1962-3 and then to 6.3 per cent in 1963-4. In 1963-4, 35.7 per cent of private investment was in housing, 15.1 per cent in agriculture, 7.9 per cent in irrigation and 12.6 per cent in industry. Private enterprise was playing a negligible part in the development of the Egyptian economy.

The problem was how to establish clearly the boundaries between the private and public sectors, for until this was done private *entrepreneurs* would be unlikely to take any risks. That India has been fairly successful in demarcating these boundaries shows that it can be done. One aspect of the problem was brought to the fore by President Nasser himself in his speech at the opening of the National Assembly's autumn session on 12 November 1964, when he said:

Some sectors of the government consider they have an exclusive right in the field of national action. But the National Charter stipulates that twenty-five per cent of domestic trade should be handled by the public sector and seventy-five per cent by the private sector. The provisions of the National Charter must be respected. . . . The object of forming consumers' cooperative societies is to prevent a sharp rise in prices, but if these societies monopolize home trade corruption is bound to occur in them.

Later the Minister of Supply, Dr Stino, produced figures to show that at least seventy-five per cent of domestic trade was in fact still in private hands. But there was no doubt that there had been unfair discrimination against private retailers. Consignments of imported cheese, for instance, had all been going to the cooperatives.

The two Five-Year Plans are extremely ambitious; their aim is to double the national income in ten years, with a rise of forty per cent in the first five. The targets for the various sectors are as follows (1959-60 = 100):

Table 17.

	1964-1965	1969-1970[a]
Heavy industry	310	445
Light industry	137	185
Services	128	213
Commerce	128	196
Transport, housing, public utilities, security and defence	122	160
Agriculture	128	159

[a]Government of the U.A.R., Five-Year Plan, Cairo, U.A.R.

The first of the Five-Year Plans assumes an overall ratio of capital invested to output of 3:1, which is low but not impossible. Similarly, the compound rate of growth for the Gross National Product is estimated at 7.2 per cent, which is high but not unattainable.

In his *Egypt in Revolution,* Charles Issawi makes some severe criticisms of the assumptions on which the Plan is based. He says:

First, the overall objectives set are often unrealistic. Secondly, there is a dearth of the basic data without which no reasonable programme, much less an overall plan, can be constructed: capital–output ratios, propensities to save, consume and import, income and price elasticities of demand and supply, technical coefficients, etc., not to mention even simpler and more fundamental data on income distribution, savings, investment and manpower resources.

Professor Issawi points out correctly that the target of doubling the national income was set first by the government and that the Plans were made to fit it. President Nasser confirmed that this was so in his speech to the National Assembly on 12 November 1964, when he announced that the 'technicians and planners' had said the national income could be doubled in twenty years. The government had insisted on ten years. The planners had come down to eighteen, and then fifteen; but the government had stuck to ten. 'The allocation of investment and manpower between the various sectors must be based largely on guesswork, and the probability of a balance being achieved is extremely low.' The estimated distribution of investment between the various sectors in the first Five-Year Plan is as follows:

Table 18.

Sector	Investment (Millions £ E)	Percent
Agriculture	224.2	13.7
Irrigation and drainage	111.7	6.8
The high dam	47.3	2.9
Industry	436.2	26.7
Electricity	138.5	8.5
Transport, communications and storage	234.2	14.3
Suez Canal	35.0	2.1
Housing	140.0	8.6
Public establishment	47.6	2.9
Services	101.7	6.2
Changes in stocks	120.0	7.3
	1,636.4	100.0

Source: Framework of the General Plan for Economic and Social Development for the Five Years 1960-1961 to 1964-1965.

As these tables show, the heaviest concentration of investment is in industry and electricity. The industrial sector is expected to generate an increasing share of the national income, and the agricultural sector share to decline. Nevertheless, it is the target for agriculture, which requires a five per cent annual increase in production, which is the most optimistic and the least likely to be attained. The cropped area will only be substantially increased after the completion of the High Dam, i.e. at the end of the second Five-Year Plan, and it is most improbable that productivity from the present area can be increased by five per cent a year. In 1961-2, the second year of the Plan, there was actually a disastrous regression, when about one third of the cotton crop was destroyed by the cotton leafworm. Value added in the agricultural sector fell from £E. 422.1 million in 1960-61 to £E. 372.3 million in 1962.

Nevertheless, despite this severe set-back, the government claims that the estimated overall rate of increase had been achieved in the first four years of the Five-Year Plan. In his report to the National Assembly on 17 November, the Prime Minister, Mr Aly Sabry, said:

Production in the foundation year of the plan, i.e. 1959-60, was estimated at £E. 2,547 million. By the end of the fourth year it reached £E. 3,600 million. This means that 91.6 per cent of the targets for the first Five-Year Plan have been fulfilled by the end of its fourth year.

Since the targets in the agricultural sector had not been reached, those in other sectors must have been exceeded. Mr Sabry declared:

A sum of £E. 929 million has been earmarked for the services sector during the first Five-Year Plan. In four years £E. 993 million was actually spent on this sector, that is, £E. 64 million more than the total allocations for the first five years. It had been decided that the services sector should represent £E. 692 million of the national income, but within the first four years it has become £E. 710 million of the national income. In the field of transport, communication and storage in the first four years, we have reached 111.5 per cent of the target for the first Five-Year Plan; in the public utilities sector, we have reached 98 per cent; and in the field of housing, 98.5 per cent.

Mr Sabry also said: 'The number of workers in the foundation year (1959-60) was about six million. It was decided to increase it to 7,015,000 by the end of the First Development Plan. I take great pleasure in announcing that by the end of the fourth year employment rose to 7,085,000.'

Foreign economic observers have often criticized this rather crude method of illustrating economic progress. By relying on national income and 'value of production' figures, it is possible to conceal wastage, inefficiency and bad planning (although, to be fair, both President Nasser and Mr Sabry have admitted freely in their speeches that these have occurred). There is no means of telling, for instance, whether with a different distribution of investment among the sectors the rate of expansion might not have been much higher. But even through the fog of dubious statistics it is possible to discern something of what has and has not been achieved.

INDUSTRIALIZATION

The rate of physical investment in industry has been high—especially during the past five or six years. Members of the government are apt to exaggerate the lack of industry in Egypt before the Revolution; Egyptian industrialization really began in the 1930s, and between 1938 and 1951 production rose by 138 per cent. But it is true that the heavily protected industrial sector was limited to a very small range of industries. As Dr Aziz Sidqi, Deputy Prime Minister for Industry and Mineral Wealth, told the National Assembly on 12 December 1964: 'In 1952 industries were limited in number and variety—a few spinning mills, some oil-pressing mills, flour mills, cement factories, etc. . . . Today the U.A.R. manufactures almost everything.' He gave as examples of the new products turned out by Egyptian industry since the Revolution: 'Ammonium sulphate, iron and steel products, rubber tyres, medicines, insecticides, dynamite, pencils, ferrous cement, white cement, sanitary installations, opaque glass, cars, lorries, television sets, refrigerators, grain board, cables, tractors, railway wagons, telephone cables, bicycles, water meters, cutlery, electricity meters, electric transformers, gas cylinders, etc.' He added that the products that were already being exported included: 'Tyres, cement, oil products, fertilizers, bicycles, yarn and fabrics and refrigerators.'

Some of the more complex products mentioned by Dr Sidqi are in fact being assembled in Egypt from imported parts rather than manufactured in the country. The buses and cars were designed in Italy (Fiat), the tractors in Yugoslavia, and the television sets in the United States (R.C.A.). But it is also true that each year more of the manufacturing process can be carried out in Egypt so that ultimately they will be wholly Egyptian products, if not designs. Foreign visitors to the Cairo Industrial Exhibition, which was shrewdly timed to coincide with the Second African Summit Conference in July 1964, and to the U.A.R. pavillion at the New York World Fair were surprised at the variety and range of the goods on display. Anyone who has lived in Egypt for the past few years will have noticed the steadily increasing choice of locally produced goods in the shops. Their quality is usually not up to the better foreign equivalents—although even when it is, Egyptians (of both the new and old regime) are inclined to disbelieve it.

But if Egypt is ever to become an industrial power, it has to export manufactured goods as well as make them. Very few Egyptian industries are yet competitive, and since the home market is almost completely protected, it is only the need to export which will make them so. One problem is that the domestic market is expanding so rapidly that in some instances Egypt has become an importer of articles that it used to export a few years ago. Any policy of starving the home market of locally manufactured consumer goods in order to export them has been rejected as inflationary. One possible course, which was being considered in the winter of 1964, was to reduce and standardize the level of consumer credit, which at present is extremely liberal. It is possible, for instance, to buy a refrigerator with a down-payment of only £E. 3 and similar monthly instalments. It is this more than anything which has enabled the new industrial working class to buy consumers' durables, and created and broadened the otherwise very narrow market for them in Egypt. But if Egypt is to export these goods on any large scale, it will have to limit domestic consumption, and the stiffening of instalment credit terms is one way of doing it, unpopular though such action would be.

The government is aware that a drive to increase exports of manufactured goods requires a radical improvement in marketing methods. The great majority of the industries producing these goods are State-owned and, except for textiles, they have mostly been established within the last ten years. Thus they are having to build up their own marketing organization from nothing. In theory they are encouraged to compete with each other in selling abroad, but the results so far have not been very satisfactory. Egyptian industry grew up behind a high protective wall, and the technique of selling in harshly competitive foreign markets is hard to acquire. Egypt's own importing is entirely controlled by the State, which is mainly guided in its choice by the need to be economical with scarce foreign currencies. There is a tendency to expect the same attitude from other countries—that is, to offer their governments a list of Egyptian goods that are available and expect them to choose. The trouble is that the export markets which Egypt particularly wants to penetrate are the industrially developed countries, where importing is in private hands and highly competitive.

At present Egypt has the best chance of increasing its exports of manufactured goods to countries which have a severe foreign exchange problem (including most of the newly independent states in Africa and Asia) and with which it has good political relations. Both these conditions are essential. A country such as Kuwait, for instance, which has all the foreign exchange it needs, is unlikely to import Egyptian manufactures in preference to those of the most technically advanced States, however pro-Egyptian its government. On the other hand, Egypt's trade with Iraq has fluctuated in direct proportion to the temperature of relations between the two countries. The recent sale to Iraq of fifty buses built by the Nasr company in Egypt was as much a demonstration of Iraqi-Egyptian unity as a commercial transaction. There is nothing wrong with this modern example of trade following the flag (which might be compared with imperial preferences) provided that the customer is reasonably satisfied.

Egypt's trade with the African States (except for the Sudan) is still only a tiny proportion of its total trade, and clearly here must lie its biggest challenge and opportunity. For here are countries which, without exception, are short of foreign exchange for their development programmes and are therefore prepared to conclude bilateral barter agreements to obtain manufactured consumer goods. Although Egypt is linked to all these States through the Organization of African Unity, it has the most chance of success where it has the best political relations. It is no accident that Egyptian exports to Algeria rose from £E. 29,000 in 1962 to £E. 875,000 in 1963, the first full year of independence, and to Tunisia from £E. 84,000 in 1962 to £E. 385,000 in 1963, when President Nasser and President Bourguiba were reconciled after a long period of estrangement.

EMPLOYMENT AND LABOUR

Employment in industry has risen steadily over the past few years. According to the Department of Public Mobilization and Statistics (Statistical Pocket-Book, 1952-63) the number of workers in industry rose from 401,000 in 1952 to 724,000 in 1963. But this eighty per cent increase in eleven years compares with a rise in the value of industrial production during the same period from £E. 313.8 million to £E. 952.6 million—which, even translated into real terms by allowing for the depreciation of the Egyptian pound, amounts to considerably more than eighty per cent. As Professor Issawi remarks:

Two general statements may safely be made about the productivity of Egyptian industry: it is rising rather rapidly and it is still very low compared with that of advanced countries.

The question is whether the government's policies have helped or hindered the increase in productivity which is vital if Egyptian industry is to become competitive. One of the socialist decrees of 1961 fixed the maximum working day in industry at seven hours; the declared object was to increase employment rapidly, and many people predicted that a sharp fall in productivity would result. Dr Sidqi has defended the policy, declaring:

The reduction affected those workers who previously worked as much as twelve hours, ten or nine hours a day. All these are now working for seven hours, but the factories operate either for the same time they did before or more according to the needs of production.

This is done by operating in shifts at many factories, and Dr Sidqi asserted that productivity had actually increased as a result of the measure, 'because productivity of a worker working nine hours is much less in the last two hours of his working day than of the seven hours he is now working.' This is impossible to confirm from the statistics that are available, but it may well be so in view of the Egyptian workers' acceptance of shift-work.

What may have had a more harmful effect on productivity are the various measures that have been taken to protect labour (or 'coddle the workers' as old-fashioned employers would say). Some managers protest despairingly that it is now virtually impossible to sack anyone, however inefficient, lazy, troublesome or unnecessary he may be. Certainly it is true that over the past few years industrial workers have gained the impression that the government is wholly on their side and that they have little to fear whatever they do. A visit to almost any factory or construction site will confirm that a high proportion of the workers are redundant. Apart from almost complete security in their jobs, workers have been given two seats on company boards of directors (out of a maximum of seven) and twenty-five per cent of the profits (ten per cent in cash and fifteen per cent in social security benefits). The share of each worker or employee in the ten per cent that is distributed directly is proportional to his wage or salary, but has a ceiling of £E. 50.

There is, however, another side to this picture. Egyptian society is paternalistic and has been so for many centuries. The country is also over-populated. Just as in the past the rich man had a host of retainers dependent upon him, so in any office or workshop there are a number of employees whose presence is strictly unnecessary—two men to bring the coffee when only one is needed, two doormen for only one door. It would have been frankly impossible to override this tradition in industry for the sake of streamlined efficiency without a major social upheaval. Paternalism does also have advantages. Egyptian trade-unions do not have the right to strike, and union officials are virtually representatives of the government. So far this system has worked reasonably well; there is no groundswell of industrial discontent, and loss of productivity from 'worker-coddling' has to be set against what might have been lost through go-slow strikes and 'walkouts.' The trouble is that this situation cannot continue for ever. Whether consciously or unconsciously, Egyptian industrial workers are aware that so far they have benefited most from the country's economic development since the Revolution. In many respects they constitute a privileged class. As one economist close to the government told the author in the winter of 1964:

During the past five years a lot has been done for the workers. Most of the new legislation has been in their favour. Now we have to reduce the costs of production in order to make our industries more competitive, which means that there can be no new benefits for the workers for the time being.

In other words there is to be a wage freeze in Egyptian industry, although since other privileges and benefits are probably more important than actual cash wages it would be more correct to call it a 'status freeze.' The workers did not have to struggle for their gains; they were decreed by the government. The freeze will similarly be imposed from above, but it would seem contrary to human nature that the workers should accept this without murmur. Although the government has great authority, and there is some understanding and acceptance among the public of the need for belt-tightening at Egypt's present stage of development, some industrial discontent may be expected in the coming years.

DISTRIBUTION OF INCOME

Again the lack of statistics makes impossible any precise estimate of the distribution of income in present-day Egypt and of the extent to which it has changed since the Revolution. But some indications can be derived from simple observation of Egyptian society and changes in the pattern of consumption. Land reform, nationalizations and sequestrations have reduced the gap between rich and poor. The multi-millionaire pashas who, like their monarch, thought nothing of gambling away a few thousand pounds every night in a Riviera casino do not exist in Egypt today; their palaces and villas are closed or have been turned into flats or hotels. Even for several years after the Revolution there was still some conspicuous consumption of the kind for which the *ancien régime* was famous—such as dinner parties for forty with a 'suffragi' behind each chair. But since the socialist decrees of 1961 this has disappeared. On the other hand, the declared aim of these decrees—that no one in Egypt should have an income of more than £E. 5,000 a year—has clearly not been achieved. There are still some families who own agricultural land, buildings, furniture, jewels, and shares worth considerably more than £E. 1 million, although the lack of outlets for private investment ensures that their incomes are not proportionately high. For obvious reasons they do not spend lavishly.

The reduction in spending by the very rich has affected the large class of servants, chauffeurs, gardeners, messengers and watchmen who worked for them. For every rich man in pre-revolutionary Egypt, there were scores who picked up the crumbs that fell from his table. Some of these have found work in the new hotels or the many foreign embassies that have opened in Cairo since the Revolution (the large foreign communities of Greeks, Italians and Levantines, now no longer in Egypt, have to some extent been replaced by a new type of more transitory foreigner—U.N.-employees, experts, engineers, etc.). Nevertheless, it is quite common to find old retainers remaining with their employers unpaid because they have nowhere else to go—like liberated slaves, whom they resemble in many ways.

Industrialization, increased industrial wages, and distribution of profits, combined with various measures to hold down the cost of living, have substantially increased the incomes of the urban working class. According to the Prime Minister, Mr Sabry: 'At the time of the Revolution, wages were estimated at £E. 349 million, in 1959-60 they reached £E. 549.5 million, and at the end of the fourth year of the Plan they were £E. 770.3 million.' The official wholesale price index showed a sharp increase from 343 in 1952 (1939 = 100) to 415 in 1956, but from then onwards held steady between 415 and 425. These figures certainly underestimate the amount of inflation because they are based on officially controlled prices which are frequently evaded. The cost of living has been rising steadily a few per cent each year for the past few years. However, the inflation has been trotting rather than galloping, and there is no doubt whatever that the mass of city-dwellers have enjoyed a substantial increase in real as well as in money income.

As is to be expected among people living at such a very low income level, most of this extra income has been spent on food. Mr Sabry himself told the National Assembly:

In 1952 we imported only 4,600 tons of meat. In 1959-60 local production amounted to 157,000 tons, and we imported 15,100 tons of livestock, meat and poultry. In 1964 local production was 189,000 tons, and imports amounted to 52,500 tons. With regard to flour, 1952 imports amounted to 144,000 tons. We imported 442,000 tons in the 1959-60 fiscal year and 693,000 tons in the 1963-4 fiscal year. In 1952 we did not import wheat, and consumption amounted to one million tons a year. This year's consumption amounted to 2,315,000 tons.

Consumption of basic foodstuffs in Egypt, such as wheat, maize, sugar, rice and tea, has been rising at the rate of between five and ten per cent a year (compared with an annual population increase of 2.5-2.8 per cent). Since the greater part of this increased consumption has been in the cities and towns, the urban working class is eating very much more than it did before. (This is borne out by the remarkable number of cheap café-restaurants selling rice, *foul, falafil,* etc., which have opened in Cairo in recent years.) In 1964-5 food imports will cost £E. 140 million. The government expects this extraordinary increase to continue and estimates that by 1970 consumption of wheat and flour will have risen to 4,700,000 tons; maize to 2,800,000 tons; and meat and fish to 464,000 tons.

The increased consumption would have been much less if the government had allowed the cost of living to rise more than it has. Price controls; reductions in house rents, bus and train fares; and food subsidies, which in 1964-5 will amount to more than £E. 55 million, have been introduced to prevent this. The chain of government retail cooperative shops has contributed much towards providing the public with meat, vegetables and groceries at reasonable prices. For this reason the cooperatives are generally popular with the public (and intensely unpopular with the private retailers) despite the long queues which are normal because supplies are limited, the frequent rudeness and inefficiency of the employees, and recently the discovery that some of them were holding back goods to sell them at a profit to the independent butchers and grocers. The government has regularly reaffirmed its policy of holding down prices by these measures although they have greatly added to its economic difficulties. In November 1964 it went further and announced that prices of essentials would be restored to their 1961 level. (A cartoon in *al-Ahram* showed two women at the end of an immense queue in front of a cooperative. One is saying to the other: 'Lucky we are at the end, because by the time we get to the front prices will have gone down.')

Liberal economists regard these 'distortions of the market' with extreme disapproval, failing to acknowledge the great humanitarian benefits that they have brought to the Egyptian urban working class. Such 'distortions' are an essential part of Nasser's doctrine that the mass of the people (workers and *fellahin*) have been deprived for so long that they deserve to be compensated. The most cogent criticism that can be made of them is that they have benefited the workers very much more than the *fellahin,* and the 'status freeze' for the workers which the government now proposes is essentially an effort to direct some of the prosperity of the towns to the countryside. The only simple way to do this is to make the townspeople pay more for home-produced food, and an indication that the government has this in mind was the decision in November 1964 to remove all price controls from home-produced, but not from imported meat, so as to encourage the *fellahin* to rear more livestock.

Foreign residents in Egypt tend to resent the U.N. statistical estimate (proudly reproduced by the government to attract tourists) that Cairo is the cheapest major capital in the world. They say that they spend as much in a month as they would in Athens, Ankara or even Beirut. The explanation is that Cairo is still very cheap for those who can subsist on Egyptian-made goods and live as far as possible in an Egyptian style (that is, eating typical Egyptian food and wearing Egyptian-made clothing). Anything imported (such as Scotch whisky at £E. 4.5 to £E. 5 a bottle) or bought on the black market is very expensive. In the winter of 1964, for example, batteries for ubiquitous transistor radios were unobtainable except on the black market at £E. 0.15 each (about 2s. 6d.). Consumers' durable goods such as refrigerators (8 cu. ft. for £E. 100) or gas heaters (£E. 35) which are produced by 100 per cent protected Egyptian industries are also expensive. Against this must be set the fact that wages are still low in Egypt (and there is a high rate of under-employment) so that anything which involves in its production a high proportion of unskilled labour is normally cheap. Foreign residents now pay their servants between £E. 12 and £E. 20 a month, but Egyptians pay half this or less. Egypt, in other words, is in that condition common to countries which are halfway between being under-developed and developed; it is both cheap and expensive at the same time, and the cost of living is much higher for the rich than for the poor.

Wages and salaries are both low, but for the fully employed wages compare favourably with salaries. In industry the minimum wage of £E. 0.25 for anyone over eighteen years of age has been generally observed, and most workers in state-owned factories earn more than this for their statutory seven-hour day, forty-two-hour week. At the Iron and Steel Factory at Helwan, for instance, unskilled workers receive between £E. 30 and £E. 35 a month, and skilled workers from £E. 60 to £E. 70. And this is apart from substantial fringe benefits such as free medical attention at the factory clinic and low-rent housing provided by the company. At the Spinning and Weaving Factory in Mehalla el-Kubra a midday meal is provided for all the 21,000 workers at seven piastres (about 1s. 2d.) to which the company contributes half the cost.

A young university graduate, on the other hand, who is fortunate enough to find immediate employment on leaving the university, may expect a salary of £E. 20 to £E. 25 a month for several years, even if he is a well-qualified doctor or engineer. In the civil service the highest grade (Under-Secretary of State) earns £E. 3,000 a year. In industry a board chairman gets £E. 4,000 a year 'compared with the £E. 30,000 formerly paid to each member of the board in some cases.' (Dr Aziz Sidqi, Speech to National Assembly, 12 December 1964.)

Some critics believe that Egypt has gone too far in its policy of reducing discrepancies, and that current salary ranges are not wide enough to provide incentives. They point out that the range is considerably wider in the Soviet Union. However, the official salary scale does not give the whole picture. During 1964 the Cairo Press revealed that a substantial number of people in the higher ranks of industry and the civil service were receiving travel and other allowances which in some cases came to more than their basic salaries. Others were holding three or four jobs and drawing salaries from each. The Ministry of Finance determined that in future total allowances should never amount to more than thirty per cent of the basic salary; but because of the difficulty of forcing senior government servants to accept such a sharp cut in income, many of the basic salaries had to be raised substantially in compensation.

MANAGEMENT, ORGANIZATION AND BUREAUCRACY

Whether or not the lack of incentive in wage and salary scales is a contributing factor, Egypt is short both of skilled top-level managers and of trained foremen in the intermediate range. The problem is made worse by the overstaffing which we have already mentioned and an ancient tradition of bureaucracy which dies very hard. Where good managers have been found the results have been remarkable, and the Egyptian contractors Othman Ahmed Othman, who have carried out seventy per cent of the work on the High Dam, the Egyptian Petroleum Organization and the Suez Canal Authority all have encouraging records. Some of the best managers have been young officer-engineers from the Egyptian army selected for their ability rather than their rank or connexions.

In a series of penetrating articles on 'Administration and the Problem of Bureaucracy,' the editor-in-chief of *al-Ahram,* Muhammad Hasanein Heykal, pointed out that after the Revolution the government was well aware of the shortcomings in the old bureaucratic system but could not dispense with it. At first it had to run the country through men who held to the old ways and methods, because it had no one else to put in their place. But as the Revolution advanced, the State tried to limit the 'bureaucratic danger' by surrounding the old guard with a new one, of which the Suez Canal Authority and the Agrarian Reform and Desert Reclamation Authority are examples. This new guard has acted as a 'spearhead of the national effort,' but inevitably it has incurred the severe hostility of the old one. Heykal concludes that the ultimate responsibility does not lie with the bureaucrats themselves, but with the political system which controls them. Bureaucrats cannot be expected to change their mentality merely because the State has changed its political colour.

In this Mr Heykal is almost certainly correct. The government has done something to improve the situation by establishing Institutes of Vocational Training and Personnel Management, as well as a Vocational

Training and Productivity Centre, with the aid of the United Nations and the International Labour Organization; but a really effective reform requires a complete change in the atmosphere of government departments. Anyone who has had to deal with the older established government ministries and enterprises will have discovered the extreme timidity and reluctance to take responsibility of all employees except the very highest. This is partly, although not entirely, the result of overstaffing. Because there is usually not enough work for all the employees, new and unnecessary regulations have to be created to occupy them. Red tape grows longer and the employees, who know instinctively that their job is really unnecessary, lose any independence of judgment that they may have had when they started. This is something that clearly cannot be changed overnight, for it is the consequence of overpopulation and underemployment. But it is also a fact that the extreme authoritarianism of Egyptian society and government does much to discourage initiative and enterprise. In cases of emergency, where something has gone radically wrong—as in 1964, when the Cairo municipal bus services had hundreds of buses idle through a lack of spare parts, or the crisis at Alexandria Port, where millions of pounds worth of essential goods were rotting on the wharves because they had not received customs clearances—drastic action is taken to put things right; but it is taken from the top by someone with special power to cut through the red tape. The system is not permanently reformed.

The whole question of bureaucracy has become more important with the nationalizations of the last five years. In one way or another, the government machine now controls most of the country's economic life, and though the government itself is aware of the dangers that this represents, it does not yet have a clear idea of what to do about it. During 1964 there were frequent rumours that State-owned companies or groups of companies (formed by the amalgamation of nationalized or semi-nationalized firms) would be made autonomous and encouraged to compete with each other. The issue of how far the profit motive should have a place in Egyptian socialism was discussed at length in the Press, but by the end of the year the government had given no clear lead in the matter.

The dominating view was that the dangers of bureaucracy and the need to associate the people more closely with the State machine could best be dealt with through the Arab Socialist Union, and in December 1964 the government administration was reorganized with the object of giving the A.S.U. some control over government departments. It will need time to see whether this reform is effective.

Another development in late 1964 was the transformation of the Civil Service Department into a Central Agency for Organization and Administration with higher status and wider powers. This has yet to prove its effectiveness, but it could be very beneficial.

CURRENCY AND BALANCE OF PAYMENTS

During the First World War the direct ties between Egypt's currency and gold were severed, and the Egyptian pound became linked to sterling. In 1947 Egypt left the sterling area, in 1948 the agreement for the automatic conversion of sterling into Egyptian pounds was ended, and Egypt's sterling balances, which stood as high as £E. 405 million in 1945, were blocked. A series of agreements over the following years enabled Egypt to draw on these balances, and it used these partly to build up its gold cover to the note issue. By the end of 1960 this gold reserve stood at £E. 60.6 million and it remained stable until some £E. 15 million were sold on the Swiss markets in January 1965 to repay some short-term credits from Western banks which had been delayed.

Since 1949 there has been no official devaluation of the Egyptian pound, but through a system of premia and discounts a *de facto* devaluation in relation to the main convertible currencies was achieved. In December 1961 the situation was regularized with a twenty per cent surcharge for import payments and a twenty per cent premium for exports, applied equally to trade with all countries, and in May 1962 a uniform premium of twenty-five per cent was applied to all bank transfers in settlement of exports and payment of services. Since December 1961 the import or export of Egyptian bank-notes has been prohibited, which means that their value on free exchange markets outside Egypt is no longer any indication of the health of the Egyptian economy.

Egypt now has a currency system which is fully controlled by the State, with all the normal advantages and disadvantages that this implies. On the one hand the Egyptian economy is insulated from external factors (such as the devaluation of sterling), and the Egyptian pound is not tied to the balance of payments. Under the pre-1948 system a deficit in the balance of payments would have automatically imposed deflation, which would effectively have disposed of Egypt's Five-Year Plans. On the other hand, there is the extreme inconvenience in a number of ways of having a currency with no international value, and there is no restraining power on the government's control of the economy.

It is certainly arguable that such a system is imperative for Egypt during its present stage of development, but the trouble is that once it is established it is extremely difficult to relax. Furthermore, like prohibition, rigid currency control makes every citizen (and every tourist) a potential criminal because of the ease and attraction of smuggling.

Once Egypt had been set on a course of breakneck development, it was inevitable that the country should suffer severe balance of payments difficulties. Free foreign exchange reserves have hovered around the $6 million mark since 1962 and the government lives from hand-to-mouth, making day-by-day decisions to allocate foreign currencies where they are most needed. The Deputy Prime Minister for Finance, Dr Kaissouny, has gone so far as to say that no developing country ought to have any substantial foreign currency reserves, because this would merely mean that resources which should be employed were lying idle. This is all very well provided that the government is realistic in its forecasts of the country's balance of payments position, but the Egyptian government has been consistently over-optimistic. The most striking example was the key estimate in the first Five-Year Plan that imports would actually decline from £E. 229.2 million in 1959-60 to £E. 214.9 million in 1964-5, whereas the entire character of the Plan made it inevitable that imports, especially of capital goods, would rise steeply. In fact they rose to £E. 238.5 million in 1961, £E. 301 million in 1962, and to the astonishing figure of £E. 398 million in 1964 (only partly inflated by the *de facto* devaluation), despite the most severe restrictions on the importing of consumer goods.

The result was that instead of improving, the balance of payments situation worsened. In the summer of 1964 a number of factories were working below capacity because of the lack of foreign exchange, which had delayed the import of essential raw materials or machine spare parts.

Table 19. Egypt's Foreign Trade (£ E. million)

	Imports	Exports
1910	23.6	28.9
1920	104.2	92.0
1930	47.5	32.9
1940	32.4	30.0
1950	216.8	175.4
1955	187.2	146.0
1956	186.1	142.3
1957	182.6	171.6
1958	240.1	166.3
1959	222.1	160.5
1960	232.5	197.8
1961	238.5	161.2
1962	301.0	158.3
1963	398.4	226.8

Source: Dept of Public Mobilization and Statistics.

The situation would have been very much worse still but for three factors. One was the recovery of cotton production after the disastrous 1961-2 season and the improved prices paid for Egyptian long staples in 1963 and 1964 (partly due to two successive failures in the Sudanese cotton harvest); another was the steady increase in Suez Canal tolls; and the third was the tourist revenue.

Suez Canal tolls have risen as more and bigger ships have used it.

Table 20.

	(£E. million)
1955	31.8
1956	29.3
1957	24.3
1958	43.0
1959	44.4
1960	50.1
1961	51.2
1962	53.7
1963	71.1
1964	77.0

Sources: Central Bank of
Egypt Research Department and
Suez Canal Authority.

The sudden increase between 1962 and 1963 is partly due to the change, as of 31 December 1962, from converting Canal receipts at the old official rate of £E. 1 = $2.87 to the new (and more realistic) rate of £E. 1 = $2.30; but further sharp increases can be expected as a result of ambitious plans to widen and deepen the Canal so that the largest tankers can pass through it. The efficiency and enterprise with which the Suez Canal Authority has been run by a young officer engineer, Mahmoud Yunes, who has consistently followed a policy of investing heavily in the improvement of the Canal to raise revenues, has been one of the outstanding achievements of the regime.

Tourism is already an important source of income for Egypt, and the potential expansion is enormous. Egypt not only has antiquities which schoolboys everywhere have heard of, but two fine and largely undeveloped coastlines, together with a climate which is superb during the spring and autumn in Lower Egypt and in Upper Egypt during the winter. It is only really oppressive in August, and even this is not enough to deter many present-day tourists—especially Americans and Scandinavians.

Dr Hatem, the Deputy Prime Minister for Culture and National Guidance, who has been in charge of the tourist drive, is undoubtedly right in believing that tourist income could be raised from its present level of about £E. 25 million to £E. 100 million in a few years, and although his heavy hotel-building programme ('a new hotel opened every month') has been expensive, its potential return in foreign currency income is greater than that of any other industry. But here, as elsewhere in the economy, an easy over-optimism and lack of planning have led to serious mistakes. In 1963-4 tourists were encouraged to come to Egypt when there were not enough completed hotels to receive them or trained staff to look after them. The 'Save Abu Simbel' campaign gave Egypt invaluable publicity throughout the world; but elderly matrons from Missouri who arrived at their hotel in Upper Egypt to find that the rooms they had booked were already occupied by elderly matrons from Ohio and that they would have to pass the night on chairs in the lounge were not mollified to be told by an Egyptian official that this was 'proof of the success of the tourist drive.' In 1964-5, there were signs that the season was not as good as the previous year; even more serious, although the number of tourists coming to Egypt in 1963 was thirty-nine per cent higher than in 1962, the total number of 'tourist nights' only rose by 1.3 per cent. The new tourists being attracted to Egypt were mostly middle-class and lower-middle-class Europeans and Americans who had a few days to spend before going on to Beirut or Athens. They paid for their inclusive tours in advance and brought little cash with them. This trend is probably inevitable, because the real expansion in the tourist market is among such people rather than the leisured rich of the kind who used to spend three months wintering in Egypt sixty years ago. But this does not seem to have been borne in mind when some of the new hotels in Egypt were planned.

FOREIGN INVESTMENTS

The gravest consequence of Egypt's chronic balance of payments difficulties is that the country has acquired a bad reputation for the payment of commercial debts. In 1963 it was still true to say that Egypt enjoyed a good reputation overall, because if payments were delayed they were always made in the end. But the delays were becoming longer, until some creditors became exasperated. One small but significant example was that many foreign booksellers stopped shipments to Egypt in 1964 because payments were two or three years behind. In July 1964 the Sudanese-Egyptian payments agreement was cancelled, and Sudanese exports to Egypt of camels and meat ceased because Egypt had failed to pay for them. Meanwhile Egypt's liabilities from interest charges and repayment of principal were piling up at an alarming rate. Payment of compensation to the Suez Canal Company of £E. 28.3 million had actually been completed one year earlier than agreed in the 1958 settlement, but there remained compensation for British, French, Belgian, Swiss, Lebanese and other nationalized and sequestrated property. As we have seen, it was persistent delay in making these payments which caused the I.B.R.D. to announce that it was making no more loans to Egypt.

The following foreign loans and credit facilities (excluding military credits) have been made available to Egypt since December 1957:

Table 21.

	(£E. million)
From Communist states	
U.S.S.R.	332.5
Czechoslovakia	62.0
East Germany	45.0
Poland	24.4
Hungary	12.0
Yugoslavia	7.0
Total	482.9
From non-Communist states	
U.S.A.	535.6
West Germany	93.0
Italy	92.9
Japan	17.0
France	10.0
Britain	5.4
Netherlands	5.0
Switzerland	4.0
Sweden	3.3
Others	6.3
Total	782.5
I.B.R.D.	19.7
International Monetary Fund	36.0
Grand total	1,321.1

These figures are, however, only estimates. No complete list of foreign aid to Egypt is available from official sources, and this one has been compiled by adding to the most recent official figures (1961) such as have since been announced in the Press and elsewhere. It is reasonably accurate, but does not give the breakdown of long-term and short-term loans—although it may be assumed that almost all the loans from Communist sources are long-term.

The greater part of American aid since 1959 has been in the form of U.S. counterpart funds related to PL 480 (that is surplus wheat, meat, chicken, etc.), and these are repayable in Egyptian currency—most of which is then re-lent to Egypt for development with interest at four per cent and repayment in thirty years. Apart from this, most of the loans from Western sources take the form of short-term credits through the banks. Egypt has generally shown a preference for buying its capital goods, wherever possible, from the Western countries rather than the Communist bloc, and this is why such a high proportion of loans and credits from the latter has not been used. By the end of 1964 however, it was clear to the government that this policy was adding to Egypt's difficulties and that more Eastern credits would have to be used.

In early 1964 Egypt received a long-term loan of £E. 25 million from the Kuwait Government and a further £E. 10 million from the Kuwaiti Arab Development Fund for the improvement of the Suez Canal. Such help provided important relief during a crucial period, but by the end of the year it was reported that Egypt was already seeking a further loan from Kuwait. One possibility that was being explored was that Egypt should make some of its repayments in the form of manufactured goods, such as underwear, pajamas or shoes, to those creditor countries like the Soviet Union and the Sudan which might prefer to have them immediately rather than wait an interminable period for repayment in convertible currency.

SAVINGS, TAXATION AND WASTE

Despite the growth of deposit banking, post-office savings and insurance since the First World War, the rate of saving in Egypt is still very low. The Prime Minister told the National Assembly on 17 November 1964: 'Savings in our society constitute not more than five per cent of national income, whereas the average rate of savings in all advanced countries is not less than twenty per cent.'

The reason for this is not, as it used to be, that Egyptians are unfamiliar with cheques and banks and prefer to hoard their money at home. A visit to any bank in Egypt shows that the banking habit has spread throughout society. Nationalization and sequestrations and the power of the Taxation Department to seize bank deposits have caused some of the wealthier classes to prefer holding their money in buildings, furniture, jewellery or *objets d'art,* but the chief reason for the low rate of saving is that the increase in the national income is all being consumed. The government's estimate is that the national income rose by 19.2 per cent in the first three years of the first Five-Year Plan and consumption by nineteen per cent. The greater part of this increase was in food consumption, and this is the normal consequence of redistributing income in favour of the working class. However, the urgent need to increase savings has made the government consider various ways of encouraging the habit among the public. It was decided in late 1964 to raise the rate of interest on post-office savings from three to 3.5 per cent and to launch a savings drive.

Since the socialist decrees of 1961, Egypt has had one of the most steeply progressive rates of taxation in the world. Income tax rises from twenty-five per cent on the £E. 1,000-1,500 group to ninety per cent on incomes over £E. 10,000. Since 1939 there have been four categories of income tax: on dividends and interest; on profits of financial, commercial and industrial enterprises; on incomes of the liberal professions; and on wages and salaries. With an exemption limit on wages of £E. 0.50 per day, a high proportion of industrial workers, employees and government servants should now be paying income tax; but the Department of Taxation has still substantially to improve the methods of collection, for evasion is widespread.

Apart from income tax, there is a land tax assessed on the rental value of agricultural land and a tax on built property. But providing by far the most important source of revenue are the indirect taxes of customs and excise duties. Although export duties have been reduced or abolished, customs duties on capital goods have been reduced, and imports of all manufactured consumer goods have either declined or ceased altogether, this has been more than offset by increased duties on and consumption of coffee, tea, tobacco and alcoholic drinks.

How far are waste and corruption a serious problem in present-day Egypt? The question is crucial, because it was these more than anything else that caused the young Egyptian nationalist's disgust with the monarch. There can be no doubt whatever that at the highest level—among Vice-Presidents, Ministers, and permanent heads of government departments—the standard of economic morality is very much higher than it was before the Revolution. President Nasser himself has dealt ruthlessly with any senior government official touched by financial scandal, and although some of his bitter enemies have tried to suggest from time to time that he or one of his Ministers is living a life of secret luxury or salting away funds in Geneva, no one seriously believes it. The net gain to the country of the public's confidence that ten per cent of every foreign loan is not going into the private pockets of government officials is immense.

Below the higher offices of the State, however, the situation has changed very little since before the Revolution. The granting of special favours in return for *baksheesh* is still a widespread practice in the police, customs and other government services. It is difficult to stamp out such a hallowed tradition, especially while salaries remain low and government officials are so strongly tempted to use their position to supplement their incomes. Moreover the immense expansion of State power has increased the opportunities for corruption. Stringent import controls, for instance, have increased the potential value of import licences, and in 1964 a serious case of bribery by businessmen of Import Department officials came to light. We have already mentioned the widespread corruption among government retail cooperatives and the effect of strict currency control in making smuggling a common practice. The thousands of residents of Egypt, both Egyptian and foreign, who still have fortunes inside the country that they wish for one reason or another to take out, will in the main not shrink from using any kind of illegal means to export their capital.

The severe restrictions on foreign travel (which are essentially a form of currency control) have enormously increased the attraction of employment likely to take anyone out of the country. The inability to travel is a severe hardship for the Egyptian upper middle classes today, and several university students from what used to be called 'good families' have told the author that they aim to join the diplomatic service for this reason alone. There is a distinct danger, indeed, that a new class will emerge in Egypt with privileges derived from office rather than property or land. The government showed some awareness of this in November 1964 when it decided, as part of its economy measures, to close down many of its representative offices abroad (commercial, tourist, etc.) which had been duplicating the work of embassies, and at home to sell government cars to the employees using them. It was revealed that the running of these cars cost the government more than £E. 1 million a year, while it had very little power to ensure that they were not being misused.

Corruption and waste are two aspects of the same problem, which is one of the most serious that the Egyptian Government has to face. Nothing would do more to undermine the Revolution than a return to the cynical self-indulgence of the governing class which was so characteristic of the Farouk era.

THE LAND AND THE FELLAH

Here man belongs to the land; it is not the land that belongs to him. (Father Henry Ayrout.)

'Know-how' is not one of the things that its [Egypt's] agriculture lacks, nor was ignorance of agricultural techniques a cause of peasant poverty. On the contrary, the *fellahin* are excellent farmers, skilled and hard-working. In these respects Egypt was not an under-developed country; it was not the land which was neglected, but its cultivators. (Doreen Warriner.)

Very few have failed to be charmed by the valley and Delta of the Lower Nile—the serene palm trees, the brilliant green clover standing against the chocolate earth and a soft blue sky, the somnolent buffaloes cooling themselves in the canals, and the overwhelming impression of ancient fertile land carefully and lovingly tended. But the civilized beauty of the Egyptian countryside should not conceal the fact that most of the people who inhabit it are as poor, hungry and diseased as anywhere on earth.

About seventy per cent of the Egyptian people are *fellahin,* but it cannot be said that the remaining thirty per cent have cared much about peasant poverty. 'They have always lived like that, so they expect nothing different' is a typical comment of an Egyptian town-dweller. The present regime, many of whose leaders, like President Nasser himself, are the sons or grandsons of *fellahin,* are aware that the miserable condition of Egypt's peasantry is the chief cause of the country's under-development. But the problem grows more serious as the heavy emphasis on industrialization widens still further the gap between town and country.

Egyptian agriculture is highly distinctive for several reasons. The land is the most productive in the world, but it is extremely limited in area (about six million acres, or three per cent of the country's total), and since the rainfall in Egypt is negligible except near the north coast, it is all irrigated. For these reasons it is expensive, highly profitable and overcrowded, and because it is irrigated rather than rain-fed, the rights of individual ownership have always been limited by the powers of the pharaoh, khedive, government or whoever has controlled the source of irrigation, the River Nile. . . .

In 1947 the *per capita* real income of Egypt's rural population was just about what it had been fifty years before, but the distribution of income had become still more uneven. The increasing population pressure combined with the relatively small increase in the cultivated area steadily to swell the number of small farmers owning less than five *feddans.*

Table 22.

Year	Small holdings (below 5 feddans)		Medium holdings (5-50 feddans)		Large holdings (above 50 feddans)	
	Landowners	Land	Landowners	Land	Landowners	Land
1894	83.3	21.7	15.4	34.3	1.3	44
1914	91.3	26.7	8.5	30.4	0.8	43.9
1930	93.1	31.6	6.3	29.7	0.6	38.7
1952	94.3	35.4	5.2	30.4	0.5	34.2

The situation was far worse even than this table suggests, however. Two *feddans* of land constitute an absolute minimum from which a *fellahin* family can make a living, and in 1952 there were 2,018,100 who owned less than one *feddan.* They were seventy-two per cent of all proprietors, and they owned only thirteen per cent of cultivable land. In addition there were about 1.5 million families (about eight million people) who owned no land at all and lived by share-cropping or casual labour. At the other end of the scale 280 proprietors owned 583,400 *feddans* (of which 178,000 *feddans* were the property of the royal family).

As it became increasingly difficult for the *fellahin* to make a living for their families from their dwindling plots of land, more and more *fellahin* were forced either to try renting or share-cropping on an additional small area, or lease out their own plot and try to find employment as labourers. In either case the trend was the same. Between 1939 and 1949 the proportion of land that was rented rose from seventeen to sixty per cent. The common impression that the typical Egyptian *fellah* was a peasant owner-cultivator had become wholly false. At the same time the demand for land had forced up the price from about £E. 200 a *feddan* before the Second World War to about £E. 800 just before the Revolution. Rents more than quadrupled, and conditions were becoming more and more unfavourable to the tenant. Moreover, rents rose more than net output, so that it became more advantageous for the landowner to lease his land than to farm it himself. Rents varied fairly widely between different estates and between different parts of the Delta and Valley, but in 1952 the average rent level for the whole country was about £E. 30 an acre, equivalent to some fifty per cent of the gross produce. An absentee owner of a 5,000-acre estate could accordingly count on a gross income of £E. 150,000, while the gross value of their produce for the vast majority who owned two *feddans* or less was under £E. 120. Net income per head of the active agricultural population in Egypt was estimated at £E. 34 in 1953, compared with an average net income for the active agricultural population in Western Europe of £E. 190. . . .

Egyptian country life is a curious mixture of drudgery and unemployment, both equally demoralizing. When there is work to be done, it is long drawn out and backbreaking. For much of the year the *fellah* suffers burning heat, but because of the perpetual dampness of the soil and mud in which he works, he is bitterly cold during the short Egyptian winter. He is also undernourished and in poor health. We have already mentioned some of the common endemic diseases of the Egyptian countryside. Although naturally of good physique, the *fellah* never fully enjoys good health after adolescence. Because there is still less perennial irrigation in Upper Egypt than in the Delta, the Upper Egyptians suffer less from the parasitic water-borne diseases than the northerners and are preferred for employment in heavy labouring work. For the same reason the women, who rarely work in the fields except as cotton pickers, enjoy better health than the men.

Eighty per cent of the *fellah's* calories come from maize bread, of which he eats up to three pounds a day. The rest of his diet consists of onions, turnip, peppers or cucumber, which he eats raw, or beans, marrows, lentils and rice which are cooked for the evening meal on a primus stove or one fuelled with dry cotton branches or maize leaves. At some seasons he will have goat's cheese, dates, melon, or a piece of sugar-cane to suck; on very rare occasions, he eats meat.

Over ninety per cent of the village houses are made of mud brick dried in the sun. The rafters are strong enough for the roof to be used as a terrace in summer and for the storage of tools, grain and firewood (a reason for the frequent fires in Egyptian villages). The house itself has two or three dank, ill-lit rooms, where the family sleeps for most of the year with its animals. The *fellahin* women are expected to do very little. They rarely help in the fields, and the family meals require little cooking or preparation. The dust and mud make cleanliness difficult, but they do not attempt to sweep or to tidy their houses, while the children are commonly filthy and covered with flies. The Nubian villages are very much cleaner in comparison.

The women do little housework, but they do nothing else. In contrast with North Africans, and still more with the Indian peasants of North and South America, they do not sew, embroider or make pottery. An effort is now being made by the Ministry of Social Affairs to start domestic industries and crafts in the villages, but after centuries of neglect these are difficult to revive.

The creators of Egypt's wealth, the *fellahin* have been oppressed, neglected and despised for so long that it is not surprising that they have become submissive and fatalistic. What they need is the opportunity to display the skill, experience and perseverance which make them potentially some of the best farmers in the world. Any agrarian reform programme in Egypt has to have this end in view.

AGRARIAN REFORM

. . . The foremost aim of the land reform measures decreed by the revolutionary leaders was frankly political. The officers believed that the large landowners were blocking any effective reforms in Egypt through their ability to influence elections in the countryside and so control parliament. The second objective was to alleviate the conditions of small landowners and landless agricultural workers; but, as we shall see, legislation in itself was able to achieve little in this direction.

The main provision of the first land reform, therefore, was to limit the size of properties to 200 *feddans*. Exceptions were allowed for companies owning land under reclamation for purposes of sale; private individuals owning and reclaiming desert land, which would be exempt from expropriation for twenty-five years; and industrial concerns and agricultural societies. At the same time family *waqfs* (or entails which vested the usufruct of the land in the heirs for ever) were abolished and the properties divided among the beneficiaries. Landowners were also allowed to transfer ownership of fifty *feddans* to each of not more than two children. In 1958 a maximum of 300 *feddans* for family holdings was decreed, and in July 1961, as part of the series of socialist measures, this was further reduced to 100 *feddans*.

In some areas of Egypt families have succeeded in retaining a degree of their influence by a judicious distribution of ownership among different branches of the family. But the influence is now localized; it does not extend to the government or, except in minor measure, to the National Assembly. On the other hand, it cannot be said that any of the large landowners have suffered anything approaching destitution. The law of 9 September 1952 permitted private sales of land due for expropriation in lots not exceeding five *feddans* to farmers owning less than that amount. There was a rush to sell (though the provision that sales should only be made to small farmers was widely evaded) and the price of land fell by fifty per cent. Further sales were prohibited on 31 October, but by then at least 150,000 *feddans* had been sold. After the second land reform of 1961, landowners were allowed until 1970 to sell any land that they held in excess of 100 *feddans*.

Under the 1952 law, landowners were to receive compensation in non-negotiable three per cent government bonds redeemable in thirty years at the rate of ten times the estimated rental value of the land, which was calculated as seven times the land tax before the reform was decreed. This has worked out to an average of slightly less than £E. 200 a *feddan,* which means that an expropriated landlord received £E. 6 a year for every *feddan* taken from him by the reform. Under the 1961 law compensation was made payable in fifteen-year four per cent negotiable bonds. Altogether, the two land reforms have achieved a significant though not very radical redistribution of income from the rich to the poor.

Redistribution of expropriated land takes time, because the Agrarian Reform Authority tries to ensure that it is done equitably. Preference is given to former tenants who own less than five *feddans* themselves and to permanent labourers, while the size of the holdings granted varies between two and three *feddans* according to the size of the family. In 1962, the government decided to expropriate, with compensation, all agricultural land owned by foreigners, and this will ultimately provide about another 140,000 *feddans* for redistribution. When, after a few more years, all the land expropriated from Egyptians and foreigners under the first and second land reforms has been redistributed, it will amount to about one million *feddans* or seventeen per cent of the total cultivated area, and it will have benefited about 250,000 families or about eight per cent of the *fellahin.*

The very large estates have disappeared, the middle class (15-20 *feddans*) and upper middle class (20-100 *feddans*) estates have remained untouched, while there has been an increase of a few per cent in the number of holdings of less than five *feddans*. The general pattern of Egyptian land ownership, with the vast majority consisting of very small properties, has not changed.

It was originally intended that the 1952 land reform should be self-financing. The beneficiaries were to pay the expropriated landlords in instalments over thirty years together with three per cent interest and fifteen per cent for the costs of administration. In fact, because the 178,000 acres owned by the royal family were expropriated without compensation but

still paid for by the beneficiaries on the same terms as the other redistributed lands, the State was making a handsome profit out of the operation
in the first years. In 1961, however, payment by the beneficiaries themselves was reduced to half the total amount paid as compensation to the
owners, the period was extended from thirty years to forty, and the interest
was halved to 1.5 per cent. The State made itself liable for the difference,
and this will amount to more than £E. 50 million by the time the operation is completed.

The instalments paid by the new owners of land invariably came to
less than the rent they had paid as tenants. In his *Land Reform in Italy and
Egypt,* published in 1956, Sir Malcolm Darling estimated the average increase in net income as fifty per cent, and this figure has been accepted by
other independent experts. In general the *fellahin* in Upper Egypt gained
most, because rents there had been much higher than in Lower Egypt.

. . . The redistribution of expropriated land will at most have benefited eight per cent of the *fellahin* when it is completed. Article 3 of the
1952 law, which decreed compulsory reduction of all agricultural rents,
benefited many more—perhaps four million of the farming population. The
new rents were calculated on the same principle as compensation for the
expropriated landlords—they were not allowed to exceed seven times the
basic land tax—and in the case of share-cropping rents, the owner's portion
was not to exceed one half of the yield after deduction of all expenses.
These measures also provided the beneficiaries with an average net increase
in income of about fifty per cent. Tenants, moreover, were given increased
security of contract, which reduced their constant fear of eviction. The 1952
law decreed that all new leases were to be made in writing and were to
cover at least three years. All existing tenancy contracts were extended for
another year, and since then two extension periods of three years each have
been provided for half the area of leased land.

Those who benefited least from the reform were the agricultural
labourers and casual workers. It is true that a statutory minimum wage rate
of eighteen piastres (about 3s.) a day for men and ten piastres (about 1s.
10d.) for others was decreed, but because of the large surplus of unemployed these measures were unenforceable. At first agricultural labourers
were actually worse off, since the break-up of the large estates caused a
sharp reduction in demand for their labour; but later they were recruited
in large numbers for work on new land reclamation projects, the High
Dam and canal building connected with it, and industrial construction.

In 1956 it was possible to say of the reduction in rents that 'this improvement in income and legal status for a very large section of the farm
population is by far the most valuable achievement of the reform, greatly
exceeding in importance the benefits of redistribution.' (Doreen Warriner,
Land Reform and Development in the Middle East.) Unfortunately, much
of this achievement was only temporary. When Miss Warriner returned to

Egypt in early 1961, she found that 'as landowners have now recovered from the initial shock, there is at present much evasion of the provisions controlling rent.' Not all was lost, because the tenants still had better security of tenure for at least half of their land, and legal rents were enforced by the cooperatives wherever these had undertaken to collect the rent themselves from the tenant and pay it to the landlord. But in general nothing had been able to prevent the overwhelming pressure of demand for a limited supply of agricultural land from forcing rents and the price of land upwards, even to above their levels before the Revolution.

Must we therefore conclude that agrarian reform in Egypt has been a failure because it has been defeated by the realities of the Egyptian economy? This is not the case, because the results achieved by the Agrarian Reform Authority *in the areas directly under its control* have pointed the way for the rest of the country.

THE SUPERVISED COOPERATIVES

Wherever small farmers acquired new land under the agrarian reform, special cooperatives were established, and these differ in many important respects from the ordinary agricultural cooperatives in the rest of the country, which are mainly concerned with credit and supply. Membership of the Agrarian Reform cooperatives was made compulsory. They advance loans to members and provide them with seed, fertilizers, livestock, and agricultural machinery, together with storage and transport of crops. Under the first Agrarian Reform decree, they were charged with undertaking the organization of cultivation 'in the most efficient manner including selection, varieties of crops, pest-control and the maintenance and improvement of irrigation.' They also sold all the main crops for the members after deducting instalments for the purchase price of the land and interest on agricultural and other loans.

These supervised cooperatives have been a striking success. In general they have been well and honestly administered under the supervision of the Ministry of Social Affairs and the Ministry of Agrarian Reform, and crop yields, especially of cotton, have risen sharply. Total cotton output by supervised cooperatives in sixteen districts increased by forty-five per cent between 1952 and 1959, compared with fifteen per cent in the rest of the country. Increases for sugar and other crops were not as high, but they were undoubtedly above the national average.

The technical advantage of the supervised cooperatives lies in their ability to use large-scale farming methods for small properties. All the land in the village is divided into large fields, each several hundred *feddans* in size and raising a single crop. The beneficiaries of the reform are then allotted a holding in three pieces with each in a different field, so that one will be under cotton, another under maize or rice, and the third under berseem (Egyptian clover). The advantage in being able to plough, irrigate, and spray with pesticide such large areas is obvious. The triennial rotation was made compulsory for all the land reform areas in 1956. Elsewhere the *fellahin* normally used a biennial rotation, as follows:

November–May: wheat or berseem (Egyptian clover).

June–July: fallow.

August–November: maize, millet or rice.

December–January: fallow or berseem.

February–November: cotton.

This produced at least three crops every two years, but it exhausted the soil. Where some progressive large landowners used a triennial rotation, yields were up to twenty per cent higher. The success of the triennial rotation in the land reform areas caused the government to make it compulsory throughout the country by Law No. 166 of 1963.

Significant social advances are registered by the supervised cooperatives because most of the profits made by them are saved or invested. One of the biggest problems of the Egyptian countryside is that if the *fellah* has a good year, he immediately spends the windfall on a new wife or in marrying off his daughter. In the reform cooperatives dividends are small, reserves are accumulated as insurance against a drop in cotton prices, and the rest of the profits are spent on socially useful purposes. In one that the author visited a new mosque, a clinic (with permanent doctor and nurse), and a social centre (with television set) had all been purchased out of profits. The houses, shops and appearance of the peasants were all well above the average in Delta villages.

In many ways supervised cooperatives are a severe restriction on the individual liberties of the peasant farmers. They go at least half-way towards collectivization or nationalization of the land. But Egypt's agricultural situation is such that no reasonable alternative really exists between controlled or supervised cooperatives and communal farms on the Chinese pattern. Voluntary cooperatives of the kind that exist elsewhere in Egypt have shown that they cannot prevent the small landowners from sinking steadily deeper into debt. They are usually dominated by a small group of the larger landlords who use them for their own benefit.

The government has accordingly decided to extend the system of supervised cooperatives by degrees all over the country. Because it is to be done gradually, this has received little publicity, but it amounts to nothing less than an agricultural revolution. If it is to be a success, it cannot be imposed on the *fellahin* against their wishes; but fortunately there is a precedent in one village outside the land reform area where the *fellahin* were won over by the obvious advantages of the scheme. The village of Nawag near Tanta in the Delta was chosen because there fragmentation of holdings had gone to extreme lengths. In a total area of 1,850 *feddans*, there were 1,585 properties and 3,500 plots, each with different drainage and irrigation schemes. The villagers were asked to accept the division of their village into several large fields, each of which—as in the supervised cooperatives—would be under one crop. They were not asked to consolidate their holdings, or alter the pattern of ownership in any way; but like all peasants, they were cautious and they first agreed only to try the experiment on a hundred *feddans*. This was such a success that the next year they agreed to extend the scheme to the whole village. A similar experiment at Minshat Sultan, a larger village in the Menufia province, has been equally successful.

At the end of 1960 the government decided in principle to extend the system of supervised cooperatives to all other agricultural cooperative societies. But nothing much more was done until 1963, when it was decided to begin in two governorates—Beni Suef in Upper Egypt and Kafr el-Sheikh in the Delta. The farmers are being persuaded to accept *tagmi'a* of their holdings (or the grouping into several large fields). The two governorates have been divided into cooperative districts with a Land Reform representative in each, and for each 1,500 *feddans* there is an inspector with two assistants who deal with an area small enough to permit personal relationships with the *fellahin*. All the land reform officials with whom the author spoke agreed that, however much they would like to have been able to insist on the consolidation of fragmented holdings, it would be fatal to force the pace. One described their method of work as 'slow penetration rather than sudden invasion.'

The extension of *tagmi'a* and supervised cooperatives throughout the country should not imply that before the scheme was begun nothing had been done for rural development apart from the rather moderately successful attempt to reduce rents and raise agricultural labourer's wages. As already mentioned, the *fellahin* have benefited substantially from new schools, rural health centres and clean drinking water. There have been three other lines of attack on rural poverty and social backwardness:

The Gamoos *(buffalo) Scheme.* For work and as a milk producer, the buffalo is invaluable to all small Egyptian farmers; indeed it produces an annual net income equal to that of one *feddan*. In 1958 a Presidential decree provided for the distribution of animals to all *fellahin* without livestock at very reduced prices, with the money payable in instalments over four years.

The Rural Credit Scheme. This was launched in 1957 by the Ministry of Social Affairs and the Agricultural and Co-operative Credit Bank (which was founded in 1931). Its purpose was to help tenant farmers, who now constitute a substantial majority of the *fellahin,* by allowing the Bank to make loans on the security of crops instead of only the land. The interest rate was not to exceed three per cent, and the crops themselves were to be marketed through the cooperatives.

The Combined Units. The idea of combined rural social centres to provide health, educational, agricultural and social services to the population of the countryside was initiated in 1938 by a voluntary body. In 1940 the new Ministry of Social Affairs took over the work, and by 1955 there were 185 of these centres in existence across Egypt with each one serving about 10,000 people. Each centre had an agricultural advisor, who was also a social worker, a doctor, a nurse-midwife and a laboratory assistant. In 1954 it was decided to recast and extend the whole scheme. The Ministries of Agriculture and Education were brought in, and the centres were expanded to include sections for hygiene, education, social affairs and agriculture, and to serve 15,000 people each. By the end of 1964 there were 300 of these serving nearly five million, and the aim has been set to raise the number to 868 and so cover the whole rural population. The villagers contribute two *feddans* of land and £E. 1,500 towards each centre. The health and social workers are carefully selected and trained and are supposed to live in a manner as similar as possible to the villagers themselves. The *fellahin* themselves are generally very well disposed towards the centres, although they tend to be more attracted by their health and welfare services than by the economic and technical advice that they are intended to provide. Shortage of money and suitable staff has prevented the system from being expanded more rapidly. It is an imaginative, idealistic but at the same time practical idea, which could do more than anything to regenerate the Egyptian countryside. The low white building of the combined centres standing close to the unfired mud bricks of the village houses provides something like a symbol of hope for the future. . . .

CONCLUSION

Redistribution of ownership, reduction of rents, increased wages, semicollectivization (or supervised cooperatives), rural development (combined centres, clinics, schools, clean water) and reclamation of marsh and desert lands are the methods which have and are being used to tackle Egypt's fundamental problem—the miserable social and economic conditions of the people who live on the land. The question is whether they are enough . . .

Egypt's social and economic problems are so daunting that some people have come to regard the country as a hopeless case—doomed to remain one of the slum quarters of the world. It is not necessary to be as pessimistic as this. In its struggle to overcome the poverty and ignorance of its people, Egypt has two great assets. Its population has been confined for several thousand years to the Valley and Delta of the Nile, dependent upon the river for its livelihood, and though this has caused its poverty and overcrowding, it has also made it cohesive and amenable to strong central government—far more so, indeed, than most other under-developed nations. For a country which has to mobilize all its resources in a frontal offensive on its economic problems, this is a priceless advantage.

The other asset is the ninety-six per cent of its territory which at present is unexploited desert. With the progress of technology there are scores of possible ways in which Egypt may be able to make use of this land. Apart from reclamation for agriculture, there is a strong possibility that the deserts contain minerals which have yet to be discovered, since only a small part of them has yet been surveyed. Coal has recently been found in commercial quantities in Central Sinai, and big deposits of iron ore, one in the Bahriyah oasis, discovered. Uranium, copper, zinc, manganese, sulphur, asbestos, and gold are all either being mined already or have been found. The best prospects for crude oil production still seem to be along the Red Sea coasts and offshore, although there is the possibility of a strike by the companies now searching the Western Desert. Dr Sidqi, the Deputy Prime Minister for Industry and Mining, has said that he expects Egypt to be producing twelve million tons a year by 1970, which would make it a net exporter of oil.

The Qattara depression scheme, which is still being surveyed, would bring the Mediterranean into the depression to produce immense quantities of cheap electricity for irrigation pumps and industry. Finally there is the strong possibility of a breakthrough in research on the distillation of sea water for agriculture, a discovery that would at once transform Egypt's economic prospects since the country has vast areas of good soil covered only by a thin layer of sand.

Emigration has never seriously been considered as a solution of Egypt's problems, because there is no country that would accept the *fellahin* in any numbers or where they could be persuaded to go. The only possible exception is the Sudan, and even this presents political difficulties that are probably insuperable. But emigration within Egypt's borders, from the Valley into the desert, is something that can be foreseen if some or all the possibilities for exploiting desert regions are achieved. For the Egyptian people even this will not be easy, since most of them dislike leaving the Valley for any length of time. But ultimately it provides the great hope of creating a prosperous and dynamic nation.

2. Egypt's Economy Analyzed

WILLY LINDER

At the end of last year [1966] Premier Soliman reported the chief economic problems of Egypt to consist in overpopulation, underemployment, the effects of misdirected investments in the past, the lack of trained cadres, the balance of payments deficits, the disproportionate increase of public and private expenditures for consumption.

With this list the Premier however mentioned only a few of the difficulties confronting Egypt's economic policy makers. He should also have cited the tremendous foreign indebtedness, the shortage of gold and foreign exchange, the problem of exchange rates and the periodic inflationary waves.

Even before the outbreak of the war with Israel, Egypt's economic foundations were extremely weak, a fact which President Nasser himself emphasized on various occasions in the past few months, preparing the population for a period of restrictions. On the other hand he has given many proofs of his lack of understanding for economic matters. The economic targets he set for the first seven-year plan were for the most part politically-inspired, with the result that they had to be cut down in the so-called "fulfillment plan" that was to become effective July 1. The new plan is actually an admission of the failure of its predecessor.

FOREIGN INDEBTEDNESS

The large foreign indebtedness can hardly be described as justified by the actual economic development. The numerous bilateral consolidation agreements which Egypt has been forced to conclude in the past few months reveal its precarious financial position; the loss of foreign exchange sources —the Suez Canal alone produced about 100 million Egyptian pounds last year—on the one hand, and the reluctance of the International Monetary Fund regarding a new loan of $60 million on the other, and finally the growing military expenditures have aggravated the financial situation still further. It is doubtful whether the authorities in Cairo have themselves a

From Willy Linder, "Egypt's Economy Analyzed," *Swiss Review of World Affairs*, July 1967, pp. 6-9. Reprinted by permission of the author and the publisher.

complete picture of their over-all indebtedness, for in addition to the long and medium-term loans which Egypt has received from individual countries and international organizations it has received numerous short-term loans the total extent of which is not clear. Of course no data are available regarding the military commitments. In 1965 President Nasser set them at $35 million a year, a figure which is surely no longer correct.

While the last official figures are already obsolete, they remain interesting as indicators of the proportions involved. They reported that on September 30, 1965, the medium and long-term foreign loans amounted to $1.84 billion, of which on that date $1.08 billion were being used and $213.9 million were already paid back, with the remaining debt amounting to about $861 million. The largest single creditor at that time was the Soviet Union which had promised loans in the amount of no less than $866.6 million, of which $347.8 million were used, while $313 million remained to be paid back. In the middle of last year the total of loans reached $1.66 billion; of this amount $993.08 were used, and $626.11 million remained to be paid back in hard currency. At this same time the Soviet Union had loaned a total of $710.68 million, of which $338.28 were used.

These figures clearly reveal the large loans made available by the USSR; by the middle of last year the total of Soviet commitments to the UAR in fact was nearly as large as all the hard-currency loans together. The Soviet Union was the source of the largest part of the loans received from the Communist East; it was followed by Poland with promises amounting to $48 million by June 30, 1966. Western financial aid to Egypt on the other hand is divided more evenly among the individual creditor nations.

Informed observers of the Egyptian scene assume that the total of foreign loans amounts to about $2.3 billion today, with $1.3 coming from the Communist East and $1 billion from the West. The extent to which the loans have actually been used is as unknown as are the due dates for the repayments. For the financial year from July 1966 to June 1967 however the amount of 80 million Egyptian pounds ($184 million) in hard currency was entered.

At the beginning of the current year the reserves in foreign exchange amounted to 20 million Egyptian pounds ($46 million) and those in gold to 40 million E. pounds ($92 million). In 1966 the Central Bank had to sell one-third of its gold reserve in order to meet the most pressing foreign exchange needs. It has been rumored that despite strict foreign exchange controls the Egyptian pounds traded abroad—as in Beirut—came not only from smuggling, but were sold by some authorities in Cairo for the purpose of obtaining convertible foreign exchange through diverse channels. Actually this would not be a very economical method of obtaining hard foreign exchange, in view of the fact that the difference between the official rate of exchange and the free rate of the Egyptian pound was still a full 100 per cent a few weeks ago.

BALANCE OF PAYMENTS IN DANGER

It must furthermore be taken into consideration that the payments deficit is bound to increase unless the Egyptian Government resorts to rigorous import restrictions, thus exposing its industries to a process of shrinkage and asking the people to further tighten its belts. The payments deficit is a result in the first place of the trade deficit, which in 1966 rose to the record level of 196 million E. pounds.

In 1965 the payments deficit was "only" 29 million pounds (against 12 million pounds in 1964). This fact is to be attributed to the favorable balance of invisibles and of capital returns, among which the revenue from the Suez Canal figured with 86 million pounds in 1965 (last year it presumably grew to nearly 100 million pounds), that is, about two-thirds of the total revenues, while the last third was produced almost exclusively by tourism. And these are the two items worst hit by the war with Israel: the closing of the Suez Canal and the paralysis of tourism will have a bad effect on the balance of current payments. Moreover, the capital returns balance shows a small surplus only because Egypt has been living on loans for the most part. Not counting the new burdens caused by the war with Israel, experts estimate the payments deficit for 1966-67 at about 80 million E. pounds, because Egypt will now have to pay—on commercial terms—for the American wheat supplies that were suspended in January, 1966. The Egyptians were in the process of negotiating the purchase of wheat within the CCC (Commodity, Cooperation, Credit) Export Credit Sales Program, on the basis of which US agricultural surpluses are disposed of through normal commercial channels; an instalment of $28 million was agreed upon and the shipping of it was to begin this month. The Russians moreover promised to supply 250,000 tons of wheat, a quantity which would cover the requirements of about two months. According to information available, they insisted on commercial terms for this transaction; but even if the Soviet Union with a view to Egypt's disastrous situation were to change this attitude, Egypt's wheat supply will continue to be a big problem.

STAGNATING EXPORTS

Egypt's principal export commodity is cotton. Of its total exports of 247 million E. pounds in 1965, 162 million were accounted for by raw cotton. This proportion increases, when textile yarns and fabrics are included, to 193 million pounds; 79 per cent of the exports therefore are in cotton and textiles. Fifty-five per cent of the cotton went to Communist countries, mostly the Soviet Union, in the last season (September 1, 1966 to March 29, 1967). This percentage has been rising in recent years as a consequence of the enormous economic engagement of the Soviet Union in Egypt, which has to be paid back mostly in raw cotton, and not at world market prices. The larger Egypt's repayments to the Soviet Union, the smaller the proportion that can be sold to hard-currency countries; thus there results a reduction of revenue in convertible foreign exchange and an increasing dependence on Eastern Communist countries for imports. As yet this situation is not catastrophic, in that the West, especially the United States, continues to be the chief source of Egyptian imports. There is a tendency however toward an increase of the payments deficit with the hard-currency countries, whereas the surplus with the Communist states, not very large to begin with, tends to shrink.

The unbalanced foreign trade is the consequence of an over-dimensioned and partly misdirected investment policy which brought about a strong increase of imports of raw materials and machines, without Egypt's being in a position to increase its exports of industrial products and durable consumer goods. This involves the big problem of an improvement of the quality of Egyptian industrial goods at prices that are competitive in the world market. It also involves the problem of the creation of a reasonably sound material and human infrastructure, especially of trained cadres. Productivity is inadequate, some factories work below capacity because as a result of import restrictions there is a lack of raw materials and of parts. Several industries dependent on foreign exchange must export their goods, because they are not competitive, to developing countries; they spend hard foreign exchange for the supply of raw materials, but receive "soft" currencies for the goods they sell.

It would undoubtedly be a mistake to describe the entire industrialization policy as a failure. But it has weaknesses which have greatly contributed to the economic difficulties, and it is the expression of an economic policy inspired not by economic, but by prestige considerations primarily. Egypt's industry moreover is today almost completely nationalized and planned. The bureaucratic suprastructure has assumed proportions in reverse ratio to its efficiency. The policy of nationalization and socialization for the rest was admittedly a means to eliminate foreign influence, as a weapon against "imperialism." The fact that under these circumstances many Egyptians still hope for foreign private investments reveals a striking lack of realism on their part.

AUSTERITY A NECESSITY

It seems inevitable for Egypt to enter a period of austerity. Under the circumstances the Government probably will have to reconsider the recommendations made by the International Monetary Fund early this year. They culminated in the recommendation of an open or veiled devaluation of the Egyptian pound to get the distorted balance of trade readjusted, and in a restrictive monetary policy, especially a reduction of public and consumer expenditures, to ease the inflationary pressure. Egypt has not had a balanced budget since the beginning of the Fifties; until the beginning of the phase of socialization properly speaking in the early Sixties to be sure the deficits remained moderate. But with the socialization and the elimination of private enterprise as well as the inauguration of an ambitious policy of industrialization the deficits increased by leaps and bounds. In the financial year 1960-61 expenditures exceeded revenues by 160 million pounds (as against 66 in the preceding year); in the financial year 1966-67 the excess amounted to 224 million pounds. The accumulated deficit in this period reached no less than 1.76 billion pounds; the internal debt increased correspondingly: in 1959-60 it was 447 million pounds, in 1962-63 1,025 million pounds, and today it presumably is far larger. As an inescapable consequence of this development the increase of the volume of money in circulation was bound to greatly encourage economic expansion, so that even severe price controls were no longer able to avoid strong inflationary waves. In 1961 the index of food prices had arrived at the level of about 300 (1939 = 100); by the end of the past year it rose to 400, without a corresponding adjustment of wages. Price increases were decreed partly also to absorb purchasing power—inflation in the service of the fight against inflation! On the other hand, industrial productivity and production increased but insufficiently. The root of the pronounced imbalance therefore is a strong disparity between global productivity and government spending policy, an overdimensioned and partly highly problematic expansion.

It is easy to see that the correction of such a situation in the turbulent atmosphere of a lost war will pose extraordinary problems because productivity will at first decrease further, state expenditures, however, in all probability will increase; the danger of a "typical" postwar inflation that might further accentuate the existing distortions is thus evident. And this in a socialist state in which as a rule public expenditures absorb a large proportion of the national income—in the case of Egypt, 60 per cent.

UNSUCCESSFUL STABILIZATION ATTEMPTS

It is not the first time that Egypt must try to stabilize its economy; but all efforts have so far been unsuccessful. There was a lack of determination to carry out the thorough reorganization required, not only because it involved a reduction of the over-ambitious aims, but because the assistance of the International Monetary Fund, which had to make available the necessary loans, was interpreted as an undesirable foreign interference. On the occasion of the first stabilization program during the socialization phase of

May, 1962, when the IMF granted a credit of $42.5 million, the Fund experts after two years had to report that practically none of the conditions tied to the stabilization had been fulfilled. And after the second stabilization program (at the beginning of 1964) for the execution of which a stand-by credit of $40 million was granted, the Fund in 1965 stated that while a few of the aims had been achieved, the principal demands had again not been met. The third attempt in December, 1965, like its predecessor came to grief over the lack of consistency; ironically during this phase of rehabilitation the economy drifted into an increasingly dangerous situation: growing foreign indebtedness, shrinking foreign exchange and gold reserves, increasing deficits in the clearing accounts, supply bottlenecks, etc. And the fourth attempt finally in the spring of 1967, that had been preceded by not very promising talks with IMF experts, petered out even before its implementation in the political turmoil engendered in Cairo in anticipation of the war against Israel.

Under these circumstances the future does not look very bright, the less so as the basic structure of the economy and the principles underlying the social and political conditions are greatly to be blamed for the development.

TOP-HEAVY PLANNING

Undoubtedly the planning institutions and administration in general are greatly overstaffed and notoriously inefficient. The hierarchy of the planning organs on the other hand is relatively simple. The plants are gathered by branches and directed by superior planning units—of which there are about twenty; the planning threads then run together on a third level in the corresponding Ministries or the Planning Ministry. The Planning Bureau itself, assisted by a committee composed of the President, Ministers and experts, is endowed with extraordinary economic powers; it holds an absolutely dominant position in the drafting and carrying-out of the plan.

The Planning Bureau obviously follows relatively modern planning techniques, in the elaboration of which such eminent economists as Ragnar Frisch and Oskar Lange have collaborated. But the infrastructure required by a planned economy, especially the statistical data, is very imperfect. Before the Middle East crisis Nasser's planned economy resembled a cracker-barrel assembly, with the instrument of "discussion" being elevated to the status of a system for the solution of economic problems. Its advocates saw in it a sort of "democratic element" mitigating the strict planning. To the planning center, whose task it is to harmonize the part-plans from bottom to top and to build in the President's political points of view, this flexibility, however, seems to apply only to a limited extent; with regard to aims it is able to decide independently to a large extent and does not consider itself bound by the information reaching it from below; it moreover has at its disposal a comprehensive control machinery.

CREATING "EMPLOYMENT"

Another pretense at democracy in planning is the parliamentary procedure. The Parliament must decide and adopt the plan; so far, however, it has out of respect for the higher will made only very small corrections. Its inferior role in this procedure can be seen from the fact that it never tried to put the frequently completely unrealistic and purely political aims on a more viable basis. With the adoption of the plan by the Parliament it becomes law, and changes can be made only via the legislative procedure.

Egypt has introduced the "right to work," which of course in view of the constant pressure of population cannot be fully realized, but which functions to the extent nevertheless of absorbing especially the academic youth into the party machinery, the planning apparatus, industry and public administration. This policy of creating employment—not work—is an attempt to bridge the gap between the growth of the population and the growth of the economy. With regard to this country's suffering from chronic underemployment one will have to have some understanding for the economic standpoint's being subordinated to the social in employment. The effect, of course, partly of pressure on productivity and partly of an increase of the bureaucratization of the economy, is highly problematical from an economic point of view.

Is it a bad sign that since 1961 government plants have no longer published any reports? The Government in any event considers it no longer necessary to enlighten the people on the situation of "its" plants, although there is a law on the books obliging it to render public account. In the absence of information it is impossible to evaluate the work of the government enterprises. And since Egypt's economy is almost completely nationalized or organized in cooperatives, with membership in the state-controlled cooperatives being gently enforced by discriminatory measures against non-members, production can be evaluated only indirectly. The unfavorable position in international cooperation as reflected in the stagnating exports in any event points to excessive costs. Well-informed sources believe that the famous steel plant at Helouan works at costs considerably above those of comparable American plants.

OIL AND EXPORTS

Before June 5 Egypt's economic strategists declared that the new discoveries of oil in the Gulf of Suez and in the western desert (El Alamein) would work a miracle; although estimates of the yields to be expected differ considerably, it is certain that in a few years they will greatly improve Egypt's situation with regard to oil and thus to foreign exchange. Prior to the war experts in Egypt declared that in the course of the next three years the output of oil would increase from the 7.1 million tons in 1965 to three times that amount. The UAR would thus become an exporter of oil. In 1965 it imported oil and oil products in the amount of 28.8 million pounds, while exports of the same brought in only 10.9 million pounds. The improvement of these terms, of course, has now become doubtful as a result of the war.

This doubt must be expressed with regard to all of Egypt's exports. The recent recommendations of a parliamentary committee for economic planning, according to which exports were to be promoted through credit priorities, a general reorganization of foreign trade administration, the creation of mixed companies and the intensification of promotion abroad will under the new circumstances have to be postponed. The proposal of a devaluation of the Egyptian pound such as the IMF experts had demanded is rejected by nearly all UAR economic policy makers; they point to the unsuccessful experiment in India and to the fact that the disparity between the official and the free rate of exchange does not suggest an overvaluation of the pound, since this disparity was to be considered exclusively as a reflection of the smuggling of currency. More convincing in the context appears the observation that the larger part of UAR exports is in agricultural products whose volume can be increased only on certain very limiting conditions by a currency manipulation. Meanwhile it is quite conceivable that the problem of an open or veiled devaluation of the pound will become more acute again in Egypt itself in connection with the economic aftermath of the war.

SUGGESTED READING

Ayrout, Henry Habib, *The Egyptian Peasant*. Boston: Beacon Press, 1963.

Collins, Robert O., *Egypt and the Sudan*. Englewood Cliffs, N.J.: Prentice-Hall, 1967.

Gerakis, Andreas S., "United Arab Republic: A Survey of Development During the First Five-Year Plan, 1960/61–1964/65," International Monetary Fund, *Staff Papers*, November 1967.

Issawi, Charles Philip, *Egypt in Revolution: An Economic Analysis*. New York: Oxford, 1963.

Kerr, Malcolm H., *Egypt Under Nasser*. New York: Foreign Policy Association, 1963.

Kardouche, George K., *The U.A.R. in Development: A Study in Expansionary Finance*. New York: Praeger, 1967.

Magdi, M. El-Kammash, *Economic Development and Planning in Egypt*. New York: Praeger, 1967.

Nasser, Gamal Abdel, *Egypt's Liberation: The Philosophy of the Revolution*. Washington, D.C.: Public Affairs Press, 1955.

O'Brien, Patrick, *The Revolution in Egypt's Economic System: From Private Enterprise to Socialism, 1952-1965*. New York: Oxford, 1966.

Saab, G. S., *The Egyptian Agrarian Reform, 1952–1962*. New York: Oxford University Press, 1967.

Sanchiz, José C., "Money and Banking in the United Arab Republic." International Monetary Fund, *Staff Papers*, July 1965.

Stevens, Georgiana G., *Egypt: Yesterday and Today*. New York: Holt, Rinehart and Winston, 1963.

Vatikiotis, Panayiotis J., *The Egyptian Army in Politics: Pattern for New Nations?* Bloomington: Indiana University Press, 1961.

Warren, C. J., "Highlights of the Agriculture and Trade of the United Arab Republic (Egypt)," *Foreign Agriculture* (January 23, 1967).

YUGOSLAVIA

Yugoslavia, a country of 100,000 square miles with a population of about 20 million, is one of the fourteen countries in the world which claim to be striving toward the establishment of a communist society built along the lines vaguely envisaged by Marx and Lenin. But Yugoslavia also claims to be a "nonaligned" country, following her "own road to socialism."

At the end of the 1940's the Yugoslavs dared to disobey the commands of Stalin, then the uncontested leader of the countries of the Communist World. Under the leadership of their war hero, Marshal Tito, the Yugoslavs were thus the first to crack the monolithic structure of what until then had been the Soviet bloc of nations. From those days until the present, Yugoslavia has gone her own way, attempting to combine the advantages of a market economy with those of centralized planning and administration and to introduce more democracy into the framework of a one-party political structure. But rights guaranteed by a constitution, official proclamations of "workers' self-management," public announcements that the Party's role is now being reduced to one of educator and advisor without powers to enforce decisions—these are not enough. Statements and proclamations in and of themselves do little good unless they are implemented. In the West, there is considerable disagreement among students of the Yugoslav system regarding the *degree* of implementation; but there is no dispute over the fact that in economic, political, and cultural liberalism, Yugoslavia is far ahead of most other communist countries, although she is surely behind when compared with the leading Western democracies.

Yugoslavia's economy today presents an interesting mixture of economic guidance and free market relations, and of Party rule and political freedom. Here one finds most means of production socially owned; but increased powers have been bestowed upon individual workers' councils, about 85 percent of all farm lands are in private hands, and in recent years Yugoslavs have been given increasing rights to establish small businesses of their own, and even to hire small numbers of workers in their private enterprises. The single slate of candidates in national and local elections has been replaced by competition among several candidates for most elective positions, but the establishment of an opposition party is at best whispered about as a future possibility. The ouster of former Vice President and Party Secretary Alexander Rankovic, unofficial leader of Yugoslavia's conservative forces, was interpreted East and West as a step in the direction of further economic decentralization and political liberalism; but the fact that, from local Party cells right up to the Party Central Committee, all votes on his demotion and subsequent expulsion from the Party were unanimous indicates that Western-type democracy has by no means won an all-out victory. And recent official statements to the effect that Yugoslavs henceforth shall be free to disagree with and to criticize anyone—even high Party officials—sound promising; but the thirty-day prison sentence given to a West German tourist in June, 1967, for publicly "supporting Israeli aggression against the Arabs" gives a slightly hollow ring to guarantees of "freedom of speech."

In the immediate pre-World War II era, Yugoslavia was truly an underdeveloped country, and whatever economic growth there was barely stayed ahead of population increase. Since the end of World War II, Yugoslavia's economy, although subject to substantial fluctuations, has advanced rapidly. Since the beginning of economic reform in the early 1950's, the average growth rate has probably exceeded 8 percent annually, which makes the Yugoslav economy one of the fastest growing in the world. With a per capita output that will surely be at least $600 per year before the end of the 1960's, Yugoslavs do not yet live in affluence; but neither do they go to bed hungry at night as do so many of the inhabitants of other developing countries.

Yugoslavia's proclaimed attempt to combine the best of two worlds into an efficiently functioning economy, and into a system that will grant maximum economic security with a minimum of surrender of freedom, is blasted by the Chinese as a sellout to "American imperialism" and as a return to capitalism. The Yugoslavs, on the other hand, refer to their system as "creative Marxism." Some of the East European countries have started to follow in Yugoslavia's footsteps; and the Soviet Union, although long opposed to Yugoslavia's "own road," has in recent years begun to look more sympathetically on the new system. Most Western Marxists outside the pro-Chinese factions of Western Communist Parties approve of the Yugoslav experiment, but there are exceptions. For instance, the co-editors of the *Monthly Review,* American Marxists Paul M. Sweezy and Leo Huberman, addressing themselves to the Yugoslavs, wrote in the March, 1964, issue of their journal: "Beware of the market; it is capitalism's secret weapon! Comprehensive planning is the heart and core of genuine socialism."

Yugoslavia's approach, more pragmatic than that of any of the other communist countries, merits the attention of the student of growth and development. The authors of our two selections, Milos Samardzija and Ivan Maksimović, are respectively Professor of Economics and Professor of Political Science at the University of Belgrade. The former concentrates in his contribution on the economic factors; the latter, on the political aspects of Yugoslavia's growth and development.

1. *Economic Development and Planning in Yugoslavia*

MILOS SAMARDZIJA

1. The historical development of Yugoslav society stretches across a short period of less than four decades. This society came into existence for the first time in the history of the Yugoslav peoples as a unified political community in 1918. From the very beginning this society has been culturally and economically heterogeneous, and was quickly entangled in acute national conflicts caused by the unitary and centralistic organization of the state. Yugoslavia was also entangled in social conflicts caused by the failure to resolve social problems. These relations had two types of effects on the life of Yugoslav society.

The unstable political community which was created quickly grew into a political dictatorship. Economically, Yugoslavia was stagnant. The process of disintegration of the traditional peasant society, and economic polarization, did not lead to the creation of a modern industrial society of a capitalist type. The participation of foreign capital was based on investment principles characteristic of investments in colonial economies.

The static character of this society was also expressed in the slow decline of the share of the agricultural population in the total population (78.9% in 1921, 75% in 1939). Yugoslavia was a typical example of a country in which the income per capita remained at a nearly constant level. The compound annual rate of growth of national product, in constant prices, between 1929 and 1939, was 1.7%. The corresponding rate of increase of population was 1.4 percent. The outbreak of World War II led to the complete political dismemberment of the Yugoslav community and to the loss of national independence.

2. A new stage in the development of Yugoslav society began after the liberation of the country in 1945. Economically, Yugoslavia found itself in complete disorganization. During the war, seven different monetary systems had been formed on the territory of Yugoslavia. Productive and transportation capacities were to a great extent disabled, and human losses amounted to more than 11 percent of the total population of 1939. The conditions for economic development, in terms of material capacities, were

From Milos Samardzija, "Economic Development and Planning in Yugoslavia," A paper presented at the March 1967 meeting of the Michigan Economic Society held in conjunction with the Michigan Academy of Science, Arts and Letters, at the University of Michigan, Ann Arbor, Michigan. Reprinted by permission of the author.

worse than they had been in 1918, since the war destruction covered the entire country, and not merely the eastern regions as had been the case in World War I.

International aid which the Allies gave to Yugoslavia made it possible for the process of reconstruction of the national economy to be finished in two years. At the beginning of 1947, planned economic development of the country began. The level of development from which Yugoslavia started in 1947 can be illustrated by the following data: the national income per capita was 170 dollars; regional discrepancies varied from $85 in Kosmet to $270 in Slovenia. Nonagricultural employment amounted to 7.4 percent of the total population.

The First Five Year Plan for the economic development of Yugoslavia, for 1947 to 1951, rested on this material basis. The central portion of the plan was concerned with the construction of an infrastructure, with particular priorities on the sector generating energy, and on ferrous metallurgy. (Annual production of electric energy in 1947 amounted to 1.4 billion kilowatt-hours; oil, about 1,000 tons; steel, about 100,000 tons.)

The period which followed liberation was particularly significant for the political and social stabilization of the country, and for laying the foundations for the socialist development of society. The federal organization of the political community, the goal of which was to make possible the national autonomy of the Yugoslav peoples, the nationalization of economic capacities (except agriculture and crafts), agrarian reform—represented a framework for the construction of a new system of guidance and management.

In all basic ways this system represented a copy of the Soviet economic system. The fact that the USSR was the only socialist country in the world was highly significant for the solution of institutional problems of societies in a transitional stage to socialism. The identity: socialism = Soviet economic system, was at that time the dominant conception of communists. This view was also shared by Yugoslav communists who, during the war, had represented the only factor for the integration of the Yugoslav peoples, and who, after the war, were the leading power in the organization of the socialist transformation of Yugoslav society.

The Yugoslav economic system at that period was based on complete centralization of management by the state, and on government planning as the basic method for the allocation of material goods and labor. This planning system was a historical form of planning which corresponded to an undeveloped economy with rudimentary market relations. What is more, even in those sectors where some types of market relations existed, they were eliminated by economic policies. At that time, the dominant conception in socialist theory was that the construction of socialism necessarily means the liquidation of market relations, and therefore that planning and the market were in principle contradictory. Physical planning and allocation of production factors, monocentrism in decision-making, and the directive character of planning decisions, were the basic characteristics of this system.

On the basis of this system were formed new relations in the material structure of production and distribution. The basic criterion for economic performance was the fulfillment of plan targets which were defined without an adequate knowledge of actual relations and capacities. A series of new circumstances made it impossible to analyze and appraise the efficacy of this system. The break in political and economic relations with the Soviet Union in 1948, accompanied by political and economic blockade; the policy of general collectivization started in 1949; the extremely unfavorable agricultural years 1950 and 1952, led in the first instance to an economic slowdown in 1949, and then to stagnation in industry and to large oscillations in agricultural production. The five year plan was extended for an additional year, since the targets could not be achieved in time. The volume of investment was decreased and concentrated on key projects. However, even the reduced plan could not be realized. The actual economic development of this period was much slower than the planned rate (the compound annual average rate of growth of gross material product, at constant prices, was 2.3%. However, if the effects of the unusually unfavorable agricultural production of 1952 are excluded, and if the period 1947-1953 is taken as the basis of comparison, then the growth rate was 4.7%).[1]

The historical conditions in which the Yugoslav economy developed between 1947 and 1952 are not an adequate basis for an evaluation of the efficiency of Soviet-type planning for the organization of economic development in Yugoslavia. This type of planning was a logical component of the economic system usually known as state, or administrative, socialism. The fact is that this type of planning has made possible the realization of priority targets of development in other socialist countries. The main target was the maximization of the rate of growth of net material product. The statistical evidence given for the Soviet Union, Bulgaria and other East European countries, between 1949 and 1959, shows rates between 8 and 11 percent.[2]

3. At the end of 1949 began the process of building a new system of management in Yugoslavia. This system is known as the Yugoslav way to socialism. What is new in this system? The socialist economic system is usually defined as a system in which the private appropriation of means of production is abolished and social ownership is created. Nationalization of means of production, however, does not, by itself, determine the social content of an economic system. The central problem of an economic system

---

[1] *Yugoslavia. Statistical Survey 1947-1964*. Belgrade: Federal Statistical Institute, 1965.

[2] United Nations: *Economic Survey of Europe in 1961*. Part II. Some Factors in Economic Growth in Europe During the Fifties. Geneva, 1964. Chapter II, p. 9.

is the social organization of labor, the role and place of social groups in economic life, and particularly their capacity to manage the means of production. To manage means to decide on the allocation and use of factors of production, and to decide on the allocation of produced goods.

Seen from the standpoint of particular social groups, the question can be formulated as follows: who is the dominant social factor in socialist society? In socialist theory, and also in critiques of socialism, that social factor is in principle identified with the state, at least in the lower, transitional phase to socialism. Even if the state receives a new form, and if a particular social group stands behind its institutions—civil servants, bureaucracy—the strengthening of the social influence of the state in economic processes in practice leads to the development of the managerial apparatus of the state and the organization of a bureaucracy (state or party) as the basic social force in the new society.

In Yugoslav theory, the starting-point for the analysis of the social content of socialism was based on the conception that the new society first of all represents a community of working people who create material wealth through their work. Thus it is these working people who must decide on the allocation and use of the goods they produce. If working people—producers —are the leading social group, then the basic question concerns the construction of an economic system in which the active role of the producers and their associations in the economic system will be strengthened, and the economic and social role of the state will decrease and gradually disappear.

In the present phase of development of socialist societies, in which forms of administrative management of the economy dominate, a contradiction between the state management of the economy and the role of the producer in economic life has been developing. This contradiction is manifested as a contradiction between the bureaucracy and the workers, and comes to the surface in the political, ideological and legal superstructure of the society.

The development of the Yugoslav economic and social system has been oriented, since 1950, in the direction of creating social forms and material bases for the development of social self-management by working people, and the gradual elimination of state and party influence on economic life. The introduction of workers' selfmanagement is the turning point of this process. The process has gone through various phases and reached its present form after a development of almost 15 years. Contemporary relations between the state and the producer in the organization of economic life were even given a legal formulation in the new Yugoslav constitution enacted in the spring of 1963.

The basic characteristics of this process are: the establishment of business autonomy in economic organizations (enterprises), and the development of a market economy as a new form of integration among enterprises in the national economy. In the particular circumstances of the Yugoslav economy it was necessary to develop the market mechanism and to create material and social conditions for its functioning. The process began with the elimination of administrative allocation of consumer goods, and the transformation of producer goods into commodities. Enterprises gradually became autonomous decision-making units. At first this autonomy was introduced in the distribution of raw materials and consumers' goods, later in the distribution of income, and finally in the allocation of investment.

In addition to the market economy, the regionalization of macroeconomic management replaced the centralized, ministerial system of management. This was achieved through decentralization of management within the state apparatus, and through the creation of local selfgovernment in the commune, which was the basic form of social and economic integration in the region. Sectoral integration of economic units was neglected throughout the entire period. This was a reaction against the centralistic and administrative procedures of the earlier period.

In this institutional organization of the economic system, the reorganization of social planning comes to the fore. It was necessary to organize a planning system consistent with decentralization of management, business autonomy of enterprises and market relations.

The introduction of the system of planning on the basis of "global proportions" in 1951 turned out to be a short-term experiment. After a series of changes in planning methodology, in which annual plans were the basis for projecting social and economic development, a new five year plan was started for the period 1957-61. These plans were no longer detailed and comprehensive national plans, but were plans of development. Development plans deal with the global distribution of gross material product, the growth rate, and detailed provisions on the volume and structure of investments.

The methodology for the preparation of these plans is being improved, although the trial and error method is still the basic method. During this period the first Yugoslav input-output table was constructed, but this table is more of a pioneering work than an analytical instrument which can be used for confirmation of the coherence of the basic indicators of the plan.

The five year plan for 1957-61 was realized in unusually favorable circumstances, among which the most significant are: the normalization of political relations with the countries of the Soviet bloc (and thus decreased investments in the armaments industry), a high share of international credits and aid (which contributed to the increase of sources of accumulation), and two unusually good agricultural years (1957 and 1959). The basic targets of the plan were achieved in four years, even though this was done with a very distorted economic structure. All this led to the formation of an optimistic conception of the possibility to organize accelerated economic development.

During 1959 and 1960, the preparation of long-range projections of Yugoslav development to 1980 began, but these were not politically approved. In the same period a new five year plan for 1961-65 was prepared. This plan was a type of linear extrapolation of the development realized from 1957 to 1960. Already at the end of 1961 it was seen that the projection was erroneous and the plan was abandoned in 1962. The preparation for a seven year plan for 1964 to 1970 began, and meanwhile the economy was organized on the basis of annual plans. This transitional period was prolonged to 1965, at which time significant changes in the organization of the economy took place. These changes are known as the Economic Reform of 1965.

The efficacy of social planning in the organization of economic development was not satisfactory during this period. Many unanswered questions which grew out of contradictory relations in the structure of the Yugoslav society (centralization-decentralization, selfmanagement-communal system-federation, economically backward-economically developed regions, unbalanced-balanced development) brought about acute debates and conflicts of interests prior to the enactment of each plan. The plans became compromises in content and, as a rule, they were not bases for development for the period for which they were enacted. In this respect, the federal plan for 1965 is a particularly illustrative example. After many months of preparations in professional political and representative bodies, the plan was accepted at the end of 1964. However, there was no social force which could have realized this plan, and the actual development during the first months of 1965 went in a different direction from the plan's targets. In March, 1965, the Federal Executive Council in practice suspended the plan, blocked prices, and began intensive preparations for economic reform.

During the entire period from 1951 to 1965 the planning system was in crisis. The idea that planning of the Soviet type is the only form of planning for a socialist society was the basis for all Yugoslav conflicts and discussions on planning. The reaction against Soviet-type planning became a reaction against planning in general. Instead of planning and social guidance in the organization of economic development, emphasis was placed on the market mechanism, on automaticity and spontaneity in the organization of economic development, on some form of socialist laissez-faire as a basis for harmonious and rational economic development. The consequence of this was that planning lost its real role in the organization of economic development, and that social coordination and channeling of development was achieved by a series of measures of economic policy which determined the distribution of the gross material product, the share of personal consumption, and the share of gross investment. The interventions of the federation took place in the sphere of investment policy through a general investment fund.

In these conditions, prices, interest rates, taxes, credits, the foreign trade and foreign exchange regime, acquired a crucial significance, and through them was created a specific form of social planning. The fact that the federal government determined not only general conditions, but also conditions for allocation and distribution, meant that in reality there was a large measure of centralization. This caused a great deal of resistance. The system of social control became increasingly ineffective and brought about direct administrative intervention, which in turn aggravated the contradictory tendencies in social life. On the one hand, forms of selfmanagement were being developed, while on the other hand tendencies of centralized and administrative intervention grew.

The economic development which was realized in this contradictory situation took place with a rate of growth of gross material produce (at constant prices) of 8.3% from 1953 to 1960, and 8% from 1961 to 1964. In the first phase, before 1960, the economic development was based on a high rate of growth of the employed labor force (from 1.8 million in 1953 to 2.9 million in 1960), and a relatively small increase in the productivity of labor (yearly rate of 3%). Investments were predominantly channeled to light and consumer goods industries. This led to the neglect of energy, raw materials production, and to some extent of the production of equipment. The structural problems became more acute.

In 1964 the rate of growth of gross national product was 12%; the newly employed labor force consisted of more than 200,000 workers. According to this data, the performance of the economy could be considered outstanding. However, that year the rate of growth of production of energy and metallurgy was only 7%, as against the average for industry of 14%. Productive capacities were used up to 70 percent, and the high rate of growth was largely realized on the basis of a heavy deficit in foreign trade. Disproportions in the productive structure, and an inadequate monetary policy, led to strong inflationary tendencies.

All these indicators are evidence of a high degree of instability in the Yugoslav economy. The development which had taken place until 1964, with contradictory relations among two types of economic management (administrative and selfmanagement), led to further economic distortions and to the increase of economic instability. It was urgent to carry out important changes in the economic system: either to construct a system based on selfmanagement consistently, or to return to centralized management of the economy. The dominant political and social forces in Yugoslavia favored the solution based on selfmanagement. This is the meaning of the economic reforms of 1965, which opened a stage in which Yugoslavs are seeking new solutions consistent with the new material and social conditions of the economy. Among the material conditions it is necessary to emphasize that the level of economic development which was achieved corresponds to a national income of 500 dollars per capita, 48 percent of the total population in agriculture, and a non-agricultural labor force of three and a half million people.

4. The process of development of the material conditions of produc-

tion required the surmounting of regional and local boundaries. The commune could no longer be the decisive factor of integration in these conditions. The problem of sectoral integration became increasingly acute, and in the past two or three years it has received new forms (association of enterprises, combination, cooperation, integration). In these conditions, the determination of rational criteria for the performance of economic activity becomes the question of the day. The problem of prices, in particular the structure of prices, becomes the central question in the distribution of enterprise revenues, and in the determination of criteria for the efficiency of performance.

The existing price system, with large disparities and administrative control, was for a long time the subject of discussions on "parity prices." This question became one of the significant questions of the economic reform. The principles for its solution set out from the idea that the Yugoslav economy represents an economic region which is too small for the organization of an economic policy based on national resources. Thus the policy of economic development is necessarily related to the policy of Yugoslavia's inclusion in the international division of labor. The success of this policy depends, to a great extent, on the economic conditions of Yugoslavia's inclusion in the world economy. Concretely, it depends on the relation between internal and foreign prices, conditions of foreign trade, and of foreign exchange. On this basis, "world prices" (Yugoslav foreign market prices) became the basis for parity prices in the Yugoslav economy. The liberalization of foreign trade and the organization of convertibility of national currency became the goals of national policy.

Important changes took place in the distribution of enterprise revenues. The largest portion of funds for investment was transferred to enterprises. (Income tax was abolished, capital tax was decreased, contributions to social investment funds were abolished, turnover tax was abolished and replaced by a sales tax paid by consumers—all these funds were transferred to the enterprise.) These changes required a complete reorganization of the banking system. In these conditions the banking system is transformed into a center for the mobilization and centralization of monetary funds of working organizations, and for the allocation of these funds in a manner that is consistent with the economic structure of Yugoslav society. This structure is expressed through the market mechanism and through the movement of prices and incomes. The next step toward market allocation and redistribution of investment is the creation of a unified market for investment funds, organized through the exchange of securities. The organization of such a capital market in the Yugoslav economic system is foreseen by the social plan of development for the period 1966-70.

The change in the structure of income distribution had as a consequence the transfer of investment funds to the disposition of enterprises to a total of 70% of all economic investments in the socialized sector. This is consistent with the goal of building socialist relations defined according to the Yugoslav conception. Special emphasis is placed on strengthening the role of the producer and of workers organizations in making decisions about the entire process of social reproduction, and thus also about the allocation of investment. It is assumed that the major part of social investment will be allocated through the market mechanism, and that such an allocation will make possible a more rational use of these funds.

For the practical application of these conceptions in the organization of Yugoslav economic life, it was necessary to change not only institutional conditions, but to create material conditions which make possible the functioning of the market mechanism as a form of rational allocation of factors of production and of produced goods. It was also necessary to create an atmosphere of confidence in the allocative function of the laissez faire economy. In the period which preceded the reform, these processes were developed by those social forces which today represent the dominant factor in the organization of the social system.

After these changes, intervention on the part of central organs has been limited to sectors which are unstable from the standpoint of the normal performance of the market economy. The goal of this intervention is to prepare the conditions for the free functioning of the market mechanism in these sectors as well. However, among these sectors, special emphasis must be given to infrastructural sectors and to the economies of backward regions. The reorganization of the economic system led to the introduction of new instruments of planned intervention, and to the definition of new goals for this intervention. First of all, the maximum rate of economic growth no longer has the character of a priority. What is sought is the optimal growth rate which will make possible economic stabilization and a constant increase of the living standard, with special emphasis on personal consumption. The increase of the share of personal consumption and personal income in the national income has become a priority goal of economic policy. The rate of growth is empirically determined on the basis of linear extrapolation, and in the social plan for 1966-70 it is projected at a level of 7.5 to 8.5 in relation to gross material product. The increase of personal income in the national income is determined at 59.7%, which represents the lower limit, and the relative participation of investment has been decreased to 21% (in 1964, 27%), which is defined in the plan as the upper limit of investment.

For these goals to be realized within the context of a freer functioning of the laws of a market economy, the measures of economic policy will be directed first of all to the stabilization of the purchasing power of money, to the creation of conditions for more liberal inclusion in the international division of labor, and for the introduction of the convertibility of the dinar. Investment is being concentrated on the modernization and activization of existing capacities, and this in branches in which Yugoslavia has comparative advantages, according to natural and human resources, in branches which serve domestic needs expanding as a result of economic growth, and in branches which are able to employ large numbers of new workers.

The policy of full employment is not defined as a goal of the development policy for the planned period. The rate of increase of new employment is projected to be two and a half to three percent per year. This means that the growth of social product will depend, to a great extent, on the success of realizing a higher level of productivity of labor. (The yearly planned rate of increase of productivity is 6 to 7 percent). In other words, this means that the goal is to intensify economic development on the basis of high productivity of labor during the planned period.

The implementation of the plan's targets will be carried out by means of some key indicators: the rate of increase of material product, the rate of increase of employment, basic proportions in the distribution of the national income. If the planned relations are realized, measures of direct intervention in economic life will not be necessary.

Whether or not the new Yugoslav system of planning, based on minimal measures of direct intervention, will be confirmed in the coming period, depends on a series of circumstances. Among these circumstances, emphasis may be placed on material conditions (whether or not the estimated material conditions for decentralized development are realistic), and on the institutional framework (in particular, whether or not the coordination of economic decisions on different levels is adequately efficient).

The basic plans in the new Yugoslav systems are the plans of enterprises. This means that in the future the plan will be constructed from the bottom ("from below to above" alternative). The preparation of regional and sectoral projections represents the first stage in the aggregation and coordination of the basic enterprise plans. The general plan represents the final stage of the coordination. General, social, plans have the character of synthetic and global plans, except in those parts where the responsibilities and tasks of the federation are defined. This does not mean that autonomous parts are not found in the general plans, parts through which active influence on the economic structure is exerted. This means that the economic actor who determined the target is himself responsible for realizing it.

The new planning system will consist of middle-term plans of four to seven years. Yearly plans will not be prepared. It is possible that plans will be revised every two or three years, at which time a new middle-term plan will be prepared, a plan which takes account of changed economic conditions.

With the measures enacted by the economic reform, Yugoslavia entered a new stage of development. This stage does not involve the creation of a new economic system, but the further and more consistent application and realization of principles on which the Yugoslav economic system has been developing since 1950. The change of institutional forms through which these principles were realized had, as a primary goal, the creation of social conditions for economic development and the creation of socialist relations.

Even though the growth rate of the social product from 1947 to 1965 has oscillated a great deal, the average rate of increase was 7.1 percent (compound annual average rate of increase of gross material product at constant prices). If J. Tinbergen's criteria for the efficiency of a developing economy are applied, then the comparison of prewar with postwar rates speaks for itself. With a lower rate of growth of population (1.1 percent yearly), an average rate of increase of 7.1 percent was realized in the postwar period, as against an average rate of increase of national product of 1.1 percent and an average rate of increase of population of 1.4 percent (between 1929 and 1939). The data clearly shows that the postwar Yugoslav economic system has found it possible to realize a relatively high rate of growth of national product even though this development was accompanied by constant changes and experiments.

2. *Constitutional Socialism in Yugoslavia*

IVAN MAKSIMOVIĆ

In Yugoslavia the process of development of democratic political forms has been astonishingly rapid, being perhaps facilitated also by specific historical circumstances. The comparative independence from external factors in organizing and waging the military struggle during World War II, the extremely independent ideological and political attitude of the Communist Party of Yugoslavia (CPY), the historical position of Yugoslavia between two cultural-political climates in the world, the specific characteristic traits of the Yugoslav peoples, among which the striving for political independence and for independent views on possible models particularly stand out—all these facts have accelerated the development of a specific outlook on the political nature of socialism. The state apparatus is most sensitive to its continuous but changing role. It recognizes that if the continuous process of political transformation is not incessantly carried out, or rather, if the state apparatus retains the monopoly of economic and political management, the individual—the working man—inevitably becomes

From Ivan Maksimović, "Constitutional Socialism in Yugoslavia," *Annals* of the American Academy of Political and Social Science, Vol. 358 (March 1965), pp. 156-159. Reprinted by permission of the author and the publisher.

the tool of the new political force of bureaucracy. The only way out of this is the process of democratization of economic life which is then followed by the democratization of political life.

It is a mutually interdependent process. Democratic forms in the sphere of economic development must impel and form the development of the new political mechanism while this mechanism must offer an opportunity for the most thorough expression of economic democracy. Both these processes necessarily lead in the long run to the elimination of forces of bureaucracy, and also of all political forms which the bureaucratic apparatus had applied—political parties and the very state apparatus of the executive administrative body of political authority—to perform the political function and factual authority "in the name of the people." The task and the substance of genuine socialist democracy is to work out a political system of *direct* democracy the organizational forms of which will enable *every individual directly to participate in the creation of political authority*—in both the horizontal and the vertical levels and structures of the political system. The forms and methods of development of direct democracy may be very specific and varied depending upon the degree of material and political maturity of socialist society, and they are constantly changing. For this reason, socialism must necessarily develop in very varied forms. However, the substance must be identical: to free the personality from the pressure of the state apparatus and its political correction, from political parties, to place the personality in a position of direct participation in the creation of elements and preconditions for this development. This is, in the briefest outline, the substance of socialist democracy without whose development—according to the Yugoslav political philosophy—there is no socialism.[1]

As far back as 1950 the above-mentioned views matured in Yugoslavia, and it began building its new social system upon this political, economic, and philosophic concept. Yugoslavia passed a law of management over economic enterprises which, in our opinion, represented a historical landmark not only of the political and economic development in Yugoslavia, but also of the contemporary tendencies of the development of socialism.

This law has opened the door to far-reaching changes in the political and economic structures of Yugoslavia which have found their legal and political elaboration only in the recently adopted Constitution, but which are still far from being perfect. The substance of this law is reflected in the fact that the state ownership of means of production is handed to workers for management, thus opening the road to a gradual realization of the

[1] Edvard Kardelj, *Socialist Democracy in Yugoslav Practice* (Oslo, 1954).

principle of economic democracy.[2] This law contains the core of the principles of self-management in all spheres of social life in Yugoslavia, one which has been rapidly expanded in the course of the following years.[3]

THE POLITICAL SYSTEM OF SELF-GOVERNMENT

In this spirit, the new constitution, passed in April 1963, seeks to emphasize and stimulate the results achieved and the experience gained in the past. Several important political and organizational solutions of the new constitution are particularly interesting in this connection.

1. The new constitution concurrently seeks to expand the sphere of direct and indirect government and influence of individuals in the horizontal direction by extending the rights of self-government from the work community—economic self-government—guaranteed under the previous constitution to the sociopolitical community. In his work community the individual participates in the administrative acts of the microcommunity while in his narrow political territory—the commune—he directly carries out the political authority backing his own interest, the interests of his work community, and the broader interests of the territorial political community: in

[2] Article 1 of this law passed on June 26, 1950 envisages that factories, mines, communications, commercial, agricultural, and other state economic enterprises be managed, in the name of the social community, by work collectives through their representative bodies: workers' councils and management committees. The workers' council is elected from among all the workers. The workers' council and its executive management committee have all the economic competencies relating to the organization and planning of production, determination of prices, and distribution of the income, cadres, and work relations in the enterprises. In the seven-year mandate period alone, that is, between 1950 and 1963, more than one million workers and employees have been members of workers' councils, this being more than 30 per cent of their total number in Yugoslavia without taking into account the statistically nonregistered bodies of workers' self-management, as well as the individuals who have been elected more than once during the past ten mandate periods. Up to 1963, inclusive self-management bodies were introduced also in social services: schools of all kinds and levels, scientific institutions, cultural-educational communities, and humanitarian institutions (The SFRY Statistic Yearbook, 1963).

[3] The political territorial counterpart of the law on workers' self-management is the General Law on the Organization of Communes and Districts of June 26, 1955— which was improved later with the series of amendments and supplements. According to this law, the entire political territory of Yugoslavia is divided into communes which are the basic "territorial-political units" of the system. The basic characteristic of the communes as the political form of authority is in that they are governed by the people's committees representative bodies elected through direct vote and delegation, which have not only a legislative function but also *all other functions of state authority*—administrative and executive functions—on their respective territories. Thus is the political and state authority decentralized into several independent and mutually connected state-social centers for passing decisions—communes. The number of these "centers" or communes amounted to 577 in 1964. Numerous communes merge into districts on the basis of economic, geographic, and sociocultural criteria.

the council of work communities and in the political council of the commune, at voters' meetings, in management bodies of other work organizations, and the like.

2. The new constitution vertically expands the sphere of the direct and indirect political influence of individuals, of work organizations, and of basic political communities. This is being achieved in several ways. First, the self-government of citizens in the commune is constituted as the political basis of the singular sociopolitical system in Yugoslavia (article 73) while the commune is granted extensive self-government rights in the sphere of political and economic life (articles 96, 99, 101, 102).[4] Second, by the fact that representative bodies of higher ranking political conglomeration—districts, republic, and federation—on the basis of general and equal suffrage are elected on the principle of communal delegation, the commune being the basic political community (articles 76, 77).[5]

3. The new constitution seeks to introduce an ever greater number of citizens of various professions in all forms of political representative engagement on the vertical and horizontal levels, and to secure their increasing interdependence. It achieves this by limiting the number of terms of the members of assemblies, councils, and executive bodies (no one may be elected for two consecutive terms), by prohibiting a person from performing representative functions at several levels concurrently (article 82), and by the limitation of the total period of representative service (article 83). This principle is known in Yugoslav literature as the "principle of rotation" of the holder of political authority.

4. The new constitution seeks to abolish or at least to reduce to a minimum the differences between the citizens as a political being and as an economic being. This is achieved by inaugurating the principle under which citizens are elected to representative bodies of sociopolitical communities on all levels ranging from the municipal up to the federal assembly, both by

---

[4] In this sense the Yugoslav self-government system differs from local self-government in the West which mostly performs "devolved" political functions on the part of parliament, and also from local self-government in the East, in socialist countries where no distinction is made between the political functions of the state and the functions of local self-government, but where jurisdiction is presupposed in favor of higher ranking state bodies. Thus, in practice, self-government bodies perform solely functions delegated from above. The new constitution of Yugoslavia solves the political jurisdiction *in favor* of communes and local bodies, granting them the constitutional right to perform all functions of the social community except those which are defined in the constitution as the specific rights of the federation and republics—articles 96 and 101 of the new constitution.

[5] As far as we know, no system of local self-government today applies this delegation system in the vertical organization of political authority. It was applied in the Soviet Union in the period from the Revolution until 1936 when it was abandoned after the adoption of Stalin's constitution. See M. Jovičić, "Communal System According to the Preliminary Draft of the New Constitution in Relation to Foreign Systems of Local Self-Government," *Archives for Law Sciences, Beograd.* No. 3/4 (1962), p. 512.

the territorial-political criterion and by the criterion of their professional activity (article 75).

Representative bodies of political authority are organized in such a way as to express and realize this requirement. In the basic political territory, in the commune, assembly consists of two chambers, the communal chamber and the chamber of the working communities. The former chamber represents man as a citizen, that is, his political being, and the latter chamber, man as the representative of the work organization, as a working man of any profession.

For the federal and republican assemblies, this idea is increasingly expanded so that in the Federal Assembly of the SFRY—in addition to the Federal Chamber, which is a chamber of elected delegates of citizens who are elected according to absolutely political criteria whose number depends upon the territory, the number of inhabitants, and the like (article 166)— we have another four chambers of delegates of the working people from work communities of communal assemblies who are elected upon the basis of their role and record in work organizations. These are the Economic Chamber, the Chamber of Education and Culture, the Chamber of Social Welfare and Health, and the Organizational Political Chamber. The laws which are passed are always the expression of the will of the representative body consisting of two houses. Together with the federal and republican chambers conceived as "political chambers" a corresponding "professional" chamber carries out the legislative functions in the sphere of specific social relations, in the sphere of economic, educational-cultural, and social-health problems, while the organizational-political chamber deals with questions from the very organization of the political system. For this reason, in contrast to other chambers, members of management bodies of work communities can only be selected to the organizational-political chamber.

5. The new constitution also seeks to transform the legislative assemblies into the highest bodies of self-management on a definite territorial basis. The constitution does not give to any of the assemblies the absolute power either in the horizontal or vertical scale of organization of authority, but the Federal Assembly is the supreme body of authority "within the rights and obligations of the federation" (article 163), and the other assemblies carry out the corresponding functions on the territories of communes, districts, socialist republics, and autonomous regions (articles 96, 105, 108). This secures the political basis of Yugoslav federalism. In addition, the assemblies are established as the real holders of authority and management by the fact that their functions contain both the legislative and executive-administrative functions of authority while they themselves are treated as unique "working and legislative bodies" in all spheres of social life. This new role is reflected also in the competencies which the constitution grants to assemblies to have, in addition to exclusively political

functions, also a whole series of functions of an economic and cultural-educational nature (article 164). It is particularly important to note the statutory provision according to which the assembly performs all these functions "directly and exclusively" and cannot devolve these rights either on its bodies and commissions or on executive and administrative bodies of authority (article 164, paragraph 1). Finally, a series of articles of the new constitution which relate to the Federal Assembly explicitly define the subordination and responsibility of executive and administrative bodies to the assembly. The assembly can pass laws and other acts independently from the initiatives and proposals of executive bodies against their opinion and substantiation (article 232). The function of members of executive and administrative bodies of the assembly is limited in time to four years, and the mandate of these functions may exceptionally—under a decision of the assembly—be prolonged for the next consecutive four years at the longest (article 236). Thus the constitution, in principle, has strongly confined bureaucracy and the independence of executive and administrative bodies from parliament.

6. Finally, the new constitution seeks to secure the juridical protection of the principles of constitutionalism as well as of constitutional provisions about legality. It achieves this by setting up a constitutional court, an institution which was unknown in the constitution of 1946. Without entering here into the great number of problems which this institution implies, we would like to point out two of its important functions. The new constitution authorizes the constitutional court to propose to the Federal Assembly the abolition of all federal laws which are not in accordance with the principles of the constitution (article 245) and to give its opinion to the Federal Assembly as to whether the republican constitution is contrary to the constitution of Yugoslavia. Second, the new constitution authorizes the constitutional court to cancel or abolish any regulation or act (except law) which is not in accordance with the constitution or the federal law. Numerous economic organizations have already availed themselves of these rights, instituting proceedings against law provisions after the adoption of the constitution.

THE PLACE AND FUNCTION OF POLITICAL PARTIES

In contrast to most constitutions in the world, to the constitution of Yugoslavia of 1946, and to the constitutional law of 1953 the new constitution of Yugoslavia explicitly deals with the main political parties in Yugoslavia, the League of Communists of Yugoslavia (LCY) and the Socialist Alliance of the Working People of Yugoslavia (SAWPY).

1. In connection with the LCY[6] the new constitution sums up in brief its political role in the new history of Yugoslavia. The constitution then determines the role and place of this political organization in the system of political democracy and social self-government. With its guiding, ideological, and political work the LCY "is the basic initiator of political activity for the protection of the achievements of the revolution of socialist relations" and especially for the enhancing of the socialist social and democratic conscience of people" (article VI).

Thus has the constitution, somehow or other in a generalized way, fixed the political function of the LCY under present conditions, which is the result of a long process of political development and evolution of the LCY. The substance of the evolution was set down as far back as at the Seventh Congress of the LCY in 1958, when the new program of the party was adopted. Without entering into details we may say that it is based upon the concept that the leading political role of the LCY in Yugoslavia—as all other political parties—will gradually disappear in the future along with the development of socialist democracy and the system of self-government. Meanwhile, the Sixth Congress of the LCY in 1952 has indicated and the Seventh Congress in 1958 has defined the elements of the gradual transient position of the LCY and its place in the system of Yugoslavia. The starting position is based upon the orientation of the party organization and party work of the LCY in the direction of the further political and economic consolidation of the system of self-government whereby the LCY retains the leading ideological and organizational role, but neither the LCY as a whole nor its individual bodies and members can be identified with the system of authority or appropriate a political monopoly in it.

This destatization and debureaucratization of functions of the LCY in relation to the apparatus of political authority in which the party hands over the direct political control to bodies of authority is accompanied also by changes as regards the method of this influence. The sixth plenum of the Central Committee of the LCY, held in 1964, in the document relating to the basic guidelines for the precongress activity, stresses that the method of party work today consists in "that social affairs are transferred to social forums where the working people including communists as members of self-government bodies and collectives publicly and democratically agree and decide every day." The new role of the LCY can be perceived also in the evaluation of two harmful tendencies of party activity identified in this same document. The first is "the bureaucratic concept" which sees in the League of Communists solely the external factor which acts from above,

---

[6] With 1,300,000 members in the first half of 1964, the LCY represents an organization which includes about 30 per cent of the entire working population in the social sector. In its composition 36.2 per cent are workers, 38.4 per cent employees, and 7.9 per cent agriculturists.

and sees in the member of the League of Communists the man who is entitled to prescribe what is socialist and what is not. This practice "underestimates and neglects the role of self-government bodies and activity of socio-political organizations as well as the obligations of the communists in them." On the other hand, this same document evaluates as harmful the underestimation and neglect of the leading political role of the League of Communists among the Communists themselves. The result, in the long run, is "the surrender of the leading role of non-socialist or bureaucratic— conservative—social forces and tendencies."

2. The largest and most numerous political organization in Yugoslavia is, however, the Socialist Alliance of the Working People of Yugoslavia—the SAWPY.[7] The constitution has defined the SAWPY as a "voluntary democratic alliance of citizens" and as "the broadest support of socio-political activity in the social self-government of the working people." The constitution has also granted very extensive political rights to the SAWPY because the citizens "discuss the socio-political questions from all spheres of social life" and "pass political conclusions as regards the solution of these questions." The constitution emphasizes that a very important function of the SAWPY is "social control," which it performs concerning the work of social bodies and bodies of social self-government, of organizations and individuals, holders of public function "particularly as regards the securing of the publicity and responsibility of their work." The constitution also grants to the SAWPY the right to take "political initiative in all spheres of social life."

The massive character of this political organization is also reflected in the fact that this is a form in which everyone may act: members of the LCY, members of the SAWPY, as well as those who are not members. The constitution stresses that the SAWPY is an "open organization." For this reason, certain Yugoslav political theoreticians see in the SAWPY something more than a political forum in the classic sense of the word. They define it as "general people's assembly," a special feature of the Yugoslav political development which introduces "significant changes into the classic structure and function of party systems, and also of political organizations in general."[8]

THE NEW CONSTITUTION AND NEW AND OLD PROBLEMS

If the new constitution of Yugoslavia has endeavored to set up the most democratic mechanism for the settlement of numerous problems in

[7] In 1963 the SAWPY had 7.545 million members, this representing about 40 per cent of the total number of inhabitants in Yugoslavia. Its work is developing today in 8,764 local organizations, 25,548 branch offices and over 20,000 sections (SFRY Statistical Yearbook 1963).

[8] Jovan Dordević, *op. cit.*, p. 96.

the sphere of politics and economics, it has certainly not been able to eliminate or settle them with the provisions of the constitution themselves. The Yugoslav Vice-President Edvard Kardelj has stressed this fact as far back as on the occasion of the inauguration of the constitution. "This is a Constitution," he said "of a socialist society which approaches with open eyes the contradictions of its own development and endeavours to set up the most democratic mechanism for their settlement."[9] Vice-President Kardelj has included among these "the contradictions between the individual and social interest," as "impartially given" and as "forms in which social progress is carried out" in the Yugoslav society.

In the settlement of contradictions emerging from the varying interests of the individual and of society, the new constitution mostly proceeded along two lines. In contrast to the constitution of 1946, it has greatly promoted and secured the socioeconomic position of the individual, of the citizen in the system, and has granted him constitutional stability. On the other hand, the new constitution has weakened the role and function of the state and administrative apparatus in the political sphere of authority and in the sphere of economic competencies, but has not abolished them.

THE ECONOMIC SYSTEM: ECONOMIC LIBERALIZATION

Yugoslavia had begun the construction of a socialist economy as a centralist, statist, planned economy in which the entire economic might was concentrated in the hands of the state apparatus and in which the political authority converged with the economic one. The process of decentralization of this power which has been evolving during the course of the last decade, especially after the new constitution, has substantially narrowed the economic function of state bodies, but has not yet abolished them.[10] In certain vital economic questions such as investment policy, insurance policy, the policy of primary and secondary distribution of the national income, the price policy, the influence of the federal bodies, the

[9] Speech at the joint session of the Federal Council and of the Council of Producers of the Federal People's Assembly, April 7, 1963.

[10] It is extremely important to establish that the new political self-government system and the process of decentralization of the economic system in Yugoslavia have not weakened, but on the contrary have considerably consolidated the dynamism and rate of the economic growth in Yugoslavia. Yugoslavia developed in the period 1948/ 1960 at the average annual rate of increase of the national product of 7.3 per cent, industry 10.2 per cent, agriculture 4.7 per cent, while the indices of the annual increase for individual periods of time amounted to 2.4 per cent (1948-1952), 8.8 per cent (1953-1956), 12 per cent (1957-1960), 14 per cent (1963-1964). ("Tendencies of the Change of the Yugoslav Economy in the Period 1952-1960," Federal Institute for Economic Planning of the SFRY and Statistical Yearbook for 1963.) Taking the eight-year period between 1952 and 1960 as a whole, the rate of the Yugoslav economic growth was the most rapid in the world.

administration is still very strong and decisive.[11] In the face of great disproportions in the development of individual economic branches, spheres, and regions in Yugoslavia and of considerable differences in technological equipment, productivity, and general and economic culture, as well as the volume of the income realized in individual spheres and branches of the Yugoslav economy,[12] the consistent implementation and realization of constitutional principles concerning the formation of "equal conditions of production," renumeration according to "work done," and unique market and free trade of products and services encounter great institutional and structural obstacles in the economic sphere, and for the time being still represent a political determination rather than actual economic possibilities and realizations. At the same time, the decentralized economic management of the economy which has proved to be an effective incentive to productivity has also displayed certain negative aspects such as the strengthening of the oligo-monopoly positions of certain branches and economic enterprises, the supremacy of the mentality of profits and interests in relation to the interest of social requirement in the activity of individual producers, and the like.

Nevertheless the resolutions which have been endorsed in the Federal Assembly lately, the draft laws which are the topic of discussion and are about to be adopted, some of the legally passed decisions—all these are aimed at the decentralization of the economic system. Among these measures we would particularly like to stress: first, those relating to the process of "change in the global distribution of available social means in favour of work organizations," and at the expense of state bodies; second, the legal abolition of all centralized social investment funds owned and controlled by the government, and the creation of an insurance and credit system which will be able in the future to develop relations with work organizations and communes upon the principles of the priority of economic criteria in relation to political owners; third, changes in the methodology of social planning and the decline of the influence of administrative bodies on prices and conditions of trade; and fourth, freeing "foreign trade

[11] Several data may illustrate these facts: (1) by means of various economic instruments the federation participated as far back as 1963 with 54.3 per cent in the total distribution of the net social product—and economic organization with 45.7 per cent (2) in 1963 the federation participated with 22.5 per cent in direct investment activity and in 1960 even with 77.1 per cent, while we have no data for its indirect influence in the current period; (3) about 70 per cent of the total volume of prices is under direct or indirect administrative control (Statistical Documents of the Federal Statistical Bureau, 1964).

[12] The average nominal net personal receipts per employed person in the socialist republics in the first half of 1964: in Montenegro 29.0, in Serbia 30.9, in Croatia 35.5, and in Slovenia 43.5 (in thousands of dinars). The Yugoslav average was 33.5. In economic branches, the discrepancy was expressed as follows: industry 33.7, agriculture 25.1, forestry 23.8, trade 38.6, crafts 31.4 (Monthly indices of the SFRY Statistical Bureau for 1964, inclusive to April).

from direct interference on the part of executive-political and administrative bodies."[13]

THE POLITICAL SYSTEM: DEBUREAUCRATIZATION AND DEPROFESSIONALIZATION

A similar process of democratization and of reduced influence of state executive bodies is being carried out also in the sphere of the political system and apparently encounters lesser obstacles than the economic system in the realization of the basic principles of the new constitution. However, this is also not a thornless path.

Let us stress in the first place the positive elements in the process. The very elections for new representative bodies in the federal and republican assembly in 1963 have shown new democratic tendencies in the spirit of the new constitution. The principle of the replacement of the current leading political personalities in bodies of authority (rotation) is being implemented and, this being equally important, numerous personalities have been included into political life who so far had not been politicians in the professional sense of the word.[14]

Significantly these nonprofessional politicians have displayed a comparatively greater independence from administrative bodies. They expressed nonconformist views and suggested solutions which were not covered in advance with the authority of political forums.

In the relationship between assemblies and their executive and administrative bodies, the present practice also shows certain shifts in the direction of the realization of constitutional principles. As a matter of fact, executive bodies are still the proponents of most of the draft laws. But the positive process is reflected in the fact that the draft laws of executive bodies are extensively discussed in assembly council and committees where they are often subject to criticisms and undergo substantial changes which executive bodies must subsequently insert in the texts. The Federal Assembly moreover has lately passed numerous resolutions to serve as future guidelines for the economic and political system, which represent the framework and limits within which the activity of executive bodies in proposing draft laws is now developing.

[13] "Resolution on the Basic Guidelines for the Further Development of the Economic System" of April 16-17, 1964, Parts I-VIII, in the booklet *Basic Problems of the Further Development of the Economic System* (Belgrade: Federal Assembly, 1964), p. 109 ff.

[14] Half of the current members of the Federal Assembly councils have had a university education, and one-third of them have graduated from vocational schools. Out of 670 deputies, 131 are women. In provincial assemblies this ratio is somewhat less favorable.

Nevertheless, even within the political system and in its further improvement in the spirit of the constitution numerous problems and obstacles are emerging which are expressed in the process of transformation of political institutions. Various factors are acting in this which do not allow for the speed and radical nature of changes which the constitution presupposes. These factors represent, in general, the existing contradictions of the individual and social interest, local communities and republics, republics and the federation, and its more profound reasons should be sought in both the economic and the historically created differences which exist in Yugoslavia and which it has not yet been possible to overcome. These factors moreover are intensified by bureaucratic tendencies of blind devotion to the state apparatus and the inclination to administrative and political pressure, instead of democratic methods of government and society. These barriers to the implementation of the new constitution have yet to be overcome.

The principle of replacement (rotation) of political representatives and leaders in bodies of authority—assemblies—is effected at a slower rate than necessary, and the composition of representative bodies still reflects the strong influence of administrative factors. The number of representatives of work organizations, especially of direct producers in representative bodies, remain insufficient. In assemblies of communes the percentage of administrative personnel is dominant. In assemblies themselves the executive and administrative bodies still have a very strong position. Thus, for example, the federal administrative bodies remain the proponents of almost all the laws and measures in the sphere of the social system: the system of pensions, distribution in institutions, the budget and tax system, and schooling. The federal administrations, moreover, have passed certain regulations which, under the new constitution, pertain to the jurisdiction of the provincial legislature.

CONCLUSION

In summary, it may be observed that the Yugoslav political practice after the adoption of the new constitution is still faced with numerous structural and institutional problems. In fact to some extent, especially in the sphere of economic relations, it lags behind the intentions and principles expressed in this document. Still, the adoption of the new constitution is a major step in the progressive development of the political system, and offers proof that the political conscience of the country will continue to serve as a powerful impetus for future progressive transformations.

SUGGESTED READING

Fisher, Jack C., *Yugoslavia: A Multinational State—Regional Difference and Administrative Response*. San Francisco: S. F. Chandler Publishing Company, 1966.

Hoffman, George W., and Neal, Fred W., *Yugoslavia and the New Communism*. New York: Twentieth Century Fund, 1962.

Nikolić, D., and Sicherl, P., "A Structural Analysis of Economic Development of Yugoslavia in the Period 1952–1962." *Czechoslovak Economic Papers*, No. 8, 1967.

Pejovich, Svetozar, *The Market-Planned Economy of Yugoslavia*. Minneapolis: University of Minnesota Press, 1966.

Pelicon, I., "Economic Relations Between Yugoslavia and Developing Countries." *Review of International Affairs*, Belgrade, No. 401 (December 20, 1966).

Shaffer, Harry G. (Ed.), *The Communist World: Marxist and Non-Marxist Views*. New York: Appleton-Century-Crofts, 1967, Ch. IV, pp. 217-288.

Stojanovich, Radmilla (Ed.), *Yugoslav Economists on Problems of a Socialist Economy*. New York: International Arts and Sciences Press, 1964.

Tito, Josip Broz, "Developing Countries." Report Submitted to the Eighth Congress of the League of Communists of Yugoslavia, December 7-13, 1964. *Review of International Affairs*, Vol. XV, No. 353 (December 20, 1964).

Tornquist, David. *Look East, Look West: The Socialist Adventure in Yugoslavia*. New York: Macmillan, 1966.

Yugoslavia's Way: The Program of the League of the Communists of Yugoslavia. Adopted by the Seventh Congress. New York: All Nations Press, 1959.